minimum unit is $100,000. Typical rates in the secondary market 5.15% one month; 5.24% three months; 5.57% six months.

BANKERS ACCEPTANCES: 5.07% 30 days; 5.08% 60 days; 5.12% 90 days; 5.15% 120 days; 5.18% 150 days; 5.35% 180 days. Offered rates at negotiable, bank-backed business credit instruments typically financing an import order.

LONDON LATE EURODOLLARS: 5 3/16%–5 1/16% one month; 5 1/4%–5 1/8% two months; 5 5/16%–5 3/16% three months; 5 11/32%–5 7/32% four months; 5 13/32%–5 9/32% five months; 5 9/16%–5 7/16% six months.

LONDON INTERBANK OFFERED RATES (LIBOR): 5.18375% one month (7/5/99 was 5.18300); 5.3100% three months; 5.5900% six months (7/5/99 was 5.58838); 5.7500% one year. British Banker's Association average of interbank offered rates for dollar deposits in the London market based on quotations at 16 major banks. Effective rate for contracts entered into two days from date appearing at top of this column.

EURO LIBOR: 2.63300% one month; 2.66300% three months; 2.85100% six months; 2.29700% one year. British Banker's Association average at interbank offered rates for euro deposits in the London market based on quotations at 16 major banks. Effective rate for contracts entered into two days from date appearing at top of this column.

EURO INTERBANK OFFERED RATES (EURIBOR): 2.633% one month; 2.663% three months; 2.851% six months; 2.971% one year. European Banking Federation-sponsored rate among 57 Euro zone banks.

FOREIGN PRIME RATES: Canada 6.25%; Germany 2.50%; Japan 1.375%; Switzerland 3.125%; Britain 5.00%. These rate indications aren't directly comparable; lending practices vary widely by location.

TREASURY BILLS: Results of the Tuesday, July 6,1999, auction of short-term U.S. government bills, sold at a discount from face value in units of $10,000 to $1 million: 4.590% 13 weeks; 4.590% 26 weeks.

OVERNIGHT REPURCHASE RATE: 4.83%. Dealer financing rate for overnight sale and repurchase of Treasury securities. Source: Telerate.

CURRENCY FUTURES

Tuesday, July 6, 1999

	Open	High	Low	Settle	Change	Lifetime High	Lifetime Low	Open Interest
JAPAN YEN (CME)-12.5 million yen; $ per yen (.00)								
Sept	.8273	.8345	.8251	.8279	− .0065	.9500	.7680	94,203
Dec	.8374	.8389	.8370	.8389	− .0066	.9600	.8257	15,278
Mr00	...	...	...	.8509	− .0065	.8931	.8369	112
Est vol 11,507; vol Fri 5,205; open int 109,594, −516.								
DEUTSCHEMARK (CME)-125,000 marks; $ per mark								
Sept	.5250	.5273	.5233	.5259	− .0006	.6300	.5233	24,160
Dec	.5285	.5305	.5285	.5295	− .0006	.6120	.5285	192
Est vol 1,947; vol Fri 2,909; open int 24,352, −325.								
CANADIAN DOLLAR (CME)-100,000 dlrs.; $ per Can $								
Sept	.6820	.6841	.6804	.6806	− .0036	.7080	.6310	58,022
Dec	.6835	.6840	.6818	.6815	− .0036	.6930	.6320	2,570
Mr00	...	...	...	.6825	− .0036	.6940	.6425	542
June	...	...	...	.6836	− .0036	.6950	.6547	185
Est vol 5,152; vol Fri 7,901; open int 61,332, +759.								
BRITISH POUND (CME)-62,500 pds.; $ per pound								
Sept	1.5666	1.5786	1.5598	1.5628	− .0172	1.6980	1.5598	64,079
Dec	1.5720	1.5720	1.5616	1.5648	− .0172	1.6760	1.5616	254
Est vol 8,240; vol Fri 7,411; open int 64,334, +2,788.								
SWISS FRANC (CME)-125,000 francs; $ per franc								
Sept	.6421	.6451	.6395	.6433	+ .0004	.7831	.6395	70,835
Dec	.6492	.6510	.6491	.6498	+ .0004	.7671	.6480	172
Est vol 6,311; vol Fri 8,734; open int 71,033, −510.								
AUSTRALIAN DOLLAR (CME)-100,000 dlrs.; $ per A.$								
Sept	.6690	.6722	.6632	.6635	− .0060	.6745	[illegible]	32,577
Est vol 1,662; vol Fri 3,410; open int [illegible]								
MEXICAN PESO (C[illegible]								
Sept	.10433	.10433	[illegible]	[illegible]	[illegible]	[illegible]	[illegible]	16,779
Dec	.09960	.09990	[illegible]	[illegible]	...	[illegible]	.06700	4,672
Mr00	.09550	.09560	[illegible]	.09550	...	.09560	.08135	3,752
Est vol 3,252; vol Fri 3,474; open int 25,214, +912.								
EURO FX (CME)-Euro 125,000; $ per Euro								
Sept	1.0244	1.0280	1.0250	1.0285	− .0012	1.2005	1.0250	45,047
Dec	1.0315	1.0351	1.0361	1.0356	− .0012	1.2059	1.0361	275
Est vol 3,917; vol Fri 9,737; open int 45,322, +206.								

S0-AIH-928

CURRENCY OPTIONS

Tuesday, July 6, 1999

PHILADELPHIA EXCHANGE

		Calls		Puts	
		Vol.	Last	Vol.	Last
British Pound					**156.13**
31,250 Brit. Pounds-European Style.					
158	Jul	16	0.23	...	...
31,250 Brit. Pounds-cents per unit.					
163	Jul	4	0.01	...	0.01
Euro					**102.46**
62,500 Euro-cents per unit.					
98	Sep	...	0.01	89	0.35
100	Sep	...	...	22	0.67
102	Sep	...	0.01	4	1.38
104	Sep	...	...	24	2.47
106	Sep	2	0.53	...	0.01
110	Sep	3	0.10	...	0.01
Japanese Yen 82.64					
6,250,000 J. Yen-100ths of a cent per unit.					
80½	Sep	...	0.01	25	0.60
6,250,000 J. Yen-EuropeanStyle.					
80½	Sep	...	0.01	20	0.53
Swiss Franc					**63.80**
62,500 Swiss Francs-cents per unit.					
67	Sep	10	0.30	...	...
68	Sep	2	0.15	...	...
Call Vol		**986**		**Open Int ....**	**39,510**
Put Vol		**3,569**		**Open Int ....**	**30,445**

SECOND EDITION

International Financial Management

The Irwin/McGraw-Hill Series in Finance, Insurance and Real Estate

Stephen A. Ross
Franco Modigliani Professor of Finance and Economics
Sloan School of Management
Massachusetts Institute of Technology
Consulting Editor

FINANCIAL MANAGEMENT

Benninga and Sarig
Corporate Finance: A Valuation Approach

Block and Hirt
Foundations of Financial Management
Ninth Edition

Brealey and Myers
Principles of Corporate Finance
Sixth Edition

Brealey, Myers, and Marcus
Fundamentals of Corporate Finance
Third Edition

Brooks
FinGame Online 3.0

Bruner
Case Studies in Finance: Managing for Corporate Value Creation
Third Edition

Chew
The New Corporate Finance: Where Theory Meets Practice
Second Edition

Graduate Management Admissions Council, Robert F. Bruner, Kenneth Eades and Robert Harris
Essentials of Finance: With an Accounting Review
Fully interactive CD-ROM derived from Finance Interactive 1997 Pre-MBA Edition
Finance Interactive: Pre-MBA Series 2000
Second Edition

Grinblatt and Titman
Financial Markets and Corporate Strategy

Helfert
Techniques of Financial Analysis: A Guide to Value Creation
Tenth Edition

Higgins
Analysis for Financial Management
Sixth Edition

Hite
A Programmed Learning Guide to Finance

Kester, Fruhan, Piper, and Ruback
Case Problems in Finance
Eleventh Edition

Nunnally and Plath
Cases in Finance
Second Edition

Ross, Westerfield, and Jaffe
Corporate Finance
Fifth Edition

Ross, Westerfield, and Jordan
Essentials of Corporate Finance
Third Edition

Ross, Westerfield, and Jordan
Fundamentals of Corporate Finance
Fifth Edition

Smith
The Modern Theory of Corporate Finance
Second Edition

White
Financial Analysis with an Electronic Calculator
Fourth Edition

INVESTMENTS

Bodie, Kane, and Marcus
Essentials of Investments
Fourth Edition

Bodie, Kane, and Marcus
Investments
Fourth Edition

Cohen, Zinbarg, and Zeikel
Investment Analysis and Portfolio Management
Fifth Edition

Corrado and Jordan
Fundamentals of Investments: Valuation and Management

Farrell
Portfolio Management: Theory and Applications
Second Edition

Hirt and Block
Fundamentals of Investment Management
Sixth Edition

Jarrow
Modelling Fixed Income Securities and Interest Rate Options

Shimko
The Innovative Investor
Excel Version

FINANCIAL INSTITUTIONS AND MARKETS

Cornett and Saunders
Fundamentals of Financial Institutions Management

Rose
Commercial Bank Management
Third Edition

Rose
Money and Capital Markets: Financial Institutions and Instruments in a Global Marketplace
Seventh Edition

Rose and Kolari
Financial Institutions: Understanding and Managing Financial Services
Fifth Edition

Santomero and Babbel
Financial Markets, Instruments, and Institutions
Second Edition

Saunders
Financial Institutions Management: A Modern Perspective
Third Edition

INTERNATIONAL FINANCE

Eun and Resnick
International Financial Management
Second Edition

Kester and Luehrman
Case Problems in International Finance
Second Edition

Levi
International Finance
Third Edition

Levich
International Financial Markets: Prices and Policies
Second Edition

REAL ESTATE

Brueggeman and Fisher
Real Estate Finance and Investments
Eleventh Edition

Corgel, Smith, and Ling
Real Estate Perspectives: An Introduction to Real Estate
Fourth Edition

Lusht
Real Estate Valuation: Principles and Applications

FINANCIAL PLANNING AND INSURANCE

Allen, Melone, Rosenbloom, and VanDerhei
Pension Planning: Pension, Profit-Sharing, and Other Deferred Compensation Plans
Eighth Edition

Crawford
Life and Health Insurance Law
Eighth Edition (LOMA)

Harrington and Niehaus
Risk Management and Insurance

Hirsch
Casualty Claim Practice
Sixth Edition

Kapoor, Dlabay, and Hughes
Personal Finance
Fifth Edition

Skipper
International Risk and Insurance: An Environmental-Managerial Approach

Williams, Smith, and Young
Risk Management and Insurance
Eighth Edition

SECOND EDITION

International Financial Management

CHEOL S. EUN
Georgia Institute of Technology

BRUCE G. RESNICK
Wake Forest University

Boston Burr Ridge, IL Dubuque, IA Madison, WI New York
San Francisco St. Louis
Bangkok Bogota Caracas Lisbon London Madrid
Mexico City Milan New Delhi Seoul Singapore Sydney
Taipei Toronto

McGraw-Hill Higher Education

A Division of The **McGraw-Hill** *Companies*

INTERNATIONAL FINANCIAL MANAGEMENT

Published by Irwin/McGraw-Hill, an imprint of The McGraw-Hill Companies, Inc. 1221 Avenue of the Americas, New York, NY, 10020. Copyright © 2001, 1998 by The McGraw-Hill Companies, Inc. All rights reserved. No part of this publication may be reproduced or distributed in any form or by any means, or stored in a data base or retrieval system, without the prior written permission of The McGraw-Hill Companies, Inc., including, but not limited to, in any network or other electronic storage or transmission, or broadcast for distance learning. Some ancillaries, including electronic and print components, may not be available to customers outside the United States.

This book was printed on acid-free paper.

3 4 5 6 7 8 9 0 KGP/KGP 0 9 8 7 6 5 4 3 2 1

ISBN 0-07-231825-2
Senior vice president and editoral director: *Robin J. Zwettler*
Publisher: *John E. Biernat*
Developmental editor: *Sarah Pearson*
Project manager: *Laura Griffin*
Production supervisor: *Rose Hepburn*
Freelance design coordinator: *Gino Cieslik*
Supplement coordinator: *Rose M. Range*
Senior/project manager new media: *Barb Block*
Compositor: *GAC Indianapolis*
Typeface: *10.5/12 Times Roman*
Printer: *Quebecor Printing Book Group/Kingsport*

Library of Congress Cataloging-in-Publication Data
Eun, Cheol S.
International financial management / Cheol S. Eun, Bruce G. Resnick.—2nd ed.
p.cm.
Includes index.
ISBN 0-07-231825-2
1. International finance.2. International business enterprises—Finance. 3. Foreign exchange.4. Financial institutions, International. I. Resnick, Bruce G.II. Title.
HG3881.E655 2001 00-027294
658.15'99 dc21

www.mhhe.com

To Elizabeth
C.S.E.

To Hillery
B.G.R.

ABOUT THE AUTHORS

Cheol S. Eun, Georgia Institute of Technology

Cheol S. Eun (Ph.D., NYU, 1981) is a professor of finance and currently holds the Thomas R. Williams Chair in International Finance at the DuPree College of Management, Georgia Institute of Technology. Before joining Georgia Tech, he taught at Kent State University, the University of Minnesota, and the University of Maryland. He also taught at the Wharton School of the University of Pennsylvania and the Esslingen University of Technology (Germany) as a visiting professor. He has published extensively on international finance issues in such major journals as the *Journal of Finance, JFQA, Journal of Banking and Finance, Journal of Portfolio Management, Management Science,* and *Oxford Economic Papers.* Currently, he is an associate editor of the *Journal of Banking and Finance, Journal of Financial Research, Global Finance Journal,* and *European Financial Management.* His research is widely quoted and referenced in various scholarly articles and textbooks in the United States as well as abroad.

Dr. Eun has taught a variety of courses at the undergraduate, graduate, and executive levels, and was the winner of the Krowe Teaching Excellence Award at the University of Maryland. He also has served as a consultant to many national and international organizations, including the World Bank and the Korean Development Institute, advising on issues relating to capital market liberalization, global capital raising, international investment, and exchange risk management. In addition, he has been a frequent speaker at academic and professional meetings held throughout the world.

Bruce G. Resnick, Wake Forest University

Bruce G. Resnick is the Joseph M. Bryan Jr. Professor of Banking and Finance at the Babcock Graduate School of Management of Wake Forest University in Winston-Salem, North Carolina. He has a D.B.A. (1979) in finance from Indiana University. Additionally, he has a M.B.A. from the University of Colorado and a B.B.A. from Wisconsin State University. Prior to coming to the Babcock School, he taught at Indiana University for ten years, the University of Minnesota for five years, and California State University for two years. He has also taught as a visiting professor at Bond University, Gold Coast, Queensland, Australia, and at the Helsinki School of Economics and Business Administration in Finland. Additionally, he served as the Indiana University resident director at the Center for European Studies at the University of Limburg, Maastricht, the Netherlands. He also served as an external examiner to the Business Administration Department of Singapore Polytechnic.

Dr. Resnick teaches M.B.A. courses at Wake Forest University. He specializes in the areas of investments, portfolio management, and international financial management. Dr. Resnick's research interests include market efficiency studies of options and financial futures markets and empirical tests of asset pricing models. In recent years, he has specialized in the optimal design of internationally diversified portfolios constructed to control for parameter uncertainty and exchange rate risk. His research articles have been published in most of the major academic journals in finance. His research is widely referenced by other researchers and textbook authors. Dr. Resnick frequently serves as a consultant in the selection and evaluation of investment managers.

BRIEF CONTENTS

CONTENTS

5 International Parity Relationships and Forecasting Foreign Exchange Rates, 99

PART TWO World Financial Markets and Institutions

6 International Banking and Money Market, 128

7 International Bond Market, 158

8 International Equity Markets, 178

9 Futures and Options on Foreign Exchange, 206

10 Currency and Interest Rate Swaps, 234

11 International Portfolio Investments, 254

PART THREE Foreign Exchange Exposure and Management

12 Management of Economic Exposure, 290

13 Management of Transaction Exposure, 312

14 Management of Translation Exposure, 338

PART FOUR Financial Management of the Multinational Firm

15 Foreign Direct Investment, 360

16 International Capital Structure and the Cost of Capital, 392

17 International Capital Budgeting, 420

18 Multinational Cash Management, 438

19 Exports and Imports, 462

20 International Tax Environment, 474

INTERNATIONAL FINANCE IN PRACTICE BOXES

PREFACE

OUR REASON FOR WRITING THIS TEXTBOOK

Both of us have been teaching international financial management to undergraduates and M.B.A. students at Georgia Institute of Technology, Wake Forest University, and at other universities we have visited for almost two decades. During this time period, we conducted many research studies, published in major finance and statistics journals, concerning the operation of international financial markets. As one might imagine, in doing this we put together an extensive set of teaching materials which we used successfully in the classroom. As the years went by, we individually relied more on our own teaching materials and notes and less on any one of the major existing textbooks in international finance (most of which we tried at some point).

As you may be aware, the scope and content of international finance have been fast evolving due to deregulation of financial markets, product innovations, and technological advancements. As capital markets of the world are becoming more integrated, a solid understanding of international finance has become essential for astute corporate decision making. Reflecting the growing importance of international finance as a discipline, we have seen a sharp increase in the demand for experts in the area in both the corporate and academic worlds.

In writing *International Financial Management,* Second Edition, our goal was to provide well-organized, comprehensive, and up-to-date coverage of the topics that take advantage of our many years of teaching and research in this area. We hope the text is challenging to students. This does not mean that it lacks readability. The text discussion is written so that a self-contained treatment of each subject is presented in a *user-friendly* fashion. The text is intended for use at both the advanced undergraduate and M.B.A. levels.

THE UNDERLYING PHILOSOPHY

International Financial Management, Second Edition, like the First Edition, was written based on two tenets: emphasis on the basics, and emphasis on a managerial perspective.

Emphasis on the Basics

We believe that any subject is better learned if one first is well grounded in the basics. Consequently, we initially devote several chapters to the fundamental concepts of international finance. After these are learned, the remaining material flows easily from them. We always bring the reader back, as the more advanced topics are developed, to their relationship to the fundamentals. By doing this, we believe students will be left with a framework for analysis that will serve them well when they need to apply this material in their careers in the years ahead.

A Managerial Perspective

The text presentation never loses sight that it is teaching students how to make managerial decisions. *International Financial Management*, Second Edition, is founded in the belief that the fundamental job of the financial manager is to maximize shareholder wealth. This belief permeates the decision-making process we present from cover to cover. To reinforce the managerial perspective, we provide numerous "real world" stories whenever appropriate.

PEDAGOGICAL FEATURES

Each chapter is organized into a common format to facilitate student reading and understanding of the material.

- At the beginning of each chapter, a **Chapter Outline** and **statement of purpose** are presented, which detail the objectives of the chapter.
- **Examples** are integrated throughout the text, providing students with immediate application of the text concepts.
- Within each chapter, extensive use is made of **graphs** to provide visual illustration of important concepts, which are followed by **numerical examples.**
- Selected chapters contain **International Finance in Practice** boxes. These real-world illustrations offer students a practical look at the major concepts presented in the chapter.
- One of the most interesting aspects of studying international finance is learning new terminology. All key terms are presented in **boldfaced type** when they are first introduced, and they are defined thoroughly in the chapter. A list of **Key Words** is presented at the end of the chapter with convenient page references.
- Some topics are by nature more complex than others. The chapter sections that contain such material are indicated by the section heading, **Supplementary Material.** These sections may be skipped without loss of continuity, enabling the instructor to easily tailor the reading assignments to the student.
- A short **Summary** concludes each chapter, providing students with a handy overview of key concepts for review.

- A set of **end-of-chapter Questions and Problems** is provided for each chapter. This material can be used by students on their own to test their understanding of the material, or as homework exercises assigned by the instructor. Questions and Problems relating to the Supplemental Material sections of the text are indicated by a supplementary icon.
- Most chapters include a **Mini Case** for student analysis of multiple concepts covered throughout the chapter. These Mini Case problems are "real world" in nature to show students how the theory and concepts in the textbook relate to the everyday world.
- At the end of each chapter a list of selected **References and Suggested Readings** is presented, allowing the student to easily locate references which provide additional information about specific topics.
- A listing of **web resources** is provided in each chapter, as well as on the Website, so students have easy and direct access to related material on the Internet.

ANCILLARY MATERIALS

The ancillary package to has been enhanced to include an **Instructor's Manual/Test Bank, Powerpoint,** and **software** available on the website to users of *International Financial Management,* Second Edition.

Instructor's Manual/Test Bank, ISBN 0072318279, contains detailed suggested answers or solutions to each question and problem; an assortment of multiple choice questions relating to each chapter for testing purposes; as well as a Software User's Manual.

Powerpoint, ISBN 0072397160. A complete set of *Powerpoint* slides has been prepared for a complete visual presentation

Software. This is available which contains Excel files, including three basic programs, for use in illustrating some of the major concepts presented in the text.

The website (www.mhhe.com/er2c) provides an overview of what the book offers, as well as downloadable supplements and related weblinks.

The three programs are as follows:

- A currency options pricing program allows students to price put and call options on foreign exchange,
- A hedging program allows the student to compare forward, money market, futures and options hedges for hedging exchange rate risk,
- A portfolio optimization program based on the Markowitz model allows for examining the benefits of international portfolio diversification.

The three programs can be used to solve certain end-of-chapter problems or assignments the instructor devises. The selected end-of-chapter problems feature a **web icon,** visually noting to students when they can use the Web software to analyze and solve selected problem material. The software is user-friendly; nevertheless a **Software User's Manual** is provided as part of the Instructor's Manual, as well as sample assignments that can be solved using the software programs.

ACKNOWLEDGMENTS

We are indebted to the many colleagues who provided insight and guidance throughout the development process. Their careful work enabled us to create a text that is current, accurate and modern in its approach. Among all who helped in this endeavor:

Victor Abraham
The Fashion Institute of Design and Merchandising

Gurdip Bakshi
University of Maryland

Robert Duvic
University of Texas, Austin

Ali Emami
University of Oregon

Hsing Fang
California State University, Los Angeles

Christine Jiang
San Francisco State University

Suk Hun Lee
Loyola University, Chicago

Atul Saxena
Mercer College

Tulin Sener
SUNY-New Paltz

Chris Stivers
University of Georgia

David Vanderlinden
University of Southern Maine

Wim Westerman
University of Groningen, The Netherlands

Many people assisted in the production of this textbook. At the risk of overlooking some individuals, we would like to acknowledge Arie Adler, Vice President of Foreign Exchange at UBS in New York, and Robert LeBien, former Senior Vice President and Managing Director of Global Trading at Security Pacific National Bank, for their feedback while writing Chapter 4 on foreign exchange trading practices. Dale R. Follmer, Manager of Accounting Operations at Eli Lilly and Company, kindly wrote the *International Finance in Practice* reading in Chapter 10. Kristen Seaver, Milind Shrikhande, Jin-Gil Jeong, Sanjiv Sabherwal, and Victor Huang provided useful inputs into the text. Professor Martin Glaum of the Giessen University (Germany) also provided valuable comments.

We also wish to thank the many professionals at Irwin/McGraw-Hill for their time and patience with us. Sarah Pearson has done a marvelous job as development editor, as has Laura Griffin as project manager.

Last, but not least, we would like to thank our families, Christine, James, and Elizabeth Eun and Donna Resnick, for their tireless love and support without which this book would not have become a reality.

We hope that you enjoy using *International Financial Management,* Second Edition. In addition, we welcome your comments for improvement. Please let us know either through Irwin/McGraw-Hill, c/o Editorial, or at our e-mail addresses provided below.

Cheol S. Eun
cheol.eun@mgt.gatech.edu

Bruce G. Resnick
bruce.resnick@mba.wfu.edu

PART ONE

1 Globalization and the Multinational Firm

2 International Monetary System

3 Balance of Payments

4 The Market for Foreign Exchange

5 International Parity Relationships and Forecasting Foreign Exchange Rates

Foundations of International Financial Management

Part one lays the macroeconomic foundation for all the topics to follow. A thorough understanding of this material is essential for understanding the advanced topics covered in the remaining sections.

Chapter 1 provides an introduction to *International Financial Management*. The chapter discusses why it is important to study international finance and distinguishes international finance from domestic finance.

Chapter 2 introduces the various types of international monetary systems under which the world economy can function and has functioned at various times. The chapter traces the historical development of the world's international monetary systems from the early 1800s to the present. Additionally, a detailed discussion of the European Monetary System of the European Union is presented.

Chapter 3 presents balance-of-payment concepts and accounting. The chapter shows that even a country must keep its "economic house in order" or else it will experience current account deficits that will undermine the value of its currency.

Chapter 4 provides an introduction to the organization and operation of the spot and forward foreign exchange market. This chapter describes institutional arrangements of the foreign exchange market and details of how foreign exchange is quoted and traded worldwide.

Chapter 5 presents the fundamental international parity relationships among exchange rates, interest rates, and inflation rates. An understanding of these parity relationships is essential for practicing financial management in a global setting.

CHAPTER ONE

Globalization and the Multinational Firm

CHAPTER OUTLINE

As the title *International Financial Management* indicates, in this book we are concerned with financial management in an international setting. Financial management is mainly concerned with how to *optimally* make various corporate financial decisions, such as those pertaining to investment, capital structure, dividend policy, and working capital management, with a view to achieving a set of given corporate objectives. In Anglo-American countries as well as in many advanced countries with well-developed capital markets, maximizing shareholder wealth is generally considered the most important corporate objective.

Why do we need to study "international" financial management? The answer to this question is straightforward: We are now living in a highly **globalized and integrated world economy**. American consumers, for example, routinely purchase oil imported from Saudi Arabia and Nigeria, TV sets and camcorders from Japan, automobiles from Germany, garments from China, shoes from Indonesia, pasta from Italy, and wine from France. Foreigners, in turn, purchase American-made aircraft, software, movies, jeans, wheat, and other products. Continued liberalization of international trade is certain to further internationalize consumption patterns around the world.

Like consumption, production of goods and services has become highly globalized. To a large extent, this has happened as a result of multinational corporations' (MNCs) relentless efforts to source inputs and locate production anywhere in the world where costs are lower and profits are higher. For example, IBM personal computers sold in the world market might have been assembled in Malaysia with Taiwanese-made monitors, Korean-made keyboards, U.S.-made chips, and preinstalled software packages that were jointly developed by U.S. and Indian engineers. It has often become difficult to clearly associate a product with a single country of origin.

Recently, financial markets have also become highly integrated. This development allows investors to diversify their investment portfolios internationally. In the words of a recent *Wall Street Journal* article, "Over the past decade, U.S. investors have poured buckets of money into overseas markets, in the form of international mutual funds. In April 1996, the total assets in these funds reached a whopping $148.14 billion, far beyond the measly $2.49 billion reported in 1985."[1] At the same time, Japanese investors are investing heavily in U.S. and other foreign financial markets in efforts to recycle their enormous trade surpluses. In addition, many major corporations of the world, such as IBM, Daimler-Benz (now, DaimlerChrysler), and Sony, have their shares cross-listed on foreign stock exchanges, thereby rendering their shares internationally tradable and gaining access to foreign capital as well. Consequently, Daimler-Benz's venture, say, in China can be financed partly by American investors who purchase Daimler-Benz shares traded on the New York Stock Exchange.

Undoubtedly, we are now living in a world where all the major economic functions—consumption, production, and investment—are highly globalized. It is thus essential for financial managers to fully understand vital international dimensions of financial management. This *global shift* is in marked contrast to 20 years ago, when the authors of this book were learning finance. At that time, most professors customarily (and safely, to some extent) ignored international aspects of finance. This attitude has become untenable since then.

WHAT'S SPECIAL ABOUT INTERNATIONAL FINANCE?

Although we may be convinced of the importance of studying international finance, we still have to ask ourselves, what's special about international finance? Put another way, how is international finance different from purely domestic finance (if such a thing exists)? Three major dimensions set international finance apart from domestic finance. They are:

1. Foreign exchange and political risks.
2. Market imperfections.
3. Expanded opportunity set.

As we will see, these major dimensions of international finance largely stem from the fact that sovereign nations have the right and power to issue currencies, formulate their own economic policies, impose taxes, and regulate movements of people, goods, and capital across their borders. Before we move on, let us briefly describe each of the key dimensions of international financial management.

Foreign Exchange and Political Risks

Suppose Mexico is a major export market for your company and the Mexican peso depreciates drastically against the U.S. dollar, as it did in December 1994. This means that your company's products can be priced out of the Mexican market, as the peso price of American imports will rise following the peso's fall. If such countries as Indonesia, Thailand, and Korea are major export markets, your company would have faced the same difficult situation in the wake of Asian currency crisis of 1997. The preceding examples suggest that when firms and individuals are engaged in cross-border transactions, they are potentially exposed to **foreign exchange risk** that they would not normally encounter in purely domestic transactions.

Currently, the exchange rates among such major currencies as the U.S. dollar, Japanese yen, British pound, and German mark fluctuate continuously in an unpredictable manner. This has been the case since the early 1970s, when fixed exchange rates were abandoned. As can be seen from Exhibit 1.1, exchange rate volatility has exploded since 1973. Exchange rate uncertainty will have a pervasive influence on all the major economic functions, that is, consumption, production, and investment.

EXHIBIT 1.1

Monthly Percentage Change in German Mark–U.S. Dollar Exchange Rate

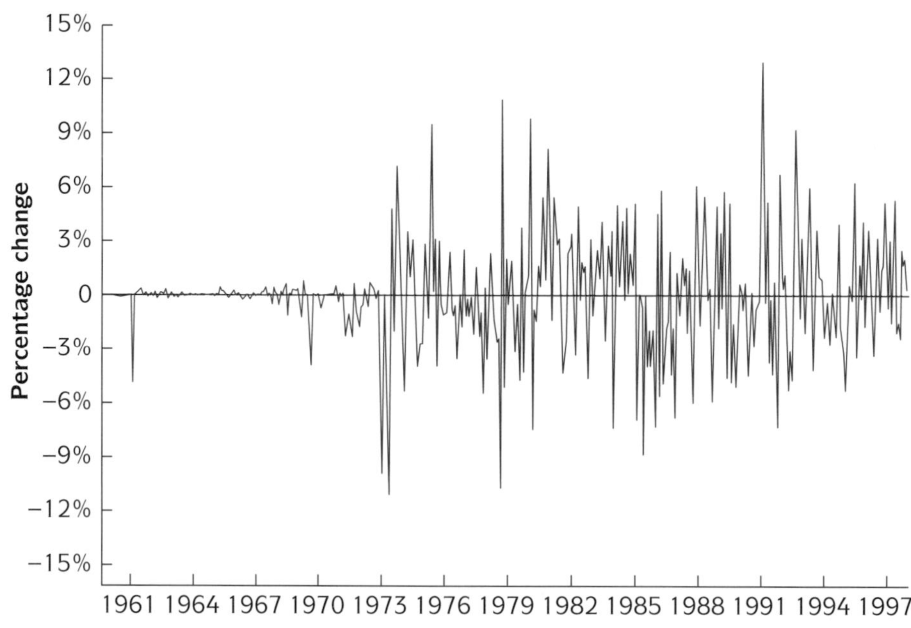

Source: International Monetary Fund, *International Financial Statistics* on CD-ROM, September 1999.

Another risk that firms and individuals may encounter in an international setting is political risk. **Political risk** ranges from unexpected changes in tax rules to outright expropriation of assets held by foreigners. Political risk arises from the fact that a sovereign country can change the "rules of the game" and the affected parties may not have effective recourse. In 1992, for example, the Enron Development Corporation, a subsidiary of a Houston-based energy company, signed a contract to build India's largest power plant. After Enron had spent nearly $300 million, the project was canceled in 1995 by nationalist politicians in the Maharashtra state who argued India didn't need the power plant. The Enron episode illustrates the difficulty of enforcing contracts in foreign countries.[2]

Market Imperfections

Although the world economy is much more integrated today than was the case 10 or 20 years ago, a variety of barriers still hamper free movements of people, goods, services, and capital across national boundaries. These barriers include legal restrictions, excessive transaction and transportation costs, and discriminatory taxation. The world markets are thus highly imperfect. As we will discuss later in this book, **market imperfections** play an important role in motivating MNCs to locate production overseas. Honda, a Japanese automobile company, for instance, decided to establish production facilities in Ohio, mainly to circumvent trade barriers. One might even say that MNCs are a gift of market imperfections.

Imperfections in the world financial markets tend to restrict the extent to which investors can diversify their portfolios. An interesting example is provided by the Nestlé Corporation, a well-known Swiss MNC. Nestlé used to issue two different classes of common stock, bearer shares and registered shares, and foreigners were only allowed to hold bearer shares. As Exhibit 1.2 shows, bearer shares used to trade for about twice the price of registered shares, which were exclusively reserved for Swiss residents.[3] This kind of price disparity is a uniquely international phenomenon that is attributable to market imperfections.

EXHIBIT 1.2 Daily Prices of Nestlé's Bearer and Registered Shares

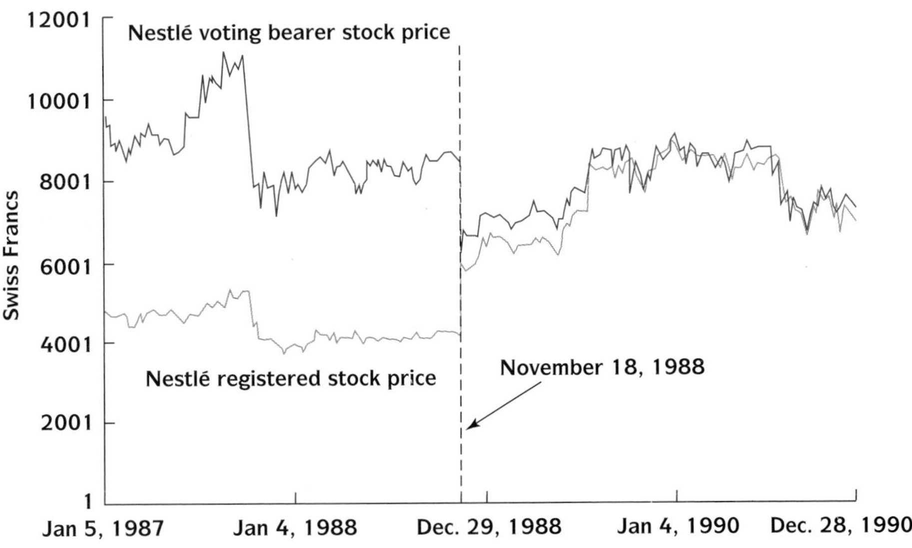

Source: Reprinted from *Journal of Financial Economics,* Volume 37, Issue 3, Claudio Loderer and Andreas Jacobs, "The Nestlé Crash," pp. 315–339, 1995, with kind permission from Elsevier Science S.A., P.O. Box 564, 1001 Lausanne, Switzerland.

On November 18, 1988, however, Nestlé lifted restrictions imposed on foreigners, allowing them to hold registered as well as bearer shares. After this announcement, the price spread between the two types of Nestlé shares narrowed drastically. As Exhibit 1.2 shows, the price of bearer shares declined sharply, whereas that of registered shares rose sharply. This implies that there was a major transfer of wealth from foreign shareholders to domestic shareholders. Foreigners holding Nestlé bearer shares were exposed to political risk in a country that is widely viewed as a haven from such risk. The Nestlé episode illustrates both the importance of considering market imperfections in international finance and the peril of political risk.

Expanded Opportunity Set

When firms venture into the arena of global markets, they can benefit from an **expanded opportunity set**. As previously mentioned, firms can locate production in any country or region of the world to maximize their performance and raise funds in any capital market where the cost of capital is the lowest. In addition, firms can gain from greater economies of scale when their tangible and intangible assets are deployed on a global basis. A real-world example showing the gains from a global approach to financial management is provided by the following excerpt from *The Wall Street Journal* (April 9, 1996):

> Another factor binding bond markets ever closer is large companies' flexibility to issue bonds around the world at will, thanks to the global swap market. At the vanguard are companies such as General Electric of the U.S. Mark VanderGriend, who runs the financing desk at Banque Paribas, says it took "about 15 minutes" to put together a four billion franc ($791.6 million) deal for GE. By raising the money in francs and swapping into dollars instantly, GE will save five hundredths of a percentage point—or about $400,000 annually on the nine-year deal. "They have such a huge requirement for capital that they are constantly looking for arbitrages," adds Mr. VanderGriend. "And they don't care much how they get there."

Individual investors can also benefit greatly if they invest internationally rather than domestically. Suppose you have a given amount of money to invest in stocks. You may invest the entire amount in U.S. (domestic) stocks. Alternatively, you may allocate the funds across domestic and foreign stocks. If you diversify internationally, the resulting international portfolio may have a lower risk or a higher return (or both) than a purely domestic portfolio. This can happen mainly because stock returns tend to covary much less across countries than within a given country. Once you are aware of overseas investment opportunities and are willing to diversify internationally, you face a much expanded opportunity set and you can benefit from it. It just doesn't make sense to play in only one corner of the sandbox.

GOALS FOR INTERNATIONAL FINANCIAL MANAGEMENT

The foregoing discussion implies that understanding and managing foreign exchange and political risks and coping with market imperfections have become important parts of the financial manager's job. *International Financial Management* is designed to provide today's financial managers with an understanding of the fundamental concepts and the tools necessary to be effective global managers. Throughout, the text emphasizes how to deal with exchange risk and market imperfections, using the various instruments and tools that are available, while at the same time maximizing the benefits from an expanded global opportunity set.

Effective financial management, however, is more than the application of the newest business techniques or operating more efficiently. There must be an underlying goal. *International Financial Management* is written from the perspective that the fundamental goal of sound financial management is shareholder wealth maximization. **Shareholder wealth maximization** means that the firm makes all business decisions and investments with an eye toward making the owners of the firm—the shareholders—better off financially, or more wealthy, than they were before.

Whereas shareholder wealth maximization is generally accepted as the ultimate goal of financial management in "Anglo-Saxon" countries, such as Australia, Canada, the United Kingdom, and especially the United States, it is not as widely embraced a goal in other parts of the world. In countries like France and Germany, for example, shareholders are generally viewed as one of the "stakeholders" of the firm, others being employees, customers, suppliers, banks, and so forth. European managers tend to consider the promotion of the firm's stakeholders' overall welfare as the most important corporate goal. In Japan, on the other hand, many companies form a small number of interlocking business groups called *keiretsu,* such as Mitsubishi, Mitsui, and Sumitomo, which arose from consolidation of family-owned business empires. Japanese managers tend to regard the prosperity and growth of their *keiretsu* as the critical goal; for instance, they tend to strive to maximize market share, rather than shareholder wealth.

It is pointed out, however, that as capital markets are becoming more liberalized and internationally integrated in recent years, even managers in France, Germany, Japan and other non-Anglo-Saxon countries are beginning to pay serious attention to shareholder wealth maximization. In Germany, for example, companies are now allowed to repurchase stocks, if necessary, for the benefit of shareholders. In accepting an unprecedented $183 billion takeover offer by Vodafone AirTouch, a leading British wireless phone company, Klaus Esser, CEO of Mannesmann of Germany cited shareholder interests: "The shareholders clearly think that this company, Mannesmann, a great company, would be better together with Vodafone AirTouch. . . . The final decision belongs to shareholders."[4]

Obviously, the firm could pursue other goals. This does not mean, however, that the goal of shareholder wealth maximization is merely an alternative, or that the firm should enter into a debate as to its appropriate fundamental goal. Quite the contrary. If the firm seeks to maximize shareholder wealth, it will most likely simultaneously be accomplishing other legitimate goals that are perceived as worthwhile. Shareholder wealth maximization is a long-run goal. A firm cannot stay in business to maximize shareholder wealth if it treats employees poorly, produces shoddy merchandise, wastes raw materials and natural resources, operates inefficiently, or fails to satisfy customers. Only a well-managed business firm that profitably produces what is demanded in an efficient manner can expect to stay in business in the long run and thereby provide employment opportunities.

Shareholders are the owners of the business; it is their capital that is at risk. It is only equitable that they receive a fair return on their investment. Private capital may not have been forthcoming for the business firm if it had intended to accomplish any other objective. As we will discuss shortly, the massive privatization that is currently taking place in developing and formerly socialist countries, which will eventually enhance the standard of living of these countries' citizens, depends on private investment. In what follows, we are going to discuss in detail: (1) the globalization of the world economy, (2) the growing role of MNCs in the world economy, and (3) the organization of the text.

GLOBALIZATION OF THE WORLD ECONOMY: RECENT TRENDS

The term "globalization" became a popular buzzword for describing business practices in the last few decades, and it appears as if it will continue to be a key word for describing business management throughout the new century. In this section, we review a few key trends of the world economy: (i) the emergence of globalized financial markets, (ii) continued trade liberalization and economic integration, and (iii) large-scale privatization of state-owned enterprises.

Emergence of Globalized Financial Markets

The 1980s and 90s saw a rapid integration of international capital and financial markets. The impetus for globalized financial markets initially came from the governments of major countries that had begun to deregulate their foreign exchange and capital markets. For example, in 1980 Japan deregulated its foreign exchange market, and in 1985 the Tokyo Stock Exchange admitted as members a limited number of foreign brokerage firms. Additionally, the London Stock Exchange (LSE) began admitting foreign firms as full members in February 1986.

Perhaps the most celebrated deregulation, however, occurred in London on October 27, 1986, and is known as the "Big Bang." On that date, as on "May Day" in 1975 in the United States, the London Stock Exchange eliminated fixed brokerage commissions. Additionally, the regulation separating the order-taking function from the market-making function was eliminated. In Europe, financial institutions are allowed to perform both investment-banking and commercial-banking functions. Hence, the London affiliates of foreign commercial banks were eligible for membership on the LSE. These changes were designed to give London the most open and competitive capital markets in the world. It has worked, and today the competition in London is especially fierce among the world's major financial centers. The United States recently repealed the Glass-Steagall Act, which restricted commercial banks from investment banking activities (such as underwriting corporate securities), further promoting competition among financial institutions. Even developing countries such as Chile, Mexico, and Korea began to liberalize by allowing foreigners to directly invest in their financial markets.

Deregulated financial markets and heightened competition in financial services provided a natural environment for financial innovations that resulted in the introduction of various instruments. Examples of these innovative instruments include currency futures and options, multicurrency bonds, international mutual funds, country funds, and foreign stock index futures and options. Corporations also played an active role in integrating the world financial markets by listing their shares across borders. Such well-known non-U.S. companies as Seagram, Sony, Toyota Motor, Fiat, Telefonos de Mexico, KLM, British Petroleum, Glaxo, and Daimler are directly listed and traded on the New York Stock Exchange. At the same time, U.S. firms such as IBM and GM are listed on the Brussels, Frankfurt, London, and Paris stock exchanges. Such cross-border listings of stocks allow investors to buy and sell foreign shares as if they were domestic shares, facilitating international investments.

Last but not least, advances in computer and telecommunications technology contributed in no small measure to the emergence of global financial markets. These technological advancements, especially Internet-based information technologies, gave investors around the world immediate access to the most recent news and information affecting their investments, sharply reducing information costs. Also, computerized order-processing and settlement procedures have reduced the costs of international transactions. Based on the U.S. Department of Commerce computer price deflator, the relative cost index of computing power declined from a level of 100 in 1960 to 15.6 in 1970, 2.9 in 1980, and only 0.5 in 1999. As a result of these technological developments and the liberalization of financial markets, cross-border financial transactions have exploded in recent years.

Trade Liberalization and Economic Integration

International trade, which has been the traditional link between national economies, continued to expand. As Exhibit 1.3 shows, the ratio of merchandise exports to GDP for the world has increased from 7.0 percent in 1950 to 13.6 percent in 1998. This implies that, over the same time period, international trade increased about twice as fast as world GDP. For some countries, international trade grew much faster; for Germany, the ratio rose from 6.2 percent to 25.2 percent, while for Taiwan it grew from 2.5 percent to 34.4 percent over the same time period. Latin American countries such as Argentina, Brazil, and Mexico have relatively low export-to-GDP ratios. This reflects the inward-looking, protectionist economic policies these countries pursued in the past. Even these once-protectionist countries are now increasingly pursuing free-market and open-economy policies because of the gains from international trade.

The principal argument for international trade is based on the **theory of comparative advantage,** which was advanced by David Ricardo in his seminal book,

EXHIBIT 1.3

Long-Term Openness in Perspective (Merchandise Exports/GDP at 1990 Prices, in Percent)

Country	1870	1913	1929	1950	1973	1998
United States	2.5	3.7	3.6	3.0	5.0	7.9
Canada	12.0	12.2	15.8	13.0	19.9	24.3
Australia	7.4	12.8	11.2	9.1	11.2	15.4
United Kingdom	12.0	17.7	13.3	11.4	14.0	19.4
Germany	9.5	15.6	12.8	6.2	23.8	25.2
France	4.9	8.2	8.6	7.7	15.4	21.0
Spain	3.8	8.1	5.0	1.6	5.0	19.3
Japan	0.2	2.4	3.5	2.3	7.9	10.1
Korea	0.0	1.0	4.5	1.0	8.2	29.4
Taiwan	0.0	2.5	5.2	2.5	10.2	34.4
Thailand	2.1	6.7	6.6	7.0	4.5	48.8
Argentina	9.4	6.8	6.1	2.4	2.1	8.4
Brazil	11.8	9.5	7.1	4.0	2.6	5.7
Mexico	3.7	10.8	14.8	3.5	2.2	13.7
World	5.0	8.7	9.0	7.0	11.2	13.6

Source: Various issues of *World Financial Markets,* JP Morgan, and *International Financial Statistics,* IMF.

Principles of Political Economy (1817). According to Ricardo, it is mutually beneficial for countries if they specialize in the production of those goods they can produce most efficiently and trade those goods among them. Suppose England produces textiles most efficiently, whereas France produces wine most efficiently. It then makes sense if England specializes in the production of textiles and France in the production of wine, and the two countries then trade their products. By doing so, the two countries can increase their combined production of textiles and wine, which, in turn, allows both countries to consume more of both goods. This argument remains valid even if one country can produce both goods more efficiently than the other country.[5] Ricardo's theory has a clear policy implication: *Liberalization of international trade will enhance the welfare of the world's citizens.* In other words, international trade is not a "zero-sum" game in which one country benefits at the expense of another country—the view held by the "mercantilists." Rather, international trade could be an "increasing-sum" game at which all players become winners.

Although the theory of comparative advantage is not completely immune to valid criticism, it nevertheless provides a powerful intellectual rationale for promoting free trade among nations. Currently, international trade is becoming further liberalized at both the global and regional levels. At the global level, the **General Agreement on Tariffs and Trade (GATT)**, which is a multilateral agreement among member countries, has played a key role in dismantling barriers to international trade. Since it was founded in 1947, GATT has been successful in gradually eliminating and reducing tariffs, subsidies, quotas, and other barriers to trade. The latest round of talks, the Uruguay Round launched in 1986, aims to (1) reduce the import tariffs worldwide by an average of 38 percent, (2) increase the proportion of duty-free products from 20 percent to 44 percent for industrialized countries, and (3) extend the rules of world trade to cover agriculture, services such as banking and insurance, and intellectual property rights. It also created a permanent **World Trade Organization (WTO)** to replace GATT. The WTO will have more power to enforce the rules of international trade. China recently opened negotiations to join WTO. China's WTO membership would further legitimize the idea of free trade.

On the regional level, formal arrangements among countries have been instituted to promote economic integration. The **European Union (EU)** is a prime example. The European Union is the direct descendent of the European Community (formerly the European Economic Community), which was established to foster economic integration among the countries of Western Europe. Today the EU includes 15 member states that have eliminated barriers to the free flow of goods, capital, and people. The member states of the EU hope this move will strengthen its economic position relative to the United States and Japan. In January 1999, 11 member countries of EU successfully adopted a single common currency, the euro, which may rival the U.S. dollar as a dominant currency for international trade and investment. The launch of the euro has spurred a rush by European companies into seeking pan-European and global alliances. Merger and acquisition (M&A) deals in Europe totaled $1.2 trillion in 1999, exceeding the figure for U.S. deals for the first time. The EU may expand in the near future to include such formerly socialist countries as Poland, Hungary, and the Czech Republic.

Whereas the economic and monetary union planned by the EU is one of the most advanced forms of economic integration, a free trade area is the most basic. In 1994, Canada, the United States, and Mexico entered into the **North American Free Trade Agreement (NAFTA)**. Canada is the United States' largest trading partner and Mexico is the third largest. In a free trade area, all impediments to trade, such as tariffs and import quotas, are eliminated among members. The terms of NAFTA call for phasing out tariffs over a 15-year period. Many observers believe that NAFTA will foster increased trade among its members, resulting in an increase in the number of jobs and the standard of living in all member countries.

INTERNATIONAL FINANCE IN PRACTICE

What Is Privatization, Anyway?

It's sweeping the world, changing the face of both the government and private sector. But what exactly is privatization, anyway? Why do countries do it? How does it work?

Here are some of the most-common questions—and answers.

What is privatization?

In the broadest sense, privatization means relying less on government to meet people's needs for goods and services, and more on private institutions such as the marketplace, the family, and voluntary organizations.

How do you do it?

Privatization takes many forms. The kind that tends to get the most attention is perhaps best described as "denationalization"—that is, when a government divests itself of a company it owns.

But there are plenty of other ways. A government might choose to delegate some functions by contracting them out to a private company; for instance, many U.S. cities pay private firms to handle municipal garbage-collecting duties. Another common way to privatize is by providing subsidies to individuals to help them purchase goods or services from the private sector. The U.S. food-stamp program is a case in point: Politicians have decided that allowing poor families to starve isn't in the national interest, but it isn't feasible to establish a vast network of state-owned farms and soup kitchens to feed them. So the government simply hands out coupons that can be used to buy food from private supermarkets.

A subtle, though pervasive, form might be termed "privatization by default." This occurs when a country's private sector grows faster than its public sector, gradually tilting the economy away from state ownership. Even though China's rulers haven't renounced communism or embarked on a massive privatization campaign, they've tolerated a certain amount of free enterprise in many areas of the economy. Because these private businesses tend to be much more vital than the bureaucratic state enterprises, they now produce more goods, employ more workers, and trade more abroad than the stagnant state sector.

Global Trends

World-wide sales of state-owned enterprises

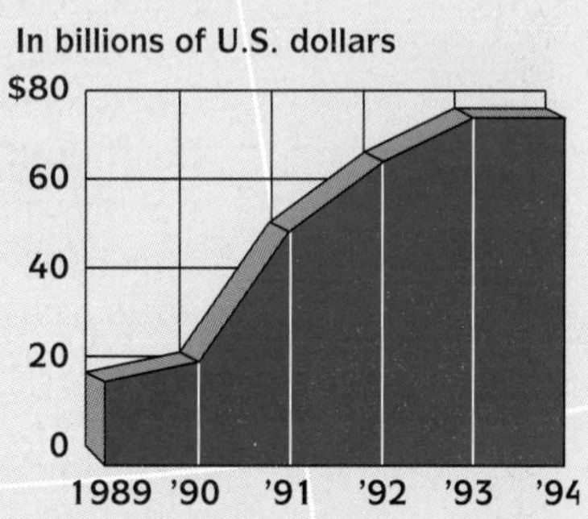

Privatization by industry, 1994

Industry	Volume ($ Millions)	% of Total
Telecommunications	$13,975.6	17.4%
Power Utilities	11,573.7	14.4
Energy	10,611.2	13.2
Tobacco	7,775.7	9.7
Insurance	7,482.1	9.3
Banking	4,465.6	5.6
Vehicles	2,094.7	2.6
Steel	1,899.1	2.4
Mining	1,661.5	2.1
Coal	1,497.4	1.9

Privatization

The economic integration and globalization that began in the 1980s is picking up speed in the 1990s via privatization. Through **privatization**, a country divests itself of the ownership and operation of a business venture by turning it over to the free market system. Privatization did not begin with the fall of the Berlin Wall; nevertheless, its pace has quickly accelerated since the collapse of communism in the Eastern Bloc countries. It is ironic that the very political and economic system that only a short while ago extolled the virtues of state ownership should so dramatically be shifting toward capitalism by shedding state-operated businesses. President Calvin

Privatization volume by region, 1994

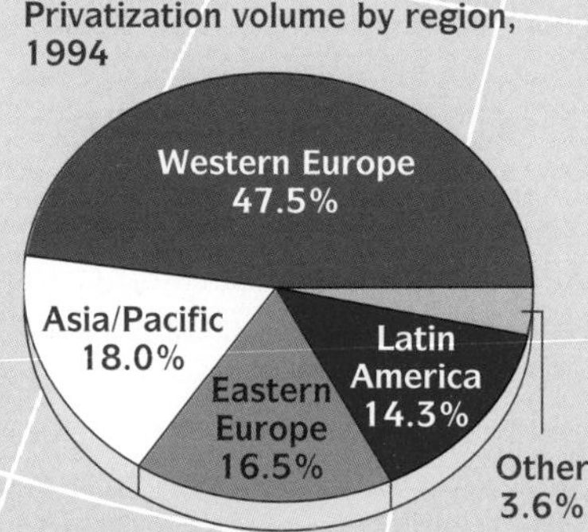

Is this a new idea?

Not exactly. Governments have been privatizing their activities in one form or another for centuries. Back in 1492, Queen Isabella and King Ferdinand of Spain hired a private contractor to seek an alternative route to India—though nobody called it privatization.

How is denationalization accomplished?

It depends on the individual country and company. Former members of the Soviet Bloc, in order to leap from socialism to capitalism as quickly as possible, typically have simply given away big chunks of state enterprises to citizens, in what is known as "mass privatization."

A common technique is to issue vouchers to the general public that can be exchanged directly for shares in a privatizing company. Often, the citizens elect to sell their shares to investment companies, which then exercise great control over the company. In other cases, the state turns over ownership directly to the workers and managers of a factory or store.

In capitalist countries privatizations tend to occur either through auctions or broad public stock offerings. Some countries, in a twist on the mass privatization concept, have also endeavored to put stock in the hands not only of wealthy investors, but also of lower-income people. Chile came up with an unusual, and highly praised, plan to allow workers to convert their vested pension interest into shares of privatized companies.

Why privatize?

Government planners try to achieve a number of goals through privatization, some of them contradictory. An oft-stated aim is to wring more efficiency out of the enterprises being privatized, and thus to make the economy in general more productive. Governments also use privatizations to raise money. Unfortunately, since buyers are willing to pay more for a monopoly, sometimes the goal of raising money gets in the way of making the economy more efficient. Another aim of privatizing, particularly in developing nations, is to invigorate and expand the local capital markets and to attract foreign capital.

Does it work?

Most available evidence shows that privatization increases a company's efficiency. The World Bank's International Finance Corp. affiliate reports that 67% of the companies it has helped privatize now report "good" profitability, up from 29% when they were still state-owned.

What's the downside?

Initially, privatization can lead to widespread layoffs of workers, as the new owners clean house to increase profits. However, proponents argue that an effective privatization program can provide more jobs over the long term because of its positive impact on the overall economy.

How much privatization has taken place so far?

Not counting voucher sales or smaller deals, roughly 2,700 state-owned enterprises were transferred to private hands in over 95 countries from 1988 to 1993, raising some $271 billion in revenue, according to the IFC.

Numbers are harder to come up with in the former Soviet Bloc. But the IFC figures 75,000 small-scale businesses have been auctioned in Russia since 1992, and 14,000 midsize and large firms have been sold. Tens of thousands of companies, likewise, have been privatized in Eastern Europe.

What are the most-active and least-active regions for privatization?

Latin America and the Caribbean accounted for 57% of the value of nonvoucher privatizations in the world during the 1988-93 period, the IFC reports. By contrast, very little privatizing has occurred in Africa and the Middle East.

Source: Michael Allen, "What Is Privatization, Anyway?," *The Wall Street Journal*, October 2, 1995, p. R4. Reprinted by permission of *The Wall Street Journal*, ©1995 Dow Jones & Company, Inc. All Rights Reserved Worldwide.

Coolidge once said that the business of America is business. One might now say that business is the business of the world.[6]

Privatization can be viewed in many ways. In one sense it is a denationalization process. When a national government divests itself of a state-run business, it gives up part of its national identity. Moreover, if the new owners are foreign, the country may simultaneously be importing a cultural influence that did not previously exist. Privatization is frequently viewed as a means to an end. One benefit of privatization for many less-developed countries is that the sale of state-owned businesses brings to the national treasury hard-currency foreign reserves. The sale proceeds are often used to pay down sovereign debt that has weighed heavily on the economy. Additionally, privatization is often seen as a cure for bureaucratic inefficiency and waste; some economists estimate that privatization improves efficiency and reduces operating costs by as much as 20 percent. The International Finance in Practice box on pages 12–13 further describes the privatization process.

There is no one single way to privatize state-owned operations. The objectives of the country seem to be the prevailing guide. For the Czech Republic, speed was the overriding factor. To accomplish privatization en masse, the Czech government essentially gave away its businesses to the Czech people. For a nominal fee, vouchers were sold that allowed Czech citizens to bid on businesses as they went on the auction block. From 1991 to 1995, more than 1,700 companies were turned over to private hands. Moreover, three-quarters of the Czech citizens became stockholders in these newly privatized firms.

In Russia, there has been an "irreversible" shift to private ownership, according to the World Bank. More than 80 percent of the country's nonfarm workers are now employed in the private sector. Eleven million apartment units have been privatized, as have half of the country's 240,000 other business firms. Additionally, via a Czech-style voucher system, 40 million Russians now own stock in over 15,000 medium- to large-size corporations that recently became privatized through mass auctions of state-owned enterprises.

For some countries, privatization has meant globalization. For example, to achieve fiscal stability, New Zealand had to open its once-socialist economy to foreign capital. Australian investors now control its commercial banks, and U.S. firms purchased the national telephone company and timber operations. While workers' rights have changed under foreign ownership and a capitalist economy, New Zealand now ranks high among the most competitive market environments. Fiscal stability has also been realized. In 1994, New Zealand's economy grew at a rate of 6 percent and inflation was under control. As can be seen from the experiences of New Zealand, privatization has spurred a tremendous increase in cross-border investment. The Bank for International Settlements reports that foreign direct investment has soared to $240 billion in 1994 from an annual level of $100 billion in the early 1990s and only $10 billion a decade earlier.

MULTINATIONAL CORPORATIONS

In addition to international trade, foreign direct investment by MNCs is a major force driving globalization of the world economy. According to a UN report, there are about 60,000 MNCs in the world with over 500,000 foreign affiliates.[7] Throughout the 1990s, foreign direct investment by MNCs grew at the annual rate of about 10 percent. In comparison, international trade grew at the rate of 3.5 percent during the same period. MNCs' worldwide sales reached $11 trillion in 1998, compared to about $7 trillion of world exports in the same year.[8] As indicated in the International Finance in Practice box on page 16, MNCs are reshaping the structure of the world economy.

A **multinational corporation** (**MNC**) is a business firm incorporated in one country that has production and sales operations in several other countries. The term suggests a firm obtaining raw materials from one national market and financial capital from another, producing goods with labor and capital equipment in a third country, and selling the finished product in yet other national markets. Indeed, some MNCs have operations in dozens of different countries. MNCs obtain financing from major money centers around the world in many different currencies to finance their operations. Global operations force the treasurer's office to establish international banking relationships, place short-term funds in several currency denominations, and effectively manage foreign exchange risk.

Exhibit 1.4 lists the top 40 of the largest 100 MNCs ranked by the size of foreign assets. The list was compiled by the United Nations Conference on Trade and Development (UNCTAD). Many of the firms on the list are well-known MNCs with household names because of their presence in consumer product markets. For example, General Motors, Royal/Dutch Shell, Toyota, Daimler-Benz, IBM, Philip Morris, British Petroleum, Unilever, Nestlé, Sony, and Siemens are names recognized by most people. By country of origin, U.S. MNCs, with 27 out of the total of 100,

EXHIBIT 1.4 The World's Top 40 MNCs Ranked by Foreign Assets, 1997 (Billions of Dollars)

Ranking by Foreign Assets	Corporation	Country	Assets		Sales	
			Foreign	Total	Foreign	Total
1	General Electric	United States	97.4	304.0	24.5	90.8
2	Ford Motor Company	United States	72.5	275.4	48.0	153.6
3	Royal Dutch/Shell Group	Netherlands/United Kingdom	70.0	115.0	69.0	128.0
4	General Motors	United States	0.0	228.9	51.0	178.2
5	Exxon Corporation	United States	54.6	96.1	104.8	120.3
6	Toyota	Japan	41.8	105.0	50.4	88.5
7	IBM	United States	39.9	81.5	48.9	78.5
8	Volkswagen Group	Germany	...	57.0	42.7	65.0
9	Nestlé SA	Switzerland	31.6	37.7	47.6	48.3
10	Daimler-Benz AG	Germany	30.9	76.2	46.1	69.0
11	Mobil Corporation	United States	30.4	43.6	36.8	64.3
12	FIAT Spa	Italy	30.0	69.1	20.2	50.6
13	Hoechst AG	Germany	29.0	34.0	24.3	30.0
14	Asea Brown Boveri (ABB)	Switzerland	...	29.8	30.4	31.3
15	Bayer AG	Germany	...	30.3	...	32.0
16	Elf Aquitaine SA	France	26.7	42.0	25.6	42.3
17	Nissan Motor Co., Ltd.	Japan	26.5	57.6	27.8	49.7
18	Unilever	Netherlands/United Kingdom	25.6	30.8	44.8	46.4
19	Siemens AG	Germany	25.6	67.1	40.0	60.6
20	Roche Holding AG	Switzerland	...	37.6	12.7	12.9
21	Sony Corporation	Japan	...	48.2	40.3	51.1
22	Mitsubishi Corporation	Japan	21.9	67.1	41.5	120.4
23	Seagram Company	Canada	21.8	22.2	9.4	9.7
24	Honda Motor Co., Ltd.	Japan	21.5	36.5	31.5	45.4
25	BMW AG	Germany	20.3	31.8	26.4	35.9
26	Alcatel Alsthom Cie	France	20.3	41.9	25.9	31.0
27	Philips Electronics N.V.	Netherlands	20.1	25.5	33.0	33.5
28	News Corporation	Australia	20.0	30.7	9.5	10.7
29	Philip Morris	United States	19.4	55.9	32.1	56.1
30	British Petroleum (BP)	United Kingdom	19.2	32.6	36.5	71.3
31	Hewlett-Packard	United States	18.5	31.7	23.8	42.9
32	Total SA	France	...	25.2	23.4	31.9
33	Renault SA	France	18.3	34.9	18.5	35.6
34	Cable and Wireless Plc	United Kingdom	...	21.6	7.8	11.5
35	Mitsui & Co., Ltd.	Japan	17.9	55.5	52.3	132.6
36	Rhone-Poulenc SA	France	17.8	27.5	11.5	15.0
37	Viag AG	Germany	17.4	32.7	15.9	27.6
38	BASF AG	Germany	...	26.8	23.9	32.2
39	Itochu Corporation	Japan	16.7	56.8	48.7	117.7
40	Nissho Iwai Corporation	Japan	16.6	40.4	32.3	75.5

Source: *World Investment Report* 1999, United Nations.

INTERNATIONAL FINANCE IN PRACTICE

Multinationals Spur Surge in Investment

The emergence of trans-national production networks is reshaping the relationship between foreign direct investment and international trade, says a report* by the United Nations Conference on Trade and Development.

It says the trend will enable economies which benefit from inward investment to grow faster and enhance their industrial competitiveness by specializing more intensively in the types of goods and services they produce. The report says the changes are reflected in surging investment inflows. These grew 40 percent last year to a record $315bn, fueled by mergers and acquisitions and investments in privatization.

Most of the world's 100 largest multinational companies said they planned to invest more abroad in the next five years. More businesses were also venturing abroad at an ever earlier stage.

The number of multinationals headquartered in highly industrialized economies has quadrupled since the late 1960s. There were now almost 40,000 multinationals worldwide, with 270,000 foreign affiliates. Their expansion was increasingly determined by advances in communications technology, making it easier to manage far-flung production networks, and by liberalization of countries' economic, trade and investment policies.

Companies no longer invested abroad just to overcome trade barriers or serve local markets. Increasingly, they decided on locations which enabled them to operate most efficiently on regional or global markets.

"In the international division of labor within firms, any part of the value-added chain can be located wherever it contributes most to a company's overall performance," the report says. "What matters are the factors that make particular locations advantageous for particular activities."

As companies' foreign subsidiaries became more specialized, they exported more to each other. More than 40 percent of total exports by the foreign affiliates of U.S. multinational companies were to each other, up from 30 percent in the late 1970s.

These developments created new opportunities for host countries to build on the comparative advantages which attracted foreign investment and to enhance their technological capacity.

The report says the advances in communications technology which are spurring the integration of manufacturing networks may reduce the need for foreign investment in many types of services, by making them easier to export worldwide.

Industrialized countries were the source of 85 percent of all investment outflows last year and absorbed 65 percent of inflows. More than a third of inflows into developing countries were accounted for by China, which attracted $37.5bn in foreign investment last year.

**Unctad World Investment Report 1996. UN sales sections in Geneva (Tel. 41 22 917 2613) and New York (Tel. 212-963 8302).*

Source: Guy de Jonquières, *Financial Times*, September 25, 1996.

FDI Inflows and Outflows: $bn

	Developed Countries		Developing Countries		Central/Eastern Europe		All Countries	
	Inflows	Outflows	Inflows	Outflows	Inflows	Outflows	Inflows	Outflows
1988–1992	139.1	193.3	36.8	15.2	1.36	0.04	177.3	208.5
1994	132.8	190.9	87.0	38.6	5.89	0.55	225.7	230.0

Source: UNCTAD

constitute the largest group. Japan ranks second with 17 MNCs in the top 100, followed by France with 13, Germany with 11, and the U.K. with 9. It is interesting to note that some Swiss firms are extremely multinational. Nestlé, for instance, derived 98.5 percent of its sales from overseas markets in 1997.

MNCs may gain from their global presence in a variety of ways. First of all, MNCs can benefit from the economy of scale by (1) spreading R and D expenditures and advertising costs over their global sales, (2) pooling global purchasing power over suppliers, (3) utilizing their technological and managerial know-how globally with minimum additional costs, and so forth. Furthermore, MNCs can use their global presence to take advantage of underpriced labor services available in certain developing countries, and gain access to special R and D capabilities residing in advanced foreign countries. MNCs can indeed leverage their global presence to boost their profit margins and create shareholder value.

ORGANIZATION OF THE TEXT

International Financial Management contains 20 chapters divided into four parts. Part One, Foundations of International Financial Management, contains five chapters on the fundamentals of international finance. This section lays the macroeconomic foundation for all the topics to follow. A thorough understanding of this material is essential for understanding the advanced topics covered in the remaining sections.

Chapter 2 introduces the student to the various types of international monetary systems under which the world economy can function and has functioned at various times. Extensive treatment is given to the differences between a fixed and a flexible exchange rate regime. The chapter traces the historical development of the world's international monetary systems from the early 1800s to the present. Additionally, a detailed discussion of the European Monetary System of the European Union is presented. Chapter 3 presents balance-of-payment concepts and accounting. The chapter is designed to show that even a national government must keep its "economic house in order" or else it will experience current account deficits that will undermine the value of its currency. This chapter also shows how the balance of payments reveals the sources of demand and supply of a country's currency. It concludes by surveying the balance-of-payments trends in major countries.

Chapter 4 provides an introduction to the organization and operation of the spot and forward foreign exchange market. It describes institutional arrangements of the foreign exchange markets and details of how foreign exchange is quoted and traded worldwide. Chapter 5, in turn, presents some of the fundamental international parity relationships among exchange rates, interest rates, and inflation rates. An understanding of these parity relationships, which are manifestations of market equilibrium, is essential for astute financial management in a global setting. Chapter 5 begins with the derivation of *interest rate parity,* showing the interrelationship between the interest rates of two countries and the spot and forward exchange rates between the same two countries. Similarly, the theory of *purchasing power parity (PPP)* is developed, showing the relationship between a change in exchange rate between two countries and the relative values of their inflation rates. The limitations of PPP are clearly detailed. The chapter concludes with a discussion of forecasting exchange rates using parity relationships and other fundamental and technical forecasting techniques.

The chapters in Part One lay the macroeconomic foundation for *International Financial Management.* Exhibit 1.5 provides a diagram that shows the text layout. The diagram shows that the discussion moves from a study of macroeconomic foundations to a study of the financial environment in which the firm and the financial manager must function. Financial strategy and decision making can be discussed intelligently only after one has an appreciation of the financial environment.

Part Two, World Financial Markets and Institutions, provides a thorough discussion of international financial institutions, financial assets, and marketplaces, and develops the tools necessary to manage exchange rate uncertainty. Chapter 6, International Banking and the Money Market, begins the section. The chapter differentiates between international and domestic bank operations and examines the institutional differences between various types of international banking offices. International banks and their clients make up the Eurocurrency market and form the

EXHIBIT 1.5 Overview of the Organization of International Financial Management

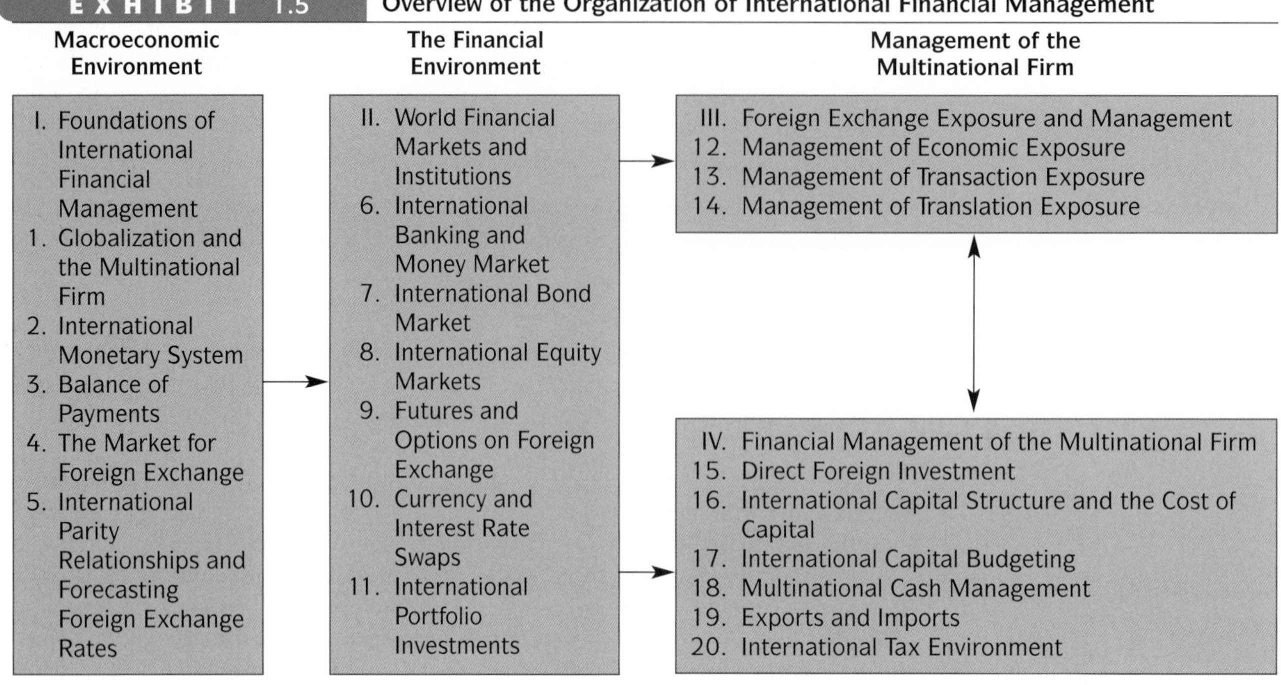

core of the international money market. The chapter includes a discussion of the features and characteristics of the major international money market instruments: forward rate agreements, Euronotes, Euro-medium-term notes, and Eurocommercial paper. The chapter concludes with an examination of the international debt crisis that severely jeopardized the economic viability of many of the world's largest banks during the past decade.

Chapter 7 distinguishes between foreign bonds and Eurobonds, which together make up the international bond market. It discusses the advantages to the issuer of sourcing funds from the international bond market as opposed to raising funds domestically. It describes both the underwriting procedure for issuing new Eurobonds as well as the procedure for trading existing international bonds in the secondary market. A discussion of the major types of international bonds is included in the chapter. The chapter concludes with a discussion of international bond ratings.

Chapter 8 covers international equity markets. There is not a separate international equity market that operates parallel to domestic equity markets. Instead, the equity shares of certain corporations have broad appeal to international investors rather than just investors from the country in which the corporation is incorporated. Chapter 8 documents the size of both developed and developing country equity markets. Various methods of trading equity shares in the secondary markets are discussed. Additionally, the chapter discusses the advantages to the firm of cross-listing equity shares in more than one country.

Chapter 9 provides an extensive treatment of exchange-traded currency futures and options contracts. The chapter covers the institutional details of trading these derivative securities and also develops basic valuation models for pricing them. We believe that derivative securities are best understood if one also understands what drives their value. How to use derivative securities is saved for Chapters 13 and 14, which examine the topics of transaction exposure and translation exposure.

Approximately 30 percent of the bonds issued in the world end up being involved in an interest rate or currency swap. Chapter 10 provides an extensive treatment of both types of swaps. The chapter provides detailed examples and real-life illustrations of swap arrangements that highlight the cash flows between counterparties and that clearly delineate the risks inherent in swap transactions. Swap pricing is also covered.

Chapter 11 covers international portfolio investment. The chapter begins by examining the benefits to the investor from diversifying his or her portfolio internationally rather than just domestically. It shows that the gains from international diversification come from the lower correlations that typically exist among international assets in comparison to those existing among domestic assets. The chapter documents the potential benefits from international diversification that are available to all national investors. An appendix to the chapter shows how the rewards from international diversification can be further enhanced by using derivative contracts to hedge the exchange rate risk in the portfolio.

Part Three, Foreign Exchange Exposure and Management, comprises three chapters, one each devoted to the topics of economic, transaction, and translation exposure management. Chapter 12 covers economic exposure, that is, the extent to which the value of the firm will be affected by unexpected changes in exchange rates. The chapter provides a way to measure economic exposure, discusses its determinants, and presents methods for managing and hedging economic exposure. Several real-life illustrations are provided.

Chapter 13 covers the management of transaction exposure that arises from contractual obligations denominated in a foreign currency. Several methods for hedging this exposure are compared and contrasted: the forward hedge, the futures hedge, the money market hedge, and the options hedge. The chapter also discusses why a MNC should hedge, a debatable subject in the minds of both academics and practitioners.

Chapter 14 covers translation exposure or, as it is sometimes called, accounting exposure. Translation exposure refers to the effect that an unanticipated change in exchange rates will have on the consolidated financial reports of a MNC. The chapter discusses, compares, and contrasts the various methods for translating financial statements denominated in foreign currencies. The chapter includes a discussion of managing translation exposure using funds adjustment and the pros and cons of using balance sheet and derivatives hedges.

Part Four, Financial Management of the Multinational Firm, covers topics on financial management practices for the MNC. The section begins with Chapter 15 on direct foreign investment, which discusses why MNCs make capital expenditures in productive capacity in foreign lands rather than just produce domestically and then export to overseas markets. The chapter also deals with an increasingly popular form of foreign investment, cross-border mergers and acquisitions. The chapter includes a full treatment of the political risk associated with foreign investment.

Chapter 16 deals with the international capital structure and the cost of capital of a MNC. An analytical argument is presented showing that the firm's cost of equity capital is lower when its shares trade internationally rather than just in the home country. Moreover, the cost of debt can be reduced if debt capital is sourced internationally. The result of international trading of equity and sourcing debt in the international bond market is a lower weighted average cost of capital, which increases the net present value of capital expenditures as well as the value of the firm.

Chapter 17 presents the adjusted present value (APV) framework of Donald Lessard, which is useful for a parent firm in analyzing a capital expenditure in foreign operations. The APV framework is a value additivity model that determines the present value of each relevant cash flow of a capital project by discounting at a rate of discount consistent with the risk inherent in the cash flow. The Lessard model is an insightful method for analyzing capital expenditures.

Chapter 18 covers issues in cash management for the MNC. The chapter begins with an illustration of a cash management system for a MNC. It is shown that if a centralized cash depository is established and if the parent firm and its foreign affiliates employ a multinational netting system, the number of foreign cash flows can be reduced, thus saving the firm money and giving the MNC better control of its cash. It is also shown that managing cash transactions through a centralized depository that administers a precautionary cash balance portfolio reduces the systemwide investment in cash. Additionally, transfer pricing strategies are explored as a means for reducing a MNC's worldwide tax liability. Further, transfer pricing strategies and other methods are considered as means for removing blocked funds from a host country.

Chapter 19 provides a brief introduction to trade financing and countertrade. Through the use of an example, a typical foreign trade transaction is traced from beginning to end. The example shows the three primary documents used in trade financing: letter of credit, time draft, and bill of lading. The example also shows how a time draft can become a negotiable money market instrument called a banker's acceptance. The chapter concludes with a discussion of countertrade transactions, which are reciprocal promises between a buyer and a seller to purchase goods or services from one another.

The text concludes with Chapter 20, which examines the international tax environment. The chapter opens with a discussion on the theory of taxation, exploring the issues of tax neutrality and tax equity. Different methods of taxation—income tax, withholding tax, value-added tax—are considered next. Income tax rates in select countries are compared, as are the withholding tax rates that exist through tax treaties between the United States and certain countries. The chapter concludes with a treatment of the organizational structures MNCs can use for reducing tax liabilities.

SUMMARY

This chapter provided an introduction to *International Financial Management.*

1. It is essential to study "international" financial management because we are now living in a highly globalized and integrated world economy. Owing to the (a) continuous liberalization of international trade and investment, and (b) rapid advances in telecommunications and transportation technologies, the world economy will become even more integrated.
2. Three major dimensions distinguish international finance from domestic finance. They are (a) foreign exchange and political risks, (b) market imperfections, and (c) an expanded opportunity set.
3. Financial managers of MNCs should learn how to manage foreign exchange and political risks using proper tools and instruments, deal with (and take advantage of) market imperfections, and benefit from the expanded investment and financing opportunities. By doing so, financial managers can contribute to shareholder wealth maximization, which is the ultimate goal of international financial management.
4. The theory of comparative advantage states that economic well-being is enhanced if countries produce those goods for which they have comparative advantages and then trade those goods. The theory of comparative advantage provides a powerful rationale for free trade. Currently, international trade is becoming liberalized at both the global and regional levels. At the global level, WTO plays a key role in promoting free trade. At the regional level, the European Union and NAFTA play a vital role in dismantling trade barriers within regions.
5. A major economic trend of the present decade is the rapid pace with which former state-owned businesses are being privatized. With the fall of communism, many Eastern Bloc countries began stripping themselves of inefficient business operations formerly run by the state. Privatization has placed a new demand on international capital markets to finance the purchase of the former state enterprises, and it has also brought about a demand for new managers with international business skills.
6. In modern times, it is not a country per se but rather a controller of capital and know-how that gives the country in which it is domiciled a comparative advantage

over another country. These controllers of capital and know-how are multinational corporations (MNCs). Today, it is not uncommon for a MNC to produce merchandise in one country on capital equipment financed by funds raised in a number of different currencies through issuing securities to investors in many countries and then selling the finished product to customers in yet other countries.

KEY WORDS

European Union (EU), 11
expanded opportunity set, 7
foreign exchange risk, 5
General Agreement on Tariffs and Trade (GATT), 11
globalized and integrated world economy, 4
market imperfections, 6
multinational corporation (MNC), 14
North American Free Trade Agreement (NAFTA), 11
political risk, 6
privatization, 12
shareholder wealth maximization, 8
theory of comparative advantage, 10
World Trade Organization (WTO), 11

QUESTIONS

1. Why is it important to study international financial management?
2. How is international financial management different from domestic financial management?
3. Discuss the three major trends that have prevailed in international business during the last two decades.
4. How is a country's economic well-being enhanced through free international trade in goods and services?
5. What considerations might limit the extent to which the theory of comparative advantage is realistic?
6. What are multinational corporations (MNCs) and what economic roles do they play?
7. Ross Perot, a former presidential candidate of the Reform Party, which is a third political party in the United States, had strongly objected to the creation of the North American Trade Agreement (NAFTA), which nonetheless was inaugurated in 1994, for the fear of losing American jobs to Mexico where it is much cheaper to hire workers. What are the merits and demerits of Perot's position on NAFTA? Considering the recent economic developments in North America, how would you assess Perot's position on NAFTA?
8. In 1995, a working group of French chief executive officers was set up by the Confederation of French Industry (CNPF) and the French Association of Private Companies (AFEP) to study the French corporate governance structure. The group reported the following, among other things: "The board of directors should not simply aim at maximizing share values as in the U.K. and the U.S. Rather, its goal should be to serve the company, whose interests should be clearly distinguished from those of its shareholders, employees, creditors, suppliers and clients but still equated with their general common interest, which is to safeguard the prosperity and continuity of the company." Evaluate the above recommendation of the working group.[9]
9. Suppose you are interested in investing in shares of Nokia Corporation of Finland, which is a world leader in wireless communication. But before you make investment decision, you would like to learn about the company. Visit the Website of CNN Financial Network (www.cnnfn.com) and collect information about Nokia, including the recent stock price history and analysts' views of the company. Discuss what you learn about the company. Also discuss how the instantaneous access to information via Internet would affect the nature and workings of financial markets.

MINI CASE

Nike's Decision

Nike, a U.S.-based company with a globally recognized brand name, manufactures athletic shoes in such Asian developing countries as China, Indonesia, and Vietnam using subcontractors, and sells the products in the U.S. and foreign markets. The company has no production facilities in the United States. In each of those Asian countries where Nike has production facilities, the rates of unemployment and underemployment are quite high. The wage rate is very low in those countries by U.S. standards; the hourly wage rate in the manufacturing sector is less than one dollar in each of those countries, compared with about $18 in the United States. In addition, workers in those countries often operate in poor and unhealthy environments and their rights are not well protected. Understandably, Asian host countries are eager to attract foreign investments like Nike's to develop their economies and raise the living standards of their citizens. Recently, however, Nike came under worldwide criticism for its practice of hiring workers for such a low pay—"next to nothing" in the words of critics—and condoning poor working conditions in host countries.

Evaluate and discuss various ethical as well as economic ramifications of Nike's decision to invest in those Asian countries.

ENDNOTES

1. Sara Calian, "Decision, Decision," *The Wall Street Journal,* June 27, 1996, p. R6.
2. Since then, Enron has renegotiated the deal with the Maharashtra state.
3. It is noted that bearer and registered shares of Nestlé had the same claims on dividends but differential voting rights. Chapter 16 provides a detailed discussion of the Nestlé case.
4. The source for this information is *The New York Times,* February 4, 2000, p. C9.
5. Readers are referred to Appendix 1A for a detailed discussion of the theory of comparative advantage.
6. Our discussion in this subsection draws heavily from the article in the special "World Business" section of *The Wall Street Journal,* October 2, 1995, entitled "Sale of the Century."
7. The source for this information is the United Nations' *World Investment Report 1999.*
8. The source of this information is *World Investment Report 1999,* The United Nations.
9. This question draws on the article by François Degeorge, "French Boardrooms Wake Up Slowly to the Need for Reform," in the Complete MBA Companion in Global Business, *Financial Times,* 1999, pp. 156–60.

WEB RESOURCES

www.wto.org/

Website of the World Trade Organization (WTO). Provides news, statistics, links to international organizations, etc.

www.worldbank.org/

Website of the World Bank. Provides more than 190 "Country at a Glance" tables, global economic prospects, etc.

www.intracen.org/

Website of the International Trade Center (ITC). ITC is the technical cooperation arm of the World Trade Organization (WTO) and the United Nations Conference on Trade and Development (UNCTAD), and supports developing economies in exports and imports.

www.ft.com/

Website of the *Financial Times,* a leading international business newspaper.

www.economist.com/

Website of *The Economist,* an international weekly journal.

www.inc.com/international

This is Inc. Online's Website for international business professionals. Particularly useful for beginners in international business.

members.xoom.com/tradeweb/genterms

Provides a glossary of terms used in world trade.

gopher://wiretap.spies.com/11/Gov/NAFTA

(no http://)

Provides text of the North American Free Trade Agreement (NAFTA).

www.citizen.org/pctrade/nafta/naftapg.html

Provides a critical review of NAFTA.

trading.wmw.com/gatt

Provides the complete text of the Generalized Agreement on Tariffs and Trade (GATT) in Adobe Acrobat (PDF) format.

www.public-policy.org/~ncpa/pd/private/privat.html

This Website of the National Center for Policy Analysis provides information on privatization.

www.cnnfn.com

Provides extensive coverage of world business and financial information and news.

REFERENCES AND SUGGESTED READINGS

Basic Finance References

Bodie, Zvi, Alex Kane, and Alan J. Marcus. *Investments,* 4th ed. New York, NY: Irwin/McGraw-Hill, 1999.

Ross, Stephen A., Randolph W. Westerfield, and Jeffrey F. Jaffee. *Corporate Finance,* 5th ed. New York, NY: Irwin/McGraw-Hill, 1999.

International Accounting References

Al Hashim, Dhia D., and Jeffrey S. Arpan. *International Dimensions of Accounting,* 2nd ed. Boston: PWS-Kent, 1988.

Meuller, Gerhard G., Helen Gernon, and Gary Meek. *Accounting: An International Perspective.* Burr Ridge, Ill.: Richard D. Irwin, 1987.

International Economics References

Baker, Stephen A. *An Introduction to International Economics.* San Diego: Harcourt Brace Jovanovich, 1990.

Husted, Steven, and Michael Melvin. *International Economics.* New York: Harper & Row, 1990.

Krugman, Paul R., and Maurice Obstfeld. *International Economics: Theory and Policy,* 2nd ed. New York: Harper Collins, 1991.

Rivera-Batiz, Francisco L., and Luis Rivera-Batiz. *International Finance and Open Economy Macroeconomics.* 2nd ed. Upper Saddle River, NJ: Prentice Hall, 1994.

APPENDIX 1A

Gains from Trade: The Theory of Comparative Advantage

The theory of comparative advantage was originally advanced by the 19th-century economist David Ricardo as an explanation for why nations trade with one another. The theory claims that economic well-being is enhanced if each country's citizens produce that which they have a comparative advantage in producing relative to the citizens of other countries, and then trade products. Underlying the theory are the assumptions of free trade between nations and that the factors of production (land, buildings, labor, technology, and capital) are relatively immobile. Consider the example described in Exhibit A.1 as a vehicle for explaining the theory.

Exhibit A.1 assumes two countries, A and B, which each produce only food and textiles, but they do not trade with one another. Country A and B each have 60,000,000 units of input. Each country presently allocates 40,000,000 units to the production of food and 20,000,000 units to the production of textiles. Examination of the exhibit shows that Country A can produce five pounds of food with one unit of production or three yards of textiles. Country B has an absolute advantage over Country A in the production of both food and textiles. Country B can produce 15 pounds of food or four yards of textiles with one unit of production. When all units of production are employed, Country A can produce 200,000,000 pounds of food and 60,000,000 yards of textiles. Country B can produce 600,000,000 pounds of food and 80,000,000 yards of textiles. Total output is 800,000,000 pounds of food and 140,000,000 yards of textiles. Without trade, each nation's citizens can consume only what they produce.

While it is clear from the examination of Exhibit A.1 that Country B has an absolute advantage in the production of food and textiles, it is not so clear that Country A (B) has a relative advantage over Country B (A) in producing textiles (food). Note that in using units of production, Country A can "trade off" one unit of production needed to produce five pounds of food for three yards of textiles. Thus, a yard of textiles has an *opportunity cost* of 5/3 = 1.67 pounds of food, or a pound of food has an opportunity cost of 3/5 = .60 yards of textiles. Analogously, Country B has an opportunity cost of 15/4 = 3.75 pounds of food per yard of textiles, or 4/15 = .27 yards of textiles per pound of food. When viewed in terms of opportunity costs it is clear that Country A is relatively more efficient in producing textiles and Country B is relatively more efficient in producing food. That is, Country A's (B's) opportunity cost for producing textiles (food) is less than Country B's (A's). A *relative efficiency* that shows up via a lower opportunity cost is referred to as a comparative advantage.

Exhibit A.2 shows that when there are no restrictions or impediments to free trade, such as import quotas, import tariffs, or costly transportation, the economic well-being of the citizens of both countries is enhanced through trade. Exhibit A.2 shows that Country A has shifted 20,000,000 units from the production of food to

EXHIBIT A.1

Input/Output without Trade

	Country A	Country B	Total
I. Units of input (000,000)			
Food	40	40	
Textiles	20	20	
II. Output per unit of input (lbs. or yards)			
Food	5	15	
Textiles	3	4	
III. Total output (lbs. or yards) (000,000)			
Food	200	600	800
Textiles	60	80	140
IV. Consumption (lbs. or yards) (000,000)			
Food	200	600	800
Textiles	60	80	140

EXHIBIT A.2

Input/Output with Free Trade

	Country A	Country B	Total
I. Units of input (000,000)			
Food	20	50	
Textiles	40	10	
II. Output per unit of input (lbs. or yards)			
Food	5	15	
Textiles	3	4	
III. Total output (lbs. or yards) (000,000)			
Food	100	750	850
Textiles	120	40	160
IV. Consumption (lbs. or yards) (000,000)			
Food	225	625	850
Textiles	70	90	160

the production of textiles where it has a comparative advantage and that Country B has shifted 10,000,000 units from the production of textiles to the production of food where it has a comparative advantage. Total output is now 850,000,000 pounds of food and 160,000,000 yards of textiles. Suppose that Country A and Country B agree on a price of 2.50 pounds of food for one yard of textiles, and that Country A sells Country B 50,000,000 yards of textiles for 125,000,000 pounds of food. With free trade, Exhibit A.2 makes it clear that the citizens of each country have increased their consumption of food by 25,000,000 pounds and textiles by 10,000,000 yards.

PROBLEMS

1. Country C can produce seven pounds of food or four yards of textiles per unit of input. Compute the opportunity cost of producing food instead of textiles. Similarly, compute the opportunity cost of producing textiles instead of food.
2. Consider the no-trade input/output situation presented in the following table for countries X and Y. Assuming that free trade is allowed, develop a scenario that will benefit the citizens of both countries.

Input/Output without Trade

	Country		
	X	Y	Total
I. Units of input (000,000)			
Food	70	60	
Textiles	40	30	
II. Output per unit of input (lbs. or yards)			
Food	17	5	
Textiles	5	2	
III. Total output (lbs. or yards) (000,000)			
Food	1,190	300	1,490
Textiles	200	60	260
IV. Consumption (lbs. or yards) (000,000)			
Food	1,190	300	1,490
Textiles	200	60	260

CHAPTER TWO

International Monetary System

CHAPTER OUTLINE

This chapter examines the **international monetary system**, which defines the overall financial environment in which multinational corporations operate. As mentioned in Chapter 1, the exchange rates among major currencies, such as the U.S. dollar, British pound, German mark, and Japanese yen, have been fluctuating since the fixed exchange rate regime was abandoned in 1973. Consequently, corporations nowadays are operating in an environment in which exchange rate changes may adversely affect their competitive positions in the marketplace. This situation, in turn, makes it necessary for many firms to carefully measure and manage their exchange risk exposure. As we will discuss shortly, however, many European countries have adopted a common currency called the **euro,** rendering intra-European trade and investment much less susceptible to exchange risk. The complex international monetary arrangements imply that for adroit financial decision making, it is essential for managers to understand, in detail, the arrangements and workings of the international monetary system.

The international monetary system can be defined as the *institutional framework within which international payments are made, movements of capital are accommodated,* and *exchange rates among currencies are determined.* It is a complex whole of agreements, rules, institutions, mechanisms, and policies regarding exchange rates, international payments, and the flow of capital. The international monetary system has evolved over time and will continue to do so in the future as the fundamental business and political conditions underlying the world economy continue to shift. In this chapter, we will review the history of the international monetary system and contemplate its future prospects. In addition, we will compare and contrast the alternative exchange rate systems, that is, fixed versus flexible exchange rates.

EVOLUTION OF THE INTERNATIONAL MONETARY SYSTEM

The international monetary system went through several distinct stages of evolution. These stages are summarized as follows:

1. Bimetallism: Before 1875.
2. Classical gold standard: 1875–1914.
3. Interwar period: 1915–1944.
4. Bretton Woods system: 1945–1972.
5. Flexible exchange rate regime: Since 1973.

We now examine each of the five stages in some detail.

BIMETALLISM: BEFORE 1875

Prior to the 1870s, many countries had **bimetallism**, that is, a double standard in that free coinage was maintained for both gold and silver. In Great Britain, for example, bimetallism was maintained until 1816 (after the conclusion of the Napoleonic Wars) when Parliament passed a law maintaining free coinage of gold only, abolishing the free coinage of silver. In the United States, bimetallism was adopted by the Coinage Act of 1792 and remained a legal standard until 1873, when Congress dropped the silver dollar from the list of coins to be minted. France, on the other hand, introduced and maintained its bimetallism from the French Revolution to 1878. Some other countries such as China, India, Germany, and Holland were on the silver standard.

The international monetary system before the 1870s can be characterized as "bimetallism" in the sense that both gold and silver were used as international means of payment and that the exchange rates among currencies were determined by either their gold or silver contents.[1] Around 1870, for example, the exchange rate between the British pound, which was fully on a gold standard, and the French franc, which was officially on a bimetallic standard, was determined by the gold content of the two currencies. On the other hand, the exchange rate between the franc and the German mark, which was on a silver standard, was determined by the silver content of the currencies. The exchange rate between the pound and the mark was determined by their exchange rates against the franc. It is also worth noting that, due to various wars and political upheavals, some major countries such as the United States, Russia, and Austria-Hungary had irredeemable currencies at one time or another during the period 1848–79. One might say that the international monetary system was less than fully *systematic* up until the 1870s.

Countries that were on the bimetallic standard often experienced the well-known phenomenon referred to as **Gresham's law**. Since the exchange ratio between the two metals was fixed officially, only the abundant metal was used as money, driving more scarce metal out of circulation. This is Gresham's law, according to which "bad" (abundant) money drives out "good" (scarce) money. For example, when gold from newly discovered mines in California and Australia poured into the market in the 1850s, the value of gold became depressed, causing overvaluation of gold under the French official ratio, which equated a gold franc to a silver franc 15½ times as heavy. As a result, the franc effectively became a gold currency.

CLASSICAL GOLD STANDARD: 1875–1914

Mankind's fondness for gold as a storage of wealth and means of exchange dates back to antiquity and was shared widely by diverse civilizations. Christopher Columbus once said, "Gold constitutes treasure, and he who possesses it has all he needs in this world." The first full-fledged **gold standard**, however, was not established until 1821 in Great Britain, when notes from the Bank of England were made fully redeemable for gold. As previously mentioned, France was effectively on the gold standard beginning in the 1850s and formally adopted the standard in 1878. The newly emergent German empire, which was to receive a sizable war indemnity from France, converted to the gold standard in 1875, discontinuing free coinage of silver. The United States adopted the gold standard in 1879, Russia and Japan in 1897.

One can say roughly that the *international* gold standard existed as a historical reality during the period 1875–1914. The majority of countries got off gold in 1914 when World War I broke out. The classical gold standard as an international monetary system thus lasted for about 40 years. During this period, London became the center of the international financial system, reflecting Britain's advanced economy and its preeminent position in international trade.

An *international* gold standard can be said to exist when, in most major countries, (1) gold alone is assured of unrestricted coinage, (2) there is two-way convertibility between gold and national currencies at a stable ratio, and (3) gold may be freely exported or imported. In order to support unrestricted convertibility into gold, banknotes need to be backed by a gold reserve of a minimum stated ratio. In addition, the domestic money stock should rise and fall as gold flows in and out of the country. The above conditions were roughly met between 1875 and 1914.

Under the gold standard, the exchange rate between any two currencies will be determined by their gold content. For example, suppose that the pound is pegged to gold at six pounds per ounce, whereas one ounce of gold is worth 12 francs. The exchange rate between the pound and the franc should then be two francs per pound. To the extent that the pound and the franc remain pegged to gold at given prices, the exchange rate between the two currencies will remain stable. There were indeed no significant changes in exchange rates among the currencies of such major countries as Great Britain, France, Germany, and the United States during the entire period. For example, the dollar–sterling exchange rate remained within a narrow range of $4.84 and $4.90 per pound. Highly stable exchange rates under the classical gold standard provided an environment that was conducive to international trade and investment.

Under the gold standard, misalignment of the exchange rate will be automatically corrected by cross-border flows of gold. In the above example, suppose that one pound is trading for 1.80 francs at the moment. Since the pound is undervalued in the exchange market, people will buy pounds with francs, but not francs with pounds. For people who need francs, it would be cheaper first to buy gold from the Bank of England and ship it to France and sell it for francs. For example, suppose that you need to buy 1,000 francs using pounds. If you buy 1,000 francs in the exchange market, it will cost you £555.56 at the exchange rate of Fr1.80/£. Alternatively, you can buy 1,000/12 ounces of gold from the Bank of England for £500:

$$\pounds 500 = (1{,}000/12) \times 6$$

Then you could ship it to France and sell it to the Bank of France for 1,000 francs. This way, you can save about £55.56.[2] Since people only want to buy, not sell, pounds at the exchange rate of Fr1.80/£, the pound will eventually appreciate to its fair value, namely, Fr2.0/£.

Under the gold standard, international imbalances of payment will also be corrected automatically. Consider a situation where Great Britain exported more to France than the former imported from the latter. This kind of trade imbalance will not persist under the gold standard. Net export from Great Britain to France will be accompanied by a net flow of gold in the opposite direction. This flow of gold will lead to a lower price level in France and, at the same time, a higher price level in Great Britain. (Recall that under the gold standard, the domestic money stock is supposed to rise or fall as the country experiences an inflow or outflow of gold.) The resultant change in the relative price level, in turn, will slow exports from Great Britain and encourage exports from France. As a result, the initial net export from Great Britain will eventually disappear. This adjustment mechanism is referred to as the **price-specie-flow mechanism**, which is attributed to David Hume, a Scottish philosopher.[3]

Despite its demise a long time ago, the gold standard still has ardent supporters among academic, business, and political circles, which view it as an ultimate hedge against price inflation. Gold has a natural scarcity and no one can increase its quantity at will. Therefore, if gold serves as the sole base for domestic money creation, the money supply cannot get out of control and cause inflation. In addition, if gold is used as the sole international means of payment, then countries' balance of payments will be regulated automatically via the movements of gold.[4]

The gold standard, however, has a few key shortcomings. First of all, the supply of newly minted gold is so restricted that the growth of world trade and investment can be seriously hampered for the lack of sufficient monetary reserves. The world economy can face deflationary pressures. Second, whenever the government finds it politically necessary to pursue national objectives that are inconsistent with maintaining the gold standard, it can abandon the gold standard. In other words, the international gold standard per se has no mechanism to compel each major country to abide by the rules of the game.[5] For such reasons, it is not very likely that the classical gold standard will be restored in the foreseeable future.

INTERWAR PERIOD: 1915–1944

World War I ended the classical gold standard in August 1914, as major countries such as Great Britain, France, Germany, and Russia suspended redemption of banknotes in gold and imposed embargoes on gold exports. After the war, many countries, especially Germany, Austria, Hungary, Poland, and Russia suffered hyperinflation. The German experience provides a classic example of hyperinflation: By the end of 1923, the wholesale price index in Germany was more than 1 trillion times as high as the prewar level. Freed from wartime pegging, exchange rates among currencies were fluctuating in the early 1920s. During this period, countries widely used "predatory" depreciations of their currencies as a means of gaining advantages in the world export market.

As major countries began to recover from the war and stabilize their economies, they attempted to restore the gold standard. The United States, which replaced Great Britain as the dominant financial power, spearheaded efforts to restore the gold standard. With only mild inflation, the United States was able to lift restrictions on gold exports and return to a gold standard in 1919. In Great Britain, Winston Churchill, the chancellor of the Exchequer, played a key role in restoring the gold standard in 1925. Besides Great Britain, such countries as Switzerland, France, and the Scandinavian countries restored the gold standard by 1928.

The international gold standard of the late 1920s, however, was not much more than a façade. Most major countries gave priority to the stabilization of domestic economies and systematically followed a policy of **sterilization of gold** by matching inflows and outflows of gold respectively with reductions and increases in domestic money and credit. The Federal Reserve of the United States, for example, kept some gold outside the credit base by circulating it as gold certificates. The Bank of England also followed the policy of keeping the amount of available domestic credit stable by neutralizing the effects of gold flows. In a word, countries lacked the political will to abide by the "rules of the game," and so the automatic adjustment mechanism of the gold standard was unable to work.

Even the façade of the restored gold standard was destroyed in the wake of the Great Depression and the accompanying financial crises. Following the stock market crash and the onset of the Great Depression in 1929, many banks, especially in Austria, Germany, and the United States, suffered sharp declines in their portfolio values, touching off runs on the banks. Against this backdrop, Britain experienced a massive outflow of gold, which resulted from chronic balance-of-payment deficits and lack of confidence in the pound sterling. Despite coordinated international efforts to rescue the pound, British gold reserves continued to fall to the point where it was impossible to maintain the gold standard. In September 1931, the British government suspended gold payments and let the pound float. As Great Britain got off gold, countries such as Canada, Sweden, Austria, and Japan followed suit by the end of 1931. The United States got off gold in April 1933 after experiencing a spate of bank failures and outflows of gold. Lastly, France abandoned the gold standard in 1936 because of the flight from the franc, which, in turn, reflected the economic and political instability following the inception of the socialist Popular Front government led by Leon Blum. Paper standards came into being when the gold standard was abandoned.

In sum, the interwar period was characterized by economic nationalism, halfhearted attempts and failure to restore the gold standard, economic and political instabilities, bank failures, and panicky flights of capital across borders. No coherent international monetary system prevailed during this period, with profoundly detrimental effects on international trade and investment.

BRETTON WOODS SYSTEM: 1945–1972

In July 1944, representatives of 44 nations gathered at Bretton Woods, New Hampshire, to discuss and design the postwar international monetary system. After lengthy discussions and bargains, representatives succeeded in drafting and signing the Articles of Agreement of the International Monetary Fund (IMF), which constitutes the core of the **Bretton Woods system**. The agreement was subsequently ratified by the majority of countries to launch the IMF in 1945. The IMF embodied an explicit set of rules about the conduct of international monetary policies and was responsible for enforcing these rules. Delegates also created a sister institution, the International Bank for Reconstruction and Development (IBRD), better known as the World Bank, that was chiefly responsible for financing individual development projects.

In designing the Bretton Woods system, representatives were concerned with how to prevent the recurrence of economic nationalism with destructive "beggar-thy-neighbor" policies and how to address the lack of clear rules of the game plaguing the interwar years. The British delegates led by John Maynard Keynes proposed an international clearing union that would create an international reserve asset called "bancor." Countries would accept payments in bancor to settle international transactions, without limit. They would also be allowed to acquire bancor by using overdraft facilities with the clearing union. On the other hand, the American delegates, headed by Harry Dexter White, proposed a currency pool to which member countries would make contributions and from which they might borrow to tide themselves over during short-term balance-of-payments deficits. Both delegates desired exchange rate stability without restoring an international gold standard. The American proposal was largely incorporated into the Articles of the Agreement of the IMF.

Under the Bretton Woods system, each country established a **par value** in relation to the U.S. dollar, which was pegged to gold at $35 per ounce. This point is illustrated in Exhibit 2.1. Each country was responsible for maintaining its exchange rate within ±1 percent of the adopted par value by buying or selling foreign exchanges as necessary. However, a member country with a "fundamental disequilibrium" may be allowed to make a change in the par value of its currency. Under the

EXHIBIT 2.1

The Design of the Gold-Exchange System

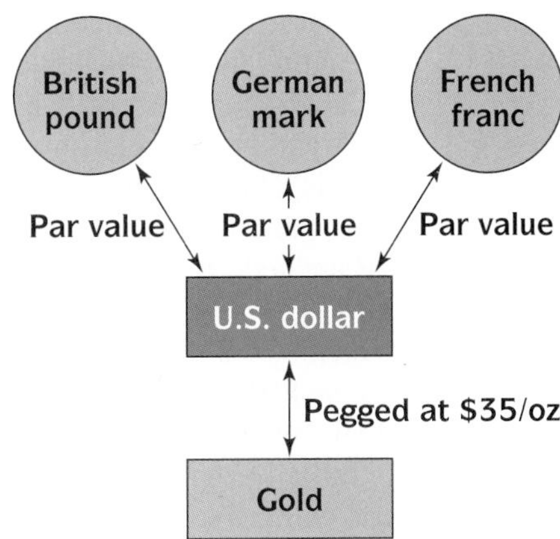

Bretton Woods system, the U.S. dollar was the only currency that was fully convertible to gold; other currencies were not directly convertible to gold. Countries held U.S. dollars, as well as gold, for use as an international means of payment. Because of these arrangements, the Bretton Woods system can be described as a dollar-based **gold-exchange standard.** A country on the gold-exchange standard holds most of its reserves in the form of currency of a country that is *really* on the gold standard.

Advocates of the gold-exchange system argue that the system economizes on gold because countries can use not only gold but also foreign exchanges as an international means of payment. Foreign exchange reserves offset the deflationary effects of limited addition to the world's monetary gold stock. Another advantage of the gold-exchange system is that individual countries can earn interest on their foreign exchange holdings, whereas gold holdings yield no returns. In addition, countries can save transaction costs associated with transporting gold across countries under the gold-exchange system. An ample supply of international monetary reserves coupled with stable exchange rates provided an environment highly conducive to the growth of international trade and investment throughout the 1950s and 1960s.

Professor Robert Triffin warned, however, that the gold-exchange system was programmed to collapse in the long run. To satisfy the growing need for reserves, the United States had to run balance-of-payments deficits continuously. Yet if the United States ran perennial balance-of-payments deficits, it would eventually impair the public confidence in the dollar, triggering a run on the dollar. Under the gold-exchange system, the reserve-currency country should run balance-of-payments deficits to supply reserves, but if such deficits are large and persistent, they can lead to a crisis of confidence in the reserve currency itself, causing the downfall of the system. This dilemma, known as the **Triffin paradox**, was indeed responsible for the eventual collapse of the dollar-based gold-exchange system in the early 1970s.

The United States began to experience trade deficits with the rest of the world in the late 1950s, and the problem persisted into the 1960s. By the early 1960s the total value of the U.S. gold stock, when valued at $35 per ounce, fell short of foreign dollar holdings. This naturally created concern about the viability of the dollar-based system. Against this backdrop, President Charles de Gaulle prodded the Bank of France to buy gold from the U.S. Treasury, unloading its dollar holdings. Efforts to remedy the problem centered on (1) a series of dollar defense measures taken by the U.S. government and (2) the creation of a new reserve asset, **special drawing rights (SDRs)**, by the IMF.

In 1963, President John Kennedy imposed the Interest Equalization Tax (IET) on U.S. purchases of foreign securities in order to stem the outflow of dollars. The IET was designed to increase the cost of foreign borrowing in the U.S. bond market. In 1965, the Federal Reserve introduced the U.S. voluntary Foreign Credit Restraint Program (FCRP), which regulated the amount of dollars U.S. banks could lend to U.S. multinational companies engaged in foreign direct investments. In 1968, these regulations became legally binding. As will be discussed in Chapter 6, such measures as IET and FCRP lent a strong impetus to the rapid growth of the Eurodollar market, which is a transnational, unregulated fund market.

To partially alleviate the pressure on the dollar as the central reserve currency, the IMF created an artificial international reserve called the SDR in 1970. The SDR, which is a basket currency comprising major individual currencies, was allotted to the members of the IMF, who could then use it for transactions among themselves or with the IMF. In addition to gold and foreign exchanges, countries could use the SDR to make international payments.

Initially, the SDR was designed to be the weighted average of 16 currencies of those countries whose shares in world exports exceeded more than 1 percent. The percentage share of each currency in the SDR was about the same as the country's share in world exports. In 1981, however, the SDR was greatly simplified to comprise only five major currencies: U.S. dollar, German mark, Japanese yen, British pound, and French franc. As Exhibit 2.2 shows, the weight for each currency is updated periodically, reflecting the relative importance of each country in the world trade of goods and services and the amount of the currencies held as reserves by the members of the IMF. Effective January 1, 1999, the IMF replaced the currency amounts of German marks and French francs in the SDR basket with equivalent amounts of the euro, based on the fixed conversion rates.

The SDR is used not only as a reserve asset but also as a denomination currency for international transactions. Since the SDR is a "portfolio" of currencies, its value tends to be more stable than the value of any individual currency included in the SDR. The portfolio nature of the SDR makes it an attractive denomination currency for international commercial and financial contracts under exchange rate uncertainty.

The efforts to support the dollar-based gold-exchange standard, however, turned out to be ineffective in the face of expansionary monetary policy and rising inflation in the United States, which were related to the financing of the Vietnam War and the Great Society program. In the early 1970s, it became clear that the dollar was overvalued, especially relative to the mark and the yen. As a result, the German and Japanese central banks had to make massive interventions in the foreign exchange market to maintain their par values. Given the unwillingness of the United States to control its monetary expansion, the repeated central bank interventions could not solve the underlying disparities. In August 1971, President Richard Nixon suspended the convertibility of the dollar into gold and imposed a 10 percent import surcharge. The foundation of the Bretton Woods system cracked under the strain.

In an attempt to save the Bretton Woods system, 10 major countries, known as the Group of Ten, met at the Smithsonian Institution in Washington, D.C., in December 1971. They reached the **Smithsonian Agreement**, according to which (1) the price of gold was raised to $38 per ounce, (2) each of the other countries revalued its currency against the U.S. dollar by up to 10 percent, and (3) the band within which

EXHIBIT 2.2

The Composition of the Special Drawing Right (SDR)

Currencies	1981–85	1986–90	1991–95	1996–2000[a]
U.S. dollar	42%	42%	40%	39%
German mark	19%	19%	21%	21%
Japanese yen	13%	15%	17%	18%
British pound	13%	12%	11%	11%
French franc	13%	12%	11%	11%

[a]The composition of the SDR changes every five years.

Source: The International Monetary Fund.

the exchange rates were allowed to move was expanded from 1 percent to 2.25 percent in either direction.

The Smithsonian Agreement lasted for little more than a year before it came under attack again. Clearly, the devaluation of the dollar was not sufficient to stabilize the situation. In February 1973, the dollar came under heavy selling pressure, again prompting central banks around the world to buy dollars. The price of gold was further raised from $38 to $42 per ounce. By March 1973, European and Japanese currencies were allowed to float, completing the decline and fall of the Bretton Woods system. Since then, the exchange rates among such major currencies as the dollar, the mark, the pound, and the yen have been fluctuating against each other.

THE FLEXIBLE EXCHANGE RATE REGIME: 1973–PRESENT

The flexible exchange rate regime that followed the demise of the Bretton Woods system was ratified after the fact in January 1976 when the IMF members met in Jamaica and agreed to a new set of rules for the international monetary system. The key elements of the **Jamaica Agreement** include;

1. Flexible exchange rates were declared acceptable to the IMF members, and central banks were allowed to intervene in the exchange markets to iron out unwarranted volatilities.
2. Gold was officially abandoned (i.e., demonetized) as an international reserve asset. Half of the IMF's gold holdings were returned to the members and the other half were sold, with the proceeds to be used to help poor nations.
3. Non-oil-exporting countries and less-developed countries were given greater access to IMF funds.

The IMF continued to provide assistance to countries facing balance-of-payments and exchange rate difficulties. The IMF, however, extended assistance and loans to the member countries on the condition that those countries follow the IMF's macroeconomic policy prescriptions. This "conditionality," which often involves deflationary macroeconomic policies and elimination of various subsidy programs, provoked resentment among the people of developing countries receiving the IMF's balance-of-payments loans.

As can be expected, exchange rates have become substantially more volatile since March 1973 than they were under the Bretton Woods system. Exhibit 2.3 summarizes the behavior of the dollar exchange rate since 1965. The exhibit shows the exchange rate between the U.S. dollar and a weighted basket of 21 other major currencies. The decline of the dollar between 1970 and 1973 represents the transition from the Bretton Woods to the flexible exchange rate system. The most conspicuous phenomena shown in Exhibit 2.3 are the dollar's spectacular rise between 1980 and 1985 and its equally spectacular decline between 1985 and 1988. These unusual episodes merit some discussion.

Following the U.S. presidential election of 1980, the Reagan administration ushered in a period of growing U.S. budget deficits and balance-of-payments deficits. The U.S. dollar, however, experienced a major appreciation throughout the first half of the 1980s because of the large-scale inflows of foreign capital caused by unusually high real interest rates available in the United States. To attract foreign investment to help finance the budget deficit, the United States had to offer high real interest rates. The heavy demand for dollars by foreign investors pushed up the value of the dollar in the exchange market.

The value of the dollar reached its peak in February 1985 and then began a persistent downward drift until it stabilized in 1988. The reversal in the exchange rate trend partially reflected the effect of the record-high U.S. trade deficit, about $160 billion in 1985, brought about by the soaring dollar. The downward trend was also

EXHIBIT 2.3

The Value of the U.S. Dollar since 1965[a]

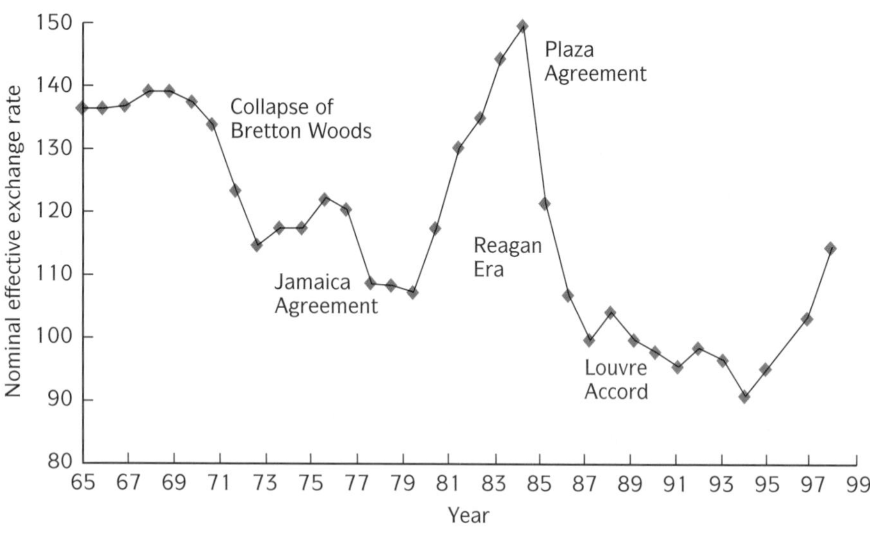

[a]The value of the U.S. dollar represents the nominal effective exchange rate index (1990 = 100) with weights derived from trade among 22 industrialized countries.

Source: International Monetary Fund, *International Financial Statistics Yearbook 1996.*

reinforced by concerted government interventions. In September 1985, the so-called G-5 countries (France, Japan, Germany, the U.K., and the United States) met at the Plaza Hotel in New York and reached what became known as the **Plaza Accord.** They agreed that it would be desirable for the dollar to depreciate against most major currencies to solve the U.S. trade deficit problem and expressed their willingness to intervene in the exchange market to realize this objective. The slide of the dollar that had begun in February was further precipitated by the Plaza Accord.

As the dollar continued its decline, the governments of the major industrial countries began to worry that the dollar may fall too far. To address the problem of exchange rate volatility and other related issues, the G-7 economic summit meeting was convened in Paris in 1987.[6] The meeting produced the **Louvre Accord**, according to which:

1. The G-7 countries would cooperate to achieve greater exchange rate stability.
2. The G-7 countries agreed to more closely consult and coordinate their macroeconomic policies.

The Louvre Accord marked the inception of the **managed-float system** under which the G-7 countries would jointly intervene in the exchange market to correct over- or undervaluation of currencies. Since the Louvre Accord, exchange rates have become relatively more stable.

THE CURRENT EXCHANGE RATE ARRANGEMENTS

Although the most actively traded currencies of the world, such as the dollar, the yen, the pound, and the mark, may be fluctuating against each other, the majority of the world's currencies are pegged to single currencies, particularly the U.S. dollar and the French franc, or baskets of currencies such as the SDR. The current exchange rate arrangements as classified by the IMF are provided in Exhibit 2.4.

As of April 1999, the largest number of countries (48), including Australia, Canada, Japan, the United Kingdom, and the United States, allow their currencies to float independently against other currencies; the exchange rates of these countries are essentially determined by market forces. Twenty-five countries, including the Czech Republic, Russia, and Singapore, adopt some forms of "managed floating" system that combines market forces and government intervention in setting the exchange rates. In contrast, 37 countries do not have their own national currencies. For example, 14 central and western African countries jointly use the CFA-franc, which is fixed to the euro through the French franc. Eight countries including Argentina, Hong Kong, and Estonia, on the other hand, maintain national currencies but they are permanently fixed to such hard currencies as the U.S. dollar or German mark. The remaining countries adopt a mixture of fixed and floating exchange-rate regimes. As is well known, the European Union has pursued Europe-wide monetary integration by first establishing the European Monetary System and then the European Monetary Union. These topics deserve a detailed discussion.

EUROPEAN MONETARY SYSTEM

According to the Smithsonian Agreement, which was signed in December 1971, the band of exchange rate movements was expanded from the original plus or minus 1 percent to plus or minus 2.25 percent. Members of the European Economic Community (EEC), however, decided on a narrower band of ±1.125 percent for their currencies. This scaled-down, European version of the fixed exchange rate system that arose concurrently with the decline of the Bretton Woods system was called the **snake**. The name "snake" was derived from the way the EEC currencies moved closely together within the wider band allowed for other currencies like the dollar.

The EEC countries adopted the snake because they felt that stable exchange rates among the EEC countries were essential for promoting intra-EEC trade and deepening economic integration. The snake arrangement was replaced by the **European Monetary System (EMS)** in 1979. The EMS, which was originally proposed by German chancellor Helmut Schmidt, was formally launched in March 1979. Among its chief objectives are:

1. To establish a "zone of monetary stability" in Europe.
2. To coordinate exchange rate policies vis-à-vis the non-EMS currencies.
3. To pave the way for the eventual European monetary union.

At the political level, the EMS represented a Franco-German initiative to speed up the movement toward European economic and political unification. All EEC member countries, except the United Kingdom and Greece, joined the EMS. The two main instruments of the EMS are the European Currency Unit and the Exchange Rate Mechanism.

The **European Currency Unit (ECU)** is a "basket" currency constructed as a weighted average of the currencies of member countries of the European Union (EU). The weights are based on each currency's relative GNP and share in intra-EU trade. The ECU serves as the accounting unit of the EMS and plays an important role in the workings of the exchange rate mechanism.

The **Exchange Rate Mechanism (ERM)** refers to the procedure by which EMS member countries collectively manage their exchange rates. The ERM is based on a "parity grid" system, which is a system of par values among ERM currencies. The par values in the parity grid are computed by first defining the par values of EMS currencies in terms of the ECU. These par values are called the ECU central rates. Currently, the ECU central rates of the German mark and the French franc are DM1.94964 per ECU and Fr6.53883 per ECU. This implies that the parity between the two member currencies should be Fr6.53883/DM1.94964 = Fr3.3539/DM. The entire parity grid can be computed by referring to the ECU central rates set by the European Commission.

EXHIBIT 2.4 Exchange Rate Arrangements and Anchors of Monetary Policy (As of April 4, 1999)[1]

Exchange Rate Regime (Number of Countries)	Monetary Policy Framework				
	Exchange Rate Anchor	Monetary Aggregate Target	Inflation Targeting Framework	Fund-Supported or Other Monetary Program	Other
Exchange arrangements with no separate legal tender (37)	**Another currency as legal tender** Kiribati Marshall Islands Micronesia Palau Panama* San Marino **ECCM**[**2] Antigua & Barbuda Dominica Grenada St. Kitts & Nevis St. Lucia St. Vincent & the Grenadines **CFA Franc Zone** **WAEMU**** Benin* Burkina Faso* Côte d'Ivoire* Guinea-Bissau Mali* Niger* Senegal* Togo **CAEMC**** Cameroon* C. African Rep. Chad* Congo, Rep. of* Equatorial Guinea Gabon*			Benin* Burkina Faso* Cameroon* Central African Rep.* Chad* Congo, Rep. of* Côte d'Ivoire* Mali* Niger* Senegal*	**Euro Area**[1,4] Austria Belgium Finland France Germany Ireland Italy Luxembourg Netherlands Portugal Spain
Currency board arrangements (8)	Argentina* Bosnia and Herzegovina* Brunei Darussalam Bulgaria* China, P.R.: Hong Kong Djibouti* Estonia* Lithuania			Argentina* Bosnia and Herzegovina* Bulgaria*	
Other conventional fixed peg arrangements (including de facto peg arrangements under managed floating) (44)	**Against a single currency (30)** Aruba Bahamas, The[5] Barbados Bahrain[6, 7] Belize Bhutan Cape Verde* China, P.R.: Mainland*[6] Comoros[8] Egypt[5, 6] El Salvador*[6] Iran[5, 6] Iraq Jordan*[6] Lebanon[6] Lesotho Macedonia, FYR*[6] Malaysia Maldives*[6] Namibia Nepal Netherlands Antilles Oman Qatar[6,7] Saudi Arabia[6,7] Syrian Arab Republic[5] Swaziland Trinidad & Tobago Turkmenistan[6] United Arab Emirates[6,7] **Against a composite (13)** Botswana[5] Burundi Fiji Kuwait Latvia Malta Morocco Myanmar[5] Samoa Seychelles Solomon Islands Tonga Vanuatu	China, P.R.: Mainland*[6]		Bangladesh Cape Verde* El Salvador*[6] Jordan*[6] Macedonia, FYR*[6] Maldives*[6]	
Pegged exchange rates within horizontal bands (8)[9]	**Within a cooperative arrangement** **ERM II (2)** Denmark Greece **Other band arrangements (6)** Croatia*[6] Cyprus Iceland Libyan A.J. Ukraine*[4]			Croatia*[6] Ukraine*[6]	
Crawling pegs (6)[6]	Angola Costa Rica Nicaragua*			Bolivia Nicaragua* Tunisia Turkey	
Exchange rates within crawling bands (9)[6,10]	Colombia Honduras Hungary Israel* Poland* Sri Lanka** Uruguay Venezuela	Sri Lanka*	Chile[5] Israel* Poland*	Uruguay*	

Managed floating with no preannounced path for exchange rate (25)		Lao PDR[5] Jamaica[4] Slovenia	Czech Republic	Azerbaijan Ethiopia Kazakhstan Kenya Kyrgyz Republic Malawi Pakistan[5] Tajikistan	Algeria[3] Belarus[3,5] Cambodia[3,5] Dominican Rep.[3,5] Mauritania Nigeria[3] Norway[3] Paraguay[3] Romania[3] Russian Federation[3] Singapore[6] Slovak Republic[3] Suriname[3] Uzbekistan[3,5]
Independently floating (48)		Gambia, The* Ghana* Guinea* Guyana* India Korea* Mauritius[6] Mongolia* Peru* Philippines* São Tomé and Príncipe*[5] Sierra Leone South Africa Switzerland Zimbabwe*	Australia Canada New Zealand Sweden United Kingdom	Albania Armenia Brazil Gambia, The* Georgia Ghana* Guinea* Guyana* Haiti Indonesia Kazakhstan Korea* Madagascar Mexico Moldova Mongolia* Mozambique Philippines* Rwanda São Tomé & Príncipe*[5] Sudan Tanzania Thailand Uganda Yemen, Rep. of Zambia[5] Zimbabwe*	Afghanistan[5,11] Congo, Dem. Rep. of[3] Ecuador[3] Eritrea[3] Guatemala[3] Japan[3] Liberia[3] Papua New Guinea[3] Somalia[5,11] United States[3]

Exchange Arrangements with No Separate Legal Tender: The currency of another country circulates as the sole legal tender or the member belongs to a monetary or currency union in which the same legal tender is shared by the members of the union.
Currency Board Arrangements: A monetary regime based on an implicit legislative commitment to exchange domestic currency for a specified foreign currency at a fixed exchange rate, combined with restrictions on the issuing authority to ensure the fulfillment of its legal obligation.
Other Conventional Fixed Peg Arrangements: The country pegs its currency (formally or de facto) at a fixed rate to a major currency or a basket of currencies where the exchange rate fluctuates within a narrow margin of at most ±1 percent around a central rate.
Pegged Exchange Rates Within Horizontal Bands: The value of the currency is maintained within margins of fluctuation around a formal or de facto fixed peg that are wider than ±1 percent around a central rate.
Crawling Pegs: The currency is adjusted periodically in small amounts at a fixed, preannounced rate or in response to changes in selective quantitative indicators.
Exchange Rates Within Crawling Bands: The currency is maintained within certain fluctuation margins around a central rate that is adjusted periodically at a fixed preannounced rate or in response to changes in selective quantitative indicators.
Managed Floating with No Preannounced Path for the Exchange Rate: The monetary authority influences the movements of the exchange rate through active intervention in the foreign exchange market without specifying, or precommitting to, a preannounced path for the exchange rate.
Independent Floating: The exchange rate is market determined, with any foreign exchange intervention aimed at moderating the rate of change and preventing undue fluctuations in the exchange rate, rather than at establishing a level for it.

**ECCM: East Caribbean Common Market; WAEMU: West African Economic and Monetary Union; CAEMC: Central African Economic and Monetary Community
Source: *International Monetary Fund, International Financial Statistics, July 1999.* Reprinted with permission.
[1]A country with * indicates that the country adopts more than one nominal anchor in conducting monetary policy.
[2]These countries also have a currency board arrangement within the common market.
[3]The country has no explicitly stated nominal anchor but rather monitors various indicators in conducting monetary policy.
[4]Until they are withdrawn in the first half of 2002, national currencies will retain their status as legal tender within their home territories.
[5]Member maintained exchange arrangements involving more than one market. The arrangement shown is that maintained in the major market.
[6]The indicated country has a de facto arrangement under a formally announced policy of managed or independent floating. In the case of Jordan, it indicates that the country has a de jure peg to the SDR but a de facto peg to the U.S. dollar. In the case of Mauritius, the authorities have a de facto policy of independent floating, with only infrequent intervention by the central bank.
[7]Exchange rates are determined on the basis of a fixed relationship to the SDR, within margins of up to ±7.25%. However, because of the maintenance of a relatively stable relationship with the U.S. dollar, these margins are not always observed.
[8]Comoros has the same arrangement with the French Treasury as do the CFA Franc Zone countries.
[9]The band width for these countries is Croatia (unspecified), Cyprus (±2.25%), Denmark (±2.25%), Greece (±15%), Iceland (±6%), Libya (±77.5%), Ukraine (Hrv 3.4–4.6 per U.S. dollar), and Vietnam (7% one-sided).
[10]The band for these countries is Colombia (±9%), Chile (±16%), Ecuador (±7.5%), Honduras (±7%), Hungary (±2.25%), Israel (symmetric band of 30%), Poland (±12.5%), Sri Lanka (±2%), Uruguay (±3%), and Venezuela (±7.5%).
[11]There is no relevant information available for the country.

When the EMS was launched in 1979, a currency was allowed to deviate from the parities with other currencies by a maximum of plus or minus 2.25 percent, with the exception of the Italian lira, for which a maximum deviation of plus or minus 6 percent was allowed. In September 1993, however, the band was widened to a maximum of plus or minus 15 percent. When a currency is at the lower or upper bound, the central banks of both countries are required to intervene in the foreign exchange markets to keep the market exchange rate within the band. To intervene in the exchange markets, the central banks can borrow from a credit fund to which member countries contribute gold and foreign reserves.

Since the EMS members were less than fully committed to coordinating their economic policies, the EMS went through a series of realignments. The Italian lira, for instance, was devalued by 6 percent in July 1985 and again by 3.7 percent in January 1990. In September 1992, Italy and the U.K. pulled out of the ERM as high German interest rates were inducing massive capital flows into Germany. Following German reunification in October 1990, the German government experienced substantial budget deficits, which were not accommodated by the monetary policy. Germany would not lower its interest rates for fear of inflation, and the U.K. and Italy were not willing to raise their interest rates (which was necessary to maintain their exchange rates) for fear of higher unemployment. Italy, however, rejoined the ERM in December 1996 in an effort to participate in the European monetary union.

Despite the recurrent turbulence in the EMS, European Union members met at Maastricht (Netherlands) in December 1991 and signed the **Maastricht Treaty**. According to the treaty, the European Union will irrevocably fix exchange rates among the member currencies by January 1, 1999, and subsequently introduce a common European currency, replacing individual national currencies. The European Central Bank, to be located in Frankfurt, Germany, will be solely responsible for the issuance of common currency and conducting monetary policy in the European Union. National central banks of individual countries then will function pretty much like regional member banks of the U.S. Federal Reserve System. Exhibit 2.5 provides a chronology of the European Union.

EXHIBIT 2.5

Chronology of the European Union

1951	The treaty establishing the European Coal and Steel Community (ECSC), which was inspired by French Foreign Minister Robert Schuman, was signed in Paris by six countries: France, Germany, Italy, Netherlands, Belgium, and Luxembourg.
1957	The treaty establishing the European Economic Community (EEC) was signed in Rome.
1968	The Custom Union became fully operational; trade restrictions among the EEC member countries were abolished and a common external tariff system was established.
1973	The U.K., Ireland, and Denmark became EC members.
1979	The European Monetary System (EMS) was established for the purpose of promoting exchange rate stability among the EC member countries.
1980	Greece became an EC member.
1986	Portugal and Spain became EC members.
1987	The Single European Act was adopted to provide a framework within which the common internal market can be achieved by the end of 1992.
1991	The Maastricht Treaty was signed and subsequently ratified by 12 member states. The treaty establishes a timetable for fulfilling the European Monetary Union (EMU). The treaty also commits the EC to political union.
1994	The European Community was renamed the European Union (EU).
1995	Austria, Finland, and Sweden became EU members.
1999	A common European currency, the euro, was adopted by 11 EU member countries.

To pave the way for the European Monetary Union (EMU), the member countries of the European Union agreed to closely coordinate their fiscal, monetary, and exchange rate policies and achieve a *convergence* of their economies. Specifically, each member country shall strive to: (1) keep the ratio of government budget deficits to gross domestic product (GDP) below 3 percent, (2) keep gross public debts below 60 percent of GDP, (3) achieve a high degree of price stability, and (4) maintain its currency within the prescribed exchange rate ranges of the ERM.

THE EURO AND THE EUROPEAN MONETARY UNION

On January 1, 1999, an epochal event took place in the arena of international finance: Eleven European countries adopted a common currency called the euro, voluntarily giving up their monetary sovereignty. The euro-11 includes Austria, Belgium, Finland, France, Germany, Ireland, Italy, Luxembourg, the Netherlands, Portugal, and Spain. Four member countries of the European Union—Denmark, Greece, Sweden, and the United Kingdom—did not join the first wave. Greece would like to join the euro group as soon as it can satisfy the preconditions for the monetary union. The other three countries deliberately chose not to adopt the euro for now.

The advent of a European single currency, which may potentially rival the U.S. dollar as a global currency, has profound implications for various aspects of international finance. In this section, we are going to (1) describe briefly the historical background for the euro and its implementation process, (2) discuss the potential benefits and costs of the euro from the perspective of the member countries, and (3) investigate the broad impacts of the euro on international finance in general.

A Brief History of the Euro

Considering that no European currency has been in circulation since the fall of the Roman Empire, the advent of the euro in January 1999 indeed qualifies as an epochal event. The Roman emperor Gaius Diocletianus, A.D. 286–301, reformed the coinage and established a single currency throughout the realm. The advent of the euro also marks the first time that sovereign countries voluntarily have given up their monetary independence to foster economic integration. The euro thus represents a historically unprecedented experiment, the outcome of which will have far-reaching implications. If the experiment succeeds, for example, both the euro and the dollar will dominate the world of international finance. In addition, a successful euro would give a powerful impetus to the political unionization of Europe.

The euro should be viewed as a product of historical evolution toward an ever deepening integration of Europe, which began in earnest with the formation of the European Economic Community in 1958. As discussed previously, the European Monetary System (EMS) was created in 1979 to establish a European zone of monetary stability; members were required to restrict fluctuations of their currencies. In 1991, the Maastricht European Council reached agreement on a draft Treaty on the European Union, which called for the introduction of a single European currency by 1999. With the launching of the euro on January 1, 1999, the European Monetary Union (EMU) was created. The EMU is a logical extension of the EMS, and the European Currency Unit (ECU) was the precursor of the euro. Indeed, ECU contracts were required by EU law to be converted to euro contracts on a one-to-one basis.

As the euro was introduced, each national currency of the euro-11 countries was *irrevocably* fixed to the euro at a conversion rate as of January 1, 1999. The conversion rates are provided in Exhibit 2.6. National currencies such as the French franc, German mark, and Italian lira are no longer independent currencies. Rather, they are just different denominations of the same currency, the euro. If one wants to find the conversion rate between a pair of national currencies, one needs to use the euro conversion rates of the two currencies. By January 1, 2002, euro notes and coins will be introduced to circulation while national bills and coins will be gradually withdrawn.

EXHIBIT 2.6

Euro Conversion Rates

1 Euro Is Equal to:	
Austrian schilling	13.7603
Belgian franc	40.3399
Dutch guilder	2.20371
Finnish markka	5.94573
French franc	6.55957
German mark	1.95583
Irish punt	0.78756
Italian lira	1936.27
Luxembourg franc	40.3399
Portuguese escudo	200.482
Spanish peseta	166.386
U.S. dollar*	1.0718
Japanese yen*	123.48
Special Drawing Rights (SDR)*	0.7866

*Represents the market exchange rates of August 9, 1999.

Source: *The Wall Street Journal.*

Once the changeover is completed by July 1, 2002, at the latest, the legal-tender status of national currencies will be canceled, leaving the euro as the sole legal tender in the euro-11 countries.

Monetary policy for the euro-11 countries will be conducted by the European Central Bank (ECB) headquartered in Frankfurt, Germany, whose primary objective is to maintain price stability. The independence of the ECB is legally guaranteed so that in conducting its monetary policy, it will not be unduly subjected to political pressure from any member countries or institutions. By and large, the ECB is modeled after the German Bundesbank, which was highly successful in achieving price stability in Germany. Willem (Wim) Duisenberg, the first president of the ECB, who previously served as the president of the Dutch National Bank, recently defined "price stability" as an inflation rate of less than 2 percent.

The national central banks of the euro-11 countries will not disappear. Together with the European Central Bank, they form the European System of Central Banks (ESCB), which is in a way similar to the Federal Reserve System of the United States. The tasks of the ESCB are threefold: (1) to define and implement the common monetary policy of the Union; (2) to conduct foreign exchange operations; and (3) to hold and manage the official foreign reserves of the euro member states. In addition, governors of national central banks will sit on the Governing Council of the ECB. Although national central banks will have to follow the policies of the ECB, they will continue to perform important functions in their jurisdiction such as distributing credit, collecting resources, and managing payment systems.

What Are the Benefits of Monetary Union?

The Euro-11 countries obviously decided to form a monetary union with a common currency because they believed the benefits from such a union would outweigh the associated costs—in contrast to those eligible countries that chose not to adopt the single currency. It is thus important to understand the potential benefits and costs of monetary union.

What are the main benefits from adopting a common currency? The most direct and immediate benefits are reduced transaction costs and the elimination of exchange-rate uncertainty. There is a popular saying in Europe that if one travels through all 15 EU countries, changing money in each country but not actually spending it, one returns home with only half the original amount. Once countries use the same currency, transactions costs will be reduced substantially. These savings will accrue to practically all economic agents, benefiting individuals, companies, and governments. Although it is difficult to estimate accurately the magnitude of foreign exchange transaction costs, a consensus estimation is around 0.4 percent of Europe's GDP.

Economic agents should also benefit from the elimination of exchange-rate uncertainty. Companies will not suffer currency loss anymore from intra–euro zone transactions. Companies that used to hedge exchange risk will save hedging costs. As price comparison becomes easier because of the common currency, consumers can benefit from comparison shopping. Increased price transparency will promote Europe-wide competition, exerting a downward pressure on prices. Reduced transaction costs and the elimination of currency risk together will have the net effect of promoting cross-border investment and trade within the euro zone. By furthering economic integration of Europe, the single currency will promote corporate restructuring via mergers and acquisitions, encourage optimal business location decisions, and ultimately strengthen the international competitive position of European companies. Thus, the enhanced efficiency and competitiveness of the European economy can be regarded as the third major benefit of the monetary union.

The advent of the common European currency also helps create conditions conducive to the development of continental capital markets with depth and liquidity comparable to those of the United States. In the past, national currencies and a localized legal/regulatory framework resulted in largely illiquid, fragmented capital markets in Europe, which prevented European companies from raising capital on competitive terms. The common currency and the integration of European financial markets are likely to pave the way for a European capital market in which both European and non-European companies can raise money at favorable rates.

Last but not least, sharing a common currency should promote political cooperation and peace in Europe. The founding fathers of the European Union, including Jean Monnet, Paul-Henri Spaak, Robert Schuman, and their successors, took a series of economic measures designed to link European countries together. They envisioned a new Europe in which economic interdependence and cooperation among regions and countries replace nationalistic rivalries which so often led to calamitous wars in the past. In this context Helmut Kohl, a former German chancellor, said that the European Monetary Union was a "matter of war and peace." If the euro proves to be successful, it will advance the political integration of Europe in a major way, eventually making a "United States of Europe" feasible. The International Finance in Practice box, "Why We Believe in the Euro," expresses a positive view of the currency.

Costs of Monetary Union

The main cost of monetary union is the loss of national monetary and exchange-rate policy independence. Suppose Finland, a country heavily dependent on the paper and pulp industries, faces a sudden drop in world paper and pulp prices. This price drop could severely hurt the Finnish economy, causing unemployment and income decline while scarcely affecting other euro zone countries. Finland thus faces an "asymmetric shock." Generally speaking, a country would be more prone to asymmetric shocks the less diversified and more trade-dependent its economy is.

If Finland maintained monetary independence, the country could consider lowering domestic interest rates to stimulate the weak economy as well as letting its currency depreciate to boost foreigners' demand for Finnish products. But because Finland has joined the EMU, the country no longer has these policy options at its disposal. Further, with the rest of the euro zone unaffected by Finland's particular problem, the ECB is not likely to tune its monetary policy to address a local Finnish shock. In other words, a common monetary policy dictated in Frankfurt cannot address asymmetric economic shocks that only affect a particular country or subregion; it can only deal with euro zone–wide shocks.

INTERNATIONAL FINANCE IN PRACTICE

Why We Believe in the Euro

By Jürgen Schrempp, CEO of DaimlerChrysler

In our company, we don't mean to waste even a day in putting the euro to work. On Jan. 1, 1999—day one for the new currency—our company will switch over completely to the euro as the internal and external unit of account. We expect to be one of the first German-based companies—perhaps *the* first—to make such a complete change. We'll also encourage our suppliers within Euroland to invoice us in euros from the very beginning. Our Euroland customers, of course, will have the option of paying in either euros or their domestic currency until 2001.

Nearly all major European companies are in favor of the single currency. But having recently agreed on a historic, transatlantic merger with Chrysler Corp. of the United States, we feel especially attuned to the forces of global competition that make the euro so essential. For our new company, DaimlerChrysler AG, and for Germany and Europe as a whole, economic and monetary union will bring substantial and lasting benefits as we take our place in the interdependent world of the 21st century.

Those benefits will take shape—indeed, are already occurring—in several realms at once. First and most fundamental is the political. The single currency will push the countries of Europe into cooperating more and more in seeking solutions to common economic problems. As they do so, they'll grow increasingly intertwined politically.

At the same time, the euro will unleash powerful market forces certain to transform the way Europeans live and work. The years ahead will bring increased efficiency, greater productivity, higher overall living standards and lower unemployment. For businesses, a common currency will reduce transaction costs—eliminating, among other things, the unnecessary waste of resources involved in dealing with several European currencies. At present, doing business across borders means having to buy and sell foreign currencies—and taking the risk that sudden changes in their relative value could upend an otherwise sound business strategy. The risks can be hedged, of course, but only at a cost that must ultimately be borne by customers.

The market forces unleashed by the euro will be felt not just by corporate managers but also by political leaders. Business executives are already working to rationalize their companies, enhancing productivity and improving labor flexibility. Elected officials, facing competition as they try to attract the investments that create jobs, will eventually lower corporate tax rates and streamline regulation. In so doing, governments will give corporations a boost, like the reduction in the cost of capital that came about as countries tightened their fiscal and monetary policies in preparation for EMU.

If, however, wage and price levels in Finland are flexible, then the country may still be able to deal with an asymmetric shock; lower wage and price levels in Finland would have economic effects similar to those of a depreciation of the Finnish currency. Furthermore, if capital flows freely across the euro zone and workers are willing to relocate to where jobs are, then again much of the asymmetric shock can be absorbed without monetary adjustments. If these conditions are not met, however, the asymmetric shock can cause a severe and prolonged recession in the affected country. In this case, monetary union will become a costly venture. According to the **theory of optimum currency areas,** originally conceived by Professor Robert Mundell of Columbia University in 1961, the relevant criterion for identifying and designing a common currency zone is the degree of factor (i.e., capital and labor) mobility within the zone; a high degree of factor mobility would provide an adjustment mechanism, providing an alternative to country-specific monetary/currency adjustments.

Considering the high degree of capital and labor mobility in the United States, one might argue that the United States approximates an optimum currency area; it would be suboptimal for each of the 50 states to issue its own currency. In contrast, unemployed workers in Helsinki, for example, are not very likely to move to Milan or Stuttgart for job opportunities because of cultural, religious, linguistic, and other barriers. The stability pact of EMU, designed to discourage irresponsible fiscal behavior in the post-EMU era, also constrains the Finnish government to restrict its budget deficit to 3 percent of GDP at most. At the same time, Finland cannot expect

These changes are mutually reinforcing. And as they take hold, Euroland companies will grow more confident about committing resources to long-term projects. A look at the level of corporate mergers in recent years shows that managers have already stepped up their strategic decision making. Europe saw 237 such deals last year, worth $250 billion, of which 25 percent were European cross-border transactions. In 1995, by contrast, there were just 100 deals, worth $168 billion—and only 17 percent were European cross-border transactions.

Euroland will be a strong base for companies striving to compete globally. In 1997 its combined population numbered 290 million, compared with 268 million for the United States and 126 million for Japan. Its combined GDP was $6.3 trillion, versus $7.8 trillion for the United States and $4.2 trillion for Japan. Euroland already trades with the rest of the world as much as the United States does, and the picture will change in favor of Europe as soon as the United Kingdom, and others who have stayed out of the first wave, join the currency union. Such a development—the sooner the better—is something we would very much welcome.

Launching the new euro is one thing; successfully managing the EMU process in the years ahead is quite another. Implementation poses major challenges. Some will be technical; others will have to do with maintaining a unity of purpose among a diverse group of nations, regions, peoples and cultures. I believe, however, that Europe possesses the unshakable political will and financial expertise needed to keep this endeavor on track.

It will help that—as we as DaimlerChrysler well know—some of the payoffs are immediate and obvious. Currently, one third of our group's revenues are earned in Deutsche marks, but nearly three quarters of our costs are incurred in that currency. That makes planning harder and running the company more complex. But with the coming of the euro, the disparity between our DM costs and DM revenues will diminish. As of January, 50 percent of our revenues will be in euros, with 80 percent of our costs incurred in the same currency.

How will the euro affect our ability to compete in the United States, our main export market outside the EU? In a word, positively. Higher productivity and a stable "home" currency will allow us to maintain a competitive pricing structure. Such long-term consistency in our business practices is something our U.S. customers have come to appreciate.

One final point. Thanks to the single market and the pending introduction of a single currency, Europe has matured both politically and economically. As a major transatlantic player, DaimlerChrysler is now in a position to communicate an important message to its business partners in that other great single-currency market, the United States. Working through the World Trade Organization and other groups, the globe has made great progress toward free and fair trade over the years. Now let us together examine opportunities for removing some of the remaining obstacles to trade between Europe and the United States. The beneficiaries will be consumers on both sides of the Atlantic.

Source: *Newsweek*, Special Issue, Winter 1998, p. 38. Reprinted with permission.

to receive a major transfer payment from Brussels, because of a rather low degree of fiscal integration among EU countries. These considerations taken together suggest that the European Monetary Union will involve significant economic costs. An empirical study by von Hagen and Neumann (1994) identified Austria, Belgium, France, Luxembourg, the Netherlands, and Germany as nations that satisfy the conditions for an optimum currency area. However, Denmark, Italy, and the United Kingdom do not. It is interesting to note that Denmark and the United Kingdom actually chose to stay out of the EMU. Von Hagen and Neumann's study suggests that Italy joined the EMU prematurely.

Prospects of the Euro: Some Critical Questions

Will the euro succeed? The first real test of the euro will come when the euro zone experiences major asymmetric shocks. A successful response to these shocks will require wage, price, and fiscal flexibility. A cautionary note is in order: Asymmetric shocks can occur even within a country. In the United States, for example, when oil prices jumped in the 1970s, oil-consuming regions such as New England suffered a severe recession, whereas Texas, a major oil-producing state, experienced a major boom. Likewise, in Italy, the highly industrialized Genoa–Milan region and the southern Mezzogiorno, an underdeveloped region, can be in very different phases of the business cycle. But these countries have managed their economies with a common national monetary policy. Although asymmetric shocks are no doubt more serious

INTERNATIONAL FINANCE IN PRACTICE

The New World Order of Finance

Global financial panics erupt every decade or so. But even by historical standards, Mexico's currency collapse ranks among the scariest. With the crisis stretching into its seventh week, investors were stampeding. Worse yet, the panic was spreading from Buenos Aires to Budapest. Even the dollar was taking an unexpected shellacking. Some were bracing for another 1987 crash—not just in Mexico City, but in New York, London, and Tokyo.

It took forceful action to stop the runaway markets before they dragged the world economy down with them: $49.8 billion in loans and guarantees for Mexico from the U.S. and its allies. Some bankers say the total could reach $53 billion or more. Certainly, this will go down as the largest socialization of market risk in international history.

Ambitious Labor

With the U.S. spreading the gospel of democracy and free-market economics throughout the developing world, Clinton and his cohorts had little choice but to assemble the megaplan. As the club of emerging-market nations expands, the rich nations' obligation to provide a safety net for poorer trading partners is growing exponentially. America and its allies must mount a collective drive to ensure global monetary and economic stability—much like their efforts to maintain geopolitical order in the post-cold-war era.

Such ambitious labor is needed because the nature of financial markets has changed since Latin America's last financial crisis in 1982. Back then, it was gunslinger bankers who lent to Latin America. Because banks could lend for the long haul and absorb losses, they were a valuable shock absorber for the financial system. When enough Latin loans eventually went bad, it still took years to craft and conclude their restructuring.

Since then, bankers have wised up. Now, others with a shorter time horizon make the emerging-market deals. This time, it was mutual-, hedge-, and pension-fund gunslingers who provided the capital. Mexico attracted $45 billion in mutual-fund cash in the past three years. And when the peso dived, fund managers bolted. In this global market, all it takes is a phone call to Fidelity to send money hurtling toward Monterey—or zooming back. And world leaders should be able to act with similar speed.

Clinton's $40 billion in loan guarantees for Mexico got nowhere because Congress objected to bailing out Wall Street. Legislators also did not like the U.S. shouldering most of the cost. They were right. Emerging markets will stay volatile, and countries and investors shouldn't expect a handout every time an economy hits a rough patch. And when a rescue is necessary, it should be global.

Bridge the Gap

Europe and Japan, after all, will benefit from a healthy Mexican economy and thus should bear the burden of supporting it in times of crisis. Likewise, Washington should be obliged to lend a hand to European or Asian allies if Poland or Indonesia come unglued. One way to keep the next crisis at bay: bridge the gap between short-term money and long-term investment needs.

In addition, emerging economies need to take steps to immunize themselves from the vagaries of a fund-dominated world. It would help a lot if more of them developed mandatory pension schemes to build up domestic savings. Along with that should come privatization. With capital so flighty, it may take hard decisions to make money stay put. But if the first world wants to encourage capitalism, it will have to underwrite it—even if the cost is huge.

Source: Reprinted from February 13, 1995 issue of *Business Week* by special permission, © 1995 by The McGraw-Hill Companies, Inc.

internationally, one should be careful not to exaggerate their significance as an impediment to monetary union. In addition, since the advent of the EMS in 1979, the EMU member countries have restricted their monetary policies in order to maintain exchange-rate stability in Europe. Considering that intra–euro zone trade accounts for about 60 percent of foreign trade of the euro-11 countries, benefits from the EMU are likely to exceed substantially the associated costs. Furthermore, leaders in political and business circles in Europe have invested substantial political capital in the success of the euro. It seems safe to predict that the euro will be a success.

Will the euro become a global currency rivaling the U.S. dollar? The U.S. dollar has been the dominant global currency since the end of the First World War, replacing the British pound as the currency of choice in international commercial and financial

EXHIBIT 2.7

Economic Comparison: Euro-11, United States, and Japan

Indicators (1997)	Euro-11	U.S.	Japan
GDP ($ billion)	6,309	7,819	4,223
Population (million)	290	268	126
International trade share	18.6%	19.6%	7.9%
Budget deficit (% of GDP)	2.5	0.3	3.4
Inflation rate	1.8%	2.4%	1.7%

Source: OECD.

transactions. Even after the dollar got off the gold standard in 1971, it retained its dominant position in the world economy. This dominance was possible because the dollar was backed by the sheer size of the U.S. economy and the relatively sound monetary policy of the Federal Reserve. Now, as can be seen from Exhibit 2.7, the euro zone is remarkably comparable to the United States in terms of population size, GDP, and international trade share. As previously discussed, there is little doubt that the ECB will pursue a sound monetary policy. Considering both the size of the euro-zone economy and the mandate of the ECB, the euro is likely to emerge as the second global currency in the near future, ending the dollar's sole dominance. The Japanese yen will be a junior partner in the dollar–euro condominium. However, the emergence of the euro as another global currency may prompt Japan and other Asian countries to explore cooperative monetary arrangements for the region.

THE MEXICAN PESO CRISIS

On December 20, 1994, the Mexican government under new president Ernesto Zedillo announced its decision to devalue the peso against the dollar by 14 percent. This decision, however, touched off a stampede to sell pesos as well as Mexican stocks and bonds. As Exhibit 2.8 shows, by early January 1995 the peso fell against the U.S. dollar by as much as 40 percent, forcing the Mexican government to float the peso. As concerned international investors reduced their holdings of emerging market securities, the peso crisis rapidly spilled over to other Latin American and Asian financial markets.

Faced with an impending default by the Mexican government and the possibility of a global financial meltdown, the Clinton administration, together with the International Monetary Fund (IMF) and the Bank for International Settlement (BIS), put together a $53 billion package to bail out Mexico.[7] As the bailout plan was put together and announced on January 31, the world's, as well as Mexico's, financial markets began to stabilize.

The Mexican peso crisis is significant in that it is perhaps the first serious international financial crisis touched off by cross-border flight of portfolio capital. International mutual funds are known to have invested more than $45 billion in Mexican securities during a three-year period prior to the peso crisis. As the peso fell, fund managers quickly liquidated their holdings of Mexican securities as well as other emerging market securities. This had a highly destabilizing, contagious effect on the world financial system. The same point is discussed in the International Finance in Practice box, "The New World Order of Finance" on page 46.

As the world's financial markets are becoming more integrated, this type of contagious financial crisis is likely to occur more often. Two lessons emerge from the peso crisis. First, it is essential to have a multinational safety net in place to safeguard the world financial system from the peso-type crisis. No single country or institution

EXHIBIT 2.8

U.S. Dollar versus Mexican Peso Exchange Rate (November 1, 1994–January 31, 1995)

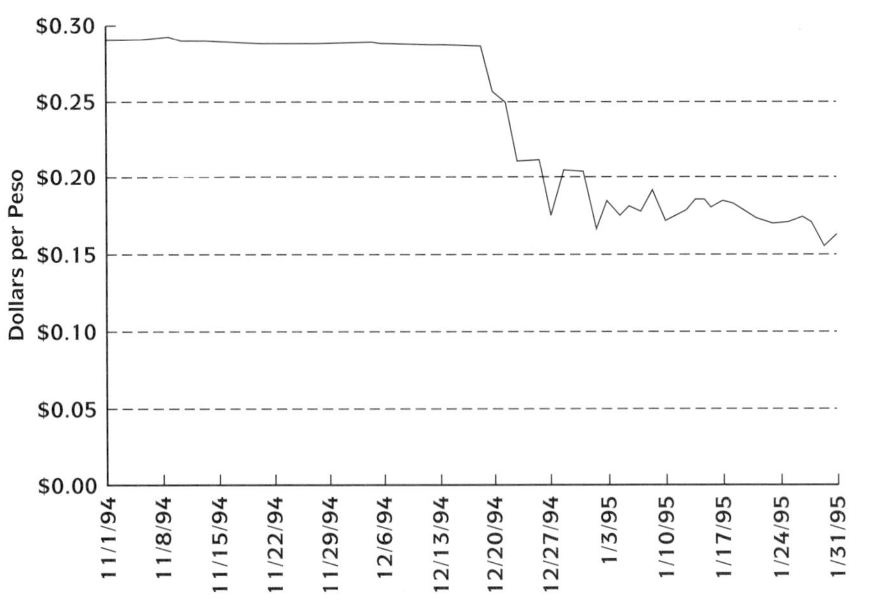

can handle a potentially global crisis alone. In addition, in the face of rapidly changing market conditions, usually slow and parochial political processes cannot cope with rapidly changing market conditions. In fact, the Clinton administration faced stiff opposition in Congress and from foreign allies when it was working out a bailout package for Mexico. As a result, early containment of the crisis was not possible. Fortunately, the G-7 countries endorsed a $50 billion bailout fund for countries in financial distress, which would be administered by the IMF, and a series of increased disclosure requirements to be followed by all countries. The reluctance of the outgoing Salinas administration to disclose the true state of the Mexican economy, that is, the rapid depletion of foreign exchange reserves and serious trade deficits, contributed to the sudden collapse of the peso.

Second, Mexico excessively depended on foreign portfolio capital to finance its economic development. In hindsight, the country should have saved more domestically and depended more on long-term rather than short-term foreign capital investments. As Professor Robert MacKinnon of Stanford University pointed out, a flood of foreign money had two undesirable effects. It led to an easy credit policy on domestic borrowings, which caused Mexicans to consume more and save less.[8] Foreign capital influx also caused a higher domestic inflation and an overvalued peso, which hurt Mexico's trade balances.

THE ASIAN CURRENCY CRISIS

On July 2, 1997, the Thai baht, which had been largely fixed to the U.S. dollar, was suddenly devalued. What at first appeared to be a local financial crisis in Thailand quickly escalated into a global financial crisis, first spreading to other Asian countries—Indonesia, Korea, Malaysia, and the Philippines—then far afield to Russia and Latin America, especially Brazil. As can be seen from Exhibit 2.9, at the height of the crisis the Korean won fell by about 50 percent in its dollar value from its precrisis level, whereas the Indonesian rupiah fell an incredible 80 percent.

EXHIBIT 2.9 Asian Currency Crisis

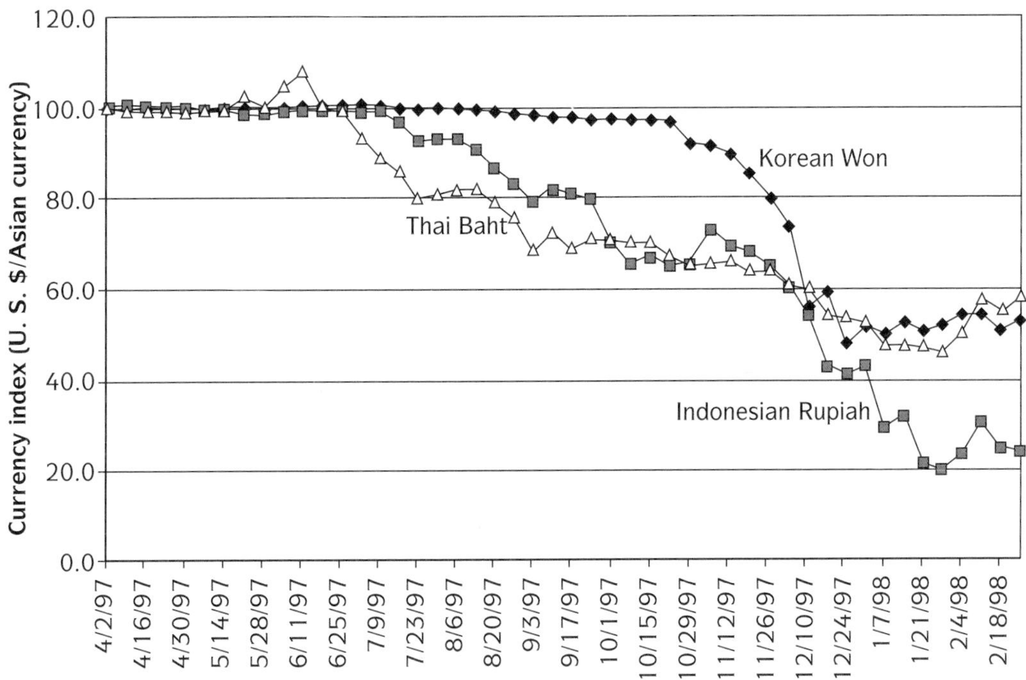

Exchange rates are indexed (U.S. $/Asian currency on 4/2/97 = 100). Exchange rates on 4/2/97: 0.00112 U.S. $/Korean won, 0.03856 U.S. $/Thai baht, and 0.00041 U.S. $/Indonesian rupiah.

The current Asian crisis is the third major currency crisis of the 1990s, preceded by the crises of the European Monetary System (EMS) of 1992 and the Mexican peso in 1994–95. The current Asian crisis, however, has turned out to be far more serious than its two predecessors in terms of the extent of contagion and the severity of resultant economic and social costs. Following the massive depreciations of local currencies, financial institutions and corporations with foreign-currency debts in the afflicted countries were driven to extreme financial distress and many were forced to default. What's worse, the currency crisis led to an unprecedentedly deep, widespread, and long-lasting recession in East Asia, a region that, for the last few decades, has enjoyed the most rapidly growing economy in the world. At the same time, many lenders and investors from the developed countries also suffered large capital losses from their investments in emerging-market securities. For example, Long Term Capital Management (LTCM), one of the largest and, until then, profitable hedge funds, experienced a near bankruptcy due to its exposure to Russian bonds. The Federal Reserve System, which feared a domino-like systematic financial failure in the United States, orchestrated a $3.5 billion bailout of LTCM in September 1998.

Considering the global effects of the Asian currency crisis and the challenges it poses for the world financial system, it would be useful to understand its origins and causes and discuss how similar crises might be prevented in the future.

Origins of the Asian Currency Crisis

Several factors are responsible for the onset of Asian currency crisis: a weak domestic financial system, free international capital flows, the contagion effects of changing market sentiment, and inconsistent economic policies. In recent years, both developing and developed countries were encouraged to liberalize their financial markets and allow free flows of capital across countries. As capital markets were liberalized, both firms and financial institutions in the Asian developing countries eagerly borrowed foreign currencies from U.S., Japanese, and European investors, who were attracted to these fast-growing emerging markets for extra returns for their portfolios. In 1996 alone, for example, five Asian countries—Indonesia, Korea, Malaysia, the Philippines, and Thailand—experienced a new inflow of private capital worth $93 billion. In contrast, there was a net outflow of $12 billion from the five countries in 1997.

Large inflows of private capital resulted in a credit boom in the Asian countries in the early and mid-1990s. The credit boom was often directed to speculations in real estate and stock markets as well as to investments in marginal industrial projects. Fixed or stable exchange rates also encouraged unhedged financial transactions and excessive risk-taking by both lenders and borrowers, who were not much concerned with exchange risk. As asset prices declined (as happened in Thailand prior to the currency crisis) in part due to the government's effort to control the overheated economy, the quality of banks' loan portfolios also declined as the same assets were held as collateral for the loans. Clearly, banks and other financial institutions in the afflicted countries practiced poor risk management and were poorly supervised. In addition, their lending decisions were often influenced by political considerations, likely leading to suboptimal allocation of resources. However, the so-called crony capitalism was not a new condition, and the East Asian economies achieved an economic miracle under the same system.

Meanwhile, the booming economy with a fixed or stable nominal exchange rate inevitably brought about an appreciation of the real exchange rate. This, in turn, resulted in a marked slowdown in export growth in such Asian countries as Thailand and Korea. In addition, a long-lasting recession in Japan and the yen's depreciation against the dollar hurt Japan's neighbors, further worsening the trade balances of the Asian developing countries. If the Asian currencies had been allowed to depreciate in real terms, which was not possible because of the fixed nominal exchange rates, such catastrophic, discrete changes of the exchange rates as observed in 1997 might have been avoided.

In Thailand, as the run on the baht started, the Thai central bank initially injected liquidity to the domestic financial system and tried to defend the exchange rate by drawing on its foreign exchange reserves. With its foreign reserves declining rapidly, the central bank eventually decided to devalue the baht. The sudden collapse of the baht touched off a panicky flight of capital from other Asian countries with a high degree of financial vulnerability. It is interesting to note from Exhibit 2.10 that the three Asian countries hardest hit by the crisis are among the most financially vulnerable as measured by (1) the ratio of short-term foreign debts to international reserve and (2) the ratio of broad money, M2 (which represents the banking sector's liabilities) to international reserve. Contagion of the currency crisis was caused at least in part by the panicky, indiscriminate flight of capital from the Asian countries for fear of a spreading crisis. Fear thus became self-fulfilling. As lenders withdrew their capital and refused to renew short-term loans, the former credit boom turned into a credit crunch, hurting creditworthy as well as marginal borrowers.

As the crisis unfolded, the International Monetary Fund (IMF) came to rescue the three hardest-hit Asian countries—Indonesia, Korea, and Thailand—with bailout plans. As a condition for the bailing out, however, the IMF imposed a set of austerity measures, such as raising domestic interest rates and curtailing government expenditures, that were designed to support the exchange rate. Since these austerity measures, contractionary in nature, were implemented when the economies had already been contracting because of a severe credit crunch, the Asian economies consequently suffered a deep, long-lasting recession. According to a recent World Bank report (1999), one-year declines in industrial production of 20 percent or more in Thailand and Indonesia are comparable to those in the United States and Germany

EXHIBIT 2.10 Financial Vulnerability Indicators

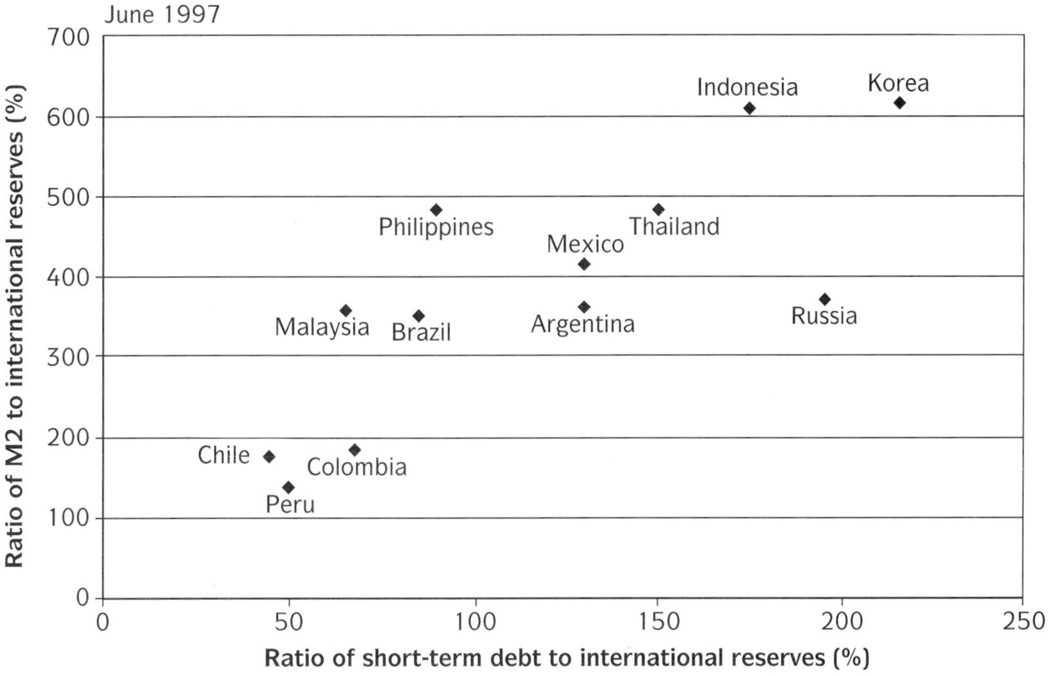

Source: The World Bank, International Monetary Fund.

during the Great Depression. One can thus argue that the IMF initially prescribed the wrong medicine for the afflicted Asian economies. The IMF bailout plans were also criticized on another ground: moral hazard. IMF bailouts may breed dependency in developing countries and encourage risk-taking on the part of international lenders. There is a sentiment that taxpayers' money should not be used to bail out "fat-cat" investors. Former U.S. senator Lauch Faircloth was quoted as saying: "Through the IMF we have privatized profits and socialized losses." No bailout, however, can be compared with the proposal to get rid of the only fire department in town so that people will be more careful about fire.

Lessons from the Asian Currency Crisis

Generally speaking, liberalization of financial markets when combined with a weak, underdeveloped domestic financial system tends to create an environment susceptible to currency and financial crises. Interestingly, both Mexico and Korea experienced a major currency crisis within a few years after joining the OECD, which required a significant liberalization of financial markets. It seems safe to recommend that countries first strengthen their domestic financial system and then liberalize their financial markets.

A number of measures can and should be undertaken to strengthen a nation's domestic financial system. Among other things, the government should strengthen its system of financial-sector regulation and supervision. One way of doing so is to sign on to the "Core Principle of Effective Banking Supervision" drafted by the Basle Committee on Banking Supervision and to monitor its compliance with the principle. In addition, banks should be encouraged to base their lending decisions solely on economic merits rather than political considerations. Furthermore, firms, financial institutions, and the government should be required to provide the public with reliable financial data in a timely fashion. A higher level of disclosure of financial information and the resultant transparency about the state of the economy will make it easier for all the concerned parties to monitor the situation better and mitigate the destabilizing cycles of investor euphoria and panic accentuated by the lack of reliable information.

Even if a country decides to liberalize its financial markets by allowing cross-border capital flows, it should encourage foreign direct investments and equity and long-term bond investments; it should not encourage short-term investments that can be reversed overnight, causing financial turmoil. As Chile has successfully implemented, some form of **"Tobin tax"** on the international flow of hot money can be useful. Throwing some sand in the wheels of international finance can have a stabilizing effect on the world's financial markets.

A fixed but adjustable exchange rate is problematic in the face of integrated international financial markets. Such a rate arrangement often invites speculative attack at the time of financial vulnerability. Countries should not try to restore the same fixed exchange-rate system unless they are willing to impose capital controls. According to the so-called "trilemma" that economists are fond of talking about, a country can attain only two of the following three conditions: (1) a fixed exchange rate, (2) free international flows of capital, and (3) an independent monetary policy. If a country would like to maintain monetary policy independence to pursue its own domestic economic goals and still would like to keep a fixed exchange rate between its currency and other currencies, then the country should restrict free flows of capital. China and India were not noticeably affected by the Asian currency crisis because both countries maintain capital controls, segmenting their capital markets from the rest of the world. Hong Kong and Argentina were less affected by the crisis for a different reason. Both countries have fixed their exchange rates permanently to the U.S. dollar via currency boards and allowed free flows of capital; in consequence, they gave up their monetary independence. A currency board is an extreme form of the fixed exchange-rate regime under which local currency is "fully" backed by the dollar (or another chosen standard currency). Hong Kong and Argentina have essentially dollarized their economies. To avoid currency crises, a country can have a really fixed exchange rate or flexible exchange rate, but not a fixed yet adjustable exchange rate, when international capital markets are integrated.

FIXED VERSUS FLEXIBLE EXCHANGE-RATE REGIMES

Since some countries, including the United States and possibly Japan, prefer flexible exchange rates, while others, notably the members of the EMS and many developing countries, would like to maintain fixed exchange rates, it is worthwhile to examine some of the arguments advanced in favor of fixed versus flexible exchange rates.

The key arguments for flexible exchange rates rest on (1) easier external adjustments and (2) national policy autonomy. Suppose a country is experiencing a balance-of-payments deficit at the moment. This means that there is an excess supply of the country's currency at the prevailing exchange rate in the foreign exchange market. Under a flexible exchange rate regime, the external value of the country's currency will simply depreciate to the level at which there is no excess supply of the country's currency. At the new exchange rate level, the balance-of-payments disequilibrium will disappear.

As long as the exchange rate is allowed to be determined according to market forces, external balance will be achieved automatically. Consequently, the government does not have to take policy actions to correct the balance-of-payments disequilibrium. With flexible exchange rates, therefore, the government can use its monetary and fiscal policies to pursue whatever economic goals it chooses. Under a fixed rate regime, however, the government may have to take contractionary (expansionary) monetary and fiscal policies to correct the balance-of-payments deficit (surplus) at the existing exchange rate. Since policy tools need to be committed to maintaining the exchange rate, the government cannot use the same policy tools to pursue other economic objectives. As a result, the government loses its policy autonomy under a fixed exchange rate regime.

A possible drawback of the flexible exchange rate regime is that exchange rate uncertainty may hamper international trade and investment. Proponents of the fixed exchange rate regime argue that when future exchange rates are uncertain, businesses tend to shun foreign trade. Since countries cannot fully benefit from international trade under exchange rate uncertainty, resources will be allocated suboptimally on a global basis. Proponents of the fixed exchange rate regime argue that fixed exchange rates eliminate such uncertainty and thus promote international trade. However, to the extent that firms can hedge exchange risk by means of currency forward or options contracts, uncertain exchange rates do not necessarily hamper international trade.

As the above discussion suggests, the choice between the alternative exchange rate regimes is likely to involve a trade-off between national policy independence and international economic integration. If countries would like to pursue their respective domestic economic goals, they are likely to pursue divergent macroeconomic policies, rendering fixed exchange rates infeasible. On the other hand, if countries are committed to promoting international economic integration (as is the case with the core members of the European Union like France and Germany), the benefits of fixed exchange rates are likely to outweigh the associated costs.

A "good" (or ideal) international monetary system should provide (1) liquidity, (2) adjustment, and (3) confidence. In other words, a good IMS should be able to provide the world economy with sufficient monetary reserves to support the growth of international trade and investment. It should also provide an effective mechanism that restores the balance-of-payments equilibrium whenever it is disturbed. Lastly, it should offer a safeguard to prevent crises of confidence in the system that result in panicked flights from one reserve asset to another. Politicians and economists should keep these three criteria in mind when they design and evaluate the international monetary system.

SUMMARY

This chapter provides an overview of the international monetary system, which defines an environment in which multinational corporations operate.

1. The international monetary system can be defined as the institutional framework within which international payments are made, the movements of capital are accommodated, and exchange rates among currencies are determined.
2. The international monetary system went through five stages of evolution: (a) bimetallism, (b) classical gold standard, (c) interwar period, (d) Bretton Woods system, and (e) flexible exchange rate regime.
3. The classical gold standard spanned 1875–1914. Under the gold standard, the exchange rate between two currencies is determined by the gold contents of the currencies. Balance-of-payments disequilibrium is automatically corrected through the price-specie-flow mechanism. The gold standard still has ardent supporters who believe that it provides an effective hedge against price inflation. Under the gold standard, however, the world economy can be subject to deflationary pressure due to the limited supply of monetary gold.
4. To prevent the recurrence of economic nationalism with no clear "rules of the game" witnessed during the interwar period, representatives of 44 nations met at Bretton Woods, New Hampshire, in 1944 and adopted a new international monetary system. Under the Bretton Woods system, each country established a par value in relation to the U.S. dollar, which was fully convertible to gold. Countries used foreign exchanges, especially the U.S. dollar, as well as gold as international means of payments. The Bretton Woods system was designed to maintain stable exchange rates and economize on gold. The Bretton Woods

system eventually collapsed in 1973 mainly because of U.S. domestic inflation and the persistent balance-of-payments deficits.

5. The flexible exchange rate regime that replaced the Bretton Woods system was ratified by the Jamaica Agreement. Following a spectacular rise and fall of the U.S. dollar in the 1980s, major industrial countries agreed to cooperate to achieve greater exchange rate stability. The Louvre Accord of 1987 marked the inception of the managed-float system under which the G-7 countries would jointly intervene in the foreign exchange market to correct over- or undervaluation of currencies.
6. In 1979, the EEC countries launched the European Monetary System (EMS) to establish a "zone of monetary stability" in Europe. The two main instruments of the EMS are the European Currency Unit (ECU) and the Exchange Rate Mechanism (ERM). The ECU is a basket currency comprising the currencies of the EMS members and serves as the accounting unit of the EMS. The ERM refers to the procedure by which EMS members collectively manage their exchange rates. The ERM is based on a parity grid that the member countries are required to maintain.
7. On January 1, 1999, eleven European countries including France and Germany adopted a common currency called the euro. The advent of a single European currency, which may eventually rival the U.S. dollar as a global vehicle currency, will have major implications for the European as well as world economy. Euro-11 countries will benefit from reduced transaction costs and the elimination of exchange rate uncertainty. The advent of the euro will also help develop continentwide capital markets where companies can raise capital at favorable rates.
8. While the core EMS members, including France and Germany, apparently prefer the fixed exchange rate regime, other major countries such as the United States and Japan are willing to live with flexible exchange rates. Under the flexible exchange rate regime, governments can retain policy independence because the external balance will be achieved by the exchange rate adjustments rather than by policy intervention. Exchange rate uncertainty, however, can potentially hamper international trade and investment. The choice between the alternative exchange rate regimes is likely to involve a trade-off between national policy autonomy and international economic integration.

KEY WORDS

bimetallism, 29
Bretton Woods system, 32
currency board, 38
Euro, 28
European Currency Unit (ECU), 37
European Monetary System (EMS), 37
Exchange Rate Mechanism (ERM), 37
gold-exchange standard, 33
gold standard, 30
Gresham's law, 29
international monetary system, 28
Jamaica Agreement, 35
Louvre Accord, 36
Maastricht Treaty, 40
managed-float system, 36
optimum currency area, 44
par value, 32
Plaza Accord, 36
price-specie-flow mechanism, 31
Smithsonian Agreement, 34
snake, 37
special drawing rights (SDR), 33
sterilization of gold, 31
Tobin tax, 52
Triffin paradox, 33

QUESTIONS

1. Explain Gresham's law.
2. Explain the mechanism that restores the balance-of-payments equilibrium when it is disturbed under the gold standard.

3. Suppose that the pound is pegged to gold at 6 pounds per ounce, whereas the franc is pegged to gold at 12 francs per ounce. This, of course, implies that the equilibrium exchange rate should be two francs per pound. If the current market exchange rate is 2.2 francs per pound, how would you take advantage of this situation? What would be the effect of shipping costs?
4. Discuss the advantages and disadvantages of the gold standard.
5. What were the main objectives of the Bretton Woods system?
6. Comment on the proposition that the Bretton Woods system was programmed to an eventual demise.
7. Explain how special drawing rights (SDR) are constructed. Also, discuss the circumstances under which the SDR was created.
8. Explain the arrangements and workings of the European Monetary System (EMS).
9. There are arguments for and against the alternative exchange rate regimes.
   a. List the advantages of the flexible exchange rate regime.
   b. Criticize the flexible exchange rate regime from the viewpoint of the proponents of the fixed exchange rate regime.
   c. Rebut the above criticism from the viewpoint of the proponents of the flexible exchange rate regime.
10. In an integrated world financial market, a financial crisis in a country can be quickly transmitted to other countries, causing a global crisis. What kind of measures would you propose to prevent the recurrence of a Asia-type crisis?
11. Discuss the criteria for a "good" international monetary system.
12. Once capital markets are integrated, it is difficult for a country to maintain a fixed exchange rate. Explain why this may be so.

MINI CASE

Will the United Kingdom join the Euro Club?

When the euro was introduced in January 1999, the United Kingdom was conspicuously absent from the list of European countries adopting the common currency. Although the current Labour government led by Prime Minister Tony Blair appears to be in favor of joining the euro club, it is not clear at the moment if that will actually happen. The opposition Tory party is not in favor of adopting the euro and thus giving up monetary sovereignty of the country. The public opinion is also divided on the issue.

Whether the United Kingdom will eventually join the euro club is a matter of considerable importance for the future of the European Union as well as that of the United Kingdom. If the United Kingdom, with its sophisticated finance industry joins, it will most certainly propel the euro into a global currency status rivaling the U.S. dollar. The United Kingdom on its part will firmly join the process of economic and political unionization of Europe, abandoning its traditional balancing role.

Investigate the political, economic, and historical situations surrounding the British participation in the European economic and monetary integration and write your own assessment of the prospect of Britain joining the euro club. In doing so, assess from the British perspective, among other things, (1) potential benefits and costs of adopting the euro, (2) economic and political constraints facing the country, and (3) the potential impact of British adoption of the euro on the international financial system, including the role of the U.S. dollar.

ENDNOTES

1. This does not imply that each individual country was on a bimetallic standard. In fact, many countries were on either a gold standard or a silver standard by 1870.
2. In this example, we ignored shipping costs. But as long as the shipping costs do not exceed £55.56, it is still advantageous to buy francs via "gold export" than via the foreign exchange market.
3. The price-specie-flow mechanism will work only if governments are willing to abide by the rules of the game by letting the money stock rise and fall as gold flows in and out. Once the government demonetizes (neutralizes) gold, the mechanism will break down. In addition, the effectiveness of the mechanism depends on the price elasticity of the demand for imports.
4. The balance of payments will be discussed in detail in Chapter 3.
5. This point need not be viewed as a weakness of the gold standard per se, but it casts doubt on the long-term feasibility of the gold standard.
6. The G-7 is composed of Canada, France, Japan, Germany, Italy, the U.K., and the United States.
7. The United States contributed $20 billion out of its Exchange Stabilization Fund, whereas IMF and BIS contributed, respectively, $17.8 billion and $10 billion. Canada, Latin American countries, and commercial banks collectively contributed $5 billion.
8. See "Flood of Dollars, Sunken Pesos," *New York Times*, January 20, 1995. p. A2g.

WEB RESOURCES

www.ex.ac.uk/~RDavies/arian/llyfr.html

Provides a comprehensive history of money.

wallstreeter.com/bankfrm.htm

Provides links to the central banks of more than 100 countries.

pacific.commerce.ubc.ca/xr/

Provides a list of all the currencies of the world with information on each country's exchange-rate regime. Also provides access to current and historic daily exchange rates.

www.tri.org.au/

Database covering the literature on exchange-rate target zones.

europa.eu.int/

Website of the European Union (EU). Provides basic information on EU, news, statistics, euro rates, and links to the EU institutions.

www.aci.net/kalliste/euro.htm

Describes the history of the euro.

www.ecb.int/

Website of the European Central Bank. Provides comprehensive coverage of the euro and links to EU central banks.

www.jpmorgan.com/emu/index.html

JPMorgan EMU information center.

REFERENCES AND SUGGESTED READINGS

Cooper, Richard N. *The International Monetary System: Essays in World Economics.* Cambridge, Mass.: MIT Press, 1987.

Eichengreen, Barry. *The Gold Standard in Theory and History.* Mathuen: London, 1985, pp. 39–48.

Friedman, Milton. *Essays in Positive Economics.* Chicago: University of Chicago Press, 1953.

Jorion, Philippe. "Properties of the ECU as a Currency Basket," *Journal of Multinational Financial Management* 1 (1991), pp. 1–24.

Machlup, Fritz. *Remaking the International Monetary System: The Rio Agreement and Beyond.* Baltimore: Johns Hopkins Press, 1968.

Mundell, Robert. "A Theory of Optimum Currency Areas." *American Economic Review* 51 (1961), pp. 657–65.

Nurkse, Ragnar. *International Currency Experience: Lessons of the Interwar Period.* Geneva: League of Nations, 1944.

Solomon, Robert. *The International Monetary System, 1945–1981.* New York: Harper & Row, 1982.

Stiglitz, Joseph. "Reforming the Global Economic Architecture: Lessons from Recent Crisis," *Journal of Finance* 54 (1999), pp. 1508–21.

Tobin, James. "Financial Globalization," unpublished manuscript presented at American Philosophical Society, 1998.

Triffin, Robert. *Gold and the Dollar Crisis.* New Haven, Conn.: Yale University Press, 1960.

CHAPTER THREE

Balance of Payments

CHAPTER OUTLINE

The term **balance of payments** is often mentioned in the news media and continues to be a popular subject of economic and political discourse around the world. It is not always clear, however, exactly what is meant by the term when it is mentioned in various contexts. This ambiguity is often attributable to misunderstanding and misuse of the term. The balance of payments, which is a statistical record of a country's transactions with the rest of the world, is worth studying for a couple of reasons.

First, the balance of payments provides detailed information concerning the demand and supply of a country's currency. For example, if the United States imports more than it exports, then this means that the supply of dollars is likely to exceed the demand in the foreign exchange market, *ceteris paribus.* One can thus infer that the U.S. dollar would be under pressure to depreciate against other currencies. On the other hand, if the United States exports more than it imports, then the dollar would be likely to appreciate.

Second, a country's balance-of-payment data may signal its potential as a business partner for the rest of the world. If a country is grappling with a major balance-of-payment difficulty, it may not be able to expand imports from the outside world. Instead, the country may be tempted to impose measures to restrict imports and discourage capital outflows in order to improve the balance-of-payment situation. On the other hand, a country experiencing a significant balance-of-payment surplus would be more likely to expand imports, offering marketing opportunities for foreign enterprises, and less likely to impose foreign exchange restrictions.

Third, balance-of-payments data can be used to evaluate the performance of the country in international economic competition. Suppose a country is experiencing trade deficits year after year. This trade data may then signal that the country's domestic industries lack international competitiveness. To interpret balance-of-payments data properly, it is necessary to understand how the balance-of-payments account is constructed.

BALANCE-OF-PAYMENTS ACCOUNTING

The balance of payments can be formally defined as *the statistical record of a country's international transactions over a certain period of time presented in the form of double-entry bookkeeping*. Examples of international transactions include import and export of goods and services and cross-border investments in businesses, bank accounts, bonds, stocks, and real estate. Since the balance of payments is recorded over a certain period of time (i.e., a quarter or a year), it has the same time dimension as national income accounting.[1]

Generally speaking, any transaction that results in a receipt from foreigners will be recorded as a credit, with a positive sign, in the U.S. balance of payments, whereas any transaction that gives rise to a payment to foreigners will be recorded as a debit, with a negative sign. Credit entries in the U.S. balance of payments result from foreign sales of U.S. goods and services, goodwill, financial claims, and real assets. Debit entries, on the other hand, arise from U.S. purchases of foreign goods and services, goodwill, financial claims, and real assets. Further, credit entries give rise to the demand for dollars, whereas debit entries give rise to the supply of dollars. Note that the demand (supply) for dollars is associated with the supply (demand) of foreign exchange.

Since the balance of payments is presented as a system of double-entry bookkeeping, every credit in the account is balanced by a matching debit and vice versa.

EXAMPLE 3.1: For example, suppose that Boeing Corporation exported a Boeing 747 aircraft to Japan Airlines for $50 million, and that Japan Airlines pays from its dollar bank account kept with Chase Manhattan Bank in New York City. Then, the receipt of $50 million by Boeing will be recorded as a credit (+), which will be matched by a debit (−) of the same amount representing a reduction of the U.S. bank's liabilities.

EXAMPLE 3.2: Suppose, for another example, that Boeing imports jet engines produced by Rolls-Royce for $30 million, and that Boeing makes payment by transferring the funds to a New York bank account kept by Rolls-Royce. In this case, payment by Boeing will be recorded as a debit (−), whereas the deposit of the funds by Rolls-Royce will be recorded as a credit (+).

As shown by the preceding examples, every credit in the balance of payments is matched by a debit somewhere to conform to the principle of double-entry bookkeeping.

Not only international trade, that is, exports and imports, but also cross-border investments are recorded in the balance of payments.

EXAMPLE 3.3: Suppose that Ford acquires Jaguar, a British car manufacturer, for $750 million, and that Jaguar deposits the money in Barclays Bank in London, which, in turn, uses the sum to purchase U.S. treasury notes. In this case, the payment of $750 million by Ford will be recorded as a debit (−), whereas Barclays' purchase of the U.S. Treasury notes will be recorded as a credit (+).

The above examples can be summarized as follows:

Transactions	Credit	Debit
Boeing's export	+$50 million	
Withdrawal from U.S. bank		−$50 million
Boeing's import		−$30 million
Deposit at U.S. bank	+$30 million	
Ford's acquisition of Jaguar		−$750 million
Barclays' purchase of U.S. securities	+$750 million	

BALANCE-OF-PAYMENTS ACCOUNTS

Since the balance of payments records all types of international transactions a country consummates over a certain period of time, it contains a wide variety of accounts. However, a country's international transactions can be grouped into the following three main types:

1. The current account.
2. The capital account.
3. The official reserve account.

The **current account** includes the export and import of goods and services, whereas the **capital account** includes all purchases and sales of assets such as stocks, bonds, bank accounts, real estate, and businesses. The **official reserve account,** on the other hand, covers all purchases and sales of international reserve assets such as dollars, foreign exchanges, gold, and special drawing rights (SDRs).

Let us now examine a detailed description of the balance-of-payments accounts. Exhibit 3.1 summarizes the U.S. balance-of-payments accounts for the year 1997 that we are going to use as an example.

The Current Account

Exhibit 3.1 shows that U.S. exports were $1,167.61 billion in 1997 while U.S. imports were $1,295.53 billion. The current account balance, which is defined as exports minus imports plus unilateral transfers, that is, (1) +(2) +(3) in Exhibit 3.1, was negative, −$166.80 billion. The United States thus had a balance-of-payments deficit on the current account in 1997. The current account deficit implies that the United States used up more output than it produced.[2] Since a country must finance its current account deficit either by borrowing from foreigners or by drawing down on its previously accumulated foreign wealth, a current account deficit represents a reduction in

EXHIBIT 3.1

A Summary of the U.S. Balance of Payments for 1997 (in $ billion)

	Credits	Debits
Current Account		
(1) Exports	1,167.61	
(1.1) Merchandise	680.28	
(1.2) Services	251.13	
(1.3) Factor income	236.20	
(2) Imports		−1,295.53
(2.1) Merchandise		−877.28
(2.2) Services		−163.72
(2.3) Factor income		−254.53
(3) Unilateral transfer	6.13	−45.01
Balance on current account [(1) + (2) + (3)]		−166.80
Capital Account		
(4) Direct investment	107.93	−119.44
(5) Portfolio investment	387.62	−79.28
(5.1) Equity securities	65.10	−37.98
(5.2) Debt securities	322.52	−41.30
(6) Other investment	194.95	−227.20
Balance on capital account [(4) + (5) + (6)]	264.57	
(7) Statistical discrepancies		−96.76
Overall balance	1.01	
Official Reserve Account		−1.01

Source: IMF, *International Financial Statistics Yearbook, 1998.*

the country's net foreign wealth. On the other hand, a country with a current account surplus acquires IOUs from foreigners, thereby increasing its net foreign wealth.

The current account is divided into four finer categories: merchandise trade, services, factor income, and unilateral transfers. **Merchandise trade** represents exports and imports of tangible goods, such as oil, wheat, clothes, automobiles, computers, and so on. As Exhibit 3.1 shows, U.S. merchandise exports were $680.28 billion in 1997 while imports were $877.28 billion. The United States thus had a deficit on the **trade balance** or a trade deficit. The trade balance represents the net merchandise export. As is well known, the United States has experienced persistent trade deficits since the early 1980s, whereas such key trading partners as Japan and Germany have generally realized trade surpluses. This continuous trade imbalance between the United States and her key trading partners set the stage for the precipitous decline of the dollar observed during the first half of the 1990s.

Services, the second category of the current account, include payments and receipts for legal, consulting, and engineering services, royalties for patents and intellectual properties, insurance premiums, shipping fees, and tourist expenditures. These trades in services are sometimes called **invisible trade.** In 1997, U.S. service exports were $251.13 billion and imports were $163.72 billion, realizing a surplus of $87.41 billion. Clearly, the U.S. performed better in services than in merchandise trade.

Factor income, the third category of the current account, consists largely of payments and receipts of interest, dividends, and other income on foreign investments that were previously made. If U.S. investors receive interest on their holdings of foreign bonds, for instance, it will be recorded as a credit in the balance of payments. On the other hand, interest payments by U.S. borrowers to foreign creditors will be recorded as debits. In 1997, U.S. residents paid out $254.53 billion to foreigners as factor income and received $236.20 billion, realizing an $18.33 billion deficit. Considering that the United States has heavily borrowed from foreigners in recent years, U.S. payments of interest and dividends to foreigners are likely to rise sharply. This can increase the U.S. current account deficit in the future, *ceteris paribus.*

Unilateral transfers, the fourth category of the current account, involve "unrequited" payments. Examples include foreign aid, reparations, official and private grants, and gifts. Unlike other accounts in the balance of payments, unilateral transfers have only one-directional flows, without offsetting flows. In the case of merchandise trade, for example, goods flow in one direction and payments flow in the opposite direction. For the purpose of preserving the double-entry bookkeeping rule, unilateral transfers are regarded as an act of buying *goodwill* from the recipients. So a country that gives foreign aid to another country can be viewed as importing goodwill from the latter. As can be expected, the United States made a net unilateral transfer of $38.88 billion, which is the receipt of transfer payments ($6.13 billion) minus transfer payments to foreign entities ($45.01 billion).

The current account balance, especially the trade balance, tends to be sensitive to exchange rate changes. When a country's currency depreciates against the currencies of major trading partners, the country's exports tend to rise and imports fall, improving the trade balance. For example, Mexico experienced continuous deficits in its trade balance of about $4.5 billion per quarter throughout 1994. Following the depreciation of the peso in December 1994, however, Mexico's trade balance began to improve immediately, realizing a surplus of about $7 billion for the year of 1995.

The effect of currency depreciation on a country's trade balance can be more complicated than the case described above. Indeed, following a depreciation, the trade balance may at first deteriorate for a while. Eventually, however, the trade balance will tend to improve over time. This particular reaction pattern of the trade balance to a depreciation is referred to as the **J-curve effect,** which is illustrated in Exhibit 3.2. The curve shows the initial deterioration and the eventual improvement of the trade balance following a depreciation. The J-curve effect received wide attention when the

EXHIBIT 3.2

A Currency Depreciation and the Time-Path of the Trade Balance: The J-Curve Effect

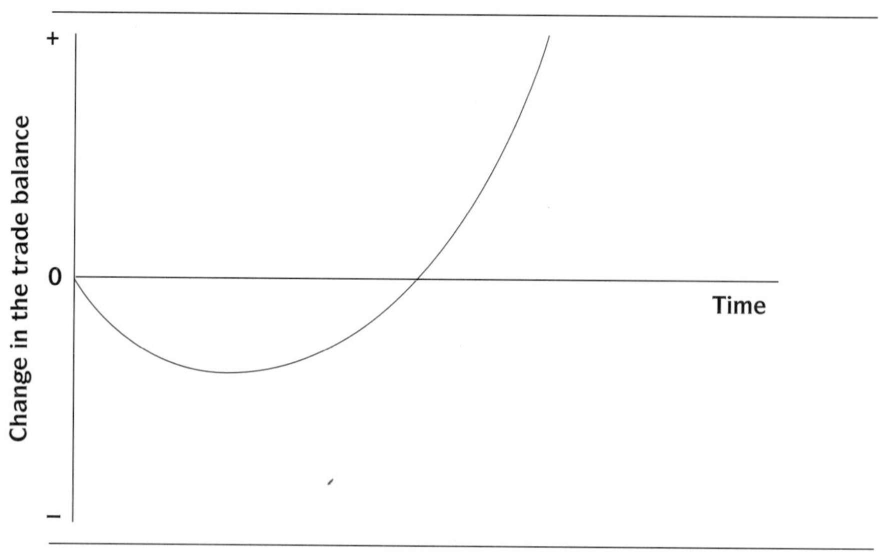

British trade balance worsened after a devaluation of the pound in 1967. Sebastian Edwards (1989) examined various cases of devaluations carried out by developing countries in the 1960s through 1980s, and confirmed the existence of the J-curve effect in about 40 percent of the cases. (See the References and Suggested Readings at the end of this chapter for more information about this study.)

A depreciation will begin to improve the trade balance immediately if imports and exports are *responsive* to the exchange rate changes. On the other hand, if imports and exports are inelastic, the trade balance will worsen following a depreciation. Following a depreciation of the domestic currency and the resultant rise in import prices, domestic residents may still continue to purchase imports because it is difficult to change their consumption habits in a short period of time. With higher import prices, the domestic country comes to spend more on imports. Even if domestic residents are willing to switch to less expensive domestic substitutes for foreign imports, it may take time for domestic producers to supply import substitutes. Likewise, foreigners' demand for domestic products, which become less expensive with a depreciation of the domestic currency, can be inelastic essentially for the same reasons. In the long run, however, both imports and exports tend to be responsive to exchange rate changes, exerting positive influences on the trade balance.

The Capital Account

The capital account balance measures the difference between U.S. sales of assets to foreigners and U.S. purchases of foreign assets. U.S. sales (or exports) of assets are recorded as credits, as they result in *capital inflow.* On the other hand, U.S. purchases (imports) of foreign assets are recorded as debits, as they lead to *capital outflow.* Unlike trades in goods and services, trades in financial assets affect future payments and receipts of factor income.

Exhibit 3.1 shows that the United States had a capital account surplus of $264.57 billion in 1997, implying that capital inflow to the United States far exceeded capital outflow. Clearly, the current account deficit was more than offset by the capital account surplus. As previously mentioned, a country's current account deficit must be paid for either by borrowing from foreigners or by selling off past foreign investments. In the absence of the government's reserve transactions, the current account balance must be equal to the capital account balance but with the opposite sign. When nothing is excluded, a country's balance of payments must necessarily balance.

The capital account can be divided into three categories: direct investment, portfolio investment, and other investment. Direct investment occurs when the investor acquires a measure of control of the foreign business. In the U.S. balance of payments, acquisition of 10 percent or more of the voting shares of a business is considered giving a measure of control to the investor.

When Honda, a Japanese automobile manufacturer, built an assembly factory in Ohio, it was engaged in **foreign direct investment (FDI).** Another example of direct investment was provided by Nestlé Corporation, a Swiss multinational firm, when it *acquired* Carnation, a U.S. firm. Of course, U.S. firms also are engaged in direct investments in foreign countries. For instance, Coca-Cola built bottling facilities all over the world. In recent years, many U.S. corporations moved their production facilities to Mexico to take advantage of lower costs of production. Generally speaking, foreign direct investments take place as firms attempt to take advantage of various market imperfections. In 1997, U.S. direct investment overseas was $119.44 billion, whereas foreign direct investment in the United States was $107.93 billion, achieving a rough equilibrium.

Firms undertake foreign direct investments when the expected returns from foreign investments exceed the cost of capital, allowing for foreign exchange and political risks. The expected returns from foreign projects can be higher than those from domestic projects because of lower wage rates and material costs, subsidized financing, preferential tax treatment, exclusive access to local markets, and the like. The volume and direction of FDI can also be sensitive to exchange rate changes. For instance, Japanese FDI in the United States soared in the latter half of the 1980s, partly because of the sharp appreciation of the yen against the dollar. With a stronger yen, Japanese firms could better afford to acquire U.S. assets that became less expensive in terms of yen. The same exchange rate movement discouraged U.S. firms from making FDI in Japan because Japanese assets became more expensive in terms of the dollar.

Portfolio investment, the second category of the capital account, mostly represents sales and purchases of foreign financial assets such as stocks and bonds that do not involve a transfer of control. International portfolio investments have boomed in recent years, partly due to the general relaxation of capital controls and regulations in many countries, and partly due to investors' desire to diversify risk globally. Portfolio investment comprises equity securities and debt securities. Equity securities include corporate shares, whereas debt securities include (1) bonds and notes, (2) money market instruments, and (3) financial derivatives like options. Exhibit 3.1 shows that in 1997, foreigners invested $387.62 billion in U.S. financial securities whereas Americans invested $79.28 billion in foreign securities, realizing a major surplus, $308.34 billion, for the United States.

Investors typically diversify their investment portfolios to reduce risk. Since security returns tend to have low correlations among countries, investors can reduce risk more effectively if they diversify their portfolio holdings internationally rather than purely domestically. In addition, investors may be able to benefit from higher expected returns from some foreign markets.[3]

The third category of the capital account is **other investment,** which includes transactions in currency, bank deposits, trade credits, and so forth. These investments are quite sensitive to both changes in relative interest rates between countries and the anticipated change in the exchange rate. If the interest rate rises in the United States while other variables remain constant, the United States will experience capital inflows, as investors would like to deposit or invest in the United States to take advantage of the higher interest rate. On the other hand, if a higher U.S. interest rate is more or less offset by an expected depreciation of the U.S. dollar, capital inflows to the United States will not materialize.[4] Since both interest rates and exchange rate expectations are volatile, these capital flows are highly reversible. In 1997, the United States experienced a net outflow of $32.25 billion in this category.

Statistical Discrepancy

Exhibit 3.1 shows that there was a statistical discrepancy of −$96.76 billion in 1997, representing omitted and misrecorded transactions. Recordings of payments and receipts arising from international transactions are done at different times and places, possibly using different methods. As a result, these recordings, upon which the balance-of-payments statistics are constructed, are bound to be imperfect. While merchandise trade can be recorded with a certain degree of accuracy at the customs houses, provisions of invisible services like consulting can escape detection. Cross-border financial transactions, a bulk of which might have been conducted electronically, are far more difficult to keep track of. For this reason, the balance of payments always presents a "balancing" debit or credit as a statistical discrepancy.[5] It is interesting to note that the sum of the balance on capital account and the statistical discrepancy is very close to the balance of current account in magnitude, −$166.80 billion. This suggests that financial transactions may be mainly responsible for the discrepancy.

When we compute the *cumulative* balance of payments including the current account, capital account, and the statistical discrepancies, we obtain the so-called **overall balance** or **official settlement balance.** All the transactions comprising the overall balance take place *autonomously* for their own sake.[6] The overall balance is significant because it indicates a country's international payment gap that must be *accommodated* with the government's official reserve transactions.

It is also indicative of the pressure that a country's currency faces for depreciation or appreciation. If, for example, a country continuously realizes deficits on the overall balance, the country will eventually run out of reserve holdings and its currency may have to depreciate against foreign currencies. In 1997, the United States had a $1.01 billion surplus on the overall balance. This means that the rest of the world had to make a net payment equal to that amount to the United States. If the United States had realized a deficit on the overall balance, the U.S. would have made a net payment to the rest of the world.

Official Reserve Account

When a country must make a net payment to foreigners because of a balance-of-payments deficit, the central bank of the country (the Federal Reserve System in the United States) should either run down its **official reserve assets,** such as gold, foreign exchanges, and SDRs, or borrow anew from foreign central banks. On the other hand, if a country has a balance-of-payments surplus, its central bank will either retire some of its foreign debts or acquire additional reserve assets from foreigners. Exhibit 3.1 shows that to absorb a $1.01 billion balance-of-payment surplus, the U.S. increased its external reserve holdings by the same amount.

The official reserve account includes transactions undertaken by the authorities to finance the overall balance and intervene in foreign exchange markets. When the United States and foreign governments wish to support the value of the dollar in the foreign exchange markets, they sell foreign exchanges, SDRs, or gold to "buy" dollars. These transactions, which give rise to the demand for dollars, will be recorded as a positive entry under official reserves. On the other hand, if governments would like to see a weaker dollar, they "sell" dollars and buy gold, foreign exchanges, and so forth. These transactions, which give rise to the supply of dollars, will be recorded as a negative entry under official reserves. The more actively governments intervene in the foreign exchange markets, the greater the official reserve entry.

Until the advent of the Bretton Woods System in 1945, gold was the predominant international reserve asset. After 1945, however, international reserve assets comprise:

1. Gold.
2. Foreign exchanges.
3. Special drawing rights (SDRs).
4. Reserve positions in the International Monetary Fund (IMF).

EXHIBIT 3.3

Composition of Total Official Reserves (in Percent)

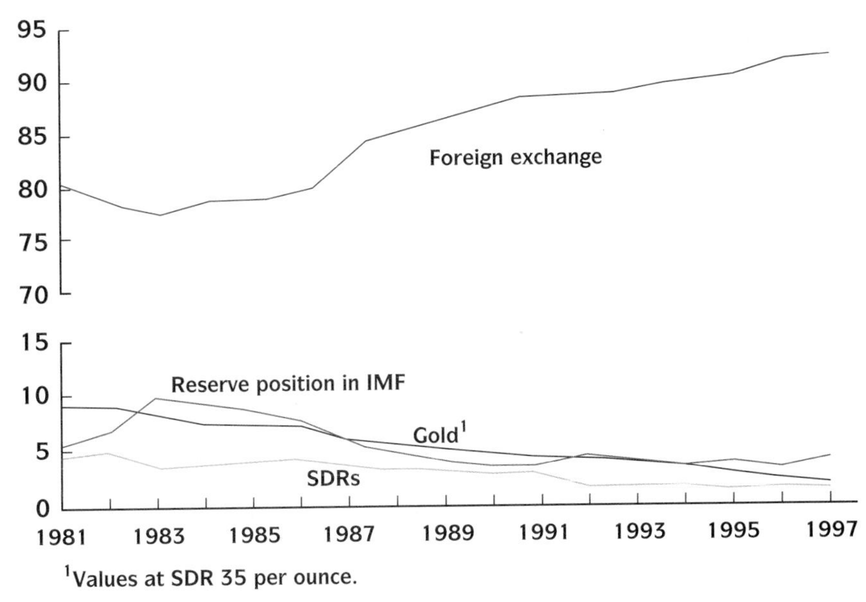

¹Values at SDR 35 per ounce.
Source: International Monetary Fund, *International Financial Statistics Yearbook,* 1998.

EXHIBIT 3.4

Currency Composition of the World's Foreign Exchange Reserves (% of Total)

Currency	1980	1997
U.S. dollar	68.6	57.1
British pound	2.9	3.4
European Currency Unit	n.a.	5.0
French franc	1.7	1.2
German mark	14.9	12.8
Japanese yen	4.4	4.9
Other	7.5	15.6

Source: IMF.

As can be seen from Exhibit 3.3, the relative importance of gold as an international means of payment has steadily declined, whereas the importance of foreign exchanges has grown substantially. As of 1997, foreign exchanges account for about 92 percent of the total reserve assets held by IMF member countries, with gold accounting for less than 5 percent of the total reserves.

As can be seen from Exhibit 3.4, the U.S. dollar's share in the world's foreign exchange reserves was 57.1 percent in 1997, followed by the German mark with a 12.8 percent share, ECU with a 5.0 percent share, and the Japanese yen with a 4.9 percent share. The dominance of the U.S. dollar may be attributable to the fact that roughly half of world trade is invoiced in dollars. Most commodities are priced in dollars. The importance of U.S. dollar as international reserve currency, however, has declined over time; in 1980, for instance, the share of U.S. dollar was 68.6 percent. This may reflect the declining dominance of the United States in the world economy and the long-run trend of the dollar to decline in exchange value due to the persistent U.S. trade deficits. In addition, once the euro establishes its credibility as a reserve currency, the dollar's share may decline further in the future.

THE BALANCE-OF-PAYMENTS IDENTITY

When the balance-of-payments accounts are recorded correctly, the combined balance of the current account, the capital account, and the reserves account must be zero, that is,

$$\text{BCA} + \text{BKA} + \text{BRA} = 0 \tag{3.1}$$

where:

BCA = balance on the current account

BKA = balance on the capital account

BRA = balance on the reserves account

The balance on the reserves account, BRA, represents the change in the official reserves.

Equation 3.1 is the **balance-of-payments identity (BOPI)** that must necessarily hold. The BOPI equation indicates that a country can run a balance-of-payments surplus or deficit by increasing or decreasing its official reserves. Under the fixed exchange rate regime, countries maintain official reserves that allow them to have balance-of-payments disequilibrium, that is, BCA + BKA is nonzero, without adjusting the exchange rate. Under the fixed exchange rate regime, the combined balance on the current and capital accounts will be equal in size, but opposite in sign, to the change in the official reserves:

$$\text{BCA} + \text{BKA} = -\text{BRA} \tag{3.2}$$

For example, if a country runs a deficit on the overall balance, that is, BCA + BKA is negative, the central bank of the country can supply foreign exchanges out of its reserve holdings. But if the deficit persists, the central bank will eventually run out of its reserves, and the country may be forced to devalue its currency. This is roughly what happened to the Mexican peso in December 1994.

Under the *pure* flexible exchange rate regime, central banks will not intervene in the foreign exchange markets. In fact, central banks do not need to maintain official reserves. Under this regime, the overall balance thus must necessarily balance, that is,

$$\text{BCA} = -\text{BKA} \tag{3.3}$$

In other words, a current account surplus or deficit must be matched by a capital account deficit or surplus, and vice versa. In a *dirty* floating exchange rate system under which the central banks discreetly buy and sell foreign exchanges, Equation 3.3 will not hold tightly.

Being an identity, Equation 3.3 does not imply a causality by itself. A current account deficit (surplus) may cause a capital account surplus (deficit), or the opposite may hold. It has often been suggested that the persistent U.S. current account deficits made it necessary for the United States to run matching capital account surpluses, implying that the former *causes* the latter. One can argue, with equal justification, that the persistent U.S. capital account surpluses, which may have been caused by high U.S. interest rates, have caused the persistent current account deficits by strengthening the value of the dollar. The issue can be settled only by careful empirical studies.

BALANCE-OF-PAYMENTS TRENDS IN MAJOR COUNTRIES

Considering the significant attention that balance-of-payments data receives in the news media, it is useful to closely examine balance-of-payments trends in some of

EXHIBIT 3.5 Balances on the Current (BCA) and Capital (BKA) Accounts of Five Major Countries: 1982–1997 ($ Billion)[a]

	China		Japan		Germany		United Kingdom		United States	
Year	BCA	BKA	BCA	BKA	BCA	BKA	BCA	BKA	BCA	BKA
1982	5.7	0.6	6.9	−11.6	4.9	−2.0	8.0	−10.6	−11.6	16.6
1983	4.2	−0.1	20.8	−19.3	4.6	−6.6	5.3	−7.1	−44.2	45.4
1984	2.0	−1.9	35.0	−32.9	9.6	−9.9	1.8	−2.8	−99.0	102.1
1985	−11.4	9.0	51.1	−51.6	17.6	−15.4	3.3	−0.7	−124.5	128.3
1986	−7.0	5.0	85.9	−70.7	40.9	−35.5	−1.3	5.0	−150.5	150.2
1987	0.3	4.5	84.4	−46.3	46.4	−24.9	−8.1	28.2	−166.5	157.3
1988	−3.8	6.2	79.2	−61.7	50.4	−66.0	−29.3	33.9	−127.7	131.6
1989	−4.3	3.8	63.2	−76.3	57.0	−54.1	−36.7	28.6	−104.3	129.5
1990	12.0	0.1	44.1	−53.2	48.3	−41.1	−32.5	32.5	−94.3	96.5
1991	13.3	1.3	68.2	−76.6	−17.7	11.5	−14.3	19.0	−9.3	3.5
1992	6.4	−8.5	112.6	−112.0	−19.1	56.3	−18.4	11.7	−61.4	57.4
1993	−11.6	13.4	131.6	−104.2	−13.9	−0.3	−15.5	21.0	−90.6	91.9
1994	6.9	23.5	130.3	−105.0	−20.9	18.9	−2.3	3.8	−132.9	127.6
1995	1.6	20.9	111.0	−52.4	−22.6	29.8	−5.9	5.0	−129.2	138.9
1996	7.2	24.5	65.9	−30.7	−13.8	12.6	−3.7	3.2	−148.7	142.1
1997	29.7	6.1	94.4	−87.8	−1.2	−2.6	6.8	−11.0	−166.8	167.8

[a]The balance on the capital account (BKA) includes statistical discrepancies.
Source: IMF, *International Financial Statistics Yearbook, 1998.*

EXHIBIT 3.6

The U.S.'s Balance-of-Payments Trend: 1982–1997

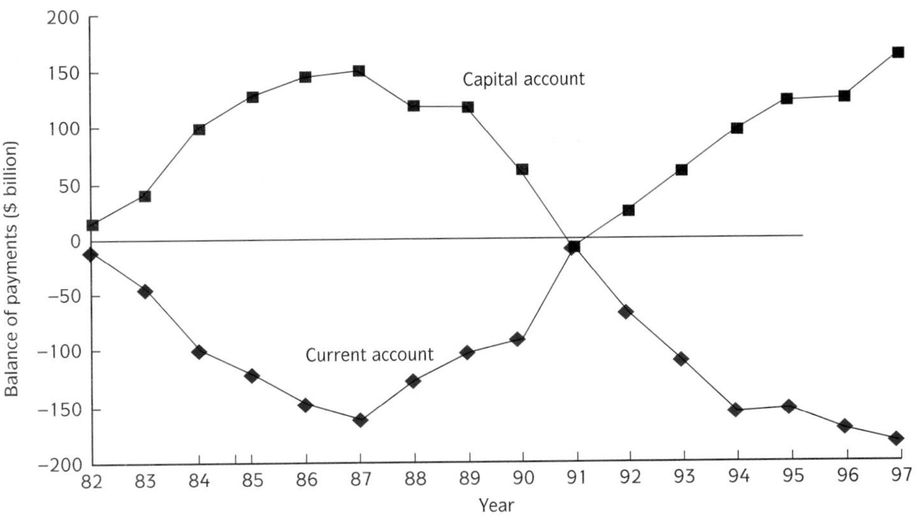

Source: IMF, *International Financial Statistics Yearbook, 1998.*

the major countries. Exhibit 3.5 provides the balance on the current account (BCA) as well as the balance on the capital account (BKA) for each of the five key countries, China, Japan, Germany, the United Kingdom, and the United States, during the period 1982–1997.

Exhibit 3.5 shows first that the United States has experienced continuous deficits on the current account since 1982 and continuous surpluses on the capital account. Clearly, the magnitude of U.S. current account deficits is far greater than any that other countries ever experienced during the 16-year sample period. The U.S. balance-of-payments trend is illustrated in Exhibit 3.6. This situation has led some politicians

INTERNATIONAL FINANCE IN PRACTICE

Will the Party Fizzle When the Sake Runs Dry?

Every twitch and twitter from American economic policy-makers is scrutinized on Wall Street for clues about the future course of policy—and hence of bond and equity markets. Yet over the next year or so, investors would be wise to watch the Bank of Japan as closely as the Fed. Japan's economic policy and performance could have a decisive influence on both the world economy and global financial markets.

International investors need to keep their eyes on two things: Japan's current-account surplus, which is shrinking at last; and the way the Bank of Japan responds as the country's stuttering economic recovery gets more firmly under way.

Japan's current-account surplus fell to $111 billion last year from almost $130 billion in 1994. Goldman Sachs, an American investment bank, forecasts that it will drop to $55 billion by 1997, or only 1.1% of GDP, compared with more than 3% at its peak (see chart). This fall has so far been driven by two factors: the strong yen has made exports less competitive, and Japanese firms which have invested in production plants elsewhere in Asia are now exporting goods back into Japan. As the economy recovers and imports pick up, this too will help to shrink the surplus.

A smaller Japanese current-account surplus should be good news for the world economy. An increase in Japanese imports will give a useful stimulus to other industrial economies just as their growth seems to be flagging. A shrinking trade surplus will also help to appease American producers and politicians who—albeit erroneously—have long claimed that Japan's trade surplus is proof that American goods are unfairly shut out of Japanese markets. It should therefore help to silence protectionist demands.

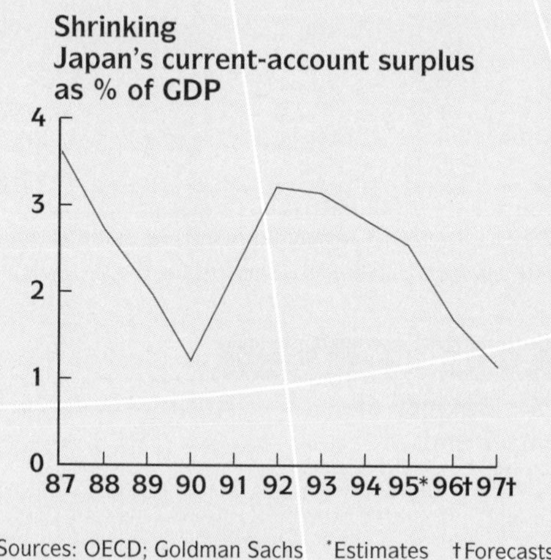

Sources: OECD; Goldman Sachs *Estimates †Forecasts

Japan's Balancing Act

This, however, is only one side of the coin. By definition, a country's overall balance of payments must balance;

and commentators to lament that Americans are living far beyond their means. As a matter of fact, the net international investment position of the United States turned negative in 1987 for the first time in decades and continued to deteriorate. The overseas debt burden of the United States—the difference between the value of foreign-owned assets in the United States and the value of U.S.-owned assets abroad—reached about $680 billion at the end of 1994, when valued by the replacement cost of the investments made abroad and at home. As recently as 1986, the United States was considered a net creditor nation, with about $35 billion more in assets overseas than foreigners owned in the United States.

Second, Exhibit 3.5 reveals that Japan has had an unbroken string of current account surpluses since 1982 despite the fact that the value of the yen rose steadily until the mid 1990s. As can be expected, during this period Japan realized continuous capital account deficits; Japan invested heavily in foreign stocks and bonds, businesses, real estates, art objects, and the like to recycle its huge, persistent current account surpluses. Consequently, Japan emerged as the world's largest creditor nation, whereas the United States became the largest debtor nation. The persistent current account disequilibrium has been a major source of friction between Japan and its key trading partners, especially the United States. In fact, Japan has often been criticized thus a current-account surplus must be matched by an equivalent capital-account deficit—ie, a net outflow of capital. So a smaller current-account surplus implies a smaller outflow of capital to the rest of the world. In recent years, the flow of surplus savings out of Japan has been an important prop to global bond and equity markets, especially in America. In 1995, Japanese net investment in foreign bonds and shares amounted to $93 billion. If this money dries up, it could have awkward repercussions.

Of course, not all of Japan's current-account surplus slops into purchases of foreign bonds and equities by financial institutions and private investors. In recent years much of the gap has been filled by the Bank of Japan, which has bought large quantities of American Treasury bonds to support the dollar.

In a move partly intended to boost private overseas portfolio investment, the government announced on February 8th a package of deregulation measures. For example, some of the restrictions on pension funds' investment in foreign securities will be eased. Few economists, however, believe that this will lead to a flood of money out of Japan. Moreover, the Japanese government is expected to issue record amounts of bonds this year and next, to finance Japan's bulging budget deficit, and these are likely to mop up a larger share of institutions' funds, leaving less to flow overseas.

There is another way to explain Japan's shrinking current-account surplus. As the economy perks up, more savings will be absorbed at home. After four years of virtual stagnation, Japan's economy is widely tipped to recover this year.

The recovery carries additional risks for international investors. At some stage it will prompt some tightening in the Bank of Japan's extremely loose monetary policy. The discount rate has been slashed to only 0.5%, and the bank has been pumping extra liquidity into the system by buying government securities, in a desperate bid to shore up the financial system and stimulate the economy. Japan's narrow measure of money supply, M1, has increased by 13% over the past 12 months—its fastest rise since the height of Japan's asset-price bubble in the late 1980s.

Easy Money

This lax monetary policy may have taken time to spur Japan's economy, but it has meanwhile aided world financial markets. It is not only domestic borrowers who have been helped by low Japanese interest rates. International investors, especially American hedge funds, have taken advantage of cheap money by borrowing in yen, swapping the proceeds into dollars, say, and then investing in higher-yielding government bonds. The exchange-rate risk on this trade is generally perceived as minimal (it is believed that the Bank of Japan, wary of letting the yen strengthen, will not allow the dollar/yen exchange rate to drop below ¥100). As a result, many investors have been eager to feast upon what appears to be a free lunch.

George Magnus, an economist at Union Bank of Switzerland, argues that such activity was probably one factor behind foreign private investors' record purchases of almost $100 billion of American Treasury bonds in the first nine months of 1995. Indeed, during that period foreigners (including central banks such as the Bank of Japan) bought more than 80% of total net American Treasury issues.

Source: Excerpted from the Economist Newspaper Group, Inc., February 17, 1996, with permission.

for pursuing **mercantilism** to ensure continuous trade surpluses.[7] Recently, however, Japan's current account surplus began to shrink. As discussed in the International Finance in Practice box, this implies, among other things, a smaller outflow of capital to the rest of the world.

Third, like the United States, the United Kingdom recently experienced continuous current account deficits, coupled with capital account surpluses. The magnitude, however, is far less than that of the United States. Germany, on the other hand, traditionally had current account surpluses. Since 1991, however, Germany has been experiencing current account deficits. This is largely due to German reunification and the resultant need to absorb more output domestically to rebuild the East German region. This has left less output available for exports.

Fourth, like Japan, China tends to have a balance-of-payment surplus on the current account. Unlike Japan, however, China tends to realize a surplus on the capital account as well. In 1997, for instance, China had a $29.7 billion surplus on the current account and, at the same time, a $6.1 billion surplus on the capital account. This implies that China's official reserve holdings must have gone up for the year. In fact, China's official reserves have increased sharply in recent years, reaching about $143 billion in 1997.

While perennial balance-of-payments deficits or surpluses can be a problem, each country need not achieve balance-of-payments equilibrium every year. Suppose a country is currently experiencing a trade deficit because of the import demand for capital goods that are necessary for economic development projects. In this case, the trade deficit can be self-correcting in the long run because once the projects are completed, the country may be able to export more or import less by substituting domestic products for foreign imports. In contrast, if the trade deficit is the result of importing consumption goods, the situation will not correct by itself. Thus, what matters is the nature and causes of the disequilibrium.

SUMMARY

1. The balance of payments can be defined as the statistical record of a country's international transactions over a certain period of time presented in the form of double-entry bookkeeping.
2. In the balance of payments, any transaction resulting in a receipt from foreigners is recorded as a credit, with a positive sign, whereas any transaction resulting in a payment to foreigners is recorded as a debit, with a minus sign.
3. A country's international transactions can be grouped into three main categories: the current account, the capital account, and the official reserve account. The current account includes exports and imports of goods and services, whereas the capital account includes all purchases and sales of assets such as stocks, bonds, bank accounts, real estate, and businesses. The official reserve account covers all purchases and sales of international reserve assets, such as dollars, foreign exchanges, gold, and SDRs.
4. The current account is divided into four subcategories: merchandise trade, services, factor income, and unilateral transfers. Merchandise trade represents exports and imports of tangible goods, whereas trade in services includes payments and receipts for legal, engineering, consulting, and other performed services and tourist expenditures. Factor income consists of payments and receipts of interest, dividends, and other income on previously made foreign investments. Lastly, unilateral transfer involves unrequited payments such as gifts, foreign aid, and reparations.
5. The capital account is divided into three subcategories: direct investment, portfolio investment, and other investment. Direct investment involves acquisitions of controlling interests in foreign businesses. Portfolio investment represents investments in foreign stocks and bonds that do not involve acquisitions of control. Other investment includes bank deposits, currency investment, trade credit, and the like.
6. When we compute the cumulative balance of payments including the current account, capital account, and the statistical discrepancies, we obtain the overall balance or official settlement balance. The overall balance is indicative of a country's balance-of-payments gap that must be accommodated by official reserve transactions. If a country must make a net payment to foreigners because of a balance-of-payments deficit, the country should either run down its official reserve assets, such as gold, foreign exchanges, and SDRs, or borrow anew from foreigners.
7. A country can run a balance-of-payments surplus or deficit by increasing or decreasing its official reserves. Under the fixed exchange rate regime, the combined balance on the current and capital accounts will be equal in size, but opposite in sign, to the change in the official reserves. Under the pure flexible exchange rate regime where the central bank does not maintain any official reserves, a current account surplus or deficit must be matched by a capital account deficit or surplus.

KEY WORDS

balance of payments, 58
balance-of-payments identity (BOPI), 66
capital account, 60
current account, 60
factor income, 61
foreign direct investment (FDI), 63
invisible trade, 61
J-curve effect, 61
mercantilism, 69
merchandise trade, 61
official reserve account, 60
official reserve assets, 64
official settlement balance, 64
other investment, 63
overall balance, 64
portfolio investment, 63
services, 61
trade balance, 61
unilateral transfer, 61

QUESTIONS

1. Define *balance of payments.*
2. Why would it be useful to examine a country's balance-of-payments data?
3. The United States has experienced continuous current account deficits since the early 1980s. What do you think are the main causes for the deficits? What would be the consequences of continuous U.S. current account deficits?
4. In contrast to the United States, Japan has realized continuous current account surpluses. What could be the main causes for these surpluses? Is it desirable to have continuous current account surpluses?
5. Comment on the following statement: "Since the United States imports more than it exports, it is necessary for the United States to import capital from foreign countries to finance its current account deficits."
6. Explain how a country can run an overall balance-of-payments deficit or surplus.
7. Explain *official reserve assets* and its major components.
8. Explain how to compute the overall balance and discuss its significance.
9. Since the early 1980s, foreign portfolio investors have purchased a significant portion of U.S. Treasury bond issues. Discuss the short-term and long-term effects of foreigners' portfolio investment on the U.S. balance of payments.
10. Describe the *balance-of-payments identity* and discuss its implications under the fixed and flexible exchange rate regimes.
11. Exhibit 3.3 indicates that in 1991, the United States had a current account deficit and at the same time a capital account deficit. Explain how this can happen.
12. Explain how each of the following transactions will be classified and recorded in the debit and credit of the U.S. balance of payments:
    a. A Japanese insurance company purchases U.S. Treasury bonds and pays out of its bank account kept in New York City.
    b. A U.S. citizen consumes a meal at a restaurant in Paris and pays with her American Express card.
    c. An Indian immigrant living in Los Angeles sends a check drawn on his LA bank account as a gift to his parents living in Bombay.
    d. A U.S. computer programmer is hired by a British company for consulting and gets paid from the U.S. bank account maintained by the British company.
13. Construct the balance-of-payment table for Japan for the year of 1998 which is comparable in format to Exhibit 3.1, and interpret the numerical data. You may consult *International Financial Statistics* published by IMF or search for useful Websites for the data yourself.

MINI CASE

Mexico's Balance-of-Payments Problem

Recently, Mexico experienced large-scale trade deficits, depletion of foreign reserve holdings, and a major currency devaluation in December 1994, followed by the decision to freely float the peso. These events also brought about a severe recession and higher unemployment in Mexico. Since the devaluation, however, the trade balance has improved.

Investigate the Mexican experiences in detail and write a report on the subject. In the report, you may:

1. Document the trend in Mexico's key economic indicators, such as the balance of payments, the exchange rate, and foreign reserve holdings, during the period 1994.1 through 1995.12.
2. Investigate the causes of Mexico's balance-of-payments difficulties prior to the peso devaluation.
3. Discuss what policy actions might have prevented or mitigated the balance-of-payments problem and the subsequent collapse of the peso.
4. Derive lessons from the Mexican experience that may be useful for other developing countries.

In your report, you may identify and address any other relevant issues concerning Mexico's balance-of-payments problem. *International Financial Statistics* published by IMF provides basic macroeconomic data on Mexico.

ENDNOTES

1. In fact, the current account balance, which is the difference between a country's exports and imports, is a component of the country's GNP. Other components of GNP include consumption and investment and government expenditure.
2. The current account balance (BCA) can be written as the difference between national output (Y) and domestic absorption, which comprises consumption (C), investment (I), and government expenditures (G):

   $$BCA = Y - (C + I + G)$$

   If a country's domestic absorption falls short of its national output, the country's current account must be in surplus.
3. Refer to Chapter 11 for a detailed discussion of international portfolio investment.
4. We will discuss the relationship between the relative interest rates and the expected exchange rate change in Chapter 5.
5. Readers might wonder how to compute the statistical discrepancies in the balance of payments. Statistical discrepancies, which represent errors and omissions, by definition, cannot be known. Since, however, the balance of payments must balance to zero when every item is included, one can determine the statistical discrepancies in the "residual" manner.
6. Autonomous transactions refer to those transactions that occur without regard to the goal of achieving the balance-of-payments equilibrium.
7. Mercantilism, which originated in Europe during the period of absolute monarchies, holds that precious metals like gold and silver are the key components of national wealth, and that a continuing trade surplus should be a major policy goal as it ensures a continuing inflow of precious metals and thus continuous increases in national wealth. Mercantilists, therefore, abhor trade deficits and argue for imposing various restrictions on imports. Mercantilist ideas were criticized by such British thinkers as David Hume and Adam Smith. Both argued that the main source of wealth of a country is its productive capacity, not precious metals.

WEB RESOURCES

www.imf.org/external/about.htm

This Website of the International Monetary Fund (IMF) discusses IMF and its role and covers a multitude of topics including Asian crisis, balance of payments, special drawing rights, etc.

www.bea.doc.gov/

Website of the Bureau of Economic Analysis, an agency of the U.S. Department of Commerce. Provides data and articles related to the key national, international, and regional aspects of the U.S. economy. Data provided includes GDP, balance of payments, etc.

REFERENCES AND SUGGESTED READINGS

Edwards, Sebastian. *Real Exchange Rates, Devaluation and Adjustment: Exchange Rate Policy in Developing Countries.* Cambridge, Mass.: MIT Press, 1989.

Grabbe, Orlin. *International Financial Markets.* New York: Elsevier, 1991.

Kemp, Donald. "Balance of Payments Concepts—What Do They Really Mean?," *Federal Reserve Bank of St. Louis Review,* July 1975, pp. 14–23.

Ohmae, Kenichi. "Lies, Damned Lies and Statistics: Why the Trade Deficit Doesn't Matter in a Borderless World," *Journal of Applied Corporate World,* Winter, 1991, pp. 98–106.

Salop, Joan, and Erich Spitaller. "Why Does the Current Account Matter?," International Monetary Fund, *Staff Papers,* March 1980, pp. 101–34.

U.S. Department of Commerce. "Report of the Advisory Committee on the Presentation of the Balance of Payments Statistics," *Survey of Current Business,* June, 1991, pp. 18–25.

Yeager, Leland. *International Monetary Relations.* New York: Harper & Row, 1965.

CHAPTER FOUR

The Market for Foreign Exchange

CHAPTER OUTLINE

Money represents purchasing power. Possessing money from your country gives you the power to purchase goods and services produced (or assets held) by other residents of your country. But to purchase goods and services produced by the residents of another country generally first requires purchasing the other country's currency. This is done by selling one's own currency for the currency of the country with whose residents you desire to transact. More formally, one's own currency has been used to buy *foreign exchange,* and in so doing the buyer has converted his purchasing power into the purchasing power of the seller's country.

The market for foreign exchange is the largest financial market in the world by virtually any standard. It is open somewhere in the world 365 days a year, 24 hours a day. Current estimates by the Bank for International Settlements (BIS) place worldwide daily trading of spot and forward foreign exchange at $1.5 trillion. London is the world's largest foreign exchange trading center. According to the 1998 triennial central bank survey, daily trading volume in the U.K. is estimated at $637 billion, a 37 percent increase over 1995. New York is the largest currency trading center in the United States. In 1998, U.S. daily turnover was $351 billion, which represents a 44 percent increase in daily trading volume over 1995. This is equivalent to more than $200 in transactions for every person on earth every business day of the year. Exhibit 4.1 presents a pie chart showing the shares of global foreign exchange turnover.

Broadly defined, the **foreign exchange (FX** or **FOREX) market** encompasses the conversion of purchasing power from one currency into another, bank deposits of foreign currency, the extension of credit denominated in a foreign currency, foreign

EXHIBIT 4.1

Shares of Reported Global Foreign Exchange Turnover, 1998

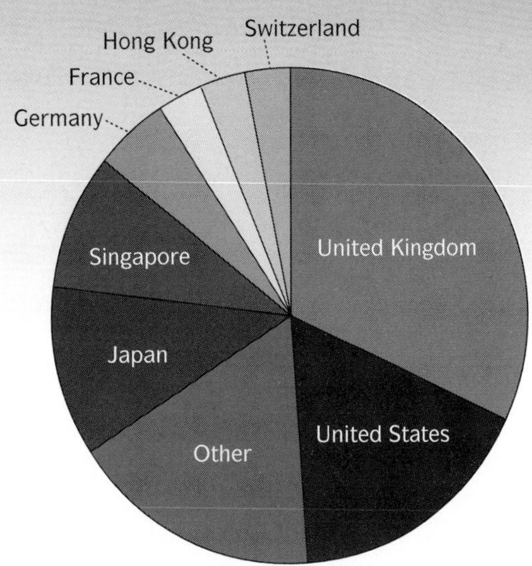

Note: Percent of total reporting foreign exchange turnover, adjusted for intracounty double-counting.

Source: Sam Y. Cross, *All About the Foreign Exchange Market in the United States,* Federal Reserve Bank of New York Website: www.ny.frb.org.

trade financing, trading in foreign currency options and futures contracts, and currency swaps. Obviously, one chapter cannot adequately cover all these topics. Consequently, we confine the discussion in this chapter to the spot and forward market for foreign exchange. In Chapter 9, we examine currency futures and options contracts, and in Chapter 10, currency swaps are discussed.

This chapter begins with an overview of the function and structure of the foreign exchange market and the major market participants that trade currencies in this market. Following is a discussion of the spot market for foreign exchange. This section covers how to read spot market quotations, derives cross-rate quotations, and develops the concept of triangular arbitrage as a means of ensuring market efficiency. The chapter concludes with a discussion of the forward market for foreign exchange. Forward market quotations are presented, the purpose of the market is discussed, and the purpose of swap rate quotations is explained.

This chapter lays the foundation for much of the discussion throughout the remainder of the text. Without a solid understanding of how the foreign exchange market works, international finance cannot be studied in an intelligent manner. As authors, we urge you to read this chapter carefully and thoughtfully.

FUNCTION AND STRUCTURE OF THE FOREX MARKET

The structure of the foreign exchange market is an outgrowth of one of the primary functions of a commercial banker: to assist clients in the conduct of international commerce. For example, a corporate client desiring to import merchandise from abroad would need a source for foreign exchange if the import was invoiced in the exporter's home currency. Alternatively, the exporter might need a way to dispose of foreign exchange if payment for the export was invoiced and received in the importer's home currency. Assisting in foreign exchange transactions of this type is one of the services that commercial banks provide for their clients, and one of the services that bank customers expect from their bank.

The spot and forward foreign exchange market is an **over-the-counter (OTC) market**; that is, trading does not take place in a central marketplace where buyers and

EXHIBIT 4.2

The Circadian Rhythms of the FX Market

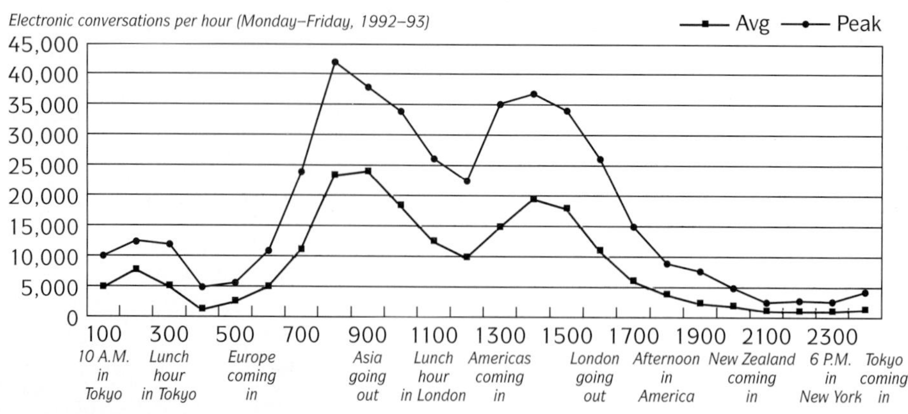

Note: Time (0100–2400 hours, Greenwich Mean Time).

Source: Sam Y. Cross, *All About the Foreign Exchange Market in the United States,* Federal Reserve Bank of New York Website: www.ny.frb.org.

sellers congregate. Rather, the foreign exchange market is a worldwide linkage of bank currency traders, nonbank dealers, and FX brokers who assist in trades connected to one another via a network of telephones, telex machines, computer terminals, and automated dealing systems. Reuters, Telerate, and Bloomberg are the largest vendors of quote screen monitors used in trading currencies. The communications system of the foreign exchange market is second to none, including industry, governments, the military, and national security and intelligence operations.

Twenty-four-hour-a-day currency trading follows the sun around the globe. Three major market segments can be identified: Australasia, Europe, and North America. Australasia includes the trading centers of Sydney, Tokyo, Hong Kong, Singapore, and Bahrain; Europe includes Zurich, Frankfurt, Paris, Brussels, Amsterdam, and London; and North America includes New York, Montreal, Toronto, Chicago, San Francisco, and Los Angeles. Most trading rooms operate over a 9- to 12-hour working day, although some banks have experimented with operating three eight-hour shifts in order to trade around the clock. Especially active trading takes place when the trading hours of the Australasia centers and the European centers overlap and when the European and North American centers overlap. More than half of the trading in the United States occurs between 8:00 A.M. and noon eastern standard time (1:00 P.M. and 5:00 P.M. Greenwich Mean Time [London]), when the European markets were still open. Certain trading centers have a more dominant effect on the market than others. For example, trading diminishes dramatically in the Australasian market segment when the Tokyo traders are taking their lunch break! Exhibit 4.2 provides a general indication of the participation level in the global FX market by showing electronic trades per hour.

FX Market Participants

The market for foreign exchange can be viewed as a two-tier market. One tier is the **wholesale** or **interbank market** and the other tier is the **retail** or **client market**. FX market participants can be categorized into five groups: international banks, bank customers, nonbank dealers, FX brokers, and central banks.

International banks provide the core of the FX market. Approximately 100 to 200 banks worldwide actively "make a market" in foreign exchange, that is, they stand willing to buy or sell foreign currency for their own account. These international banks serve their retail clients, the *bank customers,* in conducting foreign commerce or making international investment in financial assets that require foreign exchange. Bank customers broadly include MNCs, money managers, and private speculators.

According to 1998 BIS statistics, retail or bank client transactions account for approximately 18 percent of FX trading volume. The other 82 percent of trading volume is from interbank trades between international banks or nonbank dealers. *Nonbank dealers* are large nonbank financial institutions such as investment banks, whose size and frequency of trades make it cost-effective to establish their own dealing rooms to trade directly in the interbank market for their foreign exchange needs. In 1998, nonbank dealers accounted for 19 percent of interbank trading volume.

Part of the interbank trading among international banks involves adjusting the inventory positions they hold in various foreign currencies. However, most interbank trades are *speculative* or *arbitrage* transactions, where market participants attempt to correctly judge the future direction of price movements in one currency versus another or attempt to profit from temporary price discrepancies in currencies between competing dealers. Market psychology is a key ingredient in currency trading, and a dealer can often infer another's trading intention from the currency position being accumulated.

FX brokers match dealer orders to buy and sell currencies for a fee, but do not take a position themselves. Brokers have knowledge of the quotes offered by many dealers in the market. Consequently, interbank traders will use a broker primarily to disseminate as quickly as possible a currency quote to many other dealers. In recent years, since the introduction and increased usage of automated dealing systems, the use of brokers has declined because the computerized systems duplicate many of the same services at much lower fees. In 1998, 24 percent of the FX trading volume in the United States was brokered and 13 percent was done through automated trading systems.

One frequently sees or hears news media reports that the *central bank* (national monetary authority) of a particular country has intervened in the foreign exchange market in an attempt to influence the price of its currency against that of a major trading partner, or a country that it "fixes" or "pegs" its currency against. *Intervention* is the process of using foreign currency reserves to buy one's own currency in order to decrease its supply and thus increase its value in the foreign exchange market, or alternatively, selling one's own currency for foreign currency in order to increase its supply and lower its price. Recall from Chapter 2 that systematic intervention by member states of the European Union through the Exchange Rate Mechanism is a key ingredient in the operation of the European Monetary System, whose purpose is to maintain stability in the exchange rates between member states.

Central banks of major industrialized countries also frequently intervene in the foreign exchange market to influence the value of their currency relative to a trading partner. For example, intervention that successfully increases the value of one's currency against a trading partner may reduce exports and increase imports, thus alleviating persistent trade deficits of the trading partner. Central bank traders intervening in the currency market often lose bank reserves in attempting to accomplish their goal. However, there is little evidence that even massive intervention can materially affect exchange rates. The International Finance in Practice box on pages 78–79 provides an interesting account of a central bank trader for the Bank of Japan.

Correspondent Banking Relationships

The interbank market is a network of **correspondent banking relationships**, with large commercial banks maintaining demand deposit accounts with one another, called correspondent banking accounts. The correspondent bank account network allows for the efficient functioning of the foreign exchange market.

EXAMPLE 4.1: Correspondent Banking Relationship

As an example of how the network of correspondent bank accounts facilitates international foreign exchange transactions, consider U.S. Importer desiring to purchase merchandise from Dutch Exporter invoiced in guilders, at a cost of NLG1,076,250. U.S. Importer will contact his U.S. Bank and inquire about the

INTERNATIONAL FINANCE IN PRACTICE

Fearless Dealers

Central-Bank Traders Have an Advantage: Their Employers Don't Demand Profits

Tokyo—Tetsuya Nishida says his wife will be relieved when he gets his next assignment at the Bank of Japan.

Right now, the 32-year-old Mr. Nishida is a front-line soldier in the central bank's struggle to rein in the currency markets. He's one of nine currency traders at the Bank of Japan's cluttered, second-floor trading desk in downtown Tokyo. It's a grueling job; Mr. Nishida starts watching the markets when he wakes at 6 A.M. and often doesn't finish work until 11 P.M.

The past year, Mr. Nishida's trades often haven't been the least bit profitable. But that's part of his mission.

Of all central banks, the Bank of Japan has battled currency speculators the hardest. By some estimates, it bought more than $50 billion of dollars in the two years ended March 31, 1988, even though the dollar kept falling in value. With only limited success, Mr. Nishida and his colleagues were selling valuable yen in hopes of braking the dollar's fall.

A shy, conservatively dressed man, Mr. Nishida never set out to be a big-time currency trader. He was an English major at Sophia University in Japan, unlike most Bank of Japan employees, who studied law or economics at prestigious Tokyo University. When Mr. Nishida joined the central bank, he headed into the more tranquil research department. That job let him hone his English for a year at Johns Hopkins University in Baltimore.

But the Bank of Japan's tradition is to rotate employees through a wide range of departments. That's a big contrast with, say, the U.S. or West German central banks, which prefer to have lifetime currency dealers. So in June 1987, Mr. Nishida's turn came up.

Trading currencies "is just one step in one's overall career at the bank," says Zenta Nakajima, head of the foreign-exchange division at the Bank of Japan. "We don't train [dealers]. They've got to pick up expertise while they're here."

Mr. Nishida took quickly to his new setting. "This is the only place in the bank where you can get a real sense of market activities," he says. Upon awakening on a typical day, Mr. Nishida scans the newspapers and television for news of overnight markets and heads for the office. Before an 8 A.M. meeting, he reads the overnight messages from central banks around the world and phones dealers at Japanese and foreign banks in Tokyo.

Mr. Nishida won't talk about his trades, but central-bank dealers often trade in $10 million or bigger chunks. On a busy day, they can pound the market with as much as $500 million or $1 billion of total buying or selling. An advantage of working for a central bank, as opposed to a private bank, is that dealers don't have to worry about turning a profit.

"The important thing for central bankers is to be able to part with dollars or yen and not look back," says Richard Koo, senior economist at the Nomura Research Institute. "Their strength in the market comes from the fact that they can toss dollars and yen and not suffer losses." Other traders "fear those who have nothing to lose," Mr. Koo adds.

Recent market conditions suggest that the Bank of Japan's dollar-buying binge has earned some vindication. Exchange-rate stability of a sort has been achieved, and the Japanese economy is growing briskly with little threat of inflation.

As for Mr. Nishida, he says he faces plenty of stress but survives by always trying to look ahead. "I don't continue to be sorry for things already done," he says. "We may make some mistakes. But my motto is to forget about what isn't necessary."

Source: Kathryn Graven, *The Wall Street Journal*, September 23, 1988, p. R31. Reprinted by permission of *The Wall Street Journal*, © 1988 Dow Jones & Company, Inc. All Rights Reserved Worldwide.

NLG/$ exchange rate. Say U.S. Bank offers a price of NLG2.1525/$1.00. If U.S. Importer accepts the price, U.S. Bank will debit U.S. Importer's demand deposit account $500,000 = NLG1,076,250/2.1525 for the purchase of the Dutch guilders. U.S. Bank will instruct its correspondent bank in the Netherlands, Dutch Bank, to debit its correspondent bank account NLG1,076,250 and to credit that amount to Dutch Exporter's bank account. U.S. Bank will then debit its books NLG1,076,250, as an offset to the $500,000 debit to U.S. Importer's account, to reflect the decrease in its correspondent bank account balance with Dutch Bank.

This rather contrived example assumes that U.S. Bank and Dutch Exporter both have bank accounts at Dutch Bank. A more realistic interpretation is to assume that Dutch Bank represents the entire Dutch banking system. Additionally, the example implies some type of communication system between U.S. Bank and Dutch Bank. The *Society for Worldwide Interbank Financial Telecommunications* (*SWIFT*) allows international commercial banks to communicate instructions of the type in this example to one another. SWIFT is a private nonprofit message transfer system with headquarters in Brussels, with intercontinental switching centers in the Netherlands and Virginia. The *Clearing House Interbank Payments System* (*CHIPS*) in cooperation with the U.S. Federal Reserve Bank System, called Fedwire, provides a clearinghouse for the interbank settlement of U.S. dollar payments between international banks. Returning to our example, suppose U.S. Bank first needed to purchase Dutch guilders in order to have them for transfer to Dutch Exporter. U.S. Bank can use CHIPS for settling the purchase of Dutch guilders for dollars from, say, Swiss Bank, with instructions via SWIFT to Swiss Bank to deposit the Dutch guilders in its account with Dutch Bank and to Dutch Bank to transfer ownership to Dutch Exporter. The transfer between Swiss Bank and Dutch Bank would in turn be accomplished through correspondent bank accounts or through a European clearinghouse.

In August 1995, *Exchange Clearing House Limited* (*ECHO*), the first global clearinghouse for settling interbank FOREX transactions, began operation. ECHO is a multilateral netting system that on each settlement date nets a client's payments and receipts in each currency, regardless of whether they are due to or from multiple counterparties. Multilateral netting eliminates the risk and inefficiency of individual settlement. ECHO is expected to eventually reduce the current volume of interbank settlements by 90 percent.

THE SPOT MARKET

The **spot market** involves almost the immediate purchase or sale of foreign exchange. Typically, cash settlement is made two business days (excluding holidays of either the buyer or the seller) after the transaction for trades between the U.S. dollar and a non–North American currency. For regular spot trades between the U.S. dollar and the Mexican peso or the Canadian dollar, settlement takes only one business day.[1] According to BIS statistics, spot foreign exchange trading accounted for 40 percent of FX trades in 1998. Exhibit 4.3 provides a detailed analysis of foreign exchange turnover by instrument and counterparty.

Spot Rate Quotations

Spot rate currency quotations can be stated in direct or indirect terms. To understand the difference, let's refer to Exhibit 4.4. The exhibit shows currency quotations by bank dealers from Telerate and other sources as of 4:00 P.M. eastern time for Monday, July 5, and Tuesday, July 6, 1999. The first two columns provide **direct quotations** from the U.S. perspective, that is, the price of one unit of the foreign currency priced in U.S. dollars. For example, the Monday spot quote for one British pound was $1.5683. (Forward quotations for 30-, 90-, and 180-day contracts, which will be discussed in a following section, appear directly under the spot quotations for six currencies.) The second two columns provide **indirect quotations** from the U.S. perspective, that is, the price of one U.S. dollar in the foreign currency. For example, in the third column, we see that the Monday spot quote for one dollar in British pound sterling was £0.6376. Obviously, the direct quotation from the U.S. perspective is an indirect quote from the British viewpoint, and the indirect quote from the U.S. perspective is a direct quote from the British viewpoint.

EXHIBIT 4.3

Average Daily Foreign Exchange Turnover by Instrument and Counterparty

Instrument/Counterparty	Turnover in USD (000)		Percent	
Spot		*$577,737*		*40*
With reporting dealers	347,689		24	
With other financial institutions	120,708		8	
With nonfinancial customers	109,137		8	
Outright Forwards		*129,671*		*9*
With reporting dealers	49,078		3	
With other financial institutions	34,424		2	
With nonfinancial customers	46,155		3	
Foreign Exchange Swaps		*734,122*		*51*
With reporting dealers	511,719		35	
With other financial institutions	124,077		9	
With nonfinancial customers	98,289		7	
Total		$1,441,529		100

Note: Turnover is net of local and cross-border interdealer double-counting. Estimated gaps in reporting of $58,000,000 brings the total to approximately $1,500,000,000, the estimated daily average turnover figure.

Source: Tabulated from data in Table E-1 in the *Central Bank Survey of Foreign Exchange and Derivatives Market Activity*, Bank for International Settlements, Basle, May 1999.

It is common practice among currency traders worldwide to both price and trade currencies against the U.S. dollar. For example, BIS statistics indicate that in 1998, 87 percent of currency trading in the world involved the dollar on one side of the transaction. In recent years, however, the use of other currencies has been increasing, especially in dealing done by smaller regional banks. For example, in Europe many European currencies are traded against the deutsche mark. Overall, in 1998, 30 percent of all currency trading worldwide involved the deutsche mark on one side of the transaction. With respect to other major currencies, 21 percent involved the Japanese yen, 11 percent the British pound, 5 percent the French franc, 7 percent the Swiss franc, and 4 percent the Canadian dollar. Exhibit 4.5 provides a detailed analysis of foreign exchange turnover by currency. As previously noted, trading in the 11 Euro-zone currencies will cease on January 1, 2002, when trading in the euro common currency actually begins. Until then, however, trading in these 11 currencies continues, and they can be considered various denominations of the euro.

Most currencies in the interbank market are quoted in **European terms**, that is, the U.S. dollar is priced in terms of the foreign currency (an indirect quote from the U.S. perspective). By convention, however, it is standard practice to price certain currencies in terms of the U.S. dollar, or in what is referred to as **American terms** (a direct quote from the U.S. perspective). Prior to 1971, the British pound was a nondecimal currency; that is, a pound was not naturally divisible into 10 subcurrency units. Thus, it was cumbersome to price decimal currencies in terms of the pound. By necessity, the practice developed of pricing the British pound, as well as the Australian dollar, New Zealand dollar, and Irish punt, in terms of decimal currencies, and this convention continues today. To the uninitiated, this can be confusing, and it is something to bear in mind when examining currency quotations.

In this textbook, we will use the following notation for spot rate quotations. In general, $S(j/k)$ will refer to the price of one unit of currency k in terms of currency j. Thus, the American term quote from Exhibit 4.4 for British pounds on Tuesday, July 6, is $S(\$/£) = 1.5683$. The corresponding European quote is $S(£/\$) = .6376$. When the context is clear as to what terms the quotation is in, the less cumbersome S will be used to denote the spot rate.

EXHIBIT 4.4 Exchange Rates

Tuesday, July 6, 1999
Exchange Rates

The New York foreign exchange mid-range rates below apply to trading among banks in amounts of $1 million and more, as quoted at 4 p.m. Eastern time by Telerate and other sources. Retail transactions provide fewer units of foreign currency per dollar. Rates for the 11 Euro currency countries are derived from the latest dollar-euro rate using the exchange ratios set 1/1/99.

	U.S. $ equiv.		Currency per U.S. $	
Country	Tue	Mon	Tue	Mon
Argentina (Peso)	1.0005	1.0005	.9995	.9995
Australia (Dollar)	.6610	.6690	1.5129	1.4948
Austria (Schilling)	.07440	.07439	13.440	13.442
Bahrain (Dinar)	2.6525	2.6525	.3770	.3770
Belgium (Franc)	.0254	.0254	39.4020	39.4060
Brazil (Real)	.5621	.5675	1.7790	1.7620
Britain (Pound)	1.5683	1.5765	.6376	.6343
1-month forward	1.5685	1.5767	.6376	.6342
3-months forward	1.5694	1.5775	.6372	.6339
6-months forward	1.5714	1.5797	.6364	.6330
Canada (Dollar)	.6796	.6834	1.4715	1.4632
1-month forward	.6799	.6837	1.4709	1.4626
3-months forward	.6805	.6843	1.4694	1.4613
6-months forward	.6814	.6853	1.4676	1.4593
Chile (Peso)	.001943	.001937	514.55	516.15
China (Renminbi)	.1208	.1208	8.2780	8.2783
Colombia (Peso)	.0005697	.0005710	1755.31	1751.26
Czech. Rep. (Koruna)				
Commercial rate	.02829	.02829	35.352	35.352
Denmark (Krone)	.1377	.1377	7.2635	7.2635
Ecuador (Sucre)				
Floating rate	.00008400	.00008547	11905.00	11700.00
Finland (Markka)	.1722	.1722	5.8075	5.8081
France (Franc)	.1561	.1561	6.4071	6.4077
1-month forward	.1564	.1564	6.3934	6.3941
3-months forward	.1571	.1571	6.3641	6.3656
6-months forward	.1582	.1582	6.3200	6.3211
Germany (Mark)	.5235	.5234	1.9104	1.9105
1-month forward	.5246	.5245	1.9063	1.9065
3-months forward	.5270	.5269	1.8975	1.8980
6-months forward	.5307	.5306	1.8844	1.8847
Greece (Drachma)	.003147	.003156	317.75	316.81
Hong Kong (Dollar)	.1289	.1289	7.7588	7.7588
Hungary (Forint)	.004104	.004110	243.67	243.33
India (Rupee)	.02311	.02304	43.270	43.400
Indonesia (Rupiah)	.0001486	.0001478	6730.00	6765.00
Ireland (Punt)	1.2999	1.2999	.7693	.7693
Israel (Shekel)	.2449	.2451	4.0830	4.0800
Italy (Lira)	.0005288	.0005287	1891.26	1891.44
Japan (Yen)	.008193	.008263	122.05	121.02
1-month forward	.008229	.008299	121.52	120.49
3-months forward	.008304	.008373	120.43	119.43
6-months forward	.008420	.008493	118.77	117.74
Jordan (Dinar)	1.4104	1.4104	.7090	.7090
Kuwait (Dinar)	3.2552	3.2563	.3072	.3071
Lebanon (Pound)	.0006631	.0006631	1508.00	1508.00
Malaysia (Ringgit)	.2632	.2632	3.8000	3.8000
Malta (Lira)	2.4372	2.4444	.4103	.4091
Mexico (Peso)				
Floating rate	.1070	.1069	9.3470	9.3550
Netherlands (Guilder)	.4646	.4645	2.1525	2.1527
New Zealand (Dollar)	.5243	.5328	1.9073	1.8769
Norway (Krone)	.1269	.1267	7.8808	7.8928
Pakistan (Rupee)	.01939	.01946	51.575	51.375
Peru (new Sol)	.3011	.3009	3.3210	3.3230
Philippines (Peso)	.02625	.02627	38.100	38.073
Poland (Zloty)	.2556	.2551	3.9125	3.9205
Portugal (Escudo)	.005107	.005106	195.82	195.84
Russia (Ruble) (a)	.04085	.04117	24.480	24.290
Saudi Arabia (Rival)	.2666	.2666	3.7505	3.7507
Singapore (Dollar)	.5898	.5894	1.6955	1.6967
Slovak Rep. (Koruna)	.02268	.02272	44.083	44.011
South Africa (Rand)	.1655	.1660	6.0425	6.0240
South Korea (Won)	.0008562	.0008589	1168.00	1164.30
Spain (Peseta)	.006153	.006153	162.52	162.53
Sweden (Krona)	.1175	.1177	8.5083	8.4983
Switzerland (Franc)	.6386	.6378	1.5660	1.5678
1-month forward	.6408	.6400	1.5606	1.5624
3-months forward	.6453	.6444	1.5497	1.5519
6-months forward	.6518	.6509	1.5343	1.5364
Taiwan (Dollar)	.03098	.03097	32.282	32.291
Thailand (Baht)	.02719	.02712	36.775	36.870
Turkey (Lira)	.00000236	.00000237	424581.50	422688.00
United Arab (Dirham)	.2723	.2723	3.6728	3.6728
Uruguay (New Peso)				
Financial	.08776	.08787	11.395	11.380
Venezuela (Bolivar)	.001645	.001647	607.75	607.25
	—			
SDR	1.3287	1.3319	.7526	.7508
Euro	1.0238	1.0237	.9768	.9768

Special Drawing Rights (SDR) are based on exchange rates for the U.S., German, British, French, and Japanese currencies. Source: International Monetary Fund.

a-Russian Central Bank rate. Trading band lowered on 8/17/98. b-Government rate.

The Wall Street Journal daily foreign exchange data from 1996 forward may be purchased through the Readers' Reference Service (413) 592-3600.

Source: *The Wall Street Journal,* July 7, 1999, p. C14. Reprinted by permission of *The Wall Street Journal,* © 1999 Dow Jones & Company, Inc. All Rights Reserved Worldwide.

EXHIBIT 4.5

Average Daily Foreign Exchange Turnover by Currency against All Other Currencies

Currency	Turnover Stated in USD (000)	Percent
U.S. dollar	$1,260,000	87
Deutsche mark	429,952	30
Japanese yen	300,064	21
Pound sterling	157,906	11
French franc	73,330	5
Swiss franc	100,975	7
Canadian dollar	51,757	4
Australian dollar	44,209	3
ECU	20,595	1
Other EMS currencies	228,385	16
Other currencies	79,057	5
Residual	136,828	9
Total	$1,441,529	200

Note: Turnover is net of local and cross-border interdealer double-counting. Estimated gaps in reporting of $58,000,000 brings the total to approximately $1,500,000,000, the estimated daily average turnover figure. The percentage total sums to 200 percent because there are two sides to each transaction.

Source: Tabulated from data in Table E-4 in the Central Bank Survey of Foreign Exchange and Derivatives Market Activity, Bank for International Settlements, Basle, May 1999.

It should be intuitive that the American and European term quotes are reciprocals of one another. That is,

$$S(\$/£) = \frac{1}{S(£/\$)}$$
$$1.5683 = \frac{1}{.6376} \tag{4.1}$$

and

$$S(£/\$) = \frac{1}{S(\$/£)}$$
$$0.6376 = \frac{1}{1.5683} \tag{4.2}$$

The Bid-Ask Spread

Up to this point in our discussion, we have ignored the bid-ask spread in FX transactions. Interbank FX traders buy currency for inventory at the **bid price** and sell from inventory at the higher **offer** or **ask price**. Consider the Telerate quotations from Exhibit 4.4. What are they, bid or ask? In a manner of speaking, the answer is both, depending on whether one is referring to the American or European term quotes. Note the wording directly under the *Exchange Rates* title. The key to our inquiry is the sentence that reads: "Retail transactions provide fewer units of foreign currency per dollar." The word "provide" implies that the quotes in the third and fourth columns under the "Currency per U.S. $" heading are buying, or bid quotes. Thus the European term quotations are interbank bid prices.

To be more specific about the £/$ quote we have been using as an example, we can specify that it is a bid quote by writing $S(£/\$_b) = .6376$, meaning the bank dealer will bid, or pay, £0.6376 for one U.S. dollar. However, if the bank dealer is buying dollars for British pound sterling, it must be selling British pounds for U.S. dollars. This implies that the $/£ quote we have been using as an example is an ask quote, which we can designate as $S(\$/£_a) = 1.5683$. That is, the bank dealer will sell one British pound for $1.5683.

Returning to the reciprocal relationship between European and American term quotations, the recognition of the bid-ask spread implies:

$$S(\$/£_a) = \frac{1}{S(£/\$_b)} \tag{4.3}$$

In American terms, the bank dealer is asking \$1.5683 for one British pound; that means the bank dealer is willing to pay, or bid, less. Interbank bid-ask spreads are quite small. Let's assume the bid price is \$0.0005 less than the ask; thus $S(\$/£_b) = 1.5678$. Similarly, the bank dealer will want an ask price in European terms greater than its bid price. The reciprocal relationship between European and American term quotes implies:

$$\begin{aligned} S(£/\$_a) &= \frac{1}{S(\$/£_b)} \\ &= \frac{1}{1.5678} \\ &= 0.6378 \end{aligned} \tag{4.4}$$

Thus, the bank dealer's ask price of £0.6378 per U.S. dollar is indeed greater than its bid price of £0.6376.

Spot FX Trading

Examination of Exhibit 4.4 indicates that for most currencies, quotations are carried out to four decimal places in both American and European terms. However, for some currencies (e.g., the Austrian schilling, Japanese yen, Spanish peseta, South Korean won) quotations in European terms are carried out only to two or three decimal places, but in American terms the quotations may be carried out to as many as eight decimal places (see, for example, the Turkish lira).

In the interbank market, the standard-size trade among large banks in the major currencies is for the U.S.-dollar equivalent of \$10,000,000, or "ten dollars" in trader jargon. Dealers quote both the bid and the ask, willing to either buy or sell up to \$10,000,000 at the quoted prices. Spot quotations are good for only a few seconds. If a trader cannot immediately make up his mind whether to buy or sell at the proffered prices, the quotes are likely to be withdrawn.

In conversation, interbank FX traders use a shorthand abbreviation in expressing spot currency quotations. Consider the \$/£ bid-ask quotes from above, \$1.5678–\$1.5683. The "1.56" is known as the *big figure,* and it is assumed to be known by all traders. The second two digits to the right of the decimal place are referred to as the *small figure.* Since spot bid-ask spreads are typically around 5 "points," it is unambiguous for a trader to respond with "78 to 83" when asked what is his quote for British pound sterling. Similarly, "97 to 02" is a sufficient response for a quote of \$1.5097–\$1.5102, where the big figures are 1.50 and 1.51, respectively, for the bid and ask quotes.

The establishment of the bid-ask spread will facilitate acquiring or disposing of inventory. Suppose most \$/£ dealers are trading at \$1.5678–\$1.5683. A trader believing the pound will soon appreciate substantially against the dollar will desire to acquire a larger inventory of British pounds. A quote of "79 to 84" will encourage some traders to sell at the higher than market bid price, but also dissuade other traders from purchasing at the higher offer price. Analogously, a quote of "77 to 82" will allow a dealer to lower his pound inventory if he thinks the pound is ready to depreciate.

The retail bid-ask spread is wider than the interbank spread; that is, lower bid and higher ask prices apply to the smaller sums traded at the retail level. This is necessary to cover the fixed costs of a transaction that exist regardless of which tier the trade is made in.

Interbank trading rooms are typically organized with individual traders dealing in a particular currency. The dealing rooms of large banks are set up with traders dealing against the U.S. dollar in all the major currencies: the Japanese yen, German

INTERNATIONAL FINANCE IN PRACTICE

Young Traders Run Currency Markets

NEW YORK—Surrounded by flashing currency prices, ringing phones and screaming traders, Fred Scala offers his view of people who use economic analysis to forecast currency rates. "They may be right," he says, "but they don't know how to pull the trigger."

Mr. Scala knows how.

At age 27, he is Manufacturers Hanover Trust Co.'s top dealer in German marks. Yesterday morning alone, he traded about $500 million in marks, darting in and out of the market 100 times. As the dollar inched up, he bought. As it retreated, he sold. "We're mercenaries, soldiers of fortune," he says. "We have no alliances. We work for the bank."

Currency traders like Mr. Scala are riding high these days. As politicians dicker about what to do about the dollar after last month's stock-market crash, young traders at the world's top 30 to 50 banks hold day-to-day control of the currency markets. And unlike their shell-shocked counterparts at stock-trading desks, currency dealers are making nearly all the right bets.

Bravo for Lira Trader

A look at Manufacturers Hanover's trading desk shows this trading mentality in firm command. As traders arrive yesterday at 7 A.M., the lira trader, Scott Levy, gets a hero's welcome. He had bought $55 million of lira the night before, switched some of it into German marks, and benefited from a rising mark in overnight Asian trading.

"I did quite well," he tells colleagues, as he takes his seat. A Hong Kong trader woke him up at home with a 4 A.M. phone call—but helped Mr. Levy unwind his position at a profit of more than $165,000. Other traders greet him with "high five" handslaps, like a football player who has just scored a touchdown.

The next 90 minutes are consumed by a blizzard of trades with European banks. Computerized dealing systems let traders do business with London, Frankfurt or Zurich by the push of a button, without even a phone call. Typically, Manufacturers Hanover will buy "five dollars"—trader jargon for $5 million—then resell it at a razor-thin profit margin seconds later.

At 9:03 A.M., the first of the day's big news headlines hits the screen. "U.S. Commerce Under Secretary Says Dollar Is Now Competitive," a new monitor reports.

"That's good for the dollar," says Mr. Remigio. He and Mr. Scala buy $10 million at a rate of 1.7080 marks.

Moments later, a senior bank trader walks by and asks why the dollar is rising. Mr. Remigio starts to explain the new views expressed by the Commerce under secretary.

"What the hell does he know?" another trader snaps.

The issue is settled. In a flurry of four transactions, Manufacturers Hanover dumps the $10 million it just bought, and sells another $8 million as well. It gets rates ranging from 1.7088 to 1.7107 marks. The slight gain from its purchase price is infinitesimal to anyone but a currency trader. To Messrs. Scala and Remigio, it is $500 quick profit for the bank.

Difficult Stretch

About 1 P.M., the mark traders encounter their one difficult stretch of the day. They have sold dollars, expecting further drops. But the dollar is inching up. Mr. Scala twirls his phone cord around his finger and taps his feet. Mr. Remigio slams his phone down, snarling: "It's up, it's up, it's going up."

Rather than fight the momentary trend, the traders begin buying dollars. "The dollar is going uptown," Mr. Remigio declares. He holds his new positive position on the dollar for only a brief spell, but profits from it as well.

All morning, calls from incoming banks and customers light up dealers' phone boards, which hold 120 direct phone lines. Only around 11 A.M. does the most important phone line—the one in the bottom left-hand corner, begin blinking at Manufacturers Hanover's mark desk. It is the Federal Reserve Bank of New York, agent for the U.S. government. And for a moment, Mr. Scala doesn't see the line light up.

mark, French franc, Canadian dollar, Swiss franc, and British pound, plus the local currency if it is not one of the majors. Individual banks may also specialize by making a market in regional currencies or in the currencies of less-developed countries, again all versus the U.S. dollar. Additionally, banks will usually have a cross-rate desk where trades between two currencies not involving the U.S. dollar are handled. It is not uncommon for a trader of an active currency pair, such as the deutsche mark and U.S. dollar, to make as many as 1,500 quotes and 400 trades in a day.[2] In smaller

"When that line comes in, you've got to pick it up quick," Mr. Remigio chides his partner. "They could be wanting to deal."

The New York Fed in fact deals with any of a dozen big New York banks when it enters the market to buy or sell currencies, and it often doesn't let one bank know about its dealings with another. This time the Fed just wants information about the dollar. "It goes up. It goes down. It goes all around," the Fed's trader asks over the phone. "What's going on?"

Reading Fed Signals

Mr. Scala tries to offer a quick summary of market activity. Then he asks the Fed: "Is there any level you want me to call you back at?"

With his low-key question, Mr. Scala is trying to get at perhaps the most important piece of information in the foreign-exchange market. Traders' one big worry currently is that if the dollar falls too fast, the Fed and foreign central banks may barge in with big buy orders to prop up the dollar. If a trader knows what dollar rate worries the Fed, he can better prepare for any possible intervention.

"Yeah," says the Fed trader. "Call me if it gets to 1.7075."

A little later, the dollar does slip to that level. Mr. Scala calls the Fed. But instead of placing a big buy order, the Fed trader just says: "Call me back if it goes much lower."

Around this time, Manufacturers Hanover's mark traders back off from some bearish market positions they have taken against the dollar. But that is straightforward profit-taking, the traders say, unrelated to the Fed's call.

The trading frenzy continues until about noon New York time, when the European trading day ends. Only then can Manufacturers' New York traders relax. "It's like a ball and chain," complains James Young, senior sterling trader. "I can't go out to lunch."

For their efforts, the mark traders break even after making about 200 trades involving nearly $1 billion. The bank's entire currency-trading operation did better however, bringing in a profit of about $300,000 for the day.

While young traders are in the front lines, big banks like Manufacturers Hanover have top managers looking over their shoulders, setting position limits and trying to make sure the bank doesn't get stuck with unexpected losses. But the foreign-exchange market has grown so fast, and takes such a toll on traders, that there are few veterans.

Mr. Remigio, the 27-year-old No. 2 mark trader, received an M.B.A. from Hofstra University before coming to Manufacturers Hanover a couple of years ago. His colleague, Mr. Scala, has only a high-school diploma. Mr. Scala has something more valuable to the bank, though: nearly a decade of experience. He started as a broker's clerk, then advanced to trading when he was all of 20. Individual traders, many still in their 20s, earn more than $100,000 a year in salary and bonus.

The Role of Luck

But there are no illusions about succeeding on skill alone around the trading room. Within reach of nearly every trader is a good-luck charm. At the desk where Japanese yen are traded, dealers can rub the tummy of a cherubic statuette or slap a bobbing-head doll representing Japan's rising sun. It then cries out, in Japanese: "Try, you can do it!" The Japanese writing on a headband wrapped around a speaker phone reads: "We're definitely going to win!"

Traders joke that for them, 10 minutes is a long-term outlook. One of Manufacturers Hanover's economists, Marc M. Goloven, says he can sense the difference when he visits trading floors to get a feel for market trends. "When I sit down there, I can feel the tension rising," he says. "That's tough duty. I sympathize with them." His one quibble, he says, is that many traders "aren't attuned to looking at [economic] fundamentals as much as we think they should."

Down in the trading room, the traders generally agree. "I like to see what the economist thinks, but he's thinking long-term," says James Young, Manufacturer's top sterling trader. "And there are 13 floors between here and long-term."

Bank officials doubt that the dollar's decline is over. "It isn't un-American" to sell dollars and profit from the currency's decline, Mr. Young says. "It's how the game is played."

The dollar's chronic slump is worrying for the U.S. economy, adds Mr. Remigio. But there's no room at the trading desk for sentimentality. "I don't like seeing the dollar down here," he says. "My money doesn't buy as much when I travel overseas. But in trading, if the thing's going down, I'm going to sell it."

Source: Charles W. Stevens, *The Wall Street Journal,* November 5, 1987, p. 26. Excerpted from *The Wall Street Journal,* © 1987 Dow Jones & Company, Inc. All Rights Reserved Worldwide.

European banks accustomed to more regional trading, dealers will frequently quote and trade versus the deutsche mark.

A bank trading room is a noisy, active place. Currency traders are typically young, high-energy people, who are capable of interpreting new information quickly and making high-stakes decisions. The *International Finance in Practice* box on pages 84–85 entitled "Young Traders Run Currency Markets," depicts the sense of excitement and the electric atmosphere one finds in a bank dealing room.

Cross Exchange Rate Quotations

Let's ignore the transaction costs of trading temporarily while we develop the concept of a cross-rate. A **cross exchange rate** is an exchange rate between a currency pair where neither currency is the U.S. dollar. The cross exchange rate can be calculated from the U.S. dollar exchange rates for the two currencies, using either European or American term quotations. For example, the DM/£ cross-rate can be calculated from American term quotations as follows:

$$S(DM/£) = \frac{S(\$/£)}{S(\$/DM)} \tag{4.5}$$

where from Exhibit 4.4,

$$S(DM/£) = \frac{1.5683}{.5235} = 2.9958$$

That is, if £1.00 cost \$1.5683 and DM1.00 cost \$0.5235, the cost of £1.00 in deutsche marks is DM2.9958. In European terms, the calculation is

$$\begin{aligned} S(DM/£) &= \frac{S(DM/\$)}{S(£/\$)} \\ &= \frac{1.9104}{.6376} \\ &= 2.9962 \end{aligned} \tag{4.6}$$

where the difference between 2.9958 and 2.9962 is due to rounding.

Analogously,

$$\begin{aligned} S(£/DM) &= \frac{S(\$/DM)}{S(\$/£)} \\ &= \frac{.5235}{1.5683} \\ &= .3338 \end{aligned} \tag{4.7}$$

and

$$\begin{aligned} S(£/DM) &= \frac{S(£/\$)}{S(DM/\$)} \\ &= \frac{.6376}{1.9104} \\ &= .3338 \end{aligned} \tag{4.8}$$

Equations 4.5 to 4.8 imply that given N currencies, one can calculate a triangular matrix of the $N \times (N - 1)/2$ cross exchange rates. Daily in the *Financial Times* appear the 136 cross exchange rates for all pair combinations of 17 currencies and stated as $S(j/k)$ and $S(k/j)$. Exhibit 4.6 presents an example of the table for Tuesday, July 6, 1999.

Alternative Expressions for the Cross-Exchange Rate

For some purposes, it is easier to think of cross exchange rates calculated as the product of an American term and a European exchange rate rather than as the quotient of two American term or two European term exchange rates. For example, substituting $S(DM/\$)$ for $1/S(\$/DM)$ allows Equation 4.5 to be rewritten as:

$$\begin{aligned} S(DM/£) &= S(\$/£) \times S(DM/\$) \\ &= 1.5683 \times 1.9104 \\ &= 2.9961 \end{aligned} \tag{4.9}$$

where the difference from 2.9962 is due to rounding.

EXHIBIT 4.6 Exchange Cross Rates London Trading July 6, 1999)

		BFr	DKr	FFr	DM	I£	L	Fl	NKr	Es	Pta	SKr	SFr	£	C$	$	Y	€
Belgium*	(BFr)	100	18.43	16.26	4.848	1.952	4800	5.463	19.99	497.0	412.5	21.56	3.974	1.620	3.734	2.541	310.2	2.479
Denmark	(DKr)	54.26	10	8.823	2.631	1.059	2604	2.964	10.85	269.6	223.8	11.70	2.156	0.879	2.026	1.379	168.3	1.345
France*	(FFr)	61.50	11.33	10	2.982	1.201	2952	3.360	12.29	305.6	253.7	13.26	2.444	0.996	2.297	1.563	190.7	1.525
Germany*	(DM)	20.63	3.801	3.354	1	0.403	990.0	1.127	4.123	102.5	85.07	4.447	0.820	0.334	0.770	0.524	63.97	0.511
Ireland*	(I£)	51.22	9.441	8.329	2.483	1	2459	2.798	10.24	254.6	211.3	11.04	2.036	0.830	1.913	1.301	158.9	1.270
Italy*	(L)	2.083	0.384	0.339	0.101	0.041	100	0.114	0.416	10.35	8.593	0.449	0.083	0.034	0.078	0.053	6.462	0.052
Netherlands*	(Fl)	18.31	3.374	2.977	0.888	0.357	878.6	1	3.659	90.97	75.50	3.947	0.728	0.297	0.684	0.465	56.78	0.454
Norway	(NKr)	50.03	9.220	8.135	2.425	0.977	2401	2.733	10	248.6	206.3	10.79	1.988	0.811	1.868	1.271	155.2	1.240
Portugal*	(Es)	20.12	3.709	3.272	0.976	0.393	965.8	1.099	4.022	100	82.99	4.339	0.800	0.326	0.751	0.511	62.41	0.499
Spain*	(Pta)	24.24	4.469	3.942	1.175	0.473	1164	1.324	4.846	120.5	100	5.228	0.964	0.393	0.905	0.616	75.20	0.601
Sweden	(SKr)	46.38	8.548	7.541	2.249	0.905	2226	2.534	9.271	230.5	191.3	10	1.843	0.751	1.732	1.178	143.8	1.150
Switzerland	(SFr)	25.16	4.638	4.092	1.220	0.491	1208	1.375	5.030	125.1	103.8	5.425	1	0.408	0.940	0.639	78.04	0.624
UK	(£)	61.72	11.38	10.04	2.992	1.205	2962	3.372	12.34	306.7	254.6	13.31	2.453	1	2.305	1.568	191.4	1.530
Canada	(C$)	26.78	4.936	4.354	1.298	0.523	1285	1.463	5.353	133.1	110.5	5.774	1.064	0.434	1	0.680	83.06	0.664
USA	($)	39.36	7.254	6.400	1.908	0.768	1889	2.150	7.867	195.6	162.3	8.486	1.564	0.638	1.470	1	122.1	0.976
Japan	(Y)	32.24	5.942	5.243	1.563	0.629	1548	1.761	6.445	160.2	133.0	6.952	1.281	0.522	1.204	0.819	100	0.799
Euro	(€)	40.34	7.435	6.560	1.956	0.788	1936	2.204	8.064	200.5	166.4	8.698	1.603	0.654	1.506	1.025	125.1	1

Source: *Financial Times,* July 7, 1999, p. 25.

In general terms,

$$S(j/k) = S(\$/k) \times S(j/\$) \tag{4.10}$$

and, taking reciprocals of both sides of Equation 4.10 yields

$$S(k/j) = S(k/\$) \times S(\$/j) \tag{4.11}$$

The Cross-Rate Trading Desk

Earlier in the chapter, it was mentioned that most interbank trading goes through the dollar. Suppose a bank customer wants to trade out of British pound sterling into French francs. In dealer jargon, a nondollar trade such as this is referred to as a **currency against currency** trade. The bank will frequently (or effectively) handle this trade for its customer by selling British pounds for U.S. dollars and then selling U.S. dollars for French francs. At first blush, this might seem ridiculous. Why not just sell the British pounds directly for French francs? To answer this question, let's return to Exhibit 4.6 of the cross exchange rates. Suppose a bank's home currency was one of the 17 currencies in the exhibit and that it made markets in the other 16 currencies. The bank's trading room would typically be organized with 16 trading desks, each for trading one of the nondollar currencies against the U.S. dollar. A dealer needs only to be concerned with making a market in his nondollar currency against the dollar. However, if each of the 17 currencies was traded directly with the others, the dealing room would need to accommodate 136 trading desks. Or worse, individual traders would be responsible for making a market in several currency pairs, say, the DM/\$, DM/£, and DM/SF, instead of just the DM/\$. As Grabbe (1996) notes, this would entail an informational complexity that would be virtually impossible to handle.

Banks handle currency against currency trades, such as for the bank customer who wants to trade out of British pounds into French francs, at the cross-rate desk. Recall from Equation 4.10 that a $S(FF/£)$ quote can be obtained from the product of $S(\$/£)$ and $S(FF/\$)$. Recognizing transaction costs implies the following restatement of Equation 4.10:

$$S(FF/£_b) = S(\$/£_b) \times S(FF/\$_b) \tag{4.12}$$

The bank will quote its customer a selling (bid) price for the British pounds in terms French francs determined by multiplying its American term bid price for British pounds and its European term bid price (for U.S. dollars) stated in French francs.

Taking reciprocals of Equation 4.12 yields

$$S(£/FF_a) = S(£/\$_a) \times S(\$/FF_a) \tag{4.13}$$

which is analogous to Equation 4.11. In terms of our example, Equation 4.13 says the bank could alternatively quote its customer an offer (ask) price for French francs in terms of British pounds determined by multiplying its European term ask price (for U.S. dollars) stated in British pounds by its American term ask price for French francs.

Triangular Arbitrage

Certain banks specialize in making a direct market between nondollar currencies, pricing at a narrower bid-ask spread than the cross-rate spread. Nevertheless, the implied cross-rate bid-ask quotations imposes a discipline on the nondollar market makers. If their direct quotes are not consistent with cross exchange rates, a triangular arbitrage profit is possible. **Triangular arbitrage** is the process of trading out of the U.S. dollar into a second currency, then trading it for a third currency, which is in turn traded for U.S. dollars. The purpose is to earn an arbitrage profit via trading from the second to the third currency when the direct exchange rate between the two is not in alignment with the cross exchange rate.

EXAMPLE 4.2: Calculating the Cross Exchange Rate Bid-Ask Spread Let's assume (as we did earlier) that the \$/£ bid-ask prices are \$1.5678–\$1.5683 and the £/\$ bid-ask prices are £0.6376–£0.6378. Let's also assume the \$/FF bid-ask prices are \$0.1560–\$0.1561 and the FF/\$ bid-ask prices are FF6.4071–FF6.4103. These bid and ask prices and Equation 4.12 imply that $S(FF/£_b) = 1.5678 \times 6.4071 = 10.0451$. The reciprocal of $S(FF/£_b)$, or Equation 4.13, implies that $S(£/FF_a) = .6378 \times .1561 = .0996$. Analogously, Equation 4.13 suggests that $S(FF/£_a) = 1.5683 \times 6.4103 = 10.0533$, and its reciprocal implies that $S(£/FF_b) = .0995$. That is, the FF/£ bid-ask prices are FF10.0451–FF10.0533 and the £/FF bid-ask prices are £0.0995–£0.0996. Note that the cross-rate bid-ask spreads are much larger than the American or European bid-ask spreads. For example, the FF/£ bid-ask spread is FF0.0082 versus a FF/\$ spread of FF0.0032. The £/FF bid-ask spread is £0.0001 versus the \$/FF spread of \$0.0001, which is a sizable difference since a British pound is priced in excess of one dollar. The implication is that cross exchange rates *implicitly* incorporate the bid-ask spreads of the two transactions that are necessary for trading out of one nondollar currency and into another. Hence, even when a bank makes a direct market in one nondollar currency versus another, the trade is *effectively* going through the dollar because the "currency against currency" exchange rate is consistent with a cross exchange rate calculated from the dollar exchange rates of the two currencies. Exhibit 4.7 provides a more detailed presentation of cross-rate foreign exchange transactions.

EXHIBIT 4.7

Cross-Rate Foreign Exchange Transactions

	American Terms		European Terms	
Bank Quotations	**Bid**	**Ask**	**Bid**	**Ask**
British pounds	1.5678	1.5683	.6376	.6378
French francs	.1560	.1561	6.4071	6.4103

a. Bank Customer wants to sell £1,000,000 for French francs. The Bank will sell U.S. dollars (buy British pounds) for \$1.5678. The sale yields Bank Customer:

   £1,000,000 × 1.5678 = \$1,567,800.

   The Bank will buy dollars (sell French francs) for FF6.4071. The sale of dollars yields Bank Customer:

   \$1,567,800 × FF6.4071 = FF10,045,051.

   Bank Customer has effectively sold British pounds at a FF/£ bid price of

   FF10,045,051/£1,000,000 = FF10.0451/£1.00.

b. Bank Customer wants to sell FF10,000,000 for British pounds. The Bank will sell U.S. dollars (buy French francs) for FF6.4103. The sale yields Bank Customer:

   FF10,000,000 ÷ 6.4103 = \$1,559, 989.

   The Bank will buy dollars (sell British pounds) for \$1.5683. The sale of dollars yields Bank Customer:

   \$1,559,989 ÷ \$1.5683 = £994,701.

   Bank Customer has effectively bought British pounds at a FF/£ ask price of

   FF10,000,000/£994,701 = FF10.0533/£1.00.

   From parts (a) and (b), we see the currency against currency bid-ask spread for British pounds is FF10.0451–FF10.0533.

EXAMPLE 4.3 Taking Advantage of a Triangular Arbitrage Opportunity To illustrate a triangular arbitrage, assume the cross-rate trader at Deutsche Bank notices that Crédit Lyonnais is buying dollars at $S(FF/\$_b) = 6.4071$, the same as Deutsche Bank's bid price. Similarly, he observes that Barclays is offering dollars at $S(\$/£_b) = 1.5678$, also the same as Deutsche Bank. He next finds that Crédit Agricole is making a direct market between the franc and the pound, with a current ask price of $S(FF/£_a) = 10.0100$. The cross-rate formula and the American and European term quotes (as we saw above) imply that the FF/£ *bid* price should be no lower than $S(FF/£_b) = 1.5678 \times 6.4071 = 10.0451$. Yet Crédit Agricole is offering to *sell* British pounds at a rate of only 10.0100!

A triangular arbitrage profit is available if the Deutsche Bank traders are quick enough. A sale of \$5,000,000 to Crédit Lyonnais for French francs will yield FF32,035,500 = \$5,000,000 × 6.4071. The FF32,035,500 will be resold to Crédit Agricole for £3,200,350 = FF32,035,500/10.0100. Likewise, the British pounds will be resold to Barclays for \$5,017,509 = £3,200,350 × 1.5678, yielding an arbitrage profit of \$17,509.

Obviously, Crédit Agricole must raise its asking price above FF10.0100/£1.00. The cross exchange rates (from Exhibit 4.7) gave FF/£ bid-ask prices of FF10.0451–10.0533. These prices imply that Crédit Agricole can deal inside the spread and sell for less than FF10.0533, but not less than FF10.0451. An ask price of FF10.0500, for example, would eliminate the arbitrage profit. At that price, the FF32,035,500 would be resold for £3,187,612 = FF32,035,500/10.0500, which in turn would yield only \$4,997,538 = £3,187,612 × 1.5678, or a *loss* of \$2,462. In today's "high-tech" FX market, triangular arbitrage opportunities are nearly nonexistent. Exhibit 4.8 presents a diagram and a summary of this triangular arbitrage example.

EXHIBIT 4.8

Triangular Arbitrage Example

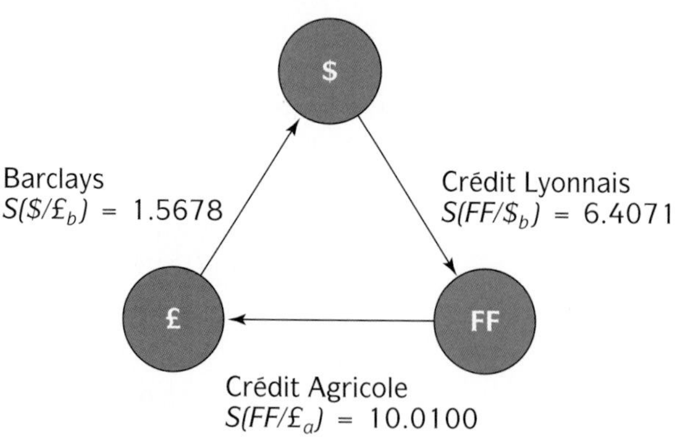

Deutsche Bank arbitrage strategy

\$	5,000,000	
×	6.4071	
FF	32,035,500	Sell U.S. dollars for French francs
÷	10.0100	
£	3,200,350	Sell French francs for British pounds
×	1.5678	
\$	5,017,509	Sell British pounds for U.S. dollars
−\$	5,000,000	
\$	17,509	Arbitrage profit

Spot Foreign Exchange Market Microstructure

Market microstructure refers to the basic mechanics of how a marketplace operates. Two recent empirical studies on FX market microstructure shed light on the operation of the spot FX marketplace. Huang and Masulis (1999) study spot FX rates on DM/$ trades over the October 1, 1992 to September 29, 1993, period. They find that bid-ask spreads in the spot FX market increase with FX exchange rate volatility and decrease with dealer competition. These results are consistent with models of market microstructure. They also find that the bid-ask spread decreases when the percentage of large dealers in the marketplace increases. They conclude that dealer competition is a fundamental determinant of the spot FX bid-ask spread.

Ito, Lyons, and Melvin (1998) study the role of private information in the spot FX market. They examine ¥/$ and DM/$ between September 29, 1994, and March 28, 1995. Their study provides evidence against the common view that private information is irrelevant, since all market participants are assumed to possess the same set of public information. Their evidence comes from the Tokyo foreign exchange market, which prior to December 21, 1994, closed for lunch between noon and 1:30 P.M. After December 21, 1994, the variance in spot exchange rates increased during the lunch period relative to the period of closed trading. This was true for both ¥/$ and DM/$ trades, but more so for the ¥/$ data, which is to be expected since ¥/$ trading is more intensive in the Tokyo FX market. Ito, Lyons, and Melvin attribute these results to a greater revelation of private information in trades being allocated to the lunch hour. This suggests that private information is, indeed, an important determinant of spot exchange rates.

THE FORWARD MARKET

In conjunction with spot trading, there is also a forward foreign exchange market. The **forward market** involves contracting today for the future purchase or sale of foreign exchange. The forward price may be the same as the spot price, but usually it is higher (at a premium) or lower (at a discount) than the spot price. Forward exchange rates are quoted on most major currencies for a variety of maturities. Bank quotes for maturities of 1, 3, 6, 9, and 12 months are readily available. Quotations on nonstandard, or broken-term, maturities are also available. Maturities extending beyond one year are becoming more frequent, and for good bank customers, a maturity extending out to 5, and even as long as 10 years, is possible.

Forward Rate Quotations

To learn how to read forward exchange rate quotations, let's examine Exhibit 4.4. Notice that **forward rate** quotations appear directly under the spot rate quotations for six major currencies (the British pound, Canadian dollar, French franc, German mark, Japanese yen, and Swiss franc). These quotes are stated as if all months have 30 days. A 90-day maturity is thus synonymous with a three-month maturity. In general, the settlement date of a three-month, or 90-day, forward transaction is three calendar months from the spot settlement date for the currency. For example, if today is September 4, 2000, and spot settlement is September 6, then the forward settlement date would be December 6, 2000, a period of 93 days from September 4.

In this textbook, we will use the following notation for forward rate quotations. In general, $F_N(j/k)$ will refer to the price of one unit of currency k in terms of currency j for delivery in N days. N equaling 30 denotes a one-month maturity based on a 360-day banker's year. Thus, N equaling 90 denotes a three-month maturity. When the context is clear, the simpler notation F will be used to denote a forward exchange rate.

Forward quotes are either direct or indirect, one being the reciprocal of the other. From the U.S. perspective, a direct forward quote is in American terms. As examples, let's consider the American term Swiss franc forward quotations in relationship to the spot rate quotation for Tuesday, July 6, 1999. We see that:

$$S(\$/SF) = .6386$$
$$F_{30}(\$/SF) = .6408$$
$$F_{90}(\$/SF) = .6453$$
$$F_{180}(\$/SF) = .6518$$

From these quotations, we can see that in American terms the Swiss franc is trading at a *premium* to the dollar, and that the premium increases out to 180 days, the further the forward maturity date is from July 6.

European term forward quotations are the reciprocal of the American term quotes. In European terms, the corresponding Swiss franc forward quotes to those stated above are:

$$S(SF/\$) = 1.5660$$
$$F_{30}(SF/\$) = 1.5606$$
$$F_{90}(SF/\$) = 1.5497$$
$$F_{180}(SF/\$) = 1.5343$$

From these quotations, we can see that in European terms the dollar is trading at a *discount* to the Swiss franc and that the discount increases out to 180 days, the further the forward maturity date is from July 6. This is exactly what we should expect, since the European term quotes are the reciprocals of the corresponding American term quotations.

Long and Short Forward Positions

One can buy (take a long position) or sell (take a short position) foreign exchange forward. Bank customers can contract with their international bank to buy or sell a specific sum of FX for delivery on a certain date. Likewise, interbank traders can establish a long or short position by dealing with a trader from a competing bank. Exhibit 4.9 graphs both the long and short positions for the 90-day Swiss franc contract, using the American quote for July 6, 1999, from Exhibit 4.4. The graph measures profits or losses on the vertical axis. The horizontal axis shows the spot price of foreign exchange on the maturity date of the forward contract, $S_{90}(\$/SF)$. If one uses the forward contract, he has "locked in" the forward price for forward purchase or sale of foreign exchange. Regardless of what the spot price is on the maturity date of the forward contract, the trader buys (if he is long) or sells (if he is short) at $F_{90}(\$/SF) = .6453$ per unit of FX. Forward contracts can also be used for speculative purposes, as the following example demonstrates.

EXAMPLE 4.4: A Speculative Forward Position It is July 6,1999. Suppose the $/SF trader has just heard an economic forecast from the bank's head economist that causes him to believe that the dollar will likely appreciate in value against the Swiss franc to a level less than the forward rate over the next three months. If he decides to act on this information, the trader will short the 90-day $/SF contract. We will assume that he sells SF5,000,000 forward against dollars. Suppose the forecast has proven correct, and on October 6, 1999, spot $/SF is trading at $0.6400. The trader can buy Swiss franc spot at $0.6400 and deliver it under the forward contract at a price of $0.6453. The trader has made a speculative profit of ($0.6453 − $0.6400) = $0.0053 per unit, as Exhibit 4.9 shows. The total profit from the trade is $26,500 = (SF5,000,000 × $0.0053). If the dollar depreciated and S_N was $0.6500, the speculator would have lost ($0.6453 − $0.6500) = −$0.0047 per unit, for a total loss of −$23,500 = (SF5,000,000 × -$0.0047).

EXHIBIT 4.9

Graph of Long and Short Position in the 90-Day Swiss Franc Contract

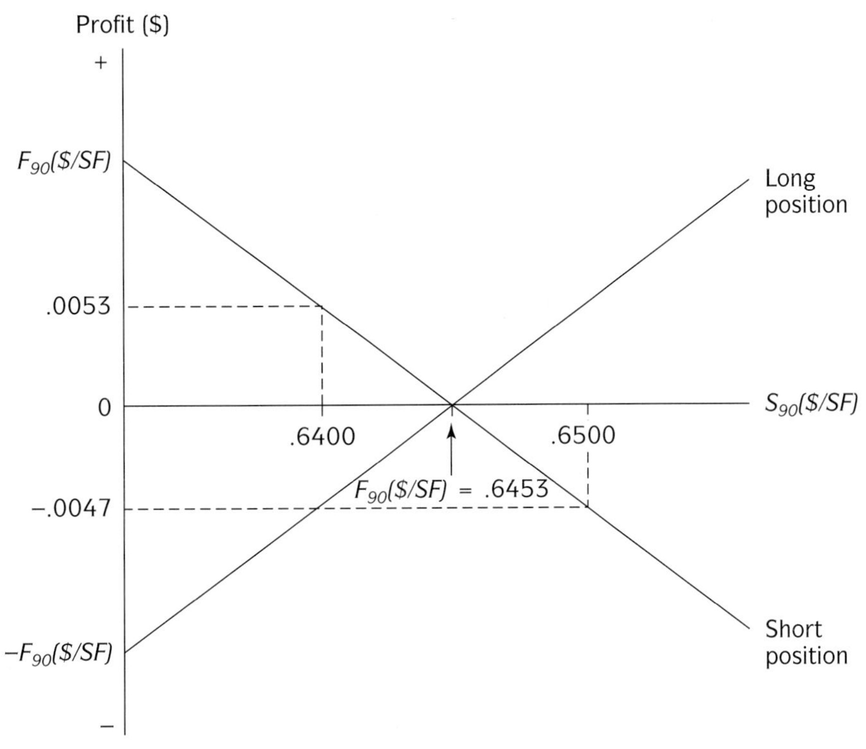

Forward Cross Exchange Rates

Forward cross exchange rate quotations are calculated in an analogous manner to spot cross-rates, so it is not necessary to provide detailed examples. In generic terms,

$$F_N(j/k) = \frac{F_N(\$/k)}{F_N(\$/j)} \tag{4.14}$$

or

$$F_N(j/k) = \frac{F_N(j/\$)}{F_N(k/\$)} \tag{4.15}$$

and

$$F_N(k/j) = \frac{F_N(\$/j)}{F_N(\$/k)} \tag{4.16}$$

or

$$F_N(k/j) = \frac{F_N(k/\$)}{F_N(j/\$)} \tag{4.17}$$

Swap Transactions

Forward trades can be classified as outright or swap transactions. In conducting their trading, bank dealers do take speculative positions in the currencies they trade, but more often traders offset the currency exposure inherent in a trade. From the bank's standpoint, an **outright forward transaction** is an uncovered speculative position in a currency, even though it might be part of a currency hedge to the bank customer on the other side of the transaction. Swap transactions provide a means for the bank to mitigate the currency exposure in a forward trade. A **swap transaction** is the simultaneous sale (or purchase) of spot foreign exchange against a forward purchase (or sale) of approximately an equal amount of the foreign currency.

Swap transactions account for approximately 51 percent of interbank FX trading, whereas outright trades are less than 9 percent. (See Exhibit 4.3.) Because interbank forward transactions are most frequently made as part of a swap transaction, bank dealers in conversation among themselves use a shorthand notation to quote bid and ask forward prices in terms of *forward points* that are either added to or subtracted from the spot bid and ask quotations.

EXAMPLE 4.5: Forward Point Quotations Recall the $/£ spot bid-ask rates of $1.5678–$1.5683 developed previously. With reference to these rates, forward prices might be displayed as:

Spot	1.5678–1.5683
One-Month	17–7
Three-Month	18–2
Six-Month	26–1

When the second number in a forward point "pair" is smaller than the first, the dealer "knows" the forward points are subtracted from the spot bid and ask prices to obtain the outright forward rates. For example, the spot bid price of $1.5678 minus .0017 (or 17 points) equals $1.5661, the 30-day forward bid price. The spot ask price of $1.5683 minus .0007 (or 7 points) equals $1.5676, the 30-day ask price. Analogously, the 90-day outright forward bid-ask rates are $1.5660–$1.5681 and the 180-day outright forward bid-ask rates are $1.5652–$1.5682.[3] The following table summarizes the calculations.

Spot	1.5678–1.5683	
	Forward Point Quotations	**Outright Forward Quotations**
One-Month	17–7	$1.5661–$1.5676
Three-Month	18–2	$1.5660–$1.5681
Six-Month	26–1	$1.5652–$1.5682

Three things are notable about the outright prices. First, the pound is trading at a forward discount to the dollar. Second, all bid prices are less than the corresponding ask prices, as they must be for a trader to be willing to make a market. Third, the bid-ask spread increases in time to maturity, as is typical. These three conditions prevail only *because* the forward points were subtracted from the spot prices. As a check, note that in points the spot bid-ask spread is 5 points, the 30-day forward bid-ask spread is 15 points, the 90-day spread is 21 points, and the 180-day spread is 30 points.

If the forward prices were trading at a premium to the spot price, the second number in a forward point pair would be larger than the first, and the trader would know to add the points to the spot bid and ask prices to obtain the outright forward bid and ask rates. For example, if the 90-day and 180-day swap points were 2–18 and 1–26, the corresponding 90-day and 180-day bid-ask rates would be $1.5680–$1.5701 and $1.5679–$1.5709. In points, the 90- and 180-day bid-ask spreads would be 21 and 30, that is, increasing in term to maturity.

Quoting forward rates in terms of forward points is convenient for two reasons. First, forward points may remain constant for long periods of time, even if the spot rates fluctuate frequently. Second, in swap transactions where the trader is attempting to minimize currency exposure, the actual spot and outright forward rates are often of no consequence. What is important is the premium or discount differential, measured in forward points. To illustrate, suppose a bank customer wants to sell dollars three months forward against British pound sterling. The bank can handle this trade for its customer and simultaneously neutralize the exchange rate risk in the trade by selling (borrowed) dollars spot against British pounds. The bank will lend the pound sterling for three months until they are needed to deliver against the dollars it has purchased forward. The dollars received will be used to liquidate the dollar loan. Implicit in this transaction is the interest rate differential between the dollar borrowing rate and the pound sterling lending rate. The interest rate differential is captured by the forward premium or discount measured in forward points. As a rule, when the interest rate of the foreign currency is greater than the interest rate of the quoting currency, the outright forward rate is less than the spot exchange rate, and vice versa. This will become clear in the following chapter on international parity relationships.

Forward Premium

It is common to express the premium or discount of a forward rate as an annualized percentage deviation from the spot rate. The forward premium (or discount) is useful for comparing against the interest rate differential between two countries, as we will see more clearly in Chapter 5 on international parity relationships. The **forward premium** or **discount** can be expressed in American or European terms. Obviously, if a currency is trading at a premium (discount) in American terms, it will be at a discount (premium) in European terms.

EXAMPLE 4.6: Calculating the Forward Premium/Discount The formula for calculating the forward premium or discount in American terms for currency *j* is:

$$f_{Nj\text{v}\$} = \frac{F_N(\$/j) - S(\$/j)}{S(\$/j)} \times \frac{360}{N} \tag{4.18}$$

When the context is clear, the forward premium will simply be stated as *f*.

As an example of calculating the forward premium, let's use the July 6 quotes from Exhibit 4.4 to calculate the 90-day forward premium or discount for the Japanese yen versus the U.S. dollar. The calculation is:

$$f_{90,¥\text{v}\$} = \frac{.008304 - .008193}{.008193} \times \frac{360}{90} = .0542$$

We see that the 90-day forward premium is .0542, or 5.42 percent. In words, we say that the Japanese yen is trading versus the U.S. dollar at a 5.42 percent premium for delivery in 90 days.

In European terms the forward premium or discount is calculated as:

$$f_{N,\$\text{v}j} = \frac{F_N(j/\$) - S(j/\$)}{S(j/\$)} \times \frac{360}{N} \tag{4.19}$$

Using the July 6 90-day European term quotations for the Japanese yen from Exhibit 4.4 yields:

$$f_{90,\$\text{v}¥} = \frac{120.43 - 122.05}{122.05} \times \frac{360}{90} = -.0531$$

We see that the 90-day forward premium is −.0531, or −5.31 percent. In words, we say that the U.S. dollar is trading versus the Japanese yen at a 5.31 percent discount for delivery in 90 days.

SUMMARY

This chapter presents an introduction to the market for foreign exchange. Broadly defined, the foreign exchange market encompasses the conversion of purchasing power from one currency into another, bank deposits of foreign currency, the extension of credit denominated in a foreign currency, foreign trade financing, and trading in foreign currency options and futures contracts. This chapter limits the discussion to the spot and forward market for foreign exchange. The other topics are covered in later chapters.

1. The FX market is the largest and most active financial market in the world. It is open somewhere in the world 24 hours a day, 365 days a year.
2. The FX market is divided into two tiers: the retail or client market and the wholesale or interbank market. The retail market is where international banks service their customers who need foreign exchange to conduct international commerce or trade in international financial assets. The great majority of FX trading takes place in the interbank market among international banks that are adjusting inventory positions or conducting speculative and arbitrage trades.
3. The FX market participants include international banks, bank customers, nonbank FX dealers, FX brokers, and central banks.
4. In the spot market for FX, nearly immediate purchase and sale of currencies takes place. In the chapter, notation for defining a spot rate quotation was developed. Additionally, the concept of a cross exchange rate was developed. It was determined that nondollar currency transactions must satisfy the bid-ask spread determined from the cross-rate formula or a triangular arbitrage opportunity exists.
5. In the forward market, buyers and sellers can transact today at the forward price for the future purchase and sale of foreign exchange. Notation for forward exchange rate quotations was developed. The use of forward points as a shorthand method for expressing forward quotes from spot rate quotations was presented. Additionally, the concept of a forward premium was developed.

KEY WORDS

American terms, 80
ask price, 82
bid price, 82
client market, 76
correspondent banking relationship, 77
cross exchange rate, 86
currency against currency, 88
direct quotation, 79
European terms, 80
foreign exchange (FX or FOREX) market, 74
forward market, 91
forward premium/discount, 95
forward rate, 91
indirect quotation, 79
interbank market, 76
offer price, 82
outright forward transaction, 93
over-the-counter (OTC) market, 75
retail market, 76
spot market, 79
spot rate, 79
swap transaction, 93
triangular arbitrage, 88
wholesale market, 76

QUESTIONS

1. Give a full definition of the market for foreign exchange.
2. What is the difference between the retail or client market and the wholesale or interbank market for foreign exchange?
3. Who are the market participants in the foreign exchange market?
4. How are foreign exchange transactions between international banks settled?
5. What is meant by a currency trading at a discount or at a premium in the forward market?
6. Why does most interbank currency trading worldwide involve the U.S. dollar?
7. Banks find it necessary to accommodate their clients' needs to buy or sell FX forward, in many instances for hedging purposes. How can the bank eliminate

the currency exposure it has created for itself by accommodating a client's forward transaction?

8. A CD/$ bank trader is currently quoting a *small figure* bid-ask of 35–40, when the rest of the market is trading at CD1.3436–CD1.3441. What is implied about the trader's beliefs by his prices?
9. What is triangular arbitrage? What is a condition that will give rise to a triangular arbitrage opportunity?

PROBLEMS

1. Using Exhibit 4.4, calculate a cross-rate matrix for the French franc, German mark, Japanese yen, and the British pound. Use the most current European term quotes to calculate the cross-rates so that the triangular matrix resulting is similar to the portion above the diagonal in Exhibit 4.6.
2. Using Exhibit 4.4, calculate the 30-, 90-, and 180-day forward cross exchange rates between the German mark and the Swiss franc using the most current quotations. State the forward cross-rates in "German" terms.
3. Restate the following one-, three-, and six-month outright forward European term bid-ask quotes in forward points.

Spot	1.3431–1.3436
One-Month	1.3432–1.3442
Three-Month	1.3448–1.3463
Six-Month	1.3488–1.3508

4. Using the spot and outright forward quotes in problem 3, determine the corresponding bid-ask spreads in points.
5. Using Exhibit 4.4, calculate the 30-, 90-, and 180-day forward premium or discount for the Canadian dollar in European terms.
6. Using Exhibit 4.4, calculate the 30-, 90-, and 180-day forward premium or discount for the British pound in American terms using the most current quotations.
7. Given the following information, what are the DM/S$ currency against currency bid-ask quotations?

	American Terms		European Terms	
Bank Quotations	Bid	Ask	Bid	Ask
Deutsche mark	.6784	.6789	1.4730	1.4741
Singapore dollar	.6999	.7002	1.4282	1.4288

8. Assume you are a trader with Deutsche Bank. From the quote screen on your computer terminal, you notice that Dresdner Bank is quoting DM1.6230/$1.00 and Credit Suisse is offering SF1.4260/$1.00. You learn that UBS is making a direct market between the Swiss franc and the mark, with a current DM/SF quote of 1.1250. Show how you can make a triangular arbitrage profit by trading at these prices. (Ignore bid-ask spreads for this problem.) Assume you have $5,000,000 with which to conduct the arbitrage. What happens if you initially sell dollars for Swiss francs? What DM/SF price will eliminate triangular arbitrage?

MINI CASE

Shrewsbury Herbal Products, Ltd.

Shrewsbury Herbal Products, located in central England close to the Welsh border, is an old-line producer of herbal teas, seasonings, and medicines. Their products are marketed all over the United Kingdom and in many parts of continental Europe as well.

Shrewsbury Herbal generally invoices in British pound sterling when it sells to foreign customers in order to guard against adverse exchange rate changes. Nevertheless, it has just received an order from a large wholesaler in central France for £320,000 of its products, conditional upon delivery being made in three months' time and the order invoiced in French francs.

Shrewsbury's controller, Elton Peters, is concerned with whether the pound will appreciate versus the franc over the next three months, thus eliminating all or most of the profit when the French franc receivable is paid. He thinks this an unlikely possibility, but he decides to contact the firm's banker for suggestions about hedging the exchange rate exposure.

Mr. Peters learns from the banker that the current spot exchange rate in FF/£ is FF7.8709; thus the invoice amount should be FF2,518,688. Mr. Peters also learns that the 90-day forward rates for the pound and the French franc versus the U.S. dollar are \$1.5458/£1.00 and FF5.0826/\$1.00, respectively. The banker offers to set up a forward hedge for selling the franc receivable for pound sterling based on the FF/£ cross forward exchange rate implicit in the forward rates against the dollar.

What would you do if you were Mr. Peters?

ENDNOTES

1. The banknote market for converting small amounts of foreign exchange, which travelers are familiar with, is different from the spot market.
2. These numbers were obtained during a discussion with the manager of the spot trading desk at the New York branch of the UBS.
3. If the 30-day forward points quotation were, say, 7–7, further elaboration from the market maker would be needed to determine if the forward points would be added or subtracted from the spot prices.

WEB RESOURCES

www.bis.org

This is the Website of the Bank for International Settlements. Many interesting reports and statistics can be obtained here. The triennial report titled *Central Bank Survey of Foreign Exchange and Derivatives Market Activity* can be downloaded for study.

http://cnnfn.com/markets/currencies

This subsite at the CNN Financial site provides a currency converter for converting one currency into another at current exchange rates.

www.ny.frb.org.

This is the Website of the Federal Reserve Bank of New York. The on-line book titled *All About the Foreign Exchange Market in the United States* can be downloaded for study. It provides a summary of many of the statistics from the BIS triennial report from the perspective of the United States.

REFERENCES AND SUGGESTED READINGS

Bank for International Settlements. *Central Bank Survey of Foreign Exchange Market and Derivatives Activity.* Basle, Switzerland: Bank for International Settlements, May 1999.

Coninx, Raymond G. F. *Foreign Exchange Dealer's Handbook,* 2nd ed. Burr Ridge, Ill.: Dow Jones-Irwin, 1986.

Copeland, Laurence S. *Exchange Rates and International Finance,* 2nd ed. Wokingham, England: Addison-Wesley, 1994.

Federal Reserve Bank of New York. *April 1995 Central Bank Survey of Foreign Exchange Market Activity.* New York: Federal Reserve Bank of New York, 1995.

"The Foreign-Exchange Market: Big," *The Economist,* September 23, 1995.

Grabbe, J. Orlin. *International Financial Markets,* 3rd ed. Englewood Cliffs, N.J.: Prentice Hall, 1996.

Graven, Kathryn. "Fearless Dealers: Central-Bank Traders Have an Advantage: Their Employers Don't Demand Profits." *The Wall Street Journal,* September 23, 1988, p. R31.

Huang, Roger D., and Ronald W. Masulis. "FX Spreads and Dealer Competition across the 24-Hour Trading Day." Review of Financial Studies 12 (1999) pp. 61–93.

International Monetary Fund. *International Capital Markets: Part I. Exchange Rate Management and International Capital Flows.* Washington, D.C.: International Monetary Fund, 1993.

Ito, Takatoshi, Richard K. Lyons, and Michael T. Melvin. "Is There Private Information in the FX Market? The Tokyo Experiment." *Journal of Finance* 53 (1998), pp. 1111–30.

Swiss Bank Corporation. *Foreign Exchange and Money Market Operations.* Basle, Switzerland: Swiss Bank Corporation, 1987.

CHAPTER FIVE

International Parity Relationships and Forecasting Foreign Exchange Rates

CHAPTER OUTLINE

This chapter examines several key international parity relationships, such as interest rate parity and purchasing power parity, that have profound implications for international financial management. Some of these are, in fact, manifestations of the *law of one price* that must hold in *arbitrage equilibrium.*[1] An understanding of these parity relationships provides insights into (1) how foreign exchange rates are determined, and (2) how to forecast foreign exchange rates.

Since **arbitrage** plays a critical role in the ensuing discussion, we should define it upfront. The term *arbitrage* can be defined as *the act of simultaneously buying and selling the same or equivalent assets or commodities for the purpose of making certain, guaranteed profits.* As long as there are profitable arbitrage opportunities, the market cannot be in equilibrium. The market can be said to be in equilibrium when no profitable arbitrage opportunities exist. Such well-known parity relationships as interest rate parity and purchasing power parity, in fact, represent arbitrage equilibrium conditions. Let us begin our discussion with interest rate parity.

INTEREST RATE PARITY

Interest rate parity (IRP) is an arbitrage condition that must hold when international financial markets are in equilibrium. Suppose that you have $1 to invest over, say, a one-year period. Consider two alternative ways of investing your fund: (1) invest domestically at the U.S. interest rate, or, alternatively, (2) invest in a foreign country, say, the U.K., at the foreign interest rate and hedge the exchange risk by selling the maturity value of the foreign investment forward. It is assumed here that you only want to consider default-free investments.

If you invest \$1 domestically at the U.S. interest rate ($i_\$$), the maturity value will be

$$\$1(1 + i_\$)$$

Since you are assumed to invest in a default-free instrument like a U.S. Treasury note, there is no uncertainty about the future maturity value of your investment in dollar terms.

To invest in the U.K., on the other hand, you carry out the following sequence of transactions:

1. Exchange \$1 for a pound amount, that is, £(1/S), at the prevailing spot exchange rate (S).[2]
2. Invest the pound amount at the U.K. interest rate ($i_£$), with the maturity value of £(1/S)(1 + $i_£$).
3. Sell the maturity value of the U.K. investment forward in exchange for a *predetermined dollar amount,* that is, \$[(1/S)(1 + $i_£$)]F, where F denotes the forward exchange rate.

When your British investment matures in one year, you will receive the full maturity value, £(1/S)(1 + $i_£$). But since you have to deliver exactly the same amount of pounds to the counterparty of the forward contract, your net pound position is reduced to zero. In other words, the exchange risk is completely hedged. Since, as with the U.S. investment, you are assured a predetermined dollar amount, your U.K. investment coupled with forward hedging is a perfect substitute for the domestic U.S. investment. Because you've hedged the exchange risk by a forward contract, you've effectively *redenominated* the U.K. investment in dollar terms. The "effective" dollar interest rate from the U.K. investment alternative is given by

$$(F/S)(1 + i_£) - 1$$

Arbitrage equilibrium then would dictate that the future dollar proceeds (or, equivalently, the dollar interest rates) from investing in the two equivalent investments must be the same, implying that

$$(1 + i_\$) = (F/S)(1 + i_£) \qquad (5.1)$$

which is a formal statement of IRP. It should be clear from the way we arrived at Equation 5.1 that IRP is a manifestation of the **law of one price (LOP)** applied to international money market instruments. The IRP relationship has been known among currency traders since the late 19th century. But it was only during the 1920s that the relationship became widely known to the public from the writings of John M. Keynes and other economists.[3]

Alternatively, IRP can be derived by constructing an **arbitrage portfolio,** which involves (1) no net investment, as well as (2) no risk, and then requiring that such a portfolio should not generate any net cash flow in equilibrium. Consider an arbitrage portfolio consisting of three separate positions:

1. Borrowing \$$S$ in the United States, which is just enough to buy £1 at the prevailing spot exchange rate (S).
2. Lending £1 in the U.K. at the U.K. interest rate.
3. Selling the maturity value of the U.K. investment forward.

Exhibit 5.1 summarizes the present and future (maturity date) cash flows, CF_0 and CF_1, from investing in the arbitrage portfolio.

EXHIBIT 5.1

Dollar Cash Flows to an Arbitrage Portfolio

Transactions	CF_0	CF_1
1. Borrow in the U.S.	\$$S$	$-S(1 + i_\$)$
2. Lend in the U.K.	−\$$S$	$S_1(1 + i_£)$
3. Sell the £ receivable forward*	0	$(1 + i_£)(F - S_1)$
Net cash flow	0	$(1 + i_£)F - (1 + i_\$)S$

*Selling the £ receivable "forward" will not result in any cash flow at the present time, that is, $CF_0 = 0$. But at the maturity, the seller will receive \$$(F - S_1)$ for each pound sold forward. S_1 denotes the future spot exchange rate.

Two things are noteworthy in Exhibit 5.1. First, the net cash flow at the time of investment is zero. This, of course, implies that the arbitrage portfolio is indeed fully self-financing; it doesn't cost any money to hold this portfolio. Second, the net cash flow on the maturity date is known with certainty. That is so because none of the variables involved in the net cash flow, that is, S, F, $i_\$$, and $i_£$, is uncertain. Since no one should be able to make certain profits by holding this arbitrage portfolio, market equilibrium requires that the net cash flow on the maturity date be zero for this portfolio:

$$(1 + i_£)F - (1 + i_\$)S = 0 \tag{5.2}$$

which, upon simple rearrangement, is the same result as Equation 5.1.

The IRP relationship is often approximated as follows:

$$(i_\$ - i_£) = (F - S)/S \tag{5.3}$$

As can be seen clearly from Equation 5.3, IRP provides a linkage between interest rates in two different countries. Specifically, the interest rate will be higher in the United States than in the U.K. when the dollar is at a forward discount, that is, $F > S$. When the dollar is at a forward discount, this implies that the dollar is expected to depreciate against the pound. If so, the U.S. interest rate should be higher than the U.K. interest rate to compensate for the expected depreciation of the dollar. Otherwise, nobody would hold dollar-denominated securities. On the other hand, the U.S. interest rate will be lower than the U.K. interest rate when the dollar is at a forward premium, that is, $F < S$. Equation 5.3 also indicates that the forward exchange rate will deviate from the spot rate as long as the interest rates of the two countries are not the same.[4]

When IRP holds, you will be indifferent between investing your money in the United States and investing in the U.K. with forward hedging. However, if IRP is violated, you will prefer one to another. You will be better off by investing in the United States (U.K.) if $(1 + i_\$)$ is greater (less) than $(F/S)(1 + i_£)$. When you need to borrow, on the other hand, you will choose to borrow where the dollar interest is lower. When IRP doesn't hold, the situation also gives rise to **covered interest arbitrage** opportunities.

Covered Interest Arbitrage

To explain the covered interest arbitrage (CIA) process, it is best to work with a numerical example.

EXAMPLE 5.1: Suppose that the annual interest rate is 5 percent in the United States and 8 percent in the U.K., and that the spot exchange rate is \$1.50/£ and the forward exchange rate, with one-year maturity, is \$1.48/£. In terms of our notation, $i_\$ = 5\%$, $i_£ = 8\%$, $S = \$1.50$, and $F = \$1.48$. Assume that the arbitrager can borrow up to \$1,000,000 or £666,667, which is equivalent to \$1,000,000 at the current spot exchange rate.

EXHIBIT 5.2

Covered Interest Arbitrage: Cash Flow Analysis

Transactions	CF_0	CF_1
1. Borrow $1,000,000	$1,000,000	−$1,050,000
2. Buy £ spot	−$1,000,000	
	£666,667	
3. Lend £666,667	−£666,667	£720,000
4. Sell £720,000 forward		−£720,000
		$1,065,600
Net cash flow	0	$15,600

Let us first check if IRP is holding under current market conditions. Substituting the given data, we find,

$$(F/S)(1 + i_£) = (1.48/1.50)(1.08) = 1.0656,$$

which is not exactly equal to $(1 + i_\$) = 1.05$. Specifically, we find that the current market condition is characterized by

$$(1 + i_\$) < (F/S)(1 + i_£). \tag{5.4}$$

Clearly, IRP is not holding, implying that a profitable arbitrage opportunity exists. Since the interest rate is lower in the United States, an arbitrage transaction should involve borrowing in the United States and lending in the U.K.

The arbitrager can carry out the following transactions:

1. In the United States, borrow $1,000,000. Repayment in one year will be $1,050,000 = $1,000,000 × 1.05.
2. Buy £666,667 spot using $1,000,000.
3. Invest £666,667 in the U.K. The maturity value will be £720,000 = £666,667 × 1.08.
4. Sell £720,000 forward in exchange for $1,065,600 = (£720,000)($1.48/£).

In one year when everything matures, the arbitrager will receive the full maturity value of his U.K. investment, that is, £720,000. The arbitrager then will deliver this pound amount to the counterparty of the forward contract and receive $1,065,600 in return. Out of this dollar amount, the maturity value of the dollar loan, $1,050,000, will be paid. The arbitrager still has $15,600 (= $1,065,600 − $1,050,000) left in his account, which is his arbitrage profit. In making this *certain profit,* the arbitrager neither invested any money out of his pocket nor bore any risk. He indeed carried out "covered interest arbitrage," which means that he borrowed at one interest rate and simultaneously lent at another interest rate, with exchange risk fully covered via forward hedging.[5] Exhibit 5.2 provides a summary of CIA transactions.

How long will this arbitrage opportunity last? A simple answer is: only for a short while. As soon as deviations from IRP are detected, informed traders will immediately carry out CIA transactions. As a result of these arbitrage activities, IRP will be restored quite quickly. To see this, let's get back to our numerical example, which induced covered interest arbitrage activities. Since every trader will (1) borrow in the United States as much as possible, (2) lend in the U.K., (3) buy the pound spot, and, at the same time, (4) sell the pound forward, the following adjustments will occur to the initial market condition described in Equation 5.4:

EXHIBIT 5.3

The Interest Rate Parity Diagram

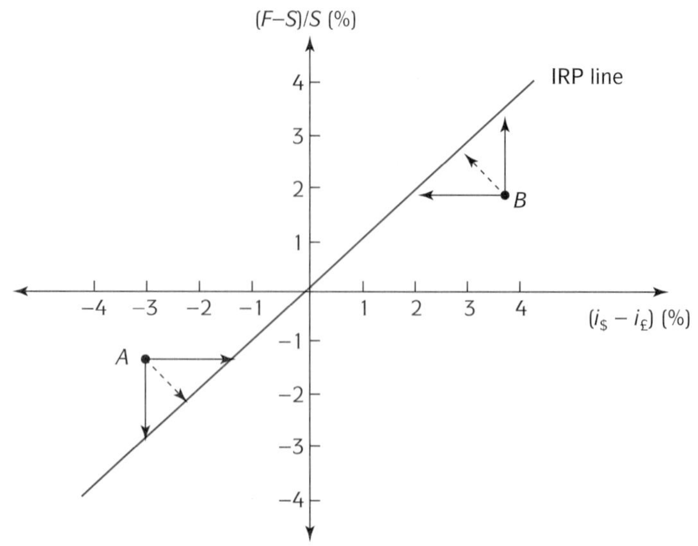

1. The interest rate will rise in the United States ($i_\$\uparrow$).
2. The interest rate will fall in the U.K. ($i_£\downarrow$).
3. The pound will appreciate in the spot market ($S\uparrow$).
4. The pound will depreciate in the forward market ($F\downarrow$).

These adjustments will raise the left hand side of Equation 5.4 and, at the same time, lower the right hand side until both sides are equalized, restoring IRP.

The adjustment process is depicted in Exhibit 5.3. The initial market condition described by Equation 5.4 is represented by point *A* in the exhibit, substantially off the IRP line.[6] CIA activities will increase the interest rate differential (as indicated by the horizontal arrow) and, at the same time, lower the forward premium/discount (as indicated by the vertical arrow). Since the foreign exchange and money markets share the burden of adjustments, the actual path of adjustment to IRP can be depicted by the dotted arrow. When the initial market condition is located at point *B*, IRP will be restored partly by an increase in the forward premium, $(F - S)/S$, and partly by a decrease in the interest rate differential, $i_\$ - i_£$.

EXAMPLE 5.2: Before we move on, it would be useful to consider another CIA example. Suppose that the market condition is summarized as follows:

Three-month interest rate in the United States: 8.0% per annum.

Three-month interest rate in Germany: 5.0% per annum.

Current spot exchange rate: DM1.60/$.

Three-month forward exchange rate: DM1.598/$.

The current example differs from the previous example in that the transaction horizon is three months rather than a year, and the exchange rates are quoted in *European* rather than American terms.

If we would like to apply IRP as defined in Equation 5.1, we should convert the exchange rates into American terms and use three-month interest rates, not annualized rates. In other words, we should use the following numerical values to check if IRP is holding:

$i_\$ = 8.0/4 = 2.0\%$ $\quad\quad i_{DM} = 5.0/4 = 1.25\%$

$S = 1/1.60 = \$.625/DM$ $\quad\quad F = 1/1.598 = \$.6258/DM$

Now, we can compute the right hand side of Equation 5.1:

$$(F/S)(1 + i_{DM}) = (.6258/.625)(1.0125) = 1.0138,$$

which is less than $(1 + i_\$) = 1.02$. Clearly, IRP is not holding and an arbitrage opportunity thus exists. Since the interest rate is lower in Germany than in the United States, the arbitrage transaction should involve borrowing in Germany and lending in the United States. Again, we assume that the arbitrager can borrow up to \$1,000,000 or the equivalent DM amount, DM 1,600,000.

The arbitrager can carry out the following transactions:

1. Borrow DM1,600,000 in Germany. Repayment in three months will be DM1,620,000 = DM1,600,000 × 1.0125.
2. Buy \$1,000,000 spot using DM1,600,000.
3. Invest \$1,000,000 in the United States. The maturity value will be \$1,020,000 in three months.
4. Buy DM1,620,000 forward in exchange for \$1,013,796 = (DM1,620,000)(\$.6258/DM).

In three months, the arbitrager will receive the full maturity value of the U.S. investment, \$1,020,000. But then, the arbitrager should deliver \$1,013,796 to the counterparty of the forward contract and receive DM1,620,000 in return, which will be used to repay the mark loan. The arbitrage profit will thus be \$6,204 (= \$1,020,000 − \$1,013,796).[7]

Interest Rate Parity and Exchange Rate Determination

Being an arbitrage equilibrium condition involving the (spot) exchange rate, IRP has an immediate implication for exchange rate determination. To see why, let us reformulate the IRP relationship in terms of the spot exchange rate:

$$S = \left[\frac{1 + i_£}{1 + i_\$}\right]F \tag{5.5}$$

Equation 5.5 indicates that given the forward exchange rate, the spot exchange rate depends on relative interest rates. All else equal, an increase in the U.S. interest rate will lead to a higher foreign exchange value of the dollar.[8] This is so because a higher U.S. interest rate will attract capital to the United States, increasing the demand for dollars. In contrast, a decrease in the U.S. interest rate will lower the foreign exchange value of the dollar.

In addition to relative interest rates, the forward exchange rate is an important factor in spot exchange rate determination. Under certain conditions the forward exchange rate can be viewed as the expected future spot exchange rate conditional on all relevant information being available now, that is,

$$F = E(S_{t+1}|I_t) \tag{5.6}$$

where S_{t+1} is the future spot rate when the forward contract matures, and I_t denotes the set of information currently available.[9] When Equations 5.5 and 5.6 are combined, we obtain,

$$S = \left[\frac{1 + i_£}{1 + i_\$}\right]E(S_{t+1}|I_t) \tag{5.7}$$

Two things are noteworthy from Equation 5.7. First, "expectation" plays a key role in exchange rate determination. Specifically, the expected future exchange rate is shown to be a major determinant of the current exchange rate; when people "expect" the exchange rate to go up in the future, it goes up now. People's expectations thus become self-fulfilling. Second, exchange rate behavior will be driven by news events. People form their expectations based on the set of information (I_t) they possess. As they receive news continuously, they are going to update their expectations continuously. As a result, the exchange rate will tend to exhibit a *dynamic* and *volatile* short-term behavior, responding to various news events. By definition, news events are unpredictable, making forecasting future exchange rates an arduous task.

When the forward exchange rate F is replaced by the expected future spot exchange rate, $E(S_{t+1})$ in Equation 5.3, we obtain:

$$(i_\$ - i_£) = E(e) \tag{5.8}$$

where $E(e)$ is the expected rate of change in the exchange rate, that is, $[E(S_{t+1}) - S_t]/S_t$. Equation 5.8 states that the interest rate differential between a pair of countries is (approximately) equal to the expected rate of change in the exchange rate. This relationship is known as the **uncovered interest rate parity.** If, for instance, the annual interest rate is 5 percent in the United States and 8 percent in the U.K., as assumed in our numerical example, the uncovered IRP suggests that the pound is expected to depreciate against the dollar by about 3 percent, that is, $E(e) = -3\%$.

Reasons for Deviations from Interest Rate Parity

Although IRP tends to hold quite well, it may not hold precisely all the time for at least two reasons: transaction costs and capital controls.

In our previous examples of CIA transactions, we implicitly assumed, among other things, that no transaction costs existed. As a result, in our first CIA example, for each dollar borrowed at the U.S. interest rate ($i_\$$), the arbitrager could realize the following amount of positive profit:

$$(F/S)(1 + i_£) - (1 + i_\$) > 0 \tag{5.9}$$

In reality, transaction costs do exist. The interest rate at which the arbitrager borrows, i^b, tends to be higher than the rate at which he lends, i^l. Likewise, there exist bid-ask spreads in the foreign exchange market. The arbirager has to buy foreign exchanges at the higher ask price and sell them at the lower bid price. Each of the four variables in Equation 5.9 can be regarded as representing the midpoint of the spread.

Because of spreads, arbitrage profit from each dollar borrowed may become nonpositive:

$$(F^b/S^a)(1 + i_£^{\,l}) - (1 + i_£^{\,b}) \leq 0 \tag{5.10}$$

where the superscripts a and b to the exchange rates, F and S, denote the ask and bid prices, respectively. This is so because

$$(F^b/S^a) < (F/S)$$
$$(1 + i_£^{\,l}) < (1 + i_£)$$
$$(1 + i_£^{\,b}) > (1 + i_\$)$$

If the arbitrage profit turns negative because of transaction costs, the current deviation from IRP does not represent a profitable arbitrage opportunity. Thus, the IRP line in Exhibit 5.4 can be viewed as included within a band around it, and only IRP deviations outside the band, such as point C, represent profitable arbitrage opportunities. IRP deviations within the band, such as point D, would not represent profitable arbitrage opportunities. The width of this band will depend on the size of transaction costs.

Another major reason for deviations from IRP is capital controls imposed by governments. For various macroeconomic reasons, governments sometimes restrict capital flows, inbound and/or outbound.[10] Governments achieve this objective by

EXHIBIT 5.4

Interest Rate Parity with Transaction Costs

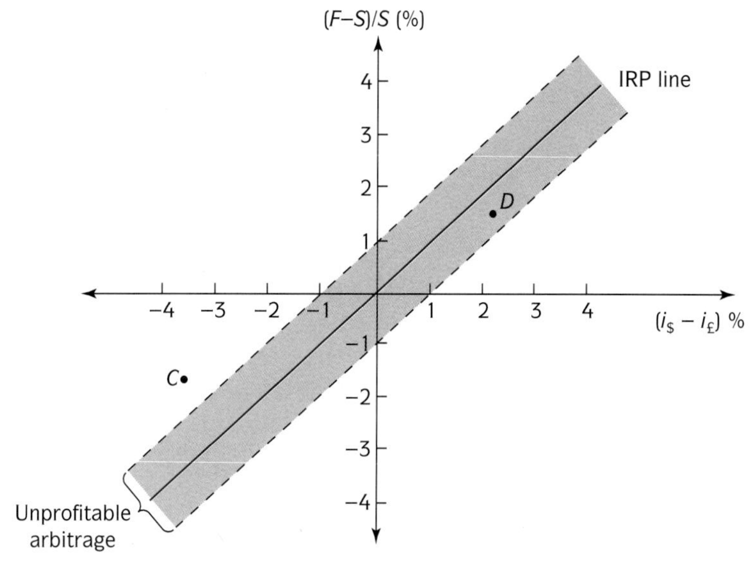

means of jawboning, imposing taxes, or even outright bans on cross-border capital movements. These control measures imposed by governments can effectively impair the arbitrage process, and, as a result, deviations from IRP may persist.

An interesting historical example is provided by Japan, where capital controls were imposed on and off until December 1980, when the Japanese government liberalized international capital flows. Otani and Tiwari (1981) investigated the effect of capital controls on IRP deviations during the period 1978–81. They computed deviations from interest rate parity (DIRP) as follows:[11]

$$\text{DIRP} = [(1 + i_{¥})S/(1 + i_{\$})F] - 1 \tag{5.11}$$

where:

$i_{¥}$ = interest rate on three-month Gensaki bonds.[12]
$i_{\$}$ = interest rate on three-month Euro-dollar deposits.
S = yen/dollar spot exchange rate in Tokyo.
F = yen/dollar three-month forward exchange rate in Tokyo.

Deviations from IRP computed as above are plotted in Exhibit 5.5. If IRP holds strictly, deviations from it would be randomly distributed, with the expected value of zero.

Exhibit 5.5, however, shows that deviations from IRP hardly hover around zero. The deviations were quite significant at times until near the end of 1980. They were the greatest during 1978. This can be attributed to various measures the Japanese government took to discourage capital inflows, which was done to keep the yen from appreciating. As these measures were removed in 1979, the deviations were reduced. They increased again considerably in 1980, however, reflecting an introduction of capital control; Japanese financial institutions were asked to discourage foreign currency deposits.

In December 1980, Japan adopted the new *Foreign Exchange and Foreign Trade Control Law,* which generally liberalized foreign exchange transactions. Not surprisingly, the deviations hover around zero in the first quarter of 1981. The empirical evidence presented in Exhibit 5.5 closely reflects changes in capital controls during the

EXHIBIT 5.5

Deviations from Interest Rate Parity: Japan, 1978–81 (in percent)

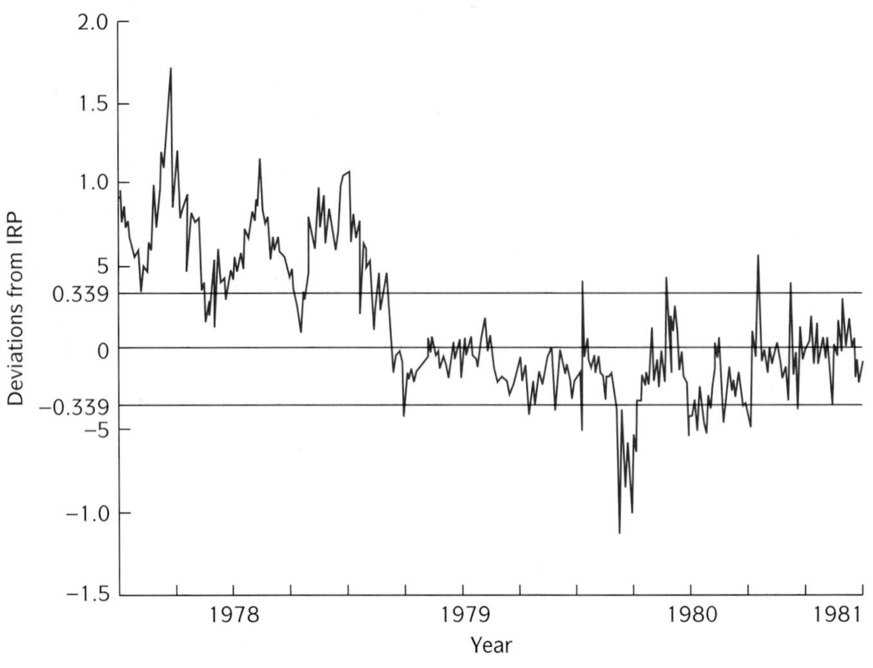

Note: Daily data were used in computing the deviations. The zone bounded by +0.339 and −0.339 represents the average width of the band around the IRP for the sample period.

Source: I. Otani and S. Tiwari, "Capital Controls and Interest Rate Parity: The Japanese Experience, 1978–81," *IMF Staff Papers* 28 (1981), pp. 793–815.

study period. This implies that deviations from IRP, especially in 1978 and 1980, do not represent unexploited profit opportunities; rather, they reflect the existence of significant barriers to cross-border arbitrage.

PURCHASING POWER PARITY

When the law of one price is applied internationally to a *standard commodity basket,* we obtain the theory of **purchasing power parity** (PPP). This theory states that the exchange rate between currencies of two countries should be equal to the ratio of the countries' price levels. The basic idea of PPP was initially advanced by classical economists such as David Ricardo in the 19th century. But it is Gustav Cassel, a Swedish economist, who popularized the PPP in the 1920s. In those years, many countries, including Germany, Hungary, and the Soviet Union, experienced hyperinflation. As the purchasing power of the currencies in these countries sharply declined, the same currencies also depreciated sharply against stable currencies like the U.S. dollar. The PPP became popular against this historical backdrop.

Let $P_\$$ be the dollar price of the standard commodity basket in the United States and $P_£$ the pound price of the same basket in the United Kingdom. Formally, PPP states that the exchange rate between the dollar and the pound should be

$$S = P_\$/P_£ \tag{5.12}$$

where S is the dollar price of one pound. PPP implies that if the standard commodity basket costs \$225 in the United States and £150 in the U.K., then the exchange rate should be \$1.50 per pound:

$\$1.50/£ = \$225/£150$

If the price of the commodity basket is higher in the United States, say, \$300, then PPP dictates that the exchange rate should be higher, that is, \$2.00/£.

To give an alternative interpretation to PPP, let us rewrite Equation 5.12 as follows:

$$P_\$ = S \times P_£$$

This equation states that the dollar price of the commodity basket in the United States, $P_\$$, must be the same as the dollar price of the basket in the U.K., that is, $P_£$ multiplied by S. In other words, PPP requires that the price of the standard commodity basket be the same across countries when measured in a common currency. Clearly, PPP is the manifestation of the law of one price applied to the standard consumption basket. As discussed in the International Finance in Practice box, Equilibrium in Currency Market?, PPP is a way of defining the equilibrium exchange rate.

The PPP relationship of Equation 5.12 is called the *absolute* version of PPP. When the PPP relationship is presented in the "rate of change" form, we obtain the *relative* version:

$$e = \pi_\$ - \pi_£ \qquad (5.13)$$

where e is the rate of change in the exchange rate and $\pi_\$$ and $\pi_£$ are the inflation rates in the United States and U.K., respectively. For example, if the inflation rate is 6 percent per year in the United States and 4 percent in the U.K., then the pound should appreciate against the dollar by 2 percent, that is, $e = 2$ percent, per year. It is noted that even if absolute PPP does not hold, relative PPP may hold.[13]

PPP Deviations and the Real Exchange Rate

Whether PPP holds or not has important implications for international trade. If PPP holds and thus the differential inflation rates between countries are exactly offset by exchange rate changes, countries' competitive positions in world export markets will not be systematically affected by exchange rate changes. However, if there are deviations from PPP, changes in nominal exchange rates cause changes in the **real exchange rates,** affecting the international competitive positions of countries. This, in turn, would affect countries' trade balances.

The real exchange rate, q, can be defined as follows:[14]

$$q = \frac{1 + \pi_\$}{(1 + e)(1 + \pi_£)} \qquad (5.14)$$

First note that if PPP holds, that is, $(1 + e) = (1 + \pi_\$)/(1 + \pi_£)$, the real exchange rate will be unity, $q = 1$. When PPP is violated, however, the real exchange rate will deviate from unity. Suppose, for example, the annual inflation rate is 5 percent in the United States and 3.5 percent in the U.K., and the dollar depreciated against the pound by 4.5 percent. Then the real exchange rate is .97:

$$q = (1.05)/(1.045)(1.035) = .97$$

In the above example, the dollar depreciated by more than is warranted by PPP, strengthening the competitiveness of U.S. industries in the world market. If the dollar depreciates by less than the inflation rate differential, the real exchange rate will be greater than unity, weakening the competitiveness of U.S. industries. To summarize,

$q = 1$: Competitiveness of the domestic country unaltered.

$q < 1$: Competitiveness of the domestic country improves.

$q > 1$: Competitiveness of the domestic country deteriorates.

INTERNATIONAL FINANCE IN PRACTICE

Equilibrium in Currency Markets?

Suppose a man climbs five feet up a sea wall, then climbs down 12 feet. Whether he drowns or not depends upon how high above sea level he was when he started. The same problem arises in deciding whether currencies are under- or over-valued. The dollar has gained almost 20% against the yen and 10% against the D-mark from its low point in April. Some pundits are already fretting about the impact of a "strong" dollar on the American economy. Yet the currency is still around 60% below its level in 1985. To predict whether the dollar has further to rise, it would help to have some idea about its "correct" value.

Economists like to talk about currency misalignments, and exchange rates being under- or over-valued. But this presumes that they know what a currency's long-term equilibrium rate is. The truth is that there is wide disagreement about how to define an equilibrium, let alone how to measure it.

The oldest method of defining long-term exchange-rate equilibrium is purchasing-power parity (PPP). This is based on the notion that goods and services should cost the same in different countries when measured in a common currency. According to this theory, the exchange rate between two currencies should, in the long run, move towards its PPP—ie, the exchange rate that equalises the prices of an identical basket of goods and services in the two countries.

A popular version of PPP is *The Economist*'s Big Mac index. Once a year we calculate PPPs by comparing the prices of a McDonald's Big Mac burger in different countries. This, along with more sophisticated estimates of PPP, signals that the dollar is still hugely under-valued against the other main currencies. For instance, the Big Mac index suggests a dollar PPP of ¥169 and DM2.07, compared with exchange rates on August 22nd of ¥97 and DM1.49. The OECD estimates the dollar's PPP at ¥181 and DM2.11. On this basis, therefore, the greenback has a lot further to climb.

But in practice PPPs have proved a poor guide to exchange-rate forecasting. Currencies can deviate from their PPP for long periods. The dollar, for example, has been under-valued relative to its PPP for most of the past 15 years. One snag is that this method ignores capital flows. That was fine when trade flows dominated foreign-currency transactions, but the value of foreign-exchange trading is now 70 times bigger than that of world trade. Today, capital flows largely determine the size of current-account balances, rather than the other way round.

The PPP is only a sustainable equilibrium exchange rate if the current account is simultaneously in balance. If, however, a country has a persistent current-account deficit, its foreign debt will rise. As a result, it will need to run a trade surplus to cover its growing debt interest payments. This will require the exchange rate to remain below its PPP.

The chart, based on an analysis by Merrill Lynch, an American securities firm, shows that there is a strong correlation between a currency's under- or over-valuation

Exhibit 5.6 plots the real "effective" exchange rates for the U.S. dollar, German mark, Japanese yen, and Mexican peso since 1970. The rates plotted in Exhibit 5.6 are, however, the real effective exchange rate "indices" computed using 1990 rates as the base, that is, 1990 = 100. The real effective exchange rate is a weighted average of bilateral real exchange rates, with the weight for each foreign currency determined by the country's share in the domestic country's international trade. The real effective exchange rate rises if domestic inflation exceeds inflation abroad and the nominal exchange rate fails to depreciate to compensate for the higher domestic inflation rate. Thus, if the real effective exchange rate rises (falls), the domestic country's competitiveness declines (improves). It is noted that the real effective exchange rate of the Mexican peso falls sharply periodically, reflecting devaluations of the peso.

Evidence on Purchasing Power Parity

As is clear from the above discussions, whether PPP holds in reality is a question of considerable importance. Considering that PPP is the manifestation of the law of one price applied to a standard commodity basket, it will hold only if the prices of constituent commodities are equalized against the dollar relative to its Big Mac, PPP and that country's current-account balance. Countries with big current-account deficits have the most under-valued currencies. The exchange rates of countries with big surpluses tend to be at a premium to their PPP. This suggests that if a country has a persistent current-account deficit, its exchange rate could remain below its PPP almost indefinitely.

Burgernomics*
Current-account balances and Big Mac PPPs

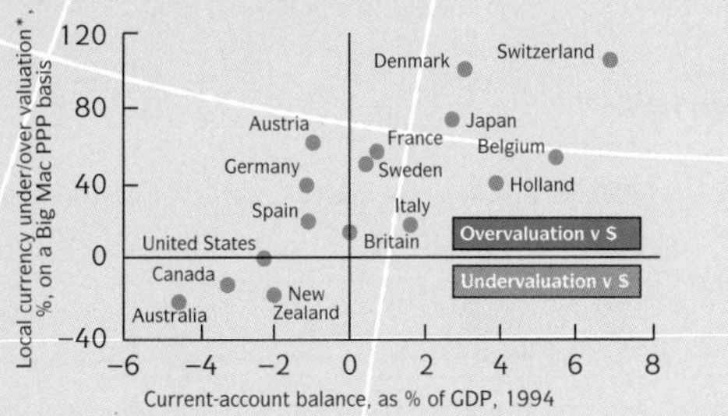

Sources: *The Economist*, OECD *Exchange rates on August 21st

FEER of the Unknown

An alternative notion of exchange-rate equilibrium tries to take account of capital flows. The so-called fundamental equilibrium exchange rate (FEER) is the rate that will generate a current-account deficit or surplus equal to the sustainable inflow or outflow of capital.

Unlike PPPs, which remain constant in real terms, FEERs will change over time in line with changes in net foreign assets or liabilities. Once an exchange rate departs from its FEER, this will affect the size of the current-account balance, the level of foreign debt, and hence the FEER itself.

John Williamson, an economist at the Institute for International Economics in Washington, DC, who pioneered the concept in the early 1980s, calculates current FEERs for the dollar at ¥105 and DM1.60. In contrast to the message from PPPs, this suggests that the dollar is already quite close to its equilibrium.

But FEERs are also flawed. Their value is sensitive to the estimated level of sustainable capital inflows. And in a world of highly mobile capital this whole concept may not make sense, since investors' asset preferences can easily shift, and will themselves depend upon the value of currencies. Moreover, some economists argue that by itself, a lower dollar will not eliminate America's current-account deficit. It will simply create inflationary pressure in America and deflationary pressure in Japan, offsetting the gain in competitiveness from a cheaper dollar. The only sure cure for America's trade gap is higher domestic savings.

This suggests a third possible yardstick for judging where the dollar may head in the longer term. If America continues to run large current-account deficits, it will flood the world with more dollar-denominated debt. To continue financing these deficits, it must either raise interest rates, or the exchange rate will have to fall by enough to make dollar assets attractive to foreigners. The implication of this is that without changes in America's monetary and fiscal policies (ie, big budget cuts to boost domestic savings), the dollar's medium-term path is likely to be down, regardless of any hypothetical notions of equilibrium.

What lessons should investors draw from all this? Mainly that economists never agree. Depending upon which of the three views on exchange rates you favour, the dollar's future path could be up, down or sideways. Indeed, given the inadequacy of economics when it comes to understanding exchange rates, terms such as "currency misalignment" and "over-valuation" should be used sparingly.

Source: The Economist Newspaper Group, Inc. August 26, 1995.

across countries in a given currency and if the composition of the consumption basket is the same across countries.

The PPP has been the subject of a series of tests, yielding generally negative results. For example, in his study of disaggregated commodity arbitrage between the United States and Canada, Richardson (1978) was unable to detect commodity arbitrage for a majority of commodity classes. Richardson reported: "The presence of commodity arbitrage could be rejected with 95 percent confidence for at least 13 out of the 22 commodity groups" (p. 346). Although Richardson did not directly test PPP, his findings can be viewed as highly negative news for PPP. If commodity arbitrage is imperfect between neighboring countries like the United States and Canada that have relatively few trade restrictions, PPP is not likely to hold much better for other pairs of countries.

Exhibit 5.7, "A Guide to World Prices," also provides evidence against commodity price parity. The price of aspirin (100 units) ranges from $2.87 in Athens to $25.40 in Rome. Likewise, a cost of a man's haircut ranges from $6.70 in Mexico City to $46.37 in Tokyo. It cost 7 times (!) more to have a haircut in Tokyo than in Mexico City. The price differential, however, is likely to persist because haircuts are

EXHIBIT 5.6 Real Effective Exchange Rates for Selected Currencies

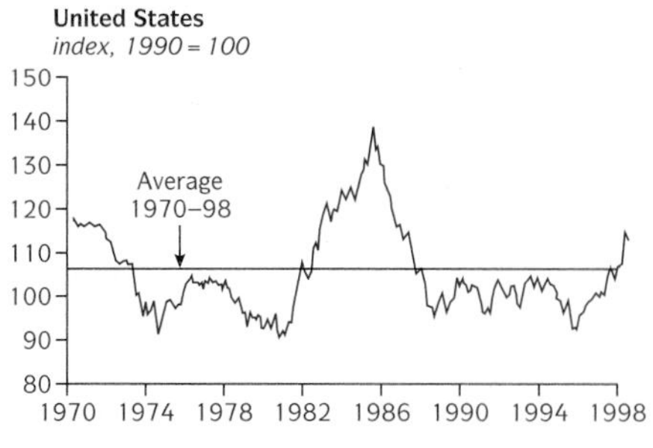

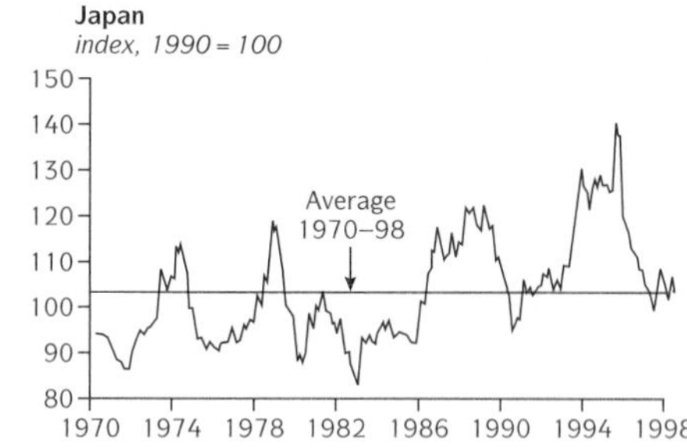

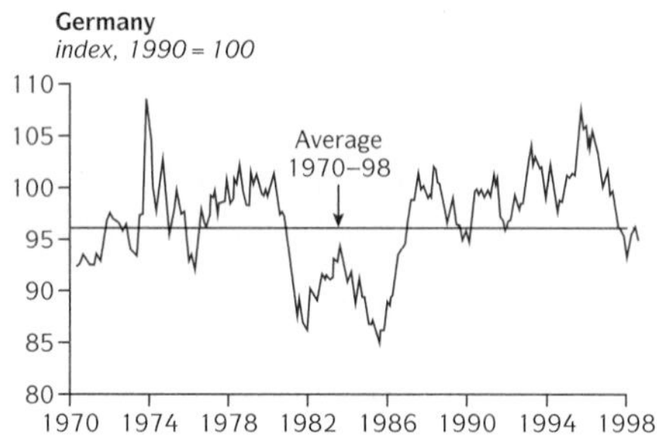

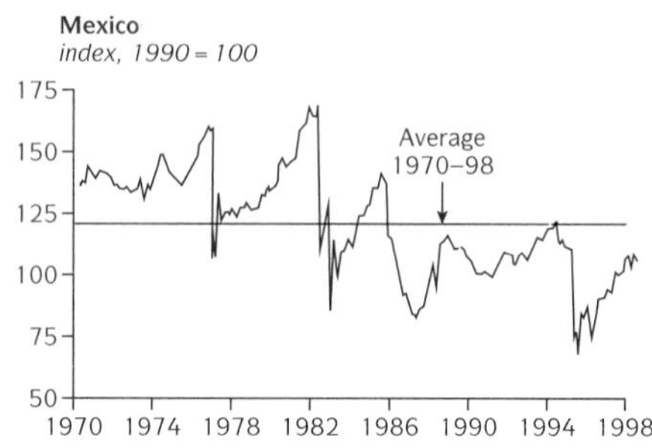

Source: www.jpmorgan.com.

EXHIBIT 5.7

A Guide to World Prices: March 1999[a]

Location	Fast Food (1 unit)	Aspirin (100.units)	Man's Haircut (1 unit)	Camera Film (24 exposures)
Athens	$4.43	$2.87	$17.76	$4.52
Copenhagen	$7.98	$5.71	$27.46	$7.81
Hong Kong	$2.65	$10.33	$36.16	$2.70
London	$5.76	$15.26	$21.28	$6.55
Los Angeles	$4.37	$7.91	$13.17	$3.49
Madrid	$4.91	$15.36	$12.56	$3.50
Mexico City	$4.50	$13.39	$6.70	$4.20
Munich	$5.52	$13.15	$23.20	$3.79
Paris	$4.76	$12.62	$20.46	$5.25
Rio de Janeiro	$2.15	$20.67	$13.95	$3.60
Rome	$4.98	$25.40	$25.79	$4.24
Sydney	$3.92	$8.54	$14.75	$4.19
Tokyo	$5.56	$17.78	$46.37	$4.03
Toronto	$4.20	$5.17	$11.43	$3.31
Vienna	$5.25	$7.55	$22.90	$3.36
Average	$4.73	$12.11	$20.93	$4.30
Standard Deviation	$1.35	$6.18	$10.26	$1.33
Coefficient of Variation[b]	0.29	0.51	0.49	0.31

[a]Prices include sales tax and value-added tax except in the United States location.

[b]The coefficient of variation is obtained from dividing the standard deviation by the average. It thus provides a measure of dispersion adjusted for the magnitude of the variable.

Source: Runzheimer International.

simply not tradable. In comparison, the price disparity for camera film is substantially less. This can be attributable to the fact that camera film is a highly standardized commodity that is actively traded across national borders.

Kravis and Lipsey (1978) examined the relationship between inflation rates and exchange rates and found that price levels can move far apart without rapid correction via arbitrage, thus rejecting the notion of integrated international commodity price structure. In a similar vein, Adler and Lehman (1983) found that deviations from PPP follow a random walk, without exhibiting any tendency to revert to PPP.

Frenkel (1981) reported that while PPP did very poorly in explaining the behavior of exchange rates between the U.S. dollar and major European currencies, it performed somewhat better in explaining the exchange rates between a pair of European currencies, such as the British pound versus the German mark, and the French franc versus the German mark. Frenkel's finding may be attributable to the fact that, in addition to the geographical proximity of the European countries, these countries belong to the European Common Market with low internal trade barriers and low transportation costs. Even among these European currencies, however, Frenkel found that relative price levels are only one of the many potential factors influencing exchange rates. If PPP holds strictly, relative price levels should be sufficient in explaining the behavior of exchange rates.

Generally unfavorable evidence about PPP suggests that substantial barriers to international commodity arbitrage exist. Obviously, commodity prices can diverge between countries up to the transportation costs without triggering arbitrage. If it costs $50 to ship a ton of rice from Thailand to Korea, the price of rice can diverge by up to $50 in either direction between the two countries. Likewise, deviations from PPP can result from tariffs and quotas imposed on international trade.

As is well recognized, some commodities never enter into international trade. Examples of such **nontradables** include haircuts, medical services, housing, and the like. These items are either immovable or inseparable from the providers of these services. Suppose a quality haircut costs $20 in New York City, but the comparable haircut only costs $7 in Mexico City. Obviously, you cannot import haircuts from Mexico. Either you have to travel to Mexico or a Mexican barber must travel to New York City, both of which, of course, are impractical in view of the travel costs and the immigration laws. Consequently, a large price differential for haircuts will persist. As long as there are nontradables, PPP will not hold in its absolute version. If PPP holds for tradables and the relative prices between tradables and nontradables are maintained, then PPP can hold in its relative version. These conditions, however, are not very likely to hold.

Even if PPP may not hold in reality, it can still play a useful role in economic analysis. First, one can use the PPP-determined exchange rate as a benchmark in deciding if a country's currency is undervalued or overvalued against other currencies. Second, one can often make more meaningful international comparisons of economic data using PPP-determined rather than market-determined exchange rates. This point is highlighted in Exhibit 5.8, "How Large Is China's Economy?"

Suppose you want to rank countries in terms of gross national product (GNP). If you use market exchange rates, you can either underestimate or overestimate the true GNP values. Exhibit 5.8 provides the GNP values of the major countries in 1992 computed using both PPP and market exchange rates. A country's ranking in terms of GNP value is quite sensitive to which exchange rate is used. China provides a striking example. When the market exchange rate is used, China ranks 10th, lagging behind such countries as Canada, Spain, and Brazil. However, when the PPP exchange rate is used, China moves up to third (!) after Japan, but ahead of Germany and France. India also moves up from 11th to 6th when the PPP exchange rate is used. In contrast, countries like Canada and Spain move down in the GNP ranking when PPP exchange rates are used.

FISHER EFFECTS

Another parity condition we often encounter in the literature is the **Fisher effect.** The Fisher effect holds that *an increase (decrease) in the expected inflation rate in a*

EXHIBIT 5.8

How Large Is China's Economy?

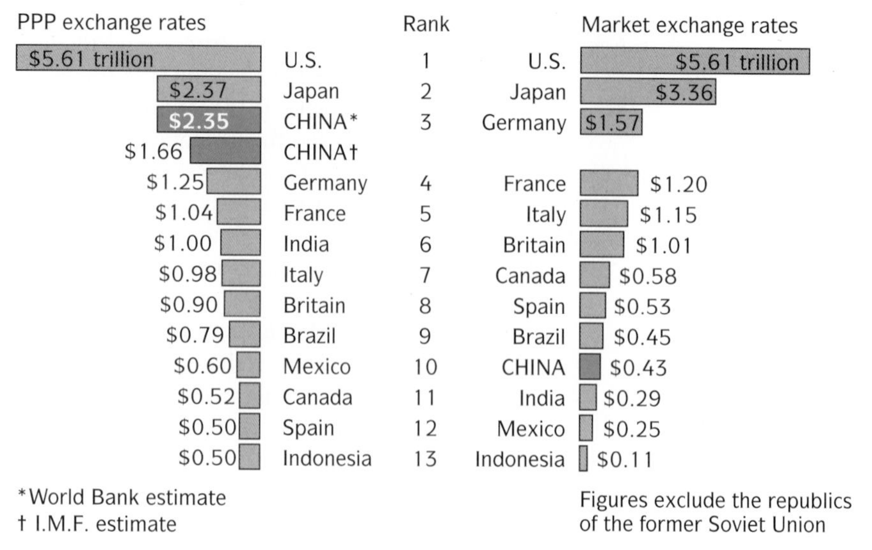

Sources: Organization for Economic Cooperation and Development, World Bank, International Monetary Fund.

Source: © 1993 by the New York Times Company.

country will cause a proportionate increase (decrease) in the interest rate in the country. Formally, the Fisher effect can be written for the United States as follows:

$$i_\$ = \rho_\$ + E(\pi_\$) \tag{5.15}$$

where $\rho_\$$ denotes the equilibrium expected "real" interest rate in the United States. IFE suggests that the nominal interest rate differential reflects the expected change in exchange rate. For instance, if the interest rate is 5 percent per year in the United States and 7 percent in the U.K., the dollar is expected to appreciate against the British pound by about 2 percent per year.[15]

For example, suppose the expected real interest rate is 2 percent per year in the United States. Given this, the U.S. (nominal) interest rate will be entirely determined by the expected inflation in the United States. If, for instance, the expected inflation rate is 4.0 percent per year, the interest rate will then be set at 6 percent. With a 6 percent interest rate, the lender will be fully compensated for the expected erosion of the purchasing power of money while still expecting to realize a 2 percent real return. Of course, the Fisher effect should hold in each country's bond market as long as the bond market is efficient.

The Fisher effect implies that the expected inflation rate is the difference between the nominal and real interest rates in each country, that is,

$$E(\pi_\$) = i_\$ - \rho_\$$$
$$E(\pi_£) = i_£ - \rho_£$$

Now, let us assume that the real interest rate is the same between countries, that is, $\rho_\$ = \rho_£$, because of unrestricted capital flows. When we substitute the above results into the relative PPP in its expectational form, that is, $E(e) = E(\pi_\$) - E(\pi_£)$, we obtain

$$E(e) = i_\$ - i_£ \tag{5.16}$$

which is known as the **international Fisher effect (IFE).**[16]

EXHIBIT 5.9

International Parity Relationships among Exchange Rates, Interest Rates, and Inflation Rates

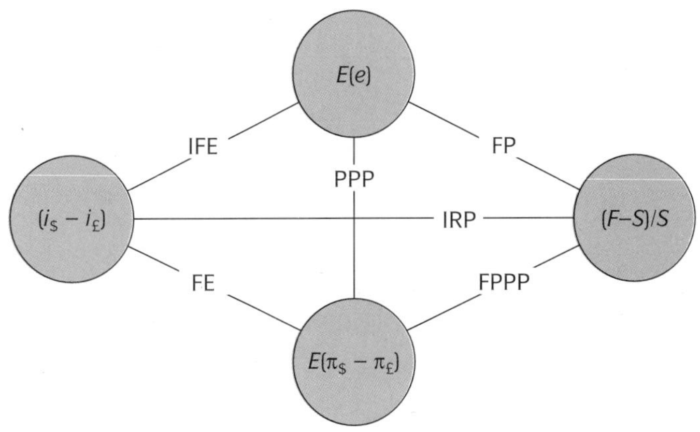

Notes:
1. With the assumption of the same real interest rate, the Fisher effect (FE) implies that the interest rate differential is equal to the expected inflation rate differential.
2. If both purchasing power parity (PPP) and forward parity (FP) hold, then the forward exchange premium or discount will be equal to the expected inflation rate differential. The latter relationship is denoted by the forward-PPP, i.e., FPPP in the exhibit.
3. IFE stands for the international Fisher effect.

Lastly, when the international Fisher effect is combined with IRP, that is, $(F - S)/S = i_{\$} - i_{£}$, we obtain

$$(F - S)/S = E(e) \tag{5.17}$$

which is referred to as **forward parity.** Forward parity states that any forward premium or discount is equal to the expected change in the exchange rate. When investors are risk-neutral, forward parity will hold as long as the foreign exchange market is informationally efficient. Otherwise, it need not hold even if the market is efficient. Exhibit 5.9 summarizes the parity relationships discussed so far.[17]

FORECASTING EXCHANGE RATES

Since the advent of the flexible exchange rate system in 1973, exchange rates have become increasingly more volatile and erratic. At the same time, the scope of business activities has become highly international. Consequently, many business decisions are now made based on forecasts, implicit or explicit, of future exchange rates. Understandably, forecasting exchange rates as accurately as possible is a matter of vital importance for currency traders who are actively engaged in speculating, hedging, and arbitrage in the foreign exchange markets. It is also a vital concern for multinational corporations that are formulating international sourcing, production, financing, and marketing strategies. The quality of these corporate decisions will critically depend on the accuracy of exchange rate forecasts.

Some corporations generate their own forecasts, while others subscribe to outside services for a fee. While forecasters use a wide variety of forecasting techniques, most can be classified into three distinct approaches:

- Efficient market approach
- Fundamental approach
- Technical approach

Let us briefly examine each of these approaches.

Efficient Market Approach

Financial markets are said to be efficient if the current asset prices fully reflect all the available and relevant information. The **efficient market hypothesis** (EMH), which is largely attributable to Professor Eugene Fama of the University of Chicago, has strong implications for forecasting.[18]

Suppose that the foreign exchange markets are efficient. This means that the current exchange rate has already reflected all relevant information, such as money supplies, inflation rates, trade balances, and output growth. The exchange rate will then change only when the market receives new information. Since news by definition is unpredictable, the exchange rate will change randomly over time. In a word, incremental changes in the exchange rate will be independent of the past history of the exchange rate. If the exchange rate indeed follows a random walk, the future exchange rate is expected to be the same as the current exchange rate, that is,

$$S_t = E(S_{t+1})$$

In a sense, the **random walk hypothesis** suggests that today's exchange rate is the best predictor of tomorrow's exchange rate.

While researchers found it difficult to reject the random walk hypothesis for exchange rates on empirical grounds, there is no theoretical reason why exchange rates should follow a pure random walk. The parity relationships we discussed previously indicate that the current forward exchange rate can be viewed as the market's consensus forecast of the future exchange rate if the foreign exchange markets are efficient, that is,

$$F_t = E(S_{t+1}|I_t)$$

To the extent that interest rates are different between two countries, the forward exchange rate will be different from the current spot exchange rate. This means that the future exchange rate should be expected to be different from the current spot exchange rate.

Those who subscribe to the efficient market hypothesis can predict the future exchange rate using either the current spot exchange rate or the current forward exchange rate. But which one is better? Researchers like Agmon and Amihud (1981) compared the performance of the forward exchange rate with that of the random walk model as a predictor of the future spot exchange rate. Their empirical findings indicate that the forward exchange rate failed to outperform the random walk model in predicting the future exchange rate; the two prediction models that are based on the efficient market hypothesis registered largely comparable performances.[19]

Predicting the exchange rates using the efficient market approach has two advantages. First, since the efficient market approach is based on market-determined prices, it is costless to generate forecasts. Both the current spot and forward exchange rates are public information. As such, everyone has free access to it. Second, given the efficiency of foreign exchange markets, it is difficult to outperform the market-based forecasts unless the forecaster has access to private information that is not yet reflected in the current exchange rate.

Fundamental Approach

The fundamental approach to exchange rate forecasting uses various models. For example, the monetary approach to exchange rate determination suggests that the exchange rate is determined by three independent (explanatory) variables: (1) relative money supplies, (2) relative velocity of monies, and (3) relative national outputs.[20] One can thus formulate the monetary approach in the following empirical form:[21]

$$s = \alpha + \beta_1(m - m^*) + \beta_2(v - v^*) + \beta_3(y^* - y) + u \qquad (5.18)$$

where:

s = natural logarithm of the spot exchange rate.
$m - m^*$ = natural logarithm of domestic/foreign money supply.
$v - v^*$ = natural logarithm of domestic/foreign velocity of money.
$y^* - y$ = natural logarithm of foreign/domestic output.
u = random error term, with mean zero.
α, β's = model parameters.

Generating forecasts using the fundamental approach would involve three steps:

Step 1: Estimation of the structural model like Equation 5.18 to determine the numerical values for the parameters such as α and β's.

Step 2: Estimation of future values of the independent variables like $(m - m^*)$, $(v - v^*)$, and $(y^* - y)$.

Step 3: Substituting the estimated values of the independent variables into the estimated structural model to generate the exchange rate forecasts.

If, for example, the forecaster would like to predict the exchange rate one year into the future, he or she has to estimate the values that the independent variables will assume in one year. These values will then be substituted in the structural model that was fitted to historical data.

The fundamental approach to exchange rate forecasting has two main difficulties. First, one has to forecast a set of independent variables to forecast the exchange rates. Forecasting the former will certainly be subject to errors and may not be necessarily easier than forecasting the latter. Second, the parameter values, that is, α and β's, that are estimated using historical data may change over time because of changes in government policies and/or the underlying structure of the economy. Either difficulty can diminish the accuracy of forecasts.

Not surprisingly, researchers found that the fundamental models failed to more accurately forecast exchange rates than either the forward rate model or the random walk model. Meese and Rogoff (1983), for example, found that the fundamental models developed based on the monetary approach did worse than the random walk model even if realized (true) values were used for the independent variables. They also confirmed that the forward rate did not do better than the random walk model. In the words of Meese and Rogoff:

> Ignoring for the present the fact that the spot rate does no worse than the forward rate, the striking feature. . . . is that none of the models achieves lower, much less significantly lower, RMSE than the random walk model at any horizon. . . . The structural models in particular fail to improve on the random walk model in spite of the fact that their forecasts are based on realized values of the explanatory variables.[22] (p. 12)

Technical Approach

The technical approach first analyzes the past behavior of exchange rates for the purpose of identifying "patterns" and then projects them into the future to generate forecasts. Clearly, the technical approach is based on the premise that *history repeats itself.* The technical approach thus is at odds with the efficient market approach. At the same time, it differs from the fundamental approach in that it does not use the key economic variables such as money supplies or trade balances for the purpose of forecasting. However, technical analysts sometimes consider various transaction data like trading volume, outstanding interests, and bid-ask spreads to aid their analyses.

An example of technical analysis is provided by the moving average crossover rule illustrated in Exhibit 5.10. Many technical analysts or chartists compute moving averages as a way of separating short- and long-term trends from the vicissitudes of daily exchange rates. Exhibit 5.10 illustrates how exchange rates may be forecast

EXHIBIT 5.10

Moving Average Crossover Rule: A Technical Analysis

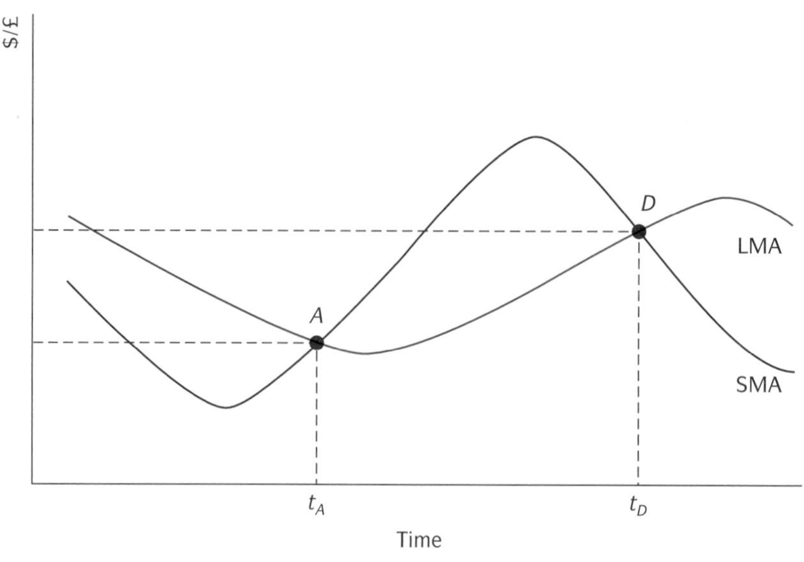

based on the movements of short- and long-term moving averages. Since the short-term moving average (SMA) weighs recent exchange rate changes more heavily than the long-term moving average (LMA), the SMA will lie below (above) the LMA when the British pound is falling (rising) against the dollar. This implies that one can forecast exchange rate movements based on the crossover of the moving averages. According to this rule, a crossover of the SMA above the LMA at point *A* signals that the British pound is appreciating. On the other hand, a crossover of the SMA below the LMA at point *D* signals that the British pound is depreciating.

While academic studies tend to discredit the validity of **technical analysis,** many traders depend on technical analyses for their trading strategies. If a trader knows that other traders use technical analysis, it can be rational for the trader to use technical analysis too. If enough traders use technical analysis, the predictions based on it can become self-fulfilling to some extent, at least in the short-run.

Performance of the Forecasters

Because predicting exchange rates is difficult, many firms and investors subscribe to professional forecasting services for a fee. Since an alternative to subscribing to professional forecasting services is to use a market-determined price such as the forward exchange rate, it is relevant to ask: *Can professional forecasters outperform the market?*

An answer to the above question was provided by Professor Richard Levich of New York University, who evaluated the performances of 13 forecasting services using the forward exchange rate as a benchmark. Under certain conditions, the forward exchange rate can be viewed as the market's consensus forecast of the future exchange rate.[23] These services use different methods of forecasting, such as econometric, technical, and judgmental. In evaluating the performance of forecasters, Levich computed the following ratio:

$$R = \text{MAE(S)/MAE(F)} \tag{5.19}$$

where:

MAE(S) = mean absolute forecast error of a forecasting service.

MAE(F) = mean absolute forecast error of the forward exchange rate as a predictor.[24]

EXHIBIT 5.11 Performance of Exchange Rate Forecasting Services

	Forecasting Services												
Currency	1	2	3	4	5	6	7	8	9	10	11	12	13
Canadian dollar	1.29	1.13	1.00	1.59	0.99	1.08	n.a.	1.47	1.17	1.03	1.47	1.74	0.80
British pound	1.11	1.24	0.91	1.44	1.09	0.98	1.05	1.09	1.27	1.69	1.03	1.22	1.01
Belgian franc	0.95	1.07	n.a.	1.33	1.17	n.a.	n.a.	0.99	1.21	n.a.	1.06	1.01	0.77
French franc	0.91	0.98	1.02	1.43	1.27	n.a.	0.98	0.92	1.00	0.96	1.03	1.16	0.70
German mark	1.08	1.13	1.07	1.28	1.19	1.35	1.06	0.83	1.19	1.07	1.13	1.04	0.76
Italian lira	1.07	0.91	1.09	1.45	1.14	n.a.	1.12	1.12	1.00	1.17	1.64	1.54	0.93
Dutch guilder	0.80	1.10	n.a.	1.41	1.06	n.a.	n.a.	0.91	1.26	1.26	1.10	1.01	0.81
Swiss franc	1.01	n.a.	1.08	1.21	1.32	n.a.	n.a.	0.86	1.06	1.04	1.04	0.94	0.63
Japanese yen	1.42	1.05	1.02	1.23	1.08	1.45	1.09	1.24	0.94	0.47	1.31	1.30	1.79

Note: Each entry represents the *R* ratio defined in Equation 5.19. If a forecasting service outperforms (underperforms) the forward exchange rate, the *R* ratio will be less (greater) than unity.

Source: Richard Levich, "Evaluating the Performance of the Forecasters," in Richard Ensor, ed., *The Management of Foreign Exchange Risk,* 2nd ed. (Euromoney Publications, 1982).

If a professional forecasting service provides more accurate forecasts than the forward exchange rate, that is, MAE(S) $<$ MAE(F), then the ratio R will be less than unity for the service. If the service fails to outperform the forward exchange rate, the ratio R will be greater than unity.

Exhibit 5.11 provides the R ratios for each service for the U.S. dollar exchange rates of nine major foreign currencies for a three-month forecasting horizon. The most striking finding presented in the exhibit is that only 24 percent of the entries, 25 out of 104, are less than unity. This, of course, means that the professional services as a whole clearly failed to outperform the forward exchange rate.[25] In other words, they failed to beat the market.

However, there are substantial variations in the performance records across individual services. In the cases of services 4 and 11, for instance, every entry is greater than unity. In contrast, for service 13, which is Wharton Econometric Forecasting Associates, the majority of entries, seven out of nine, are less than unity. It is also clear from the exhibit that the performance record of each service varies substantially across currencies. The R ratio for Wharton, for example, ranges from 0.63 for the Swiss franc to 1.79 for the Japanese yen. Wharton Associates clearly has difficulty in forecasting the dollar/yen exchange rate. Service 10, on the other hand, convincingly beat the market in forecasting the yen exchange rate, with an R ratio of 0.47! This suggests that consumers need to discriminate among forecasting services depending on what currencies they are interested in. Lastly, note that service 12, which is known to use technical analysis, outperformed neither the forward rate nor other services. This result certainly does not add credence to the technical approach to exchange rate forecasting.

SUMMARY

This chapter provides a systematic discussion of the key international parity relationships and two related issues, exchange rate determination and prediction. A thorough understanding of parity relationships is essential for astute financial management.

1. Interest rate parity (IRP) holds that the forward premium or discount should be equal to the interest rate differential between two countries. IRP represents an arbitrage equilibrium condition that should hold in the absence of barriers to international capital flows.
2. If IRP is violated, one can lock in guaranteed profit by borrowing in one currency and lending in another, with exchange risk hedged via forward contract. As a result of this covered interest arbitrage, IRP will be restored.

3. IRP implies that in the short run, the exchange rate depends on (a) the relative interest rates between two countries, and (b) the expected future exchange rate. Other things being equal, a higher (lower) domestic interest rate will lead to appreciation (depreciation) of the domestic currency. People's expectations concerning future exchange rates are self-fulfilling.
4. Purchasing power parity (PPP) states that the exchange rate between two countries' currencies should be equal to the ratio of their price levels. PPP is a manifestation of the law of one price applied internationally to a standard commodity basket. The relative version of PPP states that the rate of change in the exchange rate should be equal to the inflation rate differential between countries. The existing empirical evidence, however, is generally negative on PPP. This implies that substantial barriers to international commodity arbitrage exist.
5. There are three distinct approaches to exchange rate forecasting: (a) the efficient market approach, (b) the fundamental approach, and (c) the technical approach. The efficient market approach uses such market-determined prices as the current exchange rate or the forward exchange rate to forecast the future exchange rate. The fundamental approach uses various formal models of exchange rate determination for forecasting purposes. The technical approach, on the other hand, identifies patterns from the past history of the exchange rate and projects it into the future. The existing empirical evidence indicates that neither the fundamental nor the technical approach outperforms the efficient market approach.

KEY WORDS

arbitrage, 100
arbitrage portfolio, 101
covered interest arbitrage, 102
efficient market hypothesis, 116
Fisher effect, 113
forward parity, 115
interest rate parity, 100
international Fisher effect, 114
law of one price, 101
monetary approach, 124
nontradables, 113
purchasing power parity, 108
quantity theory of money, 124
random walk hypothesis, 116
real exchange rate, 109
technical analysis, 118
uncovered interest rate parity, 106

QUESTIONS

1. Give a full definition of *arbitrage.*
2. Discuss the implications of interest rate parity for exchange rate determination.
3. Explain the conditions under which the forward exchange rate will be an unbiased predictor of the future spot exchange rate.
4. Explain purchasing power parity, both the absolute and relative versions. What causes deviations from purchasing power parity?
5. Discuss the implications of the deviations from purchasing power parity for countries' competitive positions in the world market.
6. Explain and derive the international Fisher effect.
7. Researchers found that it is very difficult to forecast future exchange rates more accurately than the forward exchange rate or the current spot exchange rate. How would you interpret this finding?
8. Explain the random walk model for exchange rate forecasting. Can it be consistent with technical analysis?
9. Derive and explain the monetary approach to exchange rate determination.

PROBLEMS

1. Suppose that the treasurer of IBM has an extra cash reserve of $1,000,000 to invest for six months. The six-month interest rate is 8 percent per annum in the United States and 6 percent per annum in Germany. Currently, the spot exchange rate is DM1.60 per dollar and the six-month forward exchange rate is DM1.56 per dollar. The treasurer of IBM does not wish to bear any exchange risk. Where should he or she invest to maximize the return?
2. While you were visiting London, you purchased a Jaguar for £35,000, payable in three months. You have enough cash at your bank in New York City, which pays 0.35 percent interest per month, compounding monthly, to pay for the car. Currently, the spot exchange rate is $1.45/£ and the three-month forward exchange rate is $1.40/£. In London, the money market interest rate is 2.0 percent for a three-month investment. There are two alternative ways of paying for your Jaguar.
   a. Keep the funds at your bank in the United States and buy £35,000 forward.
   b. Buy a certain pound amount spot today and invest the amount in the U.K. for three months so that the maturity value becomes equal to £35,000. Evaluate each payment method. Which method would you prefer? Why?
3. Currently, the spot exchange rate is $1.50/£ and the three-month forward exchange rate is $1.52/£. The three-month interest rate is 8.0 percent per annum in the U.S. and 5.8 percent per annum in the U.K. Assume that you can borrow as much as $1,500,000 or £1,000,000.
   a. Determine whether interest rate parity is currently holding.
   b. If IRP is not holding, how would you carry out covered interest arbitrage? Show all the steps and determine the arbitrage profit.
   c. Explain how IRP will be restored as a result of covered arbitrage activities.
4. Suppose that the current spot exchange rate is FF6.25/$ and the three-month forward exchange rate is FF6.28/$. The three-month interest rate is 5.6 percent per annum in the United States and 8.8 percent per annum in France. Assume that you can borrow up to $1,000,000 or FF6,250,000.
   a. Show how to realize a certain profit via covered interest arbitrage, assuming that you want to realize profit in terms of U.S. dollars. Also determine the size of your arbitrage profit.
   b. Assume that you want to realize profit in terms of French francs. Show the covered arbitrage process and determine the arbitrage profit in French francs.
5. In the October 23, 1999 issue, *The Economist* reports that the interest rate per annum is 5.93 percent in the United States and 70.0 percent in Turkey. Why do you think the interest rate is so high in Turkey? Based on the reported interest rates, how would you predict the change of the exchange rate between the U.S. dollar and the Turkish lira?
6. As of November 1, 1999, the exchange rate between the Brazilian real and U.S. dollar was R$1.95/$. The consensus forecast for the U.S. and Brazil inflation rates for the next one-year period is 2.6 percent and 20.0 percent, respectively. What would you forecast the exchange rate to be at around November 1, 2000?

ENDNOTES

1. The law of one price prevails when the same or equivalent things are trading at the same price across different locations or markets, precluding profitable arbitrage opportunities. As we will see, many equilibrium pricing relationships in finance are obtained from imposing the law of one price, i.e., the two things that are equal to each other must be selling for the same price.
2. For notational simplicity, we delete the currency subscripts for the exchange rate notations, S and F. It is noted that here, the exchange rate represents the dollar price of one unit of foreign currency.

3. A systematic exposition of the interest rate parity is generally attributed to Keynes's *Monetary Reform* (1924).
4. It is noted that Equation 5.3 is an approximate version. The exact version is:

$$i_\$ - i_£ = \left[\frac{F - S}{S}\right](1 + i_£)$$

To determine if there exists an arbitrage opportunity, one should use the exact version of IRP.
5. The arbitrage profit is, in fact, equal to the effective interest rate differential times the amount borrowed, i.e., \$15,600 = (1.0656 − 1.05)(\$1,000,000).
6. Note that at point *A*, the interest rate differential is −3%, i.e., $i_\$ - i_£ = 5\% - 8\% = -3\%$, and the forward premium is −1.33%, i.e., $(F - S)/S = (1.48 - 1.50)/1.50 = -0.0133$, or −1.33%.
7. It is left to the readers to figure out how IRP may be restored in this example.
8. A higher U.S. interest rate ($i_\$\uparrow$) will lead to a lower spot exchange rate ($S\downarrow$) which means a stronger dollar. Note that the variable *S* represents the number of U.S. dollars per pound.
9. The set of relevant information should include money supplies, interest rates, trade balances, and so on that would influence the exchange rates.
10. Capital controls were often imposed by governments in an effort to improve the balance of payments situations and to keep the exchange rate at a desirable level.
11. Readers can convince themselves that DIRP in Equation 5.11 will be zero if IRP holds exactly.
12. Gensaki bonds, issued in the Tokyo money market, are sold with a repurchase agreement. While interest rates on Gensaki bonds are determined by market forces, they can still be affected by various market imperfections.
13. From Equation 5.12 we obtain $(1 + e) = (1 + \pi_\$)/(1 + \pi_£)$. Rearranging the above expression we obtain $e = (\pi_\$ - \pi_£)/(1 + \pi_£)$, which is approximated by $e = \pi_\$ - \pi_£$ as in Equation 5.12.
14. The real exchange rate measures the degree of deviations from PPP over a certain period of time, assuming that PPP held roughly at a starting point. If PPP holds continuously, the real exchange rate will remain unity.
15. It is noted that Equation 5.15 is an approximation. The exact version of the Fisher effect is given by $i_\$ = \rho_\$ + E(\pi_\$) + \rho_\$ E(\pi_\$)$.
16. The international Fisher effect is the same as the uncovered IRP previously discussed. While the Fisher effect should hold in an efficient market, the international Fisher effect need not hold even in an efficient market unless investors are risk-neutral. Generally speaking, the interest rate differential may reflect not only the expected change in the exchange rate but also a risk premium.
17. Suppose that the Fisher effect holds both in the United States and in the U.K., and that the real interest rate is the same in both the countries. As shown in Exhibit 5.9, the Fisher effect (FE) then implies that the interest rate differential should be equal to the expected inflation differential. Furthermore, when forward parity and PPP are combined, we obtain what might be called "forward-PPP" (FPPP), i.e., the forward premium/discount is equal to the expected inflation differential.
18. For a detailed discussion of the efficient market hypothesis, refer to Eugene Fama, "Efficient Capital Markets II," *Journal of Finance* 26 (1991), pp. 1575–1617.
19. For a detailed discussion, refer to Tamir Agmon and Yakov Amihud, "The Forward Exchange Rate and the Prediction of the Future Spot Rate," *Journal of Banking and Finance* 5 (1981) pp. 425–37.
20. For a detailed discussion of the monetary approach, see Appendix 5A.
21. For notational simplicity, we omit the time subscripts in the following equation.
22. RMSE, which stands for the root mean squared error, is the criterion that Meese and Rogoff used in evaluating the accuracy of forecasts.
23. These conditions are: (a) the foreign exchange markets are efficient, and (b) the forward exchange rate does not contain a significant risk premium.

24. The mean absolute forecast error (MAE) is computed as follows:

    $$\text{MAE} = \Sigma_i |P_i - A_i|/n$$

    where P is the predicted exchange rate, A is the actual (realized) exchange rate, and n is the number of forecasts made. The MAE criterion penalizes the over- and underestimation equally. If a forecaster has perfect foresight so that $P = A$ always, then MAE will be zero.
25. Levich found that the same qualitative result holds for different horizons like 1 month, 6 months, and 12 months.

WEB RESOURCES

www.oecd.org/std/nadata.htm

Website of Organization for Economic Co-operation and Development (OECD). Provides summary indicators for OECD countries, including PPPs, PPP-based price levels, etc.

www.oanda.com/

Provides current rates and forecasts for world's major currencies, and currency news and analysis.

www.pei-intl.com/Quotes/watch.htm

Provides daily, weekly, and monthly outlooks based on technical analysis for foreign exchange markets. Also provides such outlooks for world stock and bond markets.

www.angelfire.com/me/ozanpage/index.html

Provides numerical illustrations of foreign exchange arbitrage.

www.jpmorgan.com/market indices/currindex.html

Provides trade-weighted nominal and inflation-adjusted real exchange rates of OECD countries, as well as daily exchange rates of G-7 countries.

REFERENCES AND SUGGESTED READINGS

Abuaf, N. and P. Jorion. "Purchasing Power Parity in the Long Run." *Journal of Finance* 45 (1990), pp. 157–74.

Aliber, R. "The Interest Rate Parity: A Reinterpretation." *Journal of Political Economy* (1973), pp. 1451–59.

Adler, Michael, and Bruce Lehman. "Deviations from Purchasing Power Parity in the Long Run." *Journal of Finance* 38 (1983), pp. 1471–87.

Fisher, Irving. *The Theory of Interest,* rpt. ed. New York: Macmillan, 1980.

Frenkel, Jacob. "Flexible Exchange Rates, Prices and the Role of News: Lessons from the 1970s." *Journal of Political Economy* 89 (1981), pp. 665–705.

Frenkel, Jacob, and Richard Levich. "Covered Interest Arbitrage: Unexploited Profits?" *Journal of Political Economy* 83 (1975), pp. 325–38.

Keynes, John M. *Monetary Reform.* New York: Harcourt, Brace, 1924.

Kravis, I., and R. Lipsey. "Price Behavior in the Light of Balance of Payment Theories." *Journal of International Economics* (1978), pp. 193–246.

Levich, Richard. "Evaluating the Performance of the Forecasters," in Richard Ensor (ed.), *The Management of Foreign Exchange Risk,* 2nd ed. Euromoney Publication, 1982, pp. 121–34.

Meese, Richard, and Kenneth Rogoff. "Empirical Exchange Rate Models of the Seventies: Do They Fit Out of Sample?" *Journal of International Economics* 14 (1983), pp. 3–24.

Otani, Ichiro, and Siddharth Tiwari. "Capital Controls and Interest Rate Parity: The Japanese Experience, 1978–81." *International Monetary Fund Staff Papers* 28 (1981), pp. 793-815.

Richardson, J. "Some Empirical Evidence on Commodity Arbitrage and the Law of One Price." *Journal of International Economics* 8 (1978), pp. 341–52.

APPENDIX 5A

PURCHASING POWER PARITY AND EXCHANGE RATE DETERMINATION

Although PPP itself can be viewed as a theory of exchange rate determination, it also serves as a foundation for a more complete theory, namely, the **monetary approach.** The monetary approach, associated with the Chicago School of Economics, is based on two basic tenets: purchasing power parity and the quantity theory of money.

From the **quantity theory of money,** we obtain the following identity that must hold in each country:

$$P_\$ = M_\$V_\$/y_\$ \tag{5A.1A}$$

$$P_£ = M_£V_£/y_£ \tag{5A.1B}$$

where M denotes the money supply, V the velocity of money, measuring the speed at which money is being circulated in the economy, y the national aggregate output, and P the general price level; the subscripts denote countries. When the above equations are substituted for the price levels in the PPP Equation 5 12, we obtain the following expression for the exchange rate:

$$S = (M_\$/M_£)(V_\$/V_£)(y_£/y_\$) \tag{5A.2}$$

According to the monetary approach, what matters in the exchange rate determination are

1. The relative money supplies.
2. The relative velocities of money.
3. The relative national outputs.

All else equal, an increase in the U.S. money supply will result in a proportionate depreciation of the dollar against the pound. So will an increase in the velocity of the dollar, which has the same effect as an increased supply of dollars. But an increase in U.S. output will result in a proportionate appreciation of the dollar.

The monetary approach, which is based on PPP, can be viewed as a long-run theory, not a short-run theory, of exchange rate determination. This is so because the monetary approach does not allow for price rigidities. It assumes that prices adjust fully and completely, which is unrealistic in the short run. Prices of many commodities and services are often fixed over a certain period of time. A good example of short-term price rigidity is the wage rate set by a labor contract. Despite this apparent shortcoming, the monetary approach remains an influential theory and serves as a benchmark in modern exchange rate economics.

PART TWO

6. International Banking and Money Market
7. International Bond Market
8. International Equity Markets
9. Futures and Options on Foreign Exchange
10. Currency and Interest Rate Swaps
11. International Portfolio Investment

World Financial Markets and Institutions

Part two provides a thorough discussion of international financial institutions, assets, and marketplaces, and develops the tools necessary to manage exchange rate uncertainty.

Chapter 6 differentiates between international bank and domestic bank operations and examines the institutional differences of various types of international banking offices. International banks and their clients comprise the Eurocurrency market and form the core of the international money market.

Chapter 7 distinguishes between foreign bonds and Eurobonds, which together comprise the international bond market. The advantages of sourcing funds from the international bond market as opposed to raising funds domestically are discussed. A discussion of the major types of international bonds is included in the chapter.

Chapter 8 covers international equity markets. The chapter begins with a statistical documentation of the size of equity markets in both developed and developing countries. Various methods of trading equity shares in the secondary markets are discussed. Additionally, the chapter provides a discussion of the advantages to the firm of cross-listing equity shares in more than one country.

Chapter 9 provides an extensive treatment of exchange-traded currency futures and options contracts. Basic valuation models are developed.

Chapter 10 covers currency and interest rate swaps.

Chapter 11 covers international portfolio investment. It documents that the potential benefits from international diversification are available to all national investors.

CHAPTER SIX

International Banking and Money Market

CHAPTER OUTLINE

We begin our discussion of world financial markets and institutions in this chapter, which takes up three major topics: international banking; international money market operations, in which banks are dominant players; and the international debt crisis. The chapter starts a discussion of the services international banks provide to their clients. This is appropriate since international banks and domestic banks are characterized by different service mixes. Statistics that show the size and strength of the world's largest international banks are presented next. The first part of the chapter concludes with a discussion of the different types of bank operations that encompass international banking. The second part begins with an analysis of the Eurocurrency market, the creation of Eurocurrency deposits by international banks, and the Eurocredit loans they make. These form the foundation of the international money market. Euronotes, Eurocommercial paper, and forward rate agreements are other important money market instruments that are discussed. The chapter concludes with a history of the severe international debt crisis of only a few years ago and the dangers of private bank lending to sovereign governments.

INTERNATIONAL BANKING SERVICES

International banks can be characterized by the types of services they provide that distinguish them from domestic banks. Foremost, international banks facilitate the imports and exports of their clients by arranging trade financing. Additionally, they serve their clients by arranging for foreign exchange necessary to conduct cross-border transactions and make foreign investments. In conducting foreign exchange transactions, banks often assist their clients in hedging exchange rate risk in foreign currency receivables and payables through forward and options contracts. Since international banks have the facilities to trade foreign exchange, they generally also trade foreign exchange products for their own account.

Major distinguishing features between domestic banks and international banks are the types of deposits they accept and the loans and investments they make. Large international banks both borrow and lend in the Eurocurrency market. Additionally, they are frequently members of international loan syndicates, participating with other international banks to lend large sums to MNCs needing project financing and sovereign governments needing funds for economic development. Moreover, depending on the regulations of the country in which it operates and its organizational type, an international bank may participate in the underwriting of Eurobonds and foreign bonds, an activity allowed only for investment banks in the United States or the investment banking arms of bank holding companies. Banks that perform both traditional commercial banking functions, the subject of this chapter, and engage in investment banking activities are often called **merchant banks**.

International banks frequently provide consulting services and advice to their clients. Areas in which international banks typically have expertise are foreign exchange hedging strategies, interest rate and currency swap financing, and international cash management services. All of these international banking services and operations are covered in depth in this chapter and other chapters that make up Parts Two and Three of the text. Not all international banks provide all services, however. Banks that do provide a majority of these services are commonly known as **universal banks** or **full service banks**.

The World's Largest Banks

Exhibit 6.1 lists the world's 50 largest banks ranked by total assets as of fiscal year-end 1998. The exhibit shows the shareholder equity of each bank, its total assets, and its net income stated in millions of U.S. dollars. The exhibit indicates that 9 of the world's 50 largest banks are Japanese, 9 are U.S., 8 are French, 6 are from the U.K., 5 are German, 3 are from the Netherlands, 2 each are from Italy, Spain and Switzerland, and 1 each is from Australia, Belgium, Canada, and China.

From Exhibit 6.1, one might correctly surmise that the world's major international finance centers are Tokyo, New York, London, Paris, Frankfurt, and Zurich. London, New York, and Tokyo, however, are by far the most important international finance centers because of the relatively liberal banking regulations of their respective countries. These three financial centers are frequently referred to as *full service centers* because the major banks that operate in them usually provide a full range of services.

REASONS FOR INTERNATIONAL BANKING

The opening discussion on the services international banks provide implied some of the reasons why a bank may establish multinational operations. Rugman and Kamath (1987) provide a more formal list:

1. *Low marginal costs*—Managerial and marketing knowledge developed at home can be used abroad with low marginal costs.

EXHIBIT 6.1 The World's 50 Largest Banks (in Millions of U.S. Dollars, as of fiscal year-end 1998)

Rank	Bank	Country	Shareholder Equity	Total Assets	Net Income
1	Bank of America	U.S.	45,938	617,679	5,165
2	Citigroup	U.S.	42,708	668,641	5,807
3	HSBC Holdings	U.K.	30,587	475,546	4,782
4	Crédit Agricole Group	France	26,426	455,782	2,448
5	Chase Manhattan	U.S.	23,838	365,875	3,782
6	Industrial & Commercial Bank of China (ICBC)	China	22,213	391,213	417
7	UBS	Switzerland	21,104	684,455	2,206
8	Deutsche Bank	Germany	20,952	706,045	2,018
9	Wells Fargo	U.S.	20,759	202,475	1,950
10	Bank One	U.S.	20,560	261,496	3,108
11	Crédit Suisse Group	Switzerland	19,443	475,017	2,341
12	Bank of Tokyo-Mitsubishi	Japan	18,829	657,867	−4,127
13	ABN Amro Holding	Netherlands	17,959	504,122	2,283
14	First Union	U.S.	17,173	237,363	2,891
15	HypoVereinsbank	Germany	15,129	521,336	2,322
16	Sumitomo Bank	Japan	14,752	466,298	−1,864
17	Dai-Ichi Kangyo Bank	Japan	14,637	418,942	−483
18	Rabobank Group	Netherlands	14,607	291,353	1,157
19	NatWest Group	U.K.	14,387	297,411	2,730
20	Banque Natinoale de Paris	France	14,027	378,991	1,365
21	Fuji Bank	Japan	13,882	399,628	−2,553
22	Sanwa Bank	Japan	13,800	415,730	−1,379
23	Barclays	U.K.	13,632	353,296	2,296
24	Société Générale	France	13,336	447,487	1,199
25	Sakura Bank	Japan	12,955	387,462	−668
26	Dresdner Bank	Germany	12,563	424,620	1,111
27	Lloyds TSB Group	U.K.	12,470	240,033	3,548
28	ING Bank	Netherlands	12,411	326,813	574
29	Commerzbank	Germany	12,010	375,804	1,100
30	Halifax	U.K.	11,893	208,687	1,948
31	Crédit Mutuel	France	11,348	286,369	605
32	JP Morgan	U.S.	11,261	261,067	963
33	Norinchukin Bank	Japan	10,991	390,213	1,014
34	Industrial Bank of Japan	Japan	10,934	357,347	−1,533
35	Banco Santander	Spain	10,707	179,867	1,386
36	San Paolo-Imi	Italy	10,641	185,871	1,177
37	Groupe Caisse d'Epargne	France	10,121	235,677	422
38	Fortis Bank (proforma)	Belgium	9,879	323,567	1,183
39	Banco Bilbao Vizcaya	Spain	9,731	154,591	1,504
40	UniCredito Italiano	Italy	9,520	172,163	631
41	Fleet Financial Group	U.S.	9,409	104,382	1,532
42	National Australia Bank	Australia	9,372	136,355	1,198
43	Westdeutsche Landesbank	Germany	9,029	403,889	659
44	Abbey National	U.K.	8,995	273,492	1,760
45	Tokai Bank	Japan	8,927	253,618	108
46	Paribas	France	8,371	213,614	978
47	SunTrust Banks	U.S.	8,179	93,170	971
48	Crédit Lyonnais	France	8,103	243,708	382
49	Royal Bank of Canada	Canada	8,033	171,007	1,232
50	Groupe Banques Populaires	France	7,959	191,545	608

Source: Excerpted from *Euromoney*, June 1999, p. 209.

2. *Knowledge advantage*—The foreign bank subsidiary can draw on the parent bank's knowledge of personal contacts and credit investigations for use in that foreign market.
3. *Home nation information services*—Local firms in a foreign market may be able to obtain more complete information on trade and financial markets in the multinational bank's home nation than is otherwise obtainable from foreign domestic banks.
4. *Prestige*—Very large multinational banks have high perceived prestige, liquidity, and deposit safety that can be used to attract clients abroad.
5. *Regulation advantage*—Multinational banks are often not subject to the same regulations as domestic banks. There may be reduced need to publish adequate financial information, lack of required deposit insurance and reserve requirements on foreign currency deposits, and the absence of territorial restrictions (that is, U.S. banks may not be restricted to state of origin).
6. *Wholesale defensive strategy*—Banks follow their multinational customers abroad to prevent the erosion of their clientele to foreign banks seeking to service the multinational's foreign subsidiaries.
7. *Retail defensive strategy*—Mulitnational banks prevent erosion by foreign banks of the traveler's check, tourist, and foreign business market.
8. *Transaction costs*—By maintaining foreign branches and foreign currency balances, banks may reduce transaction costs and foreign exchange risk on currency conversion if government controls can be circumvented.
9. *Growth*—Growth prospects in a home nation may be limited by a market largely saturated with the services offered by domestic banks.
10. *Risk reduction*—Greater stability of earnings is possible with international diversification. Offsetting business and monetary policy cycles across nations reduces the country-specific risk of any one nation.

TYPES OF INTERNATIONAL BANKING OFFICES

The services and operations of international banks are a function of the regulatory environment in which the bank operates and the type of banking facility established. Following is a discussion of the major types of international banking offices, detailing the purpose of each and the regulatory rationale for its existence. The discussion moves from correspondent bank relationships, through which minimal service can be provided to a bank's customers, to a description of offices providing a fuller array of services, to those that have been established by regulatory change for the purpose of leveling the worldwide competitive playing field.[1]

Correspondent Bank

The large banks in the world will generally have a correspondent relationship with other banks in all the major financial centers in which they do not have their own banking operation. A **correspondent bank relationship** is established when two banks maintain a correspondent bank account with one another. For example, a large New York bank will have a correspondent bank account in a London bank, and the London bank will maintain one with the New York bank.

The correspondent banking system enables a bank's MNC client to conduct business worldwide through his local bank or its contacts. Correspondent banking services center around foreign exchange conversions that arise through the international transactions the MNC makes. However, correspondent bank services also include assistance with trade financing, such as honoring letters of credit and accepting drafts drawn on the correspondent bank. Additionally, a MNC needing foreign local financing for one of its subsidiaries may rely on its local bank to provide it with a letter of introduction to the correspondent bank in the foreign country.

The correspondent bank relationship is beneficial because a bank can service its MNC clients at a very low cost and without the need of having bank personnel physically located in many countries. A disadvantage is that the bank's clients may not receive the level of service through the correspondent bank that they would if the bank had its own foreign facilities to service its clients.

Representative Offices

A **representative office** is a small service facility staffed by parent bank personnel that is designed to assist MNC clients of the parent bank in dealings with the bank's correspondents. It is a way for the parent bank to provide its MNC clients with a level of service greater than that provided through merely a correspondent relationship. The parent bank may open a representative office in a country in which it has many MNC clients or at least an important client. Representative offices also assist MNC clients with information about local business practices, economic information, and credit evaluation of the MNC's foreign customers.

Foreign Branches

A **foreign branch bank** operates like a local bank, but legally it is a part of the parent bank. As such, a branch bank is subject to both the banking regulations of its home country and the country in which it operates. U.S. branch banks in foreign countries are regulated from the United States by the Federal Reserve Act and Federal Reserve Regulation K: International Banking Operations, which covers most of the regulations relating to U.S. banks operating in foreign countries and foreign banks operating within the United States.

There are several reasons why a parent bank might establish a branch bank. The primary one is that the bank organization can provide a much fuller range of services for its MNC customers through a branch office than it can through a representative office. For example, branch bank loan limits are based on the capital of the parent bank, not the branch bank. Consequently, a branch bank will likely be able to extend a larger loan to a customer than a locally chartered subsidiary bank of the parent. Additionally, the books of a foreign branch are part of the parent bank's books. Thus, a branch bank system allows customers much faster check clearing than does a correspondent bank network because the debit and credit procedure is handled internally within one organization.

Another reason a U.S. parent bank may establish a foreign branch bank is to compete on a local level with the banks of the host country. Branches of U.S. banks are not subject to domestic reserve requirements on deposits and are not required to have Federal Deposit Insurance Corporation (FDIC) insurance on deposits. Consequently, branch banks are on the same competitive level as local banks in terms of their cost structure in making loans.

Branch banking is the most popular way for U.S. banks to expand operations overseas. Most branch banks are located in Europe, in particular the United Kingdom. Many branch banks are operated as "shell" branches in offshore banking centers, a topic covered later in this section.

The most important piece of legislation affecting the operation of foreign banks in the United States is the International Banking Act of 1978 (IBA). In general, the act specifies that foreign branch banks operating in the United States must comply with U.S. banking regulations just like U.S. banks. In particular, the IBA specifies that foreign branch banks must meet the Fed reserve requirements on deposits and make FDIC insurance available for customer deposits.

Subsidiary and Affiliate Banks

A **subsidiary bank** is a locally incorporated bank that is either wholly owned or owned in major part by a foreign parent. An **affiliate bank** is one that is only partially owned but not controlled by its foreign parent. Both subsidiary and affiliate banks operate under the banking laws of the country in which they are incorporated. U.S. parent banks find subsidiary and affiliate banking structures desirable because they are allowed to underwrite securities.

Foreign-owned subsidiary banks in the United States tend to locate in the states that are major centers of financial activity, as do U.S. branches of foreign parent banks. In the United States, foreign bank offices tend to locate in the highly populous states of New York, California, Illinois, Florida, Georgia, and Texas.[2]

Edge Act Banks

Edge Act banks are federally chartered subsidiaries of U.S. banks that are physically located in the United States that are allowed to engage in a full range of international banking activities. Senator Walter E. Edge of New Jersey sponsored the 1919 amendment to Section 25 of the Federal Reserve Act to allow U.S. banks to be competitive with the services foreign banks could supply their customers. Federal Reserve Regulation K allows Edge Act banks to accept foreign deposits, extend trade credit, finance foreign projects abroad, trade foreign currencies, and engage in investment banking activities with U.S. citizens involving foreign securities. As such, Edge Act banks do not compete directly with the services provided by U.S. commercial banks.

An Edge Act bank is typically located in a state different from that of its parent in order to get around the prohibition on interstate branch banking. However, since 1979, the Federal Reserve has permitted interstate banking by Edge Act banks. Moreover, the IBA permits foreign banks operating in the United States to establish Edge Act banks. Thus, both U.S. and foreign Edge Act banks operate on an equally competitive basis.

Edge Act banks are not prohibited from owning equity in business corporations, as are domestic commercial banks. Thus, it is *through* the Edge Act that U.S. parent banks own foreign banking subsidiaries and have ownership positions in foreign banking affiliates.

Offshore Banking Centers

A significant portion of the external banking activity takes place through offshore banking centers. An **offshore banking center** is a country whose banking system is organized to permit external accounts beyond the normal economic activity of the country. The International Monetary Fund recognizes the Bahamas, Bahrain, the Cayman Islands, Hong Kong, the Netherlands Antilles, Panama, and Singapore as major offshore banking centers.

Offshore banks operate as branches or subsidiaries of the parent bank. The principal features that make a country attractive for establishing an offshore banking operation are virtually total freedom from host-country governmental banking regulations—for example, low reserve requirements and no deposit insurance, low taxes, a favorable time zone that facilitates international banking transactions, and to a minor extent, strict banking secrecy laws. It should not be inferred that offshore host governments tolerate or encourage poor banking practices, as entry is usually confined to the largest and most reputable international banks.

The primary activities of offshore banks are to seek deposits and grant loans in currencies other than the currency of the host government. Offshore banking was spawned in the late 1960s when the Federal Reserve authorized U.S. banks to establish "shell" branches, which need be nothing more than a post office box in the host country. The actual banking transactions were conducted by the parent bank. The purpose was to allow smaller U.S. banks the opportunity to participate in the growing Eurodollar market without having to bear the expense of setting up operations in a major European money center. Today there are hundreds of offshore bank branches and subsidiaries, about one-third operated by U.S. parent banks.[3] Most offshore banking centers continue to serve as locations for shell branches, but Hong Kong and Singapore have developed into full service banking centers that now rival London, New York, and Tokyo.

EXHIBIT 6.2 Organizational Structure of International Banking Offices from the U.S. Perspective

Type of Bank	Physical Location	Accept Foreign Deposits	Make Loans to Foreigners	Engage in Investment Banking	Subject to Fed Reserve Requirements	FDIC Insured Deposits	Separate Legal Equity from Parent
Domestic bank	U.S.	No	No	No	Yes	Yes	No
Correspondent bank	Foreign	N/A	N/A	Yes	No	No	N/A
Representative office	Foreign	No	No	No	Yes	Yes	No
Foreign branch	Foreign	Yes	Yes	No	No	No	No
Subsidiary bank	Foreign	Yes	Yes	Yes	No	No	Yes
Affiliate bank	Foreign	Yes	Yes	Yes	No	No	Yes
Edge Act bank	U.S.	Yes	Yes	Yes	No	No	Yes
Offshore banking center[a]	Technically Foreign	Yes	Yes	No	No	No	No
International banking facility	U.S.	Yes	Yes	No	No	No	No

[a]An offshore bank is frequently established as a branch of the U.S. parent, in which case it is not a separate legal entity, nor eligible to engage in investment banking activities.

International Banking Facilities

In 1981, the Federal Reserve authorized the establishment of **International Banking Facilities (IBF)**. An IBF is a separate set of asset and liability accounts that are segregated on the parent bank's books; it is not a unique physical or legal entity. Any U.S.-chartered depository institution, a U.S. branch or subsidiary of a foreign bank, or a U.S. office of an Edge Act bank may operate an IBF. IBFs operate as foreign banks in the United States. They are not subject to domestic reserve requirements on deposits, nor is FDIC insurance required on deposits. IBFs seek deposits from non-U.S. citizens and can make loans only to foreigners. All nonbank deposits must be nonnegotiable time deposits with a maturity of at least two business days and be of a size of at least $100,000.

IBFs were established largely as a result of the success of offshore banking. The Federal Reserve desired to return a large share of the deposit and loan business of U.S. branches and subsidiaries to the United States. IBFs have been successful in capturing a large portion of the Eurodollar business that was previously handled offshore. However, offshore banking will never be completely eliminated because IBFs are restricted from lending to U.S. citizens, while offshore banks are not.

Exhibit 6.2 summarizes the organizational structure and characteristics of international banking offices from the perspective of the United States.

CAPITAL ADEQUACY STANDARDS

A concern of bank regulators worldwide and of bank depositors is the safety of bank deposits. **Bank capital adequacy** refers to the amount of equity capital and other securities a bank holds as reserves against risky assets to reduce the probability of a bank failure. In a 1988 agreement known as the **Basle Accord**, after the Swiss city in which it is headquartered, the Bank for International Settlements (BIS) established a framework for measuring bank capital adequacy for banks in the Group of Ten countries and Luxembourg. The BIS is the central bank for clearing international transactions between national central banks, and also serves as a facilitator in reaching international banking agreements among its members.

The Basle Agreement called for a minimum bank capital adequacy ratio of 8 percent of risk-weighted assets by year-end 1992 for banks that engage in cross-border transactions. The agreement divides bank capital into two categories: Tier I Core capital, which consists of shareholder equity and retained earnings, and Tier II Supplemental capital, which consists of internationally recognized nonequity items such as preferred stock and subordinated bonds. Supplemental capital is allowed to count for no more than 50 percent of total bank capital, or no more than 4 percent of risk-weighted assets. In determining risk-weighted assets, four categories of risky assets are each weighted differently. More risky assets receive a higher weight. Government obligations are weighted at zero percent, short-term interbank assets are weighted at 20 percent, residential mortgages at 50 percent, and other assets at 100 percent. Thus, a bank with $100 million in each of the four asset categories would have the equivalent of $170 million in risk-adjusted assets. It would need to maintain $13.6 million in capital against these investments, of which no more than one-half of this amount, or $6.8 million, could be Tier II capital.

The 1988 Basle Capital Accord has been widely adopted throughout the world by national bank regulators. Nevertheless, it is not without its critics. National banking supervisors and scholars have made several criticism about the arbitrary nature of the *"rules-based"* Basle Capital Accord. Principal among these has to do with the unchanging 8 percent minimum capital assigned to risk-weighted assets. The argument is that risk is not constant throughout the business cycle. Thus, it may be preferable to require banks to keep more than the 8 percent minimum in the expansionary phase of a business cycle to guard against the more risky operating environment usually associated with an economic downturn. Additionally, the 8 percent minimum was set with the banks of industrial countries in mind. Since 1988, the Basle Capital Accord has been adopted by many developing countries that experience longer and more severe business cycles than do developed countries. Thus, in developing countries, 8 percent capital on risk-weighted assets is probably not adequate.[4]

Recognizing the deficiencies of the 1988 Accord, the Basle Committee has decided to introduce a new capital adequacy framework. Presently the Basle Committee is seeking comments on its proposed approaches. A more definitive proposal is expected in late year 2000. What appears likely is that a new capital adequacy framework will incorporate three pillars: minimum capital requirements, a supervisory review process, and the effective use of market discipline. With respect to the first pillar, a revised method for determining risk-weighted assets will likely be implemented. The proposal calls for reducing risk weights for high-quality corporate credits and the introduction of greater than 100 percent weights for certain low-quality exposures. The second pillar seeks to ensure that a bank's capital position is consistent with its overall risk profile, and will encourage supervisory intervention at the national level with the authority to require capital in excess of the minimum. The third pillar seeks to encourage high disclosure standards to enhance the role that market participants have in encouraging banks to hold adequate capital.[5]

An additional problem with the "rules-based" 1988 Basle Capital Accord has to do with the type of business in which banks now engage. Bank trading in equity, interest rate, and exchange rate derivative products has escalated in recent years. (See Chapters 9 and 10 for a discussion of derivative products.) Many of these products did not exist when the Basle Accord was drafted. Even if one ignores the problems mentioned above with the accord in safeguarding bank depositors from traditional credit risk, the capital adequacy standards are not sufficient to safeguard against the market risk from derivatives trading. For example, Barings Bank, which collapsed in 1995 due in part to the activities of a rogue derivatives trader, was considered to be a safe bank by the Basle capital adequacy standards.

A 1996 amendment to the 1988 accord requires commercial banks engaging in significant trading activity to set aside additional capital to cover the market risks inherent in their trading accounts. The amendment allows sophisticated banks to use internally developed portfolio models to assess adequate capital requirements. That is, instead of using a "rules-based" approach to determining adequate bank capital, a *"risk-focused"* approach that relies on modern portfolio theory may be used. The bank's portfolio is the monetary value of its on- and off-balance sheet trading account positions. Estimating the portfolio standard deviation of return allows the bank's value-at-risk to be calculated. **Value-at-risk (VAR)** is the loss that will be exceeded with a specified probability over a specified time horizon. The amendment requires VAR to be calculated daily according to the criterion that there be only 1 percent chance that the maximum loss over a 10 day time period will exceed the bank's capital. VAR is calculated as VAR = Portfolio Value × Daily Standard Deviation of Return × Confidence Interval Factor × $\sqrt{\text{Horizon}}$. The confidence interval factor is the appropriate z-value from the standard normal density function associated with the maximum level of loss that is tolerable. For example, the 1 percent VAR for a portfolio of $400 million with a daily portfolio standard deviation of .75 percent for a 10-day planning horizon is $22.07 million = $400 million × .0075 × 2.326 × $\sqrt{10}$, where 2.326 is the z-value associated with a one-tail 99 percent confidence interval. That is, there is only a 1 percent chance that the loss during a 10-day period will exceed $22.07 million. Assuming accurate inputs into the VAR formula, the bank would be required to maintain an equivalent amount of capital as an explicit cushion against its price risk exposure.

As an estimate of capital adequacy, VAR is only as good as the accuracy of its inputs. The true portfolio standard deviation is never known and must be estimated. Thus, implementing VAR analysis is subject to the problem of *estimation risk,* or *parameter uncertainty,* to which modern portfolio in general is subject. The Basle Committee is aware of this and other implementation problems. To address them, the capital charge for a bank that uses its own internal proprietary model to estimate VAR is the larger of the previous day's VAR, or three times the average of the daily VAR of the proceeding 60 business days.[6]

INTERNATIONAL MONEY MARKET

Eurocurrency Market

The core of the international money market is the Eurocurrency market. A **Eurocurrency** is a *time* deposit of money in an international bank located in a country different from the country that issued the currency. For example, Eurodollars are deposits of U.S. dollars in banks located outside of the United States, Eurosterling are deposits of British pound sterling in banks outside of the United Kingdom, and Euroyen are deposits of Japanese yen in banks outside of Japan. The prefix *Euro* is somewhat of a misnomer, since the bank in which the deposit is made does not have to be located in Europe. The depository bank could be located in Europe, the Caribbean, or Asia. Indeed, as we saw in the previous section, Eurodollar deposits can be made in offshore shell branches or IBFs, where the physical dollar deposits are actually with the U.S. parent bank. An "Asian dollar" market exists, with headquarters in Singapore, but it can be viewed as a major division of the Eurocurrency market.

The origin of the Eurocurrency market can be traced back to the 1950s and early 1960s, when the former Soviet Union and Soviet-bloc countries sold gold and commodities to raise hard currency. Because of anti-Soviet sentiment, these Communist countries were afraid of depositing their U.S. dollars in U.S. banks for fear that the deposits could be frozen or taken. Instead they deposited their dollars in a French bank whose telex address was EURO-BANK. Since that time, dollar deposits outside the United States have been called Eurodollars and banks accepting Eurocurrency deposits have been called **Eurobanks**.[7]

The Eurocurrency market is an *external* banking system that runs parallel to the *domestic* banking system of the country that issued the currency. Both banking systems seek deposits and make loans to customers from the deposited funds. In the United States, banks are subject to the Federal Reserve Regulation M, specifying reserve requirements on bank time deposits. Additionally, U.S. banks must pay FDIC insurance premiums on deposited funds. Eurodollar deposits, on the other hand, are not subject to these arbitrary reserve requirements or deposit insurance; hence the cost of operations is less. Because of the reduced cost structure, the Eurocurrency market, and in particular the Eurodollar market, has grown spectacularly since its inception.

The Eurocurrency market operates at the *interbank* and/or *wholesale* level. The majority of Eurocurrency transactions are interbank transactions, representing sums of $1,000,000 or more. Eurobanks with surplus funds and no retail customers to lend to will lend to Eurobanks that have borrowers but need loanable funds. The rate charged by banks with excess funds is referred to as the *interbank offered rate*; they will accept interbank deposits at the *interbank bid rate*. The spread is generally $^1/_8$ of 1 percent for most major Eurocurrencies.

London has historically been, and remains, the major Eurocurrency financial center. These days, most people have heard of the **London Interbank Offered Rate (LIBOR)**, the reference rate in London for Eurocurrency deposits. To be clear, there is a LIBOR for Eurodollars, Euro–Canadian dollars, Euroyen, and so on. In other financial centers, other reference rates are used. For example, *SIBOR* is the Singapore Interbank Offered Rate, *PIBOR* is the Paris Interbank Offered Rate, and *BRIBOR* is the Brussels Interbank Offered Rate. Obviously, competition forces the various interbank rates for a particular Eurocurrency to be close to one another.

The advent of the common euro currency on January 1, 1999, among the 11 countries of the European Union comprising the Economic and Monetary Union created a need for a new interbank offered rate designation. It also creates some confusion as to whether one is referring to the common euro currency or another Eurocurrency, such as Eurodollars. Because of this, it is starting to become common practice to refer to *international* currencies instead of Eurocurrencies and *prime* banks instead of Eurobanks. **EURIBOR** is the rate at which interbank deposits of the euro are offered by one prime bank to another in countries that comprise the EMU as well as prime banks in non-EMU EU countries and major prime banks in non-EU countries.

In the wholesale money market, Eurobanks accept Eurocurrency fixed time deposits and issue **negotiable certificates of deposit (NCDs)**. In fact, these are the preferable ways for Eurobanks to raise loanable funds, as the deposits tend to be for a lengthier period and the acquiring rate is often slightly less than the interbank rate. Denominations are at least $500,000, but sizes of $1,000,000 or larger are more typical. Rates on Eurocurrency deposits are quoted for maturities ranging from one day to several years; however, more standard maturities are for 1, 2, 3, 6, 9, and 12 months. Exhibit 6.3 shows sample Eurocurrency interest rates, and Exhibit 6.4 provides a historical perspective of Eurocurrency rates. Appendix 6A illustrates the creation of the Eurocurrency.

Exhibit 6.5 shows the year-end values in billions of U.S. dollars of international bank credit for the years 1994 through 1998. The 1998 column shows that the gross value of international bank credits was $11,048.2 billion and that interbank credits accounted for $5,563.2 billion, or about half the total. The major currencies denominating these were the U.S. dollar, the euro, and the Japanese yen.

Approximately 95 percent of wholesale Eurobank deposits come from fixed time deposits, the remainder from NCDs. There is an interest penalty for the early withdrawal of funds from a fixed time deposit. NCDs, on the other hand, being negotiable, can be sold in the secondary market if the depositor suddenly needs his funds

EXHIBIT 6.3 Eurocurrency Interest Rate Quotations: July 6, 1999

Jul 6	Short Term	7 days Notice	One Month	Three Months	Six Months	One Year
Euro	$2\frac{9}{16}$–$2\frac{1}{2}$	$2\frac{5}{8}$–$2\frac{17}{32}$	$2\frac{5}{8}$–$2\frac{17}{32}$	$2\frac{11}{16}$–$2\frac{5}{8}$	$2\frac{7}{8}$–$2\frac{13}{16}$	$3\frac{1}{32}$–$2\frac{29}{32}$
Danish Krone	$3\frac{1}{8}$–$2\frac{5}{8}$	$2\frac{31}{32}$–$2\frac{7}{8}$	$3\frac{1}{16}$–$2\frac{15}{16}$	$3\frac{3}{16}$–$3\frac{3}{32}$	$3\frac{5}{16}$–$3\frac{3}{16}$	$3\frac{7}{16}$–$3\frac{1}{4}$
Sterling	5–$4\frac{3}{4}$	5–$4\frac{13}{16}$	$5\frac{3}{32}$–$4\frac{31}{32}$	$5\frac{1}{8}$–5	$5\frac{9}{32}$–$5\frac{5}{32}$	$5\frac{7}{16}$–$5\frac{5}{16}$
Swiss Franc	$\frac{29}{32}$–$\frac{17}{32}$	$1\frac{1}{4}$–$1\frac{1}{16}$	$1\frac{5}{32}$–$1\frac{1}{32}$	$1\frac{9}{32}$–$1\frac{1}{8}$	$1\frac{17}{32}$–$1\frac{3}{8}$	$1\frac{13}{16}$–$1\frac{21}{32}$
Canadian Dollar	$4\frac{23}{32}$–$4\frac{19}{32}$	$4\frac{11}{16}$–$4\frac{9}{16}$	$4\frac{3}{4}$–$4\frac{5}{8}$	$4\frac{13}{16}$–$4\frac{5}{8}$	$5\frac{1}{16}$–$4\frac{15}{16}$	$5\frac{1}{4}$–$5\frac{3}{32}$
US Dollar	$5\frac{3}{16}$–$5\frac{1}{16}$	$5\frac{7}{32}$–$5\frac{3}{32}$	$5\frac{7}{32}$–$5\frac{1}{8}$	$5\frac{11}{32}$–$5\frac{1}{4}$	$5\frac{5}{8}$–$5\frac{17}{32}$	$5\frac{13}{16}$–$5\frac{11}{16}$
Japanese Yen	$\frac{1}{16}$–$\frac{1}{32}$	$\frac{1}{8}$–$\frac{1}{32}$	$\frac{1}{8}$–$\frac{1}{32}$	$\frac{1}{8}$–$\frac{1}{32}$	$\frac{5}{32}$–$\frac{1}{16}$	$\frac{3}{16}$–$\frac{3}{32}$
Asian $Sing	$\frac{1}{4}$– –	$2\frac{3}{16}$–1	$1\frac{29}{32}$–$\frac{29}{32}$	$2\frac{3}{16}$–$1\frac{3}{16}$	$2\frac{19}{32}$–$1\frac{11}{16}$	$2\frac{1}{2}$–$2\frac{3}{8}$

Note: Short-term rates are call for the U.S. dollar and yen, others: two days' notice.
Source: *Financial Times,* July 7, 1999, p. 25.

EXHIBIT 6.4 International Short and Long-Term Interest Rates (Weekly averages, in percentages)

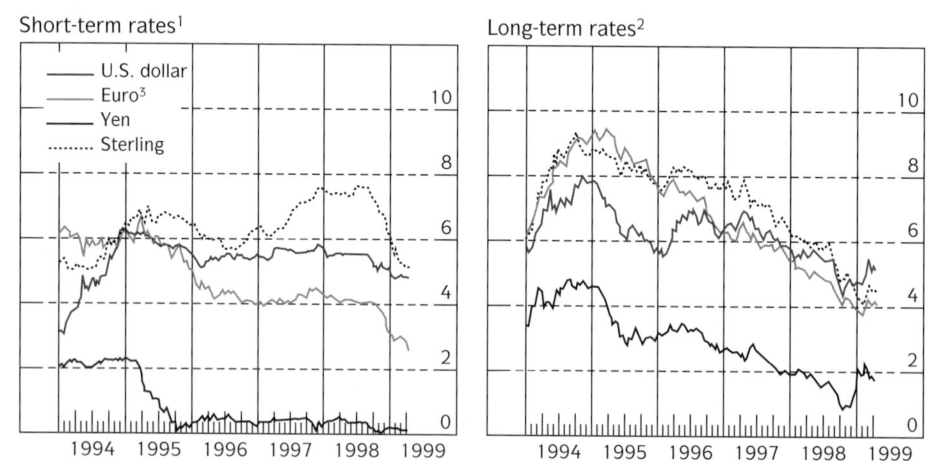

[1]Three-month Euromarket interest rates.
[2]Yields in annual terms on the basis of 10-year benchmark government bonds.
[3]EUC before 1999.
Source: *International Banking and Financial Market Developments,* Bank for International Settlements, June 1999, p. 1. Reprinted with permission.

prior to scheduled maturity. The NCD market began in 1967 in London for Eurodollars. EuroCDs for currencies other than the U.S. dollar are offered by banks in London and in other financial centers, but the secondary market for nondollar NCDs is not very liquid. Eurodollar time deposit rates are greater than the corresponding rates on U.S. domestic time deposits because Eurodollar deposits are not subject to reserve requirements or deposit insurance. In place of reserves, Eurobanks must meet the BIS capital adequacy standards discussed earlier in this chapter.

Eurocredits

Eurocredits are short- to medium-term loans of Eurocurrency extended by Eurobanks to corporations, sovereign governments, nonprime banks, or international organizations. The loans are denominated in currencies other than the home currency of the Eurobank. Because these loans are frequently too large for a single bank to handle, Eurobanks will band together to form a bank lending **syndicate** to share the risk.

The credit risk on these loans is greater than on loans to other banks in the interbank market. Thus, the interest rate on Eurocredits must compensate the bank, or

EXHIBIT 6.5

International Bank Credit (at Year-End in Billions of U.S. Dollars)

	1994	1995	1996	1997	1998
Type Credit					
Gross international bank credit	8,373.0	9,223.6	9,645.5	10,382.7	11,048.2
Interbank credit	4,133.0	4,578.6	4,630.5	5,097.7	5,563.2
Net international bank credit	4240.0	4,645.0	5,015.0	5,285.0	5,485.0

Source: *International Banking and Financial Market Developments.* Bank for International Settlements, p. 11, May 1995; p. 3, May 1996; p. 5, May 1997; p. 6, May 1998; p. 6, June 1999.

EXHIBIT 6.6

Comparison of U.S. Lending and Borrowing Rates with Eurodollar Rates on July 6, 1999[a]

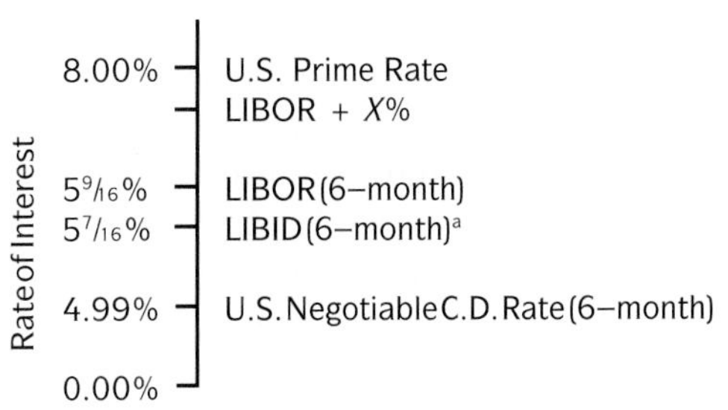

[a]LIBID denotes the London Interbank Bid rate.

banking syndicate, for the added credit risk. On Eurocredits originating in London the base lending rate is LIBOR. The lending rate on these credits is stated as LIBOR $+X$ percent, where X is the lending margin charged depending upon the creditworthiness of the borrower. Additionally, rollover pricing was created on Eurocredits so that Eurobanks do not end up paying more on Eurocurrency time deposits than they earn from the loans. Thus, a Eurocredit may be viewed as a series of shorter term loans, where at the end of each time period (generally three or six months), the loan is rolled over and the base lending rate is repriced to current LIBOR over the next time interval of the loan.

Exhibit 6.6 shows the relationship among the various interest rates we have discussed in this section. The numbers come from the *Money Rates* section of *The Wall Street Journal* (see inside front cover). On July 6, 1999, U.S. domestic banks were paying 4.99 percent for six-month NCDs and the prime lending rate, the base rate charged the bank's most creditworthy corporate clients, was 8.00 percent. This represents a spread of 3.01 percent for the bank to cover operating costs and earn a profit. By comparison, Eurobanks will accept six-month Eurodollar time deposits, say Eurodollar NCDs, at a rate of $5\frac{7}{16}$ percent or less. (We use the London Late Eurodollar bid rate, which is the afternoon closing rate in London on large deposits.) The rate charged for Eurodollar credits is LIBOR + X percent, where any lending margin less than 2.4375 percent makes the Eurodollar loan more attractive than the prime rate loan. Since lending margins typically fall in the range of $\frac{1}{4}$ percent to 3 percent, with the median rate being $\frac{1}{2}$ percent to $1\frac{1}{2}$ percent, the exhibit shows the narrow borrowing-lending spreads of Eurobankers in the Eurodollar credit market.

EXAMPLE 6.1: Rollover Pricing of a Eurocredit Teltrex International can borrow $3,000,000 at LIBOR plus a lending margin of .75 percent per annum on a three-month rollover basis from Barclays in London. Suppose that three-month LIBOR is currently $5\frac{17}{32}$ percent. Further suppose that over the second three-month interval LIBOR falls to 5⅛ percent. How much will Teltrex pay in interest to Barclays over the six-month period for the Eurodollar loan?

Solution: $3,000,000 × (.0553125 + .0075)/4 + $3,000,000 × (.05125 + .0075)/4 = $47,109.38 + $44,062.50 = $91,171.88

Forward Rate Agreements

A major risk Eurobanks face in accepting Eurodeposits and in extending Eurocredits is interest rate risk resulting from a mismatch in the maturities of the deposits and credits. For example, if deposit maturities are longer than credit maturities, and interest rates fall, the credit rates will be adjusted downward while the bank is still paying a higher rate on deposits. Conversely, if deposit maturities are shorter than credit maturities, and interest rates rise, deposit rates will be adjusted upwards while the bank is still receiving a lower rate on credits. Only when deposit and credit maturities are perfectly matched will the rollover feature of Eurocredits allow the bank to earn the desired deposit-loan rate spread.

A **forward rate agreement (FRA)** is an interbank contract that allows the Eurobank to hedge the interest rate risk in mismatched deposits and credits. A FRA involves two parties, a buyer and a seller, where the buyer agrees to pay the seller the increased interest cost on a notional amount if interest rates fall below an agreed rate, and the seller agrees to pay the buyer the increased interest cost if interest rates increase above the agreed rate. FRAs are structured to capture the maturity mismatch in standard-length Eurodeposits and credits. For example, the FRA might be on a six-month interest rate for a six-month period beginning three months from today and ending nine months from today; this would be a "three against nine" FRA. The following time line depicts this FRA example.

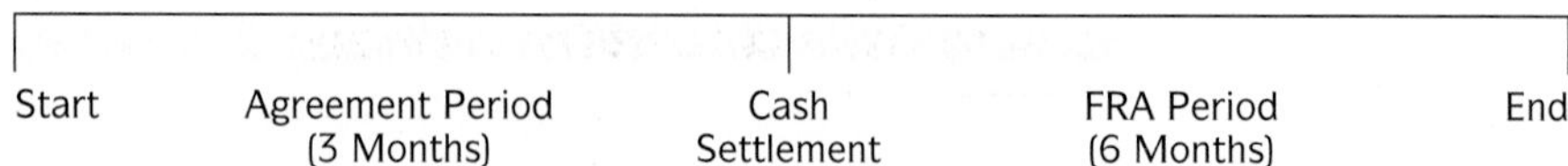

The payment amount under an FRA is calculated as the absolute value of:

Notional Amount × [(*SR* − *AR*) × *days*/360]/[1 + (*SR* × *days*/360)]

where *SR* denotes the settlement rate, *AR* denotes the agreement rate, and *days* denotes the length of the FRA period.

EXAMPLE: 6.2: Three against Six Forward Rate Agreement As an example, consider a bank that has made a three-month Eurodollar loan of $3,000,000 against an offsetting six-month Eurodollar deposit. The bank's concern is that three-month LIBOR will fall below expectations and the Eurocredit is rolled over at the new lower base rate, making the six-month deposit unprofitable.[8] To protect itself, the bank could sell a $3,000,000 "three against six" FRA. The FRA will be priced such that the agreement rate is the expected three-month dollar LIBOR in three months.

Assume *AR* is 6 percent and the actual number of days in the three-month agreement period is 91. Thus, the bank expects to receive $45,500 (= $3,000,000 × .06 × 91/360) as the base amount of interest when the Eurodollar loan is rolled over for a second three-month period. If *SR* (i.e., three-month market LIBOR) is 5⅛ percent, the bank will only receive $38,864.58 in base interest, or a shortfall of $6,635.42. Since *SR* is less than *AR*, the bank will profit from the FRA it sold. It will receive from the buyer in three months a cash settlement at the beginning of the 91-day FRA period equaling the present value of the *absolute* value of [$3,000,000 × (.05125 − .06) × 91/360] = $6,635.42. This *absolute* present value is:

$$\$3{,}000{,}000 \times [(.05125 - .06) \times 91/360]/[1 + (.05125 \times 91/360)]$$
$$= \$6{,}635.42/(1.01295)$$
$$= \$6{,}550.59$$

The sum, $6,550.59, equals the present value as of the *beginning* of the 91-day FRA period of the shortfall of $6,635.42 from the expected Eurodollar loan proceeds that are needed to meet the interest on the Eurodollar deposit. Had *SR* been greater than *AR*, the bank would have paid the buyer the present value of the excess amount of interest above what was expected from rolling over the Eurodollar credit. In this event, the bank would have effectively received the agreement rate on its three-month Eurodollar loan, which would have made the loan a profitable transaction.

FRAs can be used for speculative purposes also. If one believes rates will be less than expected, the sale of an FRA is the suitable position. In contrast, the purchase of an FRA is the suitable position if one believes rates will be greater than expected.

Euronotes

Euronotes are short-term notes underwritten by a group of international investment or commercial banks called a "facility." A client-borrower makes an agreement with a facility to issue Euronotes in its own name for a period of time, generally 3 to 10 years. Euronotes are sold at a discount from face value and pay back the full face value at maturity. Euronotes typically have maturities of from three to six months. Borrowers find Euronotes attractive because the interest expense is usually slightly less—typically LIBOR plus ⅛ percent—in comparison to syndicated Eurobank loans. The banks find them attractive to issue because they earn a small fee from the underwriting or supply the funds and earn the interest return.

Euro-Medium-Term Notes

Euro-medium-term notes (Euro MTNs) are (typically) fixed-rate notes issued by a corporation with maturities ranging from less than a year to about 10 years. Like fixed-rate bonds, Euro-MTNs have a fixed maturity and pay coupon interest on periodic dates. Unlike a bond issue, in which the entire issue is brought to market at once, a Euro-MTN issue is partially sold on a continuous basis through an issuance facility that allows the borrower to obtain funds only as needed on a flexible basis. This feature is very attractive to issuers. Euro-MTNs have become a very popular means of raising medium-term funds since they were first introduced in 1986.

Eurocommercial Paper

Eurocommercial paper, like domestic commercial paper, is an unsecured short-term promissory note issued by a corporation or a bank and placed directly with the investment public through a dealer. Like Euronotes, Eurocommercial paper is sold at a discount from face value. Maturities typically range from one to six months.

The vast majority of Eurocommercial paper is U.S. dollar-denominated. There are, however, a number of differences between the U.S. and Eurocommercial paper markets. The maturity of Eurocommercial paper tends to be about twice as long as U.S. commercial paper. For this reason, the secondary market is more active than for U.S. paper. Additionally, Eurocommercial paper issuers tend to be of much lower quality than their U.S. counterparts; consequently, yields tend to be higher.[9]

Exhibit 6.7 shows the year-end value of the Euronote and Eurocommercial paper market in billions of U.S. dollars for the years 1994 through 1998. The exhibit also shows the year-end value of Euro-medium-term notes for the years 1994 through 1996.

EXHIBIT 6.7

Size of the Euronote Market at Year-End (in Billions of U.S. dollars)

Instrument	1994	1995	1996	1997	1998
Euronotes	32.6	45.5	68.7	73.5	61.6
Euro-Medium-Term Notes	292.0	461.3	662.5	NA	NA
Eurocommercial Paper	81.5	87.0	102.9	110.4	132.9
Total	406.1	593.8	834.1	NA	NA

Source: *International Banking and Financial Market Developments,* Bank for International Settlements, Table 14, p. 46, May 1997; Table 13A, p. 70, June 1999.

Note: In 1998 the Bank for International Settlements stopped detailing statistics for Euro-medium-term notes.

INTERNATIONAL DEBT CRISIS

Certain principles define sound banking behavior. "At least five of these principles—namely, avoid an undue concentration of loans to single activities, individuals, or groups; expand cautiously into unfamiliar activities; know your counterparty; control mismatches between assets; and beware that your collateral is not vulnerable to the same shocks that weaken the borrower—remain as relevant today as in earlier times."[10] Nevertheless, violation of the first two of these principles by some of the largest international banks in the world was responsible for the **international debt crisis** (sometimes called the Third World debt crisis), which was caused by lending to the sovereign governments of some **less-developed countries (LDCs).**

History

The international debt crisis began on August 20, 1982, when Mexico asked more than 100 U.S. and foreign banks to forgive its $68 billion in loans. Soon Brazil, Argentina, and more than 20 other developing countries announced similar problems in making the debt service on their bank loans. At the height of the crisis, Third World countries owed $1.2 *trillion*!

For years it appeared as if the crisis might bring down some of the world's largest banks. On average in 1989, the World Bank estimates that 19 LDCs had debt outstanding equivalent to 53.6 percent of GNP. Interest payments alone amounted to 22.3 percent of export income. The international banking community was obviously shaken.

The source of the international debt crisis was oil. In the early 1970s, the Organization of Petroleum Exporting Countries (OPEC) became the dominant supplier of oil worldwide. Throughout this time period, OPEC raised oil prices dramatically. As a result of these price rises, OPEC amassed a tremendous amount of U.S. dollars, which was the currency generally demanded as payment from the oil-importing countries.

OPEC deposited billions in Eurodollar deposits; by 1976 the deposits amounted to nearly $100 billion. Eurobanks were faced with a huge problem of lending these funds in order to generate interest income to pay the interest on the deposits. Third World countries were only too eager to assist the eager Eurobankers in accepting Eurodollar loans that could be used for economic development *and* for payment of oil imports. The lending process became circular and known as *petrodollar recycling*: Eurodollar loan proceeds were used to pay for new oil imports; some of the oil revenues from developed and LDCs were redeposited, and the deposits were relent to Third World borrowers.

OPEC raised oil prices again in the late 1970s. The high oil prices were accompanied by high inflation and high unemployment in the industrialized countries. Tight monetary policies instituted in a number of the major industrialized countries led to a

EXHIBIT 6.8

Ten Biggest U.S. Bank Lenders to Mexico (in Billions of U.S. Dollars as of September 30, 1987)

Bank	Outstanding to Mexico	Loan Loss Reserves for Developing Country Loans
Citicorp	$2.900	$3.432
BankAmerica Corp.	2.407	1.808
Manufacturers Hanover Corp.	1.883	1.833*
Chemical New York Corp.	1.733	1.505*
Chase Manhattan Corp.	1.660	1.970
Bankers Trust New York Corp.	1.277	1.000
J. P. Morgan & Co.	1.137	1.317
First Chicago Corp.	0.898	0.930
First Interstate Bancorp.	0.689	0.500
Wells Fargo & Co.	0.587	0.760

*As of June 30, 1987.

Source: *The Wall Street Journal*, December 30, 1987. Reprinted by permission of *The Wall Street Journal*, © 1987 Dow Jones & Company, Inc. All Rights Reserved Worldwide.

global recession and a decline in the demand for commodities, such as oil, and in commodity prices. The same economic policies led to higher real interest rates, which increased the borrowing costs of the LDCs, since most of the bank borrowing was denominated in U.S. dollars and had been made on a floating-rate basis. The collapse of commodity prices and the resultant loss of income made it impossible for the LDCs to meet their debt service obligations. As an indication of the magnitude of the involvement of some of the banks in LDC loans at the height of the crisis, Exhibit 6.8 lists the 10 largest U.S. bank lenders *just* to Mexico.

Why would the international banks make such risky loans to LDC sovereign governments in the first place? One reason obviously was that they held vast sums of money in Eurodollar deposits that needed to be quickly placed to start producing interest income. Banks were simply too eager and not careful enough in analyzing the risks they were undertaking in lending to unfamiliar borrowers. Additionally, many U.S. banks claim that there was official *arm-twisting* from Washington to assist the economic development of the Third World countries. Nevertheless, had the bankers and Washington policymakers been better versed in economic history, perhaps the LDC debt crisis might have been avoided, or at least mitigated. The International Finance in Practice box on the next page presents an article documenting a clear warning by David Hume, the 18th-century Scottish economist, about the dangers of sovereign lending.

Debt-for-Equity Swaps

In the midst of the LDC debt crisis, a secondary market developed for LDC debt at prices discounted significantly from face value. The secondary market consisted of approximately 50 creditor banks, investment banks, and boutique market makers. The LDC debt was purchased for use in **debt-for-equity swaps**. As part of debt rescheduling agreements among the bank lending syndicates and the debtor nations, creditor banks would sell their loans for U.S. dollars at discounts from face value to MNCs desiring to make equity investment in subsidiaries or local firms in the LDCs. A LDC central bank would buy the bank debt from a MNC at a smaller discount than the MNC paid, but in local currency. The MNC would use the local currency to make preapproved new investment in the LDC that was economically or socially beneficial to the LDC and its populace.

Exhibit 6.9 diagrams a hypothetical debt-for-equity swap. The exhibit shows a MNC purchasing $100 million of Mexican debt (either directly or through a market maker) from a creditor bank for $60 million, that is, at a 40 percent discount from face value. The MNC then redeems the $100 million note from the Mexican central

INTERNATIONAL FINANCE IN PRACTICE

LDC Lenders Should Have Listened to David Hume

David Hume, the 18th-century Scottish philosopher-economist, is known for formulating (1) the price-specie flow mechanism of balance-of-payments adjustment, (2) the doctrine of the neutrality of money, and (3) the classical theory of interest. Not so well known are his remarks on the external debt of sovereign nations. More's the pity. For those remarks, as contained in his 1752 essay "Of Public Credit," are particularly apropos to the current problem of Third World debt. Had modern policy makers and bankers heeded his words, they might have avoided the sorry sequence of overlending, overborrowing, debt mismanagement, waste and potential default that he foresaw.

Hume thought no good could result from borrowing:

If the abuses of treasures [held by the state] be dangerous by engaging the state in rash enterprizes in confidence of its riches; the abuses of mortgaging are more certain and inevitable; poverty, impotence, and subjection to foreign powers.

Nations, presuming they can find the necessary lenders, are tempted to borrow without limit and to squander the funds on unproductive projects:

It is very tempting to a minister to employ such an expedient as enables him to make a great figure during his administration without overburthening the people with taxes or exciting any immediate clamorous against himself. The practice, therefore, of contracting debt will almost infallibly be abused in every government. It would scarcely be more imprudent to give a prodigal son a credit in every banker's shop in London than to empower a statesman to draw bills in this manner upon posterity.

Eventually, however, interest must be paid and the burden of debt service charges will fall heavily on the poor:

The taxes which are levied to pay the interest of these debts are . . . an oppression on the poorer sort.

Those same taxes "hurt commerce and discourage industry" and thus inhibit economic development and condemn the borrowing nation to continuing poverty. The debt burden will also pauperize the prosperous merchant and landowning classes that constitute the main bulwark of political freedom and stability. With the pauperization of the middle class:

No expedient at all remains for resisting tyranny: Elections are swayed by bribery and corruption alone: And the

EXHIBIT 6.9

Debt-for-Equity Swap Illustration

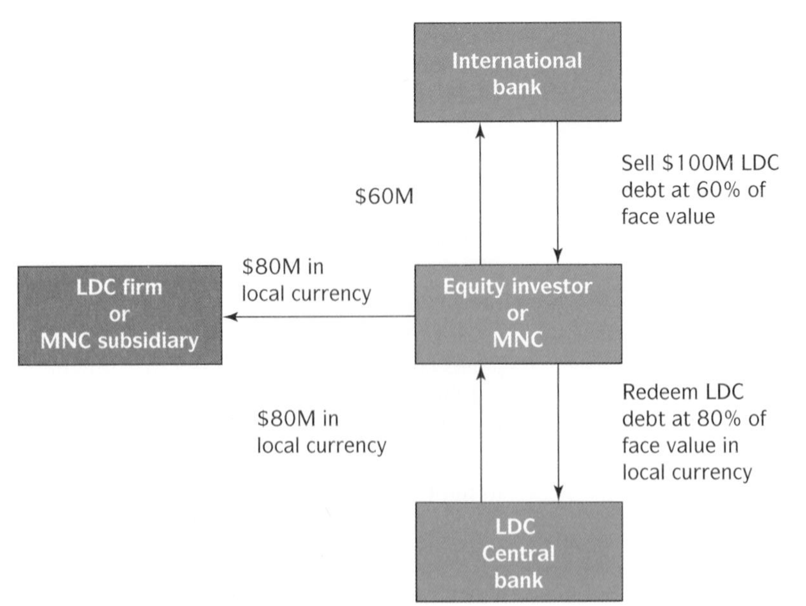

middle power between king and people being totally removed, a grievous despotism must infallibly prevail. The landowners [and merchants] despised for their oppressions, will be utterly unable to make any opposition to it.

Can one imagine a more accurate assessment of the political situation in many Third World debtor nations?

Hume even foresaw the emigration of capital and labor to escape the burden of servicing debt held by foreign banks. Referring to England, then an underdeveloped nation, he said:

As foreigners possess a great share of our national funds, they render the public, in a manner tributary to them, and may in time occasion by transport of our people and our industry.

As a country's debt expands, it eventually exceeds the taxable capacity to service it. Once this constraint is reached, Hume foresaw attempts to repudiate the debt. Contrary to Walter Wriston's dictum that sovereign nations never default, Hume argued that they would act on the belief that "either the nation must destroy public credit, or public credit will destroy the nation."

Such default, he thought, would hurt a nation's credit only temporarily. So forgetful and gullible are foreign banks that they would soon offer loans on the same generous terms and debt would flourish as before:

So great dupes are the generality of mankind that notwithstanding such a violent shock to public credit as a voluntary bankruptcy in England would occasion, it would not probably be long ere credit would again revive in as flourishing a condition as before.

Forget rational expectations, said Hume; nobody behaves rationally all the time. People are destined to be fooled over and over again:

Mankind are in all ages caught by the same baits: The same tricks played over and over again still trepan them. The heights of popularity and patriotism are still the beaten road to power and tyranny; flattery to treachery; standing armies to arbitrary governments; and the glory of God to the temporal interest of the clergy.

Because of the gullibility of lenders, "the fear of an everlasting destruction of credit . . . is a needless bugbear." In fact, a nation that has just defaulted may be a better credit risk than one that has not yet done so:

A opulent knave . . . is a preferable debtor to an honest bankrupt: For the former, in order to carry on business, may find it his interest to discharge his debts where they are not exorbitant: The latter has it not in his power.

Hume's advice to would-be creditors: Lend sparingly. For once a country has borrowed beyond its taxable capacity, it will be tempted to default. From the debtor's viewpoint, debt repudiation may seem less costly than bleeding the nation dry in a vain effort to service the debt.

Hume, although prescient, was hardly infallible. He predicted that England would default on its large and rising debt within 50 years. His prediction was never realized. England's debt-service capacity exceeded his estimate.

Source: *The Wall Street Journal*, February 21, 1989, p. A20. Reprinted by permission of *The Wall Street Journal*,
© 1989 Dow Jones & Company, Inc. All Rights Reserved Worldwide.

bank for the equivalent of $80 million in Mexican pesos at the current exchange rate. The Mexican pesos are invested in a Mexican subsidiary of the MNC or in an equity position in an LDC firm. The MNC has paid $60 million for $80 million in Mexican pesos.

During the midst of the LDC debt crisis, Latin American debt was going at an average discount of approximately 70 percent. The September 10, 1990, issue of *Barron's* quotes Brazilian sovereign debt at 21.75 cents per dollar, Mexican debt at 43.12 cents, and Argentinean debt at only 14.25 cents.

Real-life examples of debt-for-equity swaps abound. Chrysler invested $100 million in pesos in Chrysler de Mexico from money obtained from buying Mexican debt at a 56 percent discount. Volkswagen paid $170 million for $283 million in Mexican debt, which it swapped for the equivalent of $260 million of pesos. In a more complicated deal, CitiBank, acting as a market maker, paid $40 million to another bank for $60 million of Mexican debt, which was swapped with Banco de Mexico, the Mexican central bank, for $54 million worth of pesos later used by Nissan to expand a truck plant outside of Mexico City.

Who benefits from a debt-for-equity swap? All parties are presumed to, or else the swap would not have taken place. The creditor bank benefits from getting an unproductive loan off its books and at least a portion of the principal repaid. The market maker obviously benefits from earning the bid-ask spread on the discounted loan amount. The LDC benefits in two ways. The first benefit comes from being able to pay off a "hard" currency loan (generally at a discount from face value) on which it cannot meet the debt service with its own local currency. The second benefit comes from the new productive investment made in the country, which was designed to foster economic growth. The equity investor benefits from the purchase of LDC local currency needed to make the investment at a discount from the current exchange rate.

Third World countries have only been open to allowing debt-for-equity swaps for certain types of investment. The LDC obtains the local currency to redeem the hard currency loan by printing it. This obviously increases the country's money supply and is inflationary. Thus, LDCs have only allowed swaps where the benefits of the new equity investment were expected to be greater than the harm caused to the economy by increased inflation. Acceptable types of investments have been in:

1. Export-oriented industries, such as automobiles, that will bring in hard currency.
2. High-technology industries that will lead to larger exports, improve the technological base of the country, and develop the skills of its people.
3. Tourist industry, such as resort hotels, that will increase tourism and visitors bringing hard currency.
4. Low-income housing developments that will improve the standard of living of some of the populace.

The Solution: Brady Bonds

Today, most debtor nations and creditor banks would agree that the international debt crisis is effectively over. U.S. Treasury Secretary Nicholas F. Brady of the Bush administration is largely credited with designing a strategy in the spring of 1989 to resolve the problem. Brady's solution was to offer creditor banks one of three alternatives: (1) convert their loans to marketable bonds with a face value equal to 65 percent of the original loan amount; (2) convert the loans into collateralized bonds with a reduced interest rate of 6.5 percent; or, (3) lend additional funds to allow the debtor nations to get on their feet. As one can imagine, few banks chose the third alternative. The second alternative called for extending the debt maturities by 25 to 30 years and the purchase by the debtor nation of zero-coupon U.S. Treasury bonds with a corresponding maturity to guarantee the bonds and make them marketable. These bonds have come to be called **Brady bonds**.

By 1992, Brady bond agreements had been negotiated in many countries, including Argentina, Brazil, Mexico, Uruguay, Venezuela, Nigeria, and the Philippines. By August of 1992, 12 of 16 major debtor nations had reached refinancing agreements accounting for 92 percent of their outstanding private bank debt. In total, over $100 billion in bank debt has been converted to Brady bonds.

The Asian Crisis

As noted in Chapter 2, the Asian crisis began in mid-1997 when Thailand devalued the baht. Subsequently other Asian countries devalued their currencies by letting them float—ending their pegged value with the U.S. dollar. Not since the LDC debt crisis have international financial markets experienced such widespread turbulence. The troubles, which began in Thailand, soon affected other countries in the region and also emerging markets in other regions.[11]

Interestingly, the Asian crisis followed a period of economic expansion in the region financed by record private capital inflows. Bankers from the G-10 countries actively sought to finance the growth opportunities in Asia by providing businesses in the region with a full assortment of products and services. Domestic price bubbles in East Asia, particularly in real estate, were fostered by these capital inflows. The simultaneous liberalization of financial markets contributed to bubbles in financial asset prices as well. Additionally, the close interrelationships common among commercial firms and financial institutions in Asia resulted in poor investment decision making.

The risk exposure of the lending banks in East Asia was primarily to local banks and commercial firms, and not to sovereignties, as in the LDC debt crisis. It may have been implicitly assumed, however, that the governments would come to the rescue of their private banks should financial problems develop. The history of managed growth in the region at least suggested that the economic and financial system, as an integral unit, could be managed in an economic downturn. This did not turn out to be the case. The Asian crisis is the most recent, but yet another, example of banks making a multitude of poor loans.

It is doubtful if the international debt crisis or the Asian crisis has taught banks a lasting lesson about the risks of lending to sovereign governments or large amount of funds targeted to specific regions of the world. For some reason, bankers always seem willing to lend huge amounts to borrowers with a limited potential to repay. Regardless, there is no excuse for not properly evaluating the potential risks of an investment or loan. When lending to a sovereign government or making loans to private parties in distant parts of the world, the risks are unique, and a proper analysis of the economic, political, and social factors that constitute **political risk** is warranted. While this subject might fit nicely with the current discussion, we leave it instead for the next chapter on the international bond market and Chapter 15 on direct foreign investment.

SUMMARY

In this chapter, the topics of international banking, the international money market, and the Third World debt crisis were discussed. This chapter begins the textbook's six-chapter sequence on world financial markets and institutions.

1. International banks can be characterized by the types of services they provide. International banks facilitate the imports and exports of their clients by arranging trade financing. They also arrange foreign currency exchange, assist in hedging exchange rate exposure, trade foreign exchange for their own account, and make a market in currency derivative products. Some international banks seek deposits of foreign currencies and make foreign currency loans to nondomestic bank customers. Additionally, some international banks may participate in the underwriting of international bonds if banking regulations allow.
2. Various types of international banking offices include correspondent bank relationships, representative offices, foreign branches, subsidiaries and affiliates, Edge Act banks, offshore banking centers, and International Banking Facilities. The reasons for the various types of international banking offices and the services they provide vary considerably.
3. The core of the international money market is the Eurocurrency market. A Eurocurrency is a time deposit of money in an international bank located in a country different from the country that issued the currency. For example, Eurodollars, which make up the largest part of the market, are deposits of U.S. dollars in banks outside of the United States. The Eurocurrency market is headquartered in London. Eurobanks are international banks that seek Eurocurrency deposits and make Eurocurrency loans. The chapter illustrated the creation of Eurocurrency and discussed the nature of Eurocredits, or Eurocurrency loans.
4. Other main international money market instruments include forward rate agreements, Euronotes, Euro-medium-term notes, and Eurocommercial paper.
5. Capital adequacy refers to the amount of equity capital and other securities a bank holds as reserves against risky assets to reduce the probability of a bank failure. The BIS 1988 Basle Capital Accord establishes a "rules-based" framework establishing the capital charge to safeguard depositors. This framework has been widely adopted throughout the world by national bank regulators. Nevertheless, it will likely be modified in the near future to eliminate

some deficiencies. Moreover, the accord is not sufficient to safeguard against the market risk from derivatives trading by banks, which has grown rapidly in recent years. A 1996 amendment to the accord develops a "risk-focused" approach to capital adequacy for protection against the price risk exposure of its trading accounts. The amendment requires banks to determine their value-at-risk (VAR) according to the criterion that there be only a 1 percent chance that the maximum loss over a 10-day time period will exceed the bank's capital.

6. The international debt crisis was caused by international banks lending more to Third World sovereign governments than they should have. The crisis began during the 1970s when OPEC countries flooded banks with huge sums of Eurodollars that needed to be lent to cover the interest being paid on the deposits. Because of a subsequent collapse in oil prices, high unemployment, and high inflation, many less-developed countries could not afford to meet the debt service on their loans. The huge sums involved jeopardized some of the world's largest banks, in particular U.S. banks that had lent most of the money. Debt-for-equity swaps were one means by which some banks shed themselves of problem Third World debt. But the main solution was collateralized Brady bonds, which allowed the less-developed countries to reduce the debt service on their loans and extend the maturities far into the future.
7. The Asian crisis began in mid-1997. The troubles, which began in Thailand, soon affected other countries in the region and also emerging markets in other regions. Not since the LDC debt crisis have international financial markets experienced such widespread turbulence. The crisis followed a period of economic expansion in the region financed by record private capital inflows. Bankers from industrialized countries actively sought to finance the growth opportunities. The risk exposure of the lending banks in East Asia was primarily to local banks and commercial firms, and not to sovereignties, as in the LDC debt crisis. Nevertheless, the political and economic risks were not correctly assessed. The Asian crisis is the most recent example of commercial banks making a multitude of poor loans.

KEY WORDS

affiliate bank, 132
bank capital adequacy, 134
Basle Accord, 134
Brady bonds, 146
correspondent bank relationship, 131
debt-for-equity swap, 143
Edge Act bank, 133
Euro-medium-term note (Euro-MTN), 141
Eurobank, 136
Eurocommercial paper, 141
Eurocredit, 138
Eurocurrency, 136
Euronote, 141
Euro Interbank Offered Rate (EURIBOR), 137
foreign branch bank, 132
forward rate agreement (FRA), 140
full service bank, 129
International Banking Facility (IBF), 134
international debt crisis, 142
less-developed country (LDCs), 142
London Interbank Offered Rate (LIBOR), 137
merchant bank, 129
negotiable certificate of deposit (NCD), 137
offshore banking center, 133
political risk, 147
representative office, 132
subsidiary bank, 132
syndicate, 138
universal bank, 129
value-at-risk, 136

QUESTIONS

1. Briefly discuss some of the services that international banks provide their customers and the marketplace.
2. Briefly discuss the various types of international banking offices.

3. How does the deposit-loan rate spread in the Eurodollar market compare with the deposit-loan rate spread in the domestic U.S. banking system? Why?
4. What is the difference between the Euronote market, the Euro-medium-term-note market, and the Eurocommercial paper market?
5. Briefly discuss the cause and the solution(s) to the international bank crisis involving less-developed countries.
6. What warning did David Hume, the 18th-century Scottish philosopher-economist, give about lending to sovereign governments?

PROBLEMS

1. Grecian Tile Manufacturing of Athens, Georgia, borrows $1,500,000 at LIBOR plus a lending margin of 1.25 percent per annum on a six-month rollover basis from a London bank. If six-month LIBOR is 4½ percent over the first six-month interval and 5⅜ percent over the second six-month interval, how much will Grecian Tile pay in interest over the first year of its Eurodollar loan?
2. A bank sells a "three against nine" $3,000,000 FRA for a six-month period beginning three months from today and ending nine months from today. The purpose of the FRA is to cover the interest rate risk caused by the maturity mismatch from having made a three-month Eurodollar loan and having accepted a nine-month Eurodollar deposit. The agreement rate with the buyer is 5.5 percent. There are actually 183 days in the six-month period. Assume that three months from today the settlement rate is 4⅞ percent. Determine how much the FRA is worth and who pays who—the buyer pays the seller or the seller pays the buyer.
3. Assume the settlement rate in problem 2 is 6⅛ percent. What is the solution now?
4. The Fisher effect (Chapter 5) suggests that nominal interest rates differ between countries because of differences in the respective rates of inflation. According to the Fisher effect and your examination of the long-term and short-term Eurocurrency interest rates presented in Exhibit 6.4, order the five countries from highest to lowest in terms of the size of the inflation premium embedded in the nominal interest rates for 1998.
5. A bank has a $500 million portfolio of investments and bank credits. The daily standard deviation of return on this portfolio is 0.666 percent. Capital adequacy standards require the bank to maintain capital equal to its VAR calculated over a 10-day holding period. What is the capital charge for the bank?

MINI CASE

Detroit Motors' Latin American Expansion

It is September 1990 and Detroit Motors of Detroit, Michigan, is considering establishing an assembly plant in Latin America for a new utility vehicle it has just designed. The cost of the capital expenditures has been estimated at $65,000,000. There is not much of a sales market in Latin America, and virtually all output would be exported to the United States for sale. Nevertheless, an assembly plant in Latin America is attractive for at least two reasons. First, labor costs are expected to be half what Detroit Motors would have to pay in the United States to union workers. Since the assembly plant will be a new facility for a newly designed vehicle, Detroit Motors does not expect any hassle from its U.S. union in establishing the plant in Latin America. Secondly, the chief financial officer (CFO) of Detroit Motors believes that a debt-for-equity swap can be arranged with a least one of the Latin American countries that has not been able to meet its debt service on its sovereign debt with some of the major U.S. banks.

The September 10, 1990, issue of *Barron's* indicated the following prices (cents on the dollar) on Latin American bank debt:

Brazil	21.75
Mexico	43.12
Argentina	14.25
Venezuela	46.25
Chile	70.25

The CFO is not comfortable with the level of political risk in Brazil and Argentina, and has decided to eliminate them from consideration. After some preliminary discussions with the central banks of Mexico, Venezuela, and Chile, the CFO has learned that all three countries would be interested in hearing a detailed presentation about the type of facility Detroit Motors would construct, how long it would take, the number of locals that would be employed, and the number of units that would be manufactured per year. Since it is time-consuming to prepare and make these presentations, the CFO would like to approach the most attractive candidate first. He has learned that the central bank of Mexico will redeem its debt at 80 percent of face value in a debt-for-equity swap, Venezuela at 75 percent, and Chile 100 percent. As a first step, the CFO decides an analysis based purely on financial considerations is necessary to determine which country looks like the most viable candidate. You are asked to assist in the analysis. What do you advise?

ENDNOTES

1. Much of the discussion in this section follows Hultman (1990).
2. See Goldberg and Grosse (1994).
3. See Chapter 10 of Hultman (1990) for an excellent discussion of the development of offshore banking and international banking facilities.
4. The information in this paragraph is from *International Capital Markets: Developments, Prospects, and Key Policy Issues* (International Monetary Fund, Washington, D.C.), September 1998, pp. 138–41.
5. The information in this paragraph is from *A New Capital Adequacy Framework,* Bank for International Settlements, June 1999.
6. The information about the 1996 amendment is from the *Amendment to the Capital Accord of July 1988,* Bank for International Settlements, January 1996.
7. See Rivera-Batiz and Rivera-Batiz (1994) for an account of the historical origin of the Eurocurrency market.
8. Consistent with the Unbiased Expectations Hypothesis (UEH), the agreement rate *AR* is the expected rate at the beginning of the FRA period. For example, in a "three against six" FRA, the *AR* can be calculated from the forward rate that ties together current three-month LIBOR and six-month LIBOR:

   $$([1 + (6 \text{ mth LIBOR})(T_2/360)]/[1 + (3 \text{ mth LIBOR})(T_1/360)] - 1) \times 360/(T_2 - T_1)$$
   $$= f \times 360/(T_2 - T_1) = AR,$$

   where T_2 and T_1 are, respectively, the actual number of days to maturity of the six-month and three-month Eurocurrency periods and f is the forward rate. See Chapter 15 of Bodie, Kane, and Marcus (1999) for an in-depth discussion of the UEH.
9. See Dufey and Giddy (1994) for a list of the differences between the U.S. and Eurocommercial paper markets.
10. The quotation is from *International Capital Markets: Part II. Systematic Issues in International Finance* (International Monetary Fund, Washington, D.C.), August 1993, p. 2.

11. The discussion in this section closely follows the discussion on the Asian crisis found in *International Capital Markets: Developments, Prospects, and Key Policy Issues* (International Monetary Fund, Washington, D.C.), September 1998, pp. 1–6 and the Bank for International Settlements working paper titled "Supervisory Lessons to Be Drawn from the Asian Crisis," June 1999.

WEB RESOURCES

www.bis.org

This is the official Website of the Bank for International Settlements. It is quite extensive. One can download many papers on international bank policies and reports containing statistics on international banks, capital markets, and derivative securities markets. There is also Web page that provides a link to the Website of most central banks in the world.

www.euribor.org

This Website provides a brief history of the Euro common currency and a discussion of EURIBOR.

www.riskmetrics.com

This is a Website of J. P. Morgan, one of the pioneers in applying value-at-risk techniques. It has a subsite devoted to educational matters. For example, interested students can take an on-line course on market and credit risk management called "Managing Risk."

REFERENCES AND SUGGESTED READINGS

Bank for International Settlements. *Amendment to the Capital Accord of July 1988.* Basle: Bank for International Settlements, January 1996.

Bank for International Settlements. *A New Capital Adequacy Framework.* Basle: Bank for International Settlements, June 1999.

Bank for International Settlements. *Supervisory Lessons to Be Drawn from the Asian Crisis.* Basle: Bank for International Settlements, June 1999.

Baughn, William H., and Donald R. Mandich. *The International Banking Handbook*. Burr Ridge, Ill.: Dow-Jones Irwin, 1983.

Barry, Andrew. "The Lust for Latin Debt: Yield-Seeking Funds Downplay Perils in Brady Bonds." *Barron's*, August 16, 1993.

Beder, Tanya Styblo. "VAR: Seductive but Dangerous." *Financial Analysts Journal,* September/October (1995), pp. 12–24.

Bodie, Zvi, Alex Kane, and Alan J. Marcus. *Investments*, 4th ed. Boston: Irwin/McGraw Hill, 1999.

Chung, Sam Y. "Portfolio Risk Measurement: A Review of Value at Risk." *Journal of Alternative Investments* Summer (1999), pp. 34–42.

Deak, Nicholas L., and JoAnne Celusak. *International Banking*. New York: New York Institute of Finance, 1984.

Dufey, Gunter, and Ian Giddy. *The International Money Market*, 2nd ed. Englewood Cliffs, NJ: Prentice Hall, 1994.

Eng, Maximo V., Francis A. Lees, and Laurence J. Maurer. *Global Finance,* 2nd ed. Reading, MA: Addison-Wesley, 1998.

Feldstein, Martin. "A Wrong Turn in LDC Debt Management." *The Wall Street Journal*, March 5, 1989.

Goldberg, Lawrence G., and Robert Grosse. "Location Choice of Foreign Banks in the United States." *Journal of Economics and Business* 46 (1994), pp. 367–79.

Hultman, Charles W. *The Environment of International Banking*. Englewood Cliffs, NJ: Prentice Hall, 1990.

International Monetary Fund. *International Capital Markets: Part I. Exchange Rate Management and International Capital Flows.* Washington, D.C.: International Monetary Fund, April 1993.

International Monetary Fund. *International Capital Markets: Part II. Systemic Issues in International Finance.* Washington, D.C.: International Monetary Fund, August 1993.

International Monetary Fund. *International Capital Markets: Developments, Prospects, and Policy Issues.* Washington, D.C.: International Monetary Fund, September 1994.

International Monetary Fund. *International Capital Markets: Developments, Prospects, and Policy Issues.* Washington, D.C.: International Monetary Fund, August 1995.

International Monetary Fund. *International Capital Markets: Developments, Prospects, and Key Policy Issues.* Washington, D.C.: International Monetary Fund, September 1998.

Johansson, Frederik, Michael J. Seiler, and Mikael Tjarnberg. "Measuring Downside Portfolio Risk." *Journal of Portfolio Management,* Fall (1999), pp. 96–107.

Jorion, Phillipe. "Risk^2: Measuring the Risk in Value at Risk." *Financial Analysts Journal,* November/December (1996). Pp. 47–56.

Ju, Xiongwei and Neil Pearson. "Using Value-at-Risk to Control Risk Taking: How Wrong Can You Be?" *Journal of Risk* 1 (1999), pp. 5–36.

Lopez, Jose. "Regulatory Evaluation of Value-at-Risk." *Journal of Risk* 1 (1999), pp. 37–63.

Marton, Andrew. "The Debate Over Debt-for-Equity Swaps." *Institutional Investor*, February 1987, pp. 177–80.

"A Mexican Standoff on the Debt Crisis, 1982." *The Wall Street Journal*, November 30, 1989.

Mulford, David C. "Moving Beyond the Latin Debt Crisis," *The Wall Street Journal*, August 21, 1992.

Pool, John C., and Stephen C. Stamos, Jr. *International Economic Policy*. Lexington, Mass.: Lexington Books, 1989.

Reimer, Bianca. "A Way to Turn Debt from a Burden to a Boon." *Business Week*, December 22, 25, and 28, 1986.

Rivera-Batiz, Francisco L., and Luis Rivera-Batiz. *International Finance and Open Economy Macroeconomics*. 2nd ed. Upper Saddle River, NJ: Prentice Hall, 1994.

Rugman, Alan M., and Shyan J. Kamath. "International Diversification and Multinational Banking." In Sarkis J. Khoury and Alo Ghosh, eds., *Recent Developments in International Banking and Finance*. Lexington, Mass.: Lexington Books, 1987.

Saunders, Anthony. *Financial Institutions Management,* 3rd ed. Boston: Irwin/McGraw-Hill, 2000.

Shirreff, David. "Danger—Kids at Play." *Euromoney,* March (1995), pp. 43–46.

Shirreff, David. "Risk Scientists Look beyond their Silos." *Euromoney,* May (1999), pp. 32–33.

Smith, Roy C. and Ingo Walter. *Global Banking.* New York: Oxford University Press, 1997.

"Swap Shop: The Whys and Ways of the Market in LDC." *Barron's*, September 4, 1989.

Torres, Craig. " 'Bridge' Loans to Latin America Rise, But Some Wonder If the Toll Is Too High." *The Wall Street Journal*, August 25, 1993.

APPENDIX 6A

Eurocurrency Creation

As an illustration, consider the following simplified example of the creation of Eurodollars. Assume a U.S. Importer purchases \$100 of merchandise from a German Exporter and pays for the purchase by drawing a \$100 check on his U.S. checking account (demand deposit). Further assume the German Exporter deposits the \$100 check received as payment in a demand deposit in the U.S. bank (which in actuality represents the entire U.S. commercial banking system). This transaction can be represented by T accounts, where changes in assets are on the left and changes in liabilities are on the right side of the T, as follows:

U.S. Commercial Bank

Assets		Liabilities	
		Demand Deposits	
		U.S. Importer	−\$100
		German Exporter	+\$100

At this point, all that has changed in the U.S. banking system is that ownership of \$100 of demand deposits has been transferred from domestic to foreign control.

The German Exporter is not likely to leave his deposit in the form of a demand deposit for long, as no interest is being earned on this type account. If the funds are not needed for the operation of the business, the Germany Exporter can deposit the \$100 in a time deposit in a bank outside the United States and receive a greater rate of interest than if the funds were put in a U.S. time deposit. Assume the German Exporter closes out his demand deposit in the U.S. Bank and redeposits the funds in a London Eurobank. The London Eurobank credits the German Exporter with a \$100 time deposit and deposits the \$100 into its correspondent bank account (demand deposit) with the U.S. Bank (banking system). These transactions are represented as follows by T accounts:

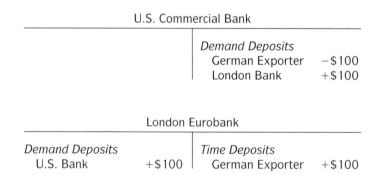

U.S. Commercial Bank

Assets		Liabilities	
		Demand Deposits	
		German Exporter	−\$100
		London Bank	+\$100

London Eurobank

Assets		Liabilities	
Demand Deposits		*Time Deposits*	
U.S. Bank	+\$100	German Exporter	+\$100

Two points are noteworthy from these transactions. First, ownership of $100 of demand deposits has again been transferred (from the German Exporter to the London Eurobank), but the entire $100 still remains on deposit in the U.S. bank. Second, the $100 time deposit of the German Exporter in the London Eurobank represents the creation of Eurodollars. This deposit exists *in addition* to the dollars deposited in the United States. Hence, no dollars have flowed out of the U.S. banking system in the creation of Eurodollars.

The London Eurobank will soon lend out the dollars, as it cannot afford to pay interest on a time deposit on which it is not earning a return. To whom will the London Eurobank lend the dollars? Most obviously to a party needing dollars for a dollar-denominated business transaction or to an investor desiring to invest in the United States. Let's assume that a Dutch Importer borrows $100 from the London Eurobank for the purpose of purchasing from a U.S. Exporter merchandise for resale in the Netherlands. The T accounts representing these transactions are as follows:

London Eurobank

Demand Deposits			
U.S. Bank	−$100		
Loans			
Dutch Importer	+$100		

U.S. Commercial Bank

		Demand Deposits	
		London Eurobank	−$100
		Dutch Importer	+$100

Dutch Importer

Demand Deposits In U.S. Bank	+$100	Loan from London Eurobank	+$100

Note from these transactions that the London Eurobank transfers ownership of $100 of its reserves held in the U.S. Commercial Bank to the Dutch Exporter in exchange for the $100 loan.

The Dutch Exporter will draw a check on its demand deposit in the U.S. Bank to pay the U.S. Exporter for the merchandise shipment. The U.S. Exporter will deposit the check in his U.S. Bank demand deposit. These transactions are represented as follows:

Dutch Importer

Demand Deposit in U.S. Bank	−$100		
Inventory	+$100		

U.S. Exporter

Inventory	−$100		
Demand Deposit in U.S. Bank	+$100		

U.S. Commercial Bank

	Demand Deposit	
	Dtuch Importer	−$100
	U.S. Exporter	+$100

The T accounts show that $100 of demand deposits in the U.S. Bank have changed ownership, going from the control of the Dutch Importer to the U.S. Exporter—or from foreign to U.S. ownership. The original $100, however, never left the U.S. banking system.

QUESTION

1. Explain how Eurocurrency is created.

CHAPTER SEVEN

International Bond Market

CHAPTER OUTLINE

This chapter continues the discussion of international capital markets and institutions, focusing on the international bond market. The chapter is designed to be useful for the financial officer of a MNC interested in sourcing new debt capital in the international bond market, as well as for the international investor interested in international fixed-income securities.

The chapter opens with a brief statistical presentation showing the size of the world's bond markets and the major currencies in which bonds are denominated. Following this are some useful definitions that describe exactly what is meant by the international bond market. The next section presents statistics that show the relative sizes of the foreign bond and Eurobond market segments. The accompanying discussion elaborates on the features that distinguish these market segments and the various types of bond instruments traded in them. An examination of the currency distribution of new international bond offerings, and the nationality and the type of borrower follows. Trading practices in the Eurobond market are discussed next. The chapter concludes with a discussion of international bond credit ratings and bond market indexes that are useful for performance analysis.

THE WORLD'S BOND MARKETS: A STATISTICAL PERSPECTIVE

Exhibit 7.1 presents an overview of the world's bond markets. It shows the amounts of domestic and international bonds outstanding denominated in the major currencies.

EXHIBIT 7.1	Amounts of Domestic and International Bonds Outstanding (As of Year-End 1998 in U.S. $Billions)					
Currency	**Domestic[a]**	**Percent**	**International**	**Percent**	**Total**	**Percent**
U.S. dollar	13,753.0	47.8	1,860.4	45.1	15,613.4	47.5
Yen	5,180.2	18.0	482.7	11.7	5,662.9	17,.2
Deutsche mark	2,004.5	7.0	425.9	10.3	2,430.4	7.4
French franc	1,227.5	4.3	219.0	5.3	1,446.5	4.4
Pound sterling	857.0	3.0	326.8	7.9	1,183.8	3.6
Other[b]	5723.3	19.9	806.8	19.6	6,530.1	19.9
Total	28,745.5	100.0	4,121.6	100.0	32,867.1	100.0

[a]OECD countries plus selected emerging markets.
[b]Including ECU.

Source: Derived from data in Tables 13B and 17, pp. 71 and 77, respectively, in *International Banking and Financial Market Developments*, Bank for International Settlements, June1999.

The exhibit shows that at year-end 1998 the face value of bonds outstanding in the world was approximately $32,867.1 billion. Domestic bonds account for the largest share of outstanding bonds, equaling $28,745.5 billion, or 87 percent, of the total.

Exhibit 7.1 shows that the U.S. dollar, the yen, and the deutsche mark are the three currencies in which the majority of domestic and international bonds are denominated. Nevertheless, proportionately more domestic bonds are denominated in the dollar (47.8 percent) and the yen (18.0 percent) than are international bonds (45.1 percent and 11.7 percent, respectively), while slightly more international bonds than domestic bonds are denominated in the deutsche mark (10.3 percent versus 7.0 percent), the French franc (5.3 percent versus 4.3 percent), and the pound sterling (7.9 percent versus 3.0 percent).

FOREIGN BONDS AND EUROBONDS

The international bond market encompasses two basic market segments: foreign bonds and Eurobonds. A **foreign bond** issue is one offered by a foreign borrower to the investors in a national capital market and denominated in that nation's currency. An example is a German MNC issuing dollar-denominated bonds to U.S. investors. A **Eurobond** issue is one denominated in a particular currency but sold to investors in national capital markets other than the country that issued the denominating currency. An example is a Dutch borrower issuing dollar-denominated bonds to investors in the U.K., Switzerland, and the Netherlands. The markets for foreign bonds and Eurobonds operate in parallel with the domestic national bond markets, and all three market groups compete with one another.[1] Obviously, the new common euro currency confuses these distinctions, and it is likely that different designations will soon develop.

Exhibit 7.2 presents the annual new offerings of international bonds for 1994 through 1997. The top portion of the exhibit subdivides annual offerings into foreign bonds and Eurobonds; the bottom portion classifies the offerings by type of issue. As the exhibit shows, new offerings of international bonds have increased steadily each year. In 1994, $428.6 billion in new bonds were issued; in 1997 the amount was $831.6 billion, a 94 percent increase.

The exhibit indicates that in any given year, over 85 percent of new international bonds are likely to be Eurobonds rather than foreign bonds. Eurobonds are known by the currency in which they are denominated, for example U.S. dollar Eurobonds, yen Eurobonds, and Swiss franc Eurobonds, or correspondingly, Eurodollar bonds, Euroyen bonds, and EuroSF bonds. Foreign bonds, on the other hand, frequently have

EXHIBIT 7.2

International Bond Offerings Classified by Market Segment and Major Instruments (U.S. $Billion)

	1994	1995	1996	1997
Market Segment				
Foreign bonds[a]	60.2	96.0	119.0	96.5
Eurobonds	368.4	371.3	589.8	735.1
Total	428.6	467.3	708.8	831.6
Instrument				
Straight-fixed rate	290.6	353.3	464.4	545.5
Floating-rate notes	96.3	78.9	165.7	213.1
Convertible issues	21.7	12.3	25.6	35.8
With equity warrants	9.9	5.8	8.8	3.1
Zero coupons	5.6	8.5	9.7	8.8
Other	4.5	8.5	34.6	25.3
Total	428.6	467.3	708.8	831.6

[a]The dollar amounts of foreign bonds were derived from information provided in the source document.

Source: *Financial Market Trends*, Organization for Economic Co-operation and Development, February 1998, Table 1, p. 62.

colorful names that designate the country in which they are issued. For example, *Yankee* bonds are dollar-denominated foreign bonds originally sold to U.S. investors, *Samurai* bonds are yen-denominated foreign bonds sold in Japan, and *Bulldogs* are pound sterling-denominated foreign bonds sold in the U.K..

Bearer Bonds and Registered Bonds

Eurobonds are usually bearer bonds. With a **bearer bond,** possession is evidence of ownership. The issuer does not keep any records indicating who is the current owner of a bond. With **registered bonds,** the owner's name is on the bond and it is also recorded by the issuer, or else the owner's name is assigned to a bond serial number recorded by the issuer. When a registered bond is sold, a new bond certificate is issued with the new owner's name, or the new owner's name is assigned to the bond serial number.

U.S. security regulations require Yankee bonds and U.S. corporate bonds sold to U.S. citizens to be registered. Bearer bonds are very attractive to investors desiring privacy and anonymity. One reason for this is that they enable tax evasion. Consequently, investors will generally accept a lower yield on bearer bonds than on registered bonds of comparable terms, making them a less costly source of funds for the issuer to service.

National Security Regulations

Foreign bonds must meet the security regulations of the country in which they are issued. This means that Yankee bonds must meet the same regulations as U.S. domestic bonds. The U.S. Securities Act of 1933 requires full disclosure of relevant information relating to a security issue. The U.S. Securities Exchange Act of 1934 established the Securities and Exchange Commission (SEC) to administer the 1933 Act. Securities sold in the United States to public investors must be registered with the SEC, and a prospectus disclosing detailed financial information about the issuer must be provided and made available to prospective investors. The expense of the registration process, the time delay it creates in bringing a new issue to market (four additional weeks), and the disclosure of information that many foreign borrowers consider private historically have made it more desirable for foreign borrowers to raise U.S. dollars in the Eurobond market. The shorter length of time in bringing a Eurodollar bond issue to market, coupled with the lower rate of interest that borrowers pay for Eurodollar bond financing in comparison to Yankee bond financing, are two major reasons why the Eurobond segment of the international bond market is roughly four times the size of the foreign bond segment. Because Eurobonds do not have to meet national security regulations, name recognition of the issuer is an extremely important factor in being able to source funds in the international capital market.

Eurobonds (or unregistered foreign bonds) sold in the United States may not be sold to U.S. citizens. To prevent this, the initial purchaser receives the bearer bond only after a 90-day waiting period and presentation of identification that one is not a U.S. citizen. Of course, nothing prevents a U.S. investor from repurchasing bearer bonds in the secondary market after 90 days.

Withholding Taxes

Prior to 1984, the United States required a 30 percent withholding tax on interest paid to nonresidents who held U.S. government or corporate bonds. Moreover, U.S. firms issuing Eurodollar bonds from the United States were required to withhold the tax on interest paid to foreigners. In 1984, the withholding tax law was repealed. Additionally, U.S. corporations were allowed to issue domestic bearer bonds to nonresidents, but Congress would not grant this privilege to the Treasury.

The repeal of the withholding tax law caused a substantial shift in the relative yields on U.S. government and Eurodollar bonds. Prior to 1984, top-quality Eurodollar bonds sold overseas traded at lower yields than U.S. Treasury bonds of similar maturities that were subject to the withholding tax. Afterwards the situation was reversed; foreign investors found the safety of registered U.S. Treasury bonds without the withholding tax more attractive than higher yields on corporate Eurodollar bond issues.

Other Recent Regulatory Changes

Two other recent changes in U.S. security regulations have had an effect on the international bond market. One is *Rule 415*, which the SEC instituted in 1982 to allow shelf registration. **Shelf registration** allows an issuer to preregister a securities issue, and then shelve the securities for later sale when financing is actually needed. Shelf registration has thus eliminated the time delay in bringing a foreign bond issue to market in the United States, but it has not eliminated the information disclosure that many foreign borrowers find too expensive and/or objectionable. In 1990, the SEC instituted *Rule 144A*, which allows qualified institutional investors in the United States to trade in private placement issues that do not have to meet the strict information disclosure requirements of publicly traded issues. Rule 144A was designed to make the U.S. capital markets more competitive with the Eurobond market. More will be mentioned about this in a later section.

Global Bonds

Global bond issues were first offered in 1989. A **global bond** issue is a very large international bond offering by a single borrower that is simultaneously sold in North America, Europe, and Asia. Global bonds follow the registration requirements of domestic bonds, but have the fee structure of Eurobonds. Global bond offerings enlarge the borrower's opportunities for financing at reduced costs. Purchasers, mainly institutional investors to date, desire the increased liquidity of the issues and have been willing to accept lower yields. The largest corporate global bond issue to date is the AT&T package of $2,000,000 of 5.625 percent notes due 2004, $3,000,000 of 6.000 percent notes due 2009, and $3,000,000 of 6.500 percent notes due 2029 issued in March 1999. The Republic of Italy issued the largest sovereign global bond issue in September 1993, a package of $2,000,000 of 6.000 percent notes due 2003 and $3,500,000 of 6.875 percent debentures due 2023. The largest emerging markets global bond issue to date is the Republic of Korea package issued April 1998 of $1,000,000 of 8.750 percent notes due 2003 and $3,000,000 of 8.875 percent bonds due 2008. The main currency denominations have been the U.S. dollar, deutsche mark, Canadian dollar, and yen. SEC Rule 415 and Rule 144A have likely facilitated global bond offerings, and more offerings in the future can be expected.[2]

TYPES OF INSTRUMENTS

The international bond market has been much more innovative than the domestic bond market in the types of instruments offered to investors. In this section, we examine the major types of international bonds. We begin with a discussion of the more standard types of instruments and conclude with the more exotic innovations that have appeared in recent years.

Straight Fixed-Rate Issues

Straight fixed-rate bond issues have a designated maturity date at which the principal of the bond issue is promised to be repaid. During the life of the bond, fixed coupon payments, which are a percentage of the face value, are paid as interest to the bondholders. In contrast to many domestic bonds, which make semiannual coupon payments, coupon interest on Eurobonds is typically paid annually. The reason is that the Eurobonds are usually bearer bonds, and annual coupon redemption is more convenient for the bondholders and less costly for the bond issuer because the bondholders are scattered geographically. Exhibit 7.2 shows that the vast majority of new international bond offerings in any year are straight fixed-rate issues. The U.S. dollar, Japanese yen, deutsche mark, and Swiss franc have been the most common currencies denominating straight fixed-rate bonds in recent years.

An example of straight-fixed rate bonds are the EUR 2,000,000 of 5.00 percent notes due in 2008, issued in March 1998 by the European Investment Bank.

Floating-Rate Notes

The first floating-rate notes were introduced in 1970. **Floating-rate notes (FRNs)** are typically medium-term bonds with coupon payments indexed to some reference rate. Common reference rates are either three-month or six-month U.S. dollar LIBOR. Coupon payments on FRNs are usually quarterly or semiannual and in accord with the reference rate. For example, consider a five-year FRN with coupons referenced to six-month dollar LIBOR paying coupon interest semiannually. At the beginning of every six-month period, the next semiannual coupon payment is *reset* to be $.5 \times (\text{LIBOR} + X \text{ percent})$ of face value, where X represents the default risk premium above LIBOR the issuer must pay based on its creditworthiness. The premium is typically no larger than 1/8 percent for top-quality issuers. As an example, if X equals 1/8 percent and the current six-month LIBOR is 6.6 percent, the next period's coupon rate on a \$1,000 face value FRN will be $.5 \times (.066 + .00125) \times \$1{,}000 = \$33.625$. If on the next reset date six-month LIBOR is 5.7 percent, the following semiannual coupon will be set at \$29.125.

Obviously, FRNs behave differently in response to interest rate risk than straight fixed-rate bonds. All bonds experience an inverse price change when the market rate of interest changes. Accordingly, the price of straight fixed-rate bonds may vary significantly if interest rates are extremely volatile. FRNs, on the other hand, experience only mild price changes between reset dates, over which time the next period's coupon payment is fixed (assuming, of course, that the reference rate corresponds to the market rate applicable to the issuer). On the reset date, the market price will gravitate back close to par value when the next period's coupon payment is reset to the new market value of the reference rate. (The actual FRN market price may deviate somewhat from exact par value because the default risk premium portion of the coupon payment is fixed at inception, whereas the credit quality of the borrower may change through time.) FRNs make attractive investments for investors with a strong need to preserve the principal value of the investment should they need to liquidate the investment prior to the maturity of the bonds. Exhibit 7.2 shows that FRNs are the second most common type of international bond issue. The U.S. dollar and the deutsche mark are the two currencies denominating most outstanding FRNs.

As an example of FRNs, in April 1989 Dresdner Finance B. V. of Amsterdam, the Netherlands, issued at 100.05 percent of face value DM1,000,000,000 of FRNs indexed to 3-month LIBOR plus 1/32 percent.

Equity-Related Bonds

There are two types of **equity-related bonds**: convertible bonds and bonds with equity warrants. A **convertible bond** issue allows the investor to exchange the bond for a predetermined number of equity shares of the issuer. The *floor-value* of a convertible bond is its straight fixed-rate bond value. Convertibles usually sell at a premium above the larger of their straight debt value and their conversion value. Additionally, investors are usually willing to accept a lower coupon rate of interest than the comparable straight fixed coupon bond rate because they find the conversion feature attractive. **Bonds with equity warrants** can be viewed as straight fixed-rate bonds with the addition of a call option (or warrant) feature. The warrant entitles the bondholder to purchase a certain number of equity shares in the issuer at a prestated price over a predetermined period of time.

Zero-Coupon Bonds

Zero-coupon bonds are sold at a discount from face value and do not pay any coupon interest over their life. At maturity the investor receives the full face value. Alternatively, some zero-coupon bonds originally sell for face value and at maturity the investor receives an amount in excess of face value to compensate the investor for the use of the money, but this is really nothing more than a semantic difference as to what constitutes "face value." Zero-coupon bonds have been denominated primarily in the U.S. dollar and the Swiss franc. Japanese investors are particularly attracted to zero-coupon bonds because their tax law treats the difference between face value and the discounted purchase price of the bond as a tax-free capital gain, whereas coupon interest is taxable. More generally, zero-coupon bonds are attractive to investors who desire to avoid the reinvestment risk of coupon receipts at possibly lower interest rates.

Examples of zero-coupon bond issues are the DM300,000,000 due in 1995 at 50 percent of face value and DM300,000,000 due in 2000 at 33 1/3 percent of face value, issued in 1985 by Commerzbank Overseas Finance B. V., chartered in the Netherlands Antilles.

Another form of zero-coupon bonds are stripped bonds. A **stripped bond** is a zero-coupon bond that results from stripping the coupons and principal from a coupon bond. The result is a series of zero-coupon bonds represented by the individual coupon and principal payments. This practice began in the early 1980s when several investment banks created stripped bonds to satisfy the demand for zero-coupon U.S. Treasury securities with various maturity dates. For example, Salomon Brothers offered CATS, which is an acronym for Certificates of Accrual for Treasury Securities. The stripped bonds are actually *receipts* representing a portion of the Treasury security held in trust. In 1985, the U.S. Treasury introduced its own product called STRIPS, for Separate Trading of Registered Interest and Principal of Securities. Investment firms are allowed under Treasury regulations to sell the stripped bonds in bearer form to non-U.S. citizens, but, as previously mentioned, the Treasury does not have this privilege. Nevertheless, the Treasury's STRIPS dominate the stripped-bond market.

Dual-Currency Bonds

Dual-currency bonds became popular in the mid-1980s. A **dual-currency bond** is a straight fixed-rate bond issued in one currency, say Swiss francs, that pays coupon interest in that same currency. At maturity, the principal is repaid in another currency, say U.S. dollars. Coupon interest is frequently at a higher rate than comparable straight fixed-rate bonds. The amount of the dollar principal repayment at maturity is set at inception; frequently, the amount allows for some appreciation in the exchange rate of the stronger currency. From the investor's perspective, a dual-currency bond includes a long-term forward contract. If the dollar appreciates over the life of the bond, the principal repayment will be worth more than a return of principal in Swiss francs. The

EXHIBIT 7.3

Typical Characteristics of International Bond Market Instruments

Instrument	Frequency of Interest Payment	Size of Coupon Payment	Payoff at Maturity
Straight fixed-rate	Annual	Fixed	Currency of issue
Floating-rate note	Quarterly or semiannual	Variable	Currency of issue
Convertible bond	Annual	Fixed	Currency of issue or conversion to equity shares
Straight fixed-rate with equity warrants	Annual	Fixed	Currency of issue plus equity shares from exercised warrants
Zero-coupon bond	None	Zero	Currency of issue
Dual-currency bond	Annual	Fixed	Dual currency
Composite currency bond	Annual	Fixed	Composite currency of issue

market value of a dual-currency bond in Swiss francs should equal the sum of the present value of the Swiss franc coupon stream discounted at the Swiss market rate of interest plus the dollar principal repayment, converted to Swiss francs at the expected future exchange rate, and discounted at the Swiss market rate of interest.

Japanese firms have been large issuers of dual currency bonds. These bonds were issued and pay coupon interest in yen with the principal reimbursement in U.S. dollars. Yen/dollar dual currency bonds could be an attractive financing method for Japanese MNCs desiring to establish or expand U.S. subsidiaries. The yen proceeds can be converted to dollars to finance the capital investment in the United States, and during the early years the coupon payments can be made by the parent firm in yen. At maturity, the dollar principal repayment can be made from dollar profits earned by the subsidiary.

Composite Currency Bonds

Composite currency bonds are denominated in a currency basket, such as SDRs or ECUs, instead of a single currency. They are frequently called *currency cocktail bonds*. They are typically straight fixed-rate bonds. A composite currency bond is an attractive type of financing for MNCs with sales receipts in a variety of currencies. From the international investor's standpoint, currency cocktail bonds are likely to have less exchange rate risk than bonds denominated in a single currency. The currency composite is a portfolio of currencies: When some currencies are depreciating, others may be appreciating, thus yielding lower variability overall.

An example of a composite currency bond issue is the ECU500,000,000 of 8.875 percent notes due in 1996, issued in 1991 by the European Bank for Reconstruction and Development.

Exhibit 7.3 summarizes the typical characteristics of the international bond market instruments discussed in this section.

CURRENCY DISTRIBUTION, NATIONALITY, AND TYPE OF ISSUER

Exhibit 7.4 provides the percentage distributions of annual new offerings of international bonds by currency for 1994 through 1997. The exhibit shows that the U.S. dollar, deutsche mark, yen, British pound sterling, Italian lira, and French franc have been the most frequently used currencies for new issues.

Exhibit 7.5 is divided into two panels that show the nationality and type of issuer of international bonds. The top panel indicates that the United States, Japan, France,

EXHIBIT 7.4

Currency Distribution of International Bond Offerings (Percent)[a]

	1994	1995	1996	1997
Currency				
U.S. dollar	37.5	38.6	43.0	45.0
Deutsche mark	7.8	15.7	14.0	16.8
Yen	13.3	12.8	8.6	4.5
Pound sterling	8.8	6.0	8.8	8.9
Swiss franc	4.8	5.6	3.3	2.6
Italian lira	5.5	3.8	4.9	5.4
Dutch guilder	3.0	3.2	2.9	2.3
Luxembourg franc	2.6	3.0	1.2	0.4
French franc	7.0	2.8	6.4	6.4
Australian dollar	1.8	2.3	1.4	0.9
ECU	2.0	1.7	0.7	1.3
Peseta	0.5	0.9	1.3	1.3
Canadian dollar	3.6	0.7	1.0	0.5
Other	1.8	2.9	2.5	3.7
Total	100.0	100.0	100.0	100.0

[a]Percentages calculated from foreign currency amount of total issues converted into U.S. dollars at constant 1990 year-end exchange rates.

Source: Derived from *Financial Market Trends* , Organization for Economic Co-operation and Development, February 1998, Table 6, p. 69.

EXHIBIT 7.5

International Bond Offerings Classified by Nationality and Type of Issuer (U.S. $Billion)

	1994	1995	1996	1997
Nationality				
Australia	12.1	10.2	19.9	13.4
Canada	23.5	15.0	22.1	22.8
France	32.4	24.6	34.8	43.6
Germany	45.9	71.1	111.5	152.1
Italy	16.3	13.6	14.1	16.1
Japan	38.6	38.8	42.3	41.6
Sweden	21.9	21.4	22.8	15.4
United Kingdom	32.8	25.6	53.4	52.2
United States	45.6	73.5	129.0	189.3
Other OECD countries	103.4	109.3	168.4	170.6
Non-OECD countries	44.0	39.9	65.6	85.9
International development organizations	12.1	17.6	24.9	28.9
Total	428.6	460.6	708.8	831.6
Type				
Governments[a]	90.5	74.2	100.5	97.5
Public enterprises	52.1	55.7	77.7	83.6
Banks	133.5	151.7	245.9	293.0
Private corporations	123.7	143.3	233.3	301.2
International organizations	28.8	35.7	51.4	56.3
Total	428.6	460.6	708.8	831.6

[a]Includes central banks and state and local governments.

Source: Derived from *Financial Market Trends*, Organization for Economic Co-operation and Development, February 1998, Table 1, p. 62 and Table 4, p. 65.

Germany, the United Kingdom, and some developing (non-OECD) countries have been major issuers of new international bonds during the past several years. In terms of type of issuer, the bottom panel of Exhibit 7.5 shows that banks and private corporations have been the largest issuers of new international bonds each year.

The International Finance in Practice box on page 166 discusses a Eurobond offering issued by Sara Lee Corporation.

INTERNATIONAL FINANCE IN PRACTICE

Sara Lee Corp. Offers 3-Year Eurobonds at 6%

Sara Lee Corp. is serving up a brand name and a shorter maturity than other recent corporate borrowers to entice buyers to its first-ever dollar Eurobonds.

The U.S. maker of consumer products, from Sara Lee cheesecake to Hanes pantyhose and Hillshire Farm meats, is selling $100 million in bonds with a 6 percent coupon.

These are three-year bonds; other corporate bond sellers including Coca-Cola Co., Unilever NV, and Wal-Mart Stores Inc., have concentrated on its five-year maturities.

"It is a well-known name and it is bringing paper to a part of the maturity curve where there is not much there," said Noel Dunn of Goldman Sachs International.

Goldman Sachs expects to find most buyers in the Swiss retail market, where "high-quality American corporate paper is their favorite buy," Dunn said.

These are the first bonds out of a $500 million Eurobond program that Sara Lee announced in August, and the proceeds will be used for general corporate purposes, said Jeffrey Smith, a spokesman for the company.

The bond is fairly priced, according to Bloomberg Fair Value analysis, which compared a bond with similar issues available in the market.

The bond offers investors a yield of 5.881 percent annually or 5.797 percent semiannually. That is 22 basis points more than they can get on the benchmark five-year U.S. Treasury note.

BFV analysis calculates that the bond is worth $100,145 on a $100,000 bond, compared with the re-offer price of $100,320. Anything within a $500 range on a $100,000 bond more or less than its BFV price is deemed fairly priced.

Sara Lee is rated "AA−" by Standard & Poor's Corp. and "A1," one notch lower, by Moody's Investors Service.

In July 1994, Sara Lee's Netherlands division sold 200 million Dutch guilders ($127 million) of three-year bonds at 35 basis points over comparable Netherlands government bonds. In January, its Australian division sold 51 million British pounds ($78 million) of bonds maturing in 2004, to yield 9.43 percent.

Source: Excerpted from Bloomburg News.

INTERNATIONAL BOND MARKET CREDIT RATINGS

Fitch IBCA, Moody's Investors Service, and Standard & Poor's (S&P) have for years provided credit ratings on domestic and international bonds. These three credit-rating organizations classify bond issues into categories based upon the creditworthiness of the borrower. The ratings are based on an analysis of current information regarding the likelihood of default and the specifics of the debt obligation.[3] The ratings only reflect creditworthiness and not exchange rate uncertainty.

It has been noted by some that a disproportionate share of international bonds have high credit ratings in comparison to domestic bonds. One explanation is that the issuers receiving low credit ratings invoke their publication rights and have had them withdrawn prior to dissemination. Kim and Stulz (1988) suggest another explanation that we believe is more likely. That is, the Eurobond market is accessible to begin with only to firms that have good credit ratings and name recognition; hence, they are rated highly. Regardless, it is beneficial to know about the ratings Fitch, Moody's and S&P assign international bond issues.

Moody's rates bonds into nine categories, from Aaa, Aa, A, Baa, and Ba down to C. Ratings of Aaa to Baa are known as *investment grade* ratings. These issues are judged not to have any speculative elements; interest payments and principal safety appear adequate at present. The future prospects of lower-rated issues cannot be considered as well assured. Within each of the nine categories, Moody's has three numeric modifiers, 1, 2, or 3, to place an issue, respectively, at the upper, middle, or lower end of the category.

Standard & Poor's rates bond issues into 11 categories, from AAA, AA, A, BBB, and BB down to D and CI. Categories AAA to BBB are investment grade ratings. Category D is reserved for bond issues that are presently in default, and the payment of interest and/or the repayment of principal is in arrears. Category CI is reserved for income bonds on which no income is being paid. Ratings for Categories AA to CCC may be modified with a plus (+) or minus (−) to reflect the relative standing of an issue to others in the category. Fitch uses ratings symbols and definitions similar to S&P's.

Exhibit 7.6 presents a guide to S&P's International Ratings for sovereigns, municipalities, corporations, utilities, and supranationals. As noted in Exhibit 7.5, sovereigns issue a sizable portion of all international bonds. In rating a sovereign government, S&P's analysis centers around an examination of the degree of *political risk* and *economic risk*. In assessing political risk, S&P examines the stability of the political system, the social environment, and international relations with other countries. Factors examined in assessing economic risk include the sovereign's external financial position, balance-of-payments flexibility, economic structure and growth, management of the economy, and economic prospects. The rating assigned a sovereign is particularly important because it usually represents the ceiling for ratings S&P will assign an obligation of an entity domiciled within that country. Exhibit 7.7 details the ratings methodology that S&P uses in rating a sovereign government.

EUROBOND MARKET STRUCTURE AND PRACTICES

Given that in any year the Eurobond segment of the international bond market accounts for approximately 80 percent of new offerings, it is beneficial to know something about the Eurobond market structure and practices.

Primary Market

A borrower desiring to raise funds by issuing Eurobonds to the investing public will contact an investment banker and ask it to serve as **lead manager** of an underwriting syndicate that will bring the bonds to market. The **underwriting syndicate** is a group of investment banks, merchant banks, and the merchant banking arms of commercial banks that specialize in some phase of a public issuance. The lead manager will usually invite comanagers to form a **managing group** to help negotiate terms with the borrower, ascertain market conditions, and manage the issuance. Exhibit 7.8 lists the names of 30 lead managers for triple-A-rated public Eurobond offerings for 1998 and the amount of the underwritings they led.

The managing group, along with other banks, will serve as **underwriters** for the issue, that is, they will commit their own capital to buy the issue from the borrower at a discount from the issue price. The discount, or **underwriting spread**, is typically in the 2 to 2.5 percent range. By comparison, the spread averages about 1 percent for domestic issues. Most of the underwriters, along with other banks, will be part of a **selling group** that sells the bonds to the investing public. The various members of the underwriting syndicate receive a portion of the spread, depending on the number and type of functions they perform. The lead manager will obviously receive the full spread, but a bank serving as only a member of the selling group will receive a smaller portion. The total elapsed time from the decision date of the borrower to issue Eurobonds until the net proceeds from the sale are received is typically five to six weeks. Exhibit 7.9 presents a tombstone (announcement) for a dollar-denominated Euronote issue and the underwriting syndicate that brought the issue to market.

Secondary Market

Eurobonds initially purchased in the **primary market** from a member of the selling group may be resold prior to their maturities to other investors in the secondary market. The **secondary market** for Eurobonds is an over-the-counter market with

EXHIBIT 7.6 S&P Debt Rating Definitions

A Standard & Poor's corporate or municipal debt rating is a current assessment of the creditworthiness of an obligor with respect to a specific obligation. This assessment may take into consideration obligors such as guarantors, insurers, or lessees.

The debt rating is not a recommendation to purchase, sell, or hold a security, inasmuch as it does not comment as to market price or suitability for a particular investor.

The ratings are based, in varying degrees, on the following considerations:

1. Likelihood of default-capacity and willingness of the obligor as to the timely payment of interest and repayment of principal in accordance with the terms of the obligation;
2. Nature of and provisions of the obligation;
3. Protection afforded by, and relative position of, the obligation in the event of bankruptcy, reorganization, or other arrangement under the laws of bankruptcy and other laws affecting creditors rights.

Investment Grade

AAA Debt rated 'AAA' has the highest rating assigned by S&P. Capacity to pay interest and repay principal is extremely strong.

AA Debt rated 'AA' has a very strong capacity to pay interest and repay principal and differs from the highest rated issues only in small degree.

A Debt rated 'A' has a strong capacity to pay interest and repay principal although it is somewhat more susceptible to the adverse effects of changes in circumstances and economic conditions than debt in higher rated categories.

BBB Debt rated 'BBB' is regarded as having an adequate capacity to pay interest and repay principal. Whereas it normally exhibits adequate protection parameters, adverse economic conditions or changing circumstances are more likely to lead to a weakened capacity to pay interest and repay principal for debt in this category than in higher rated categories.

Speculative Grade

Debt rated 'BB,' 'B,' 'CCC,' 'CC,' and 'C' is regarded as having predominantly speculative characteristics with respect to capacity to pay interest and repay principal. 'BB' indicates the least degree of speculation and 'CCC' the highest. While such debt will likely have some quality and protective characteristics, these are outweighed by large uncertainties or exposures to adverse conditions.

BB Debt rated 'BB' has less near-term vulnerability to default than other speculative issues. However, it faces major ongoing uncertainties or exposure to adverse business, financial, or economic conditions which could lead to inadequate capacity to meet timely interest and principal payments. The 'BB' rating category is also used for debt subordinated to senior debt that is assigned an actual or implied 'BBB−' rating.

B Debt rated 'B' has a greater vulnerability to default but currently has the capacity to meet interest payments and principal repayments. Adverse business, financial, or economic conditions will likely impair capacity or willingness to pay interest and repay principal. The 'B' rating category is also used for debt subordinated to senior debt that is assigned an actual or implied 'BB' or 'BB−' rating.

CCC Debt rated 'CCC' has a currently identifiable vulnerability to default, and is dependent upon favorable business, financial, and economic conditions to meet timely payment of interest and repayment of principal. In the event of adverse business, financial, or economic conditions, it is not likely to have the capacity to pay interest and repay principal. The 'CCC' rating category is also used for debt subordinated to senior debt that is assigned an actual or implied 'B' or 'B−' rating.

CC The rating 'CC' typically is applied to debt subordinated to senior debt that is assigned an actual or implied 'CCC' rating.

C The rating 'C' typically is applied to debt subordinated to senior debt that is assigned an actual or implied 'CCC−' debt rating. The 'C' rating may be used to cover a situation where a bankruptcy petition has been filed, but debt service payments are continued.

CI The rating 'CI' is reserved for income bonds on which no interest is being paid.

D Debt rated 'D' is in payment default. The 'D' rating category is used when interest payments or principal payments are not made on the date due even if the applicable grace period has not expired, unless S&P believes that such payments will be made during such grace period. The 'D' rating also will be used upon the filing of a bankruptcy petition if debt service payments are jeopardized.

Plus (+) or minus (−): The ratings from 'AA' to 'CCC' may be modified by the addition of a plus or minus sign to show relative standing within the major rating categories.

N.R. Not rated.

Debt Obligations of Issuers outside the U.S. and its territories are rated on the same basis as domestic corporate and municipal issues. The ratings measure the creditworthiness of the obligor but do not take into account currency exchange and related uncertainties.

Source: Standard & Poor's *Credit Week*, February 5, 1996, p. 64.

EXHIBIT 7.7

Standard & Poor's Sovereign Debt Rating Methodology

Political Risk

Political system
- Form of government
- Orderliness of leadership succession
- Adaptability of political institutions

Social environment
- Living standards and income distribution
- Labor market conditions
- Cultural and demographic characteristics of population

International relations
- Integration within international economic system
- Security risk

Economic Risk

External financial position
- Size and structure of gross and net external debt
- Debt service burden
- Adequacy of international reserves

Balance-of-payments flexibility
- Structure, performance, and responsiveness of the current account
- Adequacy and composition of capital flows
- Ability of policymakers to manage external payments

Economic structure and growth
- Resource endowment, level of development, and economic diversification
- Size and composition of savings and investment
- Rate and pattern of economic growth

Economic management
- Willingness and ability to ensure economic balance
- Effectiveness of fiscal, monetary, and income policies
- Structural economic reforms

Economic prospects
- Long-term economic projections, including reasonable worst-case scenario
- Cost of policy trade-offs

Source: Standard & Poor's *Sovereign Rating Criteria*, August 1992.

principal trading in London. However, important trading is also done in other major European money centers, such as Zurich, Luxembourg, Frankfurt, and Amsterdam.

The secondary market comprises market makers and brokers connected by an array of telecommunications equipment. **Market makers** stand ready to buy or sell for their own account by quoting two-way **bid** and **ask** prices. Market makers trade directly with one another, through a broker, or with retail customers. The bid-ask spread represents their only profit; no other commission is charged.

Eurobond market makers and dealers are members of the International Securities Market Association (ISMA), a self-regulatory body based in Zurich. Market makers tend to be the same investment banks, merchant banks, and commercial banks that serve as lead managers in an underwriting. **Brokers**, on the other hand, accept buy or sell orders from market makers and then attempt to find a matching party for the other side of the trade; they may also trade for their own account. Brokers charge a small commission for their services to the market maker that engaged them. They do not deal directly with retail clients.

Clearing Procedures[4]

Eurobond transactions in the secondary market require a system for transferring ownership and payment from one party to another. Two major clearing systems, Euroclear and Cedel, have been established to handle most Eurobond trades. Euroclear

EXHIBIT 7.8

Ranking of Lead Managers for Triple-A Public Eurobond Offerings (1998, in U.S. $Millions)

	Bank	Amount	Number of Issues
1	Morgan Stanley	31,886	70
2	Deutsche Bank	30,351	65
3	Merrill Lynch	28,164	101
4	ABN Amro	22,162	36
5	Goldman Sachs & Co.	22,040	27
6	Commerzbank	21,717	46
7	Salomon Smith Barney	20,940	38
8	JP Morgan	20,584	25
9	Lehman Brothers	19,171	72
10	Warburg Dillon Read	18,937	44
11	Dresdner Kleinwort Benson	18,715	44
12	HypoVereinsbank	16,703	36
13	Crédit Suisse First Boston	13,186	39
14	DG Bank Deutsche Genossenschaftsbank	12,259	32
15	HSBC	10,628	35
16	Bear Stearns	9,254	7
17	Barclays Capital	7,635	16
18	Westdeutsche Landesbank	7,584	15
19	Paribas	6,945	22
20	WGZ-Bank Westdeutsche GenossenschaftZentralbank	6,161	12
21	CDC Marchés	5,324	15
22	Crédit Agricole Indosuez	3,844	10
23	Société Générale	3,837	12
24	Bayerische Landesbank	3,775	6
25	Landesbank Sachsen	3,732	7
26	Rabobank Nederland	3,432	9
27	SGZ Sudwestdeutsche Genossenschaftszentralbank AG	2,996	10
28	Nomura Securities	2,626	5
29	RBC DS Global Markets	2,420	28
30	Chase	2,225	5

Source: *Euromoney*, February 1999, p. 82.

Clearance System is based in Brussels and is operated by Morgan Guaranty. Cedel, located in Luxembourg, was founded by a group of European banks active in the Eurobond market.

Both clearing systems operate in a similar manner, with Euroclear handling approximately twice the trading volume of Cedel. Each clearing system has a group of depository banks that physically store bond certificates. Members of either system hold cash and bond accounts. When a transaction is conducted, book entries are made that transfer book ownership of the bond certificates from the seller to the buyer and transfer funds from the purchaser's cash account to the seller's. Physical transfer of the bonds seldom takes place.

Euroclear and Cedel perform other functions associated with the efficient operation of the Eurobond market. (1) The clearing systems will finance up to 90 percent of the inventory that a Eurobond market maker has deposited within the system. (2) Additionally, the clearing systems will assist in the distribution of a new bond issue. The clearing systems will take physical possession of the newly printed bond certificates in the depository, collect subscription payments from the purchasers, and record ownership of the bonds. (3) The clearing systems will also distribute coupon payments. The borrower pays to the clearing system the coupon interest due on the portion of the issue held in the depository, which in turn credits the appropriate amounts to the bond owners' cash accounts.

EXHIBIT 7.9

Eurobond Tombstone

This announcement appears as a matter of record only

Hamburgische Landesbank

Hamburgische Landesbank – Girozentrale –

(incorporated as a credit institution under public law in the Federal Republic of Germany)

Hamburgische Landesbank London Branch

Hamburgische LB Finance (Guernsey) Limited

(incorporated in Guernsey)

U.S.$2,000,000,000

Euro Medium Term Note Programme

Guaranteed in respect of Notes issued by
Hamburgische LB Finance (Guernsey) Limited by
Hamburgische Landesbank – Girozentrale –

The Programme is rated Aa1 by Moody's and AAA by Fitch IBCA

NOW RATED Aa1 BY MOODY'S

Arrangers

Merrill Lynch International

Merrill Lynch Capital Markets Bank Limited, Frankfurt/Main Branch

Merrill Lynch Finance SA

Dealers

Credit Suisse First Boston
Hamburgische Landesbank – Girozentrale –
Merrill Lynch International
Morgan Stanley Dean Witter
Salomon Smith Barney

Deutsche Morgan Grenfell
Merrill Lynch Finance SA
J.P. Morgan Securities Ltd.
Nomura International
Warburg Dillon Read

Source: *Euromoney*, January 1999, p. 11.

INTERNATIONAL BOND MARKET INDEXES

There are several international bond market indexes. Some of the best known are the J.P. Morgan and Company Domestic Government Bond Indices and their Global Government Bond Index. J.P. Morgan publishes a government bond index for 18 individual countries: Australia, Canada, Belgium, Denmark, France, Germany, Italy, Japan, the Netherlands, Spain, Sweden, the United Kingdom, the United States, New Zealand, Ireland, Finland, Portugal, and South Africa. Each bond index includes only government bonds in five maturity categories: 1–3 years, 3–5 years, 5–7 years, 7–10 years, and 10-plus years. The Global Government Bond Index is a value-weighted representation of the 18 government bond indexes.

The J.P. Morgan Domestic and Global Government Bond Indices are widely referenced and used frequently as benchmarks of international bond market performance. The index values for six of the Domestic Government Indices, a Euro-Zone Bond Index, the 18-country Global Government Bond Index, and an Emerging Market Government Bond Index (EMBI) appear daily in *The Wall Street Journal.* Exhibit 7.10 provides an example of these indexes. Note that the index values are provided in local currency terms and in U.S. dollar terms. Additionally, 1-day, 1-month and 3-month total rates of return are provided for each index in local and U.S. dollar terms.

Exhibit 7.10 shows that *The Wall Street Journal* also publishes daily values of yields to maturity for Japanese, German, British, and Canadian Government Bonds of various terms to maturity provided by J. P. Morgan through Telerate. These data allow for comparing the term structures of interest rates from these major industrial countries with one another and with the term structure of U.S. Treasury bonds that can be found elsewhere in the *WSJ*. Another source of international bond data are the coupon rates, prices, and yields to maturity found in the daily "Benchmark Government Bonds" table in the *Financial Times*. Exhibit 7.11 provides an example.

EXHIBIT 7.10 International Bond Market Data Provided Daily in The Wall Street Journal

International Government Bonds

Prices in local currencies, from Telerate.

COUPON	MATURITY (Mo./yr.)	PRICE	CHANGE	YIELD*	COUPON	MATURITY (Mo./yr.)	PRICE	CHANGE	YIELD*
JAPAN (3 p.m. Tokyo)					**GERMANY** (5 p.m. London)				
6.60%	06/01	112.18	− 0.06	0.31%	8.00%	01/02	110.79	− 0.90	3.47%
4.10	06/04	115.36	+ 0.01	0.87	3.50	11/03	98.51	− 0.25	3.88
1.80	09/09	101.04	− 0.18	1.68	3.75	01/09	92.98	− 0.59	4.69
2.60	03/19	99.10	− 1.42	2.67	4.75	07/28	89.04	− 0.90	5.52
UNITED KINGDOM (5 p.m. London)					**CANADA** (3 p.m. Eastern Time)				
8.00%	12/00	103.98	− 0.07	5.06%	4.50	06/01	98.75	− 0.13	5.198%
6.50	12/03	104.00	− 0.34	5.47	5.50	09/02	100.25	− 0.19	5.412
5.75	12/09	104.49	− 0.95	5.19	6.00	06/08	103.35	− 0.28	5.517
6.00	12/28	119.32	− 1.37	4.77	8.00	06/27	132.76	− 0.39	5.652

*Equivalent to semi-annual compounded yields to maturity.

Total Rates of Return on International Bonds

In percent, based on J.P. Morgan Government Bonds Index, Dec. 31, 1987 = 100

	— LOCAL CURRENCY TERMS —					— U.S. DOLLAR TERMS —				
	INDEX VALUE	1 DAY	1 MO	3 MOS	SINCE 12/31	INDEX VALUE	1 DAY	1 MO	3 MOS	SINCE 12/31
Japan	198.48	− 0.48	− 0.77	+ 0.59	+ 3.80	196.82	− 0.28	− 0.98	− 0.25	− 4.08
Britain	333.46	− 0.48	− 0.40	− 2.83	− 2.61	277.27	− 0.94	− 2.76	− 4.16	− 8.21
Germany	223.91	− 0.29	− 1.41	− 2.26	− 1.19	184.08	− 0.10	− 1.94	− 6.90	− 13.75
France	297.66	− 0.35	− 1.63	− 2.74	− 1.85	247.32	− 0.16	− 2.15	− 7.36	− 14.32
Canada	309.92	− 0.19	+ 0.62	− 1.57	− 0.48	274.07	− 0.62	+ 0.61	+ 0.76	+ 4.01
Netherlands	237.83	− 0.31	− 1.53	− 2.51	− 1.43	195.23	− 0.12	− 2.05	− 7.14	− 13.96
Euro	264.26	0.00	+ 0.27	+ 0.86	+ 2.52	227.81	+ 0.19	− 0.26	− 3.93	− 10.52
Global-a	262.17	− 0.31	− 0.68	− 1.76	− 1.06	231.50	− 0.25	− 1.02	− 3.74	− 7.63
EMBI + −b	153.66	+ 0.65	+ 3.66	+ 4.09	+ 10.87	153.66	+ 0.65	+ 3.66	+ 4.09	+ 10.87

a-18 intl. gov. markets b-external-currency emerging mkt. debt, Dec. 31, 1993 = 100.

Source: *The Wall Street Journal*, July 7, 1999, p. C25. Reprinted by permission of *The Wall Street Journal*, © 1996 Dow Jones & Company, Inc. All Rights Reserved Worldwide.

EXHIBIT 7.11 International Government Bond Market Data Provided Daily in the Financial Times

WORLD BOND PRICES

BENCHMARK GOVERNMENT BONDS

Jul 6	Redemption Date	Coupon	Bid Price	Bid Yield	Day chg yield	Wk chg yield	Month chg yld	Year chg yld
Australia	01/01	8.750	105.3206	5.04	+0.03	−0.06	−0.25	−0.14
	09/09	7.500	109.5376	6.22	+0.05	−0.04	+0.03	+0.77
Austria	03/01	5.250	103.2000	3.24	+0.05	+0.01	+0.22	−0.63
	07/09	4.000	92.9700	4.91	+0.09	+0.19	+0.57	+0.13
Belgium	03/01	5.000	102.9600	3.18	+0.03	+0.03	+0.20	−0.82
	03/09	3.750	90.8000	4.96	+0.07	+0.14	+0.39	+0.13
Canada	06/01	4.500	98.7600	5.20	+0.06	−0.08	−0.06	+0.03
	06/08	6.000	103.3000	5.52	+0.02	−0.05	−0.04	+0.25
Denmark	11/00	9.000	106.9400	3.57	+0.02	+0.12	+0.13	−0.65
	11/09	6.000	106.8800	5.12	+0.07	+0.18	+0.34	+0.23
Finland	06/00	4.000	101.0100	2.89	+0.07	+0.14	+0.17	−0.76
	04/09	5.000	100.4400	4.94	+0.09	+0.21	+0.43	+0.16
France	07/01	3.000	99.5300	3.25	+0.04	−0.01	+0.24	−0.65
	04/06	7.250	117.0700	4.29	+0.09	+0.13	+0.43	−0.18
	04/09	4.000	93.9000	4.79	+0.07	+0.16	+0.38	+0.05
	04/29	5.500	99.0300	5.57	+0.05	+0.12	+0.28	+0.29
Germany	03/01	3.000	99.6900	3.19	+0.05	+0.04	+0.25	−0.61
	04/06	6.250	110.5100	4.42	+0.08	+0.14	+0.42	−0.10
	01/09	3.750	92.9300	4.69	+0.08	+0.17	+0.42	−0.01
	07/28	4.750	88.9200	5.53	+0.05	+0.12	+0.28	+0.25
Greece	05/01	9.700	103.9500	7.34	+0.08	+0.06	+0.23	−3.57
	01/09	6.300	99.7500	6.33	+0.14	+0.14	+0.50	−1.45
Ireland	10/01	6.500	106.6000	3.43	+0.08	+0.06	+0.32	−1.81
	04/10	4.000	92.0300	4.96	+0.10	+0.20	+0.46	+0.01
Italy	07/01	4.500	102.1500	3.36	+0.05	+0.03	+0.31	−0.97
	07/03	4.500	101.7500	4.02	+0.10	+0.08	+0.44	−0.49
	05/09	4.500	96.8900	4.90	+0.06	+0.13	+0.37	−0.02
	11/27	6.500	110.4000	5.75	+0.06	+0.12	+0.28	+0.30
Japan	06/01	6.600	112.1470	0.31	+0.04	−0.02	+0.08	−0.17
	06/04	4.100	115.3660	0.91	+0.07	−0.10	+0.17	−0.04
	06/09	1.800	101.3500	1.65	+0.07	−0.11	+0.05	+0.28
	03/19	2.600	99.1730	2.65	+0.09	−0.08	+0.14	+0.45
Netherlands	03/01	8.500	108.5100	3.18	+0.04	+0.02	+0.21	−0.74
	07/09	3.750	91.4900	4.84	+0.06	+0.14	+0.39	+0.14
New Zealand	02/01	8.000	104.2501	5.12	−0.03	−0.10	−0.03	−2.13
	07/09	7.000	103.4147	6.53	−0.03	−0.09	+0.07	+0.14
Norway	05/01	7.000	102.4500	5.58	+0.06	+0.17	+0.25	+0.22
	05/09	5.500	97.4000	5.85	+0.12	+0.18	+0.50	+0.39
Portugal	03/01	8.750	109.1800	3.09	+0.04	—	+0.19	−1.21
	07/09	3.950	91.7400	5.02	+0.08	+0.17	+0.40	+0.09
Spain	01/01	5.000	102.8000	3.11	+0.02	+0.01	+0.20	−1.05
	07/09	0.000	101.3200	4.95	+0.05	+0.18	+0.37	+0.09
Sweden	06/01	13.000	116.1680	4.07	+0.11	+0.17	+0.47	+0.01
	04/09	9.000	127.3370	5.33	+0.10	+0.28	+0.53	+0.48
Switzerland	10/01	5.500	107.3500	2.09	+0.04	+0.17	+0.44	−0.01
	02/09	3.250	102.3000	2.97	+0.05	+0.11	+0.30	−0.11
UK	11/01	7.000	103.4500	5.40	+0.05	—	+0.16	−1.82
	11/04	6.750	105.9400	5.46	+0.04	+0.03	+0.30	−0.55
	12/09	5.750	104.3800	5.20	+0.07	+0.10	+0.25	−0.59
	12/28	6.000	119.2200	4.78	+0.07	+0.04	−0.05	−0.78
US	04/01	5.000	99.0625	5.55	+0.01	−0.09	+0.02	+0.08
	05/04	5.250	97.9375	5.74	+0.04	−0.08	—	+0.25
	05/09	5.500	97.2188	5.88	+0.06	−0.05	+0.07	+0.38
	02/29	5.250	89.0938	6.05	+0.05	−0.01	+0.08	+0.42

London closing * New York closing   Source: Interactive Data/FT Information

Yields: Local market standard/Annualised yield basis. Yields shown for Italy exclude withholding tax at 12.5 per cent payable by nonresidents.

Source: *Financial Times*, July 7, 1999, p. 26. Reprinted with permission.

SUMMARY

This chapter introduces and discusses the international bond market. The chapter presents a statistical perspective of the market, noting its size, an analysis of the market segments, the types of instruments issued, the major currencies used to denominate international bonds, and the major borrowers by nationality and type. Trading practices of the Eurobond market are examined, as are credit ratings for international bonds and international bond market indexes.

1. At year-end 1998, there were over $28.7 trillion in domestic bonds outstanding and over $4.1 trillion in international bonds. The three major currencies that are used to denominate bonds are the U.S. dollar, yen, and deutsche mark.
2. A foreign bond issue is one offered by a foreign borrower to investors in a national capital market and denominated in that nation's currency. A Eurobond issue is one denominated in a particular currency but sold to investors in national capital markets other than the country that issues the denominating currency.
3. The Eurobond segment of the international bond market is roughly four times the size of the foreign bond segment. The two major reasons for this stem from the fact that the U.S. dollar is the currency most frequently sought in international bond financing. First, Eurodollar bonds can be brought to market more quickly than Yankee bonds because they are not offered to U.S. investors and thus do not have to meet the strict SEC registration requirements. Second, Eurobonds are typically bearer bonds that provide anonymity to the owner and thus allow a means for avoiding taxes on the interest received. Because of this feature, investors are generally willing to accept a lower yield on Eurodollar bonds in comparison to registered Yankee bonds of comparable terms, where ownership is recorded. For borrowers the lower yield means a lower cost of debt service.
4. Straight fixed-rate bonds are the most frequent type of international bond issue, and floating-rate notes are the second. Other types of issues found in the international bond market are convertible bonds, bonds with equity warrants, zero-coupon bonds, stripped bonds, dual-currency bonds, and composite currency bonds.
5. Fitch IBCA, Moody's Investors Service, and Standard & Poor's provide credit ratings on most international bond issues. It has been noted that a disproportionate share of international bonds have high credit ratings. The evidence suggests that a logical reason for this is that the Eurobond market is accessible only to firms that have good credit ratings to begin with. An entity's credit rating is usually never higher than the rating assigned the sovereign government of the country in which it resides. S&P's analysis of a sovereign includes an examination of political risk and economic risk.
6. New Eurobond issues are offered in the primary market through an underwriting syndicate hired by the borrower to bring the bonds to market. The secondary market for Eurobonds is an over-the-counter arrangement with principal trading done in London.
7. The investment banking firm of J.P. Morgan and Company provides some of the best international bond market indexes that are frequently used for performance evaluations. J.P. Morgan publishes a Domestic Government Bond Index for 18 individual countries, a Euro-Zone Government Index, a Global Government Bond Index, and an Emerging Market Bond Index..

KEY WORDS

ask price, 169
bearer bond, 160
bid price, 169
bond with equity warrants, 163
broker, 169
composite currency bond, 164
convertible bond, 163

QUESTIONS

1. Describe the differences between foreign bonds and Eurobonds. Also discuss why Eurobonds make up the lion's share of the international bond market.
2. Briefly define each of the major types of international bond market instruments, noting their distinguishing characteristics.
3. Why do most international bonds have high Moody's or Standard & Poor's credit ratings?
4. What factors does Standard & Poor's analyze in determining the credit rating it assigns a sovereign government?
5. Discuss the process of bringing a new international bond issue to market.
6. You are an investment banker advising a Eurobank about a new international bond offering it is considering. The proceeds are to be used to fund Eurodollar loans to bank clients. What type of bond instrument would you recommend that the bank consider issuing? Why?
7. What should a borrower consider before issuing dual-currency bonds? What should an investor consider before investing in dual-currency bonds?

PROBLEMS

1. Your firm has just issued five-year floating-rate notes indexed to six-month U.S. dollar LIBOR plus 1/4 percent. What is the amount of the first coupon payment your firm will pay per U.S. $1,000 of face value, if six-month LIBOR is currently 7.2 percent?
2. The discussion of zero-coupon bonds in the text gave an example of two zero-coupon bonds issued by Commerzbank. The DM300,000,000 issue due in 1995 sold at 50 percent of face value, and the DM300,000,000 due in 2000 sold at 33⅓ percent of face value; both were issued in 1985. Calculate the implied yield to maturity of each of these two zero-coupon bond issues.
3. Consider 8.5 percent Swiss franc/U.S. dollar dual-currency bonds that pay $666.67 at maturity per SF1,000 of par value. What is the implicit SF/$ exchange rate at maturity? Will the investor be better or worse off at maturity if the actual SF/$ exchange rate is SF1.35/$1.00?

MINI CASE

Sara Lee Corporation's Eurobonds

The *International Finance in Practice* boxed reading in the chapter discussed a three-year $100 million Eurobond issue by Sara Lee Corporation. The article also mentions other bond issues recently placed by various foreign divisions of Sara Lee. What thoughts do you have about Sara Lee's debt-financing strategy?

ENDNOTES

1. In this chapter the terms *market segment, market group*, and *market* are used interchangeably when referring to the foreign bond and Eurobond divisions of the international bond market.
2. The information in this paragraph comes from the 1993 *63rd Annual Report* of the Bank for International Settlements, p. 120 and International Monetary Fund (1994) *International Capital Markets: Developments and Prospects*, International Monetary Fund, pp. 67–70.
3. See Van Horne (1998) for an excellent review of the literature on default risk and bond credit ratings.
4. The discussion in this subsection follows from the corresponding discussion in Chapter 14 of Grabbe (1996).

WEB RESOURCES

www.fitchibca.com

This is the Website of Fitch IBCA, an international bond rating service. Information about Fitch and its philosophy can be found here.

www.moodys.com

This is the Website of Moody's Investor Service. Information about the investment services that Moody's provides and their bond ratings can be found here.

www.standardandpoors.com

This is the Website of Standard and Poor's, a provider of investment information, such as bond ratings. Information about S&P can be found here.

www.jpmorgan.com

This is the Website of J.P. Morgan and Company, an international investment banking firm. This is an extensive Website. Detailed information about J.P. Morgan's bond indexes can be found here.

REFERENCES AND SUGGESTED READINGS

Anderson, Torben Juul. *Euromarket Instruments*. New York: New York Institute of Finance, 1990.

Bank for International Settlements. *63rd Annual Report.* Basle: BIS, 1993.

Bank for International Settlements. *65th Annual Report.* Basle: BIS, 1995.

Dosoo, George. *The Eurobond Market*, 2nd ed. New York: Woodhead, Faulkner, 1992.

Gallant, Peter. *The Eurobond Market.* New York: Woodhead, Faulkner, 1988.

Gowland, D.H., ed. *International Bond Markets.* London: Routledge, 1991.

Grabbe, J. Orlin. *International Financial Markets*, 3rd ed. Englewood Cliffs, NJ: Prentice Hall, 1996.

International Monetary Fund. *International Capital Markets: Developments and Prospects.* Washington, D.C.: International Monetary Fund, 1991.

International Monetary Fund. *International Capital Markets: Developments and Prospects.* Washington, D.C.: International Monetary Fund, 1994.

Jones, Frank J., and Frank J. Fabozzi. *International Government Bond Markets.* Chicago: Probus, 1992.

Kim, Yong Cheol, and Rene M. Stultz. "The Eurobond Market and Corporate Financial Policy: A Test of the Clientele Hypothesis." *Journal of Financial Economics* 22 (1988), pp. 189–205.

Lederman, Jess, and Keith K. H. Park, eds. *The Global Bond Markets.* Chicago: Probus, 1991.

Van Horne, James C. *Financial Market Rates and Flows*, 5th ed. Englewood Cliffs, NJ: Prentice Hall, 1998.

CHAPTER EIGHT

International Equity Markets

CHAPTER OUTLINE

This chapter focuses on equity markets, or how ownership in publicly owned corporations is traded throughout the world. It discusses both the *primary* sale of new common stock by corporations to initial investors and how previously issued common stock is traded between investors in the *secondary* markets. This chapter is useful for understanding how companies source new equity capital and provides useful institutional information for investors interested in diversifying their portfolio internationally.

The chapter begins with an overview of the world's equity markets. Statistics are provided that show the comparative sizes and trading opportunities in various secondary equity marketplaces in both developed and developing countries. Differences in market structures are also explored, and comparative transaction costs of equity trading are presented. Following this, the discussion moves to the benefits of multiple listing of a corporation's stock on more than one national stock exchange. The related issue of sourcing new equity capital from primary investors in more than the home national market is also examined. The chapter concludes with a discussion of the factors that affect equity valuation. An examination of the historical market performances and the risks of investing in foreign national equity markets are not presented here, but rather in Chapter 11, where a strong case is made for international diversification of investment funds.

A STATISTICAL PERSPECTIVE

Before we can intelligently discuss international equity markets, it is helpful to understand where the major national equity markets are located, some information about their relative sizes, and the opportunities for trading and ownership. This section provides these background data, along with a statistical summary of emerging equity markets in Eastern Europe, the Middle East, Africa, Latin America, and Asia.

Market Capitalization of Developed Countries

At year-end 1998, total market capitalization of the world's equity markets stood at $27,462 billion. Of this amount, almost 90 percent is accounted for by the market capitalization of the major equity markets from 24 developed countries. Exhibit 8.1 shows the market capitalizations for these 24 developed countries for 1994 through 1998. As the exhibit indicates, over the five-year period, their total market capitalization increased 93 percent, from $13,211 billion to $25,554 billion.

The exhibit indicates that the growth in market capitalization was not evenly spread among the developed countries. For example, the United States registered an increase of 165 percent over the five-year period, whereas the increase in European markets was 121 percent. The Far East, however, registered an 11 percent decline when Japan was included, but a 115 percent increase when it was excluded. Japan's decrease of 33 percent over the five-year period reflects the sustained recession it has been experiencing during the current decade.

EXHIBIT 8.1

Market Capitalization of Emerging Equity Markets in Selected Developed Countries (in U.S. $ Billion)

Region or Country	1994	1995	1996	1997	1998
Europe	3,445	4,222	4,923	5,912	7,657
Austria	30	33	34	36	34
Belgium	84	105	120	137	246
Denmark	54	56	72	94	99
Finland	38	44	63	73	155
France	451	522	591	674	991
Germany	471	577	671	825	1,094
Iceland	<1	<1	1	NA	NA
Ireland	8	26	12	24	30
Italy	180	210	258	345	570
Luxembourg	29	30	33	34	35
Netherlands	283	356	379	469	603
Norway	36	45	57	67	56
Spain	155	198	243	290	402
Sweden	131	178	247	273	279
Switzerland	284	434	402	575	689
United Kingdom	1,210	1,408	1,740	1,996	2,374
Middle East	11	14	22	3	NA
Kuwait	11	14	22	3	NA
Far East	4,371	4,396	3,222	3,523	3,896
Australia	219	245	495	697	874
Hong Kong	270	304	449	413	343
Japan	3,720	3,668	3,089	2,217	2,496
New Zealand	27	32	39	90	89
Singapore	135	148	150	106	94
North America	5,397	7,224	8,970	11,877	13,994
Canada	315	366	486	568	543
United States	5,082	6,858	8,484	11,309	13,451
Total Developed Markets[a]	13,211	15,859	18,140	21,318	25,554

[a]Column total may not sum due to rounding error.

Source: Derived from various issues of *Emerging Stock Markets Factbook,* International Finance Corporation.

Market Capitalization of Developing Countries

Exhibit 8.2 presents the market capitalization of 32 emerging secondary equity markets from developing countries. In general, the International Finance Corporation classifies a stock market as "emerging" if it meets at least one of two general criteria: (1) it is located in a low- or middle-income economy as defined by the World Bank, and (2) its investable market capitalization is low relative to its most recent GDP figures.[1]

Exhibit 8.2 shows market capitalizations for 1994 through 1998. The table indicates that many emerging markets have grown significantly over the five-year period. However, many of the smaller Asian markets have declined in value as a result of the Asian crisis. The 1998 market capitalizations indicate that presently there are several tiny national equity markets in Latin America, Europe, the Middle East, and Africa. However, many of the national equity markets in Latin America (principally Brazil and Mexico) and in Asia (China, Korea, and Taiwan) have market capitalizations far in excess of the size of some of the smaller equity markets in the developed countries

EXHIBIT 8.2

Market Capitalization of Equity Markets in Developed Countries (in U.S. $ Billion)

Region or Country	1994	1995	1996	1997	1998
Latin America					
Argentina	36.9	37.8	44.7	59.3	45.3
Brazil	189.3	147.6	217.0	255.5	160.9
Chile	68.2	73.9	65.9	72.0	51.9
Colombia	14.0	17.9	17.1	19.5	13.4
Mexico	130.2	90.7	106.5	156.6	91.7
Peru	8.2	11.8	12.3	17.6	11.6
Venezuela	4.1	3.7	10.0	14.6	7.6
Asia					
China	43.5	42.0	113.8	206.4	231.3
India	127.5	127.2	122.6	128.5	105.2
Indonesia	47.2	66.6	91.0	29.1	22.1
Korea	191.8	182.0	138.8	41.9	114.6
Malaysia	199.3	222.7	307.2	93.6	98.6
Pakistan	12.3	9.3	10.6	11.0	5.4
Philippines	55.5	58.9	80.6	31.4	35.3
Sri Lanka	2.9	2.0	1.8	2.1	1.7
Taiwan	247.3	187.2	273.6	287.8	260.0
Thailand	131.5	141.5	99.8	23.5	34.9
Europe					
Czech Republic	5.9	15.7	18.1	12.8	12.0
Greece	14.9	17.1	24.2	34.2	80.0
Hungary	1.6	2.4	5.3	15.0	14.0
Poland	3.1	4.6	8.4	12.1	20.5
Portugal	16.2	18.4	24.7	39.0	63.0
Russia	0.3	0.5	3.0	16.4	20.6
Slovakia	0.1	0.8	2.3	2.2	1.0
Turkey	121.6	20.8	30.0	61.1	33.6
Mideast/Africa					
Egypt	0.8	0.7	2.5	5.9	24.3
Israel	25.1	9.2	8.0	10.7	39.6
Jordan	4.6	4.7	4.6	5.4	5.8
Morocco	0.8	NA	0.4	1.0	15.7
Nigeria	2.7	2.0	3.6	3.6	2.9
South Africa	225.7	280.5	241.6	232.1	170.3
Zimbabwe	1.8	2.0	3.6	2.0	1.3

Source: Various issues of *Emerging Stock Markets Factbook*, International Finance Corporation.

presented in Exhibit 8.1. This is indicative of investment opportunities in these emerging national markets.

Investment in foreign equity markets became common practice in the 1980s as investors became aware of the benefits of international portfolio diversification (our topic in Chapter 11). However, during the 1980s, cross-border equity investment was largely confined to the equity markets of developed countries. Only in the 1990s did world investors start to invest sizable amounts in the emerging equity markets, as the economic growth and prospects of the developing countries improved. For example, even after a horrible 1998, CDA/Wiesenberger Investment Companies Service reports that at year-end there were 179 emerging equity funds and 33 emerging fixed income funds, collectively representing 0.5 percent of investment in U.S.-based mutual funds. Only three years prior, separate emerging market fund categories did not exist as CDA/Wiesenberger classifications.

Measures of Liquidity

A liquid stock market is one in which investors can buy and sell stocks quickly at close to the current quoted prices. A measure of **liquidity** for a stock market is the turnover ratio; that is, the ratio of stock market transactions over a period of time divided by the size, or market capitalization, of the stock market. Generally, the higher the turnover ratio, the more liquid the secondary stock market, indicating ease in trading.

Exhibit 8.3 presents turnover ratio percentages for 24 equity markets of developed countries for the five years beginning with 1994. The table indicates that the turnover ratio varies considerably over time for most national equity markets. The

EXHIBIT 8.3

Turnover Ratio of Equity Markets in Developed Countries (Transactions in U.S. $/Year-End Market Capitalization in U.S. $)

Region or Country	1994	1995	1996	1997	1998
Europe					
Austria	55	79	60	69	109
Belgium	15	15	22	22	22
Denmark	51	46	48	50	NA
Finland	35	43	36	50	39
France	136	140	47	60	58
Germany	98	199	115	125	127
Iceland	4	6	8	NA	NA
Ireland	52	51	38	63	73
Italy	65	41	40	58	84
Luxembourg	<1	<1	2	2	3
Netherlands	60	70	90	61	63
Norway	24	55	62	70	77
Spain	40	30	103	156	174
Sweden	65	52	55	65	73
Switzerland	80	72	98	86	92
United Kingdom	38	36	33	42	49
Middle East					
Kuwait	19	47	88	134	NA
Far East					
Australia	43	40	48	45	47
Hong Kong	55	35	37	118	60
Japan	33	34	41	56	38
New Zealand	26	26	23	27	57
Singapore	60	41	28	60	54
North America					
Canada	51	50	55	63	69
United States	71	74	84	90	98

Source: Calculated from data from various issues of *Emerging Stock Markets Factbook,* International Financial Corporation.

table also indicates that most national equity markets had very high turnover ratios, with the great majority in excess of 50 percent turnover per year.

Exhibit 8.4 presents the turnover ratio percentages for 32 emerging stock markets for the five years from 1994 through 1998. The exhibit indicates a considerable difference in turnover ratios among the developing countries. Many of the small equity markets in each region (e.g., Chile, Colombia, Sri Lanka, Nigeria, Zimbabwe, and Morocco) have relatively low turnover ratios, indicating poor liquidity at present. Nevertheless, the larger emerging equity markets (Brazil, Korea, Taiwan, and Greece) demonstrate fairly strong liquidity. Additionally, the turnover ratios have increased (or at least stayed the same) over time for most developing countries. Comparing the ratios for 1994 and 1998 for the 32 countries indicates that 19 countries had a larger turnover ratio in 1998 than they did in 1994. Overall, liquidity in the emerging markets appears to be improving.

EXHIBIT 8.4

Turnover Ratio of Emerging Equity Markets in Selected Developing Countries (Transactions in U.S. $/Year-End Market Capitalization in U.S. $)

Region or Country	1994	1995	1996	1997	1998
Latin America					
Argentina	31	12	10	43	33
Brazil	58	54	52	80	91
Chile	8	15	13	10	9
Colombia	16	7	8	11	12
Mexico	64	38	40	34	37
Peru	38	33	31	45	24
Venezuela	23	14	13	26	20
Asia					
China	224	118	225	179	123
India	21	11	22	42	61
Indonesia	25	21	35	143	44
Korea	149	102	128	406	120
Malaysia	63	34	57	157	29
Pakistan	26	35	57	105	168
Philippines	25	25	32	63	28
Sri Lanka	24	11	7	15	16
Taiwan	289	205	172	451	340
Thailand	61	40	44	98	59
Europe					
Czech Republic	22	23	47	55	39
Greece	34	36	34	62	59
Hungary	7	23	31	51	115
Poland	168	61	66	66	28
Portugal	32	23	29	54	76
Russia	177	3	8	13	33
Slovakia	11	67	106	119	107
Turkey	100	247	123	97	204
Mideast/Africa					
Egypt	18	8	17	28	21
Israel	77	25	22	24	28
Jordan	14	11	7	9	23
Morocco	18	NA	5	9	9
Nigeria	<1	<1	2	4	<1
South Africa	7	6	11	19	34
Zimbabwe	10	7	7	27	13

Source: Calculated from data from various issues of *Emerging Stock Markets Factbook*, International Finance Corporation.

Measures of Market Concentration

As was previously mentioned, Chapter 11 will examine the benefits of constructing a diversified international portfolio. In order to construct a diversified portfolio, however, there must be opportunities for making foreign investment. The more concentrated a national equity market is in a few stock issues, the less opportunity a global investor has to include shares from that country in an internationally diversified portfolio.

Exhibit 8.5 presents the concentration ratios for 32 emerging stock markets for 1994 through 1998. The smaller the concentration percentage, the less concentrated a market is in a few stock issues. Twenty-six emerging stock markets are comparable for both years 1994 and 1998. In 1994, 13 stock markets had concentration ratios in excess of 40 percent, 5 in excess of 50 percent, and 3 in excess of 60 percent. By comparison, in 1998, 19 stock markets had concentration ratios in excess of 40 percent, 11 in excess of 50 percent and 7 in excess of 60 percent. Moreover, of the 6 stock markets represented in 1998, for which statistics were not available in 1994, 4 have concentration ratios in excess of 40 percent. Thus, one must conclude that the

EXHIBIT 8.5

Percentage of Market Capitalization Represented by the 10 Largest Stocks: Emerging Equity Markets in Developing Countries

Region or Country	1994	1995	1996	1997	1998
Latin America					
Argentina	42	48	50	52	49
Brazil	35	37	37	42	25
Chile	46	40	40	42	43
Colombia	61	39	44	50	41
Mexico	34	37	33	36	41
Peru	56	55	55	51	48
Venezuela	74	63	71	62	61
Asia					
China	17	20	19	14	18
India	19	18	20	25	33
Indonesia	30	41	51	48	61
Korea	30	35	20	39	38
Malaysia	30	29	28	36	32
Pakistan	32	38	31	67	55
Philippines	44	39	35	48	55
Sri Lanka	37	37	38	37	39
Taiwan	33	30	31	29	27
Thailand	36	36	35	48	46
Europe					
Czech Republic	NA	46	54	58	65
Greece	37	38	60	61	53
Hungary	44	31	81	85	85
Poland	47	37	53	40	65
Portugal	51	47	57	83	70
Russia	NA	NA	75	59	48
Slovakia	NA	NA	NA	77	71
Turkey	49	40	44	54	56
Mideast/Africa					
Egypt	NA	NA	33	30	21
Israel	NA	NA	NA	39	38
Jordan	46	56	59	70	71
Morocco	NA	NA	63	65	63
Nigeria	49	48	50	46	43
South Africa	26	26	27	26	27
Zimbabwe	61	64	62	67	48

Source: Various issues of *Emerging Stock Markets Factbook*, International Finance Corporation.

number of equity investment opportunities in emerging stock market countries has not been improving in recent years. These numbers are symptomatic of the Asian crisis discussed in Chapter 2.

MARKET STRUCTURE, TRADING PRACTICES, AND COSTS[2]

The **secondary** equity markets of the world serve two major purposes. They provide *marketability* and *share valuation.* Investors or traders who buy shares from the issuing firm in the **primary** market may not want to hold them indefinitely. The secondary market allows share owners to reduce their holdings of unwanted shares and purchasers to acquire the stock. Firms would have a difficult time attracting buyers in the primary market without the marketability provided through the secondary market. Additionally, competitive trading between buyers and sellers in the secondary market establishes fair market prices for existing issues.

In conducting a trade in a secondary market, public buyers and sellers are represented by an agent, known as a **broker**. The order submitted to the broker may be a market order or a limit order. A **market order** is executed at the best price available when the order is received in the market, that is, the *market price.* A **limit order** is an order *away from the market* price that is held in a **limit order book** until it can be executed at the desired price.

There are many different designs for secondary markets that allow for efficient trading of shares between buyers and sellers. Generally, however, a secondary market is structured as a dealer or agency market. In a **dealer market**, the broker takes the trade through the dealer, who participates in trades as a principal by buying and selling the security for his own account. Public traders do not trade directly with one another in a dealer market. In an **agency market**, the broker takes the client's order through the agent, who matches it with another public order. The agent can be viewed as a *broker's broker.* Other names for the agent are *official broker* and *central broker.*

Both dealer and agency structures exist in the United States. The **over-the-counter (OTC)** market is a dealer market. Almost all OTC stocks trade on the National Association of Security Dealers Automated Quotation System (NASDAQ), which is a computer-linked system that shows the **bid** (buy) and **ask** (sell) prices of all dealers in a security. As many as 20 dealers may make a market in the most actively traded issues.

In the United States, firms must meet certain listing requirements in order to have their stock traded on one of several organized stock exchanges. The two largest of these exchanges, the New York Stock Exchange (NYSE) and the American Stock Exchange (AMEX), are both national exchanges on which the stocks of the largest companies of most interest to investors are traded. Shares of firms of regional interest are traded on several regional exchanges.

The exchange markets in the United States are agency/auction markets. Each stock traded on the exchange is represented by a **specialist**, who makes a market by holding an inventory of the security. Each specialist has a designated station (desk) on the exchange trading floor where trades in his stock are conducted. Floor brokers bring the flow of public market orders for a security to the specialist's desk for execution. Serving as a dealer, the specialist is obligated to post bid and ask prices for the stock he represents and to stand willing to buy or sell for his own account at these prices. Through an auction process, the "crowd" of floor brokers may arrive at a more favorable market price for their clients between the specialist's bid and ask prices and thus transact among themselves. The specialist also holds the limit order book. In executing these orders, the specialist serves as an agent. Limit order prices receive preference in establishing the posted bid and ask prices if they are more favorable than the specialist's, and he must fill a limit order, if possible, from the flow of public orders before trading for his own account. Both the OTC and exchange markets in the United States are **continuous markets** where market and limit orders can be executed at any time during business hours.

In recent years, most national stock markets have become at least partially automated for some of the issues traded on them. The first was the Toronto Stock Exchange (TSE), which in 1977 instituted the Computer Assisted Trading System (CATS). An automated trading system electronically stores and displays public orders on a continuous basis, and allows public traders to cross orders with one another to execute a trade without the assistance of exchange personnel. A similar arrangement exists at the Tokyo Stock Exchange (also TSE), where small issues are handled by the Tokyo CATS and only large issues are paired by a *Saitori,* a floor agent, who does not trade for his account as does a specialist. Automated systems are successful largely because orders can be filled faster and fewer exchange personnel are needed. Indeed, in many countries the exchange trading floor has been completely eliminated.

Not all national stock markets provide for continuous trading. For example, the Paris Bourse was traditionally a call market. In a **call market**, an agent of the exchange accumulates, over a period of time, a batch of orders that are periodically executed by written or verbal auction throughout the trading day. Both market and limit orders are handled in this way. The major disadvantage of a call market is that traders are not certain about the price at which their orders will transact because bid and ask quotations are not available prior to the call. Today a CATS system is the primary trading system at the Paris Bourse, with only smaller issues being traded through a single daily call.

A second type of noncontinuous exchange trading system is **crowd trading**. Typically, crowd trading is organized as follows. In a trading ring, an agent of the exchange periodically calls out the name of the issue. At this point, traders announce their bid and ask prices for the issue, and seek counterparts to a trade. Between counterparts a deal may be struck and a trade executed. Unlike a call market in which there is a common price for all trades, several bilateral trades may take place at different prices. Crowd trading was once the system of trading on the Zurich Stock Exchange, but the Swiss exchange moved to an automated system in August 1996. At present, crowd trading is practiced at the Madrid Stock Exchange.

Continuous trading systems are desirable for actively traded issues, whereas call markets and crowd trading offer advantages for thinly traded issues because they mitigate the possibility of sparse order flow over short time periods. Exhibit 8.6 provides a summary of the major equity trading systems found worldwide.

Exhibit 8.7 provides a brief summary of the location and the market trading systems used at various major equity markets of the world. The exhibit also shows the typical taxes applicable to equity trades and the length of time involved in settling a trade.

EXHIBIT 8.6

Characteristics of Major Equity Trading Systems

Equity Trading System	Market Characteristics		
	Public Orders	Order Flow	Example
Dealer	Trade with dealer	Continuous	NASDAQ OTC
Agency	Agent assists with matching of public orders	Continuous or periodic	NYSE specialist system[a] (continuous) Paris Bourse (noncontinuous)
Fully automated	Electronic matching of public orders	Continuous	Toronto Stock Exchange

[a]As noted in the text, a specialist may at times also serve as a dealer.

EXHIBIT 8.7 Trading Practices and Costs of Major Equity Markets

Country	Primary Market	System	Taxes	Settlement
Argentina	Buenos Aires	Auction market; automated; OTC	.13%	Trade date + 3 days
Australia	Sydney/Melbourne	Automated national market	.15%	Trade date + 5 days
Austria	Vienna	Automated quote and market-making	.02–.1% turnonver tax	Trade date + 3 business days
Bangladesh	Dhaka	Automated	None	Trade date + 3 business days
Belgium	Brussels	Forward: automated; Cash: Call market	Fee: .03%	Forward: end of account period; Cash: trade date + 3 business days
Brazil	Sao Paulo and Rio de Janeiro	Crowd trading; automated	Fee: .035%	Trade date + 3 business days
Bulgaria	Sofia	Automated	.02%	Trade date + 3 business days
Canada	Toronto	Automated	None	Trade date + 3 business days
Croatia	Zagreb	Automated	.01–.35% on sells	Trade date + 5 business days
Czech Republic	Prague	Automated and OTC	.080–.125%; OTC: 0%	Trade date + 3 business days; OTC: Negotiable
Chile	Santiago	Major Stocks: automated; Others: crowd trading	Cumulative schedule from .50%–0%	Trade date + 2 business days
China	Shenzhen and Shanghai	Automated	Shenzhen: .385% Shanghai: .53%	Trade date + 3 days
Columbia	Bogotá	Automated	.13%	Trade date + 3 business days
Denmark	Copenhagen	Automated	None	Trade date + 3 business days
Egypt	Cairo	Automated	.0375%	Trade date + 3 business days
Finland	Helsinki	Automated	None	Trade date + 3 business days
France	Paris	Automated: 1st and large 2nd tier; Call market: 2nd and 3rd	None for foreigners	Largest stocks: last trading day; Call: trade date + 3 business days
Germany	Frankfurt	Small: official broker; Large: specialist	.04–.08%	Trade date + 2 business days
Greece	Athens	Automated	Fees: .30% on sales	Trade date + 3 business days

Hong Kong	Hong Kong	Automated	.0136%	Trade date + 2 business days
Hungary	Budapest	Automated	None	Trade date + 5 business days
India	National Stock Exchange; Bombay Stock Exchange	Automated	.50% on buys	7–15 days
Indonesia	Jakarta	Automated	Buys .043%; sells .143%	Trade date + 4 business days
Ireland	Dublin	Call; Off-floor trading	1.00% on purchases	Trade date + 5 business days
Israel	Tel Aviv	Automated (98%) and computerized call	None	Trade date + 0 (1) business days domestic (foreign)
Italy	Milan	Automated	None for nonresidents	Trade date + 5 business days
Japan	Tokyo	Automated; Floor traded (largest)	.10% sales tax	Trade date + 3 business days
Jordan	Amman	Agent posts client orders on a designated billboard	.15%	Trade date + 3 business days
Lebanon	Beirut	Call market	None	Trade date + 3 business days
Malaysia	Kuala Lumpur	Automated	.05%	Trade date + 5 (4) business days purchases (sales)
Mexico	Mexico City	Crowd trading; Automated (low volume)	.08%	Trade date + 2 business days
Morocco	Casablanca	Automated and OTC	.24% + 7% VAT on commission	Trade date + 5 business days
Netherlands	Amsterdam	Semi-specialist automatic system	.012%–.05%	Trade date + 3 business days
New Zealand	National Integrated Market	Automated	None	Trade date + 5 business days
Norway	Oslo	Automated	None	Trade date + 3 business days
Pakistan	Karachi	Automated	USD 100 per trade	Trade date + 7 business days
Peru	Lima	Integrated crowd trading	.196%	Trade date + 3 business days
Philippines	Manilla	Automated	Sales: 50%; Document tax: .0075% stock par value; Bank charges: PHP100 on buys	Trade date + 4 business days
Poland	Warsaw	Automated system supervised by specialist	.16%	Trade date + 3 business days

(continued)

EXHIBIT 8.7 Trading Practices and Costs of Major Equity Markets *(concluded)*

Country	Primary Market	System	Taxes	Settlement
Portugal	Lisbon	Automate and call market	Listed .02% OTC .05%	Trade date + 3 business days
Romania	Bucharest	Automated; OTC Automated quotation	None	Trade date + 3 business days
Russia	Moscow	OTC Automated quotation and dealer quotation	.3%	Trade date + 2 to 15 days
Singapore	Singapore	Automated	.05% (Max SGD100)	Trade date + 7 days
South Africa	Johannesburg	Automated	.25% on buys	Tuesday following trade week
South Korea	Seoul	Automated	.30%–.50% on sales	Trade date + 2 business days
Spain	Madrid	Automated and crowd trading	None	Trade date + 3 business days
Sri Lanka	Colombo	Automated	.25%	Trade date + 5 (6) business days for purchase (sale)
Sweden	Stockholm	Automated	None	Trade date + 3 business days
Switzerland	Zurich	Automated	.09%	Trade date + 3 days domestic
Taiwan	Taipei	Automated	.30% on sells	Trade date + 3 business days
Thailand	Bangkok	Automated	None	Trade date + 3 business days
Turkey	Istanbul	Automated	None	Trade date + 2 business days
United Kingdom	London	Automated dealer quotation system	.50% on purchases + GBP0.25 on trades > GBP10,000	Trade date + 5 business days
United States	New York and OTC	Specialist: NYSE and AMEX; Automated quotation: NASDAQ OTC	USD0.01 per USD300 on sale value	Trade date + 3 business days
Venezuela	Caracas	Automated	.10% + 16.5% VAT on commission + 1% on sales	Trade date + 5 to 90 days
Zimbabwe	Harare	Call market	ZWD20 per trade	Trade date + 7 business days

Source: Excerpted from *Guide to Global Equity Markets,* 8th ed., Warburg Dillon Reed, January 1999.

INTERNATIONAL EQUITY MARKET BENCHMARKS

As a benchmark of activity or performance of a given national equity market, an index of the stocks traded on the secondary exchange (or exchanges) of a country is used. Several national equity indexes are available for use by investors.

To this point, the exhibits of this chapter have presented data from stock market indexes prepared by the International Finance Corporation (IFC), a multinational financial institution that is part of the World Bank Group. The IFC was established in 1956 to facilitate the growth of its member developing countries through private-sector investment. Each year the IFC publishes its *Emerging Stock Markets Factbook,* which provides a variety of statistical data on both emerging and developed country stock markets. The *Factbook* is an excellent source that is carried by many university libraries and provides annual comparative statistics in an easy-to-read format.

The indexes prepared and published by Morgan Stanley Capital International (MSCI) are an excellent source of national stock market performance. Through its monthly publication, *Morgan Stanley Capital International Perspective,* MSCI presents return and market capitalization data for 23 national stock market indexes from developed countries. In constructing each of these indexes, an attempt is made to include equity issues representing at least 60 percent of the market capitalization of each industry within the country. The stocks in each country index are market-value weighted, that is, the proportion of the index a stock represents is determined by its proportion of the total market capitalization of all stocks in the index. Additionally, MSCI publishes a market-value-weighted World Index comprising 22 of its country indexes. The World Index includes approximately 2,600 stock issues of major corporations in the world. MSCI also publishes several regional indexes: the European, Australasia, Far East (EAFE) Index comprising approximately 1,000 stocks from 20 countries; the North American Index composed of the United States and Canada; the Far East Index (three countries); four Europe Indexes (with between 13 and 15 countries depending upon whether the U.K. and/or Switzerland are included); the Nordic Countries Index (four countries); and the Pacific Index (five countries). The EAFE Index is widely followed, and it is representative of World Index excluding North American stock market performance. Daily values of several of the MSCI country indexes and the World Index can be found in *The Wall Street Journal.* MSCI also publishes 38 industry indexes, each of which includes equity issues from the respective industry from the countries it follows.

MSCI also publishes national stock index return and historical valuation ratios for 28 emerging stock markets from developing countries covering 1,700 securities. Additionally, MSCI publishes a global and several regional emerging markets indexes. The Emerging Markets Free version of these indexes recognizes that some countries impose ownership restrictions on stocks by foreigners. In this case, the constituent national indexes are excluded or underweighted to recognize the particular restriction in order to provide an index representative of investments that can be freely made.

The Dow Jones Company (DJ) provides stock market index values and percentage change data for a number of world regional areas: the Americas, which comprise Brazil, Canada, Chile, Mexico, the United States, and Venezuela; Europe/Africa, which includes the developed Western European countries and South Africa; and the Asia/Pacific region, which includes Australia, Hong Kong, Indonesia, Japan, New Zealand, the Philippines, Singapore, South Korea, Taiwan, and Thailand. Individual country stock market indexes are provided as well as regional stock indexes and the DJ World Stock Index. The values and percentage changes of these indexes can be found daily in *The Wall Street Journal.* The data are presented in local currency terms and for comparative purposes in U.S. dollars. Exhibit 8.8 presents an example of the daily report of these indexes as found in *The Wall Street Journal.*

EXHIBIT 8.8 Example of Dow Jones Global Stock Market Indexes

Dow Jones Global Index
5:30 p.m. Thursday, August 26, 1999

Region/ Country	DJ Global Indexes, Local Currency	Pct. Chg.	In U.S. Dollars: 5:30 P.M. Index	Chg.	Pct. Chg.	12-Mo High	12-Mo Low	12-Mo Chg.	Pct. Chg.	From 12/31	Pct. Chg.
Americas			**312.18**	**− 4.22**	**− 1.33**	**325.83**	**219.47**	**+ 73.04**	**+ 30.54**	**+ 28.39**	**+ 10.00**
Brazil†	1060	− 1.51	215.74	− 1.00	− 0.46	312.23	155.25	− 22.21	− 9.33	− 22.85	− 9.58
Canada	218.55	− 1.00	168.19	− 2.32	− 1.36	175.70	117.73	+ 41.05	+ 32.29	+ 21.94	+ 15.00
Chile	223.51	+ 1.01	162.91	+ 2.00	+ 1.24	174.92	96.32	+ 49.28	+ 43.36	+ 31.97	+ 24.42
Mexico	396.70	− 0.66	130.29	− 1.57	− 1.19	147.81	60.60	+ 61.60	+ 89.68	+ 41.26	+ 46.35
U.S.	1283.16	− 1.35	1283.16	− 17.54	− 1.35	1338.32	900.71	+ 299.60	+ 30.46	+ 113.82	+ 9.73
Venezuela	322.77	+ 0.45	32.29	+ 0.13	+ 0.40	49.81	23.01	+ 7.40	+ 29.74	− 7.64	− 19.13
Latin America			**148.69**	**− 0.57**	**− 0.38**	**178.96**	**90.39**	**+ 35.16**	**+ 30.97**	**+ 20.36**	**+ 15.87**
Europe/Africa			**237.40**	**+ 0.36**	**+ 0.15**	**249.23**	**185.07**	**+ 27.62**	**+ 13.17**	**+ 2.41**	**+ 1.03**
Austria	126.77	− 0.63	102.81	− 0.43	− 0.42	113.74	93.22	− 0.18	− 0.18	− 2.52	− 2.39
Belgium	297.55	+ 1.08	241.51	+ 3.08	+ 1.29	307.75	219.37	− 4.16	− 1.69	− 47.90	− 16.55
Denmark	214.34	− 0.30	178.35	− 0.72	− 0.40	196.60	156.84	− 0.23	− 0.13	− 11.78	− 6.20
Finland	1099.62	+ 0.61	800.22	+ 6.49	+ 0.82	869.41	365.19	+ 362.55	+ 82.84	+ 195.70	+ 32.37
France	287.26	− 0.00	236.94	+ 0.49	+ 0.21	238.23	173.04	+ 41.87	+ 21.46	+ 15.93	+ 7.21
Germany	300.44	− 0.18	243.06	+ 0.07	+ 0.03	268.27	195.52	+ 15.84	+ 6.97	− 4.95	− 2.00
Greece	693.44	− 2.35	389.41	− 9.73	− 2.44	399.14	181.78	+ 173.55	+ 80.40	+ 107.42	+ 38.09
Ireland	383.44	− 0.11	303.79	+ 0.30	+ 0.10	369.89	247.45	+ 20.90	+ 7.39	− 31.86	− 9.49
Italy	309.48	+ 0.55	205.92	+ 1.56	+ 0.76	252.46	169.16	+ 5.48	+ 2.73	− 28.50	− 12.16
Netherlands	419.71	− 0.14	339.59	+ 0.25	+ 0.07	363.31	258.60	+ 35.42	+ 11.65	− 6.45	− 1.86
Norway	188.03	− 0.12	141.18	+ 0.14	+ 0.10	145.18	96.85	+ 27.04	+ 23.69	+ 25.05	+ 21.58
Portugal	314.37	+ 0.77	240.34	+ 2.35	+ 0.99	322.89	221.49	− 39.09	− 13.99	− 57.55	− 19.32
South Africa	207.32	− 0.58	93.47	0.00	0.00	101.29	57.78	+ 34.28	+ 57.90	+ 22.77	+ 32.20
Spain	399.71	− 0.12	244.77	+ 0.23	+ 0.09	293.48	194.86	+ 27.49	+ 12.65	− 25.86	− 9.55
Sweden	476.77	+ 0.36	317.44	+ 0.56	+ 0.18	317.44	190.08	+ 72.46	+ 29.58	+ 63.98	+ 25.24
Switzerland	407.03	− 0.03	259.71	+ 0.79	+ 0.22	417.95	295.28	+ 7.61	+ 2.16	− 36.21	− 9.15
United Kingdom	243.16	+ 0.03	206.48	+ 0.14	+ 0.07	217.02	162.40	+ 23.38	+ 12.77	+ 7.91	+ 3.98
Europe/Africa (ex. South Africa)			**245.69**	**+ 0.39**	**+ 0.16**	**259.05**	**191.94**	**+ 27.22**	**+ 12.46**	**+ 1.30**	**+ 0.53**
Europe/Africa (ex. U.K. & S. Africa)			**270.38**	**+ 0.53**	**+ 0.20**	**291.33**	**210.59**	**+ 29.58**	**+ 12.28**	**− 2.51**	**− 0.92**
Asia/Pacific			**108.35**	**− 1.22**	**− 1.11**	**110.67**	**62.38**	**+ 43.86**	**+ 68.02**	**+ 27.32**	**+ 33.71**
Australia	190.05	+ 0.35	157.67	+ 0.36	+ 0.23	170.99	112.56	+ 45.11	+ 40.07	+ 16.65	+ 11.81
Hong Kong	271.73	+ 0.57	272.19	+ 1.53	+ 0.57	292.81	140.39	+ 114.31	+ 72.40	+ 68.13	+ 33.39
Indonesia	226.19	− 0.77	58.52	− 1.23	− 2.06	82.35	15.47	+ 34.61	+ 144.77	+ 18.07	+ 44.66
Japan	89.78	− 1.18	100.40	− 1.71	− 1.67	103.61	57.38	+ 39.82	+ 65.73	+ 26.20	+ 35.31
New Zealand	141.91	+ 0.52	134.43	− 0.03	− 0.02	157.99	99.94	+ 20.25	+ 17.74	+ 5.03	+ 3.89
Philippines	207.26	− 1.14	135.54	− 1.43	− 1.04	175.79	60.68	+ 65.59	+ 93.76	+ 8.25	+ 6.48
Singapore	157.27	+ 0.87	150.71	+ 1.23	+ 0.82	154.66	59.89	+ 83.00	+ 122.58	+ 41.31	+ 37.75
South Korea	169.56	− 0.08	108.03	+ 0.19	+ 0.18	117.86	26.41	+ 77.47	+ 253.54	+ 46.80	+ 76.43
Taiwan	202.20	− 0.37	165.81	+ 1.63	+ 0.99	171.86	106.17	+ 50.22	+ 43.45	+ 42.52	+ 34.49
Thailand	80.28	− 1.39	49.39	− 0.79	− 1.57	59.51	20.88	+ 26.75	+ 118.21	+ 9.63	+ 24.21
Asia/Pacific (ex. Japan)			**169.78**	**+ 0.48**	**+ 0.28**	**181.77**	**91.45**	**+ 72.73**	**+ 74.94**	**+ 39.08**	**+ 29.90**
World (ex. U.S.)			**163.36**	**− 0.59**	**− 0.36**	**164.02**	**115.37**	**+ 36.34**	**+ 28.60**	**+ 16.35**	**+ 11.12**
DJ WORLD STOCK INDEX			**222.93**	**− 1.96**	**− 0.87**	**226.81**	**160.36**	**+ 50.18**	**+ 29.05**	**+ 20.14**	**+ 9.93**

Indexes based on 6/30/82 = 100 for U.S., 12/31/91 = 100 for World.
†Local currency index shown in 000s.

© 1999 Dow Jones & Co., Inc., All Rights Reserved.

Source: *The Wall Street Journal,* August 27, 1999, p. C14. Reprinted by permission of *The Wall Street Journal,* © 1999 Dow Jones & Company, Inc. All Rights Reserved Worldwide.

EXHIBIT 8.9

Major National Stock Market Indexes

Country	Index
Argentina	Merval Index
Australia	All Ordinaries
Belgium	Bel-20 Index
Brazil	Sao Paulo Bovespa
Britain	London FT 100-share
Britain	London FT 250-share
Canada	Toronto 300 Comp.
Chile	Santiago IPSA
China	Dow Jones China 88
China	Dow Jones Shanghai
China	Dow Jones Shenzhen
Europe	DJ Stoxx (Euro)
Europe	DJ Stoxx 50 (Euro)
Euro Zone	DJ Euro Stoxx (Euro)
Euro Zone	DJ Euro Stoxx 50 (Euro)
France	Paris CAC 40
Germany	Frankfurt Xetra DAX
Hong Kong	Hang Sang
India	Bombay Sensex
Italy	Milan MIBtel
Japan	Tokyo Nikkei 225
Japan	Tokyo Nikkei 300
Japan	Tokyo Topix Index
Malaysia	DJ Malaysia
Mexico	I.P.C. All-Share
Netherlands	Amsterdam AEX
Singapore	Straits Times
South Africa	Johannesburg All Share
South Korea	Composite
Spain	IBEX 35
Sweden	Stockholm General
Switzerland	Zurich Swiss Market
Taiwan	Weighted Index
United States	
American Stock Exchange Composite	
Dow Jones Industrial Average	
National Association of Security Dealers Automated Quotation Composite	
New York Stock Exchange Composite	
Russell 2000	
Standard and Poor's 500	
Wilshire 5000	
Value-Lime	

Sources: *The Wall Street Journal,* August 27, 1999, p. C14. Reprinted by permission of *The Wall Street Journal,* © 1999 Dow Jones & Company, Inc. All Rights Reserved Worldwide.

In addition to their own Dow Jones indexes, *The Wall Street Journal* also reports values and percentage changes in local currency values of the major stock market indexes of the national exchanges or markets from various countries in the world. Many of these indexes are prepared by the stock markets themselves or well-known investment advisory firms. Exhibit 8.9 presents a list of the indexes that appear daily in *The Wall Street Journal.*

World Equity Benchmark Shares

Recently, Barclays Global Fund Advisors introduced World Equity Benchmark Shares (WEBS) as vehicles to facilitate investment in country funds. WEBS are country-specific baskets of stocks designed to replicate the

MSCI country indexes of 14 countries. They trade as shares on the American Stock Exchange.

WEBS are subject to U.S. SEC and Internal Revenue Service diversification requirements. These requirements prohibit the investment of more than 50 percent of the fund in five or fewer securities, or 25 percent of the fund in a single security. Thus, for some countries, the WEB does not perfectly replicate the MSCI country fund. Nevertheless, WEBS are a low-cost, convenient way for investors to hold diversified investments in several different countries. Eleven new country WEBS are expected to start trading soon.

TRADING IN INTERNATIONAL EQUITIES

During the 1980s world capital markets began a trend toward greater global integration. Several factors account for this movement. First, investors began to realize the benefits of international portfolio diversification. Second, major capital markets became more liberalized through the elimination of fixed trading commissions, the reduction in governmental regulation, and measures taken by the European Union to integrate their capital markets. Third, new computer and communications technology facilitated efficient and fair securities trading through order routing and execution, information dissemination, and clearance and settlement.[3] Fourth, MNCs realized the benefits of sourcing new capital internationally. In this section, we explore some of the major effects that greater global integration has had on the world's equity markets. We begin by examining the cross-listing of shares.

Cross-Listing of Shares

Cross-listing refers to a firm having its equity shares listed on one or more foreign exchanges, in addition to the home country stock exchange. Cross-listing is not a new concept; however, with the increased globalization of world equity markets, the amount of cross-listing has exploded in recent years. In particular, MNCs often cross-list their shares, but non-MNCs also cross-list.

Exhibit 8.10 presents the total number of companies listed on various national stock exchanges in the world and the breakdown of the listings between domestic and foreign for 1998. The exhibit also shows the number of new listings and the domestic-foreign split for 1998. The exhibit shows that some foreign companies are listed on virtually all national stock exchanges from developed countries. Many European exchanges have a large proportion of foreign listings. In fact, the exchanges in Germany and Luxembourg have more foreign than domestic listings, while on the Brussels and Swiss bourses the foreign listings are nearly 50 percent.

A firm may decide to cross-list its shares for many reasons:

1. Cross-listing provides a means for expanding the investor base for a firm's stock, thus potentially increasing the demand for the stock. Increased demand for a company's stock may increase the market price. Additionally, greater market demand and a broader investor base improves the price liquidity of the security.
2. Cross-listing establishes name recognition of the company in a new capital market, thus paving the way for the firm to source new equity or debt capital from local investors as demands dictate.
3. Cross-listing brings the firm's name before more investor and consumer groups. Local consumers (investors) may more likely become investors in (consumers of) the company's stock (products) if the company's stock is (products are) locally available. International portfolio diversification is facilitated for investors if they can trade the security on their own stock exchange.

EXHIBIT 8.10 Total, Domestic, and Foreign Company Listings on Major National Stock Exchanges for 1998

		Total Listings			New Listings		
Region	**Exchange**	**Total**	**Domestic**	**Foreign**	**Total**	**Domestic**	**Foreign**
North and South America							
	AMEX	711	650	61	100	92	8
	Buenos Aires	131	131	0	3	3	0
	Lima	249	246	3	17	17	0
	Chicago	251	251	0	6	6	0
	Mexico	195	191	4	3	3	0
	Montreal	550	538	12	31	31	0
	NASDAQ	5,068	4,672	441	487	437	50
	NYSE	2,669	2,278	391	205	162	43
	Rio de Janeiro	583	582	1	66	66	0
	Santiago	287	287	0	5	5	0
	Sao Paulo	535	534	1	57	57	0
	Toronto	1,433	1,384	49	116	113	3
	Vancouver	1,384	NA	NA	39	NA	NA
Europe, Africa, Middle East							
	Amsterdam	356	212	144	23	22	1
	Athens	229	229	0	23	23	0
	Barcelona	392	387	5	75	73	2
	Bilbao	258	256	2	28	27	1
	Brussels	268	146	122	24	18	6
	Copenhagen	254	242	12	13	13	0
	Germany	3,525	741	2,784	997	67	930
	Helsinki	131	129	2	12	12	0
	Irish	100	79	21	6	3	3
	Istanbul	278	277	1	20	20	0
	Italy	243	239	4	22	21	1
	Johannesburg	668	642	26	101	100	1
	Lisbon	135	135	0	8	8	0
	Ljubljana	90	90	0	16	16	0
	London	2,423	1,957	466	202	169	33
	Luxembourg	276	53	223	12	2	10
	Madrid	484	479	5	113	111	2
	Oslo	235	213	22	29	27	2
	Paris	1,097	914	183	240	226	14
	Stockholm	276	258	18	36	32	4
	Switzerland	425	232	193	17	17	0
	Tehran	261	261	0	11	11	0
	Tel-Aviv	662	661	1	14	14	0
	Vienna	128	96	32	3	2	1
	Warsaw	198	198	0	57	57	0
Asia, Pacific							
	Australian	1,222	1,162	60	63	54	9
	Colombo	240	240	0	6	6	0
	Hong Kong	680	665	15	32	31	1
	Jakarta	287	287	0	6	6	0
	Korea	748	748	0	3	3	0
	Kuala Lumpur	731	728	3	28	28	0
	New Zealand	183	122	61	11	5	6
	Osaka	1,272	1,271	1	13	13	0
	Philippines	221	221	0	3	3	0
	Singapore	349	312	37	23	23	0
	Taiwan	437	437	0	35	35	0
	Thailand	418	418	0	1	1	0
	Tokyo	1,890	1,838	52	57	54	3

*NA denotes not available.

Source: Table I.1, p. 68 and Table I.2., p. 69 from *FIBV Annual Report and Statistics 1998.*

4. Cross-listing may mitigate the possibility of a hostile takeover of the firm through the broader investor base created for the firm's shares.

Cross-listing of a firm's stock obligates the firm to adhere to the securities regulations of its home country as well as the regulations of the countries in which it is cross-listed. Cross-listing in the United States means the firm must meet the accounting and disclosure requirements of the U.S. Securities and Exchange Commission. Reconciliation of a company's financial statements to U.S. standards can be a laborious process, and some foreign firms are reluctant to disclose hidden reserves. For foreign firms desiring to have their shares traded only among large institutional investors, less rigorous accounting and disclosure requirements apply under SEC Rule 144A. Rule 144A share sales are often acceptable to family-owned companies, which for privacy or tax reasons operate their business with generally unacceptable accounting standards.[4]

Yankee Stock Offerings

The introduction to this section indicated that in recent years U.S. investors have bought and sold a large amount of foreign stock. Since the beginning of the 1990s, many foreign companies, Latin American in particular, have listed their stocks on U.S. exchanges to prime the U.S. equity market for future **Yankee stock** offerings, that is, the direct sale of new equity capital to U.S. public investors. This was a break from the past for the Latin American companies, which typically sold restricted 144A shares to large investors. Three factors appear to be fueling the sale of Yankee stocks. One is the push for privatization by many Latin American and Eastern European government-owned companies. A second factor is the rapid growth in the economies of the developing countries. The third reason is the expected large demand for new capital by Mexican companies now that the North American Free Trade Agreement has been approved (and despite the meltdown of the peso in late 1994).[5]

The European Stock Market

Europe has more than 26 equity markets where at least 10 different languages are spoken and as many different accounting systems are used. The European Association of Securities Dealers Automated Quotation System (EASDAQ) can be viewed as the beginning of a truly European stock market. The EASDAQ is a pan-European stock market established in the European Union; it is not an association of multidomestic exchanges. EASDAQ is a multiple market system patterned after trading on the NASDAQ in the United States. Trading on the EASDAQ takes place among its members currently situated in the U.K., France, Germany, the Netherlands, Switzerland, Austria, Belgium, Portugal, Italy, Denmark, Finland, Greece, and Luxembourg. EASDAQ stock transactions are settled through Eurolist and Cedel. Since January 4, 1999, all trading in all securities is denominated in the euro common currency.[6]

American Depository Receipts

Foreign stocks can be traded directly on a national stock market, but most often they are traded in the form of a *depository receipt.* For example, Yankee stock issues often trade on the U.S. exchanges as **American Depository Receipts (ADRs)**. An ADR is a receipt representing a number of foreign shares that are deposited in a U.S. bank. The bank serves as the transfer agent for the ADRs, which are traded on the listed exchanges in the United States or in the OTC market. The first ADRs began trading in 1927 as a means of eliminating some of the risks, delays, inconveniences, and expenses of trading the actual shares. The ADR market has grown significantly over the years, and at mid-year 1999 there were 1,405 ADR programs, representing over $306 billion of equity in companies from at least 69 countries traded on U.S. exchanges. Similarly, on the London Stock Exchange, *Global Depository Receipts* allow foreign firms to trade, and *Singapore Depository Receipts* trade on the Singapore Stock Exchange. Exhibit 8.11 shows a tombstone for a Global Depository Receipt.

EXHIBIT 8.11

Global Depository Receipt Tombstone

COMMERCIAL INTERNATIONAL BANK
(EGYPT) S.A.E.

International Offering of
9,999,000 Global Depository Receipts

corresponding to
999,900 Shares (nominal Value of E£100 per Share)

at an
Offer price of US$11.875 per Global Depository Receipt

Seller
National Bank of Egypt

Global Co-ordinator
Co Lead Managers
Robert Fleming & Co. Limited Salomon Brothers International Limited
UBS Limited

Domestic Advisor
Commercial International Investment Company S.A.E.

ING BARINGS

July 1996

Source: *Euromoney*, October 1998, p. 127.

ADRs offer the U.S. investor many advantages over trading directly in the underlying stock on the foreign exchange. Non-U.S. investors can also invest in ADRs, and frequently do so rather than invest in the underlying stock because of the investment advantages. These advantages include:

1. ADRs are denominated in dollars, trade on a U.S. stock exchange, and can be purchased through the investor's regular broker. By contrast, trading in the underlying shares would likely require the investor to: set up an account with a broker from the country where the company issuing the stock was located; make a currency exchange; and arrange for the shipment of the stock certificates or the establishment of a custodial account.
2. Dividends received on the underlying shares are collected and converted to dollars by the custodian and paid to the ADR investor, whereas investment in the underlying shares requires the investor to collect the foreign dividends and make a currency conversion. Moreover, tax treaties between the United States and some countries lower the dividend tax rate paid by nonresident investors. Consequently, U.S. investors in the underlying shares need to file a form to get a refund on the tax difference withheld. ADR investors, however, receive the full dollar equivalent dividend, less only the applicable taxes.
3. ADR trades clear in three business days as do U.S. equities, whereas settlement practices for the underlying stock vary in foreign countries.
4. ADR price quotes are in U.S. dollars.
5. ADRs are registered securities that provide for the protection of ownership rights, whereas most underlying stocks are bearer securities.

6. An ADR investment can be terminated by trading the receipt to another investor on the exchange on which it is traded, or it can be returned to the bank depository for cash.
7. ADRs frequently represent a multiple of the underlying shares, rather than a one-for-one correspondence, to allow the ADR to trade in a price range customary for U.S. investors. A single ADR may represent more or less than one underlying share, depending on the per share value.

EXAMPLE 8.1 Daimler-Chrysler AG Stock in Daimler-Chrysler AG, the result of the merger of Daimler Benz AG, the famous German automobile manufacturer, and Chrysler Corporation, is cross-listed on the Frankfurt Stock Exchange in Germany and on the New York Stock Exchange. On the Frankfurt bourse, Daimler-Chrysler closed at a price of EUR72.65 on Friday, September 10, 1999. On the same day, Daimler-Chrysler closed in New York at \$75.75 per share. To prevent arbitrage between trading on the two exchanges, the shares have to trade at the same price when adjusted for the exchange rate. We see that this is true. The \$/EUR exchange rate on September 10 was \$1.0367/EUR1.00. Thus, EUR72.65 × \$1.0367 = \$75.32, an amount very close to the closing price in New York of \$75.75. The difference is easily explainable by the fact that the New York market closes several hours after the Frankfurt exchange, and thus market prices had changed slightly.

There are two types of ADRs: sponsored and unsponsored. *Sponsored* ADRs are created by a bank at the request of the foreign company that issued the underlying security. The sponsoring bank often offers ADR holders an assortment of services, including investment information and portions of the annual report translated into English. *Unsponsored* ADRs are usually created at the request of a U.S. investment banking firm without direct involvement by the foreign issuing firm. Consequently, the foreign company may not provide investment information or financial reports to the depository on a regular basis or in a timely manner. The depository fees of sponsored ADRs are paid by the foreign company. ADR investors pay the depository fees on unsponsored ADRs. Unsponsored ADRs may have several issuing banks, with the terms of the offering varying from bank to bank. Sponsored ADRs account for slightly more than one-half of all ADR issues.[7]

Five recent studies document some important empirical findings about the ADR market. Rosenthal (1983), using a time series of weekly, biweekly, and monthly rates of return over the time period of 1974 through 1978 for 54 ADRs, found that the ADR market was weak-form efficient. That is, abnormal trading profits are not likely from studying historical price data.

Park (1990) found that a substantial portion of the variability in (i.e., change in) ADR returns is accounted for by variation in the share price of the underlying security in the home market; however, information observed in the U.S. market is also an important factor in the ADR return-generating process.

Officer and Hoffmeister (1987) and Kao, Wei, and Vu (1991) examined ADRs as vehicles for constructing diversified equity portfolios. Officer and Hoffmeister used a sample of 45 ADRs and 45 domestic stocks. For each, they had monthly rates of return for the period 1973 through 1983. They found that as few as four ASDRs combined with four domestic stocks allowed the investor to reduce portfolio risk by as much as 25 percent with any reduction in expected return.

Kao, Wei, and Vu used 10 years of monthly return data covering the time period 1979 through 1989 for ADRs with underlying shares from the U.K., Australia, Japan, the Netherlands, and Sweden. They found that an internationally diversified portfolio of ADRs outperformed both a U.S. stock market and a world stock market benchmark on a risk-adjusted basis. Country ADR portfolios from all countries except Australia also outperformed the U.S. and world benchmarks, but only country ADR portfolios from the U.K., Japan, and the Netherlands outperformed their home country stock market benchmark.

Jayaraman, Shastri, and Tandon (1993) examine the effect of the listing of ADRs on the risk and return of the underlying stock. They find positive abnormal performance (i.e., return in excess of the expected equilibrium return) of the underlying security on the initial listing date. They interpret this result as evidence that an ADR listing provides the issuing firm with another market from which to source new equity capital. Additionally, they find an increase in the volatility of (change in) returns of the underlying stock. They interpret this result as consistent with the theory that traders with proprietary information will attempt to profit from their knowledge by taking advantage of price discrepancies caused by information differentials between the ADR and underlying security markets.

The International Finance in Practice box on page 198 discusses buying foreign shares directly and through ADRs and mutual funds.

FACTORS AFFECTING INTERNATIONAL EQUITY RETURNS

Before closing this chapter, it is beneficial to explore some of the empirical evidence about which factors influence equity returns. After all, to construct an efficiently diversified international portfolio of stocks, one must estimate the expected return and the variance of returns for each security in the investment set plus the pairwise correlation structure. It may be easier to accurately estimate these parameters if a common set of factors affect equity returns. Some likely candidates are: macroeconomic variables that influence the overall economic environment in which the firm issuing the security conducts its business; exchange rate changes between the currency of the country issuing the stock and the currency of other countries where suppliers, customers, and investors of the firm reside; and the industrial structure of the country in which the firm operates.

Macroeconomic Factors

Two recent studies have tested the influence of various macroeconomic variables on stock returns. Solnik (1984) examined the effect of exchange rate changes, interest rate differentials, the level of the domestic interest rate, and changes in domestic inflation expectations. He found that international monetary variables had only weak influence on equity returns in comparison to domestic variables. In another study, Asprem (1989) found that changes in industrial production, employment, and imports, the level of interest rates, and an inflation measure explained only a small portion of the variability of equity returns for 10 European countries, but that substantially more of the variation was explained by an international market index.

Exchange Rates

Adler and Simon (1986) examined the exposure of a sample of foreign equity and bond index returns to exchange rate changes. They found that changes in exchange rates generally explained a larger portion of the variability of foreign bond indexes than foreign equity indexes, but that some foreign equity markets were more exposed to exchange rate changes than were the respective foreign bond markets. Additionally, their results suggest that it would likely be beneficial to hedge (i.e., protect) foreign stock investment against exchange rate uncertainty.

In another study, Eun and Resnick (1988) find that the cross-correlations among major stock markets and exchange markets are relatively low, but positive. This result implies that the exchange rate changes in a given country reinforce the stock market movements in that country as well as in the other countries examined.

INTERNATIONAL FINANCE IN PRACTICE

Buying Foreign Stocks from U.S. Brokers Gets Easier

Maybe you have a hunch about Mazda's stock. Or maybe you just *know* that Peru's telephone company is going to be the next hot play from Latin America.

Until recently, it would have been difficult to make more of your idea than cocktail chatter. Neither stock is listed in any form in the U.S. and most brokers wouldn't buy shares overseas in an amount small enough for an individual investor's portfolio.

But now U.S. brokerage houses are handling more foreign stocks for small investors. Merrill Lynch & Co. now trades about 4,000 foreign stocks that aren't listed in the U.S., for retail clients—up from only around 600 two years ago, thanks to its recent acquisition of Smith New Court Securities Ltd., a British brokerage firm. Travelers Group's Smith Barney Inc. trades about 1,000 foreign issues for its retail clients, and a nest of discount brokers across the U.S. now specializes in selling foreign stocks cheap to small investors.

U.S. institutions are unwittingly helping small investors pick among foreign stocks, too. Retail brokers can trade more foreign stocks during the U.S. working day, largely because U.S. pension funds and other big investors in this country have more foreign shares to buy and sell. As a result, "more and more people are realizing that they have the access to buy foreign shares" in the U.S., says James Heitzer, an investment adviser at Renaissance Financial Securities Inc. in Atlanta, a brokerage firm that trades foreign stocks.

Be warned. Buying foreign stocks carries risks beyond those normally associated with buying domestic stocks. Financial reports, if they come at all, may not be in English. Foreign markets aren't as strictly regulated as the U.S. market. And many foreign stocks carry the risk that the currency in which they are denominated could fall against the U.S. dollar, either eroding an otherwise big gain or exacerbating a loss.

If that daunts you, consider investing overseas through other vehicles. Mutual funds hold enough different securities to keep you from holding too many of your eggs in one basket. And American depository receipts—

Industrial Structure

Studies examining the influence of industrial structure on foreign equity returns are inconclusive. In a recent study examining the correlation structure of national equity markets, Roll (1992) concluded that the industrial structure of a country was important in explaining a significant part of the correlation structure of international equity index returns. He also found that industry factors explained a larger portion of stock market variability than did exchange rate changes.

In contrast, Eun and Resnick (1984) found for a sample of 160 stocks from eight countries and 12 industries that the pairwise correlation structure of international security returns could better be estimated from models that recognized country factors rather than industry factors. Similarly, using individual stock return data for 829 firms, from 12 countries, and representing seven broad industry groups, Heston and Rouwenhorst (1994) conclude "that industrial structure explains very little of the cross-sectional difference in country return volatility, and that the low correlation between country indices is almost completely due to country specific sources of variation."

Both Rouwenhorst (1999) and Beckers (1999) examine the effect of the EMU on European equity markets and come up with opposite conclusions. Rouwenhorst concludes that country effects in stock returns have been larger than industry effects in Western Europe since 1982 and that this situation continued throughout the 1993–98 period when interest rates were converging and fiscal and monetary policies were being harmonized in the countries entering the EMU. On-the-other-hand, Beckers finds an increase in correlations between markets and between the same sector in different markets arising from the European integration of fiscal, monetary, and economic policies. He concludes that the increase in pairwise correlations in these countries represents a reduction in the diversification benefits from investing in the Euro-zone.

the restricted number of certificates that represent foreign shares but are listed on U.S. markets—are subject to the same Securities and Exchange Commission rules as U.S. stocks.

But "the advantage of buying individual [foreign] stocks is that you are making your own decisions" over a broader range of securities than are included among ADRs, says Vivian Lewis, the New York-based publisher of Global Investing, a newsletter for individuals who like to do their stock-picking overseas.

When looking for a brokerage firm to trade foreign stocks, insist on dealing only with staff that "know how to trade pink sheet stocks," Ms. Lewis says. (A U.S. investor can also open an account with a foreign brokerage house, she notes. But most foreign brokers with offices in the U.S. cater to institutional investors.)

A full-service firm has one distinct advantage over discount brokerages when it comes to picking foreign stocks: research. Merrill Lynch, for instance, offers its small clients the same foreign research that it gives U.S. institutional investors. That research comes from analysts who specialize in watching Asia, Europe, Latin America, Canada and South Africa.

To understand the value of that, consider the hassles Ms. Lewis faced when she wanted to assess Peru's telecommunications company on her own. The only English-speaker she found by phone at the company's headquarters was in the procurement department, and knew little about the company's general health. Eventually, Ms. Lewis had to call Spain and question an official of a Spanish concern that held some of the Peruvian company's shares. For such reasons, Marquette de Bary does much of its business with U.S. investors who are living abroad and know about foreign markets first hand.

Once you own a foreign stock, you will face other hurdles. The most difficult may be keeping a tab on a foreign company through financial reports that are far more lax than those in the U.S. If a foreign company with $10 million in assets has at least 500 U.S. shareholders, it must furnish the SEC with the financial statements it files in its home market. But the SEC won't do anything if those statements are false, and it won't insist that the foreign company use U.S. accounting standards.

Foreign filings usually don't provide all the information that U.S. filings must. That means you might know nothing about how a company pays its executives or how its individual units are performing. Many foreign companies don't even file statements quarterly, as U.S. companies must, but only once or twice a year.

The result can be "very messy," says Paul Broderick, operations manager at Barry Murphy. In 1993, he discovered that a Malaysian company whose shares many of his clients held was offering rights for new shares—only two days before the offering was due to expire.

Source: Excerpted from Robert Steiner, *The Wall Street Journal,* June 7, 1996, p. C1. Reprinted with permission of *The Wall Street Journal,* © 1996 Dow Jones & Company, Inc. All Rights Reserved Worldwide.

Griffin and Karolyi (1998) examine the effect of industrial structure on covariances by studying whether a difference exists in the effect between traded-goods industries and nontraded-goods industries. They find that the cross-country covariances are larger for firms within a given industry than the cross-country covariances across firms in different industries in traded-goods industries. In contrast, for nontraded-goods industries, there is little difference in cross-country covariances between firms in the same industry and those in different industries.

SUMMARY

This chapter provides an overview of international equity markets. The material is designed to provide an understanding of how MNCs source new equity capital outside of their own domestic primary market and to provide useful institutional information to investors interested in diversifying their portfolio internationally.

1. The chapter began with a statistical perspective of the major equity markets in developed countries and of emerging equity markets in developing countries. Market capitalization and turnover figures were provided for each marketplace. It was seen that most national equity markets grew substantially during the 1980s. Additionally, the turnover ratios of most emerging markets increased in recent years and the market concentration ratios decreased, indicating that investment opportunities in these markets were improving.
2. A variety of international equity benchmarks were also presented. Knowledge of where to find comparative equity market performance data is useful. Specifically, the International Finance Corporation, Morgan Stanley Capital International, and

the Dow Jones World Stock Market indexes were discussed. Also, a list of the major national stock market indexes prepared by the national exchanges or major investment advisory services was presented.

3. A considerable amount of discussion was devoted to differences in secondary equity market structures. Secondary markets were generally dealer or agency markets. Both of these types of market structure can provide for continuous market trading, but noncontinuous markets tended to be agency markets. Over-the-counter trading, specialist markets, and automated markets allow for continuous market trading. Call markets and crowd trading are each types of noncontinuous trading market systems. Trading costs—commissions and taxes—on various national equity markets were summarized in a table comparing market characteristics.
4. Cross-listing of a company's shares on foreign exchanges was extensively discussed. A firm may cross-list its shares to: establish a broader investor base for its stock; establish name recognition in foreign capital markets; and to pave the way for sourcing new equity and debt capital from investors in these markets. Yankee stock offerings, or sale of foreign stock to U.S. investors, were also discussed. Yankee shares trade on U.S. markets as American depository receipts (ADRs), which are bank receipts representing a multiple of foreign shares deposited in a U.S. bank. ADRs eliminate some of the risks, delays, inconveniences, and expenses of trading actual shares.
5. Several empirical studies that tested for factors that might influence equity returns indicate that domestic factors, such as the level of domestic interest rates and expected changes in domestic inflation, as opposed to international monetary variables, had the greatest effect on national equity returns. Industrial structure did not appear to be of primary importance. Equity returns were also found to be sensitive to own-currency exchange rate changes.

KEY WORDS

agency market, 184
American depository receipt (ADR), 194
ask price, 184
bid price, 184
broker, 184
call market, 185
continuous market, 185
cross-listing, 192
crowd trading, 185
dealer market, 184
limit order, 184
limit order book, 184
liquidity, 181
market order, 184
over-the-counter (OTC), 184
primary market, 184
secondary market, 184
specialist, 184
Yankee stock, 194

QUESTIONS

1. Get a current copy of *The Wall Street Journal* and find the *Dow Jones Global Indexes* listing in Section C of the newspaper. Examine the 12-month changes in U.S. dollars for the various national and regional indexes. How do the changes from your table compare with the 12-month changes from the sample provided in the textbook as Exhibit 8.8? Are they all of similar size? Are the same national indexes positive and negative in both listings? Discuss your findings.
2. As an investor, what factors would you consider before investing in the emerging stock market of a developing country?
3. Compare and contrast the various types of secondary market trading structures.
4. Discuss any benefits you can think of for a company to (a) cross-list its equity shares on more than one national exchange, and (b) to source new equity capital from foreign investors as well as domestic investors.

5. Why might it be easier for an investor desiring to diversify his portfolio internationally to buy depository receipts rather than the actual shares of the company?
6. Why do you think the empirical studies about factors affecting equity returns basically showed that domestic factors were more important than international factors, and, secondly, that industrial membership of a firm was of little importance in forecasting the international correlation structure of a set of international stocks?

PROBLEMS

1. On the Milan bourse, Fiat stock closed at EUR31.90 per share on Friday, September 10, 1999. Fiat trades as an ADR on the NYSE. One underlying Fiat share equals one ADR. On September 10, the $/EUR spot exchange rate was $1.0367/EUR1.00. At this exchange rate, what is the no-arbitrage U.S. dollar price of one ADR?
2. If Fiat ADRs were trading at $35 when the underlying shares were trading in Milan at EUR31.90, what could you do to earn a trading profit? Use the information in problem 1, above, to help you and assume that transaction costs are negligible.

MINI CASE

San Pico's New Stock Exchange

San Pico is a rapidly growing Latin American developing country. The country is blessed with miles of scenic beaches that have attracted tourists by the thousands in recent years to new resort hotels financed by joint ventures of San Pico businessmen and moneymen from the Middle East, Japan, and the United States. Additionally, San Pico has good natural harbors that are conducive for receiving imported merchandise from abroad and exporting merchandise produced in San Pico and other surrounding countries that lack access to the sea. Because of these advantages, many new businesses are being started in San Pico.

Presently, stock is traded in a cramped building in La Cobijio, the nation's capital. Admittedly, the San Pico Stock Exchange system is rather archaic. Twice a day an official of the exchange will call out the name of each of the 43 companies whose stock trades on the exchange. Brokers wanting to buy or sell shares for their clients then attempt to make a trade with one another. This crowd trading system has worked well for over one hundred years, but the government desires to replace it with a new modern system that will allow greater and more frequent opportunities for trading in each company, and will allow for trading the shares of the many new start-up companies that are expected to trade in the secondary market. Additionally, the government administration is rapidly privatizing many state-owned businesses in an attempt to foster their efficiency, obtain foreign exchange from the sale, and convert the country to a more capitalist economy. The government believes that it could conduct this privatization faster and perhaps at more attractive prices if it had a modern stock exchange facility where the shares of the newly privatized companies will eventually trade.

You are an expert in the operation of secondary stock markets and have been retained as a consultant to the San Pico Stock Exchange to offer your expertise in modernizing the stock market. What would you advise?

ENDNOTES

1. This definition is from the International Finance Corporation Website, www.ifc.com.
2. Much of the discussion in this section follows from Chapter 2 of Schwartz (1988).
3. See the United States General Accounting Office 1991 report, *Global Financial Markets: International Coordination Can Help Address Automation Risk.*
4. Much of the information in this paragraph is from the September 28, 1993, article in *The Wall Street Journal* by Craig Torres.
5. Much of the information in this paragraph is from the June 1, 1992, article by Michael Siconolfi and the September 28, 1993, article by Craig Torres, both in *The Wall Street Journal.*
6. The information is from the EASDAQ Website, www.easdaq.be.
7. Much of the preceding information about ADRs is from the April 16, 1990, article by Anna Merjos and the May 17, 1993, article by Edward A. Wyatt, both from *Barron's,* and the February 8, 1990, article in *The Wall Street Journal* by Tom Herman and Michael R. Sisit.

WEB RESOURCES

www.bankofny.com/adr

This is the Website of the Bank of New York Depository Receipts Services. The BNY is the largest depository of ADRs. This Website provides a wealth of information and statistics about the ADR market.

www.easdaq.be

This is the Website of the European Association of Securities Dealers Automated Quotation, the European stock market for high-growth stocks. This site provides information about the stock market, companies traded, membership, and price quotations.

www.ifc.org

This is the Website of the International Finance Corporation, the private-sector arm of the World Bank. The IFC is the world's largest source of financing for private enterprise in emerging economies. This site provides information about the IFC, its stock market indexes, and publications from the IFC that contain many useful statistics.

www.nasdaq-amex.com

This is the official Website of the NASDAQ-AMEX stock exchange. It provides information about the exchange, portfolio-monitoring software, stock-screening software, and price quotations.

www.msci.com

This is the Website of Morgan Stanley Capital International. Detailed information about the construction of MSCI's international stock market indexes is provided, as is information about index performance. One can also download index data at this site to an Excel spreadsheet.

www.nyse.com

This is the Website of the New York Stock Exchange. Information about the NYSE, its operation, membership, and listed companies is provided here. U.S. stock price quotations are available at this site.

www.tse.com

This is the Website of the Toronto Stock Exchange. Information about the exchange, its operation, membership, and listed companies is provided here. Canadian stock, futures, options, and mutual fund prices are available at this site.

REFERENCES AND SUGGESTED READINGS

Adler, Michael, and David Simon. "Exchange Rate Surprises in International Portfolios." *The Journal of Portfolio Management* 12 (1986), pp. 44–53.

Asprem, Mads. "Stock Prices, Assets Portfolios and Macroeconomic Variables in Ten European Countries." *Journal of Banking and Finance* 13 (1989), pp. 589–612.

Becker, Stan. "Investment Implications of a Single European Capital Market." *Journal of Portfolio Management,* Spring (1999), pp. 9–17.

Benos, Alexandros, and Michel Crouhy. "Changes in the Structure and Dynamics of European Securities Markets." *Financial Analysts Journal* 52 (1996), pp. 37–50.

Blackwell Publishers. *The 1992 Handbook of World Stock and Commodity Exchanges.* Oxford, UK: Blackwell Publishers, 1992.

Bodie, Zvi, Alex Kane, and Alan J. Marcus. *Investments,* 4th ed. Boston: Irwin/McGraw-Hill, 1999.

Brauchli, Marcus W., and Masayoshi Kanabayashi. "Japanese Firms Cross Holdings Prove a Hazard. *The Wall Street Journal,* October 12, 1990.

Bream, Rebecca. "Europe Gets Its Own ADR." *Euromoney,* November 1998, p. 10.

Eun, Cheol S., and Bruce G. Resnick. "Estimating the Correlation Structure of International Share Prices." *Journal of Finance* 39 (1984), pp. 1311–24.

Eun, Cheol S., and Bruce G. Resnick. "Exchange Rate Uncertainty, Forward Contracts, and International Portfolio Selection." *Journal of Finance* 43 (1988), pp. 197–215.

Foerster, Stephen R., and G. Andrew Karolyi. "The Effects of Market Segmentation and Investor Recognition on Asset Prices: Evidence from Foreign Stocks Listings in the United States." *Journal of Finance* 54 (1999), pp. 981–1013.

Griffin, John M., and G. Andrew Karolyi. "Another Look at the Role of the Industrial Structure of Markets for International Diversification Strategies." *Journal of Financial Economics* 50 (1998), pp. 351–73.

Herman, Tom, and Michael R. Sesit. "ADRs: Foreign Issues with U.S. Accents." *The Wall Street Journal,* February 8, 1990.

Heston, Steven L., and K. Geert Rouwenhorst. "Does Industrial Structure Explain the Benefits of International Diversification?" *Journal of Financial Economics* 36 (1994), pp. 3–27.

International Finance Corporation. *Emerging Stock Markets Factbook.* Washington, D.C.: International Finance Corporation, 1996.

Jayaraman, Narayanan, Kuldeep Shastri, and Kishore Tandon. "The Impact of International Cross Listings on Risk and Return: The Evidence from American Depository Receipts." *Journal of Banking and Finance* 17 (1993), pp. 91–103.

Kao, G., K. C. Wenchi, John Wei, and Joseph Vu. "Risk-Return Characteristics of the American Depository Receipts," unpublished working paper, 1991.

Karmin, Craig. "More-Efficient WEBS Provide Alternative to Closed-End Funds." *The Wall Street Journal,* July 6, 1999, p. R12.

Lederman, Jess, and Keith K. H. Parks, eds. *The Global Equity Markets.* Chicago: Probus, 1991.

Merjos, Anna. "Lure of Faraway Places: ADRs Grow in Numbers and Popularity." *Barron's,* April 16, 1990.

Miller, Darius P. "The Market Reaction to International Cross-Listings: Evidence from Depository Receipts." *Journal of Financial Economics* 51 (1999), pp. 103–23.

Muscarella, Chris J., and Michael R. Vetsuypens. "Stock Splits: Signaling or Liquidity? The Case of ADR 'solo-splits'," *Journal of Financial Economics* 42 (1996), pp. 2–26.

Officer, Dennis T., and J. Ronald Hoffmeister. "ADRs: A Substitute for the Real Thing?" *Journal of Portfolio Management,* Winter (1987), pp. 61–65.

Park, Jinwoo. *The Impact of Information on ADR Returns and Variances: Some Implications,* unpublished Ph.D. dissertation from The University of Iowa, 1990.

Parks, Keith K. H., and Antoine W. Van Agtmael, eds. *The World's Emerging Stock Markets.* Chicago: Probus, 1993.

Radcliffe, Robert C. *Investment Concepts, Analysis, Strategy,* 4th ed. New York: Harper Collins, 1994.

Roll, Richard. "Industrial Structure and the Comparative Behavior of International Stock Market Indexes." *Journal of Finance* 47 (1992), pp. 3–42.

Rosenthal, Leonard. "An Empirical Test of the Efficiency of the ADR Market." *Journal of Banking and Finance* 7 (1983) pp. 17–29.

Rouwenhorst, K. Geert. "European Equity Markets and the EMU." *Financial Analysts Journal,* May/June (1999), pp. 57–64.

Schwartz, Robert A. *Equity Markets.* New York: Harper and Row, 1988.

Siconolfi, Michael. "Foreign Firms Step Up Offerings in U.S." *The Wall Street Journal,* June 1, 1992.

Solnik, Bruno. "Capital Markets and International Monetary Variables." *Financial Analysts Journal* 40 (1984), pp. 69–73.

Torres, Craig. "Latin American Firms Break with Past, Scramble to Be Listed on U.S. Exchanges." *The Wall Street Journal,* September 28, 1993.

United States General Accounting Office. *Global Financial Markets: International Coordination Can Help Address Automation Risks.* Washington, D. C.: U.S. G.A.O., 1991.

Werner, Ingrid M., and Allan W. Kleidon. "U.K. and U.S. Trading of British Cross-Listed Stocks: An Intraday Analysis of Market Integration." *The Review of Financial Studies* 9 (1996), pp. 619–64.

Wyatt, Edward A. "Border Dispute: ADRs vs. Direct Buying of Stock." *Barron's,* May 17, 1993.

CHAPTER NINE

Futures and Options on Foreign Exchange

CHAPTER OUTLINE

On February 27, 1995, Barings PLC, the oldest merchant bank in the United Kingdom, was placed in "administration" by the Bank of England because of losses that exceeded the bank's entire $860 million in equity capital. The cause of these losses was a breakdown in Barings' risk-management system that allowed a single rogue trader to accumulate and conceal an unhedged $27 billion position in various exchange-traded futures and options contracts, primarily the Nikkei 225 stock index futures contract traded on the Singapore International Monetary Exchange. The losses occurred when the market moved unfavorably against the trader's speculative positions. The trader recently completed a prison term in Singapore for fraudulent trading. Barings was taken over by ING Group, the Dutch banking and insurance conglomerate.

As this story implies, futures and options contracts can be very risky investments, indeed, when used for speculative purposes. Nevertheless, they are also important risk-management tools. In this chapter, we introduce exchange-traded currency futures contracts, options contracts, and options on currency futures that are useful for both speculating on foreign exchange price movements and hedging exchange rate uncertainty. These contracts make up part of the foreign exchange market that was introduced in Chapter 4, where we discussed spot and forward exchange rates.

The discussion begins by comparing forward and futures contracts, noting similarities and differences between the two. We discuss the markets where futures are traded, the currencies on which contracts are written, contract specifications for the various currency contracts, and Eurodollar interest rate futures contracts. These are useful for hedging short-term dollar interest rate risk in much the same way as forward rate agreements, introduced in Chapter 6.

Next, options contracts on foreign exchange are introduced, comparing and contrasting the options and the futures markets. The exchanges where options are traded are identified and contract terms are specified. The over-the-counter options market is also discussed. Basic option-pricing boundary relationships are illustrated using actual market prices. Additionally, illustrations of how a speculator might use currency options are also provided. The chapter closes with the development of a currency option-pricing model. This chapter and the knowledge gained about forward contracts in Chapters 4 and 5 set the stage for Chapters 12, 13, and 14, which explain how these vehicles can be used for hedging foreign exchange risk.

FUTURES CONTRACTS: SOME PRELIMINARIES

In Chapter 4, a *forward contract* was defined as a vehicle for buying or selling a stated amount of foreign exchange at a stated price per unit at a specified time in the future. Both forward and futures contracts are classified as **derivative** or **contingent claim securities** because their values are derived from or contingent upon the value of the underlying security. But while a **futures** contract is similar to a forward contract, there are many distinctions between the two. A forward exchange contract is tailor-made for a client by his international bank; in contrast, a futures contract has **standardized** features and is **exchange-traded,** that is, traded on organized exchanges rather than over the counter. A client desiring a position in futures contracts contacts his broker, who transmits the order to the exchange floor where it is transferred to the trading pit. In the trading pit, the price for the order is negotiated by open outcry between floor brokers or traders.

The main standardized features are the **contract size** specifying the amount of the underlying foreign currency for future purchase or sale and the **maturity date** of the contract. A futures contract is written for a specific amount of foreign currency rather than for a tailor-made sum. Hence, a position in multiple contracts may be necessary to establish a sizable hedge or speculative position. Futures contracts have specific **delivery months** during the year in which contracts mature on a specified day of the month.

An **initial margin** must be deposited into a collateral account to establish a futures position. The initial margin is generally equal to about 2 percent of the contract value. Either cash or Treasury bills may be used to meet the margin requirement. The account balance will fluctuate through daily settlement, as the following discussion makes clear. The margin put up by the contract holder can be viewed as "good-faith" money that he will fulfill his side of the financial obligation.

The major difference between a forward contract and a futures contract is the way the underlying asset is priced for future purchase or sale. A forward contract states a price for the future transaction. By contrast, a futures contract is **settled-up,** or **marked-to-market,** daily at the settlement price. The **settlement price** is a price representative of futures transaction prices at the close of daily trading on the exchange. A buyer of a futures contract (one who holds a **long** position) in which the settlement price is higher (lower) than the previous day's settlement price has a positive (negative) settlement for the day. Since a long position entitles the owner to purchase the underlying asset, a higher (lower) settlement price means the futures price of the underlying asset has increased (decreased). Consequently, a long position in the contract is worth more (less). The change in settlement prices from one day to the next determines the settlement amount. That is, the change in settlement prices per unit of the underlying asset, multiplied times the size of the contract, equals the size of the daily settlement to be added to (or subtracted from) the long's margin account. Analogously, the seller of the futures contract (**short** position) will have his margin account increased (or decreased) by the amount the long's margin account is decreased (or increased). Thus, futures trading between the long and the short is a **zero-sum game;** that is, the sum of the long and short's

EXHIBIT 9.1

Comparison of the Differences between Futures and Forward Contracts

Trading Location
Futures: Traded competitively on an organized exchange.
Forward: Traded by bank dealers via a network of telephones, telex machines, and computerized dealing systems.

Contractual Size
Futures: Standardized amount of the underlying asset.
Forward: Tailor-made to the needs of the participant.

Settlement
Futures: Daily settlement, or marking-to-market, done by the futures clearinghouse through the participant's margin account.
Forward: Participant buys or sells the contractual amount of the underlying asset from the bank at maturity at the forward (contractual) price.

Expiration Date
Futures: Standardized delivery dates.
Forward: Tailor-made delivery date that meets the need of the investor.

Delivery
Futures: Delivery of the underlying asset is seldom made. Usually a reversing trade is transacted to exit the market.
Forward: Delivery of the underlying asset is commonly made.

Trading Costs
Futures: Bid-ask spread plus broker's commission.
Forward: Bid-ask spread plus indirect bank charges via compensating balance requirements.

daily settlement is zero. If the investor's margin account falls below a **maintenance margin** level (roughly equal to 75 percent of the initial margin), **variation margin** must be added to the account to bring it back to the initial margin level in order to keep the position open. An investor who suffers a liquidity crunch and cannot deposit additional margin money will have his position liquidated by his broker.

The marking-to-market feature of futures markets means that market participants realize their profits or suffer their losses on a day-to-day basis rather than all at once at maturity as with a forward contract. At the end of daily trading, a future contract is analogous to a new forward contract on the underlying asset at the new settlement price with a one-day shorter maturity. Because of the daily marking-to-market, the futures price will converge through time to the spot price on the last day of trading in the contract. That is, the final settlement price at which any transaction in the underlying asset will transpire is the spot price on the last day of trading. The effective price is, nevertheless, the original futures contract price, once the profit or loss in the margin account is included. Exhibit 9.1 summarizes the differences between forward and future contracts.

Two types of market participants are necessary for a derivatives market to operate: **speculators** and **hedgers.** A speculator attempts to profit from a change in the futures price. To do this, the speculator will take a long or short position in a futures contract depending upon his expectations of future price movement. A hedger, on the other hand, wants to avoid price variation by locking in a purchase price of the underlying asset through a long position in the futures contract or a sales price through a short position. In effect, the hedger passes off the risk of price variation to the speculator, who is better able, or at least more willing, to bear this risk.

Both forward and futures markets for foreign exchange are very liquid. A **reversing trade** can be made in either market that will close out, or neutralize, a position.[1] In forward markets, approximately 90 percent of all contracts result in the short making delivery of the underlying asset to the long. This is natural given the tailor-made terms of forward contracts. By contrast, only about 1 percent of currency futures contracts result in delivery. While futures contracts are useful for speculation and hedging, their standardized delivery dates are unlikely to correspond to the actual future dates when foreign exchange transactions will transpire. Thus, they are generally closed out in a reversing trade. The **commission** that buyers and sellers pay to transact in the futures market is a single amount paid up front that covers the *round-trip* transactions of initiating and closing out the position. These days, through a discount broker, the commission charge can be as little as $15 per currency futures contract.

In futures markets, a **clearinghouse** serves as the third party to all transactions. That is, the buyer of a futures contract effectively buys from the clearinghouse and the seller sells to the clearinghouse. This feature of futures markets facilitates active secondary market trading because the buyer and the seller do not have to evaluate one another's creditworthiness. The clearinghouse is made up of *clearing members.* Individual brokers who are not clearing members must deal through a clearing member to clear a customer's trade. In the event of default of one side of a futures trade, the clearing member stands in for the defaulting party, and then seeks restitution from that party. The clearinghouse's liability is limited because a contractholder's position is marked-to-market daily. Given the organizational structure, it is only logical that the clearinghouse maintains the futures margin accounts for the clearing members.

Frequently, a futures exchange may have a **daily price limit** on the futures price, that is, a limit as to how much the settlement price can increase or decrease from the previous day's settlement price. Forward markets do not have this. At present, some currency futures exchanges have daily price limits. Obviously, when the price limit is hit, trading will halt as a new market-clearing equilibrium price cannot be obtained. Exchange rules exist for expanding the daily price limit in an orderly fashion until a market-clearing price can be established.

CURRENCY FUTURES MARKETS

On May 16, 1972, trading first began at the Chicago Mercantile Exchange (CME) in currency futures contracts. Trading activity in currency futures has expanded rapidly at the CME. In 1978, only 2 million contracts were traded; this figure stood at over 30 million contracts in 1997. Most CME currency futures trade in a March, June, September, and December expiration cycle, with the delivery date being the third Wednesday of the expiration month. The last day of trading is the second business day prior to the delivery date. Regular trading in CME currency futures contracts takes place each business day from 7:20 A.M. to 2:00 P.M. Chicago time. Extended-hour trading on the $GLOBEX_2$ trading system runs from 2:30 P.M. to 7:05 A.M. Chicago time. On Sundays trading begins at 5:30 P.M. $GLOBEX_2$ is a worldwide automated order-entry and matching system for futures and options that facilitates trading after the close of regular exchange trading. Exhibit 9.2 summarizes the basic CME currency contract specifications.

The Philadelphia Board of Trade (PBOT), a subsidiary of the Philadelphia Stock Exchange, introduced currency futures trading in July 1986. The PBOT contracts trade in the same expiration cycle as the CME currency futures, plus two additional near-term months. The delivery date is also the third Wednesday of the expiration month, with the last day of trading being the preceding Friday. The trading hours of the PBOT contracts are 2:30 A.M. to 2:30 P.M. ET, except for the Canadian dollar,

EXHIBIT 9.2

Currency Futures Contract Specifications*

Currency	Contract Size	Exchange
Price Quoted in U.S. Dollars		
Australian dollar	AD100,000	CME, PBOT
Brazilian real	BR100,000	CME
British pound	£62,500	CME, PBOT
Canadian dollar	CD100,000	CME, PBOT
Deutsche mark	DM125,000	CME, PBOT
French franc	FF500,000	CME, PBOT
Japanese yen	¥12,500,000	CME, PBOT
Mexican peso	MP500,000	CME
New Zealand dollar	NE100,00	CME
South African rand	RA500,000	CME
Swiss franc	SF125,000	CME, PBOT
Euro FX	EUR125,000	CME
Cross-Rate Futures (Underlying Currency/Price Currency)		
Euro FX/British pound	EUR125,000	CME
Euro FX/Japanese yen	EUR125,000	CME
Euro FX/Swiss franc	EUR125,000	CME

*CME denotes Chicago Mercantile Exchange; PBOT denotes Philadelphia Board of Trade.

Sources: Chicago Mercantile Exchange, *Currency Futures and Options,* December 1997, *EUROFX Dollar and Crossrate Furtures and Option,* December 1998; and Philadelphia PBOT Board of Trade, *Currency Futures Contract Specifications,* January 1999.

which trades between 7:00 A.M. and 2:30 P.M. ET. Exhibit 9.2 shows the currencies and the size of the contracts traded on the PBOT. The deutsche mark and the French franc will no longer exist as national currency units for futures contracts when the euro transition period ends on July 1, 2002.

In addition to the CME and the PBOT, currency futures trading takes place on the MidAmerica Commodities Exchange, the Tokyo International Financial Futures Exchange, and the London International Financial Futures Exchange. None of these exchanges comes close to the trading volume of the CME.

BASIC CURRENCY FUTURES RELATIONSHIPS

Exhibit 9.3 shows quotations for CME futures contracts. For each delivery month for each currency, we see the opening price quotation, the high and the low quotes for the trading day (in this case July 6, 1999), and the settlement price. Each is presented in American terms, that is, $F(\$/i)$. (We use the same symbol F for futures prices as for forward prices, and explain why shortly.) For each contract, the **open interest** is also presented. This is the total number of short or long contracts outstanding for the particular delivery month. Note that the open interest is greatest for each currency in the **nearby** contract, in this case the September 1999 contract. Since few of these contracts will actually result in delivery, if we were to follow the open interest in the September contracts through time, we would see the number for each different currency decrease as the last day of trading (September 13, 1999) approaches as a result of reversing trades. Additionally, we would note increased open interest in the December 1999 contract as trading interest in the soon-to-be nearby contract picks up. In general, open interest (loosely an indicator of demand) typically decreases with the term to maturity of most futures contracts.

EXHIBIT 9.3 Chicago Mercantile Exchange Currency Futures Contract Quotations

CURRENCY						Lifetime		
	Open	High	Low	Settle	Change	High	Low	Open Interest
JAPAN Yen (CME) – 12.5 million yen; $ per yen (.00)								
Sept	.8273	.8345	.8251	.8279	– .0065	.9500	.7680	94,203
Dec	.8374	.8389	.8370	.8389	– .0066	.9600	.8257	15,278
Mr00	....	....	....	.8509	– .0065	.8931	.8369	112
Est vol 11,507; vol Fri 5,205; open int 109,594, –516.								
DEUTSCHEMARK (CME) – 125,000 marks; $ per mark								
Sept	.5250	.5273	.5233	.5259	– .0006	.6300	.5233	24,160
Dec	.5285	.5305	.5285	.5295	– .0006	.6120	.5285	192
Est vol 1,947; vol Fri 2,909; open int 24,352, –325.								
CANADIAN DOLLAR (CME) – 100,000 dlrs.; $ per Can $								
Sept	.6820	.6841	.6804	.6806	– .0036	.7080	.6310	58,022
Dec	.6835	.6840	.6818	.6815	– .0036	.6930	.6320	2,570
Mr00	....	....	....	.6825	– .0036	.6940	.6425	542
June	....	....	....	.6836	– .0036	.6950	.6547	185
Est vol 5,152; vol Fri 7,901; open int 61,332, +759.								
BRITISH POUND (CME) –62,500 pds.; $ per pound								
Sept	1.5666	1.5786	1.5598	1.5628	– .0172	1.6980	1.5598	64,079
Dec	1.5720	1.5720	1.5616	1.5648	– .0172	1.6760	1.5616	254
Est vol 8,240; vol Fri 7,411; open int 64,334, +2,788.								
SWISS FRANC (CME) – 125,000 francs; $ per franc								
Sept	.6421	.6451	.6395	.6433	+ .0004	.7831	.6395	70,835
Dec	.6492	.6510	.6491	.6498	+ .0004	.7671	.6480	172
Est vol 6,311; vol Fri 8,734; open int 71,033, –510.								
AUSTRALIAN DOLLAR (CME) – 100,000 dlrs.; $ per A.$								
Sept	.6690	.6722	.6632	.6635	– .0060	.6745	.5825	32,577
Est vol 1,662; vol Fri 3,410; open int 32,611, +1,350.								
MEXICAN PESO (CME) –500,000 new Mex. peso, $ per MP								
Sept	.10433	.10433	.10350	.10378	– 00050	.10433	.06350	16,779
Dec	.09960	.09990	.09920	.09950	....	.84345	.06700	4,672
Mr00	.09550	.09560	.09543	.09550	....	.09560	.08135	3,752
Est vol 3,252; vol Fri 3,474; open int 25,214, +912.								
EURO FX (CME) –Euro 125,000; $ per Euro								
Sept	1.0244	1.0280	1.0250	1.0285	– .0012	1.2005	1.0250	45,047
Dec	1.0315	1.0351	1.0361	1.0356	– .0012	1.2059	1.0361	275
Est vol 3,917; vol Fri 9,737; open int 45,322, +206.								

Source: *The Wall Street Journal,* July 7, 1999, p. C18. Reprinted by permission of *The Wall Street Journal,* © 1999 Dow Jones & Company, Inc. All rights Reserved Worldwide.

EXAMPLE 9.1: Reading Futures Quotations As an example of reading futures quotations, let's use the December 1999 Canadian dollar contract. From Exhibit 9.3, we see that on Tuesday, July 6, 1999, the contract opened for trading at a price of $0.6835/CD, and traded in the range of $0.6818/CD (low) to $0.6840/CD throughout the day. During its lifetime, the December 1999 contract has traded in the range of $0.6320/CD (low) to $0.6930/CD (high). The settlement ("closing") price was $0.6815/CD. The open interest, or the number of December 1999 contracts outstanding, was 2,570.

At the settlement price of \$0.6815, the holder of a long position in one contract is committing himself to paying \$68,150 for CD100,000 on the delivery day, December 15, 1999, if he actually takes delivery. Note that the settlement price decreased \$.0036 from the previous day. That is, it fell from \$0.6851/CD to \$0.6815/CD. Both the buyer and the seller of the contract would have their accounts marked-to-market by the change in the settlement prices. That is, one holding a long position from the previous day would have \$360 (= \$.0036 × CD100,000) subtracted from his margin account and the short would have \$360 added to his account. Suppose that the spot price on the last day of trading is \$.6700/CD. This will also be the final settlement price because of **price convergence.** From July 6 through December 15, the long would have a cumulative additional \$1,150 [= (\$0.6815 − \$0.6700) × CD100,000] subtracted from his margin account if he continues to hold the position open. If he takes delivery, he will pay out-of-pocket \$67,000 for the CD100,000. The effective cost, however, is \$68,150 (= \$67,000 + \$1,150), including the amount subtracted from the margin money.

Even though marking-to-market is an important economic difference between the operation of futures markets and the forward market, it has little effect on the pricing of futures contracts as opposed to the way forward contracts are priced. To see this, note the pattern of CD forward prices from the *Exchange Rates* presented in Exhibit 4.3 in Chapter 4. They go from a spot price of \$0.6796/CD to \$0.6799 (30 day) to \$0.6805 (90 day) to \$.6814 (180 day). To the extent that forward prices are an unbiased predictor of future spot exchange rates, the market is anticipating the U.S. dollar to depreciate over the next six months versus the Canadian dollar. Similarly, we see a depreciating pattern of the U.S. dollar from the pattern of settlement prices for the CD futures contracts: \$0.6806 (September) to \$0.6815 (December) to \$0.6825 (March 2000) to \$0.6836 (June). It is also noteworthy that both the forward and the futures contracts together display a chronological depreciating pattern. For example, the September futures contract price (with delivery date of September 15) and the December futures contract price (with a delivery date of December 15) fall between the 30-day forward price (with a value date of July 8) and the 180-day forward price (with a value date of January 8), displaying a (roughly) consistent depreciating pattern: \$0.6799, \$0.6806, \$0.6815, and \$0.6814, respectively. (The minor inconsistency is likely due to the fact that the forward price of \$0.6814 was obtained one hour after the futures price of \$0.6815; thus, the two are not perfectly simultaneous prices.) Thus, both the forward market and the futures market are useful for **price discovery,** or obtaining the market's forecast of the spot exchange rate at different future dates.

Example 9.1 implies that futures are priced very similarly to forward contracts. In Chapter 5, we developed the Interest Rate Parity (IRP) model, which states that the forward price for delivery at time T is

$$F_T(\$/i) = S_0(\$/i)[(1 + r_{us})/(1 + r_i)]^T \qquad (9.1)$$

We will use the same equation to define the futures price. This should work well since the similarities between the forward and the futures markets allow arbitrage opportunities if the prices between the markets are not roughly in accord.[2]

EURODOLLAR INTEREST RATE FUTURES CONTRACTS

To this point, we have considered only futures contracts written on foreign exchange. Nevertheless, future contracts are traded on many different underlying assets. One particularly important contract is the Eurodollar interest rate futures traded on the Chicago Mercantile Exchange and the Singapore International Monetary Exchange (SIMEX). The Eurodollar contract has become the most widely used futures contract for hedging short-term U.S. dollar interest rate risk. It can be used by Eurobanks as an alternative (see problem 7 at the end of this chapter) to the forward rate agreement (FRA) we considered in Chapter 6 for hedging interest risk due to a maturity mismatch between Eurodollar deposits and rollover Eurocredits. Other Eurocurrency futures contracts that trade are the Euroyen, EuroSwiss, and the EURIBOR contract, which began trading after the introduction of the euro.

The CME Eurodollar futures contract is written on a hypothetical $1,000,000 ninety-day deposit of Eurodollars. The contract trades in the March, June, September, and December cycle. The hypothetical delivery date is the third Wednesday of the delivery month. The last day of trading is two business days prior to the delivery date. The contract is a cash settlement contract. That is, the delivery of a $1,000,000 Eurodollar deposit is not actually made or received. Instead, final settlement is made through realizing profits or losses on the margin account on the delivery date based on the final settlement price on the last day of trading. Exhibit 9.4 presents an example of CME Eurodollar futures quotations. Note that contracts trade out many years into the future.

EXAMPLE 9.2: Reading Eurodollar Futures Quotations Eurodollar futures prices are stated as an index number of three-month LIBOR, calculated as: $F = 100 - \text{LIBOR}$. For example, from Exhibit 9.4 we see that the June 2000 contract (with hypothetical delivery on June 21, 2000) had a settlement price of 93.96 on Tuesday, July 6, 1999. The implied three-month LIBOR yield is thus 6.04 percent. The minimum price change is one basis point (bp). On $1,000,000 of face value, a one-basis-point change represents $100 on an annual basis. Since the contract is for a 90-day deposit, one basis point corresponds to a $25 price change.

EXAMPLE 9.3: Eurodollar Futures Hedge As an example of how this contract can be used to hedge interest rate risk, consider the treasurer of a MNC, who on July 6, 1999, learns that his firm expects to receive $20,000,000 in cash from a large sale of merchandise on June 21, 2000. The money will not be needed for a period of 90 days. Thus, the treasurer should invest the excess funds for this period in a money market instrument such as a Eurodollar deposit.

The treasurer notes that three-month LIBOR is currently 5.31 percent. (See *Money Rates* in the inside front cover.) The implied three-month LIBOR rate in the June 2000 contract is considerably higher at 6.04 percent. Additionally, the treasurer notes that the pattern of future expected three-month LIBOR rates implied by the pattern of Eurodollar futures prices suggests that it is expected to increase through time. Nevertheless, the treasurer believes that a 90-day rate of return of 6.04 percent is a decent rate to "lock in," so he decides to hedge against lower three-month LIBOR in June 2000. By hedging, the treasurer is locking in a certain return of $302,000 (= $20,000,000 × .0604 × 90/360) for the 90-day period the MNC has $20,000,000 in excess funds.

To construct the hedge, the treasurer will need to buy, or take a long position, in Eurodollar futures contracts. At first it may seem counterintuitive that a long position is needed, but remember, a decrease in the implied three-month LIBOR yield causes the Eurodollar futures price to increase. To hedge the interest rate risk in a $20,000,000 deposit, the treasurer will need to buy 20 June 2000 contracts.

Assume that on the last day of trading in the June 2000 contract three-month LIBOR is 5.50 percent. The treasurer is indeed fortunate that he chose to hedge. At 5.50 percent, a 90-day Eurodollar deposit of $20,000,000 will generate only $275,000 of interest income, or $27,000 less than at a rate of 6.04 percent. In

EXHIBIT 9.4

Chicago Mercantile Exchange Eurodollar Futures Contract Quotations

EURODOLLAR (CME)— $1 million; pts of 100%

	Open	High	Low	Settle	Chg	Yield Settle	Yield Chg	Open Interest
July	94.69	94.69	94.68	94.68	− .01	5.32	+ .01	47,417
Aug	94.62	94.63	94.62	94.63	− .01	5.37	+ .01	7,740
Sept	94.56	94.58	94.55	94.57	− .01	5.43	+ .01	597,349
Oct	94.24	94.24	94.24	94.24	− .04	5.76	+ .04	1,878
Nov	....	....	....	94.20	− .04	5.80	+ .04	415
Dec	94.13	94.15	94.11	94.13	− .04	5.87	+ .04	476,713
Mr00	94.16	94.18	94.14	94.14	− .06	5.86	+ .06	413,120
June	93.96	93.99	93.94	93.96	− .06	6.04	+ .06	272,409
Sept	93.82	93.83	93.79	93.81	− .06	6.19	+ .06	221,403
Dec	93.60	93.61	93.57	93.59	− .06	6.41	+ .06	169,156
Mr01	93.59	93.61	93.56	93.58	− .06	6.42	+ .06	128,483
June	93.52	93.55	93.50	93.52	− .05	6.48	+ .05	106,161
Sept	93.50	93.52	93.47	93.49	− .05	6.51	+ .05	87,948
Dec	93.41	93.43	93.38	93.40	− .05	6.60	+ .05	76,369
Mr02	93.45	93.46	93.41	93.44	− .05	6.56	+ .05	70,598
June	93.40	93.44	93.39	93.41	− .05	6.59	+ .05	50,207
Sept	93.39	93.41	93.36	93.38	− .05	6.62	+ .05	45,867
Dec	93.31	93.33	93.28	93.30	− .06	6.70	+ .06	47,982
Mr03	93.35	93.36	93.30	93.32	− .06	6.68	+ .06	47,197
June	93.29	93.33	93.27	93.29	− .06	6.71	+ .06	35,067
Sept	93.28	93.29	93.24	93.26	− .06	6.74	+ .06	42,418
Dec	93.19	93.20	93.15	93.16	− .07	6.84	+ .07	27,846
Mr04	93.20	93.21	93.16	93.17	− .07	6.83	+ .07	26,577
June	93.16	93.16	93.11	93.12	− .07	6.88	+ .07	14,914
Sept	....	....	....	93.08	− .07	6.92	+ .07	11,079
Dec	....	....	....	92.99	− .07	7.01	+ .07	12,331
Mr05	....	....	....	92.99	− .07	7.01	+ .07	10,147
June	....	....	....	92.95	− .07	7.05	+ .07	9,411
Sept	....	....	....	92.91	− .07	7.09	+ .07	7,461
Dec	....	....	....	92.82	− .07	7.18	+ .07	4,518
Mr06	....	....	....	92.82	− .07	7.18	+ .07	4,893
June	....	....	....	92.77	− .07	7.23	+ .07	3,703
Sept	....	....	....	92.73	− .07	7.27	+ .07	3,461
Dec	....	....	....	92.64	− .07	7.36	+ .07	3,613
Mr07	....	....	....	92.64	− .07	7.36	+ .07	3,583
June	....	....	....	92.61	− .07	7.39	+ .07	3,045
Sept	....	....	....	92.57	− .07	7.43	+ .07	2,694
Dec	....	....	....	92.48	− .07	7.52	+ .07	4,491
Mr08	....	....	....	92.49	− .07	7.51	+ .07	3,087
June	....	....	....	92.45	− .07	7.55	+ .07	3,811
Sept	....	....	....	92.42	− .07	7.58	+ .07	3,066
Dec	....	....	....	92.33	− .07	7.67	+ .07	2,303
Mr09	....	....	....	92.33	− .07	7.67	+ .07	1,247
June	....	....	....	92.30	− .07	7.70	+ .07	811

Est vol 314,779; vol Mon 360,275; open int 3,113,989 − 6,236.

Source: *The Wall Street Journal,* July 7, 1999, p. C18. Reprinted by permission of *The Wall Street Journal,* © 1999 Dow Jones & Company, Inc. All Rights Reserved Worldwide.

fact, the treasurer will have to deposit the excess funds at a rate of 5.50 percent. But the shortfall will be made up by profits from the long futures position. At a rate of 5.50 percent, the final settlement price on the June 2000 contract is 94.50 (= 100 − 5.50). The profit earned on the futures position is calculated as:

[94.50 − 93.96] × 100 bp × $25 × 20 contracts = $27,000. This is precisely the amount of the shortfall.

OPTIONS CONTRACTS: SOME PRELIMINARIES

An **option** is a contract giving the owner the right, but not the obligation, to buy or sell a given quantity of an asset at a specified price at some time in the future. Like a futures or forward contract, an option is a derivative, or contingent claim, security. Its value is derived from its definable relationship with the underlying asset—in this chapter, foreign currency, or some claim on it. An option to buy the underlying asset is a **call,** and an option to sell the underlying asset is a **put.** Buying or selling the underlying asset via the option is known as exercising the option. The stated price paid (or received) is known as the **exercise** or **striking price.** In options terminology, the buyer of an option is frequently referred to as the long and the seller of an option is referred to as the **writer** of the option, or the short.

Because the option owner does not have to exercise the option if it is to his disadvantage, the option has a price, or **premium.** There are two types of options, American and European. The names do not refer to the continents where they are traded, but rather to their exercise characteristics. A **European option** can be exercised only at the maturity or expiration date of the contract, whereas an **American option** can be exercised at any time during the contract. Thus, the American option allows the owner to do everything he can do with a European option, and more.

CURRENCY OPTIONS MARKETS

Prior to 1982, all currency option contracts were over-the-counter options written by international banks, investment banks, and brokerage houses. Over-the-counter options are tailor-made according to the specifications of the buyer in terms of maturity length, exercise price, and the amount of the underlying currency. Generally, these contracts are written for large amounts, at least $1,000,000 of the currency serving as the underlying asset. Frequently, they are written for U.S. dollars, with the deutsche mark, British pound, Japanese yen, French franc, Canadian dollar, and Swiss franc serving as the underlying currency, though options are also available on less actively traded currencies. Over-the-counter options are typically European style.

In December 1982, the Philadelphia Stock Exchange (PHLX) began trading options on foreign currency. Currently, trading is in seven major currencies and the euro against the U.S. dollar. Most trading is in *mid-month* options. These options trade in a March, June, September, and December expiration cycle with original maturities of 3, 6, 9, and 12 months, plus two near-term months so that there are always options with one-, two-, and three-month expirations. These options mature on the Friday before the third Wednesday of the expiration month. Exhibit 9.5 shows the currencies on which options are traded at the PHLX and the amount, or size, of underlying currency per contract. Note that the size of PHLX option contracts are half the corresponding futures contract size, as noted in Exhibit 9.2. The trading hours of these contracts are 2:30 A.M. to 2:30 P.M. Philadelphia time, except for the Canadian dollar, which trades between 7:00 A.M. and 2:30 P.M.

The volume of OTC currency options trading is much larger than that of organized-exchange option trading. According to the Bank for International Settlements, in 1998 the OTC volume was approximately $87 billion per day. By comparison exchange-traded currency option volume was approximately $1.9 billion per day, or about 15 million contracts per year. Nevertheless, the market for exchange-traded options is very important, even to the OTC market. As Grabbe (1996) notes, international

EXHIBIT 9.5

Philadelphia Stock Exchange Option Contract Specifications*

Currency	Contract Size	Mid-Month	Month-End	Long-Term
Premium Quoted in U.S. Dollars				
Australian dollar	AD50,000	E,A	E,A	Not Traded
British pound	£31,250	E,A	E,A	E
Canadian dollar	CD50,000	E,A	E,A	Not Traded
Deutsche mark	DM62,500	E,A	E,A	E
French franc	FF250,000	E,A	E,A	E
Japanese yen	¥6,250, 000	E,A	E,A	E
Swiss franc	SF62,500	E,A	E,A	Not Traded
Euro	EUR62,500	E,A	E,A	Not Traded
Cross Rate Options (Underlying Currency/Premium Currency)				
DM/¥	DM62,500	E	E	Not Traded
£/DM	£31,250	E	E	Not Traded

*E denotes European-style option, A denotes American style.

Source: Philadelphia Stock Exchange, *Standardized Currency Options,* www.phlx.com

banks and brokerage houses frequently buy or sell standardized exchange-traded options, which they then repackage in creating the tailor-made options desired by their clients. However, at times OTC options and forward contracts provide trading advantages over their exchange-traded counterparts, as the International Finance in Practice box on page 217 makes clear.

The PHLX trades a variety of options contracts in order to provide a more complete market. In addition to the *mid-month* contracts, *long-term* European-style contracts with original maturities of 18 to 24 months are traded in a June and December cycle. The size of these contracts and the expiration procedure date are the same as the *mid-month* contracts. Additionally, *month-end* American-style options with original maturities of one, two, and three months began trading in 1992. All other contract terms remain the same as for the *mid-month* contracts.

The PHLX also trades cross-rate European-style option contracts. Two contracts are currently offered: mark/yen and sterling/mark. The mark/yen contract is for DM62,500 with the premium quoted in Japanese yen. The sterling/mark is for £31,250 with the premium quoted in deutsche marks. These contracts have mid-month and month-end terms. Exhibit 9.5 summarizes the basic terms of these contracts.

Additionally, the PHLX established the United Currency Options Market (UCOM) in November 1994. The UCOM, which includes standardized currency options, also allows for exchange trading of currency options with custom-made contractual terms. Customized options allow users to customize the exercise price, expiration date up to two years, and the premium quotation in either units of currency or percent of underlying value for 110 currency pairs.

CURRENCY FUTURES OPTIONS

The Chicago Mercantile Exchange trades American options on the currency futures contracts it offers. With these options, the underlying asset is a futures contract on the foreign currency instead of the physical currency. Options trade on each of the currency futures contracts offered by the CME (refer to Exhibit 9.2). One futures contract underlies one options contract.

CME futures options trade with expirations in all 12 calendar months plus weekly expirations. At most, three option contracts will trade on a futures contract with a

INTERNATIONAL FINANCE IN PRACTICE

Commodities: Why Isn't Currency Turmoil Sparking Future Boom?

Market turmoil usually triggers a boom in futures and options trading as hedgers scurry to cover their risks and speculators rush in search of quick profits.

But that hasn't been true of the currency pits lately.

Despite the dollar's historic slide and currency tumult in Europe this year, listed foreign-exchange derivatives have been languishing. On the Chicago Mercantile Exchange and the Philadelphia Stock Exchange, the nation's largest forums for trading currency futures and options, business fell substantially from early 1994, measured in both trading volume and the number of contracts outstanding.

Why? Exchange-traded products simply don't seem to meet the needs of most large currency traders, such as dealers, investment funds and corporations. On the immense interbank market, where $1 trillion of currency routinely changes hands a day, trading typically takes place in multimillion dollar chunks.

On the CME, by contrast, the typical contract has an underlying value of just $125,000 or less, and even the biggest amount to no more than $250,000. On a given day, only about $12 billion in CME currency contracts change hands. That's far too small for most big players, especially in major currencies like the mark or yen. The Philadelphia currency-options market is even tinier, with the average contract commanding just $45,000 of underlying value, and the daily volume running at just $1.5 billion.

Activity on the listed foreign-exchange markets is "nothing, insignificant," says David DeRosa, a director of foreign exchange trading at Swiss Bank Corp. in New York. "If you're a real player, you have to deal in the interbank market."

Even investors who would favor using listed currency derivatives find themselves driven to private, "over-the-counter" derivatives, instead. For one thing, the OTC market's well-established bank-to-bank trading network makes executing transactions there cheaper and more efficient.

"With all the trades we'd have to do to build up a position, there's a big risk of moving the market," says Mark Fitzsimmons, senior vice president of Millburn Corp., a New York-based commodity trading advisory firm, which manages about $500 million in financial futures. "We'd rather deal on the interbank market, where we can trade 24 hours and in bulk, and get a trade done very, very quickly without distorting prices."

The OTC market also frees traders from position limits and other cumbersome exchange requirements. To complete a $100 million trade on an exchange, one large institutional investor says, "we'd have to really pay up to get it done" in fees and other costs.

What's more, the Philadelphia exchange forbids speculators and hedgers from holding more than 100,000 contracts—limiting their total positions to an average $4.5 billion. And although the CME eliminated position limits on currencies a few years ago, it still requires its customers to justify their trading strategies and imposes tough reporting requirements.

Costs and hassles aren't the only things keeping big traders out of the exchanges' currency pits. Many players also see those markets as riskier than OTC markets—particularly in turbulent times.

A big reason is the listed market's relatively small size, which makes trading thinner and more volatile. The underlying value, or open interest, of OTC currency derivatives worldwide totals $14.5 trillion, according to Swaps Monitor, a newsletter that tracks the derivatives market. By contrast, total open interest of exchange-traded currency derivatives worldwide amounts to only about $450 billion—3% of that sum. And the currency pits at the CME and Philadelphia command just $70 billion and $20 billion of open interest, respectively.

While a certain measure of volatility is desirable and even necessary for a market to remain healthy, too much turmoil tends to hurt exchange-listed products by making trading even thinner and riskier. "There is a huge liquidity concern," says Swiss Bank's Mr. DeRosa.

And since the exchanges, unlike the OTC derivatives markets, don't trade actively 24 hours a day, traders risk being left in the lurch if a big market move occurs during Asian or European trading. "People are kind of scared," says Dan O'Connell, vice president of institutional foreign-exchange at First National Bank of Chicago, a unit of First Chicago Corp. "If you put on a position, and go home overnight, prices can swing dramatically and blow you out of the water."

Source: Excerpted from Suzanne McGee, "Commodities: Why Isn't Currency Turmoil Sparking Future Boom?" *The Wall Street Journal,* April 10, 1995, p. C1. Reprinted by permission of *The Wall Street Journal,* © 1995 Dow Jones & Company, Inc. All Rights Reserved Worldwide.

particular quarterly expiration. For example, in January options with expirations in January, February, and March would trade on futures with a March expiration. These options expire on the second Friday prior to the third Wednesday of the options contract month. Regular trading takes place each business day on $GLOBEX_2$ from 7:20 A.M. to 2:00 P.M. Chicago time. Extended-hour trading on the $GLOBEX_2$ system begins at 2:30 P.M. and continues until 7:05 A.M. Chicago time. On Sundays trading begins at 5:30 P.M.

Options on currency futures behave very similarly to options on the physical currency since the futures price converges to the spot price as the futures contract nears maturity. Exercise of a futures option results in a long futures position for the call buyer or the put writer and a short futures position for the put buyer or call writer. If the futures position is not offset prior to the futures expiration date, receipt or delivery of the underlying currency will, respectively, result or be required. In addition to the PHLX and the CME, there is some limited exchange-traded currency options trading at the Belgian Futures and Options Exchange.

BASIC OPTION-PRICING RELATIONSHIPS AT EXPIRATION

To illustrate how currency options are priced, let's use quotations for PHLX options contracts presented in Exhibit 9.6. The exhibit shows that both European- and American-style options trade on the exchange. The American-style option quotations are the ones *without* a style designation specifically stated.

EXHIBIT 9.6

Philadelphia Stock Exchange Currency Options Quotations

Options
Philadelphia Exchange

		Calls		Puts	
		Vol.	Last	Vol.	Last
British Pound					156.13
31,250 Brit. Pounds-European Style					
158	Jul	16	0.23	...	...
31,250 Brit. Pounds-cents per unit.					
163	Jul	4	0.01	...	0.01
Euro					102.46
62,500 Euro-cents per unit.					
98	Sep	...	0.01	89	0.35
100	Sep	...	...	22	0.67
102	Sep	...	0.01	4	1.38
104	Sep	...	...	24	2.47
106	Sep	2	0.53	...	0.01
110	Sep	3	0.10	...	0.01
Japanese Yen					82.64
6,250,000J.Yen-100ths of a cent per unit.					
80½	Sep	...	0.01	25	0.60
6,250,000J.Yen-EuropeanStyle.					
80½	Sep	...	0.01	20	0.53
Swiss Franc					63.80
62,500 Swiss Francs-cents per unit					
67	Sep	10	0.30	...	...
68	Sep	2	0.15	...	...
Call Vol		986	Open Int		39,510
Put Vol		3,569	Open Int		30,445

Source: *The Wall Street Journal*, July 7, 1999, p. C14. Reprinted by permission of *The Wall Street Journal*, © 1999 Dow Jones & Company, Inc. All Rights Reserved Worldwide.

At expiration, a European option and an American option (which has not been previously exercised), both with the same exercise price, will have the same terminal value. For call options the time T expiration value can be stated per unit of foreign currency as:

$$C_{aT} = C_{eT} = Max[S_T - E, 0], \tag{9.2}$$

where C_{aT} denotes the value of the American call at expiration, C_{eT} is the value of the European call at expiration, E is the exercise price per unit of foreign currency, S_T is the expiration date spot price, and Max is an abbreviation for denoting the maximum of the arguments within the brackets. A call (put) option with $S_T > E(E > S_T)$ expires **in-the-money** and it will be exercised. If $S_T = E$ the option expires **at-the-money**. If $S_T < E(E < S_T)$ the call (put) option expires **out-of-the-money** and it will not be exercised.

EXAMPLE 9.4: Expiration Value of an American Call Option As an illustration of pricing Equation 9.2, consider the PHLX 67 Sep SF American call option from Exhibit 9.6. This option has a current premium, C_a, of .30 cents per SF. The exercise price is 67 cents per SF and it expires on September 10, 1999. Suppose that at expiration the spot rate is \$0.7025/SF. In this event, the call option has an exercise value of 70.25 − 67 = 3.25 cents per each of the SF62,500 of the contract, or \$2,031.25. That is, the call owner can buy SF62,500, worth \$43,906.25 (= SF62,500 × \$0.7025) in the spot market, for \$41,875 (= SF62,500 × \$0.67). On the other hand, if the spot rate is \$0.6607/SF at expiration, the call option has a negative exercise value, 66.07 − 68 = −.93 cents per SF. The call buyer is under no obligation to exercise the option if it is to his disadvantage, so he should not. He should let it expire worthless, or with zero value.

Exhibit 9.7a graphs the 67 Sep SF call option from the buyer's perspective and Exhibit 9.7b graphs it from the call writer's perspective at expiration. Note that the two graphs are mirror-images of one another. The call buyer can lose no more than the call premium but theoretically has an unlimited profit potential. The call writer can profit by no more than the call premium but theoretically can lose an unlimited amount. At an expiration spot price of $S_T = E + C_a = 67 + .30 = 67.30$ cents per SF, both the call buyer and writer break even, that is, neither earns nor loses anything.

The speculative possibilities of a long position in a call are clearly evident from Exhibit 9.7. Anytime the speculator believes that S_T will be in excess of the breakeven point, he will establish a long position in the call. The speculator who is correct realizes a profit. If the speculator is incorrect in his forecast, the loss will be limited to the premium paid. Alternatively, if the speculator believes that S_T will be less than the breakeven point, a short position in the call will yield a profit, the largest amount being the call premium received from the buyer. If the speculator is incorrect, very large losses can result if S_T is much larger than the breakeven point.

Analogously, at expiration a European put and an American put will have the same value. Algebraically, the expiration value can be stated as:

$$P_{aT} = P_{eT} = Max[E - S_T, 0] \tag{9.3}$$

where P denotes the value of the put at expiration.

EXAMPLE 9.5: Expiration Value of an American Put Option As an example of pricing Equation 9.3, consider the 104 Sep EUR American put, which has

EXHIBIT 9.7A

Graph of 67 September SF Call Option: Buyer's Perspective

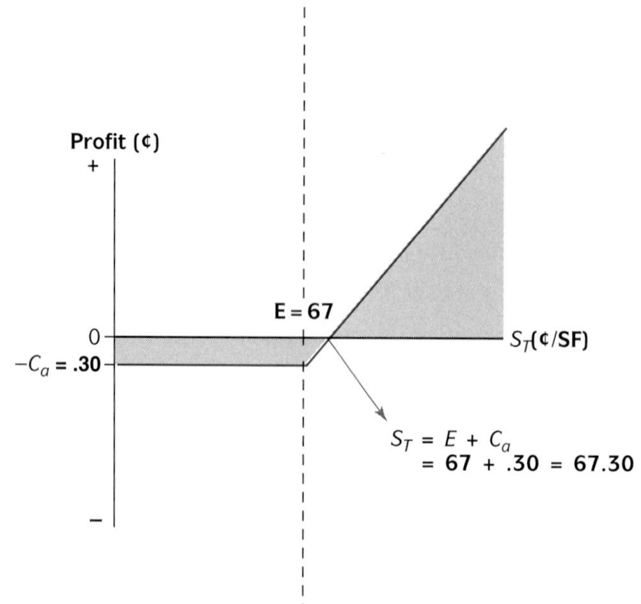

Out-of the-Money | At-the-Money | In-the-Money

EXHIBIT 9.7B

Graph of 67 September SF Call Option: Writer's Perspective

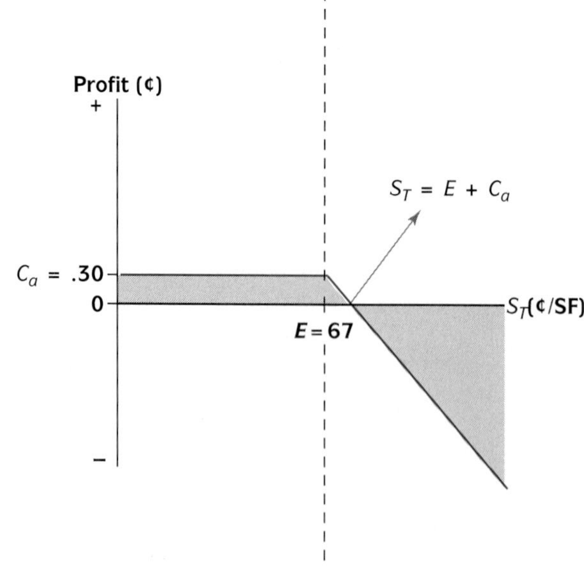

a current premium, P_a, of 2.47 cents per EUR. If S_T is \$1.0307/EUR, the put contract has an exercise value of $104 - 103.07 = .93$ cents per EUR for each of the EUR62,500 of the contract, or \$581.25. That is, the put owner can sell EUR62,500, worth \$64,418.75 (= EUR62,500 × \$1.0307) in the spot market, for \$65,000 (= EUR62,500 × \$1.04). If S_T = \$1.0425/EUR, the exercise value is $104 - 104.25 = -.25$ cents per EUR. The put buyer would rationally not exercise the put; in other words, he should let it expire worthless with zero value.

Exhibit 9.8a graphs the 68 Oct DM put from the buyer's perspective and Exhibit 9.8b graphs it from the put writer's perspective at expiration. The two graphs are mirror-images of one another. The put buyer can lose no more than the put premium and the put writer can profit by no more than the premium. The put buyer can earn a maximum profit of $E - P_a = 104 - 2.47 = 101.53$ cents per EUR if the terminal spot exchange rate is an unrealistic \$0/EUR. The put writer's maximum loss is 101.53 cents per EUR. Additionally, at $S_T = E - P_a = 101.53$ cents per EUR, the put buyer and writer both break even; neither loses nor earns anything.

The speculative possibilities of a long position in a put are clearly evident from Exhibit 9.8. Anytime the speculator believes that S_T will be less than the breakeven point, he will establish a long position in the put. If the speculator is correct, he will realize a profit. If the speculator is incorrect in his forecast, the loss will be limited to the premium paid. Alternatively, if the speculator believes that S_T will be in excess of the breakeven point, a short position in the put will yield a profit, the largest amount being the put premium received from the buyer. If the speculator is incorrect, very large losses can result if S_T is much smaller than the breakeven point.

AMERICAN OPTION-PRICING RELATIONSHIPS

An American call or put option can be exercised at any time prior to expiration. Consequently, in a rational marketplace, American options will satisfy the following basic pricing relationships at time t prior to expiration:

$$C_a \geq Max[S_t - E, 0] \tag{9.4}$$

and

$$P_a \geq Max[E - S_t, 0] \tag{9.5}$$

Verbally, these equations state that the American call and put premiums at time t will be at least as large as the immediate exercise value, or **intrinsic value,** of the call or put option. (The t subscripts are deleted from the call and put premiums to simplify the notation.) Since the owner of a long-maturity American option can exercise it on any date that he could exercise a shorter maturity option he held on a currency, or at some later date after the shorter maturity option expires, it follows that all else remaining the same, the longer term American option will have a market price at least as large as the shorter term option.

A call (put) option with $S_t > E(E > S_t)$ is referred to as trading in-the-money. If $S_t \cong E$ the option is trading at-the-money. If $S_t < E(E < S_t)$ the call (put) option is trading out-of-the-money. The difference between the option premium and the option's intrinsic value is nonnegative and sometimes referred to as the option's **time value.** For example, the time value for an American call is $C_a - [S_t - E]$. The time value exists, meaning investors are willing to pay more than the immediate exercise value, because the option may move more in-the-money, and thus become more

EXHIBIT 9.8A

Graph of 104 September EUR Put Option: Buyer's Perspective

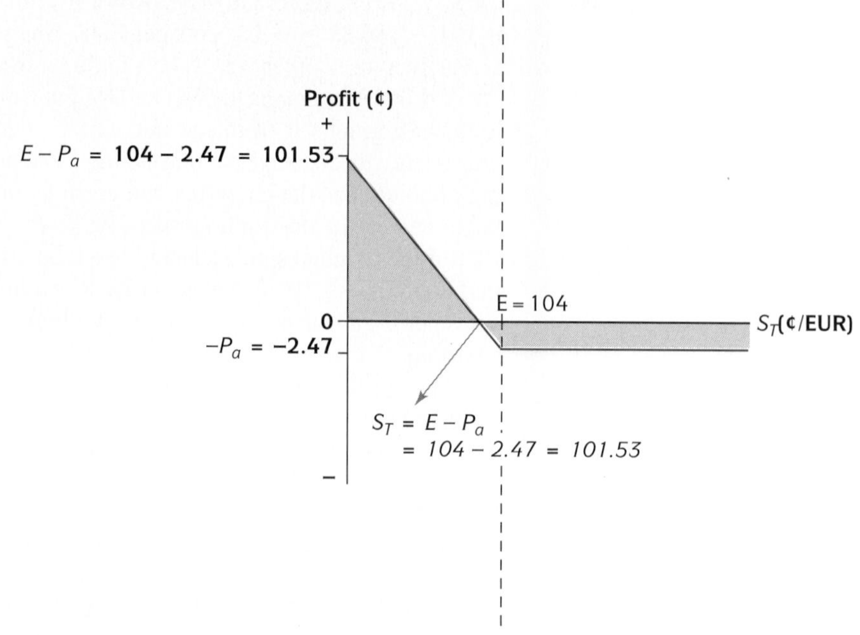

EXHIBIT 9.8B

Graph of 104 September EUR Put Option: Writer's Perspective

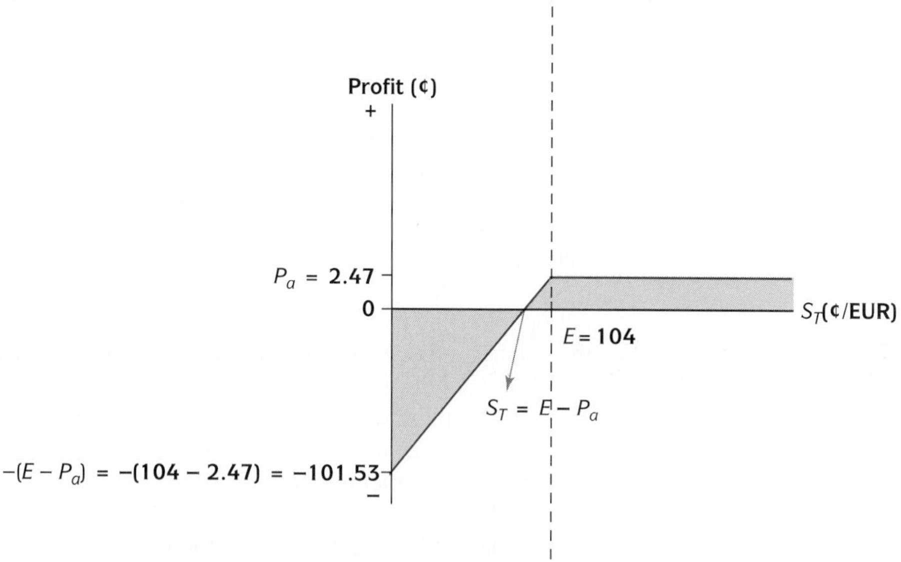

EXHIBIT 9.9

Market Value, Time Value, and Intrinsic Value of an American Call Option

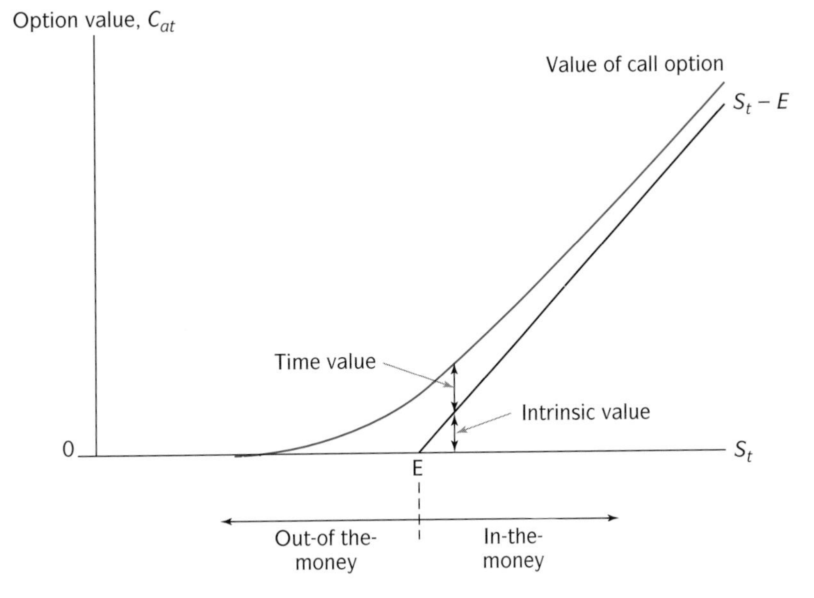

valuable, as time elapses. Exhibit 9.9 graphs the intrinsic value and time value for an American call option.

EXAMPLE 9.6: American Option Pricing Valuation Let's see if Equations 9.4 and 9.5 actually hold for the 67 Sep SF American call and the 104 Sep EUR American put options we considered. For the 67 Sep SF Call,

$$.30 \geq Max[63.80 - 67, 0] = Max[-3.20, 0] = 0.$$

Thus, the lower boundary relationship on the American call premium holds. (The spot price of 63.80 cents per SF is obtained from the beginning of the SF PHLX quotation section and may differ from the spot price listed under *Exchange Rates* in Exhibit 4.3 because it was obtained at a different time during the trading day.) For the 104 Sep EUR put,

$$2.47 \geq Max[104 - 102.46, 0] = Max[1.54, 0] = 1.54.$$

Thus, the lower boundary relationship on the American put premium holds as well.

EUROPEAN OPTION-PRICING RELATIONSHIPS

The pricing boundaries for European put and call premiums are more complex because they can only be exercised at expiration. Hence, there is a time value element to the boundary expressions. Exhibit 9.10 develops the lower boundary expression for a European call.

Exhibit 9.10 compares the cost and payoffs of two portfolios a U.S. dollar investor could make. Portfolio A involves purchasing a European call option and lending (or investing) an amount equal to the present value of the exercise price, E, at the U.S. interest rate r_{us}, which we assume corresponds to the length of the investment period. The cost of this investment is $C_e + E/(1 + r_{us})$. If at expiration, S_T is less than or equal to E, the call option will not have a positive exercise value and the call

EXHIBIT 9.10

Equation for a European Call Option Lower Boundary

	Current Time	Expiration	
		$S_T \leq E$	$S_T > E$
Portfolio A:			
Buy Call	$-C_e$	0	$S_T - E$
Lend PV of E in U.S.	$-E/(1 + r_{us})$	E	E
	$-C_e - E/(1 + r_{us})$	E	S_T
Portfolio B:			
Lend PV of one unit of currency i at rate r_i	$-S_t/(1 + r_i)$	S_T	S_T

owner will let it expire worthless. If at expiration, S_T is greater than E, it will be to the call owner's advantage to exercise the call; the exercise value will be $S_T - E > 0$. The risk-free loan will pay off the amount E regardless of which state occurs at time T.

By comparison, the U.S. dollar investor could invest in portfolio B, which consists of lending the present value of one unit of foreign currency i at the foreign interest rate r_i, which we assume corresponds to the length of the investment period. In U.S. dollar terms, the cost of this investment is $S_t/(1 + r_i)$. Regardless of which state exists at time T, this investment will pay off one unit of foreign currency, which in U.S. dollar terms will have value S_T.

It is easily seen from Exhibit 9.10 that if $S_T > E$, portfolios A and B pay off the same amount, S_T. However, if $S_T \leq E$, portfolio A has a larger payoff than portfolio B. It follows that in a rational marketplace, portfolio A will be priced to sell for at least as much as portfolio B, that is, $C_e + E/(1 + r_{us}) \geq S_t/(1 + r_i)$. This implies that

$$C_e \geq Max\left[\frac{S_t}{(1 + r_i)} - \frac{E}{(1 + r_{us})}, 0\right] \tag{9.6}$$

since the European call can never sell for a negative amount.

Similarly, it can be shown that the lower boundary pricing relationship for a European put is:

$$P_e \geq Max\left[\frac{E}{(1 + r_{us})} - \frac{S}{(1 + r_i)}, 0\right] \tag{9.7}$$

The derivation of this formula is left as an exercise for the reader. (Hint: Portfolio A involves buying a put and lending spot, portfolio B involves lending the present value of the exercise price.)

Note that both C_e and P_e are functions of only five variables: S_t, E, r_i, r_{us}, and implicitly the term to maturity. From Equations 9.6 and 9.7, it can be determined that, when all else remains the same, the call premium C_e (put premium P_e) will increase:

1. The larger (smaller) is S,
2. The smaller (larger) is E,
3. The smaller (larger) is r_i,
4. The larger (smaller) is r_{us}, and
5. The larger (smaller) r_{us} is relative to r_i.

Implicitly, both r_{us} and r_i will be larger the longer the length of the option period. When r_{us} and r_i are not too much different in size, a European FX call and put will increase in price when the option term to maturity increases. However, when r_{us} is very much larger than r_i, a European FX call will increase in price, but the put premium will decrease, when the option term to maturity increases. The opposite is true when r_i is very much greater than r_{us}.

Recall that IRP implies $F = S_t[(1 + r_{us})/(1 + r_i)]$, which in turn implies that $F/(1 + r_{us}) = S_t/(1 + r_i)$. Hence, European call and put prices on spot foreign exchange, Equations 9.6 and 9.7 can be, respectively, restated as:[3]

$$C_e \geq Max\left[\frac{(F - E)}{(1 + r_{us})}, 0\right] \tag{9.8}$$

and

$$P_e \geq Max\left[\frac{(E - F)}{(1 + r_{us})}, 0\right] \tag{9.9}$$

BINOMIAL OPTION-PRICING MODEL

The option pricing relationships we have discussed to this point have been lower boundaries on the call and put premiums, instead of exact equality expressions for the premiums. The binomial option-pricing model provides an exact pricing formula for an American call or put.[4] We will examine only a simple one-step case of the binomial model to better understand the nature of option pricing.

We want to use the binomial model to value the a PHLX 67 September SF American call from Exhibit 9.6. We see from the exhibit that the option is quoted at a premium of .30 cents. The current spot price of the SF in American terms is $S_0 = 63.86$ cents. We will further assume that the option's volatility (annualized standard deviation of the change in the spot rate) is $\sigma = 14$ percent. The volatility on SF options has varied from less than 10 percent to over 14 percent over the past three years. This call option expires in 66 days on September 10, 1999, or in $T = 66/365 = .1808$ years. The one-step binomial model assumes that at the end of the option period the SF will have appreciated to $S_{uT} = S_0 \cdot u$ or depreciated to $S_{dT} = S_0 \cdot d$, where $u = e^{\sigma \cdot \sqrt{T}}$ and $d = 1/u$. The spot rate at T will be either $67.78 = 63.86\,(1.06134)$ or $60.17 = 63.86\,(.94221)$, where $u = e^{.14 \cdot \sqrt{.1808}} = 1.06134$ and $d = 1/u = .94221$. At the exercise price of $E = 67$, the option will only be exercised at time T if the euro appreciates; its exercise value would be $C_{uT} = .78 = 67.78 - 67$. If the Euro depreciates it would not be rational to exercise the option; its value would be $C_{dT} = 0$.

The binominal option-pricing model only requires that $u > 1 + r_{us} > d$. The two-month Eurodollar bid rate is 5⅛ percent. (See *Money Rates* in the inside front cover.) Thus, $1 + r_{us} = (1.05125)^T = 1.00908$. We see that $1.06134 > 1.00908 > .94221$.

The binomial option-pricing model relies on the risk-neutral probabilities of the underlying asset increasing and decreasing in value. For our purposes, the risk-neutral probability of the euro appreciating is calculated as:

$$q = (F_0 - S_0 \cdot d)/\, S_0(u - d),$$

where F_0 is the forward (or futures) price that spans the option period. We will use the September SF futures price $F(\$/SF) = \$0.6433$ from Exhibit 9.3. Therefore,

$$q = (64.33 - 60.17)/(67.78 - 60.17) = .5466.$$

It follows that the risk-neutral probability of the SF depreciating is $1 - q = 1 - .5466 = .4534$.

Because the American call option can be exercised at any time, including time 0, the binomial call option premium is determined by:

$$
\begin{aligned}
C_0 &= Max[qC_{uT} + (1 - q)C_{dT}]/(1 + r_{us}), S_0 - E] \quad (9.10)\\
&= Max[.5466(0.78) + .4534(0)]/(1.00908), 63.86 - 67]\\
&= Max[.42, -3.14] = .42 \text{ cents per SF.}
\end{aligned}
$$

Alternatively, (if C_{uT} is positive) the binomial call price can be expressed as:

$$C_0 = Max\{[F_0 \cdot h - E((S_0 \cdot u/E)(h - 1) + 1)]/(1 + r_{us}), S_0 - E\}, \quad (9.11)$$

where $h = (C_{uT} - C_{dT})/S_0(u - d)$ is the risk-free hedge ratio. The *hedge ratio* is the size of the long (short) position the investor must have in the underlying asset per option the investor must write (buy) to have a risk-free offsetting investment that will result in the investor receiving the same terminal value at time T regardless of whether the underlying asset increases or decreases in value. For our example numbers, we see that

$$h = (.78 - 0)/(67.78 - 60.17) = .1025.$$

Thus, the call premium is:

$$
\begin{aligned}
C_0 &= Max\ \{[64.33(.1025) - 67((67.78/67)(.1025 - 1) + 1)]/(1.00908),\\
&\quad 63.86 - 67\}\\
&= Max[.42, -3.14] = .42 \text{ cents per SF.}
\end{aligned}
$$

Equation 9.11 is more intuitive than Equation 9.10 because it is in the same general form as Equation 9.8. In an analogous manner, a binomial put option-pricing model can be developed. Nevertheless, for our example, the binomial call option-pricing model yielded a price that was too large compared to the actual market price of .30 cents. This is what we might expect with such a simple model, and when using such an arbitrary value for the option's volatility. In the next section, we consider a more refined option-pricing model.

EUROPEAN OPTION-PRICING FORMULA

In the last section, we examined a simple one-step version of binomial option-pricing model. Instead, we could have assumed the stock price followed a multiplicative binomial process by subdividing the option period into many subperiods. In this case, S_T and C_T could be many different values. When the number of subperiods into which the option period is subdivided goes to infinity, the European call and put pricing formulas presented in this section obtain. Exact European call and put pricing formulas are:[5]

$$C_e = S_t e^{-r_i T} N(d_1) - E e^{-r_{us} T} N(d_2) \quad (9.12)$$

and

$$P_e = E e^{-r_{us} T} N(-d_2) - S_t e^{-r_i T} N(-d_1) \quad (9.13)$$

The interest rates r_i and r_{us} are assumed to be annualized and constant over the term to maturity T of the option contract, which is expressed as a fraction of a year.

Invoking IRP, where with continuous compounding $F = S_t e^{(r_{us} - r_i)T}$, C_e and P_e, Equations 9.12 and 9.13 can be, respectively, restated as:

$$C_e = [FN(d_1) - EN(d_2)]e^{-r_{us} T} \quad (9.14)$$

and

$$P_e = [EN(-d_2) - FN(-d_1)]e^{-r_{us} T} \quad (9.15)$$

where

$$d_1 = \frac{ln(F/E) + .5\sigma^2 T}{\sigma/\sqrt{T}}$$

and

$$d_2 = d_1 - \sigma\sqrt{T}.$$

$N(d)$ denotes the cumulative area under the standard normal density function from $-\infty$ to d_1 (or d_2). The variable σ is the annualized volatility of the exchange rate change $ln(S_{t+1}/S_t)$. Equations 9.14 and 9.15 indicate that C_e and P_e are functions of only five variables: F, E, r_{us}, T, and σ. It can be shown that both C_e and P_e increase when σ becomes larger.

The value $N(d)$ can be calculated using the NORMSDIST function of Microsoft Excel.

Equations 9.14 and 9.15 are widely used in practice, especially by international banks in trading OTC options.

EXAMPLE 9.7: The European Option Pricing Model As an example of using the European options pricing model, consider the PHLX 67 Sep SF American call option from Exhibit 9.6. We will use the European model even though the call is an American option. This is frequently done in practice, and the prices between the two option styles vary very little.[6]

The option has a premium of .30 U.S. cents per SF. The option will expire on September 10, 1999—66 days from the quotation date, or $T = 66/365 = .1808$. We will use the September futures price from Exhibit 9.3 as our estimate of $F(\$/SF) = \$0.6433$. The rate r_{us} is estimated as the annualized two-month Eurodollar bid rate of 5⅛ percent. The estimated volatility is 10.7 percent.

The values d_1 and d_2 are:

$$d_2 = \frac{ln(64.33/67) + .5(.107)^2(.1808)}{(.107)\sqrt{.1808}} = -.8713$$

and

$$d_2 = -.8713 - (.107)\sqrt{.1808} = -.9168.$$

Consequently, it can be determined that $N(-.8713) = .1918$ and $N(-.9168) = .1796$.

We now have everything we need to compute the model price:

$$\begin{aligned} C_e &= [64.33(.1918) - 67(.1796)]e^{-(.05125)(.1808)} \\ &= [12.3385 - 12.0332](.9908) \\ &= .30 \text{ cents per DM.} \end{aligned}$$

As we see, the model has done a good job of valuing the SF call. The price would obviously been higher, however, had we used a larger volatility estimate.

EMPIRICAL TESTS OF CURRENCY OPTIONS

Shastri and Tandon (1985) empirically test the American boundary relationships we developed in this chapter (Equations 9.4, 9.5, 9.6, 9.7, 9.8, and 9.9) using PHLX put and call data. They discover many violations of the boundary relationships, but conclude that nonsimultaneous data could account for most of the violations. Bodurtha and Courtadon (1986) test the immediate exercise boundary relationships (Equations 9.4 and 9.5) for PHLX American put and call options. They also find many violations when using last daily trade data. However, when they use simultaneous price data and incorporate transaction costs, they conclude that the PHLX American currency options are efficiently priced.

Shastri and Tandon (1986) also test the European option-pricing model using PHLX American put and call data. They determine that a nonmember of the PHLX could not earn abnormal profits from the hedging strategies they examine. This implies that the European option-pricing model works well in pricing American currency options. Barone-Adesi and Whaley (1987) also find that the European option-pricing model works well for pricing American currency options that are *at* or *out-of-the money,* but does not do well in pricing *in-the-money* calls and puts. For *in-the-money* options, their approximate American option-pricing model yields superior results.

SUMMARY

This chapter introduced currency futures and options on foreign exchange. These instruments are useful for speculating and hedging foreign exchange rate movements. In later chapters, it will be shown how to use these vehicles for hedging purposes.

1. Forward, futures, and options contracts are derivative, or contingent claim, securities. That is, their value is derived or contingent upon the value of the asset that underlies these securities.
2. Forward and futures contracts are similar instruments, but there are differences. Both are contracts to buy or sell a certain quantity of a specific underlying asset at some specific price in the future. Futures contracts, however, are exchange-traded, and there are standardized features that distinguish them from the tailor-made terms of forward contracts. The two main standardized features are contract size and maturity date.
3. Additionally, futures contracts are marked-to-market on a daily basis at the new settlement price. Hence, the margin account of an individual with a futures position is increased or decreased, reflecting daily realized profits or losses resulting from the change in the futures settlement price from the previous day's settlement price.
4. A futures market requires speculators and hedgers to effectively operate. Hedgers attempt to avoid the risk of price change of the underlying asset, and speculators attempt to profit from anticipating the direction of future price changes.
5. The Chicago Mercantile Exchange and the Philadelphia Board of Trade are the two largest currency futures exchanges.
6. The pricing equation typically used to price currency futures is the CIRP relationship, which is used also to price currency forward contracts.
7. Eurodollar interest rate futures contracts were introduced as a vehicle for hedging short-term dollar interest rate risk, in much the same way as forward rate agreements, introduced in Chapter 6.
8. An option is the right, but not the obligation, to buy or sell the underlying asset for a stated price over a stated time period. Call options give the owner the right to buy, put options the right to sell. American options can be exercised at any time during their life, European options can only be exercised at maturity.
9. Exchange-traded options with standardized features are traded on two exchanges. Options on spot foreign exchange are traded at the Philadelphia Stock Exchange, and options on currency futures are traded at the Chicago Mercantile Exchange.
10. Basic boundary expressions for put and call option prices were developed and examined using actual options-pricing data.
11. A European option-pricing model for put and call options was also presented and explained using actual market data.

KEY WORDS

American option, 215
at-the-money, 219
call, 215
clearinghouse, 209
commission, 209
contingent claim security, 207
contract size, 207
daily price limit, 209
delivery month, 207
derivative security, 207
European option, 215
exchange-traded, 207
exercise price, 215
futures, 207
hedger, 208
in-the-money, 219
initial margin, 207
intrinsic value, 221
long, 207
marked-to-market, 207
maintenance margin, 208
maturity date, 207
nearby, 210
open interest, 210
option, 215
out-of-the-money, 219
premium, 215
price convergence, 212
price discovery, 212
put, 215
reversing trade, 208
settled-up, 207
settlement price, 207
short, 207
speculator, 208
standardized, 207
striking price, 215
time value, 221
variation margin, 208
writer, 215
zero-sum game, 207

QUESTIONS

1. Explain the basic differences between the operation of a currency forward market and a futures market.
2. In order for a derivatives market to function, two types of economic agents are needed: hedgers and speculators. Explain.
3. Why are most futures positions closed out through a reversing trade rather than held to delivery?
4. How can the FX futures market be used for price discovery?
5. What is the major difference in the obligation of one with a long position in a futures (or forward contract) in comparison to an options contract?
6. What is meant by the terminology that an option is in-, at-, or out-of-the-money?
7. List the arguments (variables) of which an FX call or put option model price is a function. How does the call and put premium change with respect to a change in the arguments?

PROBLEMS

1. Assume today's settlement price on a CME DM futures contract is \$0.6080/DM. You have a short position in one contract. Your margin account currently has a balance of \$1,700. The next three days' settlement prices are \$0.6066, \$0.6073, and \$0.5989. Calculate the changes in the margin account from daily marking-to-market and the balance of the margin account after the third day.
2. Do problem 1 again assuming you have a long position in the futures contract.
3. Using the quotations in Exhibit 9.3, calculate the face value of the open interest in the December 1999 Swiss franc futures contract.
4. Using the quotations in Exhibit 9.3, note that the March 2000 Mexican peso futures contract has a price of \$0.09550. You believe the spot price in March will be \$0.11000. What speculative position would you enter into to attempt to profit from your beliefs? Calculate your anticipated profits, assuming you take a position in three contracts. What is the size of your profit (loss) if the futures price is indeed an unbiased predictor of the future spot price and this price materializes?
5. Do problem 4 again assuming you believe the March 2000 spot price will be \$0.08500.
6. Recall the forward rate agreement (FRA) example in Chapter 6. Show how the bank can alternatively use a position in Eurodollar futures contracts to hedge the

interest rate risk created by the maturity mismatch it has with the $3,000,000 six-month Eurodollar deposit and rollover Eurocredit position indexed to three-month LIBOR. Assume the bank can take a position in Eurodollar futures contracts maturing in three months' time that have a futures price of 94.00.

7. Use the quotations in Exhibit 9.6 to calculate the intrinsic value and the time value of the 80½ September Japanese yen American put options.
8. Assume the spot Swiss franc is $0.7000 and the six-month forward rate is $0.6950. What is the minimum price that a six-month American call option with a striking price of $0.6800 should sell for in a rational market? Assume the annualized six-month Eurodollar rate is 3 1/2 percent.
9. Do problem 8 again assuming an American put option instead of a call option.
10.  Use the European option-pricing models developed in the chapter to value the call of problem 8 and the put of problem 9. Assume the annualized volatility of the Swiss franc is 14.2 percent. This problem can be solved using the FXOPM.xls spreadsheet.
11. Use the binomial option-pricing model developed in the chapter to value the call of problem 8. The volatility of the Swiss franc is 14.2 percent.

MINI CASE

The Options Speculator

A speculator is considering the purchase of five three-month Japanese yen call options with a striking price of 96 cents per 100 yen. The premium is 1.35 cents per 100 yen. The spot price is 95.28 cents per 100 yen and the 90-day forward rate is 95.71 cents. The speculator believes the yen will appreciate to $1.00 per 100 yen over the next three months. As the speculator's assistant, you have been asked to prepare the following:

1. Diagram the call option.
2. Determine the speculator's profit if the yen appreciates to $1.00/100 yen.
3. Determine the speculator's profit if the yen only appreciates to the forward rate.
4. Determine the future spot price at which the speculator will only break even.

ENDNOTES

1. In the forward market, the investor holds offsetting positions after a reversing trade; in the futures market the investor actually exits the marketplace.
2. As a theoretical proposition, Cox, Ingersoll, and Ross (1981) show that forward and futures prices should not be equal unless interest rates are constant or can be predicted with certainty. For our purposes, it is not necessary to be theoretically specific.
3. An American option can be exercised at any time during its life. If it is not advantageous for the option owner to exercise it prior to maturity, the owner can let it behave as a European option, which can only be exercised at maturity. It follows from Equations 9.4 and 9.8 (for calls) and 9.5 and 9.9 (for puts) that a more restrictive lower boundary relationship for American call and put options are, respectively:

   $C_a \geq Max[S_t - E, (F - E)/(1 + r_{us}), 0]$ and $P_a \geq Max[E - S_t, (E - F)/(1 + r_{us}), 0]$.
4. The binomial option-pricing model was independently derived by Sharpe (1978), Rendleman, and Bartter (1979), and Cox, Ross, and Rubinstein (1979).

5. The European option pricing model was developed by Biger and Hull (1983), Garman and Kohlhagen (1983), and Grabbe (1983). The evolution of the model can be traced back to European option-pricing models developed by Merton (1973) and Black (1976).
6. Barone-Adesi and Whaley (1987) have developed an approximate American call option-pricing model that has proven quite accurate in valuing American currency call options.

WEB RESOURCES

www.belfox.be

This is the Website of the Belgian Futures and Options Exchange. It provides detailed information about the derivative products traded on it.

www.cme.com

This is the Website of the Chicago Mercantile Exchange. It provides detailed information about the futures contracts and futures options contracts traded on it.

www.liffe.com

This is the Website of the London International Financial Futures Exchange. It provides detailed information about the derivative products traded on it.

www.numa.com/ref/exchange.htm

This is the Website of Numa Directory. It provides the Website address of most all of the stock and derivative exchanges in the world.

www.phlx.com

This is the Website of the Philadelphia Stock Exchange and the Philadelphia Board of Trade. It provides detailed information about the stocks and derivative products that trade on the exchanges.

www.simex.com

This is the Website of the Singapore International Monetary Exchange. It provides detailed information about the derivative products traded on it.

REFERENCES AND SUGGESTED READINGS

Barone-Adesi, Giovanni, and Robert Whaley. "Efficient Analytic Approximation of American Option Values." *Journal of Finance* 42 (1987), pp. 301–20.

Biger, Nahum, and John Hull. "The Valuation of Currency Options." *Financial Management* 12 (1983), pp. 24–28.

Black, Fischer. "The Pricing of Commodity Contracts." *Journal of Financial Economics* 3 (1976), pp. 167–79.

——— and Myron Scholes. "The Pricing of Options and Corporate Liabilities." *Journal of Political Economy* 81 (1973), pp. 637–54.

Bodurtha, Jr., James, and George Courtadon. "Efficiency Tests of the Foreign Currency Options Market." *Journal of Finance* 41 (1986), pp. 151–62.

Chicago Mercantile Exchange. *Using Currency Futures and Options.* Chicago: Chicago Mercantile Exchange, 1992.

Cox, John C., Jonathan E. Ingersoll, and Stephen A. Ross. "The Relation between Forward Prices and Futures Prices." *Journal of Financial Economics* 9 (1981), pp. 321–46.

Cox, John C., Stephen A. Ross, and Mark Rubinstein. "Option Pricing: A Simplified Approach." *Journal of Financial Economics* 7 (1979), pp. 229–63.

Garman, Mark, and Steven Kohlhagen. "Foreign Currency Option Values." *Journal of International Money and Finance* 2 (1983), pp. 231–38.

Grabbe, J. Orlin. "The Pricing of Call and Put Options on Foreign Exchange." *Journal of International Money and Finance* 2 (1983), pp. 239–54.

——— *International Financial Markets,* 3rd ed. Englewood Cliffs, NJ: Prentice Hall, 1996.

Merton, Robert. "Theory of Rational Option Pricing." *The Bell Journal of Economics and Management Science* 4 (1973), pp. 141–83.

Philadelphia Stock Exchange. *Understanding Foreign Currency Options* and other PHLX information brochures. Philadelphia, Penn.: Philadelphia Stock Exchange, 1990.

Rendleman, Richard J. Jr., and Brit J. Bartter. "Two-State Option Pricing." *Journal of Finance* 34 (1979), pp. 1,093–1,110.

Sharpe, William F. "Chapter 14." *Investments.* Englewood Cliffs, NJ: Prentice Hall, 1978.

Shastri, Kuldeep, and Kishore Tandon. "Arbitrage Tests of the Efficiency of the Foreign Currency Options Market." *Journal of International Money and Finance* 4 (1985), pp. 455–68.

——— "Valuation of Foreign Currency Options: Some Empirical Tests." *Journal of Financial and Quantitative Analysis* 21 (1986), pp. 145–60.

Siegel, Daniel, and Diane Siegel. *Futures Markets.* Chicago: Dryden, 1990.

CHAPTER TEN

Currency and Interest Rate Swaps

CHAPTER OUTLINE

Chapter 4 introduced forward contracts as a vehicle for hedging exchange rate risk; Chapter 9 introduced futures and options contracts on foreign exchange as alternative tools to hedge foreign exchange exposure. These types of instruments seldom have terms longer than a few years, however. Chapter 9 also discussed Eurodollar futures contracts for hedging short-term U.S.-dollar-denominated interest rate risk. In this chapter, we examine interest rate swaps, both single-currency and cross-currency, which are relatively new techniques for hedging long-term interest rate risk and foreign exchange risk.

The chapter begins with some useful definitions that define and distinguish between interest rate and currency swaps. Data on the size of the interest rate and currency swap markets are presented. The next section illustrates the usefulness of interest rate swaps. The following section traces the conceptual development of currency swaps from parallel and back-to-back loans and also examines the intricacies of currency swaps. The chapter also details the risks confronting a swap dealer in maintaining a portfolio of interest rate and currency swaps and shows how swaps are priced.

TYPES OF SWAPS

In interest rate swap financing, two parties, called **counterparties,** make a contractual agreement to exchange cash flows at periodic intervals. There are two types of interest rate swaps. One is a **single-currency interest rate swap.** The name of this type is typically shortened to *interest rate swap.* The other type can be called a **cross-currency interest rate swap.** This type is usually just called a *currency swap.*

In the basic ("plain vanilla") *fixed-for-floating rate* interest rate swap, one counterparty exchanges the interest payments of a floating-rate debt obligation for the fixed-rate interest payments of the other counterparty. Both debt obligations are denominated in the same currency. Some reasons for using an interest rate swap are to better match cash inflows and outflows and/or to obtain a cost savings. There are many variants of the basic interest rate swap, some of which are discussed below.

In a **currency swap,** one counterparty exchanges the debt service obligations of a bond denominated in one currency for the debt service obligations of the other counterparty denominated in another currency. The basic currency swap involves the exchange of *fixed-for-fixed rate* debt service. Some reasons for using currency swaps are to obtain debt financing in the swapped denomination at a cost savings and/or to hedge long-term foreign exchange rate risk. The International Finance in Practice box on page 236 discusses the first currency swap.

SIZE OF THE SWAP MARKET

As the International Finance in Practice box suggests, the market for currency swaps developed first.[1] Today, however, the interest rate swap market is larger. Exhibit 10.1 provides some statistics on the size and growth in the interest rate and currency swap markets. Size is measured by **notional principal,** a reference amount of principal for

EXHIBIT 10.1

Size of Interest Rate and Currency Swap Markets: Total Notional Principal in Millions of U.S. Dollars*

Year	Total New Business	Total Outstanding
A: Interest Rate Swaps		
1987	387,856	682,888
1988	568,113	1,010,203
1989	833,535	1,539,320
1990	1,229,241	2,311,544
1991	1,621,779	3,065,065
1992	2,822,635	3,850,800
1993	4,104,666	6,177,352
1994	6,240,890	8,815,561
1995	8,698,790	12,810,736
1996	13,678,173	19,170,909
1997	17,067,106	22,291,312
1998 (end-June)	Not available	32,942,460
B: Currency Swaps		
1987	85,824	182,807
1988	122,661	316,821
1989	169,631	434,849
1990	212,763	577,535
1991	328,394	807,167
1992	301,858	860,387
1993	295,191	899,618
1994	379,303	914,885
1995	455,108	1,197,395
1996	759,051	1,559,636
1997	1,135,391	1,823,632
1998 (end-June)	Not available	2,323,581

*Notional principal is used only as a reference measure to which interest rates are applied for determining interest payments. In an interest rate swap, principal does not actually change hands. At the inception date of a swap, the market value of both sides of the swap are of equivalent value. As interest rates change, the value of the cash flows will change, and both sides may no longer be equal. This is interest rate risk. The deviation can amount to 2 to 4 percent of notional principal. Only this small fraction is subject to credit (or default) risk.

Sources: International Swaps and Derivatives Association, Inc. Various year-end surveys. End-June 1998 data from *Central Bank Survey of Foreign Exchange and Derivatives Market Activity 1998,* Bank for International Settlements, Table E-38-1 and Table E-39-1, May 1999.

INTERNATIONAL FINANCE IN PRACTICE

The World Bank's First Currency Swap

The World Bank frequently borrows in the national capital markets around the world and in the Eurobond market. It prefers to borrow currencies with low nominal interest rates, such as the deutsche mark and the Swiss franc. In 1981, the World Bank was near the official borrowing limits in these currencies but desired to borrow more. By coincidence, IBM had a large amount of deutsche mark and Swiss franc debt that it had incurred a few years earlier. The proceeds of these borrowings had been converted to dollars for corporate use. Salomon Brothers convinced the World Bank to issue Eurodollar debt with maturities matching the IBM debt in order to enter into a currency swap with IBM. IBM agreed to pay the debt service (interest and principal) on the World Bank's Eurodollar bonds, and in turn the World Bank agreed to pay the debt service on IBM's deutsche mark and Swiss franc debt. While the details of the swap were not made public, both counterparties benefited through a lower all-in cost (interest expense, transaction costs, and service charges) than they otherwise would have had. Additionally, the World Bank benefited by developing an indirect way to obtain desired currencies without going directly to the German and Swiss capital markets.[2]

determining interest payments. The exhibit indicates that both markets have grown significantly since 1987, but that the growth in interest rate swaps has been by far the more dramatic. The annual amount of new business in interest rate swaps has increased from $388 billion in 1987 to over $17 trillion in 1997, an increase of over 4,300 percent. The total amount of interest rate swaps outstanding increased from $683 billion at year-end 1987 to over $32.9 trillion by the end of June 1998, an increase of over 4,700 percent. New currency swap business grew from $86 billion in 1987 to over $1.1 trillion in 1997, a 1,200 percent increase. Total outstanding currency swaps increased 1,170 percent, from $183 billion at year-end 1987 to over $2.3 trillion by end-June 1998.

While not shown in Exhibit 10.1, at the end of June 1998, the five most common currencies used to denominate interest rate swaps were the U.S. dollar (25.5 percent of the total), Japanese yen (19.2 percent), deutsche mark (15.6 percent), French franc (9.4 percent), and British pound sterling (8.6 percent). For currency swaps, the U.S. dollar (76.8 percent of the total), Japanese yen (28.7 percent), deutsche mark (18.3 percent), British pound sterling (11.7 percent), and the French franc (9.4 percent) were the five most commonly swapped currencies.

SWAP BANK

A **swap bank** is a generic term to describe a financial institution that facilitates swaps between counterparties. A swap bank can be an international commercial bank, an investment bank, a merchant bank, or an independent operator. The swap bank serves as either a **broker** or **dealer.** As a broker, the swap bank matches counterparties but does not assume any risk of the swap. The swap broker receives a commission for this service. Today, most swap banks serve as dealers or market makers. As a market maker, the swap bank stands willing to accept either side of a currency swap, and then later lay it off, or match it with a counterparty. In this capacity, the swap bank assumes a position in the swap and therefore assumes certain risks. The dealer capacity is obviously the more risky, and the swap bank would receive a portion of the cash flows passed through it to compensate it for bearing this risk.

INTEREST RATE SWAPS

Basic Interest Rate Swap

EXAMPLE 10.1: A Plain Vanilla Interest Rate Swap As an example of a basic interest rate swap, consider the following example of a fixed-for-floating rate swap. Bank A is a AAA-rated international bank located in the United Kingdom. The bank needs $10,000,000 to finance floating-rate Eurodollar term loans to its clients. It is considering issuing five-year floating-rate notes indexed to LIBOR. Alternatively, the bank could issue five-year fixed-rate Eurodollar bonds at 10 percent. The FRNs make the most sense for Bank A, since it would be using a floating-rate liability to finance a floating-rate asset. In this manner, the bank avoids the interest rate risk associated with a fixed-rate issue. Bank A could end up paying a higher rate than it is receiving on its loans should LIBOR fall substantially.

Company B is a BBB-rated U.S. company. It needs $10,000,000 to finance a capital expenditure with a five-year economic life. It can issue five-year fixed-rate bonds at a rate of 11.75 percent in the U.S. bond market. Alternatively, it can issue five-year FRNs at LIBOR plus ½ percent. The fixed-rate debt makes the most sense for Company B because it locks in a financing cost. The FRN alternative could prove very unwise should LIBOR increase substantially over the life of the note, and could possibly result in the project being unprofitable.

A swap bank familiar with the financing needs of Bank A and Company B has the opportunity to set up a fixed-for-floating interest rate swap that will benefit each counterparty and the swap bank. The key, or necessary condition, giving rise to the swap is that a **quality spread differential (QSD)** exists. A QSD is the difference between the default-risk premium differential on the fixed-rate debt and the default-risk premium differential on the floating-rate debt. In general, the former is greater than the latter. The reason for this is that the yield curve for lower quality debt tends to be steeper than the yield curve for higher-rated debt because lenders have the option not to renew, or roll over, short-term debt. Thus, they do not need to be concerned with "locking in" a high default-risk premium. Exhibit 10.2 shows the calculation of the QSD.

Given that a QSD exists, it is possible for each counterparty to issue the debt alternative that is least advantageous for it (given its financing needs), then swap interest payments, such that each counterparty ends up with the type of interest payment desired, but at a lower all-in cost than it could arrange on its own. Exhibit 10.3 diagrams a possible scenario the swap bank could arrange for the two counterparties. The interest rates used in Exhibit 10.3 refer to the percentage rate paid per annum on the notional principal of $10,000,000.

From Exhibit 10.3, we see that the swap bank has instructed Company B to issue FRNs at LIBOR plus ½ percent rather than the more suitable fixed-rate debt at 11.75 percent. Company B passes through to the swap bank 10.50 percent (on the notional principal of $10,000,000) and receives LIBOR minus ¼ percent in return. In total, Company B pays 10.50 percent (to the swap bank) plus LIBOR + ½ percent (to the floating-rate bondholders) and receives LIBOR − ¼

EXHIBIT 10.2

Calculation of Quality Spread Differential

	Company B	Bank A	Differential
Fixed-rate	11.75%	10.00%	1.75%
Floating-rate	LIBOR + .50%	LIBOR	.50%
			QSD = 1.25%

EXHIBIT 10.3

Fixed-for-Floating Interest Rate Swap*

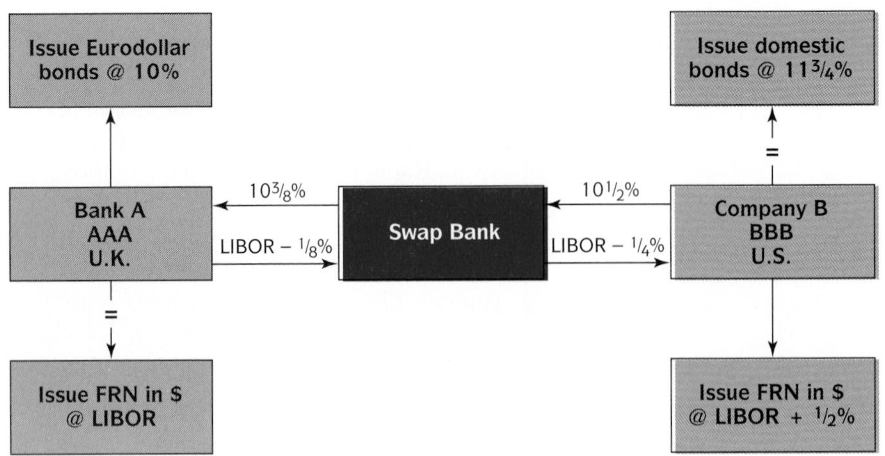

Net Cash Out Flows

	Bank A	Swap Bank	Company B
Pays	LIBOR – ⅛%	10⅜%	10½%
	10%	LIBOR – ¼%	LIBOR + ½%
Receives	–10⅜%	–10½%	–(LIBOR – ¼%)
		–(LIBOR – ⅛%)	
Net	LIBOR – ½%	– ¼%	11¼%

*Debt service expressed as a percentage of $10,000,000 notional value.

percent (from the swap bank) for an **all-in cost** (interest expense, transaction costs, and service charges) of 11.25 percent. Thus, through the swap, Company B has converted floating-rate debt into fixed-rate debt at an all-in cost ½ percent lower than the 11.75 percent fixed-rate it could arrange on its own.

Similarly, Bank A was instructed to issue fixed-rate debt at 10 percent rather than the more suitable FRNs. Bank A passes through to the swap bank LIBOR – ⅛ percent and receives 10.375 percent in return. In total, Bank A pays 10 percent (to the fixed-rate Eurodollar bondholders) plus LIBOR – ⅛ percent (to the swap bank) and receives 10.375 percent (from the swap bank) for an all-in cost of LIBOR – ½ percent. Through the swap, Bank A has converted fixed-rate debt into floating-rate debt at an all-in cost ½ percent lower than the floating-rate of LIBOR it could arrange on its own.

The swap bank also benefits because it pays out less than it receives from each counterparty to the other counterparty. Note from Exhibit 10.3 that it receives 10.50 percent (from Company B) plus LIBOR – ⅛ percent (from Bank A) and pays 10.375 percent (to Bank A) and LIBOR – ¼ percent (to Company B). The net inflow to the swap bank is ¼ percent per annum on the notional principal of $10,000,000. In sum, Bank A has saved ½ percent, Company B has saved ½ percent, and the swap bank has earned ¼ percent. This totals 1.25 percent, which equals the QSD. Thus, if a QSD exists, it can be split in some fashion among the swap parties resulting in lower all-in costs for the counterparties.

In an interest rate swap, the principal sums the two counterparties raise are not exchanged, since both counterparties have borrowed in the same currency.

The amount of interest payments that are exchanged are based on a notional sum, which may not equal the exact amount actually borrowed by each counterparty. Moreover, while Exhibit 10.3 portrays a gross exchange of interest payments based on the notional principal, in practice only the net difference is actually exchanged. For example, Company B would pay to the swap bank the net difference between 10.50 percent and LIBOR − ¼ percent on the notional value of $10,000,000.

SUPPLEMENTARY MATERIAL

EXAMPLE 10.2: Pricing the Basic Interest Rate Swap After the inception of an interest rate swap, it may become desirable for one and/or the other counterparty to get out of, or sell, the swap. The value of an interest rate swap to a counterparty should be the difference in the present values of the payment streams the counterparty will receive and pay on the notional principal. As an example, consider Company B from Example 10.1. Company B pays 10.50 percent to the swap bank and receives LIBOR − ¼ percent from the swap bank on a notional value of $10,000,000. It has an all-in cost of 11.25 percent because it has issued FRNs at LIBOR + ½ percent.

Suppose that one year later, fixed rates have fallen to 9 percent for BBB-rated issuers. Assuming a perfectly matched swap, this will also be a reset date for the FRNs. On a reset date, the present value of the future floating-rate payments Company B will receive from the swap bank based on the notional value will be $10,000,000. The present value of a hypothetical bond issue of $10,000,000 with four remaining 10.50 percent coupon payments at the new fixed rate of 9 percent is $\$10{,}485{,}960 = \$1{,}050{,}000 \times PVIFA_{9\%,4} + \$10{,}000{,}000 \times PVIF_{9\%,4}$. The value of the swap is $10,000,000 − $10,485,960 = −$485,960. Thus, Company B should be willing to pay up to $485,960 to get out of, or "sell," the swap.

CURRENCY SWAPS

Currency swaps evolved from parallel and back-to-back loans. Following the collapse of the Bretton Woods fixed exchange rate agreement, exchange rate volatility created the need among MNCs for vehicles to hedge long-term foreign exchange exposure. While parallel and back-to-back loans are useful as tools for currency risk management and cost reduction, they were created for a different purpose.

Parallel Loans

Parallel loans were originally created as a way to circumvent exchange controls the United Kingdom imposed in the early 1970s. To encourage domestic investment, the British government imposed taxes on foreign exchange transactions involving its currency to make foreign investment more expensive and thus less attractive. Through a parallel loan, these taxes could be avoided.

EXAMPLE 10.3: A Parallel Loan An example will help explain the mechanics of a parallel loan. To begin with, a parallel loan involves four parties. Consider a British parent firm with a wholly owned subsidiary in Canada. The British parent would like to fund a capital expenditure of its subsidiary by borrowing British pound sterling in the U.K. capital market at a fixed annual rate of 10 percent, then converting the proceeds to Canadian dollars. If exchange controls exist and the British parent converts pounds sterling to another currency, the transaction would be severely taxed. An alternative is for the Canadian subsidiary of the British parent to raise Canadian dollars directly in the Canadian capital market. Assume, however, the cost would be prohibitive because the subsidiary is not well known in the Canadian capital market, and that it would have to borrow at a premium of 2 percent over the normal borrowing fixed rate of 11 percent.

Suppose that an analogous situation exists for a Canadian parent and its British subsidiary. The Canadian parent can borrow in Canada at a fixed-rate of 11 percent and the subsidiary would be charged 13 percent to borrow pound sterling in the U.K. capital market.

A way around the foreign exchange controls would be for the two parent firms to each borrow in their capital markets and to relend to the other's subsidiary. The British parent would agree to lend the British subsidiary of the Canadian parent the pounds sterling it borrowed in the U.K. capital market at 10 percent, saving the British subsidiary 3 percent. The Canadian parent would borrow Canadian dollars at 11 percent and relend to the Canadian subsidiary of the British parent, saving it 2 percent. Moreover, since no currency exchanges are made, the parallel loan does not violate any foreign exchange restrictions of either country.

Exhibit 10.4 outlines the example. Note that there is a transfer of the Canadian dollar principal between the Canadian parent and the British parent's Canadian subsidiary at inception and a transfer back at the maturity date of the loan so that the Canadian parent can repay the loan. Similarly, there is a transfer of the pound sterling principal from the British parent to the Canadian parent's subsidiary in the U.K. and a transfer back at the maturity date so that the British parent can retire its loan. During the term of the loans, the Canadian subsidiary of the British parent earns revenues in Canadian dollars so that it can pay the Canadian dollar debt service to the Canadian parent to pay to the Canadian lender. Similarly, the British subsidiary of the Canadian parent earns revenues in pounds sterling so that it can pay the pound sterling debt service to the British parent to pay the British lender.

EXHIBIT 10.4

Parallel Loan

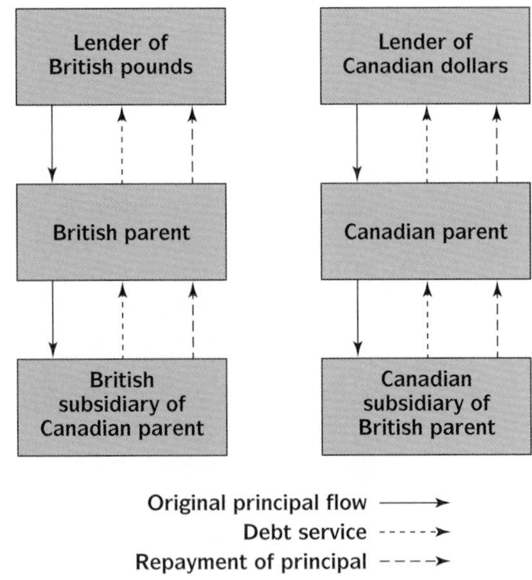

Back-to-Back Loans

EXAMPLE 10.4: A Back-to-Back Loan The **back-to-back** loan involves two parties instead of four. Continuing with Example 10.3, the British and Canadian parent firms would lend directly to one another in a back-to-back loan. As Exhibit 10.5 shows, the British parent would borrow pounds sterling in the British capital market and relend the principal sum to the Canadian parent. The Canadian parent would borrow Canadian dollars in the Canadian capital market and relend the principal sum to the British parent. It is assumed that the relending is at cost. That is, the British parent relends at its borrowing cost of 10 percent and the Canadian parent relends at its cost of 11 percent. At the maturity date of the debt, the principal sums would be reexchanged in order for the two parent firms to retire their debts in their national capital markets. Annually, each parent firm would pay to the other the annual debt service in the currency needed by the recipient to make the payment in its national capital market. In this example, the Canadian parent would pay pounds sterling to the British parent and receive Canadian dollars from the British parent.

The parent firms can obviously relend the foreign currency proceeds to a foreign subsidiary. Thus, the Canadian parent may relend the pounds sterling to its British subsidiary and the British parent may relend the Canadian dollar proceeds to its Canadian subsidiary. The major difference between a parallel loan and a back-to-back loan is the party to whom the parent firm lends.

Institutional Difficulties of Parallel and Back-to-Back Loans

Marshall and Kapner (1993) note two problems with parallel and back-to-back loans. First, both are time-consuming and expensive to establish. Time must be spent searching for a party with financial needs that mirror the other party. This search is expensive and may perhaps be fruitless. Additionally, each loan agreement is separate from the other. For example, the parallel loan agreement between the British parent and the Canadian subsidiary in the U.K. is independent of the loan agreement between the Canadian parent firm and the British subsidiary in Canada. Consequently, if one party defaults, say the Canadian subsidiary, the British subsidiary is still liable to the Canadian parent. A separate registered agreement called a *rights of set-off* must be in effect to help eliminate this problem. A currency

EXHIBIT 10.5

Back-to-Back Loan

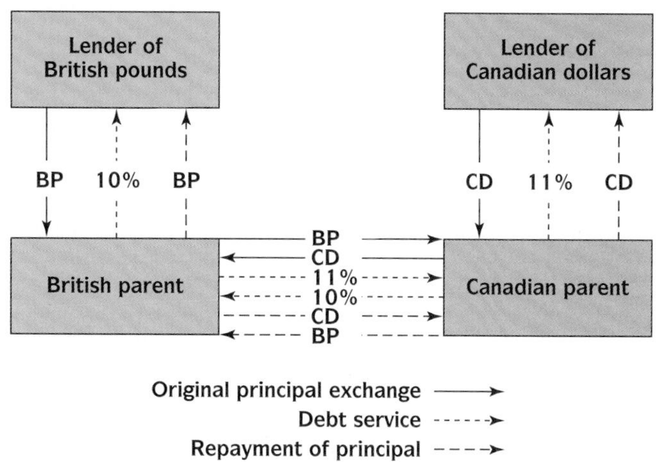

swap is a natural extension of parallel and back-to-back loans that addresses the rights of set-off as part of its basic structure.

Basic Currency Swap

EXAMPLE 10.5: A Basic Currency Swap As an example of a basic currency swap, consider the following example. A U.S. MNC desires to finance a capital expenditure of its German subsidiary. The project has an economic life of five years. The cost of the project is DM40,000,000. At the current exchange rate of DM1.60/$1.00, the parent firm could raise $25,000,000 in the U.S. capital market by issuing five-year bonds at 8 percent. The parent would then convert the dollars to deutsche marks to pay the project cost. The German subsidiary would be expected to earn enough on the project to meet the annual dollar debt service and to repay the principal in five years. The only problem with this situation is that a long-term transaction exposure is created. If the dollar appreciates substantially against the DM over the loan period, it may be difficult for the German subsidiary to earn enough in DM to service the dollar loan.

An alternative is for the U.S. parent to raise DM40,000,000 in the international bond market by issuing Euromark bonds. (The U.S. parent might instead issue deutsche mark-denominated foreign bonds in the German capital market.) However, if the U.S. MNC is not well known, it will have difficulty borrowing at a favorable rate of interest. Suppose the U.S. parent can borrow DM40,000,000 for a term of five years at a fixed rate of 7 percent. The current normal borrowing rate for a well-known firm of equivalent creditworthiness is 6 percent.

Assume a German MNC of equivalent creditworthiness has a mirror-image financing need. It has a U.S. subsidiary in need of $25,000,000 to finance a capital expenditure with an economic life of five years. The German parent could raise DM40,000,000 in the German bond market at a fixed rate of 6 percent and convert the funds to dollars to finance the expenditure. Transaction exposure is created, however, if the DM appreciates substantially against the dollar. In this event, the U.S. subsidiary might have difficulty earning enough in dollars to meet the debt service. The German parent could issue Eurodollar bonds (or alternatively, Yankee bonds in the U.S. capital market), but since it is not well known its borrowing cost would be, say, a fixed rate of 9 percent.

A swap bank familiar with the financing needs of the two MNCs could arrange a currency swap that would solve the double problem of each MNC, that is, be confronted with long-term transaction exposure or borrow at a disadvantageous rate. The swap bank would instruct each parent firm to raise funds in its national capital market where it is well known and has a **comparative advantage.** Then the principal sums would be exchanged through the swap bank. Annually, the German subsidiary would remit to its U.S. parent DM2,400,000 in interest (6 percent of DM40,000,000) to be passed through the swap bank to the German MNC to meet the DM debt service. The U.S. subsidiary of the German MNC would annually remit $2,000,000 in interest (8 percent of $25,000,000) to be passed through to the swap bank to the U.S. MNC to meet the dollar debt service. At the debt retirement date, the subsidiaries would remit the principal sums to their respective parents to be exchanged through the swap bank in order to pay off the bond issues in the national capital markets. The structure of this currency swap is diagrammed in Exhibit 10.6.

Exhibit 10.6 demonstrates that there is a cost savings for each counterparty because of their relative comparative advantage in their respective national capital markets. The currency swap also serves to contractually lock in a series of future foreign exchange rates for the debt service obligations of each counterparty.

EXHIBIT 10.6 $/DM Currency Swap

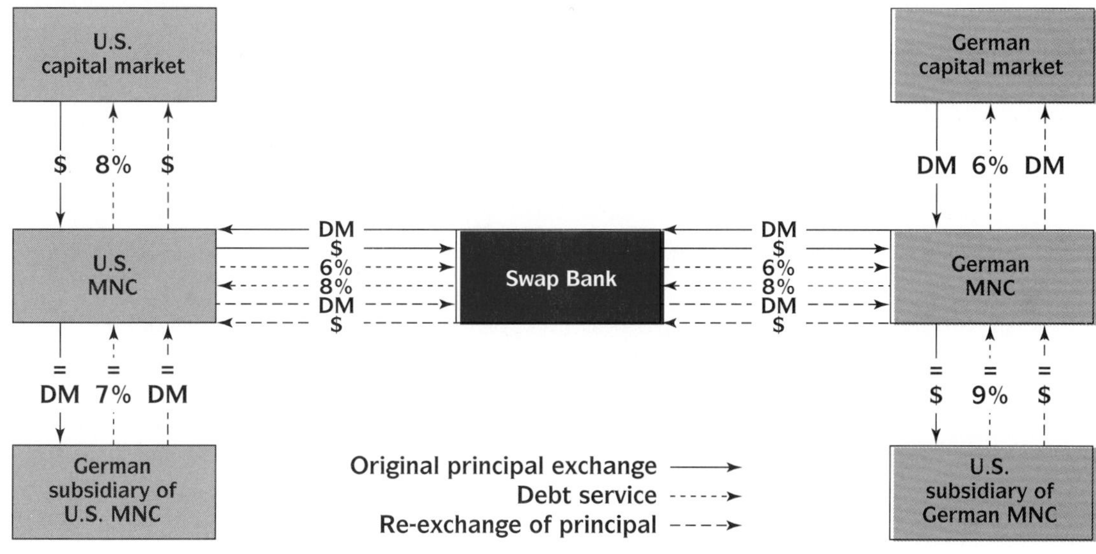

At inception, the principal sums are exchanged at the current exchange rate of DM1.60/$1.00 = DM40,000,000/$25,000,000. Each year prior to debt retirement, the swap agreement calls for the counterparties to exchange DM2,400,000 of interest on the DM debt for $2,000,000 of interest on the dollar debt; this is a contractual rate of DM1.20/$1.00. At the maturity date, a final exchange, including the last interest payments and the reexchange of the principal sums, would take place: DM42,400,000 for $27,000,000. The contractual exchange rate at year five is thus DM1.5704/$1.00. Clearly, the swap locks in foreign exchange rates for each counterparty to meet its debt service obligations over the term of the swap.

SUPPLEMENTARY MATERIAL

EXAMPLE 10.6: Equivalency of Currency Swap Debt Service Obligations To continue with Example 10.5, it superficially appears that the German counterparty is not getting as good a deal from the currency swap as the U.S. counterparty. The reasoning is that the German counterparty is borrowing at a rate of 6 percent (DM2,400,000 per year) but paying 8 percent ($2,000,000). The U.S. counterparty receives the $2,000,000 and pays DM2,400,000. This reasoning is fraught with an ill appreciation for international parity relationships, as Exhibit 10.7 is designed to show. In short, the exhibit shows that borrowing DM at 6 percent is equivalent to borrowing dollars at 8 percent.

Line 1 of Exhibit 10.7 shows the cash flows of the DM debt in millions. Line 2 shows the cash flows of the dollar debt in millions. Line 3 shows the contractual foreign exchange rates between the two counterparties that are locked in by the swap agreement. Line 4 shows the foreign exchange rate that each counterparty and the market should expect based on covered interest rate parity and the forward rate being an unbiased predictor of the expected spot rate, if we can assume that CIRP holds between the 6 percent DM rate and the 8 percent dollar rate. This appears reasonable since these rates are, respectively, the best rates

EXHIBIT 10.7

Equivalency of Currency Swap Cash Flows

	Time of Cash Flow					
	0	1	2	3	4	5
1. DM debt cash flow	40	−2.4	−2.4	−2.4	−2.4	−42.4
2. $ Debt cash flow	25	−2.0	−2.0	−2.0	−2.0	−27.0
3. Contractual FX rate	1.60	1.20	1.20	1.20	1.20	1.57
4. Implicit FX rate	1.60	1.57	1.54	1.51	1.48	1.46
5. Indifference DM cash flow	40	−3.14	−3.08	−3.02	−2.96	−39.42
6. Indifference $ cash flow	25	−1.53	−1.56	−1.59	−1.62	−29.04

Note: Lines 1 and 5 present alternative cash flows in DM that have present values of DM40,000,000 at a 6 percent discount rate. The cash flows in Line 1 are free of exchange risk if the swap is undertaken, whereas the implicit cash flows of Line 5 are not if the swap is forgone. The certain cash flows are preferable. The uncertain DM cash flows of Line 5 are obtained by multiplying the dollar cash flows of Line 2 by the corresponding implicit FX rate of Line 4. Analogously, Lines 2 and 6 present alternative cash flows in U.S. dollars that have present values of $25,000,000 at an 8 percent discount rate. The cash flows in Line 2 are free of exchange risk if the swap is undertaken, whereas the implicit cash flows of Line 6 are not if the swap if forgone. The certain cash flows are preferable. The uncertain dollar cash flows of Line 6 are obtained by dividing the DM cash flows of Line 1 by the corresponding implicit FX rate of Line 4.

available for each counterparty who is well known in its national market. According to these parity relationships $\bar{S}_t$(DM/\$) = $S_0[1.06/1.08]^t$. For example, from the exhibit DM1.54/\$1.00 = DM1.60$[1.06/1.08]^2$.

Line 5 shows the equivalent cash flows in DM that have a present value of DM40,000,000 at a rate of 6 percent. Without the currency swap, the German MNC would have to convert dollars into DM to meet the DM debt service. The expected rate at which the conversion would take place in each year is given by the implicit foreign exchange rates in Line 4. Line 5 can be viewed as a conversion of the cash flows of Line 2 via the implicit exchange rates of Line 4. That is, for year one, $2,000,000 has an expected value of DM3,140,000 at the expected exchange rate of DM1.57/$1.00. For year two, $2,000,000 has an expected value of DM3,080,000 at an exchange rate of DM1.54/$1.00. Note that the conversion at the implicit exchange rates converts *8 percent cash flows* into *6 percent cash flows.*

The lender of DM40,000,000 should be indifferent between receiving the cash flows of Line 1 or the cash flows of Line 5 from the borrower. From the borrower's standpoint, however, the cash flows of Line 1 are free of foreign exchange risk because of the currency swap, whereas the cash flows of Line 5 are not. Thus, the borrower prefers the certainty of the swap, regardless of the equivalency.

Line 6 shows in dollar terms the cash flows based on the implicit foreign exchange rates of Line 4 that have a present value of $25,000,000. Line 6 can be viewed as a conversion of the 6 percent cash flows of Line 1 into the 8 percent cash flows of Line 6 via these expected exchange rates. A lender should be indifferent between these and the cash flow stream of Line 2. The borrower will prefer to pay the cash flows of Line 2, however, because they are free of foreign exchange risk.

EXAMPLE 10.7: Pricing the Basic Currency Swap Suppose that a year after the U.S. dollar–DM swap was arranged, interest rates have decreased in the United States from 8 percent to 6.75 percent and in Germany from 6 to 5 percent. Further assume that because the U.S. rate decreased proportionately more than the German rate, the dollar appreciated versus the mark. Instead of being DM1.5704/$1.00 as expected, it is DM1.59/$1.00. One or both counterparties might be induced to sell their position in the swap to a swap dealer in order to refinance at the new lower rate.

The market value of the U.S. dollar debt is $26,064,505; this is the present value of the four remaining coupon payments of $2,000,000 and the principal of $25,000,000 discounted at 6.75 percent. Similarly, the market value of the deutsche mark debt at the new rate of 5 percent is DM41,418,380. The U.S. counterparty should be willing to sell its interest in the currency swap for $26,064,505 − DM41,418,380/1.59 = $15,209. That is, the U.S. counterparty should be willing to accept $15,209 to give up the stream of dollars it would receive under the swap agreement in return for not having to pay the DM stream. The U.S. MNC is then free to refinance the $25,000,000 8 percent debt at 6.75 percent, and perhaps enter into a new currency swap.

From the German counterparty's perspective, the swap has a value of DM41,418,380 − 1.59 × $26,064,505 = −DM24,183. The German counterparty should be willing to pay DM24,183 to "sell" the swap, that is, give up the stream of DM in return for not having to pay the dollar stream. The German MNC is then in a position to refinance the DM40,000,000 six percent debt at the new rate of 5 percent. The German firm might also enter into a new currency swap.

SWAP MARKET QUOTATIONS

Swap banks will tailor the terms of interest rate and currency swaps to customers' needs. They also make a market in generic "plain vanilla" swaps and provide current market quotations. Consider a basic U.S. dollar fixed-for-floating interest rate swap indexed to dollar LIBOR. A swap bank will typically quote a fixed-rate bid-ask spread (either semiannual or annual) in basis points (bp) above U.S. Treasuries versus six-month dollar LIBOR flat. Suppose the quote for a five-year swap with semiannual payments is T + 50bp bid and T + 80 bp ask. If five-year Treasury notes are yielding 8.00 percent, the interest rate swap bid-ask spread quotation is 8.50 − 8.80 percent. This means the swap bank will pay semiannual fixed-rate dollar payments of 8.50 percent against receiving six-month dollar LIBOR flat, or it will receive semiannual fixed-rate dollar payments at 8.80 percent against paying six-month dollar LIBOR flat.

It is convention to quote other currencies against six-month dollar LIBOR also. For example, for deutsche marks suppose the bid-ask swap quotation is 6.60 − 6.85 percent. This means the swap bank will pay semiannual fixed-rate DM payments at 6.60 percent against receiving six-month dollar LIBOR flat, or it will receive semiannual fixed-rate DM payments at 6.85 percent against paying six-month dollar LIBOR flat.

It follows that if the swap bank is quoting 8.50 − 8.80 percent in dollars and 6.60 − 6.85 percent in DM against six-month dollar LIBOR, it will enter into a currency swap in which it would pay semiannual fixed-rate dollar payments of 8.50 percent in return for receiving semiannual fixed-rate DM payments at 6.85 percent, or it will receive semiannual fixed-rate dollar payments at 8.80 percent against paying semiannual fixed-rate DM payments at 6.60 percent.

VARIATIONS OF BASIC CURRENCY AND INTEREST RATE SWAPS

There are several variants of the basic currency and interest rate swaps we have discussed. Currency swaps, for example, need not involve the swap of fixed-rate debt.

Fixed-for-floating and *floating-for-floating* currency rate swaps are also frequently arranged. Additionally, *amortizing* currency swaps incorporate an amortization feature in which periodically the amortized portions of the notional principals are reexchanged. A fixed-for-floating interest rate swap does not require a fixed-rate coupon bond. A variant is a *zero-coupon-for-floating* rate swap where the floating-rate payer makes the standard periodic floating-rate payments over the life of the swap, but the fixed-rate payer makes a single payment at the end of the swap. Another variation is the *floating-for-floating* interest rate swap. In this swap, each side is tied to a different floating rate index (e.g., LIBOR and Treasury bills) for a different frequency of the same index (such as three-month and six-month LIBOR). For a swap to be possible, a QSD must still exist. Additionally, interest rate swaps can be established on an amortizing basis, where the debt service exchanges decrease periodically through time as the hypothetical notional principal is amortized. See the International Finance in Practice box on page 247 for an interesting example of a currency swap.

RISKS OF INTEREST RATE AND CURRENCY SWAPS

Marshall and Kapner (1993) detail the risks that a swap dealer confronts. Some of the major ones are discussed here.

Interest-rate risk refers to interest rates changing unfavorably before the swap bank can lay off to an opposing counterparty the other side of an interest rate swap entered into with a counterparty. As an illustration, reconsider the interest rate swap example, Example 10.1. To recap, in that example, the swap bank earns a spread of ¼ percent. Company B passes through to the swap bank 10.50 percent per annum (on the notional principal of $10,000,000) and receives LIBOR minus ¼ percent in return. Bank A passes through to the swap bank LIBOR − ⅛ percent and receives 10.375 percent in return. Suppose the swap bank entered into the position with Company B first. If fixed rates increase substantially, say by ½ percent, Bank A will not be willing to enter into the opposite side of the swap unless it receives, say, 10.875 percent. This would make the swap unprofitable for the swap bank.

Basis risk refers to a situation in which the floating-rates of the two counterparties are not pegged to the same index. Any difference in the indexes is known as the basis. For example, one counterparty could have its FRNs pegged to LIBOR, while the other counterparty has its FRNs pegged to the U.S. Treasury bill rate. In this event, the indexes are not perfectly positively correlated and the swap may periodically be unprofitable for the swap bank. In our example, this would occur if the Treasury bill rate was substantially larger than LIBOR.

Exchange-rate risk refers to the risk the swap bank faces from fluctuating exchange rates during the time it takes for the bank to lay off a swap it undertakes with one counterparty with an opposing counterparty.

Credit risk is the major risk faced by a swap dealer. It refers to the probability that a counterparty will default. The swap bank that stands between the two counterparties is not obligated to the defaulting counterparty, only to the nondefaulting counterparty. There is a single agreement between the swap bank and each counterparty. Thus, a swap agreement avoids the rights of set-off problem of a back-to-back or parallel loan.

Mismatch risk refers to the difficulty of finding an exact opposite match for a swap the bank has agreed to take. The mismatch may be with respect to the size of the principal sums the counterparties need, the maturity dates of the individual debt issues, or the debt service dates. Textbook illustrations typically ignore these real-life problems.

Sovereign risk refers to the probability that a country will impose exchange restrictions on a currency involved in a swap. This may make it very costly, or perhaps

INTERNATIONAL FINANCE IN PRACTICE

Eli Lilly and Company: The Case of the Appreciating Yen

Eli Lilly and Company (Lilly) is an international pharmaceutical company with corporate headquarters in Indianapolis, Indiana. Lilly markets its products worldwide. Being the second largest pharmaceutical market in the world, Japan represents a particularly significant market for Lilly's products. As sales to Japan grew throughout the 1980s, Lilly became increasingly concerned about the volatility effect on overall sales and earnings performance stemming from fluctuations in the yen exchange rate.

In 1987, the company decided to investigate the possibility of developing a hedging strategy to, in effect, fix in U.S. dollars that portion of its sales to Japan. At the time of consideration, the yen was trading in the mid ¥140/$1.00 range. Not too many years earlier, the yen was trading in the ¥240–¥270/$1.00 range. If the yen were to retreat back to those levels, obviously, Lilly's sales in terms of dollars would be significantly diminished. It was Lilly's desire, therefore, to fix future sales at current exchange rates, and the way to do that of course was to borrow yen, sell the yen for dollars at the current exchange rates, and service the yen debt with the future yen sales revenues. The dollars would then be used to meet current corporate requirements, and thus the hedge would be completed.

The initial thought was for Lilly to incur yen-denominated borrowings and convert the principal into dollars for use in the United States. The future yen sales could then service the newly created yen liability. This idea, however, was not favored because it would have meant adding new debt to the company's balance sheet. The alternative would be to use the yen liability to replace existing debt. The most targetable long-term debt item in Lilly's capital structure was a $150,000,000, 10.25 percent fixed-rate Eurodollar bond issue with a 1992 maturity date. These bonds were issued primarily to allow Lilly to establish name recognition and access to the European bond markets. Unfortunately, this debt was noncallable. Had it had a call feature, the decision most likely would have been to allow for the creation of a yen liability in order to retire this higher cost long-term source of funds.

To accomplish the same result, the financial division at Lilly conceived the idea of a currency swap, which involves no exchange of borrowings. At the current exchange rate of ¥144.1, the $150 million Eurodollar issue had a yen value of ¥21.615 billion. Lilly entertained bids from a select group of investment banks to put together a uniquely structured currency swap arrangement. One of the bids was ultimately selected, and the uniqueness of the arrangement centered around the fact that Lilly would contribute to the investment bank five annual level payments in the amount of ¥4.864 billion each during the remaining five years of the life of the Eurodollar bond issue. In return, Lilly would receive dollars each year equal to the $15,375,000 coupon payments on the bond issue plus the $150,000,000 principal repayment at the end of year five. The level-contribution and variable-receipt arrangement was unique to the swap market, but essential to Lilly, in that it enabled the hedging of a level stream of future yen receipts. While the swap did not provide a complete hedge of all rate-affected sales revenue, it did eliminate the volatility associated with a significant percentage of those revenues. The other unique aspect of the arrangement was the adjustment for interest rate changes since the inception of the Eurodollar bond offering. Eurodollar rates had fallen from the 10.25 percent range to the 7.8 percent range, and yen rates had fallen similarly. To compensate the investment bank and opposite party for servicing Lilly's debt at 10.25 percent, Lilly's cost of yen contribution was grossed up to 6.2 percent from the then current yen rate of less than 4 percent. Exhibit 10.8 diagrams this interesting example of a currency swap.

impossible, for a counterparty to fulfill its obligation to the dealer. In this event, provisions exist for terminating the swap, which results in a loss of revenue for the swap bank.

To facilitate the operation of the swap market, the International Swaps and Derivatives Association (ISDA), has standardized two swap agreements. One is the "Interest Rate and Currency Exchange Agreement" that covers currency swaps, and the other is the "Interest Rate Swap Agreement" that lays out standard terms for U.S.-dollar-denominated interest rate swaps. The standardized agreements have reduced the time necessary to establish swaps and also provided terms under which swaps can be terminated early by a counterparty.

EXHIBIT 10.8 Eli Lilly's Eurodollar Bond/Yen Swap

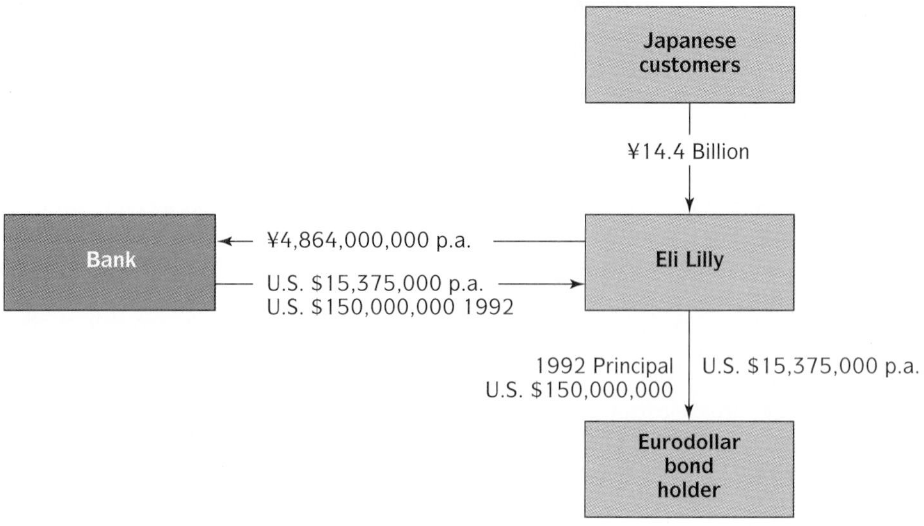

Source: Dale R. Follmer, Manager of Accounting Operations, Eli Lilly and Company.

IS THE SWAP MARKET EFFICIENT?

The two primary reasons for a counterparty to use a currency swap are to obtain debt financing in the swapped currency at an interest cost reduction brought about through comparative advantages each counterparty has in its national capital market, and/or the benefit of hedging long-run exchange rate exposure. These reasons seem straightforward and difficult to argue with, especially to the extent that name recognition is truly important in raising funds in the international bond market.

The two primary reasons for swapping interest rates are to better match maturities of assets and liabilities and/or to obtain a cost savings via the quality spread differential. In an efficient market without barriers to capital flows, the cost-savings argument through a QSD is difficult to accept. It implies that an arbitrage opportunity exists because of some mispricing of the default risk premiums on different types of debt instruments. If the QSD is one of the primary reasons for the existence of interest rate swaps, one would expect arbitrage to eliminate it over time and that the growth of the swap market would decrease. Quite the contrary has happened as Exhibit 10.1 shows; growth in interest rate swaps has been extremely large since the early 1980s. Thus, the arbitrage argument does not seem to have much merit. Indeed, Turnbull (1987) analytically shows that a QSD can exist in an efficient market. Consequently, one must rely on an argument of **market completeness** for the existence and growth of interest rate swaps. That is, all types of debt instruments are not regularly available for all borrowers. Thus, the interest rate swap market assists in tailoring financing to the type desired by a particular borrower. Both counterparties can benefit (as well as the swap dealer) through financing that is more suitable for their asset maturity structures.

CONCLUDING POINTS ABOUT SWAPS

The growth in financial swaps has been tremendous. They offer counterparties benefits and opportunities that were not previously available. Another feature of swaps is that they are off-book transactions for both the counterparties and the swap bank; that is, they do not appear as assets or liabilities on the balance sheet. The only indication that they exist is through an examination of the footnotes of the financial reports.

Swaps have become an important source of revenue for commercial banks. As swap activity increased, bank regulators became concerned that the potential liability posed by swaps might create capital adequacy problems for banks. The Federal Reserve Bank and central bankers from the Group of Ten countries and Luxembourg agreed in 1987 to a set of principles, called the Basle Accord, which standardized bank capital requirements across nations. As discussed in Chapter 6, the accord established guidelines for risk-adjusted capital requirements for off-balance-sheet activities that increase a bank's risk exposure, including swaps.

SUMMARY

This chapter provides a presentation of currency and interest rate swaps. The discussion details how swaps might be used and the risks associated with each.

1. The chapter opened with definitions of an interest rate swap and a currency swap. The basic interest rate swap is a fixed-for-floating rate swap in which one counterparty exchanges the interest payments of a fixed-rate debt obligation for the floating-interest payments of the other counterparty. Both debt obligations are denominated in the same currency. In a currency swap, one counterparty exchanges the debt service obligations of a bond denominated in one currency for the debt service obligations of the other counterparty which are denominated in another currency.
2. The function of a swap bank was discussed. A swap bank is a generic term to describe a financial institution that facilitates the swap between counterparties. The swap bank serves as either a broker or a dealer. When serving as a broker, the swap bank matches counterparties, but does not assume any risk of the swap. When serving as a dealer, the swap bank stands willing to accept either side of a currency swap.
3. An example of a basic interest rate swap was presented. It was noted that a necessary condition for a swap to be feasible was the existence of a quality spread differential between the default-risk premiums on the fixed-rate and floating-rate interest rates of the two counterparties. Additionally, it was noted that there was not an exchange of principal sums between the counterparties of an interest rate swap because both debt issues were denominated in the same currency. Interest rate exchanges were based on a notional principal.
4. Pricing an interest rate swap after inception was illustrated. It was shown that after inception, the value of an interest rate swap to a counterparty should be the difference in the present values of the payment streams the counterparty will receive and pay on the notional principal.
5. The development of the currency swap market was traced to parallel and back-to-back loans. A parallel loan involves four parties. In it, one MNC borrows and relends to another's subsidiary and vice-versa. A back-to-back loan involves only two parties. One MNC borrows and relends directly to another.
6. A detailed example of a basic currency swap was presented. It was shown that the debt service obligations of the counterparties in a currency swap are effectively equivalent to one another in cost. Nominal differences can be explained by the set of international parity relationships.
7. Pricing a currency swap after inception was illustrated. It was shown that after inception, the value of a currency swap to a counterparty should be the difference in the present values of the payment stream the counterparty will receive in one

currency and pay in the other currency, converted to one or the other currency denominations.

8. In addition to the basic fixed-for-fixed currency swap and fixed-for-floating interest rate swap, many other variants exist. One variant is the amortizing swap which incorporates an amortization of the notional principles. Another variant is a zero-coupon-for-floating rate swap in which the floating-rate payer makes the standard periodic floating-rate payments over the life of the swap, but the fixed-rate payer makes a single payment at the end of the swap. Another is the floating-for-floating rate swap. In this type of swap, each side is tied to a different floating rate index or a different frequency of the same index.
9. Reasons for the development and growth of the swap market were critically examined. It was argued that one must rely on an argument of market completeness for the existence and growth of interest rate swaps. That is, the interest rate swap market assists in tailoring financing to the type desired by a particular borrower when all types of debt instruments are not regularly available to all borrowers.

KEY WORDS

all-in cost, 238
back-to-back loan, 241
comparative advantage, 242
counterparty, 234
cross-currency interest rate swap, 234
currency swap, 235
market completeness, 248
notional principal, 235
parallel loan, 239
quality spread differential (QSD), 237
single-currency interest rate swap, 234
swap bank, 236
swap broker, 236
swap dealer, 236

QUESTIONS

1. Describe the difference between a swap broker and a swap dealer.
2. What is the necessary condition for a fixed-for-floating interest rate swap to be possible?
3. Describe the difference between a parallel loan and a back-to-back loan.
4. Discuss the basic motivations for a counterparty to enter into a currency swap.
5. How does the theory of comparative advantage relate to the currency swap market?
6. Discuss the risks confronting an interest rate and currency swap dealer.
7. Briefly discuss some variants of the basic interest rate and currency swaps diagrammed in the chapter.
8. If the cost advantage of interest rate swaps would likely be arbitraged away in competitive markets, what other explanations exist to explain the rapid development of the interest rate swap market?
9. Assume you are the swap bank in the Eli Lilly swap discussed in the chapter. Develop an example of how you might lay off the swap to an opposing counterparty.
10. Discuss the motivational difference in the currency swap presented as Example 10.5 and the Eli Lilly and Company swap discussed in the chapter.

11. Assume a currency swap in which two counterparties of comparable credit risk each borrow at the best rate available, yet the nominal rate of one counterparty is higher than the other. After the initial principal exchange, is the counterparty that is required to make interest payments at the higher nominal rate at a financial disadvantage to the other in the swap agreement? Explain your thinking.

PROBLEMS

1. Develop a different arrangement of interest payments among the counterparties and the swap bank in Example 10.1 that still leaves each counterparty with an all-in cost ½ percent below their best rate and the swap bank with a ¼ percent inflow.
2. Alpha and Beta Companies can borrow at the following rates:

	Alpha	Beta
Moody's credit rating	Aa	Baa
Fixed-rate borrowing cost	10.5%	12.0%
Floating-rate borrowing cost	LIBOR	LIBOR + 1%

   a. Calculate the quality spread differential (QSD).
   b. Develop an interest rate swap in which both Alpha and Beta have an equal cost savings in their borrowing costs. Assume Alpha desires floating-rate debt and Beta desires fixed-rate debt.
3. Company A is an AAA-rated firm desiring to issue five-year FRNs. It finds that it can issue FRNs at six-month LIBOR + ⅛ percent or at the six-month Treasury bill rate + ½ percent. Given its asset structure, LIBOR is the preferred index. Company B is an A-rated firm that also desires to issue five-year FRNs. It finds it can issue at six-month LIBOR + ⅝ percent or at the six-month Treasury bill rate + 1⅝ percent. Given its asset structure, the six-month Treasury bill rate is the preferred index. Assume a notional principal of $15,000,000. Determine the QSD and set up a floating-for-floating rate swap where the swap bank receives ⅛ percent and the two counterparties share the remaining savings equally.
4. Suppose Morgan Guaranty, Ltd. is quoting swap rates as follows: 7.75 – 8.10 percent annually against six-month dollar LIBOR for dollars and 11.25 – 11.65 percent annually against six-month dollar LIBOR for British pound sterling. At what rates will Morgan Guaranty enter into a $/£ currency swap?

5. A corporation enters into a five-year interest rate swap with a swap bank in which it agrees to pay the swap bank a fixed rate of 9.75 percent annually on a notional amount of DM15,000,000 and receive LIBOR – ½ percent. As of the second reset date, determine the price of the swap from the corporation's viewpoint assuming that the fixed rate at which it can borrow has increased to 10.25 percent.

MINI CASE

The Centralia Corporation's Currency Swap

The Centralia Corporation is a U.S. manufacturer of small kitchen electrical appliances. It has decided to construct a wholly owned manufacturing facility in Zaragoza, Spain, to manufacture microwave ovens for sale to the European Union market. The plant is expected to cost Ptas620,000,000, and to take about one year to complete. The plant is to be financed over its economic life of eight years. The borrowing capacity created by this capital expenditure is $1,700,000; the remainder of the plant will be equity financed. Centralia is not well known in the Spanish or international bond market; consequently, it would have to pay 14 percent per annum to borrow pesetas, whereas the normal borrowing rate in the Spanish capital market for well-known firms of equivalent risk is 12.5 percent. Centralia could borrow in the U.S. at a rate of 8 percent.

Study Questions

1. Suppose a Spanish MNC has a mirror-image situation and needs $1,700,000 to finance a capital expenditure of one of its U.S. subsidiaries. It finds that it must pay a 9 percent fixed rate in the United States for dollars, whereas it can borrow pesetas at 12.5 percent. The exchange rate has been forecast to be Ptas145.44/$1.00 in one year. Set up a currency swap that will benefit each counterparty.

2. Suppose that one year after the inception of the currency swap between Centralia and the Spanish MNC, the U.S. dollar fixed-rate has fallen from 8 to 6 percent and the Spanish capital market fixed-rate for pesetas has fallen from 12.5 to 11 percent. In both dollars and pesetas, determine the market value of the swap if the exchange rate is Ptas152.30/$1.00.

ENDNOTES

1. See Price, Keller, and Neilson (1983) for an account of the World Bank-IBM swap.
2. Marshall and Kapner (1993) provide a comprehensive treatment of swap financing and the development of the swap market.

WEB RESOURCES

www.isda.org

This is the Website of the International Swaps and Derivatives Association, Inc. This site describes the activities of the ISDA and provides educational information about interest rate and currency swaps, other OTC interest rate and currency derivatives, and risk management activities. Market survey data about the size of the swaps market are also provided at this site.

www.bis.org

This is the Website of the Bank for International Settlements. This site describes the activities and purpose of the BIS. Many on-line publications about foreign exchange and OTC derivatives are available at this site.

REFERENCES AND SUGGESTED READINGS

Beidleman, Carl R., ed. *Cross Currency Swaps.* Burr Ridge, Ill.: Business One Irwin, 1992.

Campbell, Tim S., and William A. Kracaw. *Financial Risk Management.* New York: Harper Collins College Publishers, 1993.

Marshall, John F., and Kenneth R. Kapner. *The Swap Market.* 2nd ed. Miami, Fla.: Kolb, 1993.

Price, John A. M., Jules Keller, and Max Neilson. "The Delicate Art of Swaps." *Euromoney,* April 1983, pp. 118–25.

Solnik, Bruno. *International Investments,* 3rd ed. Reading, Mass.: Addison-Wesley, 1996.

Smith, Clifford W., Charles W. Smithson, and Lee Macdonald Wakeman. "The Evolving Market for Swaps." *Midland Corporate Finance Journal,* Winter 1986, pp. 20–32.

________. "The Market for Interest Rate Swaps." *Financial Management,* Winter 1988, pp. 34–44.

Smithson, Charles W., Clifford W. Smith, Jr., and D. Sykes Wilford. *Managing Financial Risk.* Burr Ridge, Ill.: Irwin Professional Publishing, 1995.

Turnbull, Stuart M. "Swaps: A Zero Sum Game?" *Financial Management,* Spring 1987, pp. 15–21.

Wall, Larry D., and John J. Pringle. "Alternative Explanations of Interest Rate Swaps: A Theoretical and Empirical Analysis." *Financial Management.* Summer 1989, pp. 59–73.

CHAPTER ELEVEN

International Portfolio Investments

CHAPTER OUTLINE

In recent years, portfolio investments by individual and institutional investors in international stocks, bonds, and other financial securities have grown at a phenomenal pace, surpassing in dollar volume foreign direct investments by corporations. As Exhibit 11.1 shows, for instance, the dollar value invested in international equities (ADRs and local shares) by U.S. investors has steadily grown from a rather negligible level in the early 1980s to \$200 billion in 1990 and \$1,200 billion at the end of 1998, of which ADRs account for \$510 billion. Exhibit 11.1 also shows that foreign equities as a proportion of U.S. investors' portfolio wealth rose from about 1 percent in the early 1980s to nearly 8 percent in the late 1990s. Considering that U.S. equities account for less than 50 percent of the world equity market capitalization, the volume of international investment may further increase.

The rapid growth in international portfolio investments in recent years reflects the globalization of financial markets. The impetus for globalized financial markets initially came from the governments of major countries that began to deregulate foreign exchange and capital markets in the late 1970s. For instance, the United Kingdom dismantled the investment dollar premium system in 1979, while Japan liberalized its foreign exchange market in 1980, allowing its residents, for the first time, to freely invest in foreign securities.[1] Even developing countries such as Brazil, India, Korea, and Mexico took measures to allow foreigners to invest in their capital markets by offering country funds or directly listing local stocks on international stock exchanges. In addition, recent advances in telecommunication and computer technologies have contributed to the globalization of investments by facilitating cross-border transactions and rapid dissemination of information across national borders.

In this chapter, we are going to focus on the following issues: (1) why investors diversify their portfolios internationally, (2) how much investors can gain from

EXHIBIT 11.1

U.S. Investment in Foreign Equities

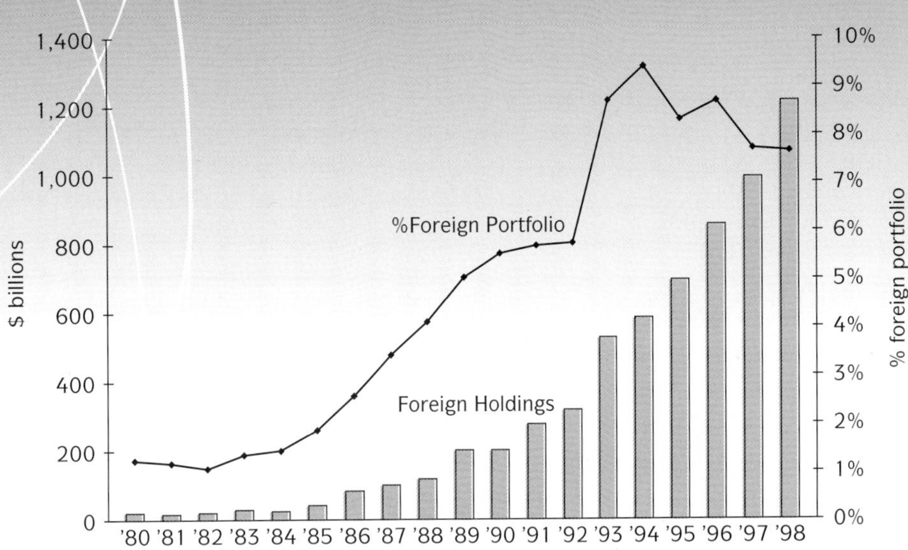

Source: Federal Reserve, June 1999.

international diversification, (3) the effects of fluctuating exchange rates on international portfolio investments, (4) whether and how much investors can benefit from investing in U.S.-based international mutual funds and country funds, and (5) the possible reasons for "home bias" in actual portfolio holdings. This chapter provides a self-contained discussion of international portfolio investment; no prior knowledge of portfolio investment theory is assumed.

INTERNATIONAL CORRELATION STRUCTURE AND RISK DIVERSIFICATION

It is clear even from casual observations that security prices in different countries don't move together very much. This suggests that investors may be able to achieve a given return on their investments at a reduced risk when they diversify their investments internationally rather than domestically. Investors diversify their portfolio holdings internationally for the same reason they may diversify domestically—to reduce risk as much as possible. As is suggested by the time-honored adage "Don't put all your eggs in one basket," most people are averse to risk and would like to diversify it away. Investors can reduce portfolio risk by holding securities that are less than perfectly correlated. In fact, the less correlated the securities in the portfolio, the lower the portfolio risk.

International diversification has a special dimension regarding **portfolio risk diversification**: Security returns are much less correlated across countries than within a country. Intuitively, this is so because economic, political, institutional, and even psychological factors affecting security returns tend to vary a great deal across countries, resulting in relatively low correlations among international securities. For instance, political turmoil in China may very well influence returns on most stocks in Hong Kong, but it may have little or no impact on stock returns in, say, Finland. On the other hand, political upheaval in Russia may affect Finnish stock returns (due to the geographic proximity and the economic ties between the two countries), with little effect on Hong Kong stock returns. In addition, business cycles are often highly asynchronous among countries, further contributing to low international correlations.

EXHIBIT 11.2 Correlations among International Stock Returns* (in U.S. Dollars)

Stock Market	AU	FR	GM	JP	NL	SW	UK	US
Australia (AU)	0.586							
France (FR)	0.286	0.576						
Germany (GM)	0.183	0.312	0.653					
Japan (JP)	0.152	0.238	0.300	0.416				
Netherlands (NL)	0.241	0.344	0.509	0.282	0.624			
Switzerland (SW)	0.358	0.368	0.475	0.281	0.517	0.664		
United Kingdom (UK)	0.315	0.378	0.299	0.209	0.393	0.431	0.698	
United States (US)	0.304	0.225	0.170	0.137	0.271	0.272	0.279	0.439

*The exhibit provides the average pairwise correlations of individual stock returns within each country in the diagonal cells and the average pairwise correlations between countries in the off-diagonal cells. The correlations were computed using the weekly returns from the period 1973–1982.

Source: C. Eun and B. Resnick, "Estimating the Correlation Structure of International Share Prices," *Journal of Finance*, December 1984, p. 1314.

Relatively low international correlations imply that investors should be able to reduce portfolio risk more if they diversify internationally rather than domestically. Since the magnitude of **gains from international diversification** in terms of risk reduction depends on the **international correlation structure**, it is useful to examine it empirically.

Exhibit 11.2 provides historical data on the international correlation structure. Specifically, the table provides the average pairwise correlations of individual stock returns within each country in the diagonal entries, and the average pairwise correlations of stock returns between countries in the off-diagonal entries. The correlations are in terms of U.S. dollars and computed using the weekly return data from the period 1973–1982. As can be seen from the table, the average *intracountry* correlation is 0.653 for Germany, 0.416 for Japan, 0.698 for the United Kingdom, and 0.439 for the United States. In contrast, the average *intercountry* correlation of the United States is 0.170 with Germany, 0.137 with Japan, and 0.279 with the United Kingdom. The average correlation of the United Kingdom, on the other hand, is 0.299 with Germany and 0.209 with Japan. Clearly, stock returns tend to be much less correlated between countries than within a country.

The international correlation structure documented in Exhibit 11.2 strongly suggests that international diversification can sharply reduce risk. According to Solnik (1974), that is indeed the case. Exhibit 11.3, adopted from the Solnik study, first shows that as the portfolio holds more and more stocks, the risk of the portfolio steadily declines, and eventually converges to the **systematic** (or nondiversifiable) **risk**. Systematic risk refers to the risk that remains even after investors fully diversify their portfolio holdings. Exhibit 11.3 shows that while a fully diversified U.S. portfolio is about 27 percent as risky as a typical individual stock, a fully diversified international portfolio is only about 12 percent as risky as a typical individual stock. This implies that when fully diversified, an international portfolio can be less than half as risky as a purely U.S. portfolio.

Exhibit 11.3 also illustrates the situation from the Swiss perspective. The figure shows that a fully diversified Swiss portfolio is about 44 percent as risky as a typical individual stock. However, this Swiss portfolio is more than three times as risky as a well-diversified international portfolio. This implies that much of the Swiss systematic risk is, in fact, unsystematic (diversifiable) risk when looked at in terms of international investment. In addition, compared with U.S. investors, Swiss investors have a lot more to gain from international diversification. In sum, Exhibit 11.3 provides rather striking evidence supporting international, as opposed to purely domestic, diversification.[2]

A cautionary note is in order here. A few studies, for example, Roll (1988) and Longin and Solnik (1995), found that international stock markets tend to move more closely together when the market volatility is higher. As was observed during the

EXHIBIT 11.3 Risk Reduction: Domestic versus International Diversification*

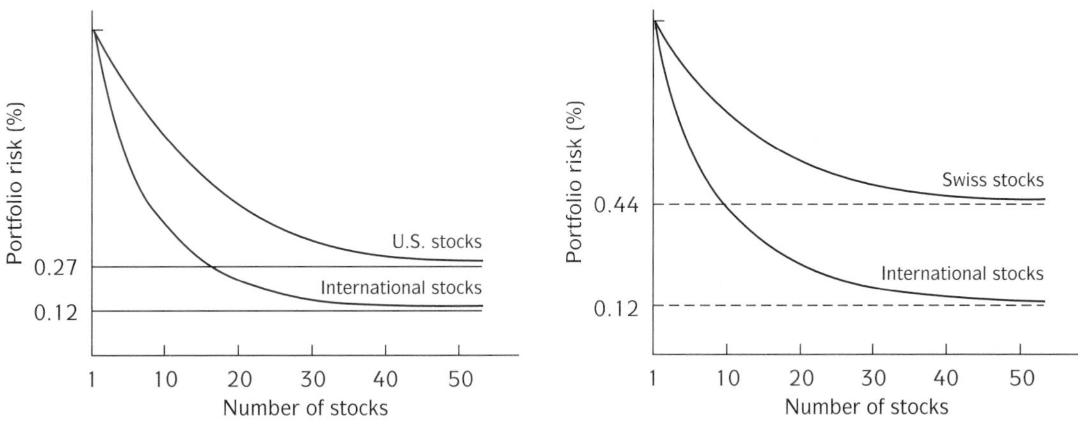

*Portfolio risk (%) represents the variance of portfolio returns divided by that of a typical individual stock.

Source: Reprinted with permission from *Financial Analysts Journal,* July/August 1974. © 1974, Financial Analysts Federation, Charlottesville, VA. All rights reserved.

October 1987 market crash, most developed markets declined together. Considering that investors need risk diversification most precisely when markets are turbulent, this finding casts some doubt on the benefits of international diversification. However, one may say that unless investors liquidate their portfolio holdings during the turbulent period, they can still benefit from international risk diversification.

OPTIMAL INTERNATIONAL PORTFOLIO SELECTION

Rational investors would select portfolios by considering returns as well as risk. Investors may be willing to assume additional risk if they are sufficiently compensated by a higher expected return. So we now expand our analysis to cover both risk and return. We are going to first examine the risk-return characteristics of major world stock markets and then evaluate the potential gains from holding **optimal international portfolios**.

Exhibit 11.4 provides summary statistics of the monthly returns, in U.S. dollars, for 11 major stock markets during the period 1980–1992.[3] Let us first examine the correlation coefficients among these markets. The correlation of the U.S. stock market with a foreign market varies from 0.24 with Japan to 0.70 with Canada. Apart from Canada, the Dutch and U.K. markets have relatively high correlations, 0.60 and 0.57, respectively, with the U.S. market. The Dutch market, in fact, has relatively high correlations with many markets: for example, 0.69 with the U.K. and 0.68 with Germany. This is likely due to a high degree of internationalization in the Dutch economy. In contrast, the Italian and Japanese markets tend to have relatively low correlations with other markets. Generally speaking, neighboring countries, such as Canada and the United States, and Germany and Switzerland, tend to exhibit the highest pairwise correlations, most likely due to a high degree of economic interdependence.

Exhibit 11.4 also provides the mean and standard deviation (SD) of monthly returns and the world beta measure for each market. The **world beta** measures the sensitivity of a national market to world market movements.[4] National stock markets have highly individualized risk-return characteristics. The mean return per month ranges from 0.79 percent (9.48 percent per year) for Canada to 1.86 percent (22.32 percent per year) for Sweden, whereas the standard deviation ranges from 4.56

EXHIBIT 11.4 Summary Statistics of the Monthly Returns for 11 Major Stock Markets: 1980.1–1992.12 (All statistics in U.S. dollars)

	Correlation Coefficient														
Stock Market	BG	CN	FR	GM	IT	JP	NL	SD	SW	UK	Mean (%)	SD (%)	β[a]	SHP	(Rank)[b]
Belgium (BG)											1.65	6.42	0.89	0.257	(4)
Canada (CN)	0.36										0.79	5.83	0.90	0.136	(11)
France (FR)	0.69	0.38									1.42	7.01	1.02	0.202	(7)
Germany (GM)	0.64	0.33	0.66								1.23	6.74	0.87	0.182	(9)
Italy (IT)	0.41	0.34	0.48	0.41							1.34	7.94	0.88	0.169	(10)
Japan (JP)	0.43	0.26	0.42	0.36	0.42						1.47	7.31	1.22	0.201	(8)
Netherlands (NL)	0.63	0.57	0.61	0.68	0.40	0.40					1.52	5.41	0.90	0.281	(2)
Sweden (SD)	0.40	0.33	0.41	0.44	0.37	0.37	0.41				1.86	7.03	0.89	0.265	(3)
Switzerland (SW)	0.62	0.41	0.63	0.72	0.32	0.38	0.65	0.50			1.19	5.86	0.84	0.203	(6)
United Kingdom (UK)	0.52	0.58	0.54	0.49	0.40	0.42	0.69	0.47	0.52		1.52	6.47	1.10	0.235	(5)
United States (US)	0.41	0.70	0.45	0.37	0.25	0.24	0.60	0.41	0.48	0.57	1.33	4.56	0.80	0.292	(1)

[a]β denotes the systematic risk (beta) of a country's stock market index measured against the world stock market index.

[b]SHP denotes the Sharpe performance measure, which is $(\bar{R}_i - \bar{R}_f)/\sigma_i$ where R_i and σ_i are, respectively, the mean and standard deviation of returns to the *i*th market. In computing the Sharpe measure, the risk-free interest rate (R_f) is assumed to be zero. Ranking of each market in terms of the Sharpe performance measure is provided in parentheses.

Source: Monthly issues of *Capital International Perspective.*

EXHIBIT 11.5

Selection of the Optimal International Portfolio

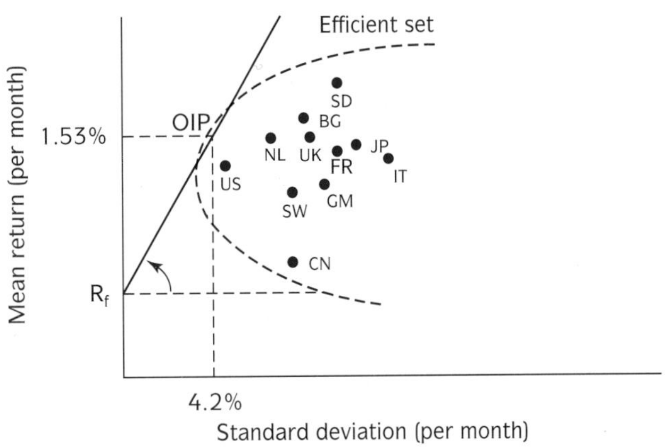

percent for the United States to 7.94 percent for Italy. Japan has the highest world beta measure, 1.22, while the United States has the lowest, 0.80. This means that the Japanese stock market is the most sensitive to world market movements and the U.S. market the least sensitive.

Lastly, Exhibit 11.4 presents the historical performance measures for national stock markets, that is,

$$\text{SHP} = (\bar{R}_i - R_f)/\sigma_i \tag{11.1}$$

where $\bar{R}_i$ and σ_i are, respectively, the mean and standard deviation of returns, and (R_f) is the risk-free interest rate. The above expression, known as the **Sharpe performance measure (SHP)**, provides a "risk-adjusted" performance measure. It represents the excess return (above and beyond the risk-free interest rate) per standard deviation risk. In Exhibit 11.4, the Sharpe performance measure is computed by assuming that the monthly risk-free interest is zero.

The computed Sharpe performance measure ranges from 0.292 for the United States to 0.136 for Canada. The U.S. market performed the best, followed by the Dutch, Swedish, and Belgian markets. The very strong performance of the U.S. stock market is mainly attributable to its low risk. Contrary to prior expectations, the stock markets of the two powerful economies of the world, Japan and Germany, have registered less than stellar performances since 1980, ranking eighth and ninth, respectively. The lackluster performance of the Canadian stock market can be attributable to the fact that it had the lowest mean return among the 11 markets considered. The Italian stock market, ranked 10th, suffers from the fact that it had the highest volatility.

Using the historical performance data represented in Exhibit 11.4, we can solve for the composition of the optimal international portfolio from the perspective of U.S. (or U.S. dollar-based) investors.[5] Exhibit 11.5 illustrates the choice of the optimal international portfolio (OIP). The result is presented in Exhibit 11.6. As can be seen from the next-to-last column of the table, U.S. investors' optimal international portfolio comprises:

Belgian market	= 14.66%
Italian market	= 0.37%
Japanese market	= 9.25%
Dutch market	= 14.15%
Swedish market	= 20.26%
U.S. market	= 41.31%
Total	= 100.00%

EXHIBIT 11.6 Composition of the Optimal International Portfolio by Investors' Domicile (Holding Period: 1980–1992)

Stock Market	From the Perspective of Investors Domiciled in											
	BG	CN	FR	GM	IT	JP	NL	SD	SW	UK	US	LC*
Belgium	0.2882	0.1441	0.2603	0.3084	0.2563	0.2211	0.2999	0.2807	0.3080	0.2039	0.1466	0.2558
Canada												
France			0.0312		0.0242							
Germany												
Italy		0.0194			0.0021			0.0287			0.0037	0.0888
Japan	0.1254	0.0906	0.1057	0.1059	0.1327	0.2569	0.1124	0.1278	0.1177	0.1141	0.0925	
Netherlands	0.2962	0.1836	0.2624	0.3372	0.2485	0.2085	0.3079	0.2204	0.3112	0.1850	0.1415	
Sweden	0.1664	0.1718	0.1886	0.2108	0.1731	0.2704	0.1922	0.1682	0.2347	0.1825	0.2026	0.2444
Switzerland	0.0277		0.0339		0.0519		0.0109		0.0284			
United Kingdom	0.0119		0.0261				0.0123	0.0661		0.2801		0.2062
United States	0.0842	0.3905	0.0918	0.0377	0.1112	0.0431	0.0644	0.1081		0.0344	0.4131	0.2048
Total	1.0000	1.0000	1.0000	1.0000	1.0000	1.0000	1.0000	1.0000	1.0000	1.0000	1.0000	1.0000

*LC column provides the composition of optimal international portfolio without considering exchange rate changes.

In their optimal international portfolio, U.S. investors allocate the largest share, 41.31 percent, of funds to their home market, followed by the Swedish, Belgian, Dutch, and Japanese markets. The Japanese market is included in the optimal portfolio mainly due to its low correlations with other markets, including the U.S. market. Five markets—Canada, France, Germany, Switzerland and U.K.—are not included in U.S. investors' optimal international portfolio.

Similarly, we can solve for the composition of the optimal international portfolio from the perspective of each of the national investors. Since the risk-return characteristics of international stock markets vary depending on the numeraire currency used to measure returns, the composition of the optimal international portfolio will also vary across national investors using different numeraire currencies. Exhibit 11.6 presents the composition of the optimal international portfolio from the currency perspective of each national investor.

For instance, the U.K. (or British pound–based) investors' optimal international portfolio comprises Belgium (20.39 percent), Japan (11.41 percent), the Netherlands (18.50 percent), Sweden (18.25 percent), the United States (3.44 percent), and the United Kingdom (28.01 percent). Like U.S. investors, U.K. investors invest heavily in their domestic market partly because the domestic market is not subject to exchange rate fluctuations and thus has a low risk. It is clear from the table that five markets, Belgium, Japan, the Netherlands, Sweden, and the United States, are most heavily represented in the optimal international portfolios. In fact, the Belgian, Japanese, Dutch, and Swedish markets are included in every national investor's optimal international portfolio and receive the largest weights. The U.S. market is included in every optimal international portfolio, except that of Swiss investors. In contrast, the Canadian and German markets are not included in any optimal portfolio, while the French and Italian markets are included in relatively few portfolios with small weights.

The last column of Exhibit 11.6 provides the composition of the optimal international portfolio in terms of the local currency (LC), constructed ignoring exchange rate changes. It is the optimal international portfolio that would have been obtained if exchange rates had not changed. As such, it can tell us the effect of currency movements on the compositions of international portfolios. The LC optimal international portfolio comprises Belgium (25.58 percent), Italy (8.88 percent), Sweden (24.44 percent), the United Kingdom (20.62 percent), and the United States (20.48 percent). Both Japan and the Netherlands, which were heavily represented in most national investors' optimal international portfolios, are not included in the LC optimal portfolio. This implies that the performances of the Japanese yen and the Dutch guilder are largely responsible for the strong demand for these markets by most national investors. Italy and the United Kingdom face the opposite situation—namely, the weak performances of the Italian lira and British pound must have been responsible for the weak demand for these two stock markets.

Having obtained optimal international portfolios, we can now evaluate the gains from holding these portfolios over purely domestic portfolios. We can measure the gains from holding international portfolios in two different ways: (1) the increase in the Sharpe performance measure, and (2) the increase in the portfolio return at the domestic-equivalent risk level. The increase in the Sharpe performance measure, ΔSHP, is given by the difference in the Sharpe ratio between the optimal international portfolio (OIP) and the domestic portfolio (DP), that is,

$$\Delta SHP = SHP(OIP) - SHP(DP) \tag{11.2}$$

ΔSHP represents the extra return per standard deviation risk accruing from international investment. On the other hand, the increase in the portfolio return at the "domestic-equivalent" risk level is measured by the difference in return between the domestic portfolio (DP) and the international portfolio (IP) that has the same risk as the domestic portfolio. This extra return, $\Delta\bar{R}$ accruing from international investment at the domestic-equivalent risk level can be computed by multiplying ΔSHP by the standard deviation of the domestic portfolio, that is,

$$\Delta\bar{R} = (\Delta\text{SHP})(\sigma_{DP}) \qquad (11.3)$$

Exhibit 11.7 presents both the measures of the gains from international investment from the perspective of each national investor. Let us first examine the results for U.S. investors. As can be seen from the last row of the table, the optimal international portfolio has a mean return of 1.53 percent per month and a standard deviation of 4.27 percent, whereas the U.S. domestic portfolio has a mean return of 1.33 percent and a standard deviation of 4.56 percent. The optimal international portfolio thus has a higher return and, at the same time, a lower risk than the domestic portfolio. This means that for U.S. investors, the optimal international portfolio completely dominates the domestic portfolio in terms of risk-return efficiency. As a result, the Sharpe performance measure increases from 0.292 to 0.358, a 23 percent increase. Alternately, U.S. investors can capture an extra return of 0.30 percent per month, or 3.60 percent per year, by holding an international portfolio at the domestic equivalent-risk, that is, at the standard deviation of 4.56 percent.

The gains from international portfolio diversification (IPD) are much larger for some national investors, especially for Canadian, French, German, Italian, and Japanese investors. Each of these national investors can increase the Sharpe ratio by more than 50 percent. German investors, for instance, can increase the Sharpe ratio by 80 percent, or can capture an extra return of 10.68 percent per year at the German-equivalent risk level by holding their optimal international portfolio. Exhibit 11.7 indicates that the gains from IPD are relatively modest for investors from Belgium, the Netherlands, the United Kingdom, and the United States. Overall, the data presented in Exhibit 11.7 suggest that, regardless of domicile and numeraire currency, investors can potentially benefit from IPD to a varying degree.[6]

EFFECTS OF CHANGES IN THE EXCHANGE RATE

The realized dollar returns for a U.S. resident investing in a foreign market will depend not only on the return in the foreign market but also on the change in the exchange rate between the dollar and the local currency. Thus, the success of foreign investment rests on the performances of both the foreign security market and the foreign currency. Formally, the rate of return in dollar terms from investing in the ith foreign market, $R_{i\$}$, is given by

$$\begin{aligned} R_{i\$} &= (1 + R_i)(1 + e_i) - 1 \\ &= R_i + e_i + R_i e_i \end{aligned} \qquad (11.4)$$

where R_i is the local currency rate of return from the ith foreign market and e_i is the rate of change in the exchange rate between the local currency and the dollar; e_i will be positive (negative) if the foreign currency appreciates (depreciates) against the dollar. Suppose that a U.S. resident just sold shares of British Petroleum (BP) she had purchased a year ago, and that the share price of BP rose 15 percent in terms of the British pound (i.e., $R = .15$), whereas the British pound depreciated 5 percent against the dollar over the one-year period (i.e., $e = -.05$). Then the rate of return, in dollar terms, from this investment will be calculated as: $R_{i\$} = (1 + .15)(1 - .05) - 1 = .0925$, or 9.25 percent.

The above expression suggests that exchange rate changes affect the risk of foreign investment as follows:

$$\text{Var}(R_{i\$}) = \text{Var}(R_i) + \text{Var}(e_i) + 2\text{Cov}(R_i,e_i) + \Delta\text{Var} \qquad (11.5)$$

EXHIBIT 11.7 Gains from International Diversification by Investor's Domicile (Monthly Returns: 1980–1992)

Investor's Domicile	Domestic Portfolio			Optimal International Portfolio			Gains from International Investment			
	Mean (%)	SD (%)	SHP	Mean (%)	SD (%)	SHP (%)	ΔSHP	(%Δ)[a]	ΔR(%)[b]	(%p.a.)[c]
Belgium	1.72	5.79	0.297	1.68	4.54	0.370	0.073	(25)	0.42	(5.04)
Canada	0.81	5.23	0.155	1.56	4.04	0.386	0.231	(149)	1.20	(14.40)
France	1.55	6.28	0.247	1.77	4.67	0.379	0.132	(53)	0.83	(9.96)
Germany	1.12	5.98	0.187	1.55	4.61	0.336	0.149	(80)	0.89	(10.68)
Italy	1.70	7.96	0.214	1.92	4.37	0.439	0.225	(105)	1.80	(21.60)
Japan	0.94	5.99	0.157	1.16	4.53	0.256	0.099	(63)	0.59	(7.08)
Netherlands	1.47	5.22	0.282	1.56	4.59	0.340	0.058	(21)	0.30	(3.60)
Sweden	2.21	7.30	0.303	1.91	4.52	0.423	0.120	(40)	0.88	(10.56)
Switzerland	1.06	4.94	0.215	1.54	4.87	0.316	0.101	(47)	0.50	(6.00)
United Kingdom	1.70	5.45	0.312	1.82	4.60	0.396	0.084	(27)	0.46	(5.52)
United States	1.33	4.56	0.292	1.53	4.27	0.358	0.066	(23)	0.30	(3.60)

[a]The number provided in parentheses represents the percentage increase in the Sharpe performance measure relative to that of the domestic portfolio, i.e., [ΔSHP/SHP(DP)] × 100, where ΔSHP denotes the difference in the Sharpe ratio between the optimal international portfolio and the domestic portfolio.

[b]This column provides the extra return accruing to the optimal international portfolio at the domestic-equivalent risk level.

[c]This column provides the annualized extra return accruing to the optimal international portfolio.

EXHIBIT 11.8 Decomposition of the Variance of International Security Returns in U.S. Dollars[a] (Monthly Data: 1978.1–1989.12)

		Components of Var (R_{is})[b]			
	$Var(R_{is})$	$Var(R_i)$	$Var(e_i)$	$2Cov(R_i,e_i)$	ΔVar
Bonds					
Canada	15.29	10.82 (70.76%)	1.72 (11.25%)	2.67 (17.46%)	0.08 (0.52%)
France	16.48	2.82 (17.11%)	12.74 (77.31%)	0.60 (3.64%)	0.32 (1.94%)
Germany	21.53	2.59 (12.03%)	13.84 (64.28%)	4.91 (22.81%)	0.19 (0.88%)
Japan	24.70	3.03 (12.27%)	15.13 (61.26%)	6.09 (24.66%)	0.45 (1.82%)
Switzerland	21.16	1.14 (5.39%)	17.64 (83.36%)	2.34 (11.06%)	0.04 (0.19%)
U.K.	27.67	8.88 (32.09%)	12.39 (44.78%)	6.08 (21.97%)	0.32 (1.16%)
U.S.	10.24	10.24 (100.00%)	0.00 (n.a.)	0.00 (n.a.)	0.00 (n.a.)
Stocks					
Canada	37.70	30.58 (81.11%)	1.72 (4.56%)	5.37 (14.24%)	0.03 (0.08%)
France	59.75	43.03 (72.02%)	12.74 (21.32%)	3.75 (6.28%)	0.23 (0.38%)
Germany	43.82	29.27 (66.80%)	13.84 (31.58%)	0.00 (0.00%)	0.71 (1.62%)
Japan	41.47	19.45 (47.24%)	15.13 (36.48%)	5.83 (14.06%)	1.06 (2.56%)
Switzerland	34.81	20.07 (57.66%)	17.64 (50.68%)	−3.76 (−10.80%)	0.86 (2.47%)
U.K.	40.96	29.27 (71.46%)	12.39 (30.25%)	−1.52 (−3.71%)	0.82 (2.00%)
U.S.	21.16	21.16 (100.00%)	0.00 (n.a.)	0.00 (n.a.)	0.00 (n.a.)

[a]The portfolio variances are computed using the monthly percentage returns.
[b]The relative contributions of individual components to the total portfolio risk appear in parentheses.

Source: Reprinted by permission, C. Eun and B. Resnick, "International Diversification of Investment Portfolios: U.S. and Japanese Perspectives," *Management Science*, Vol. 40, No. 1, January 1994. © 1994, The Institute of Management Sciences (currently INFORMS), 290 Westminster Street, Providence, RI 02903 USA.

where the ΔVar term represents the contribution of the cross-product term, R_ie_i, to the risk of foreign investment. Should the exchange rate be certain, only one term, $Var(R_i)$, would remain in the right hand side of the equation. Equation 11.5 demonstrates that exchange rate fluctuations contribute to the risk of foreign investment through three possible channels:

1. Its own volatility, $Var(e_i)$.
2. Its covariance with the local market returns, $Cov(R_ie_i)$.
3. The contribution of the cross-product term, ΔVar.

Exhibit 11.8 provides the breakdown of the variance of dollar returns into different components for both the bond and stock markets of six major foreign countries: Canada, France, Germany, Japan, Switzerland, and the United Kingdom. Let us first examine the case of bond markets. The exhibit clearly indicates that a large portion of the risk associated with investing in foreign bonds arises from exchange rate uncertainty. Consider investing in a U.K. bond. As can be seen from the exhibit, the variance of U.K. bond returns is only 8.88 percent squared in terms of the British pound, but jumps to 27.67 percent squared when measured in dollar terms. This increase in volatility is due to the volatility of the exchange rate, $Var(e_i) = 12.39$, as well as its covariance with the local bond market returns, that is $2Cov(R_i,e_i) = 6.08$. As can be expected, the cross-product term contributes little. The Swiss market provides an extreme example; the local bond market returns account for only 5.39 percent of the volatility of returns in dollar terms. This means that investing in Swiss bonds largely amounts to investing in Swiss currency.

With the exception of Canada, exchange rate volatility is much greater than bond market volatility. And without exception, exchange rate changes are found to covary *positively* with local bond market returns. Empirical evidence regarding bond markets suggests that it is essential to control exchange risk to enhance the efficiency of international bond portfolios.

Compared with bond markets, the risk of investing in foreign stock markets is, to a lesser degree, attributable to exchange rate uncertainty. Again, consider investing in the U.K. market. The variance of the U.K. stock market is 29.27 percent squared in terms of the British pound, but it increases to 40.96 percent squared when measured in terms of the U.S. dollar. The local market return volatility accounts for 71.46 percent of the volatility of U.K. stock market returns in dollar terms. In comparison, exchange rate volatility accounts for 30.25 percent of the dollar return variance, still a significant portion. Interestingly, the exchange rate covaries negatively with local stock market returns, partially offsetting the effect of exchange rate volatility. Exhibit 11.8 indicates that while exchange rates are somewhat less volatile than stock market returns, they will contribute substantially to the risk of foreign stock investments.

INTERNATIONAL BOND INVESTMENT

Although the world bond market is comparable in terms of capitalization value to the world stock market, so far it has not received as much attention in international investment literature. This may reflect, at least in part, the perception that exchange risk makes it difficult to realize significant gains from international bond diversification. It is worthwhile to explore this issue and determine if this perception has merit.

Exhibit 11.9 provides summary statistics of monthly returns, in U.S. dollar terms, on long-term government bond indexes from seven major countries: Canada, France, Germany, Japan, Switzerland, the United Kingdom, and the United States. It also presents the composition of the optimal international portfolio for U.S. (dollar-based) investors. Note that European bond markets have very high correlations. For instance, the correlation of the German bond market is 0.89 with the French as well as Swiss bond markets, while the correlation between the French and Swiss bond markets is 0.81. These high correlations reflect the fact that as a group these European currencies float against the U.S. dollar.

In the optimal international portfolio, the U.S. bond receives the largest positive weight, followed by French and Japanese bonds. The Swiss bond, however, receives a negative weight, implying that U.S. investors should have borrowed in terms of the

EXHIBIT 11.9 **Summary Statistics of the Monthly Returns to Bonds and the Composition of the Optimal International Bond Portfolio (in U.S. Dollars: 1978.1–1989.12)**

	Correlation Coefficient									Optimal International Portfolio[a]
Bond Market	CN	FR	GM	JP	SW	UK	Mean (%)	SD (%)	SHP	(Weight)
Canada (CN)							0.88	3.91	0.225	0.0218
France (FR)	0.36						0.83	4.06	0.204	0.4488
Germany (GM)	0.40	0.89					0.79	4.64	0.170	0.0204
Japan (JP)	0.27	0.68	0.64				1.07	4.97	0.215	0.2838
Switzerland (SW)	0.34	0.81	0.89	0.66			0.55	4.60	0.120	−0.4896
United Kingdom (UK)	0.40	0.52	0.56	0.51	0.54		0.94	5.26	0.179	0.0895
United States (US)	0.76	0.30	0.35	0.27	0.30	0.33	0.86	3.20	0.269	0.6254

[a]The optimal international bond portfolio is solved allowing for short sales and assuming a zero monthly risk-free interest rate. The optimal international portfolio has a mean return of 1.06% per month and standard deviation (SD) of 3.15%, with a Sharpe ratio (SHP) of 0.337.

Source: Reprinted by permission, C. Eun and B. Resnick, "International Diversification of Investment Portfolios: U.S. and Japanese Perspectives," *Management Science*, Vol. 40, No. 1, January 1994. © 1994, The Institute of Management Sciences (currently INFORMS), 290 Westminster Street, Providence, RI 02903 USA.

Swiss franc. The optimal portfolio has a monthly mean return of 1.06 percent and a standard deviation of 3.15 percent, resulting in a Sharpe performance measure of 0.337. Considering that the U.S. bond has a mean return of 0.86 percent, a standard deviation of 3.20 percent, and a Sharpe measure of 0.269, U.S. investors could have benefited modestly from holding the optimal international bond portfolio.

The preponderance of exchange risk in foreign bond investment suggests that investors may be able to increase their gains from international bond diversification if they can properly control the exchange risk. Recent studies indeed show that when investors control exchange risk by using currency forward contracts, they can substantially enhance the efficiency of international bond portfolios. Eun and Resnick (1994), for instance, show that when exchange risk is hedged, international bond portfolios tend to dominate international stock portfolios in terms of risk-return efficiency.[7]

The advent of the *euro,* the common European currency, is likely to alter the risk-return characteristics of the affected markets. Before the euro was introduced, for instance, the Italian and German bonds had quite different characteristics; the former was generally viewed as a high-risk and high-return investment, whereas the latter a low-risk and low-return investment, largely because the German mark was a hard currency while the Italian lira was a weak one. In the post-euro period, however, both German and Italian bonds (and all the other euro-zone bonds) will be denominated and transacted in the common currency, rendering nationality of bonds a much less significant factor. Although euro-zone bonds differ in terms of credit risk, their risk-return characteristics will converge to a large extent. This implies that non-euro currency bonds like British bonds would play an enhanced role in international diversification strategies as they would retain their unique risk-return characteristics.

INTERNATIONAL MUTUAL FUNDS: A PERFORMANCE EVALUATION

Currently, U.S. investors can achieve international diversification at home simply by investing in U.S.-based international mutual funds, which now number well over 300. By investing in international mutual funds, investors can (1) save any extra transaction and/or information costs they may have to incur when they attempt to invest directly in foreign markets, (2) circumvent many legal and institutional barriers to direct portfolio investments in foreign markets, and (3) potentially benefit from the expertise of professional fund managers.

These advantages of international mutual funds should be particularly appealing to small individual investors who would like to diversify internationally but have neither the necessary expertise nor the direct access to foreign markets. It is thus relevant to ask the following question: Can investors benefit from international diversification by investing in existing U.S.-based international mutual funds? To provide an answer to the above question, we are going to examine the historical performance of international mutual funds that invest a substantial portion of their assets in foreign markets.

Exhibit 11.10 provides the risk-return profiles of a sample of U.S.-based international mutual funds that have sufficient track records. Three funds—the ASA (which invests in South African gold-mining stocks), the Canadian Fund, and the Japan Fund—are single-country funds. Other funds invest more broadly. The table shows that all but one fund have a higher mean return than the U.S. stock market index, proxied by the Standard & Poor 500 Index, during the period of 1977.1–1986.12. The average mean return of the international mutual funds is 1.58 percent per month (18.96 percent per year). In comparison, the mean return on the

EXHIBIT 11.10

International Mutual Funds: A Performance Evaluation (Monthly Returns: 1977.1–1986.12)

Fund	Mean (%)	SD (%)	β_{US}	R^2	SHP[a]
ASA	1.75	11.88	0.80	0.08	0.084
Canadian Fund	0.91	4.64	0.75	0.47	0.035
International Investors	2.34	10.09	0.72	0.09	0.157
Japan Fund	1.72	7.02	0.59	0.13	0.138
Keystone International	1.14	4.29	0.69	0.47	0.091
Merrill Lynch Pacific	1.82	5.45	0.32	0.06	0.196
New Perspective	1.47	3.99	0.80	0.73	0.179
Oppenheimer Global	1.94	6.35	1.02	0.47	0.186
Putnam International	1.64	5.91	0.62	0.20	0.150
Scudder International	1.46	4.23	0.50	0.26	0.168
Sogen International	1.48	3.36	0.70	0.78	0.217
Templeton Growth	1.48	4.13	0.84	0.74	0.176
United International Growth	1.41	3.86	0.71	0.61	0.172
Average	1.58	5.78	0.69	0.39	0.150
U.S. MNC Index	1.34	4.38	0.98	0.90	0.135
S&P 500	1.17	4.25	1.00	1.00	0.099
MSCI World Index	1.46	3.80	0.70	0.61	0.186

[a]The Sharpe measure is computed using the risk-free rate of 0.752%, which is the average monthly Treasury bill rate during the sample period.

Source: C. Eun, R. Kolodny, and B. Resnick, "U.S.-Based International Mutual Funds: A Performance Evaluation." This copyrighted material is reprinted with permission from the *Journal of Portfolio Management,* 488 Madison Avenue, New York, NY 10022.

S&P 500 is 1.17 percent per month (14.04 percent per year). The standard deviation of the international mutual funds ranges from 3.36 percent to 11.88 percent, with an average of 5.78 percent. In comparison, the S&P has a standard deviation of 4.25 percent.

Exhibit 11.10 also provides the U.S. beta measures of the international funds and the associated coefficient of determination (R^2) values.[8] Note that most funds have a U.S. beta value that is much less than unity. On average, U.S. stock market movements account for less than 40 percent of the fluctuations in the international fund returns. In contrast, U.S. stock market movements are known to account for about 90 percent of the fluctuations in U.S. domestic stock fund returns.[9] These results show that the sample funds provided U.S. investors with a valuable opportunity to diversify internationally. In contrast, the U.S. MNC Index, which comprises 60 U.S. multinational corporations with the highest proportions of international revenue, has a U.S. beta value of 0.98 and an R^2 value of 90 percent. This means that the share prices of MNCs behave much like those of domestic firms, without providing effective international diversification.[10]

Lastly, Exhibit 11.10 provides the Sharpe performance measures of international mutual funds. As the table shows, 10 out of 13 international funds outperformed the U.S. stock market index based on the Sharpe measure. The same point is illustrated in Exhibit 11.11, showing that only three international funds lie below the U.S. capital market line (CML).[11] This is in sharp contrast to the findings of previous studies showing that the majority of U.S. domestic mutual funds lie below the U.S. capital market line. Against the alternative benchmark of the World Index, however, the sample funds performed rather poorly. The average SHP value for the international funds, 0.15, is substantially less than the value for the World Index, 0.186. This seems to suggest that it is desirable to invest in a world index fund if available.[12]

EXHIBIT 11.11

Performance of International Mutual Funds: 1977.1–1986.12

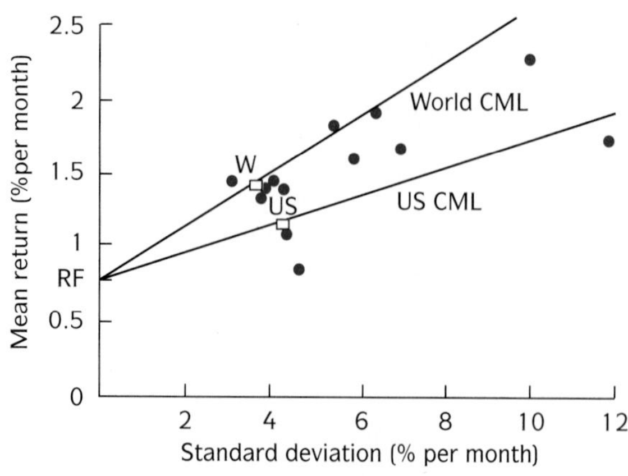

Note: Each international fund is denoted by a round dot (•). The risk-free rate (RF) is .752%, which is the average T-bill rate during the sample period. W and US, respectively, denote the MSCI World Index and the S & P 500.

SUPPLEMENTARY MATERIAL

In addition to international mutual funds, investors may achieve international portfolio diversification "at home" by investing in (1) country funds, (2) American depository receipts (ADRs), or (3) world equity benchmark shares (WEBS), without having to invest directly in foreign stock markets. In the next section, we discuss each of these instruments.

INTERNATIONAL DIVERSIFICATION THROUGH COUNTRY FUNDS

Recently, country funds have emerged as one of the most popular means of international investment in the United States as well as in other developed countries. As the name suggests, a country fund invests exclusively in stocks of a single country. Using country funds, investors can

1. Speculate in a single foreign market with minimum costs.
2. Construct their own *personal* international portfolios using country funds as building blocks.
3. Diversify into *emerging markets* that are otherwise practically inaccessible.

Many emerging markets, such as India, Brazil, China, Russia, and Turkey, still remain largely segmented. As a result, country funds often provide international investors with the most practical, if not the only, way of diversifying into these largely inaccessible foreign markets.

The majority of country funds available, however, have a *closed-end* status. Like other closed-end funds, a **closed-end country fund (CECF)** issues a given number of shares that trade on the stock exchange of the host country as if the fund were an individual stock by itself. Unlike shares of open-end mutual funds, shares of a closed-end country fund cannot be redeemed at the underlying net asset value set at the home market of the fund. Currently, about 30 countries offer CECFs, a partial list of which is provided in Exhibit 11.12. In the United States, the majority of CECFs are listed on the New York Stock Exchange, with a few listed on the American Stock Exchange.

Since the share value of a fund is set on a U.S. stock exchange, it may very well diverge from the underlying net asset value (NAV) set in the fund's home market. The

EXHIBIT 11.12 **U.S. and Home Market Betas of Closed-End Country Funds and Their Net Asset Values**

Country	Average Fund Premium (%)	Fund Share Value			Net Asset Value			Sample Period
		β_{US}	β_{HM}	R^2	β_{US}	β_{HM}	R^2	
Australia	−14.77	0.62	0.48	0.13	0.25	0.81	0.60	1986.1–90.12
Brazil	−24.72	0.11	0.16	0.02	0.32	0.65	0.60	1988.4–90.12
Canada	−6.29	0.04	0.47	0.03	−0.19	0.29	0.11	1986.6–90.12
Germany	1.80	0.73	0.53	0.11	0.15	0.69	0.40	1986.7–90.12
India	−2.66	0.87	0.26	0.04	−0.27	0.66	0.40	1988.8–90.12
Italy	−12.49	0.89	0.68	0.21	0.13	0.57	0.28	1986.3–90.12
Korea	63.17	1.00	0.63	0.19	0.24	0.76	0.62	1985.1–90.12
Malaysia	−0.36	1.34	0.60	0.24	0.58	0.68	0.79	1987.6–90.12
Mexico	−21.14	0.99	0.53	0.13	0.33	0.75	0.62	1985.1–90.12
Spain	21.57	1.56	0.28	0.14	0.39	0.75	0.65	1988.7–90.12
South Africa	12.16	0.00	0.35	0.13	0.08	0.85	0.59	1985.1–90.12
Switzerland	−7.65	0.79	0.47	0.25	0.33	0.65	0.75	1987.8–90.12
Taiwan	37.89	1.46	0.39	0.26	0.19	0.40	0.13	1987.2–90.12
Thailand	−6.86	1.20	0.44	0.14	0.63	0.85	0.75	1988.2–90.12
U.K.	−16.55	1.04	0.62	0.36	0.55	0.73	0.37	1987.8–90.12
Average		0.84	0.46	0.16	0.25	0.67	0.51	

Source: E. Chang, C. Eun, and R. Kolodny, "International Diversification through Closed-End Country Funds," *Journal of Banking and Finance* (November 1995). Reprinted with permission of Elsevier Science.

difference is known as a *premium* if the fund share value exceeds the NAV, or a *discount* in the opposite case. Exhibit 11.12 provides the magnitude of premiums/discounts for the sample CECFs. As indicated in the table, the average premium varies a great deal across funds, ranging from 63.17 percent (for the Korea Fund) to −24 percent (for the Brazil Fund). Like the Korea Fund, the Taiwan and Spain funds commanded large premiums, 37.89 percent and 21.57 percent, respectively. Like the Brazil Fund, the Mexico Fund traded at a steep discount, −21.14 percent on average. It was also observed that the fund premium/discount fluctuates widely over time. For instance, the Taiwan Fund premium varied between −25.27 percent and 205.39 percent. Most funds have traded at both a premium and a discount since their inception.[13] The behavior of the fund premium/discount implies that the risk-return characteristics of a CECF can be quite different from those of the underlying NAV.

Cash flows from CECFs are generated by the underlying assets held outside the United States. But CECFs are traded in the United States and their market values, determined in the United States, often diverge from the NAVs. This "hybrid" nature of CECFs suggests that they may behave partly like U.S. securities and partly like securities of the home market. To investigate this issue, consider the following "two-factor" market model:[14]

$$R_i = \alpha_i + \beta^{US}{}_i R_{US} + \beta^{HM}{}_i R_{HM} + e_i \tag{11.6}$$

where:

R_i = the return on the ith country fund,

R_{US} = the return on the U.S. market index proxied by the Standard & Poor 500 Index,

R_{HM} = the return on the home market of the country fund,

$\beta^{US}{}_i$ = the U.S. beta of the ith country fund, measuring the sensitivity of the fund returns to the U.S. market returns,

$\beta^{HM}{}_i$ = the home market beta of the ith country fund, measuring the sensitivity of the fund returns to the home market returns, and

e_i = the residual error term.

EXHIBIT 11.13 **Summary Statistics of the Weekly Returns for Closed-End Country Funds and Their Net Asset Values and the Compositions of Optimal Portfolios (in U.S. Dollar terms: 1989.1–1990.12)**

	Country Fund Share			Net Asset Value				Optimal Portfolio	
Country	Mean (%)	SD (%)	Correlation with U.S.	Mean (%)	SD (%)	Correlation with U.S.		CECF (Weight)	NAV (Weight)
Australia	0.46	5.64	0.12	0.01	1.78	0.25		0.0033	0.0000
Brazil	0.73	6.31	−0.01	0.29	7.55	−0.02		0.1271	0.0023
Canada	0.14	4.91	−0.31	−0.19	1.98	−0.19		0.0660	0.0000
Germany	0.78	9.70	0.22	0.38	4.67	−0.11		0.0253	0.0000
India	0.36	5.93	0.18	0.15	3.92	−0.21		0.0750	0.0882
Italy	0.44	7.00	0.22	0.39	2.20	0.25		0.0000	0.1044
Korea	−0.37	6.79	0.25	0.00	2.91	0.08		0.0000	0.0000
Malaysia	0.72	7.89	0.35	0.37	3.21	0.29		0.0000	0.0000
Mexico	1.11	6.07	0.50	0.77	2.63	0.24		0.2427	0.6026
Spain	0.39	8.76	0.40	0.03	3.08	0.29		0.0000	0.0000
South Africa	0.43	4.00	−0.13	0.36	5.06	−0.03		0.2993	0.0954
Switzerland	0.27	4.50	0.46	0.20	2.48	0.36		0.0000	0.0000
Taiwan	0.57	7.42	0.31	−0.06	7.95	0.05		0.0000	0.0000
Thailand	0.71	8.42	0.29	0.50	5.14	0.23		0.0000	0.0000
U.K.	0.35	4.01	0.44	0.27	4.08	0.23		0.0424	0.0616
U.S. Index	0.18	2.06	1.00	0.18	2.06	1.00		0.1189	0.0454
							Total =	1.0000	1.0000
							Mean =	0.58%	0.58%
							SD =	2.49%	1.81%
							SHP =	0.233	0.320

Source: E. Chang, C. Eun, and R. Kolodny, "International Diversification Through Closed-End Country Funds," *Journal of Banking and Finance* (October 1995). Reprinted with permission of Elsevier Science.

Equation 11.6 is estimated for both the CECFs and their underlying net assets; that is, we run two regressions for each fund. In the first regression, the left-hand side (dependent) variable, R_i, is the return that U.S. investors receive on the CECF share itself. In the second regression, the left-hand side variable is the return on the NAV. The estimation results are provided in Exhibit 11.12.

Exhibit 11.12 shows that CECFs tend to have substantially higher U.S. beta values than their underlying NAVs. The average U.S. beta value is 0.84 for CECFs, but is only 0.25 for the NAVs. On the other hand, the average home market beta is 0.46 for CECFs, which is compared with 0.67 for the NAVs. In the case of Korea, for example, the fund (underlying net assets) has a U.S. beta of 1.00 (0.24) and a home market beta of 0.63 (0.76). In the case of Thailand, the fund (underlying net assets) has a U.S. beta of 1.20 (0.63) and a home market beta of 0.44 (0.85). In other words, CECF returns are substantially more sensitive to the U.S. market factor and less so to the home market factor than their corresponding NAVs. This implies that CECFs behave more like U.S. securities in comparison with the NAVs.[15] However, the majority of CECFs retain significant home market betas, allowing U.S. investors to achieve international diversification to a certain extent. Also noteworthy from the table is the fact that the coefficients of determination, R^2, tend to be quite low, 0.16 on average, for CECFs. This implies that CECFs are subject to significant *idiosyncratic* (or unique) risks that are related to neither the U.S. nor home market movements.

While CECFs behave more like U.S. securities, they provide U.S. investors with the opportunity to achieve international diversification at home without incurring

EXHIBIT 11.14

Efficient Sets: Country Funds versus Net Assets: 1989.1–1990.12

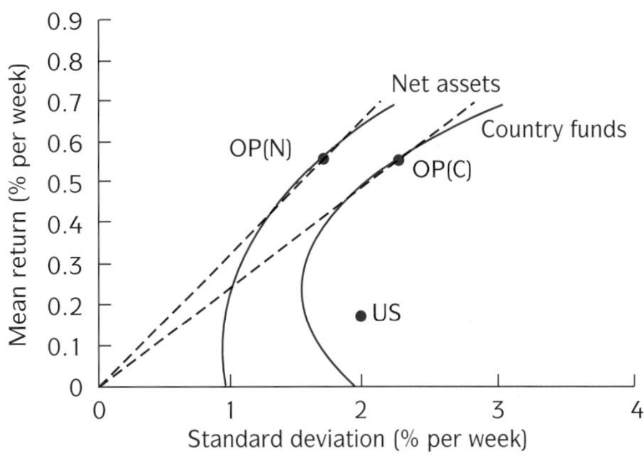

Note: OP(N) and OP(C) denote, respectively, the optimal portfolios comprising net assets and country funds. The efficient sets are illustrated by the dotted lines.

excessive transaction costs. We now estimate the potential gains from international diversification using CECFs. Exhibit 11.13 provides the risk-return characteristics of 15 sample funds, as well as the U.S. stock market index, during the sample period 1989.1–1990.12. It also presents the composition of the optimal international portfolio comprising CECFs and, for comparison purposes, the composition of the corresponding optimal portfolio comprising the NAVs.

The optimal portfolio consisting of CECFs dominates the U.S. index in terms of risk-return efficiency; the Sharpe performance measure is 0.233 for the former and 0.087 for the latter. This point can be seen clearly from Exhibit 11.14, which traces out the efficient sets, separately, for CECFs and NAVs.

The figure shows that the NAVs offer superior diversification opportunities compared to the CECFs. Consequently, those who can invest directly in foreign markets without incurring excessive costs are advised to do so. However, for the majority of investors without such opportunities, CECFs still offer a cost-effective way of diversifying internationally. Lastly, note that country funds from emerging markets receive significant weights in the optimal portfolio of CECFs. Specifically, the weight is 12.71 percent for the Brazil Fund, 7.50 percent for the India Fund, and 24.27 percent for the Mexico Fund. These emerging market funds as a whole receive about a 45 percent weight in the optimal CECF portfolio. This implies that CECFs from emerging markets can play an important role in expanding the investment opportunity set for international investors.

INTERNATIONAL DIVERSIFICATION WITH ADRS

U.S. investors can achieve international diversification at home using American depository receipts (ADRs), as well as country funds. As explained in Chapter 8, ADRs represent receipts for foreign shares held in the U.S. (depository) banks' foreign branches or custodians. Like closed-end country funds, ADRs are traded on U.S. exchanges like domestic American securities. Consequently, U.S. investors can save transaction costs and also benefit from speedy and dependable disclosures, settlements, and custody services. The International Finance in Practice box on page 272, "Live Here, Invest Abroad," describes the virtues of investing via

INTERNATIONAL FINANCE IN PRACTICE

Live Here, Invest Abroad

Global consumers, global investors. Americans' appetite for products from abroad only begins with French champagne, Swiss chocolate and Japanese televisions. American investors are flocking to buy stock in the foreign corporations that make such goods—and not only through the already well-publicized route of mutual funds. They are purchasing shares of individual companies in the form of American depository receipts, or ADRs.

ADRs of about 1,300 foreign firms trade on U.S. stock markets, with one ADR certificate equaling a given number of shares of stock. In 1993, total ADR trading volume on the New York and American exchanges and Nasdaq topped $200 billion, up from $94 billion in 1991 and $41 billion in 1988. With an average of 15 new ADRs a month, the trend shows no signs of topping out.

It's easy to comprehend the enthusiasm. Last year, Merrill Lynch's ADR Composite Index, which tracks 184 ADRs and is the only index of its kind, chalked up a 29.9 percent gain. That was far ahead of the 10.1 percent gain in the Standard & Poor's 500-stock index and just

Half a Dozen Winning ADRs

Of the 184 American depository receipts that trade on major U.S. exchanges, the six best performers over the year ended February 28 are listed below.

Company (Country)	Business	Recent Price	12-Month Price Change
Signet Group (Britain)	U.K./U.S. jewelry stores	$ 9.88	400.0%
Corimon (Venezuela)	Paints, chemicals, juices	15.50	189.4%
Fai Insurances (Australia)	Insurance	4.00	159.2%
Danka Business Sys. (Britain)	U.S./U.K. office equipment stores	43.13	143.6%
WPP Group (Britain)	Marketing/public relations	3.19	118.5%
Philips Electr. (Neth.)	Consumer electronics	27.75	108.4%

USN&WR—Basic data: Merrill Lynch International Quantitative Analysis

ADRs. It is noted that like American investors, British and European investors may achieve international diversification at home using global depository receipts (GDRs), which represent ownership claims on those foreign shares that are listed on the London Stock Exchange.

Recently, a few studies examined the potential benefits of international diversification with ADRs. Officer and Hoffmeister (1987) found that adding ADRs to a domestic portfolio had substantial risk reduction benefits. Including as few as four ADRs in a representative U.S. stock portfolio reduced risk, measured by the standard deviation of returns, by as much as 25 percent without reducing the expected return. They also found that ADRs tend to have very low beta exposure to the U.S. stock market. During the sample period 1973–1983, ADRs were found to have an average U.S. beta of only 0.264.

Wahab and Khandwala (1993) found similar results. They reported that when investors hold an equally weighted portfolio of seven ADRs and the S&P 500, the annualized standard deviation of daily returns drops from 30.2 percent (for a purely domestic portfolio) to 17.5 percent. They also reported that most of the nonsystematic risk of the portfolio is eliminated by adding only seven ADRs to the S&P 500. Adding ADRs beyond seven did not reduce the portfolio risk materially, regardless of portfolio weights.

slightly below the average 30.2 percent return for international stock funds. Some ADRs enjoyed triple-digit returns. From March 1, 1993, to Feb. 28, 1994, for example, the ADR price of the Signet Group, the U.K.'s largest retailer of fine jewelry, surged 400 percent to $9.38.

"U.S. stocks are increasingly pricey and precarious," explains Mark Coler, publisher of the *Global Portfolio* (800-582-9854; $195 for a one-year trial subscription), an ADR newsletter that compiles brokerage reports but doesn't make its own recommendations. "Many foreign shares still have some big gains ahead as a global economic recovery takes hold."

To buy ADRs, you don't have to dial overseas; all it takes is a quick call to a broker. ADRs are issued by the U.S. banks that hold the underlying foreign shares in custody and are sold in U.S. dollars through brokers, just like stocks.

Watch the News

ADRs open the door to a new world, but staying abreast of currency fluctuations and economic and political developments is a must. When Mexico's top presidential candidate was assassinated last week, for example, the ADR price of Teléfonos de México, the national telephone company, dropped by more than 6 percent overnight.

Many foreign firms, moreover, tell shareholders—including those back home—as little as possible. About 70 percent of foreign companies offering ADRs choose not to file financial statements with the Securities and Exchange Commission. Executive pay, lines of business and insider trading thus remain mysteries, and shareholders rarely get prospectuses or quarterly income reports. As a result, these companies' ADRs trade on the "pink sheets" segment of the over-the-counter market, a realm exempt from the rules of the bigger exchanges.

Big Feet

Prices can be hard to track in that thinly traded part of the market, but that doesn't mean the companies are fly-by-nights or start-ups. Most pink-sheeted ADRs are bigfoot entities like Nestlé, Mitsubishi and Deutsche Bank that simply reject the arduous process of conforming to U.S. standards.

For investors who want to learn more, Chicago-based Morningstar Inc., a publisher of mutual fund reports, plans a late April start-up, *Morningstar American Depository Receipts* (800-876-5005; biweekly; $35 for a three-month trial subscription). The report will probe 700 ADRs, including about 300 pink sheeters and all of the others, with up to 10 years of data, business summaries and market snapshots, as well as a list of the five mutual funds owning the greatest number of a company's shares.

Investors hungry for foreign fare sans stomachache can dine at foreign stock mutual funds. "Overseas funds probably won't see quite as much action this year, but the good ones are still likely to outperform the U.S. market," says Michael Stolper, publisher of the *Mutual Fund Monthly* newsletter (800-426-6502; $49 annually). Two that Stolper recommends are GAM International, (800) 426-4685, and Janus Worldwide, (800) 525-3713. GAM, a nine-year-old fund, has had an average annual return of 25.6 percent. Janus Worldwide had a 1993 return of 28.4 percent—champagne and chocolate performance by any measure.

Copyright, April 4, 1994, *U.S. News & World Report.*

Considering that the majority of ADRs are from such developed countries as Australia, Japan, and the United Kingdom, U.S. investors have a limited opportunity to diversify into emerging markets using ADRs. However, in a few emerging markets like Mexico, investors can choose from several ADRs. In this situation, investors should consider the relative advantages and disadvantages of ADRs and CECFs as a means of international diversification. Compared with ADRs, CECFs are likely to provide more complete diversification. As shown previously, however, the potential gains from investing in them tend to be reduced by premiums/discounts.

INTERNATIONAL DIVERSIFICATION WITH WEBS

In April 1996, the American Stock Exchange (AMEX) introduced a class of securities called **World Equity Benchmark Shares (WEBS).** In essence, WEBS are exchange-traded open-end country funds that are designed to closely track foreign stock market indexes. Currently, there are 17 WEBS tracking the Morgan Stanley Capital International (MSCI) indexes for the following individual countries: Australia, Austria, Belgium, Canada, France, Germany, Hong Kong, Italy, Japan,

Malaysia, Mexico, the Netherlands, Singapore, Spain, Sweden, Switzerland, and the United Kingdom. The AMEX had previously introduced a similar security for the U.S. market, Standard & Poor's Depository Receipts (SPDRs) known as "spiders," that is designed to track the S&P 500 Index. Using *index shares* like WEBS and spiders, investors can trade a whole stock market index as if it were a single stock. Being open-end funds, WEBS trade at prices that are very close to their net asset values.

A recent study by Khorana, Nelling, and Trester (1998) found that WEBS indeed track the underlying MSCI country indexes very closely. For example, the average correlation of daily returns between WEBS and the underlying country indexes is 0.97. They also found that the average correlation of WEBS with the S&P 500 Index is quite low, 0.22, which makes WEBS an excellent tool for international risk diversification. For those investors who desire international equity exposure, WEBS may well serve as a major alternative to such traditional tools as international mutual funds, ADRs, and closed-end country funds.

WHY HOME BIAS IN PORTFOLIO HOLDINGS?

As previously documented, investors can potentially benefit a great deal from international diversification. The actual portfolios that investors hold, however, are quite different from those predicted by the theory of international portfolio investment. Recently, various researchers, such as French and Porteba (1991), Cooper and Kaplanis (1994), Tesar and Werner (1993), and Glassman and Riddick (1993), documented the extent to which portfolio investments are concentrated in domestic equities.

Exhibit 11.15, which is adopted from Cooper and Kaplanis (1994), shows the extent of **home bias in portfolio holdings**. U.S. investors, for instance, invested 98 percent of their funds in domestic equities as of 1987 when the U.S. stock market accounted for only 36.4 percent of the world market capitalization value. Relatively speaking, French investors seem to invest more internationally—they put 35.6 percent of their funds in foreign equities and 64.4 percent in domestic equities. Considering, however, that the French share in the world market value is only 2.6 percent, French investors also display a striking degree of home bias in their portfolio holdings.

EXHIBIT 11.15

The Home Bias in Equity Portfolios: December 1987

Country	Share in the World Market Value (%)	Proportion of Domestic Equities in the Portfolio (%)
France	2.6	64.4
Germany	3.2	75.4
Italy	1.9	91.0
Japan	43.7	86.7
Spain	1.1	94.2
Sweden	0.8	100.0
United Kingdom	10.3	78.5
United States	36.4	98.0
	Total = 100.0	

Source: Ian Cooper and Evi Kaplanis, "Home Bias in Equity Portfolios, Inflation Hedging, and International Capital Market Equilibrium," *Review of Financial Studies* 7 (1994) pp. 45–60. Reprinted by permission of Oxford University Press.

This home bias in actual portfolio holdings obviously runs counter to the strand of literature, including Grubel (1968), Levy and Sarnat (1970), Solnik (1974), Lessard (1976), and Eun and Resnick (1988), that collectively established a strong case for international diversification. This points to the following possibilities. First, domestic securities may provide investors with certain extra services, such as hedging against domestic inflation, that foreign securities do not. Second, there may be barriers, formal or informal, to investing in foreign securities that keep investors from realizing gains from international diversification. In what follows, we are going to examine possible reasons for the home bias in portfolio holdings.[16]

First, consider the possibility that investors face country-specific inflation risk due to the violations of purchasing power parity and that domestic equities may provide a hedging service against domestic inflation risk. In this case, investors who would like to hedge domestic inflation risk may allocate a disproportionate share of their investment funds to domestic equities, resulting in home bias. This, however, is not a likely scenario. Those investors who are averse to inflation risk are likely to invest in domestic risk-free bonds rather than domestic equities, as the latter tends to be a poor hedge against inflation.[17] In addition, a study by Cooper and Kaplanis (1994) rules out inflation hedging as a primary cause for home bias.

Second, the observed home bias may reflect institutional and legal restrictions on foreign investments. For example, many countries restrict foreigners' ownership share of domestic firms. In Finland, foreigners could own at most 30 percent of the shares outstanding of any Finnish firm. In Korea, foreigners' ownership proportion was restricted to 20 percent of any Korean firm. As a result, foreigners had to pay premiums for local shares, which may reduce the gains from investing in those restricted markets. At the same time, some institutional investors may not invest more than a certain fraction of their funds overseas under the so-called *prudent man rule*. For example, Japanese insurance companies and Spanish pension funds may invest at most 30 percent of their funds in foreign securities. These inflow and outflow restrictions may contribute to the home bias in actual portfolio holdings.

Third, extra taxes and transaction/information costs for foreign securities can inhibit cross-border investments, giving rise to home-bias. Investors often have to pay withholding taxes on dividends from foreign securities for which they may or may not receive tax credits in their home country. Transaction costs can be higher for foreign securities partly because many foreign markets are relatively thin and illiquid and partly because investment in foreign securities often involves transactions in foreign exchange markets. What's more, as argued by Merton (1987), investors tend not to hold securities with which they do not feel familiar. To the extent that investors feel familiar with domestic securities, but not with foreign securities, they are going to allocate funds to domestic, but not to foreign, securities. It is even possible that some investors may not be fully aware of the potential gains from international investments. The International Finance in Practice box on page 276, "Stay-at-Home Shareholders," further discusses the home-bias phenomenon.

The observed home bias in asset holdings is likely to reflect a combination of some of the factors mentioned above. Considering the ongoing integration of international financial markets, coupled with the active financial innovations introducing new financial products such as country funds and international mutual funds, home bias may be substantially mitigated in the near future.

INTERNATIONAL FINANCE IN PRACTICE

Stay-at-Home Shareholders

Pick up any investment newsletter these days and you will read about the joys of international investing. European investors, the story goes, should venture overseas before recession drags down continental bourses; Americans should flee before Wall Street's bubble bursts; all rich-country investors should rush into emerging markets, where shares are cheap after a dismal 1995. Many will no doubt be lured by these promises of easy pickings. But the case for diversifying has little to do with market fashion.

Despite the much-vaunted integration of the global economy, the things that can send a country's stockmarket reeling are still often unique to its own economy. By buying stakes in each other's economies, the world's investors should be able to pool their risks, thereby lowering them without sacrificing returns. One way to measure these potential gains is to compare two imaginary portfolios: a giant global mutual fund (unit trust) and one that invests solely in domestic securities. Using past stock-market returns, and—crucially—adjusting for risk, one can gauge how much better off a global investor would be than a parochial one.

The chart shows such a comparison for a British investor. It compares the combinations of risks and returns that could have been attained using British assets in 1970–95 with those on investments in the Group of Seven countries as a whole. For any given level of risk, the punter could have earned more from an international portfolio.

Karen Lewis, an economist at the University of Pennsylvania's Wharton business school, has made similar calculations for America.* She reckons that, on various

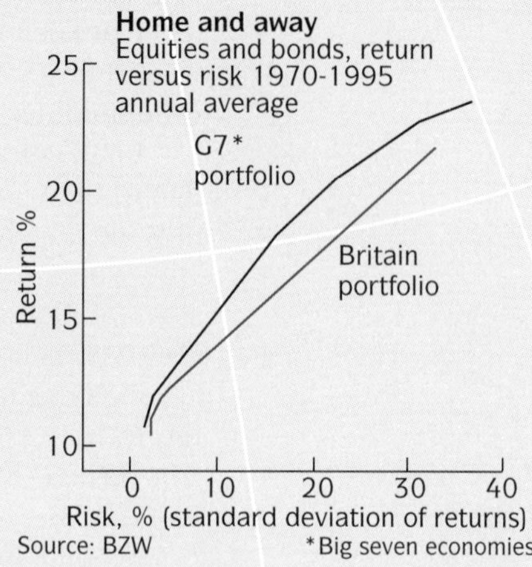

Source: BZW *Big seven economies

assumptions about how people feel about risk and about consuming today instead of tomorrow, an American who invested globally in 1969–93 would have been between 10% and 50% better off than one who stayed at home. Her estimates, like the British example, are based only on the gains from investing in other G7 countries. A portfolio that also included emerging markets, which are far less correlated with rich ones than the rich ones are with each other, should offer even bigger rewards.

Economists have been aware of these opportunities for decades. Yet investors have been slow to cash in. Studies have found that, as recently as the early 1990s, Americans kept more than 90% of their assets at home,

SUMMARY

This chapter discusses the gains from international portfolio diversification, which has emerged as a major form of cross-border investment in the 1980s, rivaling foreign direct investment by firms.

1. International portfolio investment (IPI) has been growing rapidly in recent years due to (a) the deregulation of financial markets, and (b) the introduction of such investment vehicles as international mutual funds, country funds, and internationally cross-listed stocks, which allow investors to achieve international diversification without incurring excessive costs.
2. Investors diversify to reduce risk; the extent to which the risk is reduced by diversification depends on the covariances among individual securities comprising the portfolio. Since security returns tend to covary much less across countries than within a country, investors can reduce portfolio risk more by diversifying internationally than purely domestically.

even though their securities markets accounted for less than half of the world's capitalisation.

The bias towards domestic investment is even more striking when you consider human capital. Skills constitute a big share of most people's wealth, and their value is tied to the domestic economy's fortunes. A dedicated diversifier should therefore bet against his own country's equities, not invest in them.

Given these reasons to invest abroad, why are investors so fond of native shares? Economists have plenty of theories. For instance, investors may shun foreign shares because of cost: investing in many different markets can be expensive, especially after allowing for securities taxes and other capital controls.

But this explanation hardly solves the puzzle. Hurdles such as these have all been falling for years, yet the home-country bias has persisted. Between 1980 and 1990, for example, the share of rich countries' pension assets invested abroad barely budged. (Britain, however, has been an exception: the foreign share of its pension funds' investments went from about a tenth to a quarter during the decade.) Moreover, studies have found that, at least in rich countries, foreigners tend to turn over their shares even more often than domestic investors, casting doubt on the theory that they are deterred by excessive trading costs.

The Grass Is Greener

In a recent paper, Jun-Koo Kang and Rene Stultz, economists at the University of California-Riverside and Ohio State University, respectively, argue that investing overseas can be expensive even if explicit transaction costs are low.[†] Foreign investors may have less information than domestic ones about certain kinds of firms,—say, smaller ones. Knowing this, investors will shun shares in those companies. To test the idea, the economists looked at foreign equity investments in Japan between 1975 and 1991. They found that foreign investors were much more likely than domestic ones to prefer firms that, for example, were big and had little debt.

The study shows that, once foreigners decide to shun part of a country's market, they do best by also shying away from the country as a whole. Moreover, the best way to learn about foreign markets is probably to set up networks there to gather information and trade shares. This involves large fixed costs—which may explain why investors stay out of some countries altogether, but do a lot of trading in any they enter. Now that rich-country institutional investors have begun to incur these costs by putting down global roots, international equity investing should take off.

Besides these less tangible barriers, explicit barriers to foreign capital may still play a role in keeping investors out of some emerging markets. In another new paper, Ms. Lewis finds that the combined effect of capital controls and (for complicated reasons) non-tradable goods can go a long way towards explaining why investors shun some countries.[**]

It appears, therefore, that foreign investment has been hampered, at least until recently, by many of the factors that common sense would suggest: capital controls, opaque markets, and the high cost for fund managers of setting up overseas. In the past few years, these barriers have been falling—especially in emerging markets, where the gains from diversifying are biggest. So investors should soon start gobbling up foreign shares in record numbers. If they do not, economists may have to diversify into other theories.

*"Consumption, Stock Returns, and the Gains from International Risk-Sharing." NBER Working Paper No. 5410, January 1996.

[†]"Why Is There a Home Bias? An Analysis of Foreign Portfolio Equity Ownership in Japan." Unpublished, February 1996.

**"What Can Explain the Apparent Lack of International Consumption Risk Sharing?" Forthcoming in *Journal of Political Economy*, April 1996.

Source: *The Economist*, February 17, 1996, p. 75. © 1996 The Economist Newspaper Group, Inc.

3. In a full-fledged risk-return analysis, investors can gain from international diversification in terms of "extra" returns at the "domestic-equivalent" risk level. Empirical evidence indicates that regardless of domicile and the numeraire currency used to measure returns, investors can capture extra returns when they hold their optimal international portfolios.
4. Foreign exchange rate uncertainty contributes to the risk of foreign investment through its own volatility as well as through its covariance with local market returns. Generally speaking, exchange rates are substantially more volatile than bond market returns but less so than stock market returns. This suggests that investors can enhance their gains from international diversification, especially in the case of bond investment, when they hedge exchange risk using, say, forward contracts.
5. U.S.-based international mutual funds that investors actually held did provide investors with an effective global risk diversification. In addition, the majority of

them outperformed the U.S. stock market index in terms of the Sharpe performance measure. Closed-end country funds (CECFs) also provided U.S. investors with an opportunity to achieve international diversification at home. CECFs, however, were found to behave more like U.S. securities in comparison with their underlying net asset values (NAVs).

6. Despite sizable potential gains from international diversification, investors allocate a disproportionate share of their funds to domestic securities, displaying so-called home bias. Home bias is likely to reflect imperfections in the international financial markets such as excessive transaction/information costs, discriminatory taxes for foreigners, and legal/institutional barriers to international investments.

KEY WORDS

closed-end country fund (CECF), 268
gains from international diversification, 256
home bias in portfolio holdings, 274
international correlation structure, 256
optimal international portfolios, 257
portfolio risk diversification, 255
Sharpe performance measure (SHP), 259
systematic risk, 256
world beta, 257
World Equity Benchmark Shares (WEBS), 273

QUESTIONS

1. What factors are responsible for the recent surge in international portfolio investment?
2. Security returns are found to be less correlated across countries than within a country. Why can this be?
3. Explain the concept of the world beta of a security.
4. Explain the concept of the Sharpe performance measure.
5. Explain how exchange rate fluctuations affect the return from a foreign market, measured in dollar terms. Discuss the empirical evidence on the effect of exchange rate uncertainty on the risk of foreign investment.
6. Would exchange rate changes always increase the risk of foreign investment? Discuss the condition under which exchange rate changes may actually reduce the risk of foreign investment.
7. Evaluate a home country's multinational corporations as a tool for international diversification.
8. Discuss the advantages and disadvantages of closed-end country funds (CECFs) relative to American depository receipts (ADRs) as a means of international diversification.
9. Why do you think closed-end country funds often trade at a premium or discount?
10. Why do investors invest the lion's share of their funds in domestic securities?
11. What are the advantages of investing via international mutual funds?
12. Discuss how the advent of the euro would affect international diversification strategies.

PROBLEMS

1. Suppose you are a euro-based investor who just sold Microsoft shares that you had bought six months ago. You had invested 10,000 euros to buy Microsoft shares for $120 per share; the exchange rate was $1.15 per euro. You sold the

stock for $135 per share and converted the dollar proceeds into euro at the exchange rate of $1.06 per euro. First, determine the profit from this investment in euro terms. Second, compute the rate of return on your investment in euro terms. How much of the return is due to the exchange rate movement?

2. Mr. James K. Silber, an avid international investor, just sold a share of Rhone-Poulenc, a French firm, for FF50. The share was bought for FF42 a year ago. The exchange rate is FF5.80 per U.S. dollar now and was FF6.65 per dollar a year ago. Mr. Silber received FF4 as a cash dividend immediately before the share was sold. Compute the rate of return on this investment in terms of U.S. dollars.

3. In the above problem, suppose that Mr. Silber sold FF42, his principal investment amount, forward at the forward exchange rate of FF6.15 per dollar. How would this affect the dollar rate of return on this French stock investment? In hindsight, should Mr. Silber have sold the French franc amount forward or not? Why or why not?

4. Japan Life Insurance Company invested $10,000,000 in pure-discount U.S. bonds in May 1995 when the exchange rate was 80 yen per dollar. The company liquidated the investment one year later for $10,650,000. The exchange rate turned out to be 110 yen per dollar at the time of liquidation. What rate of return did Japan Life realize on this investment in yen terms?

5. At the start of 1996, the annual interest rate was 6 percent in the United States and 2.8 percent in Japan. The exchange rate was 95 yen per dollar at the time. Mr. Jorus, who is the manager of a Bermuda-based hedge fund, thought that the substantial interest advantage associated with investing in the United States relative to investing in Japan was not likely to be offset by the decline of the dollar against the yen. He thus concluded that it might be a good idea to borrow in Japan and invest in the United States. At the start of 1996, in fact, he borrowed ¥1,000 million for one year and invested in the United States. At the end of 1996, the exchange rate became 105 yen per dollar. How much profit did Mr. Jorus make in dollar terms?

6. From Exhibit 11.3 we obtain the following data in dollar terms:

Stock Market	Return (Mean)	Risk (SD)
United States	1.33% per month	4.56%
United Kingdom	1.52% per month	6.47%

The correlation coefficient between the two markets is 0.57. Suppose that you invest equally, that is, 50 percent in each of the two markets. Determine the expected return and standard deviation risk of the resulting international portfolio.[18]

7. Suppose you are interested in investing in the stock markets of seven countries—i.e., Canada, France, Germany, Japan, Switzerland, the United Kingdom, and the United States—the same seven countries that appear in Exhibit 11.9. Specifically, you would like to solve for the optimal (tangency) portfolio comprising the above seven stock markets. In solving the optimal portfolio, use the input data (i.e., correlation coefficients, means, and standard deviations) provided in Exhibit 11.4. The risk-free interest rate is assumed to be 0.5% per month and you can take a short position in any stock market. What are the optimal weights for each of the seven stock markets? This problem can be solved using the EFFPORT.XLS spreadsheet.

MINI CASE

Solving for the Optimal International Portfolio

Suppose you are a financial adviser and your client, who is currently investing only in the U.S. stock market, is considering diversifying into the U.K. stock market. At the moment, there are neither particular barriers nor restrictions on investing in the U.K. stock market. Your client would like to know what kind of benefits can be expected from doing so. Using the data provided in problem 6, solve the following problems:

1. Graphically illustrate various combinations of portfolio risk and return that can be generated by investing in the U.S. and U.K. stock markets with different proportions. Two extreme proportions are (a) investing 100 percent in the United States with no position in the U.K. market, and (b) investing 100 percent in the U.K. market with no position in the U.S. market.
2. Solve for the optimal international portfolio comprising the U.S. and U.K. markets. Assume that the monthly risk-free interest rate is 0.5 percent and that investors can take a short (negative) position in either market.
3. What is the extra return that U.S. investors can expect to capture at the U.S.-equivalent risk level? Also trace out the efficient set. Appendix 11.B provides an example.

ENDNOTES

1. Under the investment dollar premium system, U.K. residents had to pay a premium over the prevailing commercial exchange rate when they bought foreign currencies to invest in foreign securities. Since the premium increased the cost of cross-border portfolio investments, U.K. investors were discouraged from investing overseas.
2. In Solnik's study, international portfolios were fully hedged against exchange risk and, as a result, both U.S. and Swiss investors faced the same risk in international portfolios, which was essentially determined by local stock market risks. The Solnik study also compared international diversification across countries versus across industries and found the former to be a superior strategy.
3. All the statistics in Exhibit 11.4 were computed using returns to the stock market indexes rather than individual stocks.
4. Formally, the world beta is defined as $\beta_i = \sigma_{iW}/\sigma_W^2$, where σ_{iW} is the covariance between returns to the ith market and the world market index, and σ_W^2 is the variance of the world market return. If, for example, the world beta of a market is 1.2, it means that as the world market moves up and down by 1 percent, the market goes up and down by 1.2%.
5. The optimal international portfolio can be solved by maximizing the Sharpe ratio, i.e., SHP = $[E(R_p) - R_f]/\sigma_p$, with respect to the portfolio weights. Refer to the Appendix 11B for a detailed discussion.
6. In analyzing the gains from international investments, it was implicitly assumed that investors fully bear exchange risk. As will be discussed later, investors can hedge exchange risk using, say, forward contracts, therefore enhancing the gains. It is also pointed out that the preceding analyses are strictly "ex-post" in the sense that the risk-return characteristics of securities are assumed to be known to investors. In reality, of course, investors will have to estimate these characteristics, and estimation errors may lead to an inefficient allocation of funds.
7. For further discussion of exchange risk hedging, readers are referred to Appendix 11A.
8. The U.S. beta measures the sensitivity of the fund returns to the U.S. stock market returns. The coefficient of determination (R^2) measures the fraction of the variance of fund returns that can be explained by the U.S. market returns.
9. See, for example, Sharpe (1966), pp. 127–28.

10. This result is consistent with Jacquillat and Solnik's study (1978), showing that multinational corporations of various countries have very low exposure (beta) to foreign stock market indexes.
11. The capital market line (CML) is the straight line obtained by connecting the risk-free interest rate and the market portfolio.
12. The capital asset pricing model (CAPM) suggests that if the world market portfolio is indeed mean-variance efficient, then the expected return on a portfolio will be determined by its world beta. This, in turn, implies that if investors hold parochial portfolios that are less than fully diversified globally, they are bearing some diversifiable risk for which there will be no compensation in terms of extra returns. Under this situation it would be optimal for investors to hold the world market portfolio, proxied by a world index fund, together with the risk-free asset, to achieve the desired combination of risk and return.
13. A recent study by Bonser-Neal, Brauer, Neal, and Wheatley (1990) suggests that the country fund premium/discount reflects the barriers to direct portfolio investment in the home countries of the funds. They found that whenever these barriers were lowered, the fund premium declined.
14. The returns to the home market, R_{HM}, employed in Equation 11.6 is, in fact, the "residual" obtained from regressing the home market returns on the U.S. market returns. U.S. investors who wish to diversify risk internationally will value exposure to the "pure" (or, orthogonal) foreign market risk, i.e., β_{HM}.
15. This finding is consistent with the Bailey and Lim (1992) study showing that CECFs act more like U.S. securities than foreign stock market indexes.
16. For a survey of this issue, readers are referred to Uppal (1992).
17. Fama and Schwert (1975) showed that common stocks are a perverse hedge against domestic inflation in that returns to common stocks are significantly negatively correlated with the inflation rate. In comparison, bond returns are positively correlated with the inflation rate.
18. The mean return on the portfolio is simply the weighted average of the returns on the individual securities that are included in the portfolio. The portfolio variance, on the other hand, can be computed using the following formula:

    $$\text{Var}(R_p) = \Sigma_i \Sigma_j x_i x_j \sigma_{ij}$$

    where x_i represents an investment weight for the ith security, and σ_{ij} denotes the variances and covariances among individual securities. In the case where the portfolio is comprised of two securities, its variance is computed as follows:

    $$\text{Var}(R_p) = x_1^2\sigma_1^2 + x_2^2\sigma_2^2 + 2x_1x_2\sigma_{12}$$

    The standard deviation, of course, is the square root of the variance. It is also noted that the covariance σ_{ij} is related to the correlation coefficient ρ_{ij} via $\sigma_{ij} = \rho_{ij}\sigma_i\sigma_j$, where σ_i is the standard deviation of returns on the ith security.

WEB RESOURCES

www.adr.com/

This Web site managed by J.P. Morgan & Co., Inc., is a comprehensive source of information on American depository receipts.

wallstreeter.com/adrframe.htm

Provides an elaborate explanation of American Depository Receipts (ADRs) and a detailed countrywise list of ADRs traded on U.S. exchanges.

websontheweb.com/enhanced/index.html

Provides details of the World Equity Benchmark Shares (WEBS) traded on the American Stock Exchange.

www.riskview.com/html-inf/home2.html

Provides global equity data and risk analysis, including historical returns and volatilities, forecast volatilities and correlations, Value at Risk (VaR), etc.

www.sbam.com/framasia.htm

Provides details of Salomon Brothers Asia Growth Fund.

www.anakonda.com/Hedgefunds.htm

Provides information on various aspects of domestic and offshore hedge funds.

REFERENCES AND SUGGESTED READINGS

Adler, Michael, and Bernard Dumas. "International Portfolio Choice and Corporation Finance: A Synthesis." *Journal of Finance* 38 (1983), pp. 925–84.

Bailey, Warren, and J. Lim. "Evaluating the Diversification Benefits of the New Country Funds." *Journal of Portfolio Management* 18 (1992), pp. 74–80.

Bonser-Neal, C., G. Brauer, R. Neal, and S. Wheatley. "International Investment Restriction and Closed-End Country Fund Prices." *Journal of Finance* 45 (1990), pp. 523–47.

Chuppe, T., H. Haworth, and M. Watkins. "Global Finance: Causes, Consequences and Prospects for the Future." *Global Finance Journal* 1 (1989), pp. 1–20.

Cooper, Ian, and Evi Kaplanis. "Home Bias in Equity Portfolios, Inflation Hedging, and International Capital Market Equilibrium," *Review of Financial Studies* 7 (1994), pp. 45–60.

Cumby, R., and J. Glen. "Evaluating the Performance of International Mutual Funds." *Journal of Finance* 45 (1990), pp. 497–521.

Errunza, Vihang, Ked Hogan, and Mao-Wei Hung. "Can the Gains from International Diversification Be Achieved without Trading Abroad?" Forthcoming in *Journal of Finance* (1999).

Eun, Cheol, and Bruce Resnick. "Exchange Rate Uncertainty, Forward Contracts and International Portfolio Selection." *Journal of Finance* 43 (1988), pp. 197–215.

Eun, Cheol, and Bruce Resnick. "International Diversification of Investment Portfolios: U.S. and Japanese Perspectives." *Management Science* 40 (1994), pp. 140–61.

Eun, Cheol, and Bruce Resnick. "International Equity Investments with Selective Hedging Strategies." *Journal of International Financial Markets, Institutions and Money* 7 (1997), pp. 21–42.

Eun, Cheol, Richard Kolodny, and Bruce Resnick. "Performance of U.S.-Based International Mutual Funds." *Journal of Portfolio Management* 17 (1991), pp. 88–94.

Fama, Eugene, and W. G. Schwert. "Asset Returns and Inflation." *Journal of Financial Economics* 5 (1975), pp. 115–46.

French, K., and J. Poterba. "Investor Diversification and International Equity Markets." *American Economic Review* 81 (1991), pp. 222–26.

Glassman, Debra, and Leigh Riddick. "Why Empirical Portfolio Models Fail: Evidence That Model Misspecification Creates Home Asset Bias," unpublished manuscript, 1993.

Grubel, H. G. "Internationally Diversified Portfolios." *American Economic Review* 58 (1968), pp. 1299–1314.

Jacquillat, B., and B. Solnik. "Multinationals Are Poor Tools for Diversification." *Journal of Portfolio Management* 4 (1978), pp. 8–12.

Jorion, Philippe. "Asset Allocation with Hedged and Unhedged Foreign Stocks and Bonds." *Journal of Portfolio Management* 15 (Summer 1989), pp. 49–54.

Larsen, Glen, Jr., and Bruce Resnick. "The Optimal Construction of Internationally Diversified Equity Portfolios Hedged Against Exchange Rate Uncertainty." Forthcoming in *European Financial Management.*

Lessard, D. "World, Country and Industry Relationship in Equity Returns: Implications for Risk Reduction through International Diversification." *Financial Analyst Journal* 32 (1976), pp. 22–28.

Longin, Francois, and Bruneo Solnik. "Is the Correlation in International Equity Returns Constant?: 1960–1990." *Journal of International Money and Finance* 14 (1995), pp. 3–26.

Merton, R. "A Simple Model of Capital Market Equilibrium with Incomplete Information." *Journal of Finance* 42 (1987), pp. 483–510.

Officer, Dennis, and Ronald Hoffmeister. "ADRs: A Substitute for the Real Thing?" *Journal of Portfolio Management* (Winter, 1987), pp. 61–65.

Roll, Richard. "The International Crash of 1987." *Financial Analyst Journal* 44, (1988), pp. 19–35.

Sener, T. "Objectives of Hedging and Optimal Hedge Ratios: U.S. vs. Japanese Investors." *Journal of Multinational Financial Management* 8 (1998), pp. 137–53.

Sharpe, W. "Mutual Fund Performance." *Journal of Business*, A Supplement, No. 1, Part 2 (1966), pp. 119–38.

Solnik, Bruno. "Why Not Diversify Internationally?" *Financial Analyst Journal* 20 (1974), pp. 48–54.

Tesar, L., and I. Werner. "Home Bias and High Turnover," unpublished manuscript, 1993.

Uppal, Raman. "The Economic Determinants of the Home Country Bias in Investors' Portfolios: A Survey." *Journal of International Financial Management and Accounting* 4 (1992), pp. 171–89.

Wahab, Mahmood, and Amit Khandwala. "Why Not Diversify Internationally with ADRs?" *Journal of Portfolio Management* (Winter 1993), pp. 75–82.

APPENDIX 11A

International Investment with Exchange Risk Hedging

Consider a simple exchange risk hedging strategy in which the U.S. (or the dollar-based) investor sells the expected foreign currency proceeds forward. In dollar terms, it amounts to exchanging the "uncertain" dollar return, $(1 + \bar{R}_i)(1 + e_i) - 1$, for the "certain" dollar return, $(1 + \bar{R}_i)(1 + f_i) - 1$, where $\bar{R}_i$ is the expected rate of return on the ith foreign market, whether bond or stock, in terms of the foreign currency, and f_i $(= (F - S)/S)$ is the forward exchange premium. As defined previously, e_i denotes the rate of change of the spot exchange rate.

Although the expected foreign investment proceeds will be converted into U.S. dollars at the known forward exchange rate under this strategy, the unexpected foreign investment proceeds will have to be converted into U.S. dollars at the uncertain future spot exchange rate. The dollar rate of return under the hedging (H) strategy is thus given by

$$\begin{aligned} R_{i\$\mathrm{H}} &= [1 + \bar{R}_i](1 + f_i) + [R_i + \bar{R}_i](1 + e_i) - 1 \\ &= R_i + f_i + R_i e_i + \bar{R}_i(f_i - e_i) \end{aligned} \tag{11A.1}$$

Since the third and fourth terms of the above equation are likely to be small in magnitude, the following approximation can be made:

$$R_{i\$\mathrm{H}} \approx R_i + f_i \tag{11A.2}$$

The above approximation result indicates that the effect of uncertain exchange rates on the dollar return from foreign investment can be largely removed by entering into a forward exchange contract.

Moreover, the empirical results presented in Exhibit 11.8 generally suggests that

$$\mathrm{Var}(R_{i\$\mathrm{H}}) < \mathrm{Var}(R_{i\$}), \text{ and}$$
$$\mathrm{Cov}(R_{i\$\mathrm{H}}, R_{j\$\mathrm{H}}) < \mathrm{Cov}(R_{i\$}, R_{j\$})$$

given that f_i is a constant. To the extent that the forward exchange premium is roughly an unbiased predictor of the future exchange rate change, that is, f_i is about equal to e_i as discussed in Chapter 5, hedging offers a potential of reducing risk without adversely affecting return. As mentioned in the text, the existing empirical evidence indicates that investors can indeed enhance the gains from international diversification by hedging exchange risk.

APPENDIX 11B

Solving for the Optimal Portfolio

Here we explain how to solve for the optimal portfolio of risky securities when there exists a risk-free asset paying a certain risk-free interest rate, R_f. Once we assume that investors prefer more wealth to less and are averse to risk, we can solve for the "optimal" portfolio by maximizing the ratio (θ) of the excess portfolio return to the standard deviation risk. In other words,

$$\text{Max } \theta = [\bar{R}_p - R_f]/\sigma_p \tag{11B.1}$$

where $\bar{R}_p$ is the expected rate of return on the portfolio and σ_p is the standard deviation of the portfolio returns.

The expected portfolio return, $\bar{R}_p$, is just the weighted average of the expected returns to individual assets, $\bar{R}_i$, included in the portfolio, that is,

$$\bar{R}_p = \Sigma_i x_i \bar{R}_i \tag{11B.2}$$

where x_i denotes a fraction of wealth invested in the ith individual asset; the sum of fractions should add up to one, that is, $\Sigma_i x_i = 1$. The portfolio risk, σ_p, on the other hand, is related to the variances and covariances of individual asset returns as follows:

$$\sigma_p = [\Sigma_i \Sigma_j x_i x_j \sigma_{ij}]^{1/2} \tag{11B.3}$$

where σ_{ij} denotes the covariance of returns to the ith and jth assets. What's inside the bracket is the variance of portfolio return.

Now let us consider a simple case where the portfolio includes only two risky assets, A and B. In this case, the risk and return of the portfolio will be determined as follows:

$$\bar{R}_p = x_A \bar{R}_A + x_B \bar{R}_B \tag{11B.4}$$

$$\sigma_p = [x_A^2 \sigma_A^2 + x_B^2 \sigma_B^2 + 2x_A x_B \sigma_{AB}]^{1/2} \tag{11B.5}$$

Suppose we now want to solve for the optimal portfolio using the two assets. We then first substitute Equations 11B.4 and 11B.5 in Equation 11B.1 and maximize θ with respect to the portfolio weights x's to obtain the following solution:

$$x_A = \frac{[\bar{R}_A - R_f]\sigma_B^2 - [\bar{R}_B - R_f]\sigma_{AB}}{[\bar{R}_A - R_f]\sigma_B^2 + [\bar{R}_B - R_f]\sigma_A^2 - [\bar{R}_A - R_f + \bar{R}_B - R_f]\sigma_{AB}}$$

$$x_B = 1 - x_A \tag{11B.6}$$

EXAMPLE Suppose we are trying to construct the optimal international portfolio using the U.S. (US) and Japanese (JP) stock market indexes. From Exhibit 11.4 we obtain the following data (in percentage per month) for the two stock markets:

$$\bar{R}_{US} = 1.33;\ \sigma_{US}^2 = 20.79$$
$$\bar{R}_{JP} = 1.47;\ \sigma_{JP}^2 = 53.44$$
$$\sigma_{US,JP} = \sigma_{US}\sigma_{JP}\rho_{US,JP} = (4.56)(7.31)(0.24) = 8.0$$

Assuming the monthly risk-free rate is zero, we can substitute the given data into Equation 11B.6 to obtain

$$x_{US} = \frac{(1.33)(53.44) - (1.47)(8)}{(1.33)(53.44) + (1.47)(20.79) - (1.33 + 1.47)(8)}$$
$$= .7486$$
$$x_{JP} = 1 - x_{US} = 1 - .7486 = .2514$$

The optimal international portfolio thus comprises 74.86 percent in the U.S. market and 25.14 percent in the Japanese market. The expected return and risk of the optimal portfolio can be computed as follows:

$$\bar{R}_{OP} = (.7486)(1.33\%) + (.2514)(1.47\%) = 1.37\%$$
$$\sigma_{OP} = [(.7486)^2\,(20.79) + (.2514)^2\,(53.44) + 2(.7486)(.2514)(8)]^{1/2}$$
$$= 4.25\%$$

The Sharpe performance measure of the optimal international portfolio is .322 (= 1.37/4.25), which is compared with the Sharpe measure of .292 for the U.S. market. One can thus compute the extra return from holding the optimal international portfolio at the U.S. domestic-equivalent risk level as follows:

$$\Delta R_{US} = (\Delta \text{SHP})(\ \sigma_{US}) = (.322 - .292)(4.56) = .137\%$$

or 1.64 percent per year.

PART THREE

12. Management of Economic Exposure

13. Management of Transaction Exposure

14. Management of Translation Exposure

Foreign Exchange Exposure and Management

Part three is composed of three chapters covering the topics of economic, transaction, and translation exposure management, respectively.

Chapter 12 covers economic exposure, that is, the extent to which the value of the firm will be affected by unexpected changes in exchange rates. The chapter provides a way to measure economic exposure, discusses its determinants, and presents methods for managing and hedging economic exposure.

Chapter 13 covers the management of transaction exposure that arises from contractual obligations denominated in a foreign currency. Several methods for hedging this exposure are compared and contrasted. The chapter also includes a discussion of why a MNC should hedge, a debatable subject in the minds of both academics and practitioners.

Chapter 14 covers translation exposure or, as it is sometimes called, accounting exposure. Translation exposure refers to the effect that an unanticipated change in exchange rates will have on the consolidated financial reports of a MNC. The chapter discusses, compares, and contrasts the various methods for translating financial statements denominated in foreign currencies, and includes a discussion of managing translation exposure using funds adjustment and the pros and cons of using balance sheet and derivatives hedges.

CHAPTER TWELVE

Management of Economic Exposure

CHAPTER OUTLINE

As business becomes increasingly global, more and more firms find it necessary to pay careful attention to foreign exchange exposure and to design and implement appropriate hedging strategies. Suppose, for example, that the U.S. dollar substantially depreciates against the Japanese yen, as it often has since the mid-eighties. This change in the exchange rate can have significant economic consequences for both U.S. and Japanese firms. For example, it can adversely affect the competitive position of Japanese car makers in the highly competitive U.S. market by forcing them to raise dollar prices of their cars by more than their U.S. competitors do. The same change in exchange rate, however, will tend to strengthen the competitive position of import-competing U.S. car makers. On the other hand, should the dollar appreciate against the yen (as it did in the early 1980s), it would bolster the competitive position of Japanese car makers at the expense of U.S. makers. A real-world example of the effect of exchange rate changes is provided in the International Finance in Practice box on page 294, "U.S. Firms Feel the Pain of Peso's Plunge."

Changes in exchange rates can affect not only firms that are directly engaged in international trade but also purely domestic firms. Consider, for example, a U.S. bicycle manufacturer that sources only domestic materials and sells exclusively in the U.S. market, with no foreign-currency receivables or payables in its accounting book. This seemingly purely domestic U.S. firm can be subject to foreign exchange exposure if it competes against imports, say, from a Taiwanese bicycle manufacturer. When the Taiwanese dollar depreciates against the U.S. dollar, this is likely to lead to a lower U.S. dollar price of Taiwanese bicycles, boosting their sales in the United States, thereby hurting the U.S. manufacturer.

Changes in exchange rates may affect not only the operating cash flows of a firm by altering its competitive position but also dollar (home currency) values of the firm's assets and liabilities. Consider a U.S. firm that has borrowed Swiss francs. Since the dollar amount needed to pay off the franc debt depends on the dollar/franc exchange rate, the U.S. firm can gain or lose as the Swiss franc depreciates or appreciates against the dollar. A classic example of the peril of facing currency exposure is provided by Laker Airways, a British firm founded by Sir Freddie Laker, which pioneered the concept of mass-marketed, low-fare air travel. The company heavily borrowed U.S. dollars to finance acquisitions of aircraft while it derived more than half of its revenue in sterling. As the dollar kept appreciating against the British pound (and most major currencies) throughout the first half of the 1980s, the burden of servicing the dollar debts became overwhelming for Laker Airways, forcing it to default.

The preceding examples suggest that exchange rate changes can systematically affect the value of the firm by influencing its operating cash flows as well as the domestic currency values of its assets and liabilities. In a study examining the exposure of U.S. firms to currency risk, Jorion (1990) documented that a significant relationship exists between stock returns and the dollar's value. Recent studies, such as Choi and Prasad (1995) and Simkins and Laux (1996), also documented that U.S. stock returns are sensitive to exchange rate movements.

Exhibit 12.1, which is excerpted from the Simkins and Laux study, provides an estimate of the U.S. industries' market betas as well as the "forex" betas. The market and forex betas measure the sensitivities of an industry portfolio against the U.S. stock market index and the dollar exchange rate index, respectively. As Exhibit 12.1 shows, the forex beta varies greatly across industry lines; it ranges from −1.272 for

EXHIBIT 12.1

Exchange Rate Exposure of U.S. Industry Portfolios[a]

Industry	Market Beta[b]	Forex Beta[c]
1. Aerospace	0.999	0.034
2. Apparel	1.264	0.051
3. Beverage	1.145	−0.437
4. Building materials	1.107	0.604
5. Chemicals	1.074	−0.009
6. Computers, office equipment	0.928	0.248
7. Electronics, electrical equipment	1.202	0.608*
8. Food	1.080	−0.430
9. Forest and paper products	1.117	0.445
10. Furniture	0.901	1.217*
11. Industrial and farm equipment	1.125	0.473
12. Metal products	1.081	−0.440
13. Metals	1.164	0.743*
14. Mining and crude oil	0.310	−0.713
15. Motor vehicles and parts	0.919	1.168*
16. Petroleum refining	0.515	−0.746*
17. Pharmaceuticals	1.124	−1.272*
18. Publishing and printing	1.154	0.567
19. Rubber and plastics	1.357	0.524
20. Science, photo, and control equipment	0.975	−0.437*
21. Cosmetics	1.051	0.417
22. Textiles	1.279	1.831*
23. Tobacco	0.898	−0.768*
24. Toys, sporting goods	1.572	−0.660
25. Transportation equipment	1.613	1.524*

[a]The market and forex (foreign exchange) betas are obtained from regressing the industry portfolio (monthly) returns, constructed from the *Fortune* 500 companies, on the U.S. stock market index returns and the rate of change in the dollar exchange rate index over the sample period 1.1989–12.93.

[b]For every industry portfolio the market beta is statistically significant at the 1% level.

[c]The forex beta is significant for some industry portfolios and insignificant for others. Those forex betas that are significant at 10% or higher are denoted by (*).

Source: Betty Simkins and Paul Laux, "Derivatives Use and the Exchange Rate Risk of Investing in Large U.S. Corporations," Case Western Reserve University Working Paper (1996).

pharmaceuticals to 1.831 for textiles. A negative (positive) forex beta means that stock returns tend to move down (up) as the dollar appreciates. Out of the 25 total industries studied, 10 were found to have a significant exposure to exchange rate movements.

THREE TYPES OF EXPOSURE

Before we get into the important issue of how to measure and manage economic exposure, let us briefly discuss different types of exposure. It is conventional to classify foreign currency exposures into three types:

- Economic exposure
- Transaction exposure
- Translation exposure

Economic exposure can be defined as the extent to which the value of the firm would be affected by unanticipated changes in exchange rates. Any anticipated changes in exchange rates would have been already discounted and reflected in the firm's value. As we will discuss later in this chapter, changes in exchange rates can have a profound effect on the firm's competitive position in the world market and thus on its cash flows and market value.

Transaction exposure, a subject to be discussed in Chapter 13, can be defined as the sensitivity of "realized" domestic currency values of the firm's contractual cash flows *denominated* in foreign currencies to unexpected exchange rate changes. Since settlements of these contractual cash flows affect the firm's domestic currency cash flows, transaction exposure is sometimes regarded as a short-term economic exposure. Transaction exposure arises from fixed-price contracting in a world where exchange rates are changing randomly.

On the other hand, **translation exposure**, which will be discussed in Chapter 14, refers to the potential that the firm's consolidated financial statements can be affected by changes in exchange rates. Consolidation involves translation of subsidiaries' financial statements from local currencies to the home currency. Consider a U.S. multinational firm that has subsidiaries in the United Kingdom and Japan. Each subsidiary will produce financial statements in local currency. To consolidate financial statements worldwide, the firm must translate the subsidiaries' financial statements in local currencies into the U.S. dollar, the home currency. As we will see later, translation involves many controversial issues. Resultant translation gains and losses represent the accounting system's attempt to measure economic exposure *ex post*. It does not provide a good measure of *ex ante* economic exposure. In the remainder of this chapter, we will focus on how to measure and manage economic exposure.

HOW TO MEASURE ECONOMIC EXPOSURE

Currency risk or uncertainty, which represents random changes in exchange rates is not the same as the currency exposure, which measures "what is at risk." Under certain conditions, a firm may not face any exposure at all, that is, nothing is at risk, even if the exchange rates change randomly. Suppose your company maintains a vacation home for employees in the British countryside and the local price of this property is always moving together with the pound price of the U.S. dollar. As a result, whenever the pound depreciates against the dollar, the local currency price of this property goes up by the same proportion. In this case, your company is not exposed to currency risk even if the pound/dollar exchange rate fluctuates randomly. The British asset your company owns has an embedded hedge against exchange risk, rendering the dollar price of the asset *insensitive* to exchange rate changes.

EXHIBIT 12.2

Channels of Economic Exposure

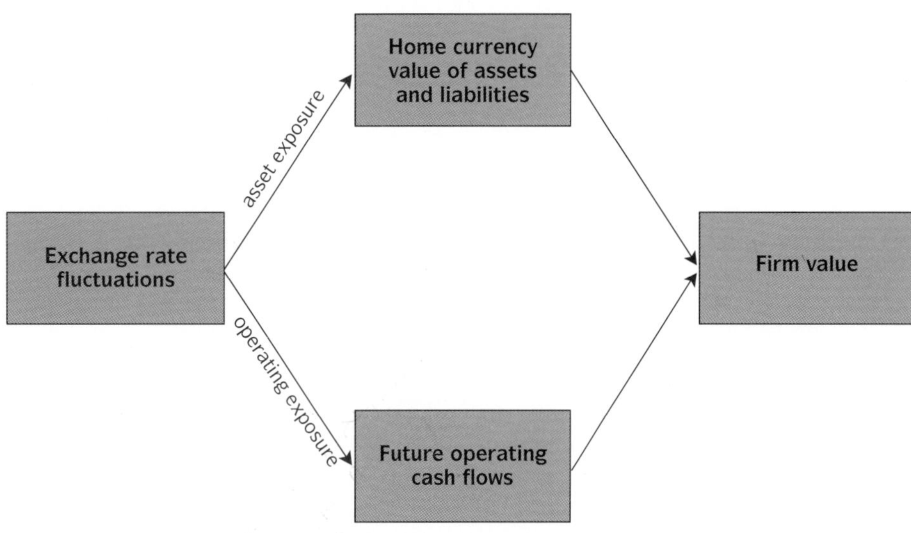

Consider an alternative situation in which the local (pound) price of your company's British asset barely changes. In this case, the dollar value of the asset will be highly *sensitive* to the exchange rate since the former will change as the latter does. To the extent that the dollar price of the British asset exhibits "sensitivity" to exchange rate movements, your company is exposed to currency risk. Similarly, if your company's operating cash flows are sensitive to exchange rate changes, the company is again exposed to currency risk.

Exposure to currency risk thus can be properly measured by the *sensitivities* of (1) the future home currency values of the firm's assets (and liabilities) and (2) the firm's operating cash flows to random changes in exchange rates. The same point is illustrated by Exhibit 12.2; assets include the tangible assets (property, plant and equipment, inventory) as well as financial assets. Let us first discuss the case of asset exposure. For expositional convenience, assume that dollar inflation is nonrandom. Then, from the perspective of the U.S. firm that owns an asset in Britain, the exposure can be measured by the coefficient (b) in regressing the dollar value (P) of the British asset on the dollar/pound exchange rate (S).[1]

$$P = a + b \times S + e \qquad (12.1)$$

where a is the regression constant and e is the random error term with mean zero, that is, $E(e) = 0$; $P = SP^*$, where P^* is the local currency (pound) price of the asset.[2] It is obvious from the above equation that the regression coefficient b measures the sensitivity of the dollar value of the asset (P) to the exchange rate (S). If the regression coefficient is zero, that is, $b = 0$, the dollar value of the asset is independent of exchange rate movements, implying no exposure. Based on the above analysis, one can say that *exposure is the regression coefficient.* Statistically, the **exposure coefficient**, b, is defined as follows:

$$b = \frac{\text{Cov}(P, S)}{\text{Var}(S)}$$

where Cov(P,S) is the covariance between the dollar value of the asset and the exchange rate, and Var(S) is the variance of the exchange rate.

Next, we show how to apply the exposure measurement technique using numerical examples. Suppose that a U.S. firm has an asset in Britain whose local currency

INTERNATIONAL FINANCE IN PRACTICE

U.S. Firms Feel the Pain of Peso's Plunge

Foreign-exchange traders and investors aren't the only Americans feeling the pain of the two-week plunge in the value of the Mexican peso.

For U.S. companies that are paid in pesos or that own substantial assets in Mexico, the recent 37% decline in the currency's value is a vivid example of just how quickly and substantially changes in the value of foreign currency can affect sales and profits.

And for the hundreds of companies that see Mexico as a ticket for expansion, the peso's fall is another reminder that foreign markets aren't anything like those at home. The Mexican financial crisis forces U.S. companies to "pay attention to the direction of the economy in any country they invest in," says Serge Ratmiroff, senior manager, international services, at Deloitte & Touche in Chicago.

The impact of the peso's fall on those that do business in the Mexican currency is striking. A U.S. company that sold widgets for 345 pesos early last month received about $100. Now, 345 pesos is valued at between $60 and $65. Meanwhile, as the value of the peso declines, prices of U.S. exports will rise, making them less affordable for Mexican buyers.

Ford Motor Co., for instance, said the peso's problems could dent its growth in exports to Mexico next year. Ford sent 27,000 to 28,000 vehicles to Mexico in 1994, up from a few hundred in 1992. It had hoped those sales would double over time with the aid of the North American Free Trade Agreement. But the auto maker's chairman and chief executive officer, Alexander Trotman, noted Tuesday that the cost of Ford autos "in peso terms has gone up enormously." Ford continues to build more than 200,000 vehicles a year in Mexico, but its Mexican output excludes such hot-sellers as the Mustang sports coupe, which is imported from the U.S. While wages should fall at its Mexican plants, at least in dollar terms, a spokesman said the company wouldn't see much gain from that because most of the parts used to assemble cars in Mexico actually are made in the U.S.

Other companies are feeling the impact immediately. Toy maker Mattel Inc. said yesterday that it will take an eight-cent-a-share charge for the fourth quarter because the peso's decline has reduced the value of its Mexican inventory and receivables. The charge means that despite a 35% jump in world-wide sales, Mattel's record earnings for the year will be on the "conservative" side of analysts' estimates.

Metalclad Corp., a Newport Beach, Calif., company with waste-oil recycling and landfill operations in Mexico, said the peso's plunge may wipe out its hopes for a profitable fiscal third quarter, ending Feb. 28. And Pilgrim's Pride, a Pittsburg, Texas, chicken producer, expects to take a substantial write-down for its first quarter ended Dec. 31, as it marks down its $120 million in assets in Mexico. A spokesman for Goodyear Tire & Rubber Co. in Akron, Ohio, said the company has "seen tire business fall off in Mexico because dealers don't want to sell the product at less than what they bought it for."

For many big U.S. companies, however, the swings are just another day in the currency markets. Mexico is a relatively small international market, though it accounts for about 9% of U.S. exports. Many companies say they do business in dollars or have otherwise hedged against currency changes, and won't feel any immediate financial impact. Further, those who manufacture there should see lower labor costs while some businesses, like trucking and hotels, contend they will benefit from increasing U.S. imports and tourism.

Still, some firms are putting expansion plans on hold and even large companies expect exports to Mexico to fall off this year as Mexican buyers adjust to the higher prices of U.S. goods. After all, that's part of Mexico's goal in letting the peso's value fall in relation to the dollar. "The whole purpose of what they're doing is to try to reduce the level of imports and increase Mexican exports," says Sidney Weintraub of the Center for Strategic and International Studies, a Washington think tank.

A drop in product sales to Mexico would be felt particularly in Texas, which exported about $20.38 billion in goods to its southern neighbor in 1993—nearly half the U.S. exports to Mexico. The state comptroller's office is predicting that exports will grow another 5% to 7% this year, but rise just 3% a year in 1996 and beyond, in part, because currency changes will curtail demand.

Source: Reprinted with permission of *The Wall Street Journal,* © 1995 Dow Jones & Company, Inc. All Rights Reserved Worldwide.

price is random. For simplicity, let us assume that there are three possible states of the world, with each state equally likely to occur. The future local currency price of this British asset as well as the future exchange rate will be determined, depending on the realized state of the world. First, consider Case 1, described in Panel A of Exhibit 12.3.

EXHIBIT 12.3

Measurement of Currency Exposure

State	Probability	P^*	S	$P(=SP^*)$	Parameters
A. Case 1					
1	1/3	£ 980	\$1.40	\$1,372	Cov(P,S) = 34/3
2	1/3	£1,000	\$1.50	\$1,500	Var(S) = .02/3
3	1/3	£1,070	\$1.60	\$1,712	***b* = £1,700**
Mean			\$1.50	\$1,528	
B. Case 2					
1	1/3	£1,000	\$1.40	\$1,400	Cov(P,S) = 0
2	1/3	£ 933	\$1.50	\$1,400	Var(S) = .02/3
3	1/3	£ 875	\$1.60	\$1,400	***b* = 0**
Mean			\$1.50	\$1,400	
C. Case 3					
1	1/3	£1,000	\$1.40	\$1,400	Cov(P,S) = 20/3
2	1/3	£1,000	\$1.50	\$1,500	Var(S) = .02/3
3	1/3	£1,000	\$1.60	\$1,600	***b* = £1,000**
Mean			\$1.50	\$1,500	

EXHIBIT 12.4

Computations of Regression Parameters: Case 1

1. Computation of Means

$$\bar{P} = \sum_i q_i P_i = \frac{1}{3}(1{,}372 + 1{,}500 + 1{,}712) = 1{,}528$$

$$\bar{S} = \sum_i q_i S_i = \frac{1}{3}(1.40 + 1.50 + 1.60) = 1.50$$

2. Computation of Variance and Covariance

$$\text{Var}(S) = \sum_i q_i (S_i - \bar{S})^2$$
$$= \frac{1}{3}[(1.40-1.50)^2 + (1.50 - 1.50)^2 + (1.60 - 1.50)^2]$$
$$= 0.02/3$$

$$\text{Cov}(P,S) = \sum_i q_i (P_i - \bar{P})(S_i - \bar{S})$$
$$= \frac{1}{3}[(1{,}372 - 1{,}528)(1.40 - 1.50) + (1{,}500 - 1{,}528)(1.50 - 1.50) + (1{,}712 - 1{,}528)(1.60 - 1.50)]$$
$$= 34/3$$

3. Computation of the Exposure Coefficient

$$b = \text{Cov}(P,S)/\text{Var}(S) = (34/3)/(0.02/3) = 1{,}700$$

Note: q_i denotes the probability for the ith state.

Case 1 indicates that the local currency price of the asset (P^*) and the dollar price of the pound (S) are positively correlated, so that depreciation (appreciation) of the pound against the dollar is associated with a declining (rising) local currency price of the asset. The dollar price of the asset on the future (liquidation) date can be \$1,372, or \$1,500 or \$1,712, depending on the realized state of the world.

When we compute the parameter values for Case 1, we obtain Cov(P,S) = 34/3, Var(S) = 0.02/3, and thus b = £1,700. This pound amount, £1,700, represents the sensitivity of the future dollar value of the British asset to random changes in exchange rate. This finding implies that the U.S. firm faces a substantial exposure to currency risk. Note that the magnitude of the exposure is expressed in British pounds. For illustration, the computations of the parameter values for Case 1 are shown in Exhibit 12.4.

Next, consider Case 2. This case indicates that the local currency value of the asset is clearly negatively correlated with the dollar price of the British pound. In fact, the effect of exchange rate changes is exactly offset by movements of the local currency price of the asset, rendering the dollar price of the asset totally insensitive to exchange rate changes. The future dollar price of the asset will be uniformly \$1,400 across the three states of the world. One thus can say that the British asset is effectively *denominated* in terms of the dollar. Although this case is clearly unrealistic, it shows that uncertain exchange rates or exchange risk does not necessarily constitute exchange exposure. Despite the fact that the future exchange rate is uncertain, the U.S. firm has nothing at risk in this case. Since the firm faces no exposure, no hedging will be necessary.

We now turn to Case 3, where the local currency price of the asset is fixed at £1,000. In this case, the U.S. firm faces a "contractual" cash flow that is *denominated* in pounds. This case, in fact, represents an example of the special case of economic exposure, transaction exposure. Intuitively, what is at risk is £1,000, that is, the exposure coefficient, b, is £1,000. Readers can confirm this by going through the same kind of computations as shown in Exhibit 12.4. Measurement of transaction exposure is thus very simple. The exposure coefficient, b, is the same as the magnitude of the contractual cash flow fixed in terms of foreign currency.

Once the magnitude of exposure is known, the firm can hedge the exposure by simply selling the exposure forward. In Case 3, where the asset value is fixed in terms of local currency, it is possible to completely eliminate the variability of the future dollar price of the asset by selling £1,000 forward. In Case 1, however, where the local currency price of the asset is random, selling £1,700 forward will not completely eliminate the variability of the future dollar price; there will be a residual variability that is independent of exchange rate changes.

Based on regression Equation 12.1, we can decompose the variability of the dollar value of the asset, Var(P), into two separate components: exchange rate-related and residual. Specifically,

$$\text{Var}(P) = b^2\text{Var}(S) + \text{Var}(e) \tag{12.2}$$

The first term in the right hand side of the equation, $b^2\text{Var}(S)$, represents the part of the variability of the dollar value of the asset that is related to random changes in the exchange rate, whereas the second term, Var(e), captures the residual part of the dollar value variability that is independent of exchange rate movements.

The consequences of hedging the exposure by forward contracts are illustrated in Exhibit 12.5. Consider Case 1, where the firm faces an exposure coefficient (b) of £1,700. If the firm sells £1,700 forward, the dollar proceeds that the firm will receive are given by

$$\$1{,}700(F - S)$$

where F is the forward exchange rate and S is the spot rate realized on the maturity date. Note that for each pound sold forward, the firm will receive a dollar amount equal to ($F - S$). In Exhibit 12.5, the forward exchange rate is assumed to be \$1.50, which is the same as the expected future spot rate. Thus, if the future spot rate turns out to be \$1.40 under state 1, the dollar proceed from the forward contract will be \$170 = 1,700(1.50 − 1.40). Since the dollar value (P) of the asset is \$1,372 under state 1, the dollar value of the hedged position (HP) will be \$1,542 (= \$1,372 + \$170) under state 1.

As shown in part A of Exhibit 12.5, the variance of the dollar value of the hedged position is only 392(\$)^2, whereas that of the unhedged position is 19,659(\$)^2. This result implies that much of the uncertainty regarding the future dollar value of the asset is associated with exchange rate uncertainty. As a result, once the exchange exposure is hedged, most of the variability of the dollar value of the asset is eliminated. The

EXHIBIT 12.5

Consequences of Hedging Currency Exposure

Future Quantities	State 1	State 2	State 3	Variance
A. Case 1 (b = £1,700)				
Local currency asset price (P^*)	980	1,000	1,070	
Exchange rate (S)	1.40	1.50	1.60	
Dollar value ($P = SP^*$)	1,372	1,500	1,712	19,659
Proceeds from forward contract	170	0	−170	
Dollar value of hedged position (HP)	1,542	1,500	1,542	392
B. Case 3 (b = £1,000)				
Local currency asset price (P^*)	1,000	1,000	1,000	
Exchange rate (S)	1.40	1.50	1.60	
Dollar value ($P = SP^*$)	1,400	1,500	1,600	6,667
Proceeds from forward contract	100	0	−100	
Dollar value of hedged position (HP)	1,500	1,500	1,500	0

Note: In both cases, the forward exchange rate (F) is assumed to be \$1.50/£. Proceeds from the forward contract are computed as $\$b(F - S)$. Recall that each of the three states is equally likely to happen, i.e., $q_i = 1/3$ for each state.

residual variability of the dollar value of the asset that is independent of exchange rate changes, Var(e), is equal to 392(\$)^2.

Let us now turn to Case 3 where the local currency price of the asset is fixed. In this case, complete hedging is possible in the specific sense that there will be no residual variability. As shown in part B of Exhibit 12.5, the future dollar value of the asset, which is totally dependent upon the exchange rate, has a variance of 6,667(\$)^2. Once the firm hedges the exposure by selling £1,000 forward, the dollar value of the hedged position (HP) becomes nonrandom, and is \$1,500 across the three states of the world. Since the asset now has a constant dollar value, it is effectively *redenominated* in terms of the dollar.

OPERATING EXPOSURE: DEFINITION

While many managers understand the effects of random exchange rate changes on the dollar value of their firms' assets and liabilities denominated in foreign currencies, they often do not fully understand the effect of volatile exchange rates on operating cash flows. As the economy becomes increasingly globalized, more firms are subject to international competition. Fluctuating exchange rates can seriously alter the relative competitive positions of such firms in domestic and foreign markets, affecting their operating cash flows.

Unlike the exposure of assets and liabilities (such as accounts payable and receivable, loans denominated in foreign currencies, and so forth) that are listed in accounting statements, the exposure of operating cash flows depends on the effect of random exchange rate changes on the firm's competitive position, which is not readily measurable. This difficulty notwithstanding, it is important for the firm to properly manage **operating exposure** as well as **asset exposure.** In many cases, operating exposure may account for a larger portion of the firm's total exposure than contractual exposure. Formally, operating exposure can be defined as the *extent to which the firm's operating cash flows would be affected by random changes in exchange rates.*

ILLUSTRATION OF OPERATING EXPOSURE

Before we discuss what determines operating exposure and how to manage it, it is useful to illustrate the exposure using a simple example. Suppose that a U.S. computer

EXHIBIT 12.6

Projected Operations for Albion Computers PLC: Benchmark Case ($1.60/£)

Sales (50,000 units at £1,000/unit)	£50,000,000
Variable costs (50,000 units at £650/unit)[a]	32,500,000
Fixed overhead costs	4,000,000
Depreciation allowances	1,000,000
Net profit before tax	£12,500,000
Income tax (at 50%)	6,250,000
Profit after tax	6,250,000
Add back depreciation	1,000,000
Operating cash flow in pounds	£ 7,250,000
Operating cash flow in dollars	$11,600,000

[a]The unit variable cost, £650, comprises £330 for the locally sourced inputs and £320 for the imported input, which is priced in dollars, i.e., $512. At the exchange rate of $1.60/£ the imported part costs £320.

company has a wholly owned British subsidiary, Albion Computers PLC, that manufactures and sells personal computers in the U.K. market. Albion Computers imports microprocessors from Intel, which sells them for $512 per unit. At the current exchange rate of $1.60 per pound, each Intel microprocessor costs £320. Albion Computers hires British workers and sources all the other inputs locally. Albion faces a 50 percent income tax rate in the U.K.

Exhibit 12.6 summarizes projected operations for Albion Computers, assuming that the exchange rate will remain unchanged at $1.60 per pound. The company expects to sell 50,000 units of personal computers per year at a selling price of £1,000 per unit. The unit variable cost is £650, which comprises £320 for the imported input and £330 for the locally sourced inputs. Needless to say, the pound price of the imported input will change as the exchange rate changes, which, in turn, can affect the selling price in the U.K. market. Each year, Albion incurs fixed overhead costs of £4 million for rents, property taxes, and the like, regardless of output level. As the exhibit shows, the projected operating cash flow is £7,250,000 per year, which is equivalent to $11,600,000 at the current exchange rate of $1.60 per pound.

Now, consider the possible effect of a depreciation of the pound on the projected dollar operating cash flow of Albion Computers. Assume that the pound may depreciate from $1.60 to $1.40 per pound. The dollar operating cash flow may change following a pound depreciation due to:

1. The **competitive effect**: A pound depreciation may affect operating cash flow in pounds by altering the firm's competitive position in the marketplace.
2. The **conversion effect**: A given operating cash flow in pounds will be converted into a lower dollar amount after the pound depreciation.

To get a feel of how the dollar operating cash flow may change as the exchange rate changes, consider the following cases with varying degrees of realism:

Case 1: No variables change, except the price of the imported input.

Case 2: The selling price as well as the price of the imported input changes, with no other changes.

Case 3: All the variables change.

In Case 1, which is illustrated in Exhibit 12.7, the unit variable cost of the imported input rises to £366 (= $512/$1.40) following the pound depreciation, with no other changes. Following the depreciation, the total variable costs become £34.8 million, lowering the firm's before-tax profit from £12.5 million (for the benchmark case) to £10.2 million. Considering that the firm faces a 50 percent income tax rate,

EXHIBIT 12.7

Projected Operations for Albion Computers PLC: Case 1 ($1.40/£)

Sales (50,000 units at £1,000/unit)	£50,000,000
Variable costs (50,000 units at £696/unit)	34,800,000
Fixed overhead costs	4,000,000
Depreciation allowances	1,000,000
Net profit before tax	£10,200,000
Income tax (at 50%)	5,100,000
Profit after tax	5,100,000
Add back depreciation	1,000,000
Operating cash flow in pounds	£ 6,100,000
Operating cash flow in dollars	$ 8,540,000

EXHIBIT 12.8

Projected Operations for Albion Computers PLC: Case 2 ($1.40/£)

Sales (50,000 units at £1,143/unit)	£57,150,000
Variable costs (50,000 units at £696/unit)	34,800,000
Fixed overhead costs	4,000,000
Depreciation allowances	1,000,000
Net profit before tax	£17,350,000
Income tax (at 50%)	8,675,000
Profit after tax	8,675,000
Add back depreciation	1,000,000
Operating cash flow in pounds	£ 9,675,000
Operating cash flow in dollars	$13,545,000

depreciation of the pound will lower the net operating cash flow from £7.25 million (for the benchmark case) to £6.1 million. In terms of dollars, Albion's projected net operating cash flow changes from $11.6 million to $8.54 million as the exchange rate changes from $1.60 per pound to $1.40 per pound. Albion may be forced not to raise the pound selling price because it faces a British competitor that manufactures similar products using only locally sourced inputs. An increase in selling price can potentially lead to a sharp decline in unit sales volume. Under this kind of competitive environment, Albion's costs are responsive to exchange rate changes, but the selling price is not. This asymmetry makes the firm's operating cash flow sensitive to exchange rate changes, giving rise to operating exposure.

In Case 2, which is analyzed in Exhibit 12.8, the selling price as well as the price of the imported input increases following the pound depreciation. In this case, Albion Computers does not face any serious competition in the British market and faces a highly inelastic demand for its products. Thus, Albion can raise the selling price to £1,143 (to keep the dollar selling price at $1,600 after the pound depreciation) and still maintain the sales volume at 50,000 units. Computations presented in Exhibit 12.8 indicate that the projected operating cash flow actually increases to £9,675,000, which is equivalent to $13,545,000. Compared with the benchmark case, the dollar operating cash flow is higher when the pound depreciates. This case shows that a pound depreciation need not always lead to a lower dollar operating cash flow.

We now turn to Case 3 where the selling price, sales volume, and the prices of both locally sourced and imported inputs change following the pound depreciation. In particular, we assume that both the selling price and the price of locally sourced inputs increase at the rate of 8 percent, reflecting the underlying inflation rate in the U.K. As a result, the selling price will be £1,080 per unit and the unit variable cost of locally sourced inputs will be £356. Since the price of the imported input is £366, the combined unit variable cost will be £722. Facing an **elastic demand** for its products,

EXHIBIT 12.9

Projected Operations for Albion Computers PLC: Case 3 ($1.40/£)

Sales (40,000 units at £1,080/unit)	£43,200,000
Variable costs (40,000 units at £722/unit)	28,880,000
Fixed overhead costs	4,000,000
Depreciation allowances	1,000,000
Net profit before tax	£ 9,320,000
Income tax (at 50%)	4,660,000
Profit after tax	4,660,000
Add back depreciation	1,000,000
Operating cash flow in pounds	£ 5,660,000
Operating cash flow in dollars	$ 7,924,000

EXHIBIT 12.10 **Summary of Operating Exposure Effect of Pound Depreciation on Albion Computers PLC**

Variables	Benchmark Case	Case 1	Case 2	Case 3
Exchange rate ($/£)	1.60	1.40	1.40	1.40
Unit variable cost (£)	650	696	696	722
Unit sales price (£)	1,000	1,000	1,143	1,080
Sales volume (units)	50,000	50,000	50,000	40,000
Annual cash flow (£)	7,250,000	6,100,000	9,675,000	5,660,000
Annual cash flow ($)	11,600,000	8,540,000	13,545,000	7,924,000
Four-year present value ($)[a]	33,118,000	24,382,000	38,671,000	22,623,000
Operating gains/losses ($)[b]		−8,736,000	5,553,000	−10,495,000

[a]The discounted present value of dollar cash flows was computed over a four-year period using a 15 percent discount rate. A constant cash flow is assumed for each of four years.

[b]Operating gains or losses represent the present value of change in cash flows, which is due to pound depreciation, from the benchmark case.

sales volume declines to 40,000 units per year after the price increase. As Exhibit 12.9 shows, Albion's projected operating cash flow is £5.66 million, which is equivalent to $7.924 million. The projected dollar cash flow under Case 3 is lower than that of the benchmark case by $3.676 million.

Exhibit 12.10 summarizes the projected operating exposure effect of the pound depreciation on Albion Computers PLC. For expositional purposes it is assumed here that a change in exchange rate will have effects on the firm's operating cash flow for four years. The exhibit provides, among other things, the four-year present values of operating cash flows for each of the three cases as well as for the benchmark case. The proper discount rate for Albion's cash flow is assumed to be 15 percent. The exhibit also shows the operating gains or losses computed as the present value of changes in operating cash flows (over a four-year period) from the benchmark case that are due to the exchange rate change. In Case 3, for instance, the firm expects to experience an operating loss of $10,495,000 due to the pound depreciation.

DETERMINANTS OF OPERATING EXPOSURE

Unlike contractual (i.e., transaction) exposure, which can readily be determined from the firm's accounting statements, operating exposure cannot be determined in the same manner. A firm's operating exposure is determined by (1) the structure of the markets in which the firm sources its inputs, such as labor and materials, and sells its products, and (2) the firm's ability to mitigate the effect of exchange rate changes by adjusting its markets, product mix, and sourcing.

To highlight the importance of market structure in determining operating exposure, consider a hypothetical company, Ford Mexicana, a subsidiary of Ford, which imports cars from the parent and distributes them in Mexico. If the dollar appreciates against the Mexican peso, Ford Mexicana's costs go up in peso terms. Whether this creates operating exposure for Ford critically depends on the structure of the car market in Mexico. For example, if Ford Mexicana faces competition from Mexican car makers whose peso costs did not rise, it will not be able to raise the peso price of imported Ford cars without risking a major reduction in sales. Facing a highly elastic demand for its products, Ford Mexicana cannot let the **exchange rate change pass through** the peso price. As a result, an appreciation of the dollar will squeeze the profit of Ford Mexicana, subjecting the parent firm to a high degree of operating exposure.

In contrast, consider the case in which Ford Mexicana faces import competition only from other U.S. car makers like General Motors and Chrysler rather than from local producers. Since peso costs of those other imported U.S. cars will be affected by a dollar appreciation in the same manner, the competitive position of Ford Mexicana will not be adversely affected. Under this market structure, the dollar appreciation is likely to be reflected in higher peso prices of imported U.S. cars pretty quickly. As a result, Ford will be able to better maintain its dollar profit, without being subject to a major operating exposure.

Generally speaking, a firm is subject to high degrees of operating exposure when *either* its cost *or* price is sensitive to exchange rate changes. On the other hand, when *both* the cost *and* price are sensitive or insensitive to exchange rate changes, the firm has no major operating exposure.

Given the market structure, however, the extent to which a firm is subject to operating exposure depends on the firm's ability to stabilize cash flows in the face of exchange rate changes. Even if Ford faces competition from local car makers in Mexico, for example, it can reduce exposure by starting to source Mexican parts and materials, which would be cheaper in dollar terms after the dollar appreciation. Ford can even start to produce cars in Mexico by hiring local workers and sourcing local inputs, thereby making peso costs relatively insensitive to changes in the dollar/peso exchange rate. In other words, the firm's flexibility regarding production locations, sourcing, and financial hedging strategy is an important determinant of its operating exposure to exchange risk.

Before we discuss how to hedge operating exposure, it is important to recognize that changes in nominal exchange rates may not always affect the firm's competitive position. This is the case when a change in exchange rate is exactly offset by the inflation differential. To show this point, let us again use the example of Ford Mexicana competing against local car makers. Suppose that the annual inflation rate is 4 percent in the United States and 15 percent in Mexico. For simplicity, we assume that car prices appreciate at the same pace as the general domestic inflation rate in both the United States and Mexico. Now, suppose that the dollar appreciates about 11 percent against the peso, offsetting the inflation rate differential between the two countries. This, of course, implies that purchasing power parity is holding.

Under this situation the peso price of Ford cars appreciates by about 15 percent, which reflects a 4 percent increase in the dollar price of cars and an 11 percent appreciation of the dollar against the peso. Since the peso prices of both Ford and locally produced cars rise by the same 15 percent, the 11 percent appreciation of the dollar will not affect the competitive position of Ford vis-à-vis local car makers. Ford thus does not have operating exposure.

If, however, the dollar appreciates by more than 11 percent against the peso, Ford cars will become relatively more expensive than locally produced cars, adversely affecting Ford's competitive position. Ford is thus exposed to exchange risk. Since purchasing power parity does not hold very well, especially in the short run, exchange

EXHIBIT 12.11

Exchange Rate Pass-through Coefficients for U.S. Manufacturing Industries

Industry Code (SIC)	Industry	Pass-Through Coefficient
20	Food and kindred products	0.2485
22	Textile mill products	0.3124
23	Apparels	0.1068
24	Lumber and wood products	0.0812
25	Furniture and fixtures	0.3576
28	Chemicals and allied products	0.5312
30	Rubber and plastic products	0.5318
31	Leather products	0.3144
32	Stone, glass, concrete products	0.8843
33	Primary metal industries	0.2123
34	Fabricated metal products	0.3138
35	Machinery, except electrical	0.7559
36	Electrical and electronic machinery	0.3914
37	Transportation equipment	0.3583
38	Measurement instruments	0.7256
39	Miscellaneous manufacturing	0.2765
Average		0.4205

Source: Jiawen Yang. "Exchange Rate Pass-through in U.S. Manufacturing Industries," *Review of Economic and Statistics* 79 (1997), pp. 95–104.

rate changes are likely to affect the competitive positions of firms that are sourcing from different locations but selling in the same markets.

Before we move on, it would be useful to examine the relationship between exchange rate changes and the price adjustments of goods. Facing exchange rate changes, a firm may choose one of the following three pricing strategies: (1) pass the cost shock fully to its selling prices (complete pass-through), (2) fully absorb the shock to keep its selling prices unaltered (no pass-through), or (3) do some combination of the two strategies described above (partial pass-through). Import prices in the United States do not fully reflect exchange rate changes, exhibiting a partial pass-through phenomenon.

In a recent study, Yang (1997) investigated exchange rate pass-through in U.S. manufacturing industries during the sample period 1980–1991 and found that the pricing behavior of foreign exporting firms is generally consistent with partial pass-through. Exhibit 12.11, constructed based on the Yang study, provides the pass-through coefficients for different industries; the coefficient would be 1 for complete pass-through and 0 for no pass-through. As can be seen from the exhibit, the pass-through coefficient ranges from 0.0812 for SIC 24 (lumber and wood products) to 0.8843 for SIC 32 (stone, glass, and concrete products). The average coefficient is 0.4205, implying that when the U.S. dollar appreciates or depreciates by 1 percent, import prices of foreign products change, on average, by about 0.42 percent. It is noteworthy that partial pass-through is common but varies a great deal across industries. Import prices would be affected relatively little by exchange rate changes in industries with low product differentiation and thus high demand elasticities. In contrast, in industries with a high degree of product differentiation and thus low demand elasticities, import prices will tend to change more as the exchange rates change.

MANAGING OPERATING EXPOSURE

As the economy becomes increasingly globalized, many firms are engaged in international activities such as exports, cross-border sourcing, joint ventures with foreign

INTERNATIONAL FINANCE IN PRACTICE

The Strong Yen and Toyota's Choice

Facing a strong yen in recent years that made Japanese exports more expensive, Toyota, Japan's biggest car maker, chose to shift production from Japan to U.S. manufacturing facilities, where the cost of production is lower. Toyota plans to boost U.S. production by about 50 percent by 1996 compared with 1993. Consequently, Toyota expects that its exports to the United States will decline by about 30 percent over the same period. The car maker also plans to double its production of engines at its Georgetown, Kentucky, plant. In addition to substantially boosting car production at its Georgetown factory, Toyota is also shifting production of all its pickup trucks sold in the United States from Japan to Fremont, California.

As a result, American-built vehicles will account for more than 60 percent of Toyota's U.S. sales in 1996 (about 800,000 units) compared with 46 percent in 1993. Toyota also will boost its exports from America to about 80,000 vehicles by 1996, an increase of about 60 percent from the 50,000 units exported in 1993. The company expects U.S. jobs will grow by 23 percent to 6,000 workers by 1996 at its Georgetown plant. At the same time, procurement of U.S. parts and materials will rise about 40 percent to $6.45 billion from $4.65 billion in 1993.

In addition to shifting production and sourcing to the United States, Toyota is using attractive lease deals to help close the price gap on imports. Since the company doesn't have to raise monthly leasing fees in step with the rising yen, the cars remain more attractive to U.S. consumers, although the company risks taking losses upon resale.

Although shifting production to the United States helps Toyota to get out of the dollar/yen problem and maintain its market share in the United States, it adds to the excess capacity problem of Toyota and leads to underutilization of domestic plants and job losses. A persistent strong yen can result in *hollowing out* of the Japanese economy, as some worry.

Source: Reprinted by permission of *The Wall Street Journal*, © 1994 Dow Jones & Company, Inc. All Rights Reserved Worldwide.

partners, and establishing production and sales affiliates abroad. The cash flows of such firms can be quite sensitive to exchange rate changes. The objective of managing operating exposure is to stabilize cash flows in the face of fluctuating exchange rates.

Since a firm is exposed to exchange risk mainly through the effect of exchange rate changes on its competitive position, it is important to consider exchange exposure management in the context of the firm's long-term strategic planning. For example, in making such strategic decisions as choosing where to locate production facilities, where to purchase materials and components, and where to sell products, the firm should consider the currency effect on its overall future cash flows. Managing operating exposure is thus not a short-term tactical issue. The firm can use the following strategies for managing operating exposure:

1. Selecting low-cost production sites.
2. Flexible sourcing policy.
3. Diversification of the market.
4. Product differentiation and R&D efforts.
5. Financial hedging.

Selecting Low-Cost Production Sites

When the domestic currency is strong or expected to become strong, eroding the competitive position of the firm, it can choose to locate production facilities in a foreign country where costs are low due to either the undervalued currency or underpriced factors of production. Recently, Japanese car makers, including Nissan and Toyota, have been increasingly shifting production to U.S. manufacturing facilities in order to mitigate the negative effect of the strong yen on U.S. sales. German car makers such as Daimler Benz and BMW also decided to establish manufacturing facilities in the United States for the same reason. A real world example is provided by the International Finance in Practice box on page 303, "The Strong Yen and Toyota's Choice."

Also, the firm can choose to establish and maintain production facilities in multiple countries to deal with the effect of exchange rate changes. Consider Nissan, which has manufacturing facilities in the United States and Mexico, as well as in Japan. Multiple manufacturing sites provide Nissan with a great deal of flexibility regarding where to produce, given the prevailing exchange rates. While the yen appreciated substantially against the dollar, the Mexican peso depreciated against the dollar in recent years. Under this sort of exchange rate development, Nissan may choose to increase production in the United States, and especially in Mexico, in order to serve the U.S. market. This is, in fact, how Nissan has reacted to the rising yen in recent years. Maintaining multiple manufacturing sites, however, may prevent the firm from taking advantage of economies of scale, raising its cost of production. The resultant higher cost can partially offset the advantages of maintaining multiple production sites.

Flexible Sourcing Policy

Even if the firm has manufacturing facilities only in the domestic country, it can substantially lessen the effect of exchange rate changes by sourcing from where input costs are low. In the early 1980s when the dollar was very strong against most major currencies, U.S. multinational firms often purchased materials and components from low-cost foreign suppliers in order to keep themselves from being priced out of the market.

Facing the strong yen in recent years, many Japanese firms are adopting the same practices. It is well known that Japanese manufacturers, especially in the car and consumer electronics industries, depend heavily on parts and intermediate products from such low-cost countries as Thailand, Malaysia, and China. Flexible sourcing need not be confined just to materials and parts. Firms can also hire low-cost guest workers from foreign countries instead of high-cost domestic workers in order to be competitive. For example, Japan Airlines is known to heavily hire foreign crews to stay competitive in international routes in face of the rising yen.

Diversification of the Market

Another way of dealing with exchange exposure is to **diversify the market** for the firm's products as much as possible. Suppose that General Electric (GE) is selling power generators in Mexico as well as in Germany. Reduced sales in Mexico due to the dollar appreciation against the peso can be compensated by increased sales in Germany due to the dollar depreciation against the mark. As a result, GE's overall cash flows will be much more stable than would be the case if GE sold only in one foreign market, either Mexico or Germany. As long as exchange rates do not always move in the same direction, the firm can stabilize its operating cash flows by diversifying its export market.

It is sometimes argued that the firm can reduce currency exposure by diversifying across different business lines. The idea is that although each individual business may be exposed to exchange risk to some degree, the firm as a whole may not face a significant exposure. It is pointed out, however, that the firm should not get into new lines of business solely to diversify exchange risk because conglomerate expansion can bring about inefficiency and losses. Expansion into a new business should be justified on its own right.

R&D Efforts and Product Differentiation

Investment in R&D activities can allow the firm to maintain and strengthen its competitive position in the face of adverse exchange rate movements. Successful R&D efforts allow the firm to cut costs and enhance productivity. In addition, R&D efforts can lead to the introduction of new and unique products for which competitors offer no close substitutes. Since the demand for unique products tends to be highly inelastic, the firm would be less exposed to exchange risk. At the same time, the firm can strive to create a perception among consumers that its product is indeed different from those offered by competitors. Once the firm's product acquires a unique identity, its demand is less likely to be price-sensitive.

Financial Hedging

While not a substitute for the long-term, **operational hedging** approaches discussed above, **financial hedging** can be used to stabilize the firm's cash flows. For example, the firm can lend or borrow foreign currencies on a long-term basis. Or, the firm can use currency forward or options contracts and roll them over if necessary. It is noted that existing financial contracts are designed to hedge against nominal, rather than real, changes in exchange rates. Since the firm's competitive position is affected by real changes in exchange rates, financial contracts can at best provide an approximate hedge against the firm's operating exposure. However, if operational hedges, which involve redeployment of resources, are costly or impractical, financial contracts can provide the firm with a flexible and economical way of dealing with exchange exposure.

ILLUSTRATED MINI CASE

Exchange Risk Management at Merck[3]

To examine how companies actually manage exchange risk exposure, we choose Merck & Co. Incorporated, a major U.S. pharmaceutical company, and study its approach to overall exchange exposure management. While Merck's actual hedging decision reflects its own particular business situation, the basic framework for dealing with currency exposure can be informative for other firms.

Merck & Co. primarily develops, produces, and markets health care pharmaceuticals. As a multinational company that operates in more than 100 countries, Merck had worldwide sales of $6.6 billion in 1989, and it controlled about a 4.7 percent market share worldwide. Merck's major foreign competitors are European firms and emerging Japanese firms. Merck is among the most internationally oriented U.S. pharmaceutical companies, with overseas assets accounting for about 40 percent of the firm's total and with roughly 50 percent of its sales overseas.

As is typical in the pharmaceutical industry, Merck established overseas subsidiaries. These subsidiaries number about 70 and are responsible for finishing imported products and marketing in the local markets of incorporation. Sales are denominated in local currencies, and thus, the company is directly affected by exchange rate fluctuations. Costs are incurred partly in the U.S. dollar for basic manufacturing and research and partly in terms of local currency for finishing, marketing, distribution, and so on. Merck found that costs and revenues were not matched in individual currencies mainly because of the concentration of research, manufacturing, and headquarters operations in the United States.

To reduce the currency mismatch, Merck first considered the possibility of redeploying resources in order to shift dollar costs to other currencies. The company, however, decided that relocating employees and manufacturing and research sites was not a practical and cost-effective way of dealing with exchange exposure. Having decided that operational hedging was not appropriate, Merck considered the alternative of financial hedging. Merck developed a five-step procedure for financial hedging:

1. Exchange forecasting.
2. Assessing strategic plan impact.
3. Hedging rationale.
4. Financial instruments.
5. Hedging program.

Step 1: Exchange Forecasting

The first step involves reviewing the likelihood of adverse exchange movements. The treasury staff estimates possible ranges for dollar strength or weakness over the five-year planning horizon. In doing so, the major factors expected to influence exchange rates, such as the U.S. trade deficit, capital flows, the U.S. budget deficit, and government policies regarding exchange rates, are considered. Outside forecasters are also polled on the outlook for the dollar over the planning horizon.

Step 2: Assessing Strategic Plan Impact

Once the future exchange rate ranges are estimated, cash flows and earnings are projected and compared under the alternative exchange rate scenarios, such as strong dollar and weak dollar. These projections are made on a five-year cumulative basis rather than on a year-to-year basis because cumulative results provide more useful information concerning the magnitude of exchange exposure associated with the company's long-range plan.

Step 3: Deciding Whether to Hedge

In deciding whether to hedge exchange exposure, Merck focused on the objective of maximizing long-term cash flows and on the potential effect of exchange rate movements on the firm's ability to meet its strategic objectives. This focus is ultimately intended to maximize shareholder wealth. Merck decided to hedge for two main reasons. First, the company has a large portion of earnings generated overseas while a disproportionate share of costs is incurred in dollars. Second, volatile cash flows can adversely affect the firm's ability to implement the strategic plan, especially investments in R&D that form the basis for future growth. To succeed in a highly competitive industry, the company needs to make a long-term commitment to a high level of research funding. But the cash flow uncertainty caused by volatile exchange rates makes it difficult to justify a high level of research spending. Management decided to hedge in order to reduce the potential effect of volatile exchange rates on future cash flows.

Step 4: Selecting the Hedging Instruments

The objective was to select the most cost-effective hedging tool that accommodated the company's risk preference. Among various hedging tools, such as forward currency contracts, foreign currency borrowing, and currency options, Merck chose currency options because it was not willing to forgo the potential gains if the dollar depreciated against foreign currencies as it has been doing against major currencies since the mid-eighties. Merck regarded option costs as premiums for the insurance policy designed to preserve its ability to implement the strategic plan.

Step 5: Constructing a Hedging Program

Having selected currency options as the key hedging vehicle, the company still had to formulate an implementation strategy regarding the term of the hedge, the strike price of the currency options, and the percentage of income to be covered. After simulating the outcomes of alternative implementation strategies under various exchange rate scenarios, Merck decided to (1) hedge for a multiyear period using long-dated options contracts, rather than hedge year-by-year, to protect the firm's strategic cash flows, (2) not use far out-of-money options to save costs, and (3) hedge only on a partial basis, with the remainder self-insured.

To help formulate the most cost-effective hedging program, Merck developed a computer-based model that simulates the effectiveness of various hedging strategies. Exhibit 12.12 provides an example of simulation results, comparing distributions of hedged and unhedged cash flows. Obviously, the hedged cash flow distribution has a higher mean and a lower standard deviation than the unhedged cash flow distribution. As we will discuss in Chapter 13, hedging may not only reduce risk but also increase

EXHIBIT 12.12

Cash Flows Unhedged versus Hedged

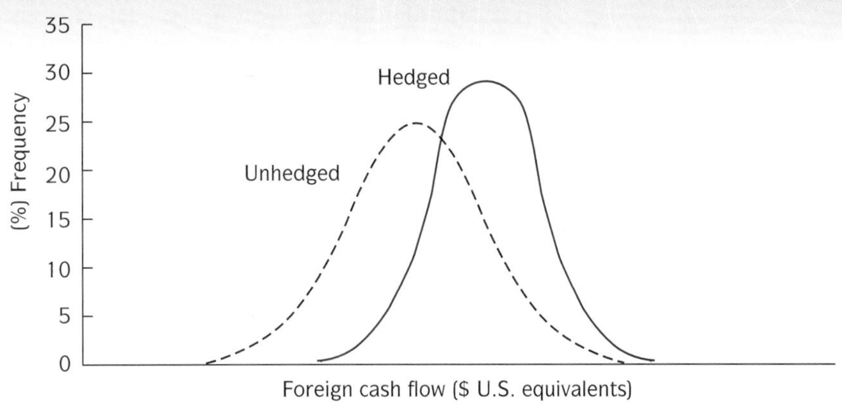

Source: J. Lewent and J. Kearney, "Identifying, Measuring, and Hedging Currency Risk at Merck." Reprinted with permission from the Bank of America *Journal of Applied Corporate Finance,* Winter 1990.

cash flows if a reduced risk lowers the firm's cost of capital and tax liabilities. In this scenario, hedging is preferred to no hedging.

SUMMARY

In this chapter, we discussed how to measure and manage economic exposure to exchange risk. We also examined how companies manage currency risk in the real world.

1. Exchange rate changes can systematically affect the value of the firm by influencing the firm's operating cash flows as well as the domestic currency values of its assets and liabilities.
2. It is conventional to classify foreign currency exposure into three classes: economic exposure, transaction exposure, and translation exposure.
3. Economic exposure can be defined as the extent to which the value of the firm would be affected by unexpected changes in exchange rates. Transaction exposure is defined as the sensitivity of realized domestic currency values of the firm's contractual cash flows denominated in foreign currencies to unexpected exchange rate changes. Translation exposure, on the other hand, refers to the potential that the firm's consolidated financial statements can be affected by changes in exchange rates.
4. If the firm has an asset in a foreign country, its exposure to currency risk can be properly measured by the coefficient in regressing the dollar value of the foreign asset on the exchange rate. Once the magnitude of exposure is known, the firm can hedge the exposure simply by selling the exposure forward.
5. Unlike the exposure of assets and liabilities that are listed in accounting statements, operating exposure depends on the effect of random exchange rate changes on the firm's future cash flows, which are not readily measurable. Despite this difficulty, it is important to properly manage operating exposure since operating exposure may account for a larger portion of the firm's total exposure than contractual exposure.
6. A firm's operating exposure is determined by (a) the structure of the markets in which the firm sources its inputs and sells its products, and (b) the firm's ability to mitigate the effect of exchange rate changes on its competitive position by adjusting markets, product mix, and sourcing.

7. Since a firm is exposed to exchange risk mainly via the effect of exchange rate changes on its competitive position, it is important to consider exchange exposure management in the context of the firm's overall long-term strategic plan. The objective of exposure management is to stabilize cash flow in the face of fluctuating exchange rates.
8. To manage operating exposure, the firm can use various strategies, such as (a) choosing low-cost production sites, (b) maintaining flexible sourcing policy, (c) diversification of the market, (d) product differentiation, and (e) financial hedging using currency options and forward contracts.

KEY WORDS

asset exposure, 297
competitive effect, 298
conversion effect, 298
diversification of the market, 304
economic exposure, 292
elasticity of demand, 299
exchange rate pass-through, 301
exposure coefficient, 293
financial hedges, 305
flexible sourcing policy, 304
operating exposure, 297
operational hedges, 305
product differentiation, 304
transaction exposure, 292
translation exposure, 292

QUESTIONS

1. How would you define economic exposure to exchange risk?
2. Explain the following statement: "Exposure is the regression coefficient."
3. Suppose that your company has an equity position in a French firm. Discuss the condition under which dollar/franc exchange rate uncertainty does not constitute exchange exposure for your company.
4. Explain the competitive and conversion effects of exchange rate changes on the firm's operating cash flow.
5. Discuss the determinants of operating exposure.
6. Discuss the implications of purchasing power parity for operating exposure.
7. General Motors exports cars to Spain, but the strong dollar against the peseta hurts sales of GM cars in Spain. In the Spanish market, GM faces competition from Italian and French car makers, such as Fiat and Renault, whose currencies remain stable relative to the peseta. What kind of measures would you recommend so that GM can maintain its market share in Spain?
8. What are the advantages and disadvantages to a firm of financial hedging of its operating exposure compared to operational hedges (such as relocating its manufacturing site)?
9. Discuss the advantages and disadvantages of maintaining multiple manufacturing sites as a hedge against exchange rate exposure.
10. Evaluate the following statement: "A firm can reduce its currency exposure by diversifying across different business lines."
11. Exchange rate uncertainty may not necessarily mean that firms face exchange risk exposure. Explain why this may be the case.

PROBLEMS

1. Suppose that you hold a piece of land in the city of London that you may want to sell in one year. As a U.S. resident, you are concerned with the dollar value of the land. Assume that, if the British economy booms in the future, the land will be worth £2,000, and one British pound will be worth $1.40. If the British economy

slows down, on the other hand, the land will be worth less, say, £1,500, but the pound will be stronger, say, \$1.50/£. You feel that the British economy will experience a boom with a 60 percent probability and a slowdown with a 40 percent probability.

a. Estimate your exposure (b) to the exchange risk.
b. Compute the variance of the dollar value of your property that is attributable to exchange rate uncertainty.
c. Discuss how you can hedge your exchange risk exposure and also examine the consequences of hedging.

2. A U.S. firm holds an asset in France and faces the following scenario:

	State 1	State 2	State 3	State 4
Probability	25%	25%	25%	25%
Spot rate	\$.30/FF	\$.25/FF	\$.20/FF	\$.18/FF
P^*	FF1,500	FF1,400	FF1,300	FF1,200
P	\$450	\$350	\$260	\$216

In the above table, P^* is the French franc price of the asset held by the U.S. firm and P is the dollar price of the asset.

a. Compute the exchange exposure faced by the U.S. firm.
b. What is the variance of the dollar price of this asset if the U.S. firm remains unhedged against this exposure?
c. If the U.S. firm hedges against this exposure using a forward contract, what is the variance of the dollar value of the hedged position?

MINI CASE

Economic Exposure of Albion Computers PLC

Consider Case 3 of Albion Computers PLC discussed in the chapter. Now, assume that the pound is expected to depreciate to \$1.50 from the current level of \$1.60 per pound. This implies that the pound cost of the imported part, that is, Intel's microprocessors, is £341 (=\$512/\$1.50). Other variables, such as the unit sales volume and the U.K. inflation rate, remain the same as in Case 3.

a. Compute the projected annual cash flow in dollars.
b. Compute the projected operating gains/losses over the four-year horizon as the discounted present value of change in cash flows, which is due to the pound depreciation, from the benchmark case presented in Exhibit 12.4.
c. What actions, if any, can Albion take to mitigate the projected operating losses due to the pound depreciation?

ENDNOTES

1. Our discussion in this section draws on Adler and Dumas (1984) who clarified the notion of currency exposure.
2. In addition, the covariance between the random error (residual) term and the exchange rate is zero, i.e., $Cov(S,e)=0$, by construction.
3. This case is adopted from Lewent and Kearney (1990).

WEB RESOURCES

www.stern.nyu.edu/rigiddy/fxrisk.htm

Deals with management of foreign exchange risk and economic exposure.

REFERENCES AND SUGGESTED READINGS

Adler, Michael, and Bernard Dumas. "Exposure to Currency Risk: Definition and Measurement." *Financial Management*, Spring (1984), pp. 41–50.

Allayannis, George. "Exchange Rate Exposure Revisited." Working Paper, Stern School of Business, New York University, 1996.

Bartov, Eli, and Gordon Bodnar. "Firm Valuation, Earnings Expectations, and the Exchange-Rate Exposure Effect." *Journal of Finance* 49, 1994, pp. 1755–85.

Dornbusch, Rudiger. "Exchange Rates and Prices." *American Economic Review* 77, 1987, pp. 93–106.

Dufey, Gunter, and S. L. Srinivasulu. "The Case for Corporate Management of Foreign Exchange Risk." *Financial Management*, Winter (1983), pp. 54–62.

Eaker, Mark. "The Numeraire Problem and Foreign Exchange Risk." *Journal of Finance*, May 1981, pp. 419–27.

Flood, Eugene, and Donald Lessard. "On the Measurement of Operating Exposure to Exchange Rates: A Conceptual Approach." *Financial Management* 15, Spring (1986), pp. 25–36.

Glaum, M., M. Brunner, and H. Himmel. "The DAX and the Dollar: The Economic Exchange Rate Exposure of German Corporations." Working Paper, Europa-Universitat Viadrina, 1998.

Hekman, Christine R. "Don't Blame Currency Values for Strategic Errors." *Midland Corporate Finance Journal*, Fall (1986), pp. 45–55.

Jacque, Laurent. "Management of Foreign Exchange Risk: A Review Article." *Journal of International Business Studies*, Spring (1981), pp. 81–100.

Jorion, Philippe. "The Exchange-Rate Exposure of U.S. Multinationals." *Journal of Business* 63 (1990), pp. 331–45.

Lessard, Donald, and S. B. Lightstone. "Volatile Exchange Rates Can Put Operations at Risk." *Harvard Business Review*, July/August 1986, pp. 107–14.

Lewent, Judy, and John Kearney. "Identifying, Measuring and Hedging Currency Risk at Merck." *Journal of Applied Corporate Finance*, Winter (1990), pp. 19–28.

Pringle, John, and Robert Connolly. "The Nature and Causes of Foreign Currency Exposure." *Journal of Applied Corporate Finance*, Fall (1993), pp. 61–72.

Simkins, Berry, and Paul Laux. "Derivatives Use and the Exchange Rate Risk of Investing in Large U.S. Corporations." Case Western Reserve University Working Paper (1996).

Wihlborg, Clas. "Economics of Exposure Management of Foreign Subsidiaries of Multinational Corporations." *Journal of International Business Studies*, Winter (1980), pp. 9–18.

Yang, Jiawen. "Exchange Rate Pass-through in U.S. Manufacturing Industries." *Review of Economics and Statistics* 79 (1997), pp. 95–104.

CHAPTER 13

Management of Transaction Exposure

CHAPTER OUTLINE

As discussed in Chapter 12, the firm is subject to **transaction exposure** when it faces *contractual* cash flows that are fixed in foreign currencies. Suppose that a U.S. firm sold its product to a German client on three-month credit terms and invoiced DM1 million. When the U.S. firm receives DM1 million in three months, it will have to convert (unless it hedges) the marks into dollars at the spot exchange rate prevailing on the maturity date, which cannot be known in advance. As a result, the dollar receipt from this foreign sale becomes uncertain; should the mark appreciate (depreciate) against the dollar, the dollar receipt will be higher (lower). This situation implies that if the firm does nothing about the exposure, it is effectively speculating on the future course of the exchange rate.

For another example of transaction exposure, consider a Japanese firm entering into a loan contract with a Swiss bank that calls for the payment of SF100 million for principal and interest in one year. To the extent that the yen/Swiss franc exchange rate is uncertain, the Japanese firm does not know how much yen it will take to buy SF100 million spot in one year's time. If the yen appreciates (depreciates) against the Swiss franc, a smaller (larger) yen amount will be needed to pay off the SF-denominated loan.

These examples suggest that whenever the firm has foreign-currency-denominated receivables or payables, it is subject to transaction exposure, and their settlements are likely to affect the firm's cash flow position. Furthermore, in view of the fact that firms are now more frequently entering into commercial and financial contracts denominated in foreign currencies, judicious management of transaction exposure has become an important function of international financial management. Unlike economic exposure, transaction exposure is well defined: The magnitude of transaction exposure is the same as the amount of foreign currency that is receivable or payable. This chapter will thus focus on alternative ways of hedging transaction exposure using various financial contracts and *operational techniques:*

Financial contracts

- Forward market hedge
- Money market hedge
- Option market hedge
- Swap market hedge

Operational techniques

- Choice of the invoice currency
- Lead/lag strategy
- Exposure netting

Before we discuss how to manage transaction exposure, however, it is useful to introduce a particular business situation that gives rise to exposure. Suppose that Boeing Corporation exported a Boeing 747 to British Airways and billed £10 million payable in one year. The money market interest rates and foreign exchange rates are given as follows:

The U.S. interest rate:	6.10% per annum.
The U.K. interest rate:	9.00% per annum.
The spot exchange rate:	$1.50/£.
The forward exchange rate:	$1.46/£ (1-year maturity).

Let us now look at the various techniques for managing this transaction exposure.

FORWARD MARKET HEDGE

Perhaps the most direct and popular way of hedging transaction exposure is by currency forward contracts. Generally speaking, the firm may sell (buy) its foreign currency receivables (payables) forward to eliminate its exchange risk exposure. In the above example, in order to hedge foreign exchange exposure, Boeing may simply sell forward its pounds receivable, £10 million for delivery in one year, in exchange for a given amount of U.S. dollars. On the maturity date of the contract, Boeing will have to deliver £10 million to the bank, which is the counterparty of the contract, and, in return, take delivery of $14.6 million ($1.46 × 10 million), regardless of the spot exchange rate that may prevail on the maturity date. Boeing will, of course, use the £10 million that it is going to receive from British Airways to fulfill the forward contract. Since Boeing's pound receivable is exactly offset by the pound payable (created by the forward contract), the company's net pound exposure becomes zero.

Since Boeing is assured of receiving a given dollar amount, $14.6 million, from the counterparty of the forward contract, the dollar proceeds from this British sale will not be affected at all by future changes in the exchange rate. This point is illustrated in Exhibit 13.1. Once Boeing enters into the forward contract, exchange rate uncertainty becomes irrelevant for Boeing. Exhibit 13.1 also illustrates how the dollar proceeds from the British sale will be affected by the future spot exchange rate when exchange exposure is not hedged. The exhibit shows that the dollar proceeds under the forward hedge will be higher than those under the unhedged position if the future spot exchange rate turns out to be less than the forward rate, that is, F = $1.46/£, and the opposite will hold if the future spot rate becomes higher than the forward rate. In the latter case, Boeing forgoes an opportunity to benefit from a strong pound.

Suppose that on the maturity date of the forward contract, the spot rate turns out to be $1.40/£, which is less than the forward rate, $1.46/£. In this case, Boeing would have received $14.0 million, rather than $14.6 million, had it not entered into

EXHIBIT 13.1

Dollar Proceeds from the British Sale: Forward Hedge versus Unhedged Position

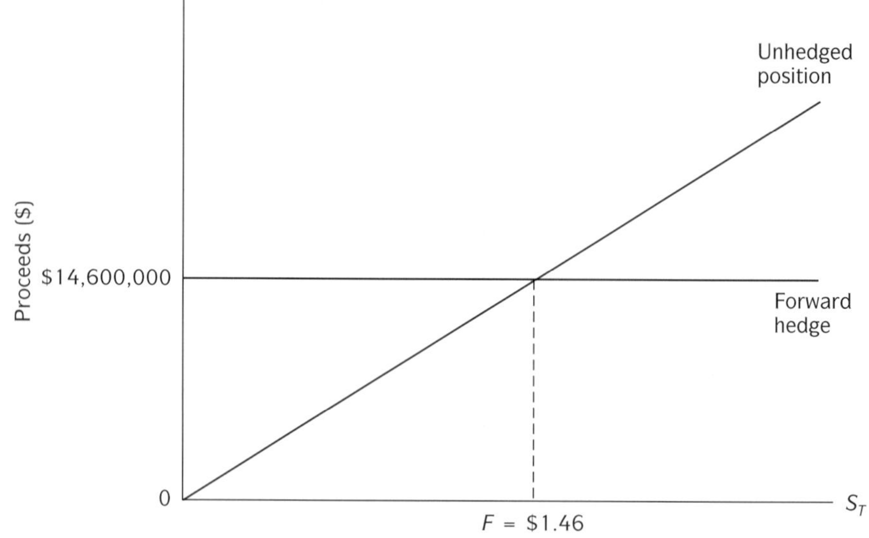

EXHIBIT 13.2

Gains/Losses from Forward Hedge

Spot Exchange Rate on the Maturity Date (S_T)	Receipts from the British Sale: Unhedged Position	Receipts from the British Sale: Forward Hedge	Gains/Losses from Hedge[b]
$1.30	$13,000,000	$14,600,000	$1,600,000
$1.40	$14,000,000	$14,600,000	$ 600,000
$1.46[a]	$14,600,000	$14,600,000	0
$1.50	$15,000,000	$14,600,000	−$ 400,000
$1.60	$16,000,000	$14,600,000	−$1,400,000

[a]The forward exchange rate (F) is $1.46/£ in this example.
[b]The gains/losses are computed as the proceeds under the forward hedge minus the proceeds from the unhedged position at the various spot exchange rates on the maturity date.

the forward contract. Thus, one can say that Boeing gained $0.6 million from forward hedging. Needless to say, Boeing will not always gain in this manner. If the spot rate is, say, $1.50/£ on the maturity date, then Boeing could have received $15.0 million by remaining unhedged. Thus, one can say *ex post* that forward hedging cost Boeing $0.40 million.

The gains and losses from forward hedging can be illustrated as in Exhibits 13.2 and 13.3. The gain/loss is computed as follows:

$$\text{Gain} = (F - S_T) \times £10 \text{ million} \quad (13.1)$$

Obviously, the gain will be positive as long as the forward exchange rate is greater than the spot rate on the maturity date, that is, $F > S_T$, and the gain will be negative (that is, a loss will result) if the opposite holds. As Exhibit 13.3 shows, the firm theoretically can gain as much as $14.6 million when the pound becomes worthless, which, of course, is unlikely, whereas there is no limit to possible losses.

It is important, however, to note that the above analysis is *ex post* in nature, and that no one can know for sure what the future spot rate will be beforehand. The firm must decide whether to hedge or not to hedge *ex ante*. To help the firm decide, it is useful to consider the following three alternative scenarios:

EXHIBIT 13.3

Illustration of Gains and Losses from Forward Hedging

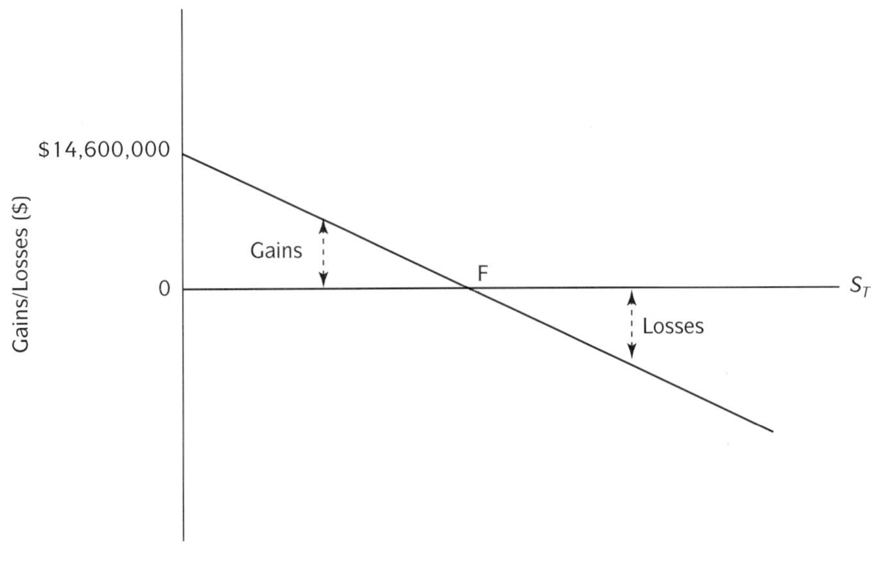

1. $\bar{S}_T \approx F$
2. $\bar{S}_T < F$
3. $\bar{S}_T > F$

where $\bar{S}_T$ denotes the firm's expected spot exchange rate for the maturity date.

Under the first scenario, where the firm's expected future spot exchange rate, $\bar{S}_T$, is about the same as the forward rate, F, the "expected" gains or losses are approximately zero. But forward hedging eliminates exchange exposure. In other words, the firm can eliminate foreign exchange exposure without sacrificing any expected dollar proceeds from the foreign sale. Under this scenario the firm would be inclined to hedge as long as it is averse to risk. Note that this scenario becomes valid when the forward exchange rate is an unbiased predictor of the future spot rate.[1]

Under the second scenario, where the firm's expected future spot exchange rate is less than the forward rate, the firm expects a positive gain from forward hedging. Since the firm expects to increase the dollar proceeds while eliminating exchange exposure, it would be even more inclined to hedge under this scenario than under the first scenario. The second scenario, however, implies that the firm's management dissents from the market's consensus forecast of the future spot exchange rate as reflected in the forward rate.

Under the third scenario, on the other hand, where the firm's expected future spot exchange rate is more than the forward rate, the firm can eliminate exchange exposure via the forward contract only at the cost of reduced expected dollar proceeds from the foreign sale. Thus, the firm would be less inclined to hedge under this scenario, other things being equal. Despite lower expected dollar proceeds, however, the firm may still end up hedging. Whether the firm actually hedges or not depends on the degree of risk aversion; the more risk averse the firm is, the more likely it is to hedge. From the perspective of a hedging firm, the reduction in the expected dollar proceeds can be viewed implicitly as an "insurance premium" paid for avoiding the hazard of exchange risk.

The firm can use a currency futures contract, rather than a forward contract, to hedge. However, a futures contract is not as suitable as a forward contract for hedging purpose for two reasons. First, unlike forward contracts that are tailor-made to the firm's specific needs, futures contracts are standardized instruments in terms of contract size, delivery date, and so forth. In most cases, therefore, the firm can only hedge approximately. Second, due to the marking-to-market property, there are interim cash flows prior to the maturity date of the futures contract that may have to be invested at uncertain interest rates. As a result, exact hedging again would be difficult.

MONEY MARKET HEDGE

Transaction exposure can also be hedged by lending and borrowing in the domestic and foreign money markets. Generally speaking, the firm may borrow (lend) in foreign currency to hedge its foreign currency receivables (payables), thereby matching its assets and liabilities in the same currency. Again using the same example presented above, Boeing can eliminate the exchange exposure arising from the British sale by first borrowing in pounds, then converting the loan proceeds into dollars, which then can be invested at the dollar interest rate. On the maturity date of the loan, Boeing is going to use the pound receivable to pay off the pound loan. If Boeing borrows a particular pound amount so that the maturity value of this loan becomes exactly equal to the pound receivable from the British sale, Boeing's net pound exposure is reduced to zero, and Boeing will receive the future maturity value of the dollar investment.

The first important step in money market hedging is to determine the amount of pounds to borrow. Since the maturity value of borrowing should be the same as the pound receivable, the amount to borrow can be computed as the discounted present value of the pound receivable, that is, £10 million/(1.09) = £9,174,312. When Boeing borrows £9,174,312, it then has to repay £10 million in one year, which is equivalent to its pound receivable. The step-by-step procedure of money market hedging can be illustrated as follows:

Step 1: Borrow £9,174,312 in the U.K.

Step 2: Convert £9,174,312 into $13,761,468 at the current spot exchange rate of $1.50/£

Step 3: Invest $13,761,468 in the United States.

Step 4: Collect £10 million from British Airways and use it to repay the pound loan.

Step 5: Receive the maturity value of the dollar investment, that is, $14,600,918 = $13,761,468(1.061), which is the guaranteed dollar proceeds from the British sale.

Exhibit 13.4 provides a cash flow analysis of money market hedging. The table shows that the net cash flow is zero at the present time, implying that, apart from possible transaction costs, the money market hedge is fully self-financing. The table also clearly shows how the £10 million receivable is exactly offset by the £10 million

EXHIBIT 13.4

Cash Flow Analysis of a Money Market Hedge

Transaction	Current Cash Flow	Cash Flow at Maturity
1. Borrow pounds	£ 9,174,312	−£10,000,000
2. Buy dollar spot with pounds	$13,761,468 −£ 9,174,312	
3. Invest in the United States	−$13,761,468	$14,600,918
4. Collect pound receivable		£10,000,000
Net cash flow	0	$14,600,918

payable (created by borrowing), leaving a net cash flow of \$14,600,918 on the maturity date.[2]

The maturity value of the dollar investment from the money market hedge turns out to be nearly identical to the dollar proceeds from forward hedging. This result is no coincidence. Rather, this is due to the fact that the interest rate parity (IRP) condition is approximately holding in our example. If the IRP is not holding, the dollar proceeds from money market hedging will not be the same as those from forward hedging. As a result, one hedging method will dominate another. In a competitive and efficient world financial market, however, any deviations from IRP are not likely to persist.

OPTIONS MARKET HEDGE

One possible shortcoming of both forward and money market hedges is that these methods completely eliminate exchange exposure. Consequently, the firm has to forgo the opportunity to benefit from favorable exchange rate changes. To elaborate on this point, let us assume that the spot exchange rate turns out to be \$1.60 per pound on the maturity date of the forward contract. In this instance, forward hedging would cost the firm \$1.4 million in terms of forgone dollar receipts (see Exhibit 13.2). If Boeing had indeed entered into a forward contract, it would regret its decision to do so. With its pound receivable, Boeing ideally would like to protect itself only if the pound weakens, while retaining the opportunity to benefit if the pound strengthens. Currency options provide such a *flexible* "optional" hedge against exchange exposure. Generally speaking, the firm may buy a foreign currency call (put) option to hedge its foreign currency payables (receivables).

To show how the options hedge works, suppose that in the over-the-counter market Boeing purchased a put option on 10 million British pounds with an exercise price of \$1.46 and a one-year expiration. Assume that the option premium (price) was \$0.02 per pound. Boeing thus paid \$200,000 (= \$0.02 × 10 million) for the option. This transaction provides Boeing with the right, but not the obligation, to sell up to £10 million for \$1.46/£, regardless of the future spot rate.

Now assume that the spot exchange rate turns out to be \$1.30 on the expiration date. Since Boeing has the right to sell each pound for \$1.46, it will certainly exercise its put option on the pound and convert £10 million into \$14.6 million. The main advantage of options hedging is that the firm can decide whether to exercise the option based on the realized spot exchange rate on the expiration date. Recall that Boeing paid \$200,000 upfront for the option. Considering the time value of money, this upfront cost is equivalent to \$212,200 (= \$200,000 × 1.061) as of the expiration date. This means that under the options hedge, the net dollar proceeds from the British sale become \$14,387,800:

$$\$14{,}387{,}800 = \$14{,}600{,}000 - \$212{,}200$$

Since Boeing is going to exercise its put option on the pound whenever the future spot exchange rate falls below the exercise rate of \$1.46, it is assured of a "minimum" dollar receipt of \$14,387,800 from the British sale.

Next, consider an alternative scenario where the pound appreciates against the dollar. Assume that the spot rate turns out to be \$1.60 per pound on the expiration date. In this event, Boeing would have no incentive to exercise the option. It will rather let the option expire and convert £10 million into \$16 million at the spot rate. Subtracting \$212,200 for the option cost, the net dollar proceeds will become \$15,787,800 under the option hedge. As suggested by these scenarios, the options hedge allows the firm to *limit the downside risk while preserving the upside potential.* The firm, however, has to pay for this flexibility in terms of the option premium.

EXHIBIT 13.5

Dollar Proceeds from Options Hedge

Future Spot Exchange Rate (S_T)	Exercise Decision	Gross Dollar Proceeds	Option Cost	Net Dollar Proceeds
\$1.30	Exercise	\$14,600,000	\$212,200	\$14,387,800
\$1.40	Exercise	\$14,600,000	\$212,200	\$14,387,800
\$1.46	Neutral	\$14,600,000	\$212,200	\$14,387,800
\$1.50	Not exercise	\$15,000,000	\$212,200	\$14,787,800
\$1.60	Not exercise	\$16,000,000	\$212,200	\$15,787,800

Note: The exercise exchange rate (E) is \$1.46 in this example.

EXHIBIT 13.6

Dollar Proceeds from the British Sale: Option versus Forward Hedge

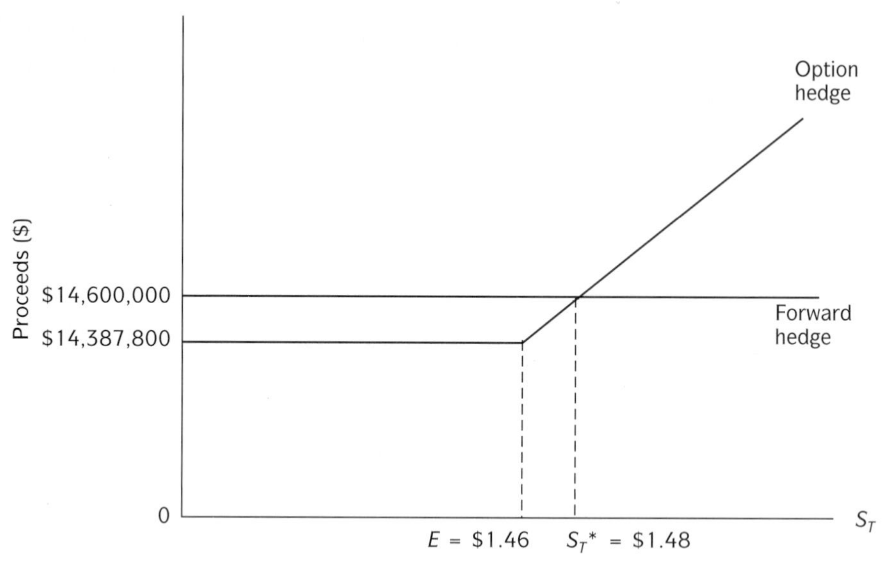

There rarely exist free lunches in finance! Note that neither the forward nor the money market hedge involves any upfront cost.

Exhibit 13.5 provides the net dollar proceeds from the British sale under options hedging for a range of future spot exchange rates. The same results are illustrated in Exhibit 13.6. As Exhibit 13.6 shows, the options hedge sets a "floor" for the dollar proceeds. The future dollar proceeds will be at least \$14,387,800 under the option hedge. Boeing thus can be said to have an insurance policy against the exchange risk hazard; the upfront option cost, \$200,000, Boeing incurred can be explicitly regarded as an insurance premium. When a firm has an account payable rather than a receivable, in terms of a foreign currency, the firm can set a "ceiling" for the future dollar cost of buying the foreign currency amount by buying a call option on the foreign currency amount.

Exhibit 13.6 also compares the dollar proceeds from forward and options hedges. As indicated in the exhibit, the options hedge dominates the forward hedge for future spot rates greater than \$1.48 per pound, whereas the opposite holds for spot rates lower than \$1.48 per pound. Boeing will be indifferent between the two hedging methods at the "break-even" spot rate of \$1.48 per pound.

The break-even spot rate, which is useful for choosing a hedging method, can be determined as follows:

$$\$(10{,}000{,}000)S_T - \$212{,}200 = \$14{,}600{,}000$$

EXHIBIT 13.7 Boeing's Alternative Hedging Strategies: A Summary

Strategy	Transactions	Outcomes
Forward market hedge	1. Sell £10,000,000 forward for U.S. dollars now. 2. In one year, receive £10,000,000 rate from the British client and deliver it to the counterparty of the forward contract.	Assured of receiving $14,600,000 in one year; future spot exchange becomes irrelevant.
Money market hedge	1. Borrow £9,174,312 and buy $13,761,468 spot now. 2. In one year, collect £10,000,000 from the British client and pay off the pound loan using the amount.	Assured of receiving $13,761,468 now or $14,600,918 in one year; future spot exchange rate becomes irrelevant.
Options market hedge	1. Buy a put option on £10,000,000 for an upfront cost of $200,000. 2. In one year, decide whether to exercise the option upon observing the prevailing spot exchange rate.	Assured of receiving at least $14,387,800 or more if the future spot exchange rate exceeds the exercise exchange rate; Boeing controls the downside risk while retaining the upside potential.

By solving the equation for S_T, we obtain the break-even spot rate, $S_T^* = \$1.48$. The break-even analysis suggests that if the firm's expected future spot rate is greater (less) than the break-even rate, then the options (forward) hedge might be preferred.

Unlike the forward contract, which has only one forward rate for a given maturity, there are multiple exercise exchange rates (prices) for the options contract. In the preceding discussion, we worked with an option with an exercise price of $1.46. Considering that Boeing has a pound receivable, it is tempting to think that it would be a good idea for Boeing to buy a put option with a higher exercise price, thereby increasing the minimum dollar receipt from the British sale. But it becomes immediately clear that the firm has to pay for it in terms of a higher option premium. Again, there is no free lunch. Choice of the exercise price for the options contract ultimately depends on the extent to which the firm is willing to bear exchange risk. For instance, if the firm's objective is only to avoid very unfavorable exchange rate changes (that is, a major depreciation of the pound in Boeing's example), then it should consider buying an out-of-money put option with a low exercise price, saving option costs. The three alternative hedging strategies are summarized in Exhibit 13.7.

CROSS-HEDGING MINOR CURRENCY EXPOSURE

If a firm has receivables or payables in major currencies such as the British pound, German mark, and Japanese yen, it can easily use forward, money market, or options contracts to manage its exchange risk exposure. In contrast, if the firm has positions in minor currencies such as the Korean won, Portuguese escudo, and Czech koruna, it may be either very costly or impossible to use financial contracts in these currencies. This is because financial markets of developing countries are relatively underdeveloped and often highly regulated. Facing this situation, the firm may consider using **cross-hedging** techniques to manage its minor currency exposure. Cross-hedging involves hedging a position in one asset by taking a position in another asset.

Suppose a U.S. firm has an account receivable in Korean won and would like to hedge its won position. If there were a well-functioning forward market in won, the firm would simply sell the won receivable forward. But the firm finds it impossible to do so. However, since the won/dollar exchange rate is highly correlated with the yen/dollar exchange rate, the U.S. firm may sell a yen amount, which is equivalent to the won receivable, forward against the dollar thereby cross-hedging its won exposure. Obviously, the effectiveness of this cross-hedging technique would depend on the stability and strength of the won/yen correlation. A study by Aggarwal and Demaskey (1997) indicates that Japanese yen derivative contracts are fairly effective in cross-hedging exposure to minor Asian currencies such as the Indonesian rupiah, Korean won, Philippine peso, and Thai bhat. Likewise, German mark derivatives can be effective in cross-hedging exposures in some Central and East European currencies such as the Czech koruna, Estonian kroon and Hungarian forint.

Another study by Benet (1990) suggests that commodity futures contracts may be used effectively to cross-hedge some minor currency exposures. Suppose the dollar price of the Mexican peso is positively correlated to the world oil price. Note that Mexico is a major exporter of oil, accounting for roughly 5 percent of the world market share. Considering this situation, a firm may use oil futures contracts to manage its peso exposure. The firm can sell (buy) oil futures if it has peso receivables (payables). In the same vein, soybean and coffee futures contracts may be used to cross-hedge a Brazilian real exposure. Again, the effectiveness of this cross-hedging technique would depend on the strength and stability of the relationship between the exchange rate and the commodity futures prices.

HEDGING CONTINGENT EXPOSURE

In addition to providing a flexible hedge against exchange exposure, options contracts can also provide an effective hedge against what might be called **contingent exposure.** Contingent exposure refers to a situation in which the firm may or may not be subject to exchange exposure. Suppose General Electric (GE) is bidding on a hydroelectric project in Quebec Province, Canada. If the bid is accepted, which will be known in three months, GE is going to receive C$100 million to initiate the project. Since GE may or may not face exchange exposure depending on whether its bid will be accepted, it faces a typical contingent exposure situation.[3]

It is difficult to deal with contingent exposure using traditional hedging tools like forward contracts. Suppose that GE sold C$100 million forward to hedge the contingent exposure. If GE's bid is accepted, then GE will have no problem because it will have C$100 million to fulfill the forward contract. However, if the bid is rejected, GE now faces an unhedged short position in Canadian dollars. Clearly, a forward contract does not provide a satisfactory hedge against contingent exposure. A "do-nothing" policy does not guarantee a satisfactory outcome either. The problem with this policy is that if GE's bid is accepted, the firm ends up with an unhedged long position in Canadian dollars.

An alternative approach is to buy a three-month put option on C$100 million. In this case, there are four possible outcomes:

1. The bid is accepted and the spot exchange rate turns out to be less than the exercise rate: In this case, the firm will simply exercise the put option and convert C$100 million at the exercise rate.
2. The bid is accepted and the spot exchange rate turns out to be greater than the exercise rate: In this case, the firm will let the put option expire and convert C$100 million at the spot rate.
3. The bid is rejected and the spot exchange rate turns out to be less than the exercise rate: In this case, although the firm does not have Canadian dollars, it will exercise the put option and make a profit.

EXHIBIT 13.8

Contingent Exposure Management: The Case of GE Bidding for a Quebec Hydro-electric Project

	Bid Outcome	
Alternative Strategies	**Bid Accepted**	**Bid Rejected**
Do nothing	*An unhedged long position in C$100 million*	No exposure
Sell C$ forward	No exposure	*An unhedged short position in C$100 million*
Buy a put option on C$[a]	If the future spot rate becomes less than the exercise rate, $(S_T < E)$	
	Convert C$100 million at the exercise price	Exercise the option and make a profit
	If the future spot rate becomes greater than the exercise rate, $(S_T > E)$	
	Let the option expire and convert C$100 million at the spot exchange rate	Simply let the option expire

[a]If the future spot rate turns out to be equal to the exercise price, i.e. $S_T = E$, GE will be indifferent between (i) exercising the option and (ii) letting the option expire and converting C$100 million at the spot rate.

4. The bid is rejected and the spot rate turns out to be greater than the exercise rate: In this case, the firm will simply let the put option expire.

The above scenarios indicate that when the put option is purchased, each outcome is adequately covered; the firm will not be left with an unhedged foreign currency position. Again, it is stressed that the firm has to pay the option premium upfront. The preceding discussion is summarized in Exhibit 13.8.

HEDGING RECURRENT EXPOSURE WITH SWAP CONTRACTS

Firms often have to deal with a "sequence" of accounts payable or receivable in terms of a foreign currency. Such recurrent cash flows in a foreign currency can best be hedged using a currency swap contract, which is an agreement to exchange one currency for another at a predetermined exchange rate, that is, the swap rate, on a sequence of future dates. As such, a swap contract is like a portfolio of forward contracts with different maturities. Swaps are very flexible in terms of amount and maturity; the maturity can range from a few months to 20 years.

Suppose that Boeing is scheduled to deliver an aircraft to British Airways at the beginning of each year for the next five years, starting in 1996. British Airways, in turn, is scheduled to pay £10,000,000 to Boeing on December 1 of each year for five years, starting in 1996. In this case, Boeing faces a sequence of exchange risk exposures. As previously mentioned, Boeing can hedge this type of exposure using a swap agreement by which Boeing delivers £10,000,000 to the counterparty of the contract on December 1 of each year for five years and takes delivery of a predetermined dollar amount each year. If the agreed swap exchange rate is $1.50/£, then Boeing will receive $15 million each year, regardless of the future spot and forward rates. Note that a sequence of five forward contracts would not be priced at a uniform rate,

\$1.50/£; the forward rates will be different for different maturities. In addition, longer-term forward contracts are not readily available.

HEDGING THROUGH INVOICE CURRENCY

While such financial hedging instruments as forward, money market, swap, and options contracts are well known, hedging through the choice of invoice currency, an operational technique, has not received much attention. The firm can *shift, share,* or *diversify* exchange risk by appropriately choosing the currency of invoice. For instance, if Boeing invoices \$15 million rather than £10 million for the sale of the aircraft, then it does not face exchange exposure anymore. Note, however, that the exchange exposure has not disappeared; it has merely shifted to the British importer. British Airways now has an account payable denominated in U.S. dollars.

Instead of shifting the exchange exposure entirely to British Airways, Boeing can share the exposure with British Airways by, for example, invoicing half of the bill in U.S. dollars and the remaining half in British pounds, that is, \$7.5 million and £5 million. In this case, the magnitude of Boeing's exchange exposure is reduced by half. As a practical matter, however, the firm may not be able to use risk shifting or sharing as much as it wishes to for fear of losing sales to competitors. Only an exporter with substantial market power can use this approach. In addition, if the currencies of both the exporter and the importer are not suitable for settling international trade, neither party can resort to risk shifting/sharing to deal with exchange exposure.

The firm can diversify exchange exposure to some extent by using currency basket units such as the SDR and ECU as the invoice currency. Often, multinational corporations and sovereign entities are known to float bonds denominated either in the SDR or in the ECU. For example, the Egyptian government charges for the use of the Suez Canal using the SDR. Obviously, these currency baskets are used to reduce exchange exposure. As previously noted, the SDR comprises five individual currencies, the U.S. dollar, the German mark, the Japanese yen, the British pound, and the French franc. Because the SDR is a portfolio of currencies, its value should be substantially more stable than the value of any individual constituent currency.[4] Currency basket units can be a useful hedging tool especially for long-term exposure for which no forward or options contracts are readily available.

HEDGING VIA LEAD AND LAG

Another operational technique the firm can use to reduce transaction exposure is leading and lagging foreign currency receipts and payments. To "lead" means to pay or collect early, whereas to "lag" means to pay or collect late. The firm would like to lead soft currency receivables and lag hard currency receivables to avoid the loss from depreciation of the soft currency and benefit from the appreciation of the hard currency. For the same reason, the firm will attempt to lead the hard currency payables and lag soft currency payables.

To the extent that the firm can effectively implement the **lead/lag strategy,** the transaction exposure the firm faces can be reduced. However, a word of caution is in order. Suppose, concerned with the likely depreciation of sterling, Boeing would like British Airways to prepay £10 million. Boeing's attempt to lead the pound receivable may encounter difficulties. First of all, British Airways would like to lag this payment, which is denominated in the soft currency (the pound), and thus has no incentive to prepay unless Boeing offers a substantial discount to compensate for the prepayment. This, of course, reduces the benefits of collecting the pound receivable early. Second, pressing British Airways for prepayment can hamper future sales efforts by Boeing. Third, to the extent that the original invoice price, £10 million, incorporates the expected depreciation of the pound, Boeing is already partially protected against the depreciation of the pound.

The lead/lag strategy can be employed more effectively to deal with intrafirm payables and receivables, such as material costs, rents, royalties, interests, and dividends, among subsidiaries of the same multinational corporation. Since managements of various subsidiaries of the same firm are presumably working for the good of the entire firm, the lead/lag strategy can be applied more aggressively.

EXPOSURE NETTING

In 1984, Lufthansa, a German airline, signed a contract to buy $3 billion worth of aircraft from Boeing and entered into a forward contract to purchase $1.5 billion forward for the purpose of hedging against the expected appreciation of the dollar against the German mark. This decision, however, suffered from a major flaw: A significant portion of Lufthansa's cash flows was also dollar-denominated. As a result, Lufthansa's net exposure to the exchange risk might not have been significant. Lufthansa had a so-called natural hedge. In 1985, the dollar depreciated substantially against the mark and, as a result, Lufthansa experienced a major foreign exchange loss from settling the forward contract. This episode shows that when a firm has both receivables and payables in a given foreign currency, it should consider hedging only its net exposure.

So far, we have discussed exposure management on a currency-by-currency basis. In reality, a typical multinational corporation is likely to have a portfolio of currency positions. For instance, a U.S. firm may have an account payable in German marks and, at the same time, an account receivable in Swiss francs. Considering that the mark and franc move against the dollar almost in lockstep, the firm can just wait until these accounts become due and then buy marks spot with francs. It can be wasteful and unnecessary to buy marks forward and sell francs forward. In other words, if the firm has a portfolio of currency positions, it makes sense to hedge residual exposure rather than hedge each currency position separately.

If the firm would like to apply exposure netting aggressively, it helps to centralize the firm's exchange exposure management function in one location. Many multinational corporations are using a **reinvoice center,** a financial subsidiary, as a mechanism for centralizing exposure management functions. All the invoices arising from intrafirm transactions are sent to the reinvoice center, where exposure is netted. Once the residual exposure is determined, then foreign exchange experts at the center determine optimal hedging methods and implement them.

SHOULD THE FIRM HEDGE?

We have discussed how the firm can hedge exchange exposure if it wishes. We have not discussed whether the firm should try to hedge to begin with. As can be seen from the International Finance in Practice box on page 324, "To Hedge or Not to Hedge," there hardly exists a consensus on whether the firm should hedge. Some would argue that exchange exposure management at the corporate level is redundant when stockholders can manage the exposure themselves. Others would argue that what matters in the firm valuation is only systematic risk; corporate risk management may only reduce the total risk. These arguments suggest that corporate exposure management would not necessarily add to the value of the firm.

INTERNATIONAL FINANCE IN PRACTICE

To Hedge or Not to Hedge

"Most value-maximising firms do not hedge." Thus Merton Miller and Christopher Culp, two economists at the University of Chicago, said in a recent article[1] about Metallgesellschaft, a firm that saw its value plunge after its oil-price hedging strategy came a cropper. Yet the vast majority of firms that use derivatives do so to hedge. Last year's survey of big American non-financial companies by the Wharton School and Chase Manhattan bank found that, of those firms that used derivatives (about one-third of the sample), some 75% said they did so to hedge commitments. As many as 40% of the derivatives users said they sometimes took a view on the direction of markets, but only 8% admitted to doing so frequently.

To justify speculation, managers ought to have good reason to suppose that they can consistently outwit firms for which playing the financial markets is a core business. Commodity businesses, such as oil or grain companies taking positions on the direction of their related commodity markets, may have such reason, but non-financial firms taking bets on interest rates or foreign-exchange rates almost certainly do not—though some claim to make a profit on it. But why might hedging be wrong?

In the 1950s, Merton Miller and Franco Modigliani, another financial economist, demonstrated that firms make money only if they make good investments—the kind that increase their operating cash flows. Whether those investments are financed through debt, equity or retained earnings is irrelevant. Different methods of financing simply determine how a firm's value is divided between its various sorts of investors (eg, shareholders or bondholders), not the value itself. This surprising insight helped win each of them a Nobel prize. If they are right, it has crucial implications for hedging. For if methods of financing and the character of financial risks do not matter, managing them is pointless. It cannot add to the firm's value; on the contrary, as derivatives do not come free, using them for hedging might actually lower that value. Moreover, as Messrs Miller and Modigliani showed, if investors want to avoid the financial risks attached to holding shares in a firm, they can diversify their portfolio of holdings. Firms need not manage their financial risks; investors can do it for themselves.

In recent years, other academics have challenged the Miller-Modigliani thesis—at least in its pure form—and demonstrated that hedging can sometimes add value. That is because firms may be able to manage certain risks internally in ways that cannot be replicated by outside investors. Some investors may not want, or be able, to hold diversified share portfolios (for instance, if the firm is family-owned). It may be possible to use derivatives to reduce profits in good years and raise them in bad years in order to cut the firm's average tax bill. Hedging can also be used to prevent the firm getting into financial difficulties, or even going bust.

Recently, another view has been winning converts. According to Kenneth Froot, David Sharfstein and Jeremy Stein, three Boston-based economists, firms should hedge to ensure they always have sufficient cash flow to fund their planned investment programme.[2] Otherwise some potentially profitable investments may be missed because of inefficiencies in the bond and equity markets that prevent the firm raising the funds, or the reluctance of managers to tap these markets when internal cash is tight. Merck, an American pharmaceuticals firm, has helped to pioneer the use of derivatives to ensure that investment plans—particularly in R&D—can always be financed. In a paper explaining the firm's strategy, Judy Lewent and John Kearney observed that "our experience, and that of the [drugs] industry in general, has been that

While the above arguments against corporate risk management may be valid in a "perfect" capital market, one can make a case for it based on various market imperfections:

1. Information asymmetry: Management knows about the firm's exposure position much better than stockholders. Thus, the management of the firm, not its stockholders, should manage exchange exposure.
2. Differential transaction costs: The firm is in a position to acquire low-cost hedges; transaction costs for individual stockholders can be substantial. Also, the firm has hedging tools like the reinvoice center that are not available to stockholders.

cash-flow and earnings uncertainty caused by exchange-rate volatility leads to a reduction in research spending."[3]

Though apparently simple, such a strategy has some intriguing implications. As Messrs Froot, Scharfstein and Stein point out, the factors that cause cash flow to fall below expectations may also cut the number of profitable investment opportunities, so lessening the need to hedge. For instance, an oil company's cash flow may suffer due to a fall in oil prices. However, that fall in prices also reduces the value of investing in developing new oil fields. With fewer profitable projects to invest in, the firm will need less cash to finance investment.

All About Cash Flow

Rene Stulz, an economist at Ohio State University, sees even more powerful implications.[4] He says that there are only a couple of good reasons why a firm should hedge. One is to cut its tax bills, which is likely to happen only if the firm's profits tend to yo-yo between lower and higher tax bands. The other one is being unable to get cash when it needs it, or facing a serious risk of running short. By this rule, reckons Mr. Stulz, a firm with little debt or with highly-rated debt has no need to hedge, as the risk of it getting into financial trouble is tiny. If he is right, many of America's biggest hedgers—including some of those that have revealed losses on derivatives, such as Procter & Gamble—may be wasting their energies, or worse. By contrast, Mr. Stulz thinks that if a firm is highly geared, hedging can boost its value significantly. Indeed, during the leveraged buy-out craze of the 1980s, when firms were taken over by buying off shareholders and loading up on debt, tough risk-management requirements were standard in any borrowing arrangement.

Messrs. Culp and Miller, of the University of Chicago, take this argument a step further in defending the management of Metallgesellschaft from some of the wilder accusations of recklessness (a matter that is now before the American courts). Instead of analysing the firm's hedging strategy (which involved selling oil for up to ten years ahead and hedging this exposure with futures contracts) in terms of its effectiveness in reducing risk, Messrs. Culp and Miller argue that the company had no need to reduce its risk-exposure because it had no reason to suppose it could not get hold of cash if needed. After all, the mighty Deutsche Bank, as its principal creditor and controlling shareholder, was behind the firm, ensuring that it could not go bust; and, as it turned out, it did not. Rather, the aim of the hedging strategy was to exploit what Metallgesellschaft thought was its superior understanding of the relationship between spot prices and futures prices—risky but not obviously foolish.

Not everyone agrees that firms with little debt should not hedge. Myron Scholes, an economist at Stanford University, reaches the opposite conclusion: firms with little debt could reduce their riskiness by hedging, and so be able to borrow more and rely less on equity. Equity can be expensive compared with debt; it is inherently riskier, offering no guaranteed payout, so investors require a higher average return on it than they do on bonds. Ultimately, through risk-reducing hedging and borrowing, more firms might be able to remain (or become) privately owned, reckons Mr. Scholes. But to do this well, managers will need a very good understanding of the risks to which their firm is exposed, and of opportunities to hedge.

However, the way firms typically use derivatives to reduce the cost of capital is different from that described above. Rather than hedge and borrow more, they substitute for traditional debt a hybrid of bonds and options and/or futures that will pay off in certain circumstances, thus lowering capital costs. This is speculation dressed up as prudence, because if events take an unexpected turn, capital costs go up by at least the cost of the options.

[1]"Hedging in the Theory of Corporate Finance: A Reply to our Critics." By Christopher Culp and Merton Miller. *Journal of Applied Corporate Finance;* Spring 1995.

[2]"A Framework for Risk Management." By Kenneth Froot, David Scharfstein and Jeremy Stein. *Harvard Business Review;* November 1994.

[3]"Identifying, Measuring and Hedging Currency Risk at Merck." By Judy Lewent and John Kearney. In *The New Corporate Finance,* edited by Donald Chew, McGraw-Hill; 1993.

[4]"Rethinking Risk Management" By Rene Stulz. Ohio State University working paper; 1995.

Source: *Economist,* February 10, 1996, pp. PS10–12. © 1996 The Economist Newspaper Group, Inc. Reprinted with permission.

3. Default costs: If default costs are significant, corporate hedging would be justifiable because it will reduce the probability of default. Perception of a reduced default risk, in turn, can lead to a better credit rating and lower financing costs.
4. Progressive corporate taxes: Under progressive corporate tax rates, stable before-tax earnings lead to lower corporate taxes than volatile earnings with the same average value. This happens because under progressive tax rates, the firm pays more taxes in high-earning periods than it saves in low-earning periods.

The last point merits elaboration. Suppose the country's corporate income tax system is such that a tax rate of 20 percent applies to the first $10 million of corporate

EXHIBIT 13.9

Tax Savings from Hedging Exchange Risk Exposure

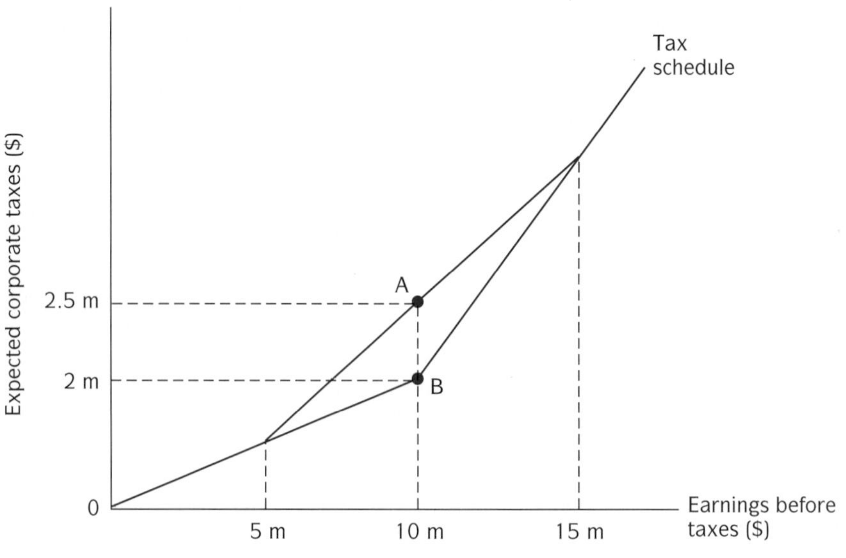

earnings and a 40 percent rate applies to any earnings exceeding \$10 million. Firms thus face a simple progressive tax structure. Now consider an exporting firm that expects to earn \$15 million if the dollar depreciates, but only \$5 million if the dollar appreciates. Let's assume that the dollar may appreciate or depreciate with equal chances. In this case, the firm's expected tax will be \$2.5 million:

$$\begin{aligned}\text{Expected tax} &= \tfrac{1}{2}[(.20)(\$5{,}000{,}000)] + \tfrac{1}{2}[(.20)(\$10{,}000{,}000) \\ &\quad + (.40)(\$5{,}000{,}000)] \\ &= \$2{,}500{,}000\end{aligned}$$

Now consider another firm, B, that is identical to firm A in every respect except that, unlike firm A, firm B aggressively and successfully hedges its risk exposure and, as a result, it can expect to realize certain earnings of \$10,000,000, the same as firm A's expected earnings. Firm B, however, only expects to pay \$2 million as taxes. Obviously, hedging results in a \$500,000 tax saving. Exhibit 13.9 illustrates this situation.

While not every firm is hedging exchange exposure, many firms are engaged in hedging activities, suggesting that corporate risk management is relevant to maximizing the firm's value. To the extent that for various reasons, stockholders themselves cannot properly manage exchange risk, the firm's managers can do it for them, contributing to the firm's value. Some corporate hedging activities, however, might be motivated by managerial objectives; managers may want to stabilize cash flows so that the risk to their human capital can be reduced.

WHAT RISK MANAGEMENT PRODUCTS DO FIRMS USE?

In a recent survey, Jesswein, Kwok, and Folks (1995) documented the extent of knowledge and use of foreign exchange risk management products by U.S. corporations. Based on a survey of *Fortune* 500 firms, they found that the traditional forward contract is the most popular product. As Exhibit 13.10 shows, about 93 percent of respondents of the survey used forward contracts. This old, traditional instrument has not been supplanted by recent "fancy" innovations. The next commonly used

EXHIBIT 13.10

A Survey of Knowledge and Use of Foreign Exchange Risk Management Products[a]

Type of Product	Heard of (Awareness)	Used (Adoption)
Forward contracts	100.0%	93.1%
Foreign currency swaps	98.8	52.6
Foreign currency futures	98.8	20.1
Exchange-traded currency options	96.4	17.3
Exchange-traded futures options	95.8	8.9
Over-the-counter currency options	93.5	48.8
Cylinder options	91.2	28.7
Synthetic forwards	88.0	22.0
Synthetic options	88.0	18.6
Participating forwards, etc.	83.6	15.8
Forward exchange agreements, etc.	81.7	14.8
Foreign currency warrants	77.7	4.2
Break forwards, etc.	65.3	4.9
Compound options	55.8	3.8
Lookback options, etc.	52.1	5.1
Average across products	84.4%	23.9%

[a]The products are ranked by the percentages of respondents who have heard of products. There are 173 respondents in total.

Source: Kurt Jesswein, Chuck Kwok, and William Folks, Jr., "Corporate Use of Innovative Foreign Exchange Risk Management Products." *Columbia Journal of World Business* (Fall 1995).

instruments are foreign currency swaps (52.6 percent) and over-the-counter currency options (48.8 percent). Such recent innovations as compound options (3.8 percent) and lookback options (5.1 percent) are among the least extensively used instruments. These findings seem to indicate that most U.S. firms meet their exchange risk management needs with forward, swap, and options contracts.

The Jesswein, Kwok, and Folks survey also shows that, among the various industries, the finance/insurance/real estate industry stands out as the most frequent user of exchange risk management products. This finding is not surprising. This industry has more finance experts who are skillful at using derivative securities. In addition, this industry handles mainly financial assets, which tend to be exposed to exchange risk. The survey further shows that the corporate use of foreign exchange risk management products is positively related to the firm's degree of international involvement. This finding is not surprising either. As the firm becomes more internationalized through cross-border trade and investments, it is likely to handle an increasing amount of foreign currencies, giving rise to a greater demand for exchange risk hedging.

SUMMARY

1. The firm is subject to a transaction exposure when it faces contractual cash flows denominated in foreign currencies. Transaction exposure can be hedged by financial contracts like forward, money market, and options contracts, as well as by such operational techniques as the choice of invoice currency, lead/lag strategy, and exposure netting.
2. If the firm has a foreign-currency-denominated receivable (payable), it can hedge the exposure by selling (buying) the foreign currency receivable (payable) forward. The firm can *expect* to eliminate the exposure without incurring costs as long as the forward exchange rate is an unbiased predictor of the future spot rate. The firm can achieve equivalent hedging results by lending and borrowing in the domestic and foreign money markets.

3. Unlike forward and money market hedges, currency options provide flexible hedges against exchange exposure. With the options hedge, the firm can limit the downside risk while preserving the upside potential. Currency options also provide the firm with an effective hedge against contingent exposure.
4. The firm can shift, share, and diversify exchange exposure by appropriately choosing the invoice currency. Currency basket units such as the SDR and ECU can be used as an invoice currency to partially hedge long-term exposure for which financial hedges are not readily available.
5. The firm can reduce transaction exposure by leading and lagging foreign currency receipts and payments, especially among its own affiliates.
6. When a firm has a portfolio of foreign currency positions, it makes sense only to hedge the residual exposure rather than hedging each currency position separately. The reinvoice center can help implement the portfolio approach to exposure management.
7. In a perfect capital market where stockholders can hedge exchange exposure as well as the firm, it is difficult to justify exposure management at the corporate level. In reality, capital markets are far from perfect, and the firm often has advantages over the stockholders in implementing hedging strategies. There thus exists room for corporate exposure management to contribute to the firm value.

KEY WORDS

contingent exposure, 320
cross-hedging, 319
exposure netting, 323
forward market hedge, 313
hedging through invoice currency, 322
lead/lag strategy, 322
money market hedge, 316
options market hedge, 317
reinvoice center, 323
transaction exposure, 312

QUESTIONS

1. How would you define *transaction exposure?* How is it different from economic exposure?
2. Discuss and compare hedging transaction exposure using the forward contract versus money market instruments. When do alternative hedging approaches produce the same result?
3. Discuss and compare the costs of hedging by forward contracts and options contracts.
4. What are the advantages of a currency options contract as a hedging tool compared with the forward contract?
5. Suppose your company has purchased a put option on the German mark to manage exchange exposure associated with an account receivable denominated in that currency. In this case, your company can be said to have an "insurance" policy on its receivable. Explain in what sense this is so.
6. Recent surveys of corporate exchange risk management practices indicate that many U.S. firms simply do not hedge. How would you explain this result?
7. Should a firm hedge? Why or why not?
8. Using an example, discuss the possible effect of hedging on a firm's tax obligations.
9. Explain *contingent exposure* and discuss the advantages of using currency options to manage this type of currency exposure.
10. Explain cross-hedging and discuss the factors determining its effectiveness.

PROBLEMS

The spreadsheet TRNSEXP.EXC may be used in solving parts of problems 2, 3, 4, and 6.

1. Cray Research sold a supercomputer to the Max Planck Institute in Germany on credit and invoiced DM 10 million payable in six months. Currently, the six-month forward exchange rate is DM1.50/$ and the foreign exchange adviser for Cray Research predicts that the spot rate is likely to be DM1.43/$ in six months.
   a. What is the expected gain/loss from a forward hedge?
   b. If you were the financial manager of Cray Research, would you recommend hedging this DM receivable? Why or why not?
   c. Suppose the foreign exchange adviser predicts that the future spot rate will be the same as the forward exchange rate quoted today. Would you recommend hedging in this case? Why or why not?

2. IBM purchased computer chips from NEC, a Japanese electronics concern, and was billed ¥250 million payable in three months. Currently, the spot exchange rate is ¥105/$ and the three-month forward rate is ¥100/$. The three-month money market interest rate is 8 percent per annum in the United States and 7 percent per annum in Japan. The management of IBM decided to use a money market hedge to deal with this yen account payable.
   a. Explain the process of a money market hedge and compute the dollar cost of meeting the yen obligation.
   b. Conduct a cash flow analysis of the money market hedge.

3. You plan to visit Geneva, Switzerland, in three months to attend an international business conference. You expect to incur a total cost of SF5,000 for lodging, meals, and transportation during your stay. As of today, the spot exchange rate is $0.60/SF and the three-month forward rate is $0.63/SF. You can buy the three-month call option on SF with an exercise price of $0.64/SF for the premium of $0.05 per SF. Assume that your expected future spot exchange rate is the same as the forward rate. The three-month interest rate is 6 percent per annum in the United States and 4 percent per annum in Switzerland.
   a. Calculate your expected dollar cost of buying SF5,000 if you choose to hedge by a call option on SF.
   b. Calculate the future dollar cost of meeting this SF obligation if you decide to hedge using a forward contract.
   c. At what future spot exchange rate will you be indifferent between the forward and option market hedges?
   d. Illustrate the future dollar cost of meeting the SF payable against the future spot exchange rate under both the options and forward market hedges.

4. McDonnell Douglas just signed a contract to sell a DC-10 aircraft to Air France. Air France will be billed FF50 million payable in one year. The current spot exchange rate is $0.20/FF and the one-year forward rate is $0.19/FF. The annual interest rate is 6.0 percent in the United States and 9.5 percent in France. McDonnell Douglas is concerned with the volatile exchange rate between the dollar and the franc and would like to hedge exchange exposure.
   a. It is considering two hedging alternatives: sell the franc proceeds from the sale forward or borrow francs from Crédit Lyonnaise against the franc receivable. Which alternative would you recommend? Why?
   b. Other things being equal, at what forward exchange rate would McDonnell Douglas be indifferent between the two hedging methods?

5. Suppose that Baltimore Machinery sold a drilling machine to a Swiss firm and gave the Swiss client a choice of paying either $10,000 or SF15,000 in three months.

a. In the example, Baltimore Machinery effectively gave the Swiss client a free option to buy up to $10,000 dollars using Swiss francs. What is the "implied" exercise exchange rate?
b. If the spot exchange rate turns out to be $0.62/SF, which currency do you think the Swiss client will choose to use for payment? What is the value of this free option for the Swiss client?
c. What is the best way for Baltimore Machinery to deal with exchange exposure?

6. Princess Cruise Company (PCC) purchased a ship from Mitsubishi Heavy Industry for 500 million yen payable in one year. The current spot rate is ¥124/$ and the one-year forward rate is ¥110/$. The annual interest rate is 5 percent in Japan and 8 percent in the United States. PCC can also buy a one-year call option on yen at the strike price of $.0081 per yen for a premium of .014 cents per yen.
   a. Compute the future dollar costs of meeting this obligation using the money market and forward hedges.
   b. Assuming that the forward exchange rate is the best predictor of the future spot rate, compute the expected future dollar cost of meeting this obligation when the option hedge is used.
   c. At what future spot rate do you think PCC may be indifferent between the option and forward hedge?

MINI CASE

CHASE OPTIONS, INC.: HEDGING FOREIGN CURRENCY EXPOSURE THROUGH CURRENCY OPTIONS

HARVEY A. PONIACHEK

This case study briefly reviews the foreign currency options market and hedging. It presents several international transactions that require currency options hedging strategies by the corporations involved.

The Currency Options Market

Foreign currency options include options on spot exchange, options on foreign currency futures and futures-style option.[1] Foreign currency options can be transacted over-the-counter and on organized exchanges.

The market for currency options is comprised of an interbank market that consists of London, New York, and Tokyo. Markets for over-the-counter (OTC) currency options began to develop in the early 1980s. Transactions over-the-counter mainly involve the U.S. dollar against the major currencies, including the pound sterling, the German mark, the Japanese yen, and others. Over-the-counter options offer corporations tailor-made accommodation transactions in terms of size and maturity.

The main currency traded on the exchange-based markets include the DM, the yen, the Australian dollar, the Canadian dollar, the ECU, and the Swiss franc. Currency options in the United States are traded in standardized contracts that generally correspond to the features of the International Money Market (IMM) of the Chicago Mercantile Exchange currency futures contracts. Option prices are usually quoted in cents (or a fraction thereof) per unit of foreign currency. Currency options are listed

Copyright © Harvey A. Poniachek, 1990. This case was prepared for classroom discussions at New York University, Stern School of Business, Graduate Division.

[1]See for instance J. Orlin Grabbe, *International Financial Markets,* 2nd Ed., Elsevier, New York, 1991, Ch. 6, "Foreign Currency Options."

on the Philadelphia Stock Exchange, the IMM, the CBOE (Chicago Board of Exchange), the LIFFE (London International Financial Futures Exchange), and several other exchanges.

American-style currency options on spot exchange are traded over-the-counter at the Philadelphia Stock Exchange (PHLX) in the amount of one-half the size of the IMM futures contracts. Options on currency futures—traded on the Chicago Mercantile Exchange (CME)—provide options on exchange traded currency futures contracts. All currency traded options on currency futures are American-type contracts.

Markets for foreign exchange options increased in breadth in recent years. International activity has expanded due to the high volatility of exchange rates, which has created a continuing need for hedging. The proliferation of market activity in currency options around the world led to the emergence of new centers and the establishment of links among different exchanges in different time zones. See Appendix on pages 334–336 for information on where currency options are traded, contract size and volume of business.

Fundamentals of Options

A foreign currency option contract is an agreement between the buyer and the seller, where the seller grants the buyer the right to buy or sell a currency under certain conditions. The buyer of a call or put pays the seller a price, called the premium, for the right of buying or selling a specific amount of a currency at a pre-agreed upon price, known as the exercise price or strike price, during a specific period of time, or on a specific date, called the expiration date or maturity date. Foreign currency options limit the risk of the options buyer to the premium paid, but provide the buyer with unlimited potential gain. The option seller's gain is limited to its premium, but its loss is unlimited.

There are American and European options. Exchange traded currency options are all American style, whereas over-the-counter currency options are primarily European-style options. An American option affords the holder the right to exercise at any time before maturity, whereas a European option allows the holder the right to exercise only at maturity. In an option on a futures currency contract, the underlying asset is not a spot asset, but a futures contract on the currency. Acquiring an option on the futures implies that the holder obtains a long position in the currency futures.

In summary, currency options are characterized by several features: the currency option type (American or European), the expiration date, the strike price, premium, and the type of underlying instrument (spot or future). Option valuation or pricing is determined by models that are based on the Black-Scholes principles, and by the application of several variables:

1. The spot price of the underlying currency (e.g., the price of dollar per yen).
2. The strike price of the option,
3. The maturity,
4. The volatility of the underlying currency, and
5. The interest rates in both countries (e.g., in the U.S. and Japan when the option price on yen is determined).

Hedging with Currency Options

The currency options market is rapidly becoming the preferred venue for corporations wishing to hedge their foreign currency exposure. The surge in demand for currency options has come from translation exposure—as defined according to Financial Accounting Standards Board (FASB) 52 requirements. In addition, the increased internationalization of the U.S. economy in the late 1980s has given rise to greater international involvement and currency exposure. These factors contributed to the growth of the over-the-counter options markets. Unlike organized exchange markets traded options, OTC options offer customized maturities, contract size and strike prices, do not involve the extra cost and inconvenience of posting and satisfying minimum margin requirements and have no brokerage fees.

Foreign currency forwards and options are imperfect substitutes for hedging of currency exposure. Forward currency hedging locks the firm into a rigid position, whereby the firm needs to perform the forward contract or else be in default. By entering into a forward contract the hedger could not enjoy favorable future developments in the currency market. Options are most suitable for hedging foreign currency denominated transactions that might not occur (e.g., competitive bidding for a construction project abroad that might not be awarded). In addition, hedging through options provides the potential for enjoying favorable market circumstances. Currency options have the advantage over forward exchange contracts because they allow corporations to benefit from favorable currency movements and limit the extent of currency losses. The option markets allow the trading of volatility; that is, taking a view on how volatile the underlying currency will be.

Currency options can be used to hedge foreign currency exposure under a variety of circumstances that involve transactions denominated in foreign currencies or attempts to enhance international competitiveness:

1. Anticipated currency transactions where the company seeks to take a view on the exchange rate trend (e.g., account payables or account receivables denominated in foreign exchange, dividend flows from foreign subsidiaries or investments). If the company doesn't have a view it should use forward exchange hedging.
2. Uncertain currency transactions (e.g., bids on international projects denominated in a foreign currency, portfolio hedges where the timing of the sale of securities due to interest rate conditions is difficult to determine ahead of time).
3. Economic exposure (e.g., circumstances where a company's market position stands to be hurt by foreign competition if its currency rises in value in relation to others).

The three most favored currency options strategies include:

1. BUYING AN OPTION. Allows unlimited upside potential and caps downside exposure.
2. SELLING AN OPTION. Caps upside potential but allows unlimited downside exposure.
   Buying an option and selling a put provides the hedger with a comparable outcome. For instance, buying a dollar call against a yen implies that the buyers could exercise the option by buying dollars and paying yen. Alternatively, by buying a yen put against dollars, the hedger could exercise by delivering yen and getting paid dollars. Both options require that the hedger pays yen and obtains dollars.
3. BUY-SELL OPTIONS. Caps upside potential and downward exposure, and it is generally obtained at zero cost.

Devising Hedging Strategies

The Assignment

You are a member of Chase Options, Inc., who was asked to participate in designing hedging strategies for the following transactions:

TABLE 1 Currency Options Quotations

Row	Currency Exchange Rates: Contract	Spot	Forward	Interest Rate: U.S.	Foreign	Option Type	Strike Price
1	DM/$	1.67	1.6725	8.3	8.5106	PUT	1.7
2	DDM/$	1.67	1.6725	8.3	8.5106	CALL	1.647
3	$/STG	1.7	1.6818	8.2	14.8657	CALL	1.7
4	A$/$	0.785	0.76	8.25	14.7892	PUT	0.72
5	A$/$	0.785	0.76	8.25	14.7892	CALL	0.8025
6	DM/STG	2.8921	2.8845	7.9091	14.8811	PUT	2.8845
7	YEN/$	120.0	116.5	8.7	7.1318	PUT	128.15

Row	Maturity	Premium per FC	Premium per Dollar	Hedging Ratio: Delta	Gamma	Theta
1	272	0.0164	0.0466	0.3387	0.039	0.00003
2	272	0.0164	0.0452	0.423	0.041	0.00003
3	60	0.0176	0.006105	0.388	0.098	0.00008
4	195	0.007211	0.0128	0.206	0.037	0.00007
5	195	0.007234	0.0115			
6	14	0.0161	0.001936	0.494	0.281	0.00085
7	731	0.000127	1.9595	0.188	0.019	N.A.

ANTICIPATED CURRENCY TRANSACTIONS

1. A U.S. company expects DM 100 million in repatriated profits from its German subsidiary on March 20, 1991. The company believes that the dollar has reached a long-term low at the current level DM/$1.6700; however, it doesn't want to lock in a forward exchange contract because of uncertainty concerning the impact of the German reunification on the currency market. The company doesn't want to exchange at greater than DM/$1.7000 (e.g., 1.7200). Design a hedging strategy by using currency options and utilizing the rates available in Table 1 (Row 1). Examine the implications of hedging instead with a forward contract. Consider whether strategy (III) B (3) listed below is applicable for this transaction. Utilize the date in Table 1 (Row 2).
2. A U.S. firm has bought industrial equipment from a U.K. firm for £5 million payable in 60 days. The firm believes that UK's political and economic uncertainty might drive the pound sterling down significantly. Design a hedging strategy for the corporation by employing either forward currency contracts or currency options and utilizing the data listed in Table 1 (Row 3).

UNCERTAIN CURRENCY TRANSACTIONS

3. A U.S. fund manager who bought 100 million in Australian dollar (A$) bonds when the A$ was at US$/A$0.72 is worried that the A$ might depreciate because of disappointing Australian economic performance. He decides to set A$/$0.72 as the maximum downside loss that he wants to risk from the current level of A$/$0.7850 (spot). The fund manager doesn't mind foregoing profit opportunities from a further upward move in the A$ and is uncertain how long he will hold the bonds. He sets the year end as his time horizon. By utilizing Table 1 (Rows 4 and 5) data, which hedging strategy should the fund manager adopt?
4. A German company is bidding on a contract in the U.K. The bid is estimated at £40 million and they anticipate a profit margin of 30 percent on the

project. Hence, they will need to repatriate £12 million in profit, but they worry that the new U.K. economic trends could hurt the pound sterling exchange rate. Determine how the German company could hedge their potential exposure. Utilize Table 1 (Row 6) for data.

ECONOMIC HEDGING

5. In late 1987 American Motors Corporation (AMC) believed that with the yen exchange rate at ¥/$120 the corporation was competitive vis-à-vis its Japanese rivals. However, if the dollar is to rise again, AMC believed that it could lose 5–10 percent of its sales for every 10 percent strengthening of the dollar. Propose a hedging policy for AMC by utilizing the data in Table 1 (Row 7). What is the cost of your recommendation and what is the company's break-even point?

CROSS HEDGING

6. Multinational corporation B has borrowed DM to finance expansion of its German subsidiary. The German subsidiary sells 89 percent of its products to an Italian customer who pays in lira. Company B is exposed to the depreciation of the lira and the appreciation of the DM. Design a hedging strategy for the parent.
7. Multinational corporation B has lira sales, but because of high interest rates on lira denominated funds, hedging with lira options could be less favorable than hedging with DM options. Which hedging strategy would you consider as the most feasible?

APPENDIX

Currency Futures and Options

Currency Futures and Options: Exchanges, Contracts, and Volume of Trades (1988–89)

		Volume of Contracts Traded	
			1989
Exchange/Type	Face Value of Contract	1988	Jan.–Oct.
		(in thousands of contracts)	
United States			
Chicago Mercantile Exchange (CME)			
Currency			
Futures			
Eurodollar (three months)[a]	$1,000,000	21,705	35,862
Pound sterling[a]	£25,000	2,616	2,148
Canadian dollar	Can$100,000	1,409	1,108
Deutsche mark[a]	DM 125,000	5,662	6,729
Japanese yen[a]	¥12,500,000	6,433	6,762
Swiss franc	Sw F 125,000	5,283	5,194
French franc	F250,000	4	2
Australian dollar	$A 100,000	76	104
Options			
Eurodollar	$1,000,000	2,600	5,181
Pound sterling	£25,000	543	350
Deutsche mark	DM 125,000	2,734	3,164
Swiss franc	Sw F 125,000	1,070	1,305
Japanese yen	¥12,500,000	2,945	2,780
Canadian dollar	Can$100,000	314	246
Australian dollar	$A 100,000	7	21

(continued)

APPENDIX **Currency Futures and Options**

Currency Futures and Options: Exchanges, Contracts, and Volume of Trades, (1988–89) ***(continued)***

Exchange/Type	Face Value of Contract	Volume of Contracts Traded	
			1989
		1988	Jan.–Oct.
		(in thousands of contracts)	
Philadelphia Stock Exchange (PHLX)			
Currency[b]			
Options			
Australian dollar	$A 100,000	351	673
Canadian dollar	CAN$100,000	317	424
European currency unit	ECU 125,000	1	9
French franc	F 500,000	252	86
Japanese yen	¥12,500,000	2,921	2,876
Pound sterling	£62,500	1,283	409
Swiss franc	Sw F 125,000	1,067	919
United Kingdom			
London International Financial Futures Exchange (LIFFE)			
Currency			
Futures			
Eurodollar (three-month)	$1,000,000	1,662	1,850
Pound sterling (three-month)	£500,000	3,555	6,049
Japanese yen	¥12,500,000	3	3
Swiss franc	Sw F 125,000	3	1
Pound sterling	£25,000	7	5
Deutsche mark	DM 125,000	4	2
Euromark		n.t.	712
Options			
Eurodollar (three-month)	$1,000,000	77	71
Pound sterling (three-month)	£500,000	446	709
Pound/U.S. dollar		10	1
Pound sterling	£25,000	446	709
France			
March} © Terme d'Instruments Financiers (MATIF)			
Currency			
Futures			
Euro-deutsche mark		n.t.	481
The Netherlands			
European Options Exchange (EOE)			
Currency			
Options			
U.S. dollar/guilder and pound sterling/guilder	$10,000 £10,000		412
Australia			
Sydney Futures Exchange			
Currency			
Futures			
Australian dollar		22	5
Options			
Australian dollar		3	—

(continued)

APPENDIX Currency Futures and Options

Currency Futures and Options: Exchanges, Contracts, and Volume of Trades, (1988–89) *(concluded)*

Exchange/Type	Face Value of Contract	Volume of Contracts Traded 1988	1989 Jan.–Oct.
		(in thousands of contracts)	
New Zealand			
New Zealand Futures Exchange			
Currency			
Futures			
U.S. Dollar	$50,000	19	4
N.Z. dollar	$NZ 100,000	n.t.	2
Singapore			
Singapore International Monetary Exchange (SIMEX)			
Currency			
Futures			
Deutsche mark	DM 125,000	98	23
Eurodollar	$1,000,000	1,881	3,406
Euro-yen		n.t.	58
Japanese yen	¥23,500,000	221	275
Pound sterling	£62,500	3	3
Options			
Deutsche mark	DM 125,000	12	1
Eurodollar	$1,000,000	11	10
Japanese yen	¥12,500,000	61	2

[a]CME Eurodollar, pound sterling, deutsche mark, and Japanese yen contracts are listed on a mutual offset link with SIMEX in Singapore.
[b]American volume.
n.t. = not traded; $A = Australian dollar; Can$ = Canadian dollar; DM = deutsche mark; ECU = European Currency Unit; F = French franc; HK$ = Hong Kong dollar; ¥ = Japanese yen; $NZ = New Zealand dollar; f. = Netherland guilder; £ = pound sterling; SKr = Swedish Krone; and $ = U.S. dollar. Options volume is puts and calls combined. 1989 covers January to October.
Sources: International Monetary Fund, International Capital Markets; Developments and Prospects, Washington, DC. April 1990.

ENDNOTES

1. As mentioned in Chapter 5, the forward exchange rate will be an unbiased predictor of the future spot rate if the exchange market is informationally efficient and the risk premium is not significant. Empirical evidence indicates that the risk premium, if it exists, is generally not very significant. Unless the firm has private information that is not reflected in the forward rate, it would have no reason for disagreeing with the forward rate.
2. In the case where the firm has an account payable denominated in pounds, the money market hedge calls for borrowing in dollars, buying pounds spot, and investing at the pound interest rate.
3. These days, it is not unusual for the exporter to let the importer choose the currency of payment. For example, Boeing may allow British Airways to pay either $15 million or £10 million. To the extent that Boeing does not know in advance which currency it is going to receive, it faces a contingent exposure. Given the future spot exchange rate, British Airways will choose to pay with a cheaper currency. It is noteworthy that in this example, Boeing provided British Airways with a free option to buy up to $15 million using pounds (which is equivalent to an option to sell pounds for dollars) at the implicit exercise rate of $1.50/£.
4. The ECU may not be as effective an instrument as the SDR for risk diversification, as the former exclusively comprises European currencies that tend to covary substantially among themselves.

WEB RESOURCES

www.gsm.uci.edul~jorion/pachet/case.html

A case study by Prof. Philippe Jorion; presents the situation of a company with transaction exposure to the Deutsche mark/dollar exchange rate.

www.florin.com/v4/valore4.html

Discusses issues related to currency risk management

REFERENCES AND SUGGESTED READINGS

Aggarwal, R., and A. Demaskey. "Cross-hedging Currency Risks in Asian Emerging Markets Using Derivatives in Major Currencies." *Journal of Portfolio Management,* Spring (1997), pp. 88–95.

Aubey, R., and R. Cramer. "Use of International Currency Cocktails in the Reduction of Exchange Rate Risk." *Journal of Economics and Business,* Winter (1977), pp. 128–34.

Benet, B. "Commodity Futures Cross-Hedging of Foreign Exchange Exposure." *Journal of Futures Markets,* Fall (1990), pp. 287–306.

Beidelman, Carl, John Hillary, and James Greenleaf. "Alternatives in Hedging Long-Date Contractual Foreign Exchange Exposure." *Sloan Management Review,* Summer (1983), pp. 45–54.

Dufey, Gunter, and S. Srinivasulu. "The Case for Corporate Management of Foreign Exchange Risk." *Financial Management,* Winter (1983), pp. 54–62.

Folks, William. "Decision Analysis for Exchange Risk Management." *Financial Management,* Winter (1972), pp. 101–12.

Giddy, Ian. "The Foreign Exchange Option as a Hedging Tool." *Midland Corporate Finance Journal,* Fall (1983), pp. 32–42.

Jesswein, Kurt, Chuck C. Y. Kwok, and William Folks, Jr. "Corporate Use of Innovative Foreign Exchange Risk Management Products." *Columbia Journal of World Business,* Fall (1995), pp. 70–82.

Khoury, Sarkis, and K. H. Chan. "Hedging Foreign Exchange Risk: Selecting the Optimal Tool." *Midland Corporate Finance Journal,* Winter (1988), pp. 40–52.

Levi, Maurice. *International Finance.* New York: McGraw-Hill, 1990.

Smithson, Charles. "A LEGO Approach to Financial Engineering: An Introduction to Forwards, Futures, Swaps and Options." *Midland Corporate Finance Journal,* Winter (1987), pp. 16–28.

Stulz, Rene, and Clifford Smith. "The Determinants of Firms' Hedging Policies." *Journal of Financial and Quantitative Analysis,* December 1985, pp. 391–405.

CHAPTER FOURTEEN

Management of Translation Exposure

CHAPTER OUTLINE

This chapter concludes our discussion of foreign exchange exposure and management. In it we discuss translation exposure. **Translation exposure,** also frequenting called *accounting exposure,* refers to the effect that an unanticipated change in exchange rates will have on the consolidated financial reports of a MNC. When exchange rates change, the value of a foreign subsidiary's assets and liabilities denominated in a foreign currency change when they are viewed from the perspective of the parent firm. Consequently, there must be a mechanical means for handling the consolidation process for MNCs that logically deals with exchange rate changes.

This chapter presents the basic methods of handling translation adjustments. We present an example of a simple consolidation using the different methods for handling translation adjustments so that the effects of the various methods can be compared. Special consideration is given to recently prescribed methods of the Financial Accounting Standards Board (FASB), the authoritative body in the United States that specifies accounting policy for U.S. business firms and certified public accounting firms. However, translation methods used in other major developed countries are also briefly examined.

We use an illustrated mini case to explore at length the impact of exchange rate changes on the consolidation process according to the currently prescribed FASB statement. Following this, the relationships between translation exposure and economic exposure and translation exposure and transaction exposure are addressed. Next, the need for, and methods for, managing translation exposure are examined. The chapter concludes with a discussion of an empirical analysis of the effect on firm value of a change in translation methods.

TRANSLATION METHODS

Four methods of foreign currency translation have been used in recent years: the current/noncurrent method, the monetary/nonmonetary method, the temporal method, and the current rate method.

Current/Noncurrent Method

The **current/noncurrent** method of foreign currency translation was generally accepted in the United States from the 1930s until 1975, when FASB 8 became effective. The underlying principle of this method is that assets and liabilities should be translated based on their maturity. Current assets and liabilities, which by definition have a maturity of one year or less, are converted at the current exchange rate. Noncurrent assets and liabilities are translated at the historical exchange rate in effect at the time the asset or liability was first recorded on the books. Under this method, a foreign subsidiary with current assets in excess of current liabilities will cause a translation gain (loss) if the local currency appreciates (depreciates). The opposite will happen if there is negative net working capital in local terms in the foreign subsidiary.

Most income statement items under this method are translated at the average exchange rate for the accounting period. However, revenue and expense items that are associated with noncurrent assets or liabilities, such as depreciation expense, are translated at the historical rate that applies to the applicable balance sheet item.

Monetary/Nonmonetary Method

According to the **monetary/nonmonetary** method, all monetary balance sheet accounts (for example, cash, marketable securities, accounts receivable, notes payable, accounts payable) of a foreign subsidiary are translated at the current exchange rate. All other (nonmonetary) balance sheet accounts, including stockholders' equity, are translated at the historical exchange rate in effect when the account was first recorded. In comparison to the current/noncurrent method, this method differs substantially with respect to accounts such as inventory, long-term receivables, and long-term debt. The underlying philosophy of the monetary/nonmonetary method is that monetary accounts have a similarity because their value represents a sum of money whose currency equivalent after translation changes each time the exchange rate changes. This method classifies accounts on the basis of similarity of attributes rather than similarity of maturities.

Under this method, most income statement accounts are translated at the average exchange rate for the period. However, revenue and expense items associated with nonmonetary accounts, such as cost of goods sold and depreciation, are translated at the historical rate associated with the balance sheet account.

Temporal Method

Under the **temporal** method, monetary accounts such as cash, receivables, and payables (both current and noncurrent) are translated at the current exchange rate. Other balance sheet accounts are translated at the current rate, if they are carried on the books at current value; if they are carried at historical costs, they are translated at the rate of exchange on the date the item was placed on the books. Since fixed assets and inventory are usually carried at historical costs, the temporal method and the monetary/nonmonetary method will typically provide the same translation. Nevertheless, the underlying philosophies of the two methods are entirely different. Under current value accounting, all balance sheet accounts are translated at the current exchange rate.

Under the temporal method, most income statement items are translated at the average exchange rate for the period. Depreciation and cost of goods sold, however, are translated at historical rates if the associated balance sheet accounts are carried at historical costs.

EXHIBIT 14.1 Comparison of Effect of Translation Methods on Financial Statement Preparation after Appreciation from DM 3.00 to DM 2.00 = $1.00

	Local Currency	Current/ Noncurrent	Monetary/ Nonmonetary	Temporal	Current Rate
Balance Sheet					
Cash	DM 2,100	$1,050	$1,050	$1,050	$1,050
Inventory					
(Current value = DM1,800)	1,500	750	500	900	750
Net fixed assets	3,000	1,000	1,000	1,000	1,500
Total assets	DM 6,600	$2,800	$2,550	$2,950	$3,300
Current liabilities	DM 1,200	$ 600	$ 600	$ 600	$ 600
Long-term debt	1,800	600	900	900	900
Common stock	2,700	900	900	900	900
Retained earnings	900	700	150	550	360
CTA	—	—	—	—	540
Total liabilities and equity	DM 6,600	$2,800	$2,550	$2,950	$3,300
Income Statement					
Sales revenue	DM10,000	$4,000	$4,000	$4,000	$4,000
COGS	7,500	3,000	2,500	3,000	3,000
Depreciation	1,000	333	333	333	400
Net operating income	1,500	667	1,167	667	600
Income tax (40%)	600	267	467	267	240
Profit after tax	900	400	700	400	360
Foreign exchange gain (loss)	—	300	(550)	150	—
Net income	900	700	150	550	360
Dividends	0	0	0	0	0
Addition to retained earnings	DM 900	$ 700	$ 150	$ 550	$ 360

Current Rate Method

Under the **current rate** method, all balance sheet accounts are translated at the current exchange rate, except for stockholders' equity. This is the simplest of all translation methods to apply. The common stock account and any additional paid-in capital are carried at the exchange rates in effect on the respective dates of issuance. Year-end retained earnings equal the beginning balance of retained earnings plus any additions for the year. A "plug" equity account named **cumulative translation adjustment (CTA)** is used to make the balance sheet balance, since translation gains or losses do not go through the income statement according to this method.

Under the current rate method, income statement items are to be translated at the exchange rate at the dates the items are recognized. Since this is generally impractical, an appropriately weighted average exchange rate for the period may be used for the translation.

EXAMPLE 14.1: Comparison of Translation Methods Exhibit 14.1 uses an example to present a comparison of the effect of the different translation methods on financial statement preparation. The example assumes that the balance sheet and income statement of a German subsidiary, which keeps its books in deutsche marks, is translated into U.S. dollars, the reporting currency of the MNC.

Exhibit 14.1 first presents the balance sheet and income statement in deutsche marks, from which it can be seen that both additions to retained earnings and accumulated retained earnings are both DM900,000. (The example as-

EXHIBIT 14.1 Comparison of Effects of Translation Methods on Financial Statement Preparation after Depreciation from DM 3.00 to DM 4.00 = $1.00 *(concluded)*

	Local Currency	Current/ Noncurrent	Monetary/ Nonmonetary	Temporal	Current Rate
Balance Sheet					
Cash	DM 2,100	$525	$525	$525	$525
Inventory					
(Current value = DM1,800)	1,500	375	500	450	375
Net fixed assets	3,000	1,000	1,000	1,000	750
Total assets	DM 6,600	$1,900	$2,025	$1,975	$1,650
Current liabilities	DM 1,200	$300	$300	$300	$300
Long-term debt	1,800	600	450	450	450
Common stock	2,700	900	900	900	900
Retained earnings	900	100	375	325	257
CTA	—	—	—	—	(257)
Total liabilities and equity	DM 6,600	$1,900	$2,025	$1,975	$1,650
Income Statement					
Sales revenue	DM10,000	$2,857	$2,857	$2,857	$2,857
COGS	7,500	2,143	2,500	2,143	2,143
Depreciation	1,000	333	333	333	286
Net operating income	1,500	381	24	381	428
Income tax (40%)	600	152	10	152	171
Profit after tax	900	229	14	229	257
Foreign exchange gain (loss)	—	(129)	361	96	—
Net income	900	100	375	325	257
Dividends	0	0	0	0	0
Addition to retained earnings	DM 900	$100	$375	$325	$257

sumes that the subsidiary is at the end of its first year of operation.) The historical exchange rate is DM3.00/$1.00. The next four columns show the translated statements after an assumed appreciation of the mark to DM2.00/$1.00. The average exchange for the period is thus DM2.50/$1.00. As can be seen from the exhibit, total assets vary from $2,550,000 under the monetary/nonmonetary method, which has a foreign exchange loss of $550,000 passed through the income statement, to $3,300,000 under the current rate method, which has an effective foreign exchange gain of $540,000 carried in the cumulative translation adjustment (CTA) account.

Under the temporal method, it is assumed that the firm carries its inventory at the current market value of DM1,800,000 instead of at the historical value of DM1,500,000. Note that the temporal method and the monetary/nonmonetary methods would both translate inventory to a value of $500,000 if the subsidiary was assumed to carry inventory at its historical value under the temporal method.

Exhibit 14.1 also shows the translated balance sheet and income statements after an assumed depreciation of the mark from DM3.00/$1.00 to DM4.00/$1.00. The average exchange rate for the period is thus DM3.50/$1.00. As the exhibit shows, total assets vary from $1,650,000 under the current rate method, which has an effective foreign exchange loss of $257,000 carried in the CTA account, to $2,025,000 under the monetary/nonmonetary method, which has a foreign exchange gain of $361,000.

FINANCIAL ACCOUNTING STANDARDS BOARD STATEMENT 8

FASB 8 became effective on January 1, 1976. Its objective was to measure in dollars an enterprise's assets, liabilities, revenues, or expenses that are denominated in a foreign currency according to generally accepted accounting principles. FASB 8 is essentially the temporal method of translation as previously defined, but there are some subtleties. For example, according to the temporal method, revenues and expenses are to be measured at the average exchange rate for the period. In practice, MNCs prepare monthly statements. What is done is to cumulate the monthly figures to obtain the total for the year.

FASB 8 ran into acceptance problems from the accounting profession and MNCs from the very beginning. The temporal method requires taking foreign exchange gains or losses through the income statement, as was demonstrated in Example 14.1. Consequently, reported earnings could, and did, fluctuate substantially from year to year, which was irritating to corporate executives.

Additionally, many MNCs did not like translating inventory at historical rates, which was required if the firm carried the inventory at historical values, as most did, and do. It was felt that it would be much simpler to translate at the current rate.

FINANCIAL ACCOUNTING STANDARDS BOARD STATEMENT 52

Given the controversy surrounding FASB 8, a proposal was put on the agenda of the FASB in January 1979 to consider all features of FASB 8. Subsequently, in February 1979, a task force was established with representatives of the board, the International Accounting Standards Committee, and the accounting standards bodies from Canada and the United Kingdom. After many meetings and hearings, FASB 52 was issued in December 1981, and all U.S. MNCs were required to adopt the statement for fiscal years beginning on or after December 15, 1982.

The stated objectives of FASB 52 are to:

a. Provide information that is generally compatible with the expected economic effects of a rate change on an enterprise's cash flows and equity; and
b. Reflect in consolidated statements the financial results and relationships of the individual consolidated entities as measured in their functional currencies in conformity with U.S. generally accepted accounting principles.[1]

Many discussions of FASB 52 claim that it is a current rate method of translation. This, however, is a misnomer, as FASB 52 requires the current rate method of translation in some circumstances and the temporal method in others. Which method of translation is prescribed by FASB 52 depends upon the functional currency used by the foreign subsidiary whose statements are to be translated. The **functional currency** is defined in FASB 52 as "the currency of the primary economic environment in which the entity operates."[2] Normally, that is the local currency of the country in which the entity conducts most of its business. However, under certain circumstances, the functional currency may be the parent firm's home country currency or some third-country currency. Exhibit 14.2 summarizes the method for determining the functional currency.

The **reporting currency** is defined as the currency in which the MNC prepares its consolidated financial statements. That currency is usually the currency in which the parent firm keeps its books, which in turn is usually the currency of the country in which the parent is located and conducts most of its business. However, the reporting currency could be some third currency. For our purposes in this chapter, the terms reporting currency and parent currency will be used synonymously, and will be assumed to be the U.S. dollar.

EXHIBIT 14.2

Salient Economic Factors for Determining the Functional Currency

Cash Flow Indicators

Foreign Currency: Foreign entity's cash flows are primarily in foreign currency and they do not directly affect the parent firm's cash flows.

Parent's Currency: Foreign entity's cash flows directly affect the parent's cash flows and are readily available for remittance to the parent firm.

Sales Price Indicators

Foreign Currency: Sales prices for the foreign entity's products are generally not responsive on a short-term basis to exchange rate changes, but are determined more by local competition and government regulation.

Parent's Currency: Sales prices for the foreign entity's products are responsive on a short-term basis to exchange rate changes, where sales prices are determined through worldwide competition.

Sales Market Indicators

Foreign Currency: There is an active local sales market for the foreign entity's products.

Parent's Currency: The sales market is primarily located in the parent's country or sales contracts are denominated in the parent's currency.

Expense Indicators

Foreign Currency: Factor of production costs of the foreign entity are primarily local costs.

Parent's Currency: Factor of production costs for the foreign entity are primarily, and on a continuing basis, costs for components obtained from the parent's country.

Financing Indicators

Foreign Currency: Financing of the foreign entity is primarily denominated in the foreign currency and the debt service obligations are normally handled by the foreign entity.

Parent's Currency: Financing of the foreign entity is primarily from the parent, with debt service obligations met by the parent, or the debt service obligations incurred by the foreign entity are primarily made by the parent.

Intercompany Transactions and Arrangements Indicators

Foreign Currency: There is a low volume of intercompany transactions and a minor interrelationship of operations between the foreign entity and the parent. However, the foreign entity may benefit from competitive advantages of the parent, such as patents or trademarks.

Parent's Currency: There is a large volume of intercompany transactions and an extensive interrelationship of operations between the foreign entity and the parent. Moreover, if the foreign entity is only a shell company for carrying accounts that could be carried on the parent's books, the function currency would generally be the parent's currency.

Source: Excerpted from *Foreign Currency Translation, Statement of Financial Accounting Standards No. 52,* Paragraph 42, Financial Accounting Standards Board, Stamford, CT, October 1981. Used by permission.

The Mechanics of the FASB 52 Translation Process

The actual translation process prescribed by FASB 52 is a two-stage process. First, it is necessary to determine in which currency the foreign entity keeps its books. If the local currency in which the foreign entity keeps its books is not the functional currency (and, as shown in Exhibit 14.3, it does not have to be), remeasurement into the functional currency is required. *Remeasurement* is intended "to produce the same result as if the entity's books had been maintained in the functional currency."[3] The temporal method of translation is used to accomplish the remeasurement. Second, when the foreign entity's functional currency is not the same as the parent's currency, the foreign entity's books are *translated* from the functional currency into the reporting currency using the current rate method. Obviously, translation is not required if the foreign entity's functional currency is the same as the reporting currency.

Highly Inflationary Economies

In highly inflationary economies, FASB 52 requires that the foreign entity's financial statements be remeasured from the local currency "as if the functional currency were the reporting currency" using the temporal translation method.[4] A highly inflationary economy is defined as "one that has cumulative inflation of approximately 100 percent or more over a 3-year period."[5] The purpose of this requirement is to prevent large important balance sheet accounts, carried at historical values, from having insignificant values once translated into the reporting currency at the current rate. We know, according to relative purchasing power parity, that a currency from a higher inflationary economy will depreciate relative to the currency of a lower inflationary economy at approximately the differential of the two countries' inflation rates. Hence, for example, the fixed asset account of a foreign entity in a highly inflationary economy, carried on the books in the local currency, would soon lose value relative to the reporting currency, and translate into a relatively insignificant amount in comparison to its true book value. Exhibit 14.3 presents a diagram of the two-stage translation process prescribed by FASB 52. For comparison purposes, Exhibit 14.4 presents foreign currency translation methods used in other major developed countries.

EXHIBIT 14.3

FASB 52 Two-Stage Translation Process[a]

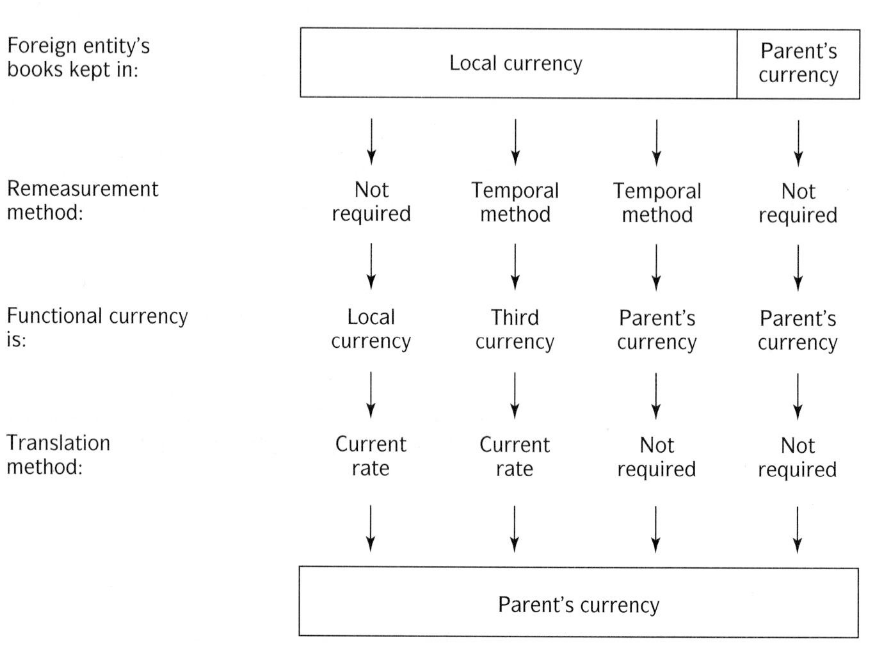

[a]The translation process prescribed by FASB 52 is a two-stage process. First, if the local currency in which the foreign entity keeps its books is not the functional currency, remeasurement by the temporal method is required. Second, when the foreign entity's functional currency is not the same as the parent's currency, the foreign entity's books are translated from the functional currency into the reporting currency using the current rate method. If the foreign entity is in a highly inflationary economy, FASB 52 requires that the local currency be remeasured into the parent's currency.

Source: Derived from J. S. Arpan and L. H. Radenbaugh, *International Accounting and Multinational Enterprises,* 2nd ed. (New York: Wiley, 1985), Exhibit 5.2, p. 136, and Andrew A. Haried, Leroy F. Imdieke, and Ralph E. Smith, *Advanced Accounting,* 6th ed. (New York: Wiley, 1994), Illustration 15-3, p. 562.

EXHIBIT 14.4 Foreign-Currency Translation Methods Used in Other Major Developed Countries

Japan

Receivables and payables in foreign currencies must be translated into yen at the end of the accounting period. Both translation gains or losses and realized foreign exchange gains or losses are treated as taxable income or loss and flow through earnings. Historical exchange rates that existed at the transaction date are generally used to record revenue, costs, and expenses resulting from foreign currency transactions.

Short-term foreign currency receivables and payables are translated at the prevailing yearend rate. Long-term foreign currency receivables and payables are translated at the historical rate, except in unusual circumstances. Securities, inventories, and fixed assets are translated at the rate in effect when they were acquired (historical rate).

Any change in the method of translating foreign currencies requires prior approval by tax regulators.

Germany

As of yearend 1992, a common treatment of foreign-currency translation had not been implemented. All translation methods are, in principle, acceptable.

A broad variety of practices are followed, including the (1) current/noncurrent, (2) monetary/nonmonetary, (3) temporal, (4) closing, and (5) current rate methods. Some companies flow translation gains or losses through stockholders' equity, while others flow the impact of foreign-currency translation through the profit and loss account.

France

Many different methods of foreign-currency translation are followed.

GROUP ACCOUNTS:

Most companies appear to use the closing exchange rate for balance sheet translations (translation gains and losses impact shareholders' equity) and the average exchange rate for the income statement.

Differences between income statement and balance sheet translation gains and losses (if different exchange rates are used) would flow through shareholders' equity.

INDIVIDUAL ACCOUNTS:

Detailed rules govern foreign-currency translation in individual company accounts. These give rise to long-term deferred charges and credits.

Unsettled monetary assets and liabilities denominated in a foreign currency must be restated to their closing value at the balance sheet date. Foreign exchange gains are recorded as long-term deferred credits and released when the account is settled.

Foreign exchange losses result in the following entries: (1) The original account is adjusted and a deferred charge appears on the balance sheet; (2) a balance sheet provision is set up, and the income statement is debited.

Foreign-currency translation policies may differ. Some firms only provide against unrealized foreign exchange losses if they exceed unrealized foreign exchange gains. These deferred exchange gains and losses could be offset against each other with the difference applied to the risk provision.

(continued)

ILLUSTRATED MINI CASE

Consolidation of Accounts According to FASB 52: The Centralia Corporation

We use a mini case to illustrate consolidating the balance sheet of a MNC according to FASB 52. The basic information is provided in Exhibit 14.5, which shows the unconsolidated balance sheets for Centralia Corporation, a U.S. parent firm, and its two wholly owned affiliates located in Mexico and Spain. Centralia Corporation is a midwestern manufacturer of small kitchen electrical appliances. The Mexican manufacturing affiliate has been established to cater to the Mexican market, which is expected to expand rapidly under NAFTA. Similarly, the Spanish manufacturing affiliate was established to handle demand in the European Union. The functional currency of the Mexican affiliate is the peso and the peseta is the functional currency for the Spanish affiliate. The reporting currency is the U.S. dollar. The initial exchange rates assumed in the example are: $1.00 = CD1.3333 = Ps3.00 = Ptas140.00 = FF5.60.

The nonconsolidated balance sheets and the footnotes to the statements indicate that the Mexican affiliate owes the parent firm Ps900,000, which is carried on the parent's books as a $300,000 accounts receivable at the current exchange rate

EXHIBIT 14.4 **Foreign-Currency Translation Methods Used in Other Major Developed Countries *(concluded)***

Canada

Foreign exchange gains and losses may be treated differently for book and tax purposes.

REALIZED GAINS AND LOSSES:

The excess of realized foreign exchange gains of a capital nature over realized losses is treated as a capital gain; three-quarters of this capital gain is included in taxable income.

In cases where foreign exchange losses exceed gains, three-quarters of the loss is deductible from other taxable gains. Foreign exchange gains and losses arising from current business transactions of a taxpayer are fully included in income or fully deductible on an accrual basis.

UNREALIZED GAINS AND LOSSES:

Unrealized gains and losses resulting from foreign currency translation are ignored for tax purposes.

However, for accounting purposes (1) unrealized gains or losses related to short-term assets or liabilities are recognized in the current period, and (2) unrealized gains or losses related to long-term assets or liabilities are deferred and amortized over the remaining life of the assets or liability.

Italy

REALIZED GAINS AND LOSSES:

Income, receipts, and expenditures in foreign currency are translated at the exchange rates that existed on the transaction date. These realized gains and losses flow through the income statement.

UNREALIZED GAINS AND LOSSES:

The average exchange rate of the last month of the accounting period is used for foreign-currency translation. Items denominated in foreign currency are originally recorded at the exchange rate that existed on the transaction date.

Unrealized foreign currency translation gains and losses flow through a special provision, impacting shareholders' equity.

United Kingdom

Foreign-currency translation adjustments are disclosed for both individual and group (consolidated) accounts. In cases of consolidation, companies prepare a set of translation accounts for (1) the individual firms within the group and (2) the group as a whole.

INDIVIDUAL COMPANY:

Foreign-currency transactions are generally translated into the home currency of each company using the average rate method. Nonmonetary assets are not restated.

Currency differences flow through the profit and loss account (separately from ongoing businesses) and are shown as discontinued operations. Exchange rate gains and losses related to foreign currency hedging pass through reserves.

GROUP ACCOUNTS:

The average rate/net investment method is commonly used, although the temporal method is also acceptable. Consolidated accounts are prepared in the currency in which the parent company is based.

Investments in the foreign enterprises are represented by the net worth held by the parent. Exchange rate gains or losses that impact the group accounts pass through reserves, with no impact on the group profit and loss account.

Source: © 1993 by Goldman Sachs. By Gabrielle Napolitano, an employee of Goldman Sachs.

of Ps3.00/$1.00. Additionally, the $2,200,000 investment of the parent firm in the Mexican affiliate is the translated amount of Ps6,600,000 of equity on the Mexican affiliate's books. Similarly, the $1,660,000 investment of the parent in the Spanish affiliate is the translated amount of Ptas232,400,000 of equity on the Spanish affiliate's books. The footnotes also show that the parent firm has CD200,000 deposited in a Canadian bank, carried as $150,000 in the cash account, and the Spanish affiliate has a FF1,400,000 loan outstanding from a French bank, translated at Ptas25/FF1.00, and carried at Ptas35,000,000 as part of its Ptas154,000,000 of notes payable.

Exhibit 14.6 shows the process of consolidating the balance sheets for Centralia Corp. and its affiliates. Of importance is to note that *both* intracompany debt *and* investment net out in the consolidation. That is, the Ps900,000 owed by the Mexican affiliate to the parent is not reflected in the consolidated accounts receivable nor in the accounts payable. When this debt is eventually paid, in effect it will be the same as taking money out of one company pocket and putting it into another. In a similar vein, the investment of the parent in each affiliate cancels with the net worth of each affiliate. The parent owns the affiliates, and in turn, the shareholders' investment represents ownership of the parent firm. In this manner, the shareholders own the entire MNC.

EXHIBIT 14.5 Nonconsolidated Balance Sheet for Centralia Corporation and Its Mexican and Spanish Affiliates, December 31, 1997 (in 000 Currency Units)

	Centralia Corp. (Parent)	Mexican Affiliate	Spanish Affiliate
Assets			
Cash	$ 950[a]	Ps 1,800	Ptas 105,000
Accounts receivable	1,750[b]	2,700	133,000
Inventory	3,000	4,500	210,000
Investment in Mexican affiliate	2,200[c]	—	—
Investment in Spanish affiliate	1,660[d]	—	—
Net fixed assets	9,000	13,800	560,000
Total assets	$18,560	Ps22,800	Ptas1,008,000
Liabilities and Net Worth			
Accounts payable	$ 1,800	Ps 3,000[b]	Ptas 173,600
Notes payable	2,200	5,100	154,000[e]
Long-term debt	7,110	8,100	448,000
Common stock	3,500	4,800[c]	168,000[d]
Retained earnings	3,950	1,800[c]	64,400[d]
Total liabilities and net worth	$18,560	Ps22,800	Ptas1,008,000

[a]The parent firm has a deposit of CD200,000 in a Canadian bank. This sum is carried on the parent firm's books at $150,000, translated at CD1.3333/$1.00.
[b]The parent firm is owed Ps900,000 by the Mexican affiliate. This sum is included in the parent's accounts receivable as $300,000. The remainder of the parent's (Mexican affiliate's) accounts receivable (payable) are denominated in dollars (pesos).
[c]The Mexican affiliate is wholly owned by the parent firm. It is carried on the parent firm's books at $2,200,000. This represents the sum of the common stock (PS4,800,000) and retained earnings (Ps1,800,000) on the Mexican affiliate's books, translated at Ps3.00/$1.00.
[d]The Spanish affiliate is wholly owned by the parent firm. It is carried on the parent firm's books at $1,660,000. This represents the sum of the common stock (Ptas168,000,000) and the retained earnings (Ptas64,400,000) on the Spanish affiliate's books, translated at Ptas140/$1.00.
[e]The Spanish affiliate has outstanding notes payable of FF1,400,000 (× Ptas25/FF1.00 = Ptas35,000,000) from a French bank. This loan is carried on the Spanish affiliate's books as part of the Ptas154,000,000 = Ptas35,000,000 + Ptas119,000,000.

The consolidation presented in Exhibit 14.6 is rather simplistic. It is nice and neat from the standpoint that the consolidated balance sheet, in fact, balances. That is, total assets equal total liabilities and net worth. Implicit in the example are that the current exchange rates used are the same as those used when the affiliates were originally established; that is, they have not changed from that time. Thus, the example is not very realistic even though it properly presents the mechanics of the consolidation process under FASB 52. After all, the central purpose of a translation method is to deal in some systematic way with exchange rate *changes.*

To determine the effect that exchange rate changes will have on the consolidated balance sheet of a MNC, it is useful to prepare a translation exposure report. A **translation exposure report** shows, for each account that is included in the consolidated balance sheet, the amount of foreign exchange exposure that exists for each foreign currency in which the MNC has exposure. Continuing with our example of Centralia Corporation and its affiliates, we know from Exhibit 14.5 that the MNC has foreign exchange exposure from the Mexican peso, Spanish peseta, Canadian dollar, and French franc. A change in any one of these currency exchange rates versus the reporting currency will have an effect on the consolidated balance sheet if there exists a net translation exposure for that currency.

Exhibit 14.7 presents the translation exposure report for Centralia. The report shows, for each exposure currency, the amount of exposed assets and exposed liabilities denominated in that currency, and the net difference, or net exposure. For the Canadian dollar the net exposure is a positive CD200,000; for the Mexican peso a positive Ps7,500,000; for the Spanish peseta a positive Ptas267,400,000; and for the French franc a negative FF1,400,000. A positive net exposure means there are more exposed assets than liabilities, and vice-versa for negative net exposure. When the exchange rate of an exposure currency depreciates against the reporting currency,

EXHIBIT 14.6 Consolidated Balance Sheet for Centralia Corporation and Its Mexican and Spanish Affiliates, December 31, 1997 (in $000): Pre-Exchange Rate Change

	Centralia Corp. (Parent)	Mexican Affiliate	Spanish Affiliate	Consolidated Balance Sheet
Assets				
Cash	$ 950[a]	$ 600	$ 750	$ 2,300
Accounts receivable	1,450[b]	900	950	3,300
Inventory	3,000	1,500	1,500	6,000
Investment in Mexican affiliation	—[c]	—	—	—
Investment in Spanish affiliation	—[d]	—	—	—
Net fixed assets	9,000	4,600	4,000	17,600
Total assets				$29,200
Liabilities and Net Worth				
Accounts payable	$1,800	$ 700[b]	$1,240	$ 3,740
Notes payable	2,200	1,700	1,100[e]	5,000
Long-term debt	7,110	2,700	3,200	13,010
Common stock	3,500	—[c]	—[d]	3,500
Retained earnings	3,950	—[c]	—[d]	3,950
Total liabilities and net worth				$29,200

[a]This sum includes CD200,000 the parent firm has on deposit in a Canadian bank, carried on the books as $150,000. CD200,000/(CD1.3333/$1.00) = $150,000.

[b]$1,750,000 − $300,000 (= Ps900,000/(Ps3.00/$1.00)) intracompany loan = $1,450,000.

[c,d]The investment in the affiliates cancels with the net worth of the affiliates in the consolidation.

[e]The Spanish affiliate owes a French bank FF1,400,000 (× Ptas25/FF1.00 = Ptas35,000,000). This is carried on the books as part of the Ptas154,000,000 = Ptas35,000,000 + Ptas119,000,000. Ptas154,000,000/(Ptas140/$1.00) = $1,100,000.

EXHIBIT 14.7 Translation Exposure Report for Centralia Corporation and Its Mexican and Spanish Affiliates, December 31, 1997 (in 000 Currency Units)

	Canadian Dollar	Mexican Peso	Spanish Peseta	French Franc
Assets				
Cash	CD200	PS 1,800	Ptas 105,000	FF 0
Accounts receivable	0	2,700	133,000	0
Inventory	0	4,500	210,000	0
Net fixed assets	0	13,800	560,000	0
Exposed assets	CD200	Ps22,800	Ptas1,008,000	FF 0
Liabilities				
Accounts payable	CD 0	Ps 2,100	Ptas 173,600	FF 0
Notes payable	0	5,100	119,000	1,400
Long-term debt	0	8,100	448,000	0
Exposed liabilities	CD 0	Ps15,300	Ptas 740,600	FF1,400
Net exposure	CD200	Ps 7,500	Ptas 267,400	(FF1,400)

exposed assets fall in translated value by a greater (smaller) amount than exposed liabilities if there is positive (negative) net exposure. Analogously, when an exposure currency appreciates against the reporting currency, exposed assets increase in translated value by a smaller (greater) amount than exposed liabilities if there is negative (positive) net exposure. Consequently, the consolidation process will not result in a consolidated balance sheet that balances after an exchange rate change.

To show the effect on the consolidation process after an exchange rate change, let's perform the consolidation of the nonconsolidated balance sheets from Exhibit 14.5 once again, assuming this time that exchange rates have changed from $1.00 = CD1.3333 = Ps3.00 = Ptas140.00 = FF5.60 to $1.00 = CD1.3333 = Ps3.00 =

EXHIBIT 14.8 **Consolidated Balance Sheet for Centralia Corporation and Its Mexican and Spanish Affiliates, December 31, 1997 (in $000): Post-Exchange Rate Change**

	Centralia Corp. (Parent)	Mexican Affiliate	Spanish Affiliate	Consolidated Balance Sheet
Assets				
Cash	$ 950[a]	$ 600	$ 700	$ 2,250
Accounts receivable	1,450[b]	900	887	3,237
Inventory	3,000	1,500	1,400	5,900
Investment in Mexican affiliate	—[c]	—	—	—
Investment in Spanish affiliate	—[d]	—	—	—
Net fixed assets	9,000	4,600	3,733	17,333
Total Assets				$28,720
Liabilities and Net Worth				
Accounts payable	$1,800	$700[b]	$1,157	$ 3,657
Notes payable	2,200	1,700	1,043[e]	4,943
Long-term debt	7,110	2,700	2,987	12,797
Common stock	3,500	—[c]	—[d]	3,500
Retained earnings	3,950	—[c]	—[d]	3,950
CTA	—	—	—	(127)
Total liabilities and net worth				$28,720

[a]This includes CD200,000 the parent firm has in a Canadian bank, carried as $150,000. CD200,000/(CD1.3333/$1.00) = $150,000.
[b]$1,750,000 − $300,000 (= Ps900,000/(Ps3.00/$1.00)) intracompany loan = $1,450,000.
[c, d]Investment in affiliates cancels with the net worth of the affiliates in the consolidation.
[e]The Spanish affiliate owes a French bank FF1,400,000 (× Ptas26.79/FF1.00 = Ptas37,506,000). This is carried on the books, after the exchange rate change, as part of Ptas156,506,000 = Ptas37,506,000 + Ptas119,000,000. Ptas156,506,000/(Ptas150/$1.00) = $1,043,373.

Ptas150.00 = FF5.60. We are assuming that only the Spanish peseta has changed (depreciated) versus all other currencies in order to keep the example simple so as to better be able to decipher the effect of an exchange rate change.

To get an overview of the effect of the exchange rate change, recall from Exhibit 14.7 that there is a positive net exposure of Ptas267,400,000. This implies that after the 6.67 percent depreciation from Ptas140/$1.00 to Ptas150/$1.00, the exposed assets denominated in pesetas will have fallen in translated value by $127,333 more than the exposed liabilities denominated in pesetas. This can be calculated as follows:

$$\frac{\text{Net exposure currency } i}{S_{\text{new}}(i/\text{reporting})} - \frac{\text{Net exposure currency } i}{S_{\text{old}}(i/\text{reporting})}$$

$$= \text{Reporting currency imbalance.}$$

For our example,

$$\frac{\text{Ptas}267{,}400{,}000}{\text{Ptas}150/\$1.00} - \frac{\text{Ptas}267{,}400{,}000}{\text{Ptas}140/\$1.00} = -\$127{,}333$$

In other words, the net translation exposure of Ptas267,400,000 in dollars is currently $1,910,000 when translated at the current exchange rate of Ptas140/$1.00. A 6.67 percent depreciation of the peseta to Ptas150/$1.00 will result in a translation loss of $127,333 = Ptas267,400,000 ÷ 140 × .0667.

Exhibit 14.8 shows the consolidation process and consolidated balance sheet for Centralia Corporation and its two foreign affiliates after the depreciation of the peseta. Note that the values for the accounts are the same as in Exhibit 14.6 for the parent firm and the Mexican affiliate. However, the values of the accounts of the Spanish affiliate are different because of the exchange rate change. In order for the consolidated balance sheet to now balance, it is necessary to have a "plug" equity account with a balance of −$127,333. As before, we referred to this special equity account as the cumulative translation adjustment account, or CTA account. The balance of this account at any time represents the accumulated total of all past translation adjustments. FASB

52 handles the effect of exchange rate changes as an adjustment to equity rather than as an adjustment to net income because "exchange rate changes have an indirect effect on the net investment that may be realized upon sale or liquidation, but . . . prior to sale or liquidation, that effect is so uncertain and remote as to require that translation adjustments arising currently should not be reported as part of operating results."[6]

MANAGEMENT OF TRANSLATION EXPOSURE

Translation Exposure versus Transaction Exposure

In Chapter 13, we discussed transaction exposure and ways to manage it. It is interesting to note that some items that are a source of transaction exposure are also a source of translation exposure, and some are not. Exhibit 14.9 presents a transaction exposure report for Centralia Corporation and its two affiliates. Items that create transaction exposure are receivables or payables that are denominated in a currency other than the currency in which the unit transacts its business, or cash holdings denominated in a foreign currency. From the exhibit, it can be seen that the parent firm has two sources of transaction exposure. One is the CD200,000 deposit that it has in a Canadian bank. Obviously, if the Canadian dollar depreciates, the deposit will be worth less to Centralia Corporation once converted to U.S. dollars. Previously, it was noted that this deposit was also a translation exposure; it is, in fact, for the same reason that it is a transaction exposure. The Ps900,000 accounts receivable the parent holds on the Mexican affiliate is also a transaction exposure, but it is not a translation exposure because of the netting of intracompany payable and receivables. The FF1,400,000 notes payable the Spanish affiliate owes the French bank is both a transaction and a translation exposure.

It is, generally, not possible to eliminate both translation and transaction exposure. In some cases, the elimination of one exposure will also eliminate the other. But in other cases, the elimination of one exposure actually creates the other. Since transaction exposure involves real cash flows, we believe it should be considered the most important of the two. That is, one would not want to create transaction exposure at the expense of minimizing or eliminating translation exposure. As previously noted, the translation process has no direct effect on reporting currency cash flows, and will only have a realizable effect on net investment upon the sale or liquidation of the assets.

Centralia Corporation and its affiliates can take certain measures to reduce its transaction exposure and to simultaneously reduce its translation exposure. One step the parent firm can take is to convert its Canadian dollar cash deposits into U.S. dollar deposits. Secondly, the parent firm can request payment of the Ps900,000 owed to it by the Mexican affiliate. Third, the Spanish affiliate has enough cash to pay off the FF1,400,000 loan to the French bank. If these three steps are taken, all transactions exposure for the MNC will be eliminated. Moreover, translation exposure will be reduced. This can be seen from Exhibit 14.10, which presents a revision of Exhibit 14.7, the translation exposure report for Centralia Corporation and its affiliates. Exhibit 14.10 shows that there is no longer any translation exposure associated with the Canadian dollar or the French franc. Additionally, the exhibit shows that the net

EXHIBIT 14.9

Transaction Exposure Report for Centralia Corporation and Its Mexican and Spanish Affiliates, December 31, 1997

Affiliate	Amount	Account	Translation Exposure
Parent	CD200,000	Cash	Yes
Parent	Ps900,000	Accounts receivable	No
Spanish	FF1,400,000	Notes payable	Yes

exposure has been reduced from Ps7,500,000 to Ps6,600,000 for the peso and from Ptas267,400,000 to Ptas232,400,000 for the peseta.

Hedging Translation Exposure

Exhibit 14.10 indicates that there is still considerable translation exposure with respect to changes in the exchange rate of the Mexican peso and the Spanish peseta against the U.S. dollar. There are two methods for dealing with this remaining exposure, if one feels compelled to attempt to control accounting changes in value of net investment.

Balance Sheet Hedge

Note that translation exposure is not entity specific; rather, it is currency specific. Its source is a mismatch of net assets and net liabilities denominated in the same currency. A **balance sheet hedge** eliminates the mismatch. Using the Spanish peseta as an example, Exhibit 14.10 shows that there are Ptas232,400,000 more exposed assets than liabilities. If the Spanish affiliate, or more practically the parent firm or the Mexican affiliate, had Ptas232,400,0000 more liabilities, or less assets, denominated in pesetas, there would not be any translation exposure with respect to the Spanish peseta. A perfect balance sheet hedge would have been created. A change in the Ptas/$ exchange rate would no longer have any effect on the consolidated balance sheet since the change in value of the assets denominated in pesetas would completely offset the change in value of the liabilities denominated in pesetas. Nevertheless, if the parent firm or the Mexican affiliate increased its liabilities through, say, peseta-denominated borrowings to affect the balance sheet hedge, it would simultaneously be creating transaction exposure in the peseta, if the new liability could not be covered from peseta cash flows generated by the Spanish affiliate.

Derivatives Hedge

According to Exhibit 14.7, we determined that when the net exposure for the Spanish peseta was Ptas267,400,000, a depreciation from Ptas140/$1.00 to Ptas150/$1.00 would create a paper loss of stockholders' equity equal to $127,333. According to the revised translation exposure report shown as Exhibit 14.10, the same depreciation in the peseta will result in an equity loss of $110,667, still a sizable amount. (The calculation of this amount is left as an exercise for the reader.) If one desires, a derivative product, such as a forward contract, can be used to attempt to hedge this potential loss. We use the word "attempt" because as the following example demonstrates, using a **derivatives hedge** to control translation exposure really involves speculation about foreign exchange rate changes.

EXHIBIT 14.10

Revised Translation Exposure Report for Centralia Corporation and Its Mexican and Spanish Affiliates, December 31, 1997 (in 000 Currency Units)

	Canadian Dollar	Mexican Peso	Spanish Peseta	French Franc
Assets				
Cash	CD0	Ps 900	Ptas 70,000	FF0
Accounts receivable	0	2,700	133,000	0
Inventory	0	4,500	210,000	0
Net fixed assets	0	13,800	560,000	0
Exposed assets	CD0	Ps21,900	Ptas973,000	FF0
Liabilities				
Accounts payable	CD0	Ps 2,100	Ptas173,600	FF0
Notes payable	0	5,100	119,000	0
Long-term debt	0	8,100	448,000	00
Exposed liabilities	CD0	Ps15,300	Ptas740,600	FF0
Net exposure	CD0	Ps 6,600	Ptas232,400	FF0

EXAMPLE 14.2: Hedging Translation Exposure with a Forward Contract
To see how a forward contract can be used to hedge the \$110,667 potential translation loss in equity, assume that the forward rate coinciding with the date of the consolidation is Ptas145/\$1.00. If the expected spot rate on the consolidation date is forecast to be Ptas150/\$1.00, a forward sale of Ptas481,400,000 will "hedge" the risk:

$$\frac{\text{Potential translation loss}}{F(\text{reporting/functional}) - \text{Expected}[S(\text{reporting/functional})]}$$

$$= \text{forward contract position in functional currency,}$$

$$\frac{\$110{,}667}{1/(\text{Ptas}145/\$1.00) - 1/(\text{Ptas}150/\$1.00)} = \text{Ptas}481{,}401{,}451.$$

The purchase of Ptas481,401,451 at the expected spot price will cost \$3,209,343. The delivery of Ptas481,401,451 under the forward contract will yield \$3,320,010, for a profit of \$110,667. If everything goes as expected, the \$110,667 profit from the forward hedge will offset the equity loss from the translation adjustment. Note, however, that the hedge will not provide a certain outcome because the size of the forward position is based on the expected future spot rate. Consequently, the forward position taken in pesetas is actually a speculative position. If the realized spot rate turns out to be less than Ptas145/\$1.00, a loss from the forward position will result. Moreover, the hedging procedure violates the hypothesis of the forward rate being the market's unbiased predictor of the future spot rate.

Translation Exposure versus Operating Exposure

As noted, an unhedged depreciation in the peseta will result in an equity loss. Such a loss, however, would only be a paper loss. It would not have any direct effect on reporting currency cash flows. Moreover, it would only have a realizable effect on net investment in the MNC if the affiliate's assets were sold or liquidated. However, as was discussed in Chapter 12, the depreciation of the local currency may, under certain circumstances, have a favorable operating effect. A currency depreciation may, for example, allow the affiliate to raise its sales price because the prices of imported competitive goods are now relatively higher. If costs do not rise proportionately and unit demand remains the same, the affiliate would realize an operating profit as a result of the currency depreciation. It is substantive issues such as these, which result in realizable changes in operating profit, that management should concern itself with.

EMPIRICAL ANALYSIS OF THE CHANGE FROM FASB 8 TO FASB 52

Garlicki, Fabozzi, and Fonfeder (1987) empirically tested a sample of MNCs to determine if there was a change in value when the firms were required to switch from FASB 8 to FASB 52. FASB 8 calls for recognizing translation gain or loss immediately in net income. FASB 52 calls for recognizing translation gains or losses in the cumulative translation adjustment account on the balance sheet. Consequently, the change in the translation process had an effect on reported earnings. "Despite the impact of the change...on reported earnings, the actual cash flow of multinationals would not be affected *if managers were not making suboptimal decisions based on accounting rather than economic considerations under Statement 8.* In such circumstances, the mandated switch...should not change the value of the firm."[7]

The researchers tested their hypothesis concerning a change in value on the initial exposure draft date and on the date FASB 52 was adopted. They found that there was no significant positive reaction to the change or perceived change in the foreign currency translation process. The results suggest that market agents do not react to cosmetic earnings changes that do not affect value. Other researchers have found similar results when investigating other accounting changes that had only a cosmetic effect on earnings. The results of Garlicki, Fabozzi, and Fonfeder also underline the futility of attempting to manage translation gains and losses.

SUMMARY

In this chapter, we have discussed the nature and management of translation exposure. Translation exposure relates to the effect that an unanticipated change in exchange rates will have on the consolidated financial reports of a MNC.

1. The four recognized methods for consolidating the financial reports of an MNC include the current/noncurrent method, the monetary/nonmonetary method, the temporal method, and the current rate method.
2. An example comparing and contrasting the four translation methods was presented under the assumptions that the foreign currency had appreciated and depreciated. It was noted that under the current rate method the gain or loss due to translation adjustment does not affect reported cash flows, as it does with the other three translation methods.
3. The old translation method prescribed by the Financial Accounting Standards Board, FASB 8, was discussed and compared with the present prescribed process, FASB 52.
4. In implementing FASB 52, the functional currency of the foreign entity must be translated into the reporting currency in which the consolidated statements are reported. The local currency of a foreign entity may not always be its functional currency. If it is not, the temporal method of translation is used to remeasure the foreign entity's books into the functional currency. The current rate method is used to translate from the functional currency to the reporting currency. In some cases, a foreign entity's functional currency may be the same as the reporting currency, in which case translation is not necessary.
5. Foreign currency translation methods used in other major developed countries were briefly summarized in Exhibit 14.4. As the exhibit shows, a broad variety of methods are used in practice.
6. A mini case illustrating the translation process of the balance sheet of a parent firm with two foreign wholly owned affiliates according to FASB 52 was presented. This was done assuming the foreign exchange rates had not changed since the inception of the businesses, and again after an assumed change, to more thoroughly show the effects of balance sheet consolidation under FASB 52. When a net translation exposure exists, a cumulative translation adjustment account is necessary to bring balance to the consolidated balance sheet after an exchange rate change.
7. Two ways to control translation risk were presented: a balance sheet hedge and a derivatives "hedge." Since translation exposure does not have an immediate direct effect on operating cash flows, its control is relatively unimportant in comparison to transaction exposure, which involves potential real cash flow losses. Since it is, generally, not possible to eliminate both translation and transaction exposure, it is more logical to effectively manage transaction exposure, even at the expense of translation exposure.

KEY WORDS

balance sheet hedge, 351
cumulative translation adjustment (CTA), 340
current/noncurrent method, 339
current rate method, 340
derivatives hedge, 351
functional currency, 342
monetary/nonmonetary method, 339
reporting currency, 342
temporal method, 339
translation exposure, 338
translation exposure report, 347

QUESTIONS

1. Explain the difference in the translation process between the monetary /nonmonetary method and the temporal method.
2. How are translation gains and losses handled differently according to the current rate method in comparison to the other three methods, that is, the current/noncurrent method, the monetary/nonmonetary method, and the temporal method?
3. Identify some instances under FASB 52 when a foreign entity's functional currency would be the same as the parent firm's currency.
4. Describe the remeasurement and translation process under FASB 52 of translating into the reporting currency the books of a wholly owned affiliate that keeps its books in the local currency of the country in which it operates, which is different than its functional currency.
5. It is, generally, not possible to completely eliminate both translation exposure and transaction exposure. In some cases, the elimination of one exposure will also eliminate the other. But in other cases, the elimination of one exposure actually creates the other. Discuss which exposure might be viewed as the most important to effectively manage, if a conflict between controlling both arises. Also, discuss and critique the common methods for controlling translation exposure.

PROBLEMS

1. Assume that FASB 8 is still in effect instead of FASB 52. Construct a translation exposure report for Centralia Corporation and its affiliates that is the counterpart to Exhibit 14.7 in the text. Centralia and its affiliates carry inventory and fixed assets on the books at historical values.
2. Assume that FASB 8 is still in effect instead of FASB 52. Construct a consolidated balance sheet for Centralia Corporation and its affiliates after a depreciation of the Spanish peseta from Ptas140.00/$1.00 to Ptas150.00/$1.00 that is the counterpart to Exhibit 14.8 in the text. Centralia and its affiliates carry inventory and fixed assets on the books at historical values.
3. In Example 14.2, a forward contract was used to establish a derivatives "hedge" to protect Centralia from a translation loss if the peseta depreciated from Ptas140/$1.00 to Ptas150/$1.00. Assume that an over-the-counter call option on the dollar with a strike price of Ptas145 can be purchased for Ptas1.50. Show how the potential translation loss can be "hedged" with an option contract.

MINI CASE

Sundance Sporting Goods, Inc.

Sundance Sporting Goods, Inc., is a U.S. manufacturer of high-quality sporting goods—principally golf, tennis, and other racquet equipment, and also lawn sports, such as croquet and badminton—with administrative offices and manufacturing facilities in Chicago, Illinois. Sundance has two wholly owned manufacturing affiliates, one in Mexico and the other in Canada. The Mexican affiliate is located in Mexico City and services all of Latin America. The Canadian affiliate is in Toronto and serves only Canada. Each affiliate keeps its books in its local currency, which is also the functional currency for the affiliate. The current exchange rates are: \$1.00 = CD1.25 = Ps3.30 = A1.00 = ¥105 = W800. The nonconsolidated balance sheets for Sundance and its two affiliates appear in the accompanying table.

Nonconsolidated Balance Sheet for Sundance Sporting Goods, Inc. and Its Mexican and Canadian Affiliates, December 31, 1997 (in 000 currency units)

	Sundance, Inc. (Parent)	Mexican Affiliate	Canadian Affiliate
Assets			
Cash	\$ 1,500	Ps 1,420	CD 1,200
Accounts receivable	2,500[a]	2,800[e]	1,500[f]
Inventory	5,000	6,200	2,500
Investment in Mexican affiliate	2,400[b]	—	—
Investment in Canadian affiliate	3,600[c]	—	—
Net fixed assets	12,000	11,200	5,600
Total assets	\$27,000	Ps21,620	CD10,800
Liabilities and Net Worth			
Accounts payable	\$3,000	Ps 2,500[a]	CD 1,700
Notes payable	4,000[d]	4,200	2,300
Long-term debt	9,000	7,000	2,300
Common stock	5,000	4,500[b]	2,900[c]
Retained earnings	6,000	3,420[b]	1,600[c]
Total liabilities and net worth	\$27,000	Ps21,620	CD10,800

[a]The parent firm is owed Ps1,320,000 by the Mexican affiliate. This sum is included in the parent's accounts receivable as \$400,000, translated at Ps3.30/\$1.00. The remainder of the parent's (Mexican affiliate's) accounts receivable (payable) are denominated in dollars (pesos).
[b]The Mexican affiliate is wholly owned by the parent firm. It is carried on the parent firm's books at \$2,400,000. This represents the sum of the common stock (Ps4,500,000) and retained earnings (Ps3,420,000) on the Mexican affiliate's books, translated at Ps3.30/\$1.00.
[c]The Canadian affiliate is wholly owned by the parent firm. It is carried on the parent firm's books at \$3,600,000. This represents the sum of the common stock (CD2,900,000) and the retained earnings (CD1,600,000) on the Canadian affiliate's books, translated at CD1.25/\$1.00.
[d]The parent firm has outstanding notes payable of ¥126,000,000 due a Japanese bank. This sum is carried on the parent firm's books as \$1,200,000, translated at ¥105/\$1.00. Other notes payable are denominated in U.S. dollars.
[e]The Mexican affiliate has sold on account A120,000 of merchandise to an Argentine import house. This sum is carried on the Mexican affiliate's books as Ps396,000, translated at A1.00/Ps3.30. Other accounts receivable are denominated in Mexican pesos.
[f]The Canadian affiliate has sold on account W192,000,000 of merchandise to a Korean importer. This sum is carried on the Canadian affiliate's books as CD300,000, translated at W800/CD1.25. Other accounts receivable are denominated in Canadian dollars.

You joined the International Treasury division of Sundance six months ago after spending the last two years receiving your MBA degree. The corporate treasurer has asked you to prepare a report analyzing all aspects of the translation exposure faced by Sundance as a MNC. She has also asked you to address in your analysis the relationship between the firm's translation exposure and its transaction exposure. After performing a forecast of future spot rates of exchange, you decide that you must do the following before any sensible report can be written.

a. Using the current exchange rates and the nonconsolidated balance sheets for Sundance and its affiliates, prepare a consolidated balance sheet for the MNC according to FASB 52.

b. i. Prepare a translation exposure report for Sundance Sporting Goods, Inc., and its two affiliates.

ii. Using the translation exposure report you have prepared, determine if any reporting currency imbalance will result from the change in exposure currency exchange rates. Your forecast is that exchange rates will change from \$1.00 = CD1.25 = Ps3.30 = A1.00 = ¥105 = W800 to \$1.00 = CD1.30 = Ps3.30 = A1.03 = ¥105 = W800.

c. Prepare a second consolidated balance sheet for the MNC using the exchange rates you expect in the future. Determine how any reporting currency imbalance will affect the new consolidated balance sheet for the MNC.

d. i. Prepare a transaction exposure report for Sundance and its affiliates. Determine if any transaction exposures are also translation exposures.

ii. Investigate what Sundance and its affiliates can do to control its transactions and translation exposure. Determine if any of the translation exposure should be hedged.

ENDNOTES

1. See FASB 52, paragraph 4.
2. See FASB 52, paragraph 5.
3. See FASB 52, paragraph 10.
4. See FASB 52, paragraph 11.
5. See FASB 52, paragraph 11.
6. See FASB 52, paragraph 111.
7. Garlicki, Fabozzi, and Fonfeder (1987).

WEB RESOURCES

www.duni

This Website illustrates translation and transaction exposure as reported in the current annual report of a Swedish multinational firm.

REFERENCES AND SUGGESTED READINGS

Arpan, J. S., and L. H. Radenbaugh. *International Accounting and Multinational Enterprises,* 2nd ed. New York: Wiley, 1985.

Coopers & Lybrand. *Foreign Currency Translation and Hedging.* New York: Coopers & Lybrand, February 1994.

Financial Accounting Standards Board. *Accounting for the Translation of Foreign Currency Transactions and Foreign Currency Financial Statements, Statement of Financial Accounting Standards No. 8,* Stamford, CT: Financial Accounting Standards Board, October 1975.

Financial Accounting Standards Board. *Foreign Currency Translation, Statement of Financial Accounting Standards No. 52.* Stamford, CT: Financial Accounting Standards Board, December 1981.

Garlicki, T. Dessa, Frank J. Fabozzi, and Robert Fonfeder. "The Impact of Earnings under FASB 52 on Equity Returns." *Financial Management* 16 (1987), pp. 36–44.

Haried, Andrew A., Leroy F. Imdieke, and Ralph E. Smith. *Advanced Accounting,* 6th ed. New York: Wiley, 1994.

Napolitano, Gabrielle. *International Accounting Standards: A Primer.* New York: Goldman, Sachs & Co., November 24, 1993.

PART FOUR

15. Foreign Direct Investment

16. International Capital Structure and the Cost of Capital

17. International Capital Budgeting

18. Multinational Cash Management

19. Exports and Imports

20. International Tax Environment

Financial Management of the Multinational Firm

Part four covers topics on financial management practices for the MNC.

Chapter 15 discusses why MNCs make capital expenditures in productive capacity in foreign lands rather than just producing domestically and then exporting to overseas markets.

Chapter 16 deals with the international capital structure and the cost of capital of a MNC. An analytical argument is presented showing that the firm's cost of capital is lower when its shares trade internationally, and if debt capital is sourced internationally.

Chapter 17 presents the adjusted present value (APV) framework of Donald Lessard that is useful for the parent firm to analyze a capital expenditure in foreign operations.

Chapter 18 covers issues in cash management for the MNC. The chapter shows that if a MNC establishes a centralized cash depository and a multilateral system, the number of foreign cash flow transactions can be reduced, saving it money and giving it better control of its cash.

Chapter 19 provides a brief introduction to trade financing and counter-trade. An example of a typical foreign trade transaction explains the three primary documents that are used in trade financing: letter of credit, time draft, and bill of lading.

Chapter 20 on the international tax environment opens with a discussion of the theory of taxation. Different methods of taxation are considered, and income tax rates in select countries are compared.

CHAPTER FIFTEEN

Foreign Direct Investment

CHAPTER OUTLINE

In the early 1980s, Honda, a Japanese automobile company, built an assembly plant in Marysville, Ohio, and began to produce cars for the North American market. These cars were substitutes for imports from Japan. As the production capacity at the Ohio plant expanded, Honda began to export its U.S.-manufactured cars to other markets, including its home market, Japan. A few key factors seem to have motivated Honda to make investments in America. First, Honda wanted to circumvent trade barriers imposed on Japanese automobile manufacturers; under the 1981 *Voluntary Restraint Agreement,* Japanese manufacturers were not allowed to increase their automobile exports to the U.S. market. Second, direct investments in America might have been an integral part of Honda's overall corporate strategy designed to bolster its competitive position vis-à-vis its domestic rivals, such as Toyota and Nissan. Following Honda's lead, Toyota and Nissan themselves subsequently made direct investments in America.

It is noteworthy that the Japanese government had been urging the automobile companies to begin production in the United States. In the early 1980s, Japan exported about two million cars a year to the United States, compared to about 20,000 cars imported from the United States. The Japanese government wished to forestall the kind of protectionist sentiment that led to U.S. import quotas on Japanese-made TVs. When TV import quotas were introduced in 1977, virtually all Japanese TV makers were forced to build plants in the United States.

Honda's decision to build a plant in Ohio was welcomed by the United Auto Workers (UAW), an American labor union, which regarded the plant as a major job opportunity for its members. Honda also received several forms of assistance from the state of Ohio, including improved infrastructure around the plant site, access to the Transportation Research Center operated by Ohio State University, abatement of property taxes, and setting up a special foreign trade zone that allowed Honda to import automobile parts from Japan at a reduced tariff rate.

Firms become *multinational* when they undertake **foreign direct investments (FDI).** FDI often involves the establishment of new production facilities in foreign countries such as Honda's Ohio plant. FDI may also involve acquisitions of existing foreign businesses. An example is provided by Ford, which recently acquired effective control of Mazda, a Japanese car manufacturer, as well as Jaguar, a British automobile company. Whether FDI involves a **greenfield investment** (that is, building brand-new production facilities) or **cross-border acquisition** of an existing foreign business, it affords the multinational corporation (MNC) a measure of *control.* FDI thus represents an internal organizational expansion by MNCs.

According to a recent UN survey, the world FDI stock grew about twice as fast as worldwide exports of goods and services, which themselves grew faster than the world GDP by about 50 percent.[1] Indeed, FDI by MNCs now plays a vital role in linking national economies and defining the nature of the emerging global economy. By undertaking FDI on a global basis, such MNCs as Sony, Toyota, Royal Dutch Shell, IBM, GM, Coca-Cola, McDonald's, Daimler-Benz, Bayer, and Nestlé have established their presence worldwide and become familiar household names. These MNCs deploy their formidable resources, tangible and intangible, irrespective of national boundaries, to pursue profits and bolster their competitive positions.

In this chapter, we discuss competing theories of FDI for the purpose of understanding the reasons firms undertake it. We also discuss in detail an increasingly popular mode of FDI, namely, cross-border acquisitions. In addition, we are going to discuss an extra dimension in FDI that would not particularly matter in domestic investments: how to measure and manage political risk associated with FDI. Once a MNC acquires a production facility in a foreign country, its operation will be subject to the "rules of the game" set by the host government. Political risk ranges from (unexpected) restrictions on the repatriation of foreign earnings to outright confiscation of foreign-owned assets. Needless to say, it is essential to the welfare of MNCs to effectively manage political risk. Before we discuss these issues, however, let us briefly review the global trends in FDI in recent years.

GLOBAL TRENDS IN FDI

The recent trends in **FDI flows** are presented in Exhibit 15.1 and Exhibit 15.2. FDI flows represent new additions to the existing stock of FDI. As the exhibits show, during the five-year period 1994–98, total annual worldwide FDI flows amounted to about $430 billion on average. As can be expected, several developed countries are the dominant sources of FDI *outflows.* During the five-year period 1994–98, the United States, on average, invested about $97 billion per year overseas, far more than any other country. France, Germany, Japan, the Netherlands, and the United Kingdom, on average, each invested more than $20 billion per year overseas. After these "big six" come Canada ($16.5 billion), Switzerland ($14.7 billion), Sweden ($11.5 billion), Spain ($8.9 billion), and Italy ($8.2 billion). The developed countries mentioned above account for about 90 percent of the total worldwide FDI outflows during this five-year period. This implies that MNCs domiciled in these countries should have certain comparative advantages in undertaking overseas investment projects. It is interesting to note that China, a developing country, began to undertake FDI, albeit on a modest scale.

Exhibits 15.1 and 15.2 also show FDI *inflows* by country. During the five-year period 1994–1998, the United States received the largest amount of FDI inflows, (96.6 billion per year on average, among all countries. The next most popular destinations of FDI flows were China ($39.9 billion), the United Kingdom ($31.1 billion), France ($22.5 billion), the Netherlands ($15.1 billion), Sweden ($11.3 billion), Canada ($11.0 billion), Germany ($10.8 billion), Mexico ($10.8 billion), and Spain ($8.1 billion). These 10 countries account for about 60 percent of the total worldwide FDI inflows, suggesting these countries must have locational advantages for FDI over other

EXHIBIT 15.1 Foreign Direct Investment—Outflows (Inflows) in Billions of Dollars

Country	1994	1995	1996	1997	1998	Annual Average
Australia	2.5	3.8	5.9	5.9	2.5	4.1
	(4.6)	(12.7)	(5.1)	(8.6)	(6.6)	(7.5)
Canada	9.3	11.5	12.9	22.0	26.6	16.5
	(8.2)	(9.3)	(9.4)	(11.5)	(16.5)	(11.0)
China	2.0	2.0	2.1	2.6	1.6	2.1
	(33.8)	(35.8)	(40.2)	(44.2)	(45.5)	(39.9)
France	24.4	15.8	30.4	35.6	40.6	29.4
	(15.6)	(23.7)	(22.0)	(23.2)	(28.0)	(22.5)
Germany	18.9	39.1	50.8	40.3	86.6	47.1
	(7.1)	(12.0)	(5.6)	(9.6)	(19.9)	(10.8)
Italy	5.6	6.9	6.0	10.2	12.1	8.2
	(2.1)	(4.9)	(3.5)	(3.7)	(2.6)	(3.4)
Japan	18.5	22.6	23.4	26.0	24.2	22.9
	(0.9)	(0.1)	0.2)	(3.2)	(3.2)	(1.5)
Mexico	1.0	0.3	0.0	1.1	1.4	2.6
	(12.4)	(9.5)	(9.2)	(12.8)	(10.2)	(10.8)
Netherlands	17.7	20.0	31.6	21.5	38.3	25.8
	(7.3)	(12.2)	(14.8)	(9.4)	(31.9)	(15.1)
Spain	3.9	4.1	5.5	12.5	18.4	8.9
	(9.4)	(6.8)	(6.7)	(6.4)	(11.3)	(8.1)
Sweden	6.7	11.2	4.7	12.6	22.5	11.5
	(6.4)	(14.5)	(5.1)	(10.9)	(19.4)	(11.3)
Switzerland	10.8	12.2	16.2	16.7	17.4	14.7
	(4.1)	(3.6)	(3.1)	(4.9)	(3.7)	(3.9)
United Kingdom	34.0	44.4	35.1	63.6	114.2	58.3
	(9.3)	(20.4)	(25.8)	(37.0)	(63.1)	(31.1)
United States	73.3	92.1	74.8	110.0	132.8	96.6
	(45.1)	(58.8)	(76.5)	(109.3)	(193.4)	(96.6)
World	284.9	358.6	379.9	475.1	648.9	429.5
	(253.5)	(328.9)	(358.9)	(464.3)	(643.9)	(409.9)

Source: Adapted from *World Investment Report 1999,* UNCTAD.

countries. In contrast to its substantial role as an originating country of FDI outlfows, Japan plays a relatively minor role as a host of FDI inflows; Japan received only $1.5 billion worth of FDI, on average, per year during the period 1994–1998, reflecting a variety of legal, economic, and cultural barriers to foreign investment in Japan.

It is noteworthy that FDI flows into China have dramatically increased in recent years. The amount of inflow increased from $3.5 billion in 1990 to 45.5 billion in 1998. By 1993, China had emerged as the second most important host country for FDI, trailing only the United States. MNCs might have been lured to invest in China not only by lower labor and material costs but also by the desire to preempt the entry of rivals into China's potentially huge market.

Among developing countries, Mexico is another country that experienced substantial FDI inflows, $10.8 billion on average per year. It is well known that MNCs are investing in Mexico, a low-cost country, to serve the North American as well as Mexican markets. It is also noteworthy that MNCs invested heavily, $8.1 billion per year, in Spain, where the costs of production are relatively low compared to other European countries such as France and Germany. Most likely, MNCs invested in Spain to gain a foothold in the huge single market created by the European Union, of which Spain is a member country.

Now, let us turn our attention to **FDI stocks,** which are the accumulation of previous FDI flows. The overall cross-border production activities of MNCs are best

EXHIBIT 15.2

Average Foreign Direct Investments per Year (Billions of Dollars)

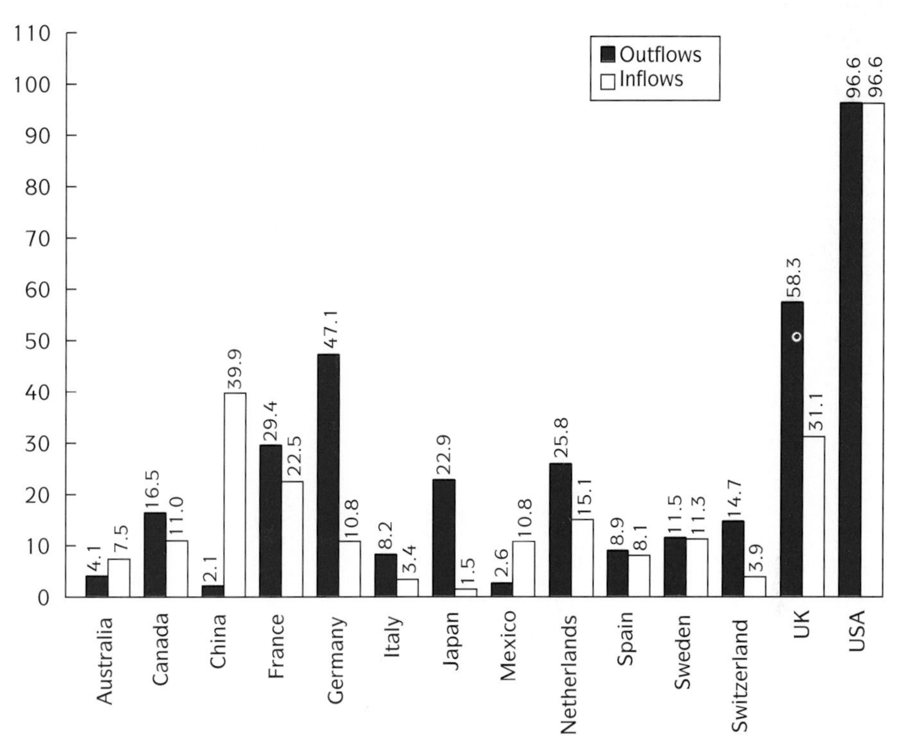

Source: Adapted from *World Investment Report 1999,* UNCTAD.

captured by FDI stocks. Exhibit 15.3 provides a summary of FDI stocks, both outward and inward, by country. As the exhibit shows, the total worldwide FDI stock, which was about $514 billion in 1980, rose to $4,117 billion in 1998. In the case of the United States, FDI outward stock rose from $220 billion in 1980 to $993 billion in 1998. As of 1998, the United States, the U.K., Germany, Japan, the Netherlands, France, Switzerland, and Canada held the most outward FDI stocks. For FDI inward stock, on the other hand, the United States, the U.K., China, Germany, France, and the Netherlands are the most important hosts. Exhibit 15.4 shows the direction of FDI stocks among the three major economic centers, that is, the United States, the European Union, and Japan. Clearly, much of the FDI stocks are concentrated in these three major economic centers.

WHY DO FIRMS INVEST OVERSEAS?

Why do firms locate production overseas rather than exporting from the home country or licensing production to a local firm in the host country? In other words, why do firms seek to extend corporate *control* overseas by forming multinational corporations? Unlike the theory of international trade or the theory of international portfolio investment, we do not have a well-developed, comprehensive theory of FDI. But several theories can shed light on certain aspects of the FDI phenomenon. Many of the existing theories, such as Kindleberger (1969) and Hymer (1975), emphasize various *market imperfections,* that is, imperfections in product, factor, and capital markets, as the key motivating forces driving FDI.

In what follows, we are going to discuss some of the key factors that are important in firms' decisions to invest overseas:

EXHIBIT 15.3

Foreign Direct Investment—Outward (Inward) Stocks in Billions of Dollars

Country	1980	1985	1990	1995	1998
Australia	2.3	6.7	30.1	41.3	62.2
	(13.2)	(25.0)	(75.8)	(104.2)	(104.9)
Canada	22.6	40.9	78.9	110.4	156.6
	(54.2)	(64.7)	(113.1)	(116.8)	(141.8)
China	0.0	0.1	2.5	17.3	22.1
	(0.0)	(3.4)	(14.1)	(129.0)	(261.1)
France	23.6	37.1	110.1	200.9	242.3
	(22.6)	(33.4)	(86.5)	(162.4)	(179.2)
Germany	43.1	59.9	151.6	235.0	390.1
	(36.6)	(36.9)	(111.2)	(134.0)	(228.8)
Italy	7.3	16.3	56.1	86.7	170.7
	(8.9)	(18.9)	(58.0)	(64.7)	(105.4)
Japan	19.6	43.9	201.4	305.5	296.1
	(3.3)	(4.7)	(9.9)	(17.8)	(30.3)
Mexico	0.1	0.5	0.6	2.7	5.8
	(9.0)	(14.8)	(27.9)	(61.3)	(60.8)
Netherlands	42.1	47.8	109.1	158.6	263.0
	(19.2)	(24.9)	(73.7)	(102.6)	(169.5)
Spain	1.2	2.1	14.9	34.3	68.4
	(5.1)	(8.9)	(66.3)	(128.9)	(118.9)
Sweden	5.6	12.4	49.5	61.6	93.5
	(3.6)	(5.1)	(12.5)	(32.8)	(53.8)
Switzerland	21.5	21.4	65.7	108.3	176.7
	(8.5)	(10.1)	(33.7)	(43.1)	(60.1)
United Kingdom	80.4	100.3	230.8	319.0	498.6
	(63.0)	(64.0)	(218.0)	(244.1)	(326.8)
United States	220.2	251.0	435.2	705.6	993.6
	(83.0)	(184.6)	(394.9)	(564.6)	(875.0)
World FDI Stock	514.2	679.4	1,667.6	2,657.9	4,117.1

Source: Adapted from various issues of *World Investment Report,* UNCTAD.

- Trade barriers
- Imperfect labor market
- Intangible assets
- Vertical integration
- Product life cycle
- Shareholder diversification services

Trade Barriers

International markets for goods and services are often rendered imperfect by acts of governments. Governments may impose tariffs, quotas, and other restrictions on exports and imports of goods and services, hindering the free flow of these products across national boundaries. Sometimes, governments may even impose complete bans on the international trade of certain products. Governments regulate international trade to raise revenue, protect domestic industries, and pursue other economic policy objectives.

Facing barriers to exporting its products to foreign markets, a firm may decide to move production to foreign countries as a means of circumventing the trade barriers. A classic example for trade barrier-motivated FDI is Honda's investment in Ohio. Since the cars produced in Ohio would not be subject to U.S. tariffs and quotas,

EXHIBIT 15.4

FDI Stock among Triad Members and Their Clusters (Billions of Dollars)

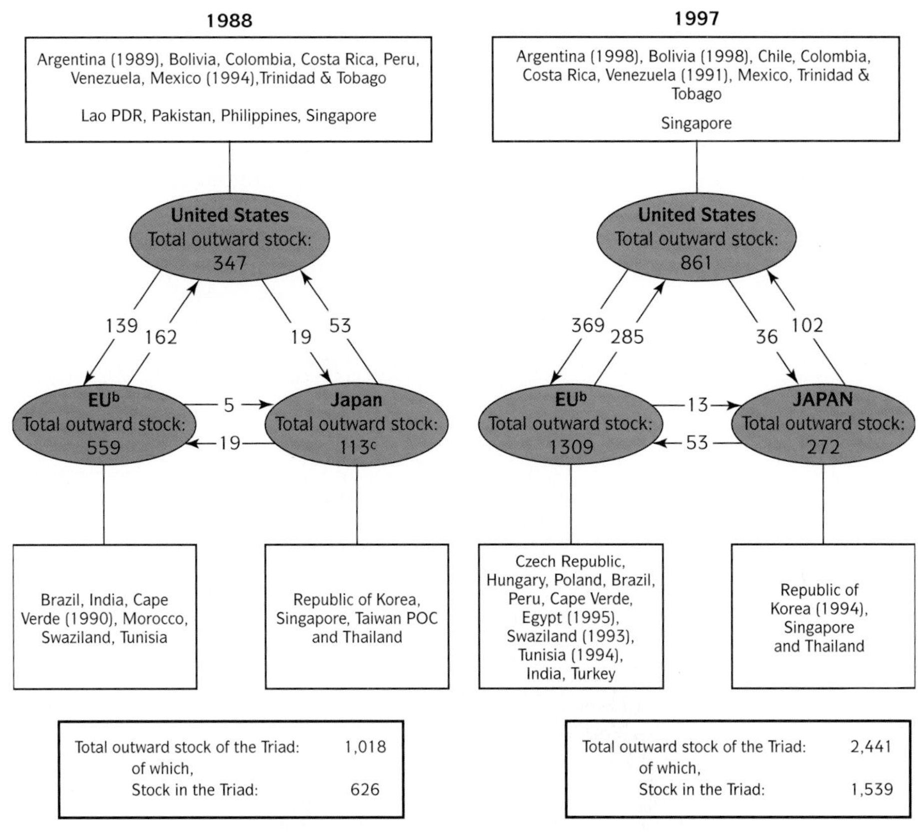

[a] The host countries in which the Triad member accounts for at least 30 percent of total FDI inflows during a three-year period in the latter half of the 1980s/beginning of the 1990s or total inward FDI stock in 1988 are selected for the 1988 chart; and at least 30 percent of total FDI inflows during a three-year period in the mid-1990s or total inward FDI stock in 1997 for the 1997 chart. In cases where data are available for years other than those stated in the respective charts, those years are indicated in parenthesis.
[b] Includes Austria (1996 instead of 1997), Denmark (1996 instead of 1997), Finland (1991 instead of 1988, and 1996 instead of 1997), Germany (1996 instead of 1997), Italy, Netherlands (1996 instead of 1997), Sweden (1996 instead of 1997), and United Kingdom that account for more than 90 percent of the EU outward stock. Denmark is not included for 1988 due to unavailability of data.
[c] Cumulative flows on a balance-of-payment basis since 1968.

Source: UNCTAD, FDI/TNC database.

Honda could circumvent these barriers by establishing production facilities in the United States. The recent surge in FDI in countries like Mexico and Spain can be explained, at least in part, by the desire of MNCs to circumvent external trade barriers set up by NAFTA and the European Union.

Trade barriers can also arise *naturally* from transportation costs. Such products as mineral ore and cement that are bulky relative to their economic values may not be suitable for exporting because high transportation costs will substantially reduce profit margins. In these cases, FDI can be made in the foreign markets to reduce transportation costs.

Imperfect Labor Market

Suppose Samsung, a Korean conglomerate, would like to build production facilities for its consumer electronics products to serve the North American markets. Samsung could locate its production facilities anywhere in North America if the firm is concerned only with circumventing trade barriers imposed by NAFTA.

EXHIBIT 15.5

Labor Costs around the Globe (1997)

Country	Average Hourly Cost ($)
Germany	28.28
Belgium	22.82
Sweden	22.24
Japan	19.37
United States	18.24
France	17.97
Italy	16.74
Canada	16.55
Australia	16.00
United Kingdom	15.47
Spain	12.16
Israel	12.05
Korea	7.22
Taiwan	5.89
Hong Kong	5.42
Mexico	1.75

Source: U.S. Department of Labor, Bureau of Labor Statistics, September 1998.

Samsung chose to locate its production facilities in northern Mexico rather than in Canada or the United States, mainly because it wanted to take advantage of the lower costs of labor in Mexico.

Labor services in a country can be severely underpriced relative to its productivity because workers are not allowed to freely move across national boundaries to seek higher wages. Among all factor markets, the labor market is the most imperfect. Severe imperfections in the labor market lead to persistent wage differentials among countries. Exhibit 15.5 provides the hourly labor costs in the manufacturing sector for selected countries as surveyed by the U.S. Labor Department (in 1997). Compared with Germany, hourly compensation for factory workers is about $10 less in the United States. Substantially lower labor costs in the United States might have motivated, at least in part, such German car manufacturers as Daimler and BMW to establish production facilities in Alabama and South Carolina, respectively. The hourly compensation is only $1.75 in Mexico.

When workers are not mobile because of immigration barriers, firms themselves should move to the workers in order to benefit from the underpriced labor services. This is one of the main reasons MNCs are making FDIs in less developed countries such as Mexico, China, India, and Southeast Asian countries like Thailand, Malaysia, and Indonesia, where labor services are underpriced relative to their productivity.

Intangible Assets

Coca-Cola has invested in bottling plants all over the world rather than, say, licensing local firms to produce Coke. Coca-Cola chose FDI as a mode of entry into foreign markets for an obvious reason—it wanted to protect the formula for its famed soft drink. If Coca-Cola licenses a local firm to produce Coke, it has no guarantee that the secrets of the formula will be maintained. Once the formula is leaked to other local firms, they may come up with similar products, which will hurt Coca-Cola's sales. This possibility is known as the *boomerang* effect. In the 1960s, Coca-Cola, which had bottling plants in India, faced strong pressure from the Indian government to reveal the Coke formula as a condition for continued operations in India. Instead of revealing the formula, Coca-Cola chose to withdraw from India.[2]

MNCs may undertake overseas investment projects in a foreign country, despite the fact that local firms may enjoy inherent advantages. This implies that MNCs should have significant advantages over local firms. Indeed, MNCs often enjoy comparative advantages due to special **intangible assets** they possess. Examples include technological, managerial and marketing know-how, superior R&D capabilities, and brand names. These intangible assets are often hard to package and sell to foreigners. In addition, the property rights in intangible assets are difficult to establish and protect, especially in foreign countries where legal recourse may not be readily available. As a result, firms may find it more profitable to establish foreign subsidiaries and capture returns directly by *internalizing* transactions in these assets. The internalization theory can help explain why MNCs, not local firms, undertake investment projects in foreign countries.

A strand of literature, including Caves (1971) and Magee (1976), places special emphasis on the role of market imperfections for intangible assets in motivating firms to undertake FDI. According to the **internalization theory** of FDI, firms that have intangible assets with a *public good* property tend to invest directly in foreign countries in order to use these assets on a larger scale and, at the same time, avoid the misappropriations of intangible assets that may occur while transacting in foreign markets through a market mechanism.[3]

Vertical Integration

Suppose Royal Dutch Shell purchases a significant portion of crude oil for its refinery facilities from a Saudi oil company that owns the oil fields. In this situation, Royal Dutch Shell can experience a number of problems. For example, Royal Dutch Shell, the downstream firm, would like to hold the crude oil price down, whereas the Saudi oil company, an upstream firm, would like to push the price up. If the Saudi company has stronger bargaining power, Royal Dutch Shell may be forced to pay a higher price than it would like to, adversely affecting the firm's profits. In addition, as the world's demand for refined oil fluctuates, one of the two firms may have to bear excessive risk. The conflicts between the upstream and downstream firms can be resolved, however, if the two firms form a vertically integrated firm. Obviously, if Royal Dutch Shell controls the oil fields, the problems will disappear.

Generally speaking, MNCs may undertake FDI in countries where inputs are available in order to secure the supply of inputs at a stable price. Furthermore, if MNCs have monopolistic/oligopolistic control over the input market, this can serve as a barrier to entry to the industry. Many MNCs involved in extractive/natural resources industries tend to directly own oil fields, mine deposits, and forests for these reasons. Also, MNCs often find it profitable to locate manufacturing/processing facilities near the natural resources in order to save transportation costs. It would be costly to bring bulky bauxite ore to the home country and then extract the aluminum.

Although the majority of vertical FDIs are *backward* in that FDI involves an industry abroad that produces inputs for MNCs, foreign investments can take the form of *forward* vertical FDI when they involve an industry abroad that sells a MNC's outputs. As is well known, U.S. car makers found it difficult to market their products in Japan. This is partly because most car dealers in Japan have a long and close business relationship with the Japanese car makers and are reluctant to carry foreign imports. To overcome this problem, U.S. car makers began to build their own network of dealerships in Japan to help sell their cars. This is an example of forward vertical FDI.

Product Life Cycle

According to Raymond Vernon (1966), firms undertake FDI at a particular stage in the life cycle of the products that they initially introduced. Vernon observed that throughout the 20th century, the majority of new products, such as computers,

INTERNATIONAL FINANCE IN PRACTICE

Linear Sequence in Manufacturing: Singer & Company

Singer was one of the first United States—based companies that internationalized its operations. In August 1850, I.M. Singer invented a sewing machine and established I.M. Singer & Company in New York in 1851 to manufacture and sell the machines in the United States. To protect this innovative product, Singer had applied for and obtained domestic and some foreign patents by 1851. Until 1855, the company concentrated on fine-tuning its operations in the domestic market.

The first step towards internationalizing took place in 1855, when Singer & Co. sold its French patent for the single thread machine to a French merchant for a combination of lump-sum payment and royalties. This proved to be a bad experience for Singer as the French merchant was reluctant to pay royalties and handled competitors' products, leading to disputes and discouraging Singer from selling foreign patents to independent businesspersons. By 1856, Singer stopped granting territorial rights to independents in the domestic market due to bad experiences and began establishing its own sales outlets. Independent agents were not providing user instructions to buyers and failed to offer servicing. They were also reluctant to risk their capital by providing instalment payments as well as carrying large inventories.

Learning from its domestic problems, Singer used franchised agents as a mode of entry abroad; they sold and advertised the company's product in a given region. By 1858, Singer had independent businesspersons as foreign agents in Rio de Janeiro and elsewhere. Between September 1860 and May 1861, the company exported 127 machines to agents in Canada, Cuba, Curacao, Germany, Mexico, Peru, Puerto Rico, Uruguay, and

televisions, and mass-produced cars, were developed by U.S. firms and first marketed in the United States. According to Vernon's **product life-cycle theory,** when U.S. firms first introduce new products, they choose to keep production facilities at home, close to customers. In the early stage of the product life cycle, the demand for the new product is relatively insensitive to the price and thus the pioneering firm can charge a relatively high price. At the same time, the firm can continuously improve the product based on feedback from its customers at home.

As demand for the new product develops in foreign countries, the pioneering U.S. firm begins to export to those countries. As the foreign demand for the product continues to grow, U.S. firms, as well as foreign firms, may be induced to start production in foreign countries to serve local markets. As the product becomes standardized and mature, it becomes important to cut the cost of production to stay competitive. A foreign producer operating in a low-cost country may start to export the product to the United States. At the same time, cost considerations may induce the U.S. firms to set up production facilities in a low-cost foreign country and export the product back to the United States. In other words, FDI takes place when the product reaches maturity and cost becomes an important consideration. FDI can thus be interpreted as a *defensive* move to maintain the firm's competitive position against its domestic and foreign rivals. The International Finance in Practice box, "Linear Sequence in Manufacturing: Singer & Company," provides an interesting historical example supporting the product life-cycle view of FDI.

The product life-cycle theory predicts that over time the United States switches from an exporting country of new products to an importing country. The dynamic changes in the international trade pattern are illustrated in Exhibit 15.6. The prediction of the product life-cycle theory is consistent with the pattern of dynamic changes observed for many products. For instance, personal computers (PCs) were first de-

Venezuela. Due to its domestic experience, Singer sped up the linear sequence, sometimes simultaneously using both franchised agents and its own sales outlets.

Singer also started extending its policy of establishing sales outlets to foreign markets. By 1861, it had salaried representatives in Glasgow and London. They established additional branches in England, to each of which the machines were sold on commission. By 1862, Singer was facing competition in England from imitators. Foreign sales of Singer machines increased steadily as the company was able to sell machines abroad at prices lower than in the United States because of the undervaluation of the dollar. In 1863, Singer opened a sales office in Hamburg, Germany, and later in Sweden. By 1866, the European demand for Singer machines surpassed supplies and competitors were taking advantage of Singer's inability to supply the machines. After the Civil War, the United States currency appreciated; at the same time, wages in the United States began to rise, increasing manufacturing costs and affecting firms' international competitiveness. As a result, some United States firms started establishing factories abroad.

In 1868, Singer established a small assembly factory in Glasgow, with parts imported from the United States. The venture proved to be successful and, by 1869, Singer decided to import tools from the United States to manufacture all parts in Glasgow. By 1874, partly due to the recession at home, Singer was selling more than half of its output abroad. Then, Singer started replacing locally financed independent agents with salaried-plus-commission agents. By 1879, its London regional headquarters had 26 offices in the United Kingdom and one each in Paris, Madrid, Brussels, Milan, Basel, Capetown, Bombay, and Auckland.

By the 1880s, the company had a strong foreign sales organization, with the London regional headquarters taking the responsibility for sales in Australia, Asia, Africa, the southern part of South America, the United Kingdom, and a large part of the European continent. The Hamburg office was in charge of northern and middle Europe, while the New York office looked after sales in the Caribbean, Mexico, the northern part of South America and Canada. By 1881, the capacity in Singer's three factories in Glasgow was insufficient to meet demand. Therefore, in 1882, Singer established a modern plant in Kilbowie near Glasgow with the latest United States machine tools and with a capacity equivalent to that of its largest factory in the United States. In 1883, Singer set up manufacturing plants in Canada and Australia. Through experience, Singer learned that it could manufacture more cost effectively in Scotland than in the United States for sales in Europe and other markets.

Source: World Investment Report 1996, UNCTAD, p. 77.

veloped by U.S. firms (such as IBM and Apple Computer) and exported to overseas markets. As PCs became a standardized commodity, however, the United States became a net importer of PCs from foreign producers based in such countries as Japan, Korea, and Taiwan, as well as foreign subsidiaries of U.S. firms.

It should be pointed out that Vernon's theory was developed in the 1960s when the United States was the unquestioned leader in R&D capabilities and product innovations. Increasingly, product innovations are taking place outside the United States, and new products are introduced simultaneously in many advanced countries. Production facilities may be located in multiple countries from the inception of a new product. The international system of production is becoming too complicated to be explained by a simple version of the product life-cycle theory.

Shareholder Diversification Services

If investors cannot effectively diversify their portfolio holdings internationally because of barriers to cross-border capital flows, firms may be able to provide their shareholders with indirect diversification services by making direct investments in foreign countries. When a firm holds assets in many countries, the firm's cash flows are internationally diversified. Thus, shareholders of the firm can indirectly benefit from international diversification even if they are not directly holding foreign shares. Capital market imperfections thus may motivate firms to undertake FDI.

Although shareholders of MNCs may indirectly benefit from corporate international diversification, it is not clear that firms are motivated to undertake FDI for the purpose of providing shareholders with diversification services. Considering the fact that many barriers to international portfolio investments have been dismantled in recent years, enabling investors to diversify internationally by themselves, capital market imperfections as a motivating factor for FDI are likely to become less relevant.

EXHIBIT 15.6

The Product Life Cycle

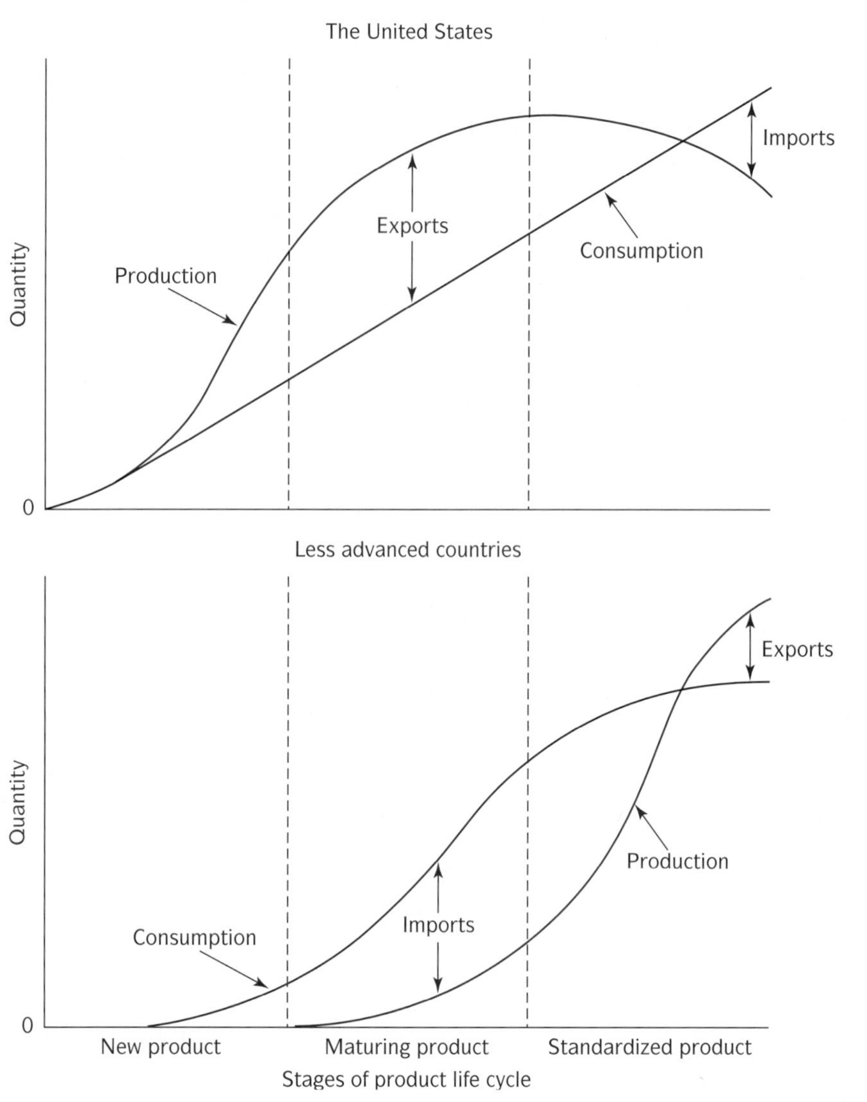

CROSS-BORDER ACQUISITIONS

As previously mentioned, FDI can take place either through *greenfield investments,* which involve building new production facilities in a foreign country, or through *cross-border acquisitions,* which involve buying existing foreign businesses. In recent years, a growing portion of FDI has taken the form of cross-border acquisitions, accounting for roughly 50 percent of FDI flows in terms of dollar amount. In 1998, for instance, British Petroleum purchased Amoco, a U.S. oil company, for $55 billion. Daimler-Benz of Germany acquired Chrysler, the third largest U.S. car company, for $40.5 billion. And Hoechst, a major German pharmaceutical company, acquired Rhone-Poulenc SA (Life Sciences), a French company, for $21.2 billion. Exhibit 15.7 lists major cross-border mergers and acquisition (M&A) deals with a value of above $2.0 billion that were consummated in 1998. The rapid increase in cross-border

EXHIBIT 15.7 Cross-Border M&A Deals with Values of More Than $2 billion Announced in 1998

Deal Value (Billion Dollars)	Acquiring Company	Home Economy	Industry of Acquiring Company	Acquired Company	Host Economy	Industry of Acquired Company
55.0	British Petroleum Co PLC (BP)	United Kingdom	Petroleum expl/ref/dist	Amoco Corp.	United States	Petroleum expl/ref/dist
40.5	Daimler-Benz AG	Germany	Automotive	Chrysler Corp.	United States	Automotive
31.8	ZENECA Group PLC	United Kingdom	Pharmaceuticals	Astra AB	Sweden	Pharmaceuticals
21.2	Hoechst AG-Life Sciences Divs	Germany	Chemicals/pharmaceuticals	Rhone-Poulenc AG-Life Sciences	France	Pharmaceuticals
12.6	Scottish Power PLC	United Kingdom	Electric utility	PacificCorp	United States	Utilities
11.5	Total SA	France	Petroleum expl/ref/dist	Petrofina SA	Belgium	Petroleum expl/ref/dist
10.3	Universal Studios Inc.	United States	Media	PolyGram NV(Philips Electrn)	Netherlands	Media
9.1	Deutsche Bank AG	Germany	Banking	Bankers Trust New York Corp.	United States	Banking
9.0	Northern Telecom Ltd(BCE Inc)	Canada	Telecommunications	Bay Networks Inc	United States	Data networking prods
8.8	Texas Utilities Co	United States	Electric and gas utility	Energy Group PLC	United Kingdom	Electric utility;coal mining
8.6	VIAG AG	Germany	Diversified	Alusuisse-Lonza AG	Switzerland	Chemicals
6.9	Enso Oy	Finland	Paper,lumber,chemicals	Stora Kopparbergs Bergslags AB	Sweden	Forestry; pulp products
6.9	Teleglobe Inc	Canada	Telecommunications	Excel Communications Inc	United States	Telecommunications
6.1	Astra AB	Sweden	Pharmaceuticals	Astra Merck Inc(Merck & Co)	United States	Pharmaceuticals
5.9	Suez Lyonnaise des Eaux	France	Diversified	Societe Generale de Belgique	Belgium	Banking
5.3	Total SA	France	Petroleum expl/ref/dist	Petrofina SA	Belgium	Petroleum expl/ref/dist
5.1	Aeropuertos Argentina 2000	United States	Airports	Argentina-Airports(33)	Argentina	Own,operate airports
5.1	Alcatel Alsthom CGE	France	Telecommunications	DSC Communications Corp.	United States	Telecommunications
5.0	British Telecomm-Worldwide Ast	United Kingdom	Telecommunications	AT&T-Worldwide Assets,Ops	United States	Telecommunications
5.0	Investor Group	Spain	Investor group	TELESP(Telebrás/Brazil)	Brazil	Telecommunications
4.7	Hong Kong Monetary Authority	Hong Kong, China	Government agency	HSBC Holdings PLC	United Kingdom	Banking
4.6	Pearson PLC	United Kingdom	Publishing	Simon & Schuster-Educ,Prof	United States	Publishing
4.1	B&Q PLC(Kingfisher PLC)	United Kingdom	Trading	Castorama Dubois	France	Trading
3.8	National Grid Co PLC	United Kingdom	Electric utility	New England Electric System	United States	Electric utility
3.7	Akzo Nobel NV	Netherlands	Chemicals	Courtaulds PLC	United Kingdom	Chemicals
3.6	Owens-Illinois Inc	United States	Glass,plastic containers	BTR PLC-Global Packaging &	Australia	Packaging
3.2	AXA-UAP	France	Insurance	Royale Belge SA	Belgium	Insurance
3.2	Electricite de France {EDF}	France	Electric utility	London Electricity(Entergy Po)	United Kingdom	Electric utility
3.1	Investor Group	Portugal	Investor group	Telesp Celular Participacoes	Brazil	Telecommunications
3.0	Bass PLC	United Kingdom	Food and beverages	Saison Holdings BV	Netherlands	Tourism
2.9	Canadian National Railway Co	Canada	Railroad services	Illinois Central Corp.	United States	Railroad services
2.8	Metro AG(Metro Holding AG)	Germany	Trading	Metro-Holding-Wrldwd Whl	Denmark	Trading
2.8	Koninklijke Ahold NV	Netherlands	Trading	Giant Food Inc	United States	Trading
2.6	Bowater Inc	United States	Paper and lumber	Avenor Inc	Canada	Paper,pulp,lumber
2.5	Union Pacific Resources Group	United States	Petroleum expl/ref/dist	Norcen Energy Resources Ltd	Canada	Petroleum expl/ref/dist
2.5	Ciba Specialty Chemicals Hldgs	Switzerland	Chemicals	Allied Colloids Group PLC	United Kingdom	Chemicals
2.4	Enron Corp.	United States	Own,operate gas pipelines	Wessex Water PLC	United Kingdom	Utilities
2.4	Shareholders	Australia	Investor group	Coca-Cola Beverages(Coca-Cola)	United Kingdom	Food and beverages
2.4	Telecom Italia(IT Treasury)	Italy	Telecommunications	Telekom Austria	Austria	Telecommunications
2.3	Anglo American Corp of SA ltd	South Africa	Diversified	Minorco SA	Luxembourg	Mining
2.3	MCI Communications Corp.	United States	Telecommunications services	Embratel(Telebrás/Brazil)	Brazil	Telecommunications
2.1	Marsh & McLennan Cos Inc	United States	Insurance	Sedgwick Group PLC	United Kingdom	Insurance
2.1	Boston Scientific Corp.	United States	Catheters	Schneider Worldwide	Switzerland	Catheters
2.1	ABN-AMRO Holding NV	Netherlands	Banking	Banco Real SA	Brazil	Banking

Source: *World Investment Report 1999,* UNCTAD, p. 436. Reprinted with permission.

acquisitions can be attributed to the ongoing liberalization of capital markets and the integration of the world economy.

Firms may be motivated to engage in cross-border M&A deals to bolster their competitive positions in the world market by acquiring special assets from other firms or using their own assets on a larger scale. A recent United Nations study aptly discusses why firms choose M&As as a mode of investment.[4]

> Mergers and acquisitions are a popular mode of investment for firms wishing to protect, consolidate and advance their global competitive positions, by selling off divisions that fall outside the scope of their core competence and acquiring strategic assets that enhance their competitiveness. For those firms, "ownership" assets acquired from another firm, such as technical competence, established brand names, and existing supplier networks and distribution systems, can be put to immediate use towards better serving global customers, enhancing profits, expanding market share and increasing corporate competitiveness by employing international production networks more efficiently.

The International Finance in Practice box, "DaimlerChrysler: The First Global Car Colossus," page 374, provides a real-world example involving the merger deal between Daimler, a German car company, and Chrysler, the third largest U.S. car marker. As mentioned in the box, the combined company expects to cut costs by as much as $3 billion annually and fill product and geographic gaps. Anticipating the synergistic gains, stock prices of both companies rose upon the announcement of a $40.5 billion deal.

Cross-border acquisitions of businesses are a politically sensitive issue, as most countries prefer to retain local control of domestic firms. As a result, although countries may welcome greenfield investments, as they are viewed as representing new investment and employment opportunities, foreign firms' bids to acquire domestic firms are often resisted and sometimes even resented. Whether or not cross-border acquisitions produce **synergistic gains** and how such gains are divided between acquiring and target firms are thus important issues from the perspective of shareholder welfare and public policy. Synergistic gains are obtained when the value of the combined firm is greater than the stand-alone valuations of the individual (acquiring and target) firms.[5] If cross-border acquisitions generate synergistic gains and both the acquiring and target shareholders gain wealth at the same time, one can argue that cross-border acquisitions are mutually beneficial and thus should not be thwarted both from a national and global perspective.

Synergistic gains may or may not arise from cross-border acquisitions, depending on the motive of acquiring firms. In general, gains will result when the acquirer is motivated to take advantage of the market imperfections mentioned earlier. In other words, firms may decide to acquire foreign firms to take advantage of mispriced factors of production and to cope with trade barriers.

As previously mentioned, imperfections in the market for *intangible assets* can also play a major role in motivating firms to undertake cross-border acquisitions. According to the internalization theory, a firm with intangible assets that have a public good property such as technical and managerial know-how may acquire foreign firms as a platform for using its special assets on a larger scale and, at the same time, avoid the misappropriation that may occur while transacting in foreign markets through a market mechanism. Cross-border acquisitions may also be motivated by the acquirer's desire to acquire and internalize the target firm's intangible assets. In this *backward-internalization* case, the acquirer seeks to create wealth by appropriating the rent generated from the economy of scale obtained from using the target's intangible assets on a global basis. The internalization thus may proceed *forward* to internalize the acquirer's assets, or *backward* to internalize the target's assets.

Reflecting the increased importance of cross-border acquisitions as a mode of FDI, several researchers investigated the effects of cross-border acquisitions. Doukas and Travlos (1988) investigated the impact of international acquisitions on the stock

EXHIBIT 15.8 Average Wealth Gains from Cross-Border Acquisitions: Foreign Acquisitions of U.S. Firms

Country of Acquirer	Number of Cases	R&D/Sales (%)		Average Wealth Gains (in Million U.S. $)		
		Acquirer	Target	Acquirer	Target	Combined
Canada	10	0.21	0.65	14.93	85.59	100.53
Japan	15	5.08	4.81	227.83	170.66	398.49
U.K.	46	1.11	2.18	−122.91	94.55	−28.36
Other	32	1.63	2.80	−47.46	89.48	42.02
All	103	1.66	2.54	−35.01	103.19	68.18

Source: Reprinted from *Journal of Banking and Finance* 20, C. Eun, R. Kolodny, and C. Scheraga, "Cross-Border Acquisitions and Shareholder Wealth: Tests of the Synergy and Internalization Hypotheses," pp. 1559–1582, © 1996 with kind permission from Elsevier Science-NL, Sara Burgerhartstreet 25, 1055 KV Amsterdam, The Netherlands.

prices of U.S. bidding firms. The study shows that shareholders of U.S. bidders experience significant positive abnormal returns when firms expand into new industries and geographic markets. When firms already have operations in the target firm's country, U.S. shareholders experience no significant abnormal returns. Harris and Ravenscraft (1991), on the other hand, studied shareholder wealth gains for U.S. firms acquired by foreign firms. They conclude that U.S. targets experience higher wealth gains when they are acquired by foreign firms than when acquired by U.S. firms.

Morck and Yeung (1992) also investigate the effect of international acquisitions on the stock prices of U.S. firms. They show that U.S. acquiring firms with information-based intangible assets experience a significantly positive stock price reaction upon foreign acquisition. This is consistent with the findings of their earlier work (1991) that the market value of the firm is positively related to its multinationality because of the firm's intangible assets, such as R&D capabilities, with public good nature. It is not the multinationality per se that contributes to the firm's value. Their empirical findings support the (forward-) internalization theory of FDI.

Eun, Kolodny, and Scheraga (1996), on the other hand, directly measure the magnitude of shareholders' gains from cross-border acquisitions, using a sample of major foreign acquisitions of U.S. firms that took place during the period 1979–90. Their findings are summarized in Exhibit 15.8. First, the exhibit shows that U.S. target shareholders realized significant wealth gains, $103 million on average, regardless of the nationality of acquirers. Second, the wealth gains to foreign acquiring shareholders, however, varied greatly across acquiring countries. Shareholders of British acquirers experienced significant wealth reduction, −$123 million on average, whereas Japanese shareholders experienced major wealth increases, $228 million on average. Canadian acquisitions of U.S. firms produced modest wealth increases for their shareholders, $15 million on average.

Third, cross-border acquisitions are generally found to be synergy generating corporate activities. Shareholders of the "paired" sample of U.S. targets and foreign acquirers experienced positive combined wealth gains, $68 million, on average. Synergistic gains, however, vary a great deal across acquiring countries. Japanese acquisitions generated large combined gains, $398 million, on average, which were shared by target shareholders (43 percent) and acquiring shareholders (57 percent).[6] In contrast, British acquisitions produced a somewhat negative combined wealth gain, −$28 million on average, and caused a wealth transfer from acquiring to target shareholders.

Eun, Kolodny, and Scheraga argue that the significant gains for Japanese acquirers can be attributed to the successful internalization of the R&D capabilities of their targets, which have a much higher R&D intensity on average than the targets of

INTERNATIONAL FINANCE IN PRACTICE

DaimlerChrysler: The First Global Car Colossus

The champagne was on ice at the Dorchester Hotel in London. Earlier in the day on May 6, the board of Chrysler Corp. and the management board of Daimler Benz approved a historic merger, creating a $130 billion automotive colossus known as DaimlerChrysler AG. The chief executives of two of the world's largest auto makers, Chrysler's Robert J. Eaton and Daimler's Jürgen Schrempp, strode across the room and sealed the largest merger in automotive history—and the third-largest deal ever—with a handshake. The mood was electric as the assembled executives prepared to pop the cork on a pact that would send shock waves around the world. "Both men were enormously energized," says a source close to the deal.

And why not? It looks like a marriage made in automotive heaven. In one bold stroke, the pending merger of Daimler and Chrysler dramatically changes the landscape of the global auto industry. By combining forces, Daimler, Germany's biggest industrial concern, and Chrysler, America's No. 3 carmaker, bring a range of hot-selling models and formidable financial muscle under one garage roof. Simply said, DaimlerChrysler is set to transform the way the auto industry operates worldwide.

The megadeal, which was set to be formally announced on May 7, unites two of the world's most profitable auto companies—with combined 1997 net earnings of $4.6 billion. And if ever a merger had the potential for that elusive quality—synergy—this could be the one. Mercedes-Benz passenger cars are synonymous with luxury and sterling engineering. Chrysler is renowned for its low-cost production of trucks, minivans, and sport-utility vehicles. Chrysler is almost wholly domestic, and Mercedes is increasing global sales—albeit within the confines of the luxury-car market. By spreading Chrysler's production expertise to Daimler operations and merging both product-development forces, the new company could cut costs by up to $3 billion annually—including $1.1 billion in purchasing costs, analysts say.

But DaimlerChrysler is about more than cutting costs and filling product and geographic gaps. It's about the emergence of a new category of global carmaker at a critical moment in the industry—when there is plant capacity to build at least 15 million more vehicles each year than will be sold. And overcapacity is expected to balloon to 18.2 million vehicles by 2002 as Asia continues to decline, predicts Standard & Poor's DRI, a division of The McGraw-Hill Companies. Consolidation is inevitable; from about 40 auto companies now, to about 20 in the next century, says DRI analyst Sam Fiorani.

DaimlerChrysler, then, may be the first member of the 21st century 20. "The Mercedes-Chrysler deal sanctions the concept of auto mergers and is a major catalyst for more," says Joseph S. Phillippi, auto analyst for Lehman Brothers Inc. Eaton, in an Apr. 27 interview with *Business Week*, predicted that Western auto makers with the wherewithal would snap up the troubled auto makers of South Korea and Southeast Asia. General Motors Corp., for example, is considering a big stake in Korea's beleaguered Daewoo. In Europe, auto makers such as Volvo, Fiat, PSA (Peugeot/Citröen), and Renault are ripe for takeover.

DaimlerChrysler will have the wherewithal. It will have $130 billion in annual sales and assets totaling $120 billion. It will have factories on four continents.

Indeed, both partners were giants in their own right. So why merge? Top executives at the two companies came to realize that if they continue to go it alone, their companies could survive as strong regional players—but might be forced onto the shoulder in a global industry. "There are world forces at work that are driving consolidation," Eaton said in the April interview. "Two factors are huge: the worldwide excess capacity in autos and the Asian economic crisis."

Eaton and Schrempp hatched their stunning plan in secret meetings over the past nine months in Germany and Detroit. Daimler was represented by Goldman, Sachs & Co. and Deutsche Bank, while CS First Boston represented Chrysler. The estimated $40 billion deal is being financed by a stock swap of two Chrysler shares for every one Daimler share. It will leave Chrysler shareholders with 43% of the combined entity, while Daimler stockholders control 57%, say sources familiar with the deal. That will make DaimlerChrysler a German company for tax and accounting benefits, these sources say.

acquirers from other countries. Thus, the desire to "backward" internalize the target's intangible assets appears to be an important driving force for Japanese acquisition programs in the United States. This supports the backward-internalization hypothesis.[7] In the case of British acquisitions, the average combined wealth gain was negative, and the acquiring shareholders lost substantial wealth. It thus appears that the

But the company will have dual headquarters. A source close to Daimler says that Daimler and Chrysler headquarters will remain in Stuttgart and Auburn Hills, Mich., for some time to come. "Can you imagine Daimler leaving Stuttgart? Can you imagine Chrysler leaving Detroit?" It will also have CO-CEOS—to start. After three years, however, Eaton is expected to retire, allowing Schrempp to take full control, says sources familiar with the arrangement.

Investors immediately applauded—pushing Chrysler shares up 7³/₈ to 48¹³/₁₆ on May 6. "Chrysler has the trucks, vans, and SUVS, and Daimler has the luxury cars," says Seth M. Glickenhaus of Glickenhaus & Co., an investment firm that holds 8 million Chrysler shares. "There are enormous synergies in product."

One of the biggest opportunities is for the paired company to plunge into new markets that neither could assay alone. Neither has much of a presence in Latin America or Asia, although Daimler does sell heavy trucks there. Chrysler's inexpensive small cars will give Daimler a vehicle to drive into emerging markets. "With our [upscale] product portfolio, we will never be a mass marketer," says a source close to Daimler. "There are some markets where [Mercedes] will never be able to have an impact."

The first venture of the new merged company likely will be a barebones little car, smaller than Chrysler's subcompact Neon model, to sell in Asia and Latin America. "We would like a sub-Neon vehicle for the international market," says Eaton. "We started looking at projects four years ago, and it's something we're looking at harder now." Ironically, such a car may be powered by engines to be made in Brazil in a joint venture between Chrysler and BMW—Mercedes' archival in Germany. BMW declines to comment on the DaimlerChrysler union.

Indeed, most rivals are too stunned to react. Both Ford and GM declined to comment. On the other hand, many industry watchers immediately questioned whether the enormously divergent cultures of Auburn Hills and Stuttgart won't get in the way of all that synergy. "I can't imagine two more different cultures," says Furman Selz auto analyst Maryann N. Keller.

Chrysler's brushes with bankruptcy forged a culture dedicated to speedy product development, lean operations, and flashy design. Daimler remains a buttoned-down, engineering-driven bureaucracy known for conservatively styled products. "The reaction here is shock, excitement, enthusiasm, and concern," says one Chrysler exec.

Schrempp and Eaton are certainly an odd couple. Eaton, 58, is a Kansas-born engineer who worked his way up the ranks at GM before replacing Lee Iacocca as Chrysler chairman in 1993. His soft-spoken manner belies his reputation as a savvy manager. When he took the job at Chrysler, Motown observers expected that his rival, Robert A. Lutz, would bolt. Yet Eaton and Lutz came together to drive Chrysler to record sales and profits. Lutz, 66, now vice-chairman, is expected to retire soon.

Schrempp, who once trained as an auto mechanic, is also an engineer who climbed the corporate ladder to become CEO in 1995 after 28 years with Daimler. After he won the top post, he forced out his rival for the job, Helmut Werner, who had engineered a turnaround with hot products, like the M-class sport utility vehicles and SLK roadster, and youthful, irreverent marketing.

Can Chrysler and Mercedes live together? It could be tough because they will want to protect their vastly different brands. The Mercedes network "is not the kind of distribution system that Chrysler wants or needs, or even could use," says Keller. Nor is it likely that a Mercedes sedan will one day roll down a Chrysler line. "People buy Mercedes because they think they're made by guys in white coats," says Keller. "That image better not be contaminated by the idea that it's being built by a bunch of guys in Indiana."

So how will Chrysler and Mercedes help each other without losing their identities? Chrysler's slowly improving quality could take a quantum leap forward with help from Daimler engineers. And Daimler's diesel engines, for example, could help Chrysler in its efforts to sell subcompacts and minivans in Europe and elsewhere. Chrysler, for its part, has the industry's best supplier relations, while Daimler still relies on strong-arm techniques to get lower prices from its suppliers. Together, they can save on warehousing and logistics for cars and spare parts in both Europe and the U.S. They also can jointly make internal components like air-conditioning systems and door latches and pool their resources in developing basic technology.

Well before anyone knows if DaimlerChrysler is a success, however, its very existence could reshape the industry. Look for auto makers to scramble for partners to ensure survival as one of the 21st century 20. How that plays out is anybody's guess. "The odd man out here seems to be the Japanese," says Phillippi of Lehman Brothers. "Nissan and Honda in particular have only two legs to stand on: North America and Japan." That won't be enough in this race.

By Bill Vlasic.
Source: *Business Week*, May 18, 1998, pp. 40–43. Reprinted with permission.

managers of British firms often undertook negative NPV projects when they acquired U.S. firms. It is well known that corporate acquisitions can be driven by managers who pursue growth and diversification at the expense of shareholders' interests. As Jensen pointed out (1986), managers may benefit by expanding the firm beyond the size that maximizes shareholder wealth for various reasons.[8]

POLITICAL RISK AND FDI

In assessing investment opportunities in a foreign country, it is important for a parent firm to take into consideration the risk arising from the fact that investments are located in a foreign country. A sovereign country can take various actions that may adversely affect the interests of MNCs. In this section, we are going to discuss how to measure and manage **political risk,** which refers to the potential losses to the parent firm resulting from adverse political developments in the host country. Political risks range from the outright expropriation of foreign assets to unexpected changes in the tax laws that hurt the profitability of foreign projects.

Political risk that firms face can differ in terms of the incidence as well as the manner in which political events affect them. Depending on the incidence, political risk can be classified into two types:

1. *Macro risk,* where all foreign operations are affected by adverse political developments in the host country.
2. *Micro risk,* where only selected areas of foreign business operations or particular foreign firms are affected.

The communist victory in China in 1949 is an example of macro risk, whereas the predicament of Enron in India, which we will discuss shortly, is an example of micro risk.

Depending on the manner in which firms are affected, political risk can be classified into three types:[9]

1. *Transfer risk,* which arises from uncertainty about cross-border flows of capital, payments, know-how, and the like.
2. *Operational risk,* which is associated with uncertainty about the host country's policies affecting the local operations of MNCs.
3. *Control risk,* which arises from uncertainty about the host country's policy regarding ownership and control of local operations.

Examples of transfer risk include the unexpected imposition of capital controls, inbound or outbound, and withholding taxes on dividend and interest payments. Examples for operational risk, on the other hand, include unexpected changes in environmental policies, sourcing/local content requirements, minimum wage law, and restriction on access to local credit facilities. Lastly, examples of control risk include restrictions imposed on the maximum ownership share by foreigners, mandatory transfer of ownership to local firms over a certain period of time (fade-out requirements), and the nationalization of local operations of MNCs.

Recent history is replete with examples of political risk. As Mao Ze-dong took power in China in 1949, his communist government nationalized foreign assets with little compensation. The same happened again when Castro took over Cuba in 1960. Even in a country controlled by a noncommunist government, strong nationalist sentiments can lead to the expropriation of foreign assets. For example, when Gamal Nasser seized power in Egypt in the early 1950s, he nationalized the Suez Canal, which was controlled by British and French interests. Politically, this move was immensely popular throughout the Arab world. The International Finance in Practice box, "Stories Past and Present," provides other historical examples showing how foreign investments can be decimated by nationalistic actions in a host country.

As Exhibit 15.9 shows, the frequency of expropriations of foreign-owned assets peaked in the 1970s, when as many as 30 countries were involved in expropriations each year. Since then, however, expropriations have dwindled to practically nothing. This change reflects the popularity of *privatization,* which, in turn, is attributable to

EXHIBIT 15.9

Frequency of Expropriations of Foreign-Owned Assets

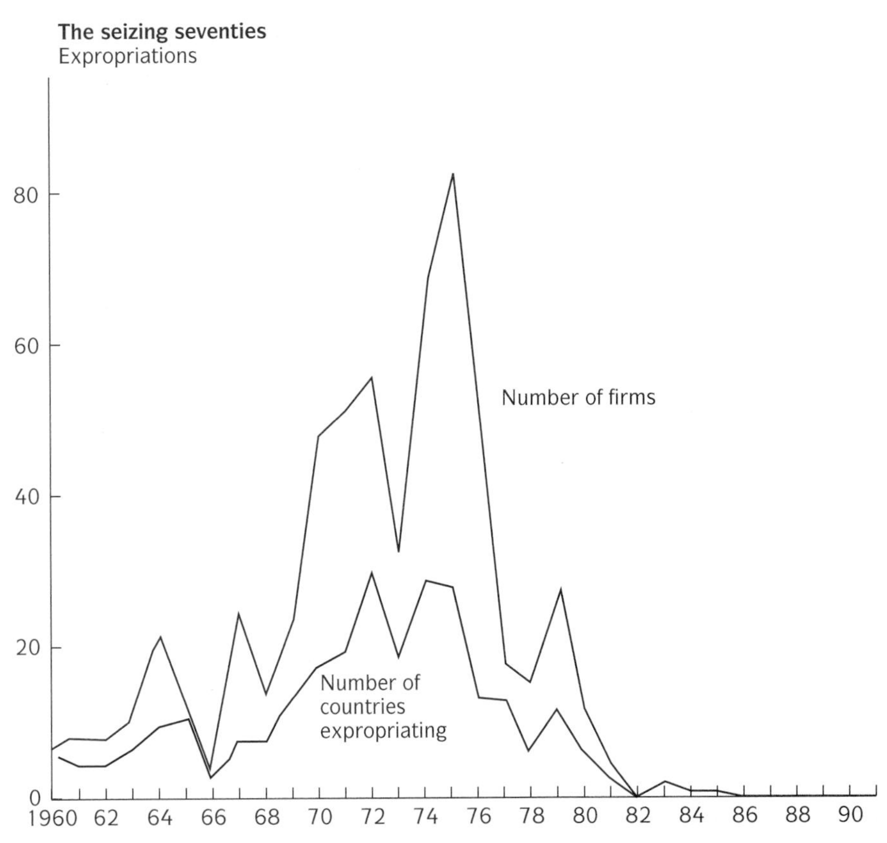

Source: *The Economist,* March 27, 1993, p. 19. © 1993 The Economist Newspaper Group, Inc. Reprinted with permission.

widespread failures of state-run enterprises and mounting government debts around the world.

This, however, does not mean that political risk is a thing of the past. In 1992, the Enron Development Corporation, a subsidiary of the Houston-based energy company, signed a contract to build the largest-ever power plant in India, requiring a total investment of $2.8 billion. Severe power shortages have been one of the bottlenecks hindering India's economic growth. After Enron had spent nearly $300 million, the project was canceled by Hindu nationalist politicians in the Maharastra state where the plant was to be built. Subsequently, Maharastra invited Enron to renegotiate its contract. If Enron had agreed to renegotiate, it may have had to accept a lower profitability for the project. As can be seen from the Enron fiasco, the lack of an effective means of enforcing contracts in a foreign country is clearly a major source of political risk associated with FDI.

Political risk is not easy to measure. When Enron signed the contract to build a power plant in India, it perhaps could not have anticipated the victory of the Hindu nationalist party. Many businesses domiciled in Hong Kong are nervous about the intentions of Beijing in the post-1997 era. Once Hong Kong reverts to Chinese jurisdiction, the rules of the game may change. Difficult as it may be, MNCs still have to measure political risk for foreign projects under consideration. Experts of political risk analysis evaluate, often subjectively, a set of key factors such as:[10]

- *The host country's political and government system:* Whether the host country has a political and administrative infrastructure that allows for

INTERNATIONAL FINANCE IN PRACTICE
Stories Past and Present

An old story: Brazilian Tramways

The first electric trams in Brazil were built in 1891 by Thomson-Houston Company of Lynn, Massachusetts, which the following year became the General Electric Company. GE went on to build most of the early electric lines in Brazil and throughout Latin America, often retaining ownership. Other players soon entered the field, and, by 1907, a Canadian group had created South America's first great tramway empire, holding most of the lines in Rio de Janeiro and São Paulo as well as an assortment of telephone, gas, and water companies. The Canadians were bitterly and publicly opposed by a powerful Brazilian family, the Guinles, who also sought control of utilities in the major cities. The dispute profoundly affected the attitudes of Brazilians toward foreign-owned tramways. As a result of street riots and large-scale destruction of equipment in the city of Salvador, the Canadians curtailed their expansion efforts and in 1912 consolidated their assets into Brazilian Traction, Light & Power.

American & Foreign Power, the GE affiliate, eventually joined the fray and acquired 333 utilities in Brazil alone, with tramway systems in 13 Brazilian cities. By 1933, however, rising anti-Yankee sentiment led to freezing of tram fares at their 1909 level. A number of small companies shut down. Others switched to closed cars to increase fare collections. These cars were distinctly unpopular with riders because of the heat (and perhaps because of the better fare collection).

Still, on the eve of World War II, North American companies operated roughly two-thirds of Brazil's tramway systems. The lethal combination of parts shortages, increased hydroelectric power costs, and the effect of inflation on fixed fares led companies to cut back on service and, in some cases, to leave the business. In 1947, Brazilian Traction sold its São Paulo system to the municipal transport board, which then proceeded to raise fares by 250%. Rioting citizens pleaded for the foreigners and low rates. But, by 1950, a new president had vowed to rid Brazil of foreign corporations. AFP and most other foreign investors were quite willing by this point to sell their unprofitable tram systems to the Brazilians. By 1960, only Brazilian Traction's Rio system remained foreign owned; this last holdout went the way of the rest when it was acquired by the state in January 1965.

A recent story: Bangkok Toll Road

To help relieve Bangkok's horrible traffic congestion, a Japanese-led consortium was granted a 30-year concession to build a 12-mile toll road in the city. Just as part of the road was about to be opened in 1993, the Thai Expressway and Rapid Transit Authority (ETA) balked at the 30-baht toll that had been specified in the contract. Hesitating to absorb the proposed 10-baht toll reduction, the private consortium delayed opening the completed sections of road, and it halted further construction when its lenders suspended credit. Claiming to fear riots on the part of frustrated motorists who were angered at being unable to use the expressway, the ETA obtained a court order to force the road open and insisted on reopening negotiations to settle this and a number of other outstanding issues. Kumagai Gumi, the lead investor, reportedly with more than $100 million exposure, and its bankers, with still more at stake, cried foul, publicly accusing the Thai government of nationalizing the project. Eventually, Kumagai sold its 65% interest. And all this occurred in a country that is viewed as being very hospitable to foreign direct investment.

Source: Reprinted by permission of *Harvard Business Review.* From "Is Foreign Infrastructure Still Risky?" by Louis T. Wells and Eric S. Gleason, Sept./Oct. 1995. © 1995 by the President and Fellows of Harvard College; all rights reserved.

effective and streamlined policy decisions has important implications for political risk. If a country has too many political parties and frequent changes in government (like Italy, for example), government policies may become inconsistent and discontinuous, creating political risk.

- *Track records of political parties and their relative strength:* Examination of the ideological orientations and historical track records of political parties would reveal a great deal about how they would run the economy. If a party has a strong nationalistic ideology and/or socialist beliefs, it may implement policies that are detrimental to foreign interests. On the other hand, a party that subscribes to a liberal and market-oriented ideology is not very likely to take actions to damage the interests of foreign concerns. If the former party is more popular than the latter party and thus more likely to win the next general election, MNCs will bear more political risk.

- *Integration into the world system:* If a country is politically and economically isolated and segmented from the rest of the world, it would be less willing to observe the rules of the game. North Korea, Iraq, Libya, and Cuba are examples. If a country is a member of major international organizations, such as the EMS, OECD and WTO, it is more likely to abide by the rules of the game, reducing political risk. In the same vein, if China is admitted to the World Trade Organization (WTO), MNCs operating in China may face less political risk.
- *The host country's ethnic and religious stability:* As can be seen from recent civil war in Bosnia, domestic peace can be shattered by ethnic and religious conflicts, causing political risk for foreign business. Additional examples are provided by Rwanda, Northern Ireland, Turkey, Israel, Sri Lanka, and Quebec.
- *Regional security:* Real and potential aggression from a neighboring country is obviously a major source of political risk. Kuwait is a recent example. Countries like South Korea and Taiwan may potentially face the same risk depending on the future course of political developments in East Asia. Israel and its Arab neighbors still face this risk as well.
- *Key economic indicators:* Often political events are triggered by economic situations. Political risk thus is not entirely independent of economic risk. For example, persistent trade deficits may induce a host country's government to delay or stop interest payments to foreign lenders, erect trade barriers, or suspend the convertibility of the local currency, causing major difficulties for MNCs. Severe inequality in income distribution (for example, in many Latin American countries) and deteriorating living standards (as in Russia) can cause major political disturbances.

MNCs may use in-house experts to do the analysis. But often, MNCs use outside experts who provide professional assessments of political risks in different countries. For example, Morgan Stanley offers an in-depth analysis of country/political risks using a variety of data sources, including government and private sector publications, statistics provided by international organizations, newspaper articles, and on-site due diligence in countries with government officials and the private sector. Exhibits 15.10 and 15.11 provide such an analysis for two countries, South Korea and Hungary.

Euromoney also provides such an assessment twice a year.[11] As Exhibit 15.12 shows, *Euromoney* provides country ratings by political risk, credit rating, economic performance, and other factors. It also provides the overall country risk ranking based on an opinion poll of economists and political analysts, plus market data and debt figures. **Country risk** is a broader measure of risk than political risk, as the former encompasses political risk, credit risk, and other economic performances. As of March 1999, countries like Switzerland, Germany, Luxembourg, and the United States were considered practically free of political risk. In contrast, countries like Israel, China, India, Mexico, Brazil, and Argentina were rated as having substantial political risk, while countries such as Indonesia, Russia, and Yugoslavia were rated as among the most politically risky countries. Exhibit 15.12 shows that the ranking of countries by political risk closely coincides with that by overall country risk.

Let us now turn to the issue of how to manage political risk. First, MNCs can take a conservative approach to foreign investment projects when faced with

EXHIBIT 15.10 Political Risk Analysis: South Korea

Moody's: A1; S&P: A+, Outlook: Positive

Strengths	Weaknesses
Political	
■ Smooth transition to democracy (1987). ■ Integrated into global and regional organizations.	■ Still a young democracy. ■ More radical opposition party. ■ Cost of potential unification with North Korea. ■ Difficult labor relations. ■ Anti-Western sentiment among students.
Economic	
■ Well-diversified economy. ■ Strong manufacturing sector. ■ Fast growth. ■ Prudent fiscal management. ■ Low unemployment. ■ Well-diversified and competitive exports. ■ Increasing foreign investment. ■ Very favorable debt profile.	■ Lacks natural resources and oil. ■ Some foreign exchange controls. ■ Financial sector needs reforms. ■ Low foreign exchange reserves. ■ Wage hikes eroding competitiveness.

Key Ratios (%)	1987	1988	1989	1990	1991
External Debt/Current Account Earnings	63	44	40	41	46
Debt Service/Current Account Earnings	17	10	9	11	10
Current Account Balance/GDP	7.5	8.1	2.4	−0.9	−3.1
Import Cover (Mos.)	1.1	3.1	3.2	2.7	2.2
Budget Balance (% of GDP)	1.5	2.1	0.3	0.4	−1.1

Source: IFS, World Bank Debt Tables, IIF, Monthly Statistical Bulletin of the Bank of Korea, Morgan Stanley Credit Research.

South Korea's economy is one of the most dynamic in the world. Economic fundamentals remain strong, and a well-developed industry geared toward exports has made South Korea's economy one of the fastest growing in the world during the past decade. Exports are diversified and competitive, and foreign portfolio investment has increased greatly following recent financial deregulation and easing of foreign exchange controls. Sound fiscal policy is evidenced by budget surpluses, unemployment is low and, by developing country standards, inflation is moderate. External debt at US$39 billion, or 46% of current account earnings, and the debt service ratio of 10% are very favorable. The country's few weaknesses include a lack of natural resources, dependence on imported oil and a financial system that needs to be deregulated, modernized and brought to world standards. The development of the financial sector is a requirement for the further development of the domestic economy and export sector and more effective macroeconomic management.

It is in the political area that the greatest risks lie. Despite great progress (a smooth transition to democracy through presidential elections in 1987), at times the political climate is uncertain as South Korea is still a young democracy and the main opposition party is radical. Anti-Western sentiment is prevalent among students and some labor demonstrators. Labor relations have been difficult, with major strikes occurring every spring. Although the military threat from North Korea has significantly diminished, the financial and social cost of a prospective reunification can be great. Finally, per capita income is still well below that of developed countries.

political risk. When a foreign project is exposed to political risk, the MNC can explicitly incorporate political risk into the capital budgeting process and adjust the project's NPV accordingly. The firm may do so either by reducing expected cash flows or by increasing the cost of capital. The MNC may undertake the foreign project only when the adjusted NPV is positive. It is important here to recognize that political risk may be diversifiable to some extent. Suppose that a MNC has assets in, say, 30 different countries. Since the political risks in different countries may not be positively correlated, the political risk associated with a single country may be diversifiable to some extent. To the extent that political risk is diversifiable, a major adjustment to the NPV may not be necessary. This consideration also suggests that MNCs can use geographic diversification of foreign investments as a means of reducing political risk. Put simply, don't put all your eggs in one basket.

EXHIBIT 15.11 Political Risk Analysis: Hungary

Moody's: Ba1; S&P: BB+, Outlook: Positive

Strengths	Weaknesses
Political	
■ Smooth transition to multiparty system. ■ Pro-reform government and opposition. ■ Associate member of the EEC. ■ Ethnically homogeneous. ■ Labor is accommodative of reform.	■ Located in an unstable region. ■ Uncertainty about relations with Slovakia.
Economic	
■ Economic reform progressing rapidly. ■ Much-eased foreign exchange controls. ■ Significantly liberalized trade system. ■ Successful redirection of trade from East to West. ■ OECD accounts for 70% of trade. ■ Rapid accumulation of foreign exchange reserves. ■ Improved current account performance. ■ Rapid increase in foreign investment. ■ Rapidly improving debt profile.	■ Reliance on imported oil. ■ Major economic restructuring to be completed. ■ Poor budgetary performance. ■ High and growing unemployment.

Key Ratios (%)	1987	1988	1989	1990	1991
External Debt/Current Account Earnings	327	299	266	218	177
Debt Service/Current Account Earnings	63	54	47	44	32
Current Account Balance/GDP	−3.4	−2.9	−5.0	0.8	0.8
Import Cover (Mos.)	3.9	3.5	2.5	2.1	5.2
Budget Balance (% of GDP)	−3.3	−0.2	−2.1	0.9	−4.1

Source: IFS, World Bank Debt Tables, IIF, National Bank of Hungary, Morgan Stanley Credit Research

Hungary is unique as it is the only Eastern Bloc country to have made a smooth transition to a market economy without splitting or violence. The transition to a multiparty democracy was completed with the general elections in 1990. Hungary enjoys stability in a region torn by ethnic violence. Currently, the only threat to stability may come from the possible mistreatment of ethnic Hungarians in Slovakia after the Czechoslovak split. Hungary's willingness to pay has been very strong even during difficult times.

Hungary's economic transformation and resilience in the face of the collapse of Soviet trade are very impressive. During the past two years, the process of economic reform, started in 1968, has accelerated to develop a dynamic private sector, restructure the state sector and liberalize trade. The private sector now represents 30% of GDP, from only 10% in 1989. The trade system has been liberalized, with 90% of imports free of licensing and tariffs have been lowered significantly. In light of the collapse of the Soviet Union and its economic difficulties, redirection of trade toward the West has been very successful with convertible currency exports increasing 45% in 1991 and 21% in the first seven months of 1992, and the OECD countries accounting for 70% of the trade. The current account continues to be in surplus, and the country has been able to attract more than half of all foreign investment in Eastern Europe. The debt profile has improved very quickly, with the debt ratio falling from 343% in 1986 to 177% in 1991. The debt service ratio has also improved from 85% in 1986 to 32% in 1991. On the negative side, the restructuring of the economy translates into a severe recession (GDP fell 10.2% in 1991 and is expected to fall another 5% this year) and high unemployment (currently about 11%).

Second, once a MNC decides to undertake a foreign project, it can take various measures to minimize its exposure to political risk. For example, an MNC can form a joint venture with a local company. The idea is that if the project is partially owned by a local company, the foreign government may be less inclined to expropriate it since the action will hurt the local company as well as the MNC. The MNC may also consider forming a consortium of international companies to undertake the foreign project. In this case, the MNC can reduce its exposure to political risk and, at the same time, make expropriation more costly to the host government. Understandably, the host government may not wish to take actions that will antagonize many countries at the same time. Alternatively, MNCs can use local debt to finance the foreign

EXHIBIT 15.12

Country Risk Rankings

Rank	Country	Country Risk	Political Risk	Credit Rating	Economic Performance
	Weighting:	100	25	10	25
1	Luxembourg	98.48	24.28	10.00	25.00
2	Switzerland	98.36	24.88	10.00	23.85
3	Norway	95.43	23.96	10.00	21.90
4	United States	94.92	25.00	10.00	20.28
5	Netherlands	94.22	24.51	10.00	19.71
6	Germany	94.04	24.87	10.00	19.55
7	France	93.68	24.78	10.00	19.27
8	Austria	93.30	23.96	10.00	19.35
9	Denmark	93.24	23.32	9.38	20.96
10	Belgium	91.18	23.27	9.17	18.76
11	Japan	90.94	23.81	9.58	18.88
12	Finland	90.91	22.52	9.58	19.22
13	United Kingdom	90.87	24.72	10.00	16.52
14	Sweden	90.33	22.54	8.96	19.24
15	Ireland	90.12	22.66	9.79	17.69
16	Canada	90.09	23.48	8.96	17.72
17	Singapore	88.88	23.41	9.58	18.62
18	Australia	87.79	21.89	8.75	18.02
19	Italy	87.62	22.52	8.96	16.57
20	New Zealand	86.90	21.70	9.06	16.20
21	Spain	86.72	22.33	9.17	15.63
22	Iceland	84.47	20.22	7.81	17.30
23	Portugal	84.41	21.91	9.17	14.18
24	Bermuda	81.49	20.91	8.96	19.62
25	Taiwan	79.74	20.38	8.75	14.27
26	Hong Kong	76.73	18.68	6.88	15.75
31	Israel	70.62	15.97	6.25	12.82
39	Hungary	65.75	17.39	5.00	10.74
42	Poland	62.06	15.99	4.79	10.54
43	Czech Republic	61.96	16.58	5.83	9.97
44	South Korea	61.63	15.91	4.17	12.03
45	China	56.51	15.32	6.04	9.46
47	Mexico	55.18	13.35	3.13	9.27
55	Argentina	52.90	12.09	2.92	9.64
60	India	50.90	13.17	3.13	7.34
88	Indonesia	36.37	6.52	8.42	5.71
125	Ukraine	29.85	3.17	0.63	4.05
161	Russia	20.86	3.02	0.31	3.67
171	Yugoslavia	15.25	0.92	0.00	3.83
180	North Korea	1.28	0.00	0.00	0.26

Source: *Euromoney*, March 1999, pp. 97–100. Adapted with permission.

project. In this case, the MNC has an option to repudiate its debt if the host government takes actions to hurt its interests.

Third, MNCs may purchase insurance against the hazard of political risk. Such insurance policies, which are available in many advanced countries, are especially useful for small firms that are less well equipped to deal with political risk on their own. In the United States, the **Overseas Private Investment Corporation (OPIC),** a federally owned organization, offers insurance against (1) the inconvertibility of foreign currencies, (2) expropriation of U.S.-owned assets overseas, (3) destructions of U.S.-owned physical properties due to war, revolution, and other violent political events in foreign countries, and (4) loss of business income due to political violence. OPIC's primary goal is to encourage U.S. private investments in the economies of developing countries. Alternatively, MNCs may also purchase tailor-made insurance policies from private insurers such as Lloyd's of London.

When the political risk faced by a MNC can be fully covered by an insurance contract, the MNC can subtract the insurance premium from the expected cash flows from the project in computing its NVP. The MNC then can use the usual cost of capital, which would be used to evaluate domestic investment projects, in discounting the expected cash flows from foreign projects. Lastly, it is pointed out that many countries have concluded bilateral or multilateral investment protection agreements, effectively eliminating most political risk. As a result, if a MNC invests in a country that signed the investment protection agreement with the MNC's home country, it need not be overly concerned with political risk.

SUMMARY

This chapter discusses various issues associated with foreign direct investments (FDI) by MNCs, which play a key role in shaping the nature of the emerging global economy.

1. Firms become *multinational* when they undertake FDI. FDI may involve either the establishment of new production facilities in foreign countries or acquisitions of existing foreign businesses.
2. During the recent five-year period 1994–98, total annual worldwide FDI flows amounted to about $430 billion on average. The United States is the largest recipient, as well as initiator, of FDI. Besides the United States, France, Germany, Japan, and the United Kingdom are the leading sources of FDI outflows, whereas the United Kingdom, China, France, and the Netherlands are the major destinations for FDI in recent years.
3. Most existing theories of FDI put emphasis on various market imperfections, that is, imperfections in product, factor, and capital markets, as the key motivating forces driving FDI.
4. The *internalization* theory of FDI holds that firms that have intangible assets with a public good property tend to invest directly in foreign countries in order to use these assets on a larger scale and, at the same time, avoid the misappropriations that may occur while transacting in foreign markets through a market mechanism.
5. According to Raymond Vernon's product life-cycle theory, when firms first introduce new products, they choose to produce at home, close to their customers. Once the product becomes standardized and mature, it becomes important to cut production costs to stay competitive. At this stage, firms may set up production facilities in low-cost foreign countries.
6. In recent years, a growing portion of FDI has taken the form of cross-border acquisitions of existing businesses. *Synergistic* gains may arise if the acquirer is motivated to take advantage of various market imperfections.
7. Imperfections in the market for intangible assets, such as R&D capabilities, may play a key role in motivating cross-border acquisitions. The internalization may proceed *forward* to internalize the acquirer's intangible assets or *backward* to internalize the target's intangible assets.
8. In evaluating political risk, experts focus their attention on a set of key factors such as the host country's political/government system, historical records of political parties and their relative strengths, integration of the host country into the world political/economic system, the host country's ethnic and religious stability, regional security, and key economic indicators.

9. In evaluating a foreign investment project, it is important for the MNC to consider the effect of political risk, as a sovereign country can change the *rules of the game.* The MNC may adjust the cost of capital upward or lower the expected cash flows from the foreign project. Or, the MNC may purchase insurance policies against the hazard of political risks.

KEY WORDS

country risk, 379
cross-border acquisitions, 361
FDI flows, 361
FDI stocks, 362
foreign direct investments (FDI), 360
greenfield investments, 361
intangible assets, 367
internalization theory, 367
Overseas Private Investment Corporation (OPIC), 382
political risk, 376
product life-cycle theory, 368
synergistic gains, 372

QUESTIONS

1. Recently, many foreign firms from both developed and developing countries acquired high-tech U.S. firms. What might have motivated these firms to acquire U.S. firms?
2. Japanese MNCs, such as Toyota, Toshiba, and Matsushita, made extensive investments in Southeast Asian countries like Thailand, Malaysia, and Indonesia. In your opinion, what forces are driving Japanese investments in this region?
3. Since NAFTA was established, many Asian firms, especially those from Japan and Korea, have made extensive investments in Mexico. Why do you think these Asian firms decided to build production facilities in Mexico?
4. How would you explain the fact that China emerged as the second most important recipient of FDI after the United States in recent years?
5. Explain the internalization theory of FDI. What are the strengths and weaknesses of the theory?
6. Explain Vernon's product life-cycle theory of FDI. What are the strengths and weaknesses of the theory?
7. Why do you think the host country tends to resist cross-border acquisitions rather than greenfield investments?
8. How would you incorporate political risk into the capital budgeting process of foreign investment projects?
9. Explain and compare forward versus backward internalization.
10. What could be the reason for the negative synergistic gains for British acquisitions of U.S. firms?
11. Define *country risk.* How is it different from political risk?
12. What are the advantages and disadvantages of FDI as compared to a licensing agreement with a foreign partner?
13. What operational and financial measures can a MNC take to minimize the political risk associated with a foreign investment project?
14. Study the experience of Enron in India and discuss what we can learn from it for the management of political risk.
15. Discuss the different ways political events in a host country may affect local operations of a MNC.
16. What factors would you consider in evaluating the political risk associated with making FDI in a foreign country.

17. *Mini Project:* Suppose you are hired as a political consultant by Coca-Cola, which is considering investing in the bottling facilities in four countries: Mexico, Argentina, China, and Russia. Pick a country out of the four and analyze the political risk associated with investing there. Prepare a final report to Coca-Cola using a similar format as Exhibit 15.10.

MINI CASE

Enron in India

BY PROF. AMEETA JAISWAL-DALE
University of St. Thomas

Ms. Rebecca Mark, CEO of Enron International, a wholly owned subsidiary of Enron Corp., has earned all the accolades showered on her, especially those by her toughest adversarial negotiators. In March 1995 contemplating the future of Enron from the plush Corporate Office in Houston, she anticipates her most proselytized overseas Foreign Direct Investment project come to a successful closure—*Dhabol Power Project, Maharastra, India,* targeted for commercial use in December 1998. Ms. Mark was the chief negotiator and driving force of the project in India, personally choosing the precise site of the project after driving along the rugged coastline of the Western Ghats for six hours in the heat and dust of India. The site of the Dhabol Power Plant sits high on a remote volcanic bluff overlooking the azure Arabian Sea, seven hours' drive south of Bombay.

EXHIBIT 1

Enron Corporation (Snap shot in 1995)

Revenues	$ millions	9,189
	% change from 1994	2.28
Profits	$ millions	520
	% change from 1994	4.8
Assets	$ millions	13,239
Stockholder's Equity	$ millions	3,165

Source: Moody's Investor Services.

On August 3, 1995, Ms. Mark obtained word from Dhabol Power Company, India, that the project had come to a halt by the order of the government of Maharastra. Taken by surprise, Enron Corp. decides to view the situation up close and Ms. Mark made immediate plans to leave for India.

Enron's Imperative for Foreign Direct Investment

As recently as late summer 1995, Rebecca Mark mused over the path she had tread since 1991. Rebecca Mark had risen in the company ranks rapidly since her entry as a newly recruited MBA less than a decade ago. She saw the opportunity of tremendous growth for Enron Corp. in various projects of expansion abroad, particularly in Latin America and Asia. She helped to shape the company's strategy of international expansion abroad and implemented its execution, while rising to the coveted post of the Chief Executive of the then Enron Development Corp. (now Enron International). She spearheaded these development projects in rapidly growing economies that needed new energy sources to fuel economic growth and satisfy the growing consumer demand for cheap energy.

Enron's foreign direct investments diversified the company's operations. From a regional Texan company providing pipelines for transporting natural gas, Enron Corp. became an industry leader in the development of energy infrastructure. The company is now ranked by *Fortune* as the world's third largest in the industry of developers of energy infrastructure. This success has brought increased market share, higher share prices, rapid growth and visibility to the top management.

Besides *Dhabol* there are other Enron projects for overseas energy infrastructure that Ms. Mark has left her mark upon. Enron's international development portfolio includes *EcoElectrica,* the Puerto Rican liquefied natural gas (LNG) project, as in *Dhabol India,* to commence operations in 1999; the oil gasification power project in *Sardinia,* also slated for operation in 1999, and the 1875-mile-long *natural gas pipeline from Bolivia to Brazil* currently under construction. The LNG projects are a first for both the host countries and Enron Corp.

These projects have made Enron a leader in power and pipeline among its peers. Riding the high wave of confidence, the company has now launched new services for third parties in emerging markets.

As far an Enron was concerned these uncharted territories offered great promise. And given the competition they were to soon face in the deregulated U.S. market, the timing was perfect to undertake Foreign Direct Investment in Asia and Latin America. Enron took the plunge with two other strong U.S. companies. They formed a joint venture for investment in India. The team members are Enron Corp. with 79.93 percent of equity stake; Bechtel Enterprises Inc.; and General Electric's Financial Services with 10.036 percent each.

Ms. Mark saw tremendous opportunity in India and did not hesitate to take the sacred Indian cow by the horns. And what a sacred cow it turned out to be! Little did she know what was lying in wait for her. She required tenacity, negotiating skills, and more to weather uncharted seas. The *Dhabol* project put Enron in the international spotlight for the prickly issues of Foreign Direct Investment and political risk from host countries.[1]

The Enron case had become a benchmark for multinationals interested in investing in India. The outcome of the Enron case was viewed by many as a "litmus test" of the country's willingness to deal with foreign firms.

India: The Host Country and Political Risk

The story begins in 1991 with Enron's plans to build a private power plant in India at the invitation of the central government. Indian bureaucrats visited Enron's Houston headquarters in May 1992 as they shopped for potential investors. Enron had a project in place to develop massive natural gas reserves in the Persian Gulf State of Qatar, a project of $5 billion. A natural gas based power plant on the West Coat along the Arabian Sea in India, which would become a "cost effective client" of the *Qatar project.* Thus was conceived the first phase of the *Dhabol* Power Plant, south of Bombay, in the state of Maharastra. There seemed to be a mutual advantage for both parties.

- Enron found a cost-effective client for its Qatar project and gained entry into one of the larger Asian markets to build, own and operate a power station.
- India obtained the largest Foreign Direct Investment to date with financing in place.

Construction began on the project in 1995 with the backing of Prime Minister Rao's central government in New Delhi. The terms of the project were negotiated between Enron and the central government of India.

The Chronology of Events

The following is a brief chronology of the progress of the *Dhabol* project soon after the accord was signed between Enron and the Indian government in New Delhi.

- December 1993: Enron and its partners sign a power purchase agreement with the state of Maharastra, negotiated with India's central government. Same political parties are in power at both the central and state levels.
- March 1995: Construction began with massive bulldozers of Betchel Enterprises Inc. scraping out a spectacular sight from the red rock and scrub of the Western Ghats. In 1995 agreement was signed with Qatar General Petroleum Corp. to produce 5 million tons/year of LNG beginning in 2001, proposing to ship 2 million tons/year to feed the *Dhabol* project.
- August 3, 1995: Construction stopped by the government of the state of Maharastra after state elections brings a new nationalistic political party to power. Prime Minister Rao's political party loses its majority in the state elections. The newly elected state government declares the 1993 agreement untenable and "unconstitutional." Mr. Manohar Joshi, the new chief minister of Maharastra, called the deal against the interests of the state of Maharastra and its people. He indicated that he reserved the right to renegotiate new terms.

The Particular Elements of Political Risk

Although Prime Minister Rao's government in New Delhi completely supported the *Dhabol* project, the support proved to be insufficient for a company undertaking FDI.

[1] Later, Ms. Rebecca Mark was quoted as saying, "It's not an experience I would look forward to repeating any place in the world" and again, "It's been difficult, but hopefully the problems are solved for anyone else looking at India." *The Wall Street Journal,* Dec. 11, 1996.

There were countless other matters to deal with as in any developing country. For example, the legacy of colonial British India—a massive antiquated bureaucracy—and banks afraid to lend money, lack of roads, and housing and port facilities, all of which Enron had to supply.

Starting May 1992 both Enron and India painfully slogged through unexplored territories. R. Vasudevan, Indiana's power secretary, notes, "We were completely uninitiated into the mysteries of negotiating a power deal. It is like learning to play a violin solo in public. Every dissonant note gets heard." (*The Wall Street Journal,* 04/27/95.) And there were several dissonant notes on both sides.

Enron felt that they were being treated like guinea pigs and scapegoats for everything. Enron officials did not enjoy flying constantly to New Delhi for brief meetings with feudal bureaucrats after having waited endlessly in the corridors of government offices. Nor did they relish obtaining the countless number of approvals, at different bureaucratic levels and often redundant, to obtain clearance for a given procedure. For example, in order to use explosives for construction purposes in *Dhabol,* Enron was required to visit the central Indian town of Nagpur, where the colonial British Raj once stored munitions. Clearly that practice continues after 50 years of the country's independence.

Unlike other developed countries, India does not have a "single window clearance" for important projects—this is the Indian way to discourage concentration of political power in any one given agency.

And yet because of New Delhi's backing of the *Dhabol,* Bank of America and ABN-Amro Bank of Netherlands agreed to provide badly needed financing.[2] Most banks were leery because the Mexican financial crisis had recently unraveled.

After all these painful negotiations on both sides, the project had barely begun when the dissonant notes of the violin turned to violent protests. Soon after work commenced on the *Dhabol* project, elections were held to the lower more powerful house of the legislature. Two pro nationalistic political parties were elected to power—the Bharatiya Janata Party (BJP Party) obtained a majority in the Lower House of the Indian legislature and the Shiv Sena won the majority in the state of Maharastra. They together reviewed the agreement between Enron and New Delhi and found that several concessions, quite uncalled for, were granted by New Delhi to Enron Corp.

The major points of disaccord as reported in the Indian and foreign press (notably *The Wall Street Journal*) were:

- Categorization of *Dhabol* as a "fast track" project, thus making it eligible for "private negotiations" with the central government as compared to open public bidding.
- Pricing of electricity when *Dhabol* becomes operational.
- Amount of electricity purchased by the state government of Maharastra and the central government of New Delhi.
- Final responsibility of covering the inevitable fluctuations in foreign exchange rates.
- Environmental and nationalistic concerns of foreign ownership.

To its credit the Indian press attempted to impartially present the views of all the parties concerned.

[2]The presence of Bechtel Enterprises, Inc. as a partner in Dhabol may have influenced the West Coast Bank of America to provide the much needed financing. Bechtel, headquartered in San Francisco, no doubt has strong financial ties to the Bank of America. Bechtel, a private construction company, also has some politically influential members on its board of directors—George Schultz, former U.S. Secretary, Caspar Weinberger, former U.S. defense secretary, Carla Hills, and so on.

Old Insecurities of the Colonial Raj and Political Risk

It would appear that some of the old insecurities and fears of the colonial British Raj and the Independence movement calling for self-sufficiency, had begun to resurface. The fears were very real and recent—the industrial accident on the factory premises of the American firm, Union Carbide in Bhopal, India, in 1984. The lethal gas leak at the plant that killed thousands and injured thousands more. Injuries ranged from all respiratory ailments to eye and limb infections. Compensation of victims was long in coming and inadequate, often ending in the wrong hands. Union Carbide, the Indian government, and the Indian Justice Department (where Union Carbide was battling the numerous litigation cases) all pointed fingers at each other. However, it was the victims, the poor shantytown day laborers, that paid the price in health and future employment.

As information on the *Dhabol* project of Enron became public, it obtained top billing in the press—the memory of Union Carbide is only too recent! Other American companies cited were IBM and Coca-Cola. Both firms had been asked to leave India during the government of Mrs. Indira Gandhi in the 1970s mainly because of their refusal to transfer technology and reinvest profits in India. However, both Coca-Cola and IBM were invited back to the country and have become an integral part of the local economy.[3]

It is a well known fact that during economically and politically troubled times foreign investment attracts undue attention. The foreign firms in the fast food and consumer goods sectors are particularly vulnerable. These firms are the most visible and offer the greatest threat to any nation's established traditions and culture, thus attracting the greatest wrath—be it in India or elsewhere. And yet, strangely enough they usually have the patronage and support of a large proportion of the local population.

The slogan of the day to express the nation's ire against the perceived foreign invasion became, *"Give us computer chips, not potato chips."*

Doubtless, Ms. Rebecca Mark was observing this edifying scenario of massive contradictions from her five-star hotel when she landed in India during that hot and sultry month of August in 1995. Cast as a robber baron by certain segments of the press, she was renegotiating the Enron contract with the state government with minimal support of the central government in this election year.[4]

Ms. Mark had her job cut out for her. However, she was also aware of the fact that she has an impressive array of predecessors and followers to count upon. India had either already allowed or was now poised to allow several projects of foreign direct investment in various forms from a variety of firms. The following is a partial list.

3M
AES Corp. of Virginia
Asea Brown Boveri AG
Carlson Co.'s
CMS Energy of Michigan
Coca-Cola
Cogentrix Energy of North Carolina
Colgate
Eli Lilly
Exxon Corp.
Glaxo
Hong Kong's China Light & Power
IBM
ICI
Johnson & Johnson
Kellogg Co.
McDonald's
Merrill Lynch
Morgan Stanley

[3]Both Coca-Cola and IBM are now much better corporate citizens in their host country than a few years ago. They, like many others, have learned to play the win-win game instead of the zero sum game.

[4]The September 24, 1995, issue of the *New York Times* reported, "When Ms. Mark left her New Delhi hotel on a recent afternoon to visit the India Gate, a soldiers' memorial that is one of the capital's principal landmarks, it was a surprise to find her surrounded by well-wishers. One man, Rakesh Aggarwal, a New Delhi lawyer sightseeing with his family, put it simply: "Personally, I think India needs power."

Motorola
Nestlé
Pepsi
Royal Dutch/Shell Group
Shakey's International Ltd.
Texas Instruments
TGI Friday's

Firms showing interest in investing in the near future included:

Oman Oil Co.

Kuwait Petroleum Corp.

Saudi Aramco

Rebecca Mark felt that she was in good company amongst these peers. However, after the Maharastra government's decision on August 3, 1995, and given all the pitfalls of political risk involved, was it worthwhile for Enron to pursue this project any further?

QUESTIONS FOR DISCUSSION:

1. Foreign Direct Investment
   a. What are the particular challenges faced by foreign companies investing in India?
   b. Are there financially more efficient ways to achieve the same objective without undertaking FDI?
2. Political Risk
   a. What were the various elements of Political Risk faced by Enron in India?
   b. What could Enron have done differently to avoid this Political Risk in order to safeguard its FDI in India?

ENDNOTES

1. Source: *World Investment Report 1998,* UNCTAD, United Nations.
2. Coca-Cola reentered the Indian market as India gradually liberalized its economy, improving the climate for foreign investments.
3. Examples of public goods include public parks, lighthouses, and radio/TV broadcasting services. Once these goods are produced, it is difficult to preclude the public from using them, whether they are paying or not.
4. Source: *World Investment Report 1996,* UNCTAD, p. 7.
5. Synergistic gains may arise if the combined companies can save on the costs of production, marketing, distribution, and R&D and redeploy the combined assets to the highest value projects.
6. This result is quite different from the findings of studies of domestic acquisitions showing that target shareholders capture the lion's share of synergistic gains.
7. Japanese acquirers themselves are highly R&D intensive. This suggests that Japanese acquisitions of U.S. firms may generate technological synergies, and that Japanese firms may be capable of using U.S. target firms' technical know-how.
8. For example, managers' payments are often positively related to the size of the assets they control, not just profits.
9. Our discussion here draws on Kobrin (1979) and Root (1972).
10. Our discussion here draws heavily on Morgan Stanley's system of evaluating political risk.
11. Each year, *Euromoney* publishes its country risk ranking in the March and September issues.

WEB RESOURCES

asiarisk.com/

Provides country risk reports and economic indicators for some Asian countries.

www.wasa.shh.fi/institut/natekon/kurser/internet/lecture4.htm

Provides a discussion on the role of foreign direct investment (FDI) in the development process and examines FDI in East Asia in detail.

members.aol.com/idealmaker/home.htm

This Website of a mergers and acquisitions adviser discusses various aspects of a merger or acquisition.

REFERENCES AND SUGGESTED READINGS

Aharoni, Yair. "The Foreign Investment Decision Process," *Harvard Business School,* 1966.

Caves, Richard. *Multinational Enterprise and Economic Analysis.* Cambridge, MA: Harvard University Press, 1982.

Doukas, John, and Nicholas Travlos. "The Effect of Corporate Multinationalism on Shareholders' Wealth: Evidence from International Acquisitions." *Journal of Finance* 43 (1988), pp. 1161–75.

Dunning, John. *Economic Analysis and the Multinational Enterprise.* New York: Praeger, 1975.

The Economist. "Multinationals, a Survey," March 27, 1993, pp. 4–20.

Harris, Robert, and David Ravenscraft. "The Role of Acquisitions in Foreign Direct Investment: Evidence from the U.S. Stock Market." *Journal of Finance* 46 (1991), pp. 825–44.

Hymer, Stephen. *The International Operations of National Firms: A Study of Direct Foreign Investment.* Cambridge, MA: MIT Press, 1976.

Kang, Jun-Koo. "The International Market for Corporate Control: Mergers and Acquisitions of U.S. Firms by Japanese Firms." *Journal of Financial Economics* 35 (1993), pp. 345–71.

Kindleberger, Charles. *American Business Abroad.* New Haven, CT: Yale University Press, 1969.

Kobrin, Stephen. "Political Risk: A Review and Reconsideration." *Journal of International Business Studies* 10 (1979), pp. 67–80.

Mandel, Robert. "The Overseas Private Investment Corporation and International Investment." *Columbia Journal of World Business* 19 (1984), pp. 89–95.

Magee, Stephen. "Information and the Multinational Corporation: An Appropriability Theory of Direct Foreign Investment." In Jagdish N. Bhagwati (ed.), *The New International Economic Order.* Cambridge, MA: MIT Press, 1977.

Morck, Randall, and Bernard Yeung. "Why Investors Value Multinationality." *Journal of Business* 64 (1991), pp. 165–87.

_______. "Internalization: An Event Study Test." *Journal of International Economics* 33 (1992), pp. 41–56.

Ragazzione, Giorgio. "Theories of Determinants of Direct Foreign Investment." IMF Staff Papers 20 (1973), pp. 471–98.

Root, Franklin. "Analyzing Political Risks in International Business." In *The Multinational Enterprise in Transition,* ed. A. Kapoor and Philip Grub. Princeton: Darwin Press, pp. 354–65.

Rugman, Alan. "Internalization Is Still a General Theory of Foreign Direct Investment." Weltwirtschaftliche Archiv. 121 (1985), pp. 570–76.

Rummel, R. J. and David Heenan. "How Multinationals Analyze Political Risk." *Harvard Business Review* 56 (1978), pp. 67–76.

Vernon, Raymond. "International Investment and International Trade in the Product Cycle." *Quarterly Journal of Economics* 80 (1966), pp. 190–207.

_______. "The Product Cycle Hypothesis in a New International Environment." *Oxford Bulletin of Economics and Statistics* 41 (1979), pp. 255–67.

CHAPTER SIXTEEN

International Capital Structure and the Cost of Capital

CHAPTER OUTLINE

Recently, many major firms throughout the world have begun to internationalize their capital structure by raising funds from foreign as well as domestic sources. As a result, these corporations are becoming *multinational* not only in the scope of their business activities but also in their **capital structure.** This trend reflects not only a conscious effort on the part of firms to lower the cost of capital by international sourcing of funds but also the ongoing liberalization and deregulation of international financial markets that make them accessible for many firms.

If international financial markets were completely integrated, it would not matter whether firms raised capital from domestic or foreign sources because the cost of capital would be equalized across countries. If, on the other hand, these markets are less than fully integrated, firms may be able to create value for their shareholders by issuing securities in foreign as well as domestic markets.

As discussed in Chapter 8, cross-listing of a firm's shares on foreign stock exchanges is one way a firm operating in a segmented capital market can lessen the negative effects of segmentation and also internationalize the firm's capital structure.[1] For example, IBM, Sony, and British Petroleum are simultaneously listed and traded on the New York, London, and Tokyo stock exchanges. By internationalizing its corporate ownership structure, a firm can generally increase its share price and lower its cost of capital. The International Finance in Practice box, "U.S. Welcomes the Alien Invasion," page 396, illustrates the rising popularity of raising capital internationally.

In this chapter, we examine various implications of internationalizing the capital structure for the firm's cost of capital and market value. We also study existing restrictions on foreign ownership of domestic firms and their effects on the firm's cost of capital. We are ultimately concerned with the MNC's ability to obtain capital at the lowest possible cost so that it can profitably take on the largest number of capital projects and maximize shareholders' wealth. We begin the chapter with a review of cost of capital concepts and basic asset pricing theory.

COST OF CAPITAL

The **cost of capital** is the minimum rate of return an investment project must generate in order to pay its financing costs. If the return on an investment project is equal to the cost of capital, undertaking the project will leave the firm's value unaffected. When a firm identifies and undertakes an investment project that generates a return exceeding its cost of capital, the firm's value will increase. It is thus important for a value-maximizing firm to try to lower its cost of capital.

When a firm has both debt and equity in its capital structure, its financing cost can be represented by the **weighted average cost of capital.** It can be computed by weighting the after-tax borrowing cost of the firm and the cost of equity capital, using the capital structure ratio as the weight. Specifically,

$$K = (1 - \lambda)K_l + \lambda(1 - \tau)i \tag{16.1}$$

where:

K = weighted average cost of capital,

K_l = cost of equity capital for a levered firm,

i = before-tax cost of debt capital (i.e., borrowing),

τ = marginal corporate income tax rate, and

λ = debt-to-total-market-value ratio.

In general, both K_l and i increase as the proportion of debt in the firm's capital structure increases.[2] At the optimal combination of debt and equity financing, however, the weighted average cost of capital (K) will be the lowest. Firms may have an incentive to use debt financing to take advantage of the tax-deductibility of interest payments. In most countries, interest payments are tax deductible, unlike dividend payments. The debt financing, however, should be balanced against possible bankruptcy costs associated with higher debt. A trade-off between the tax advantage of debt and potential bankruptcy costs is thus a major factor in determining the optimal capital structure.

Choice of the optimal capital structure is important, since a firm that desires to maximize shareholder wealth will finance new capital expenditures up to the point where the marginal return on the last unit of new invested capital equals the weighted marginal cost of capital of the last unit of new financing to be raised. Consequently, for a firm confronted with a fixed schedule of possible new investments, any policy that lowers the firm's cost of capital will increase the profitable capital expenditures the firm takes on and increase the wealth of the firm's shareholders. Internationalizing the firm's cost of capital is one such policy.

Exhibit 16.1 illustrates this point. The value-maximizing firm would undertake an investment project as long as the internal rate of return (IRR) on the project exceeds the firm's cost of capital. When all the investment projects under consideration are ranked in descending order in terms of the IRR, the firm will face a negatively sloped IRR schedule, as depicted in the exhibit. The firm's optimal capital expenditure will then be determined at the point where the IRR schedule intersects the cost of capital.

Now, suppose that the firm's cost of capital can be reduced from K^l under the local capital structure to K^g under an internationalized capital structure. As the exhibit illustrates, the firm can then increase its profitable investment outlay from I^l to I^g,

EXHIBIT 16.1

The Firm's Investment Decision and the Cost of Capital

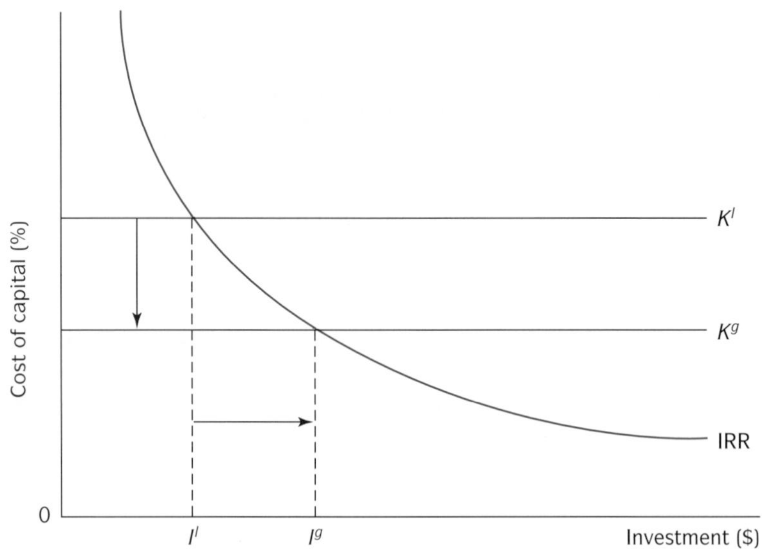

Note: K^l and K^g represent, respectively, the cost of capital under local and international capital structures; IRR represents the internal rate of return on investment projects; I^l and I^g represent the optimal investment outlays under the alternative capital structures.

contributing to the firm's value. It is important, however, to note that a reduced cost of capital increases the firm's value not only through increased investments in new projects but also through revaluation of the cash flows from existing projects.

COST OF CAPITAL IN SEGMENTED VERSUS INTEGRATED MARKETS

The main difficulty in computing the financing cost (K) of a firm is related to the cost of equity capital (K_e). The cost of equity capital is the expected return on the firm's stock that investors require. This return is frequently estimated using the **Capital Asset Pricing Model (CAPM).** The CAPM states that the equilibrium expected rate of return on a stock (or more generally any security) is a linear function of the systematic risk inherent in the security. Specifically, the CAPM-determined expected rate of return for the ith security is:

$$\bar{R}_i = R_f + (\bar{R}_M - R_f)\beta_i \tag{16.2}$$

where R_f is the risk-free rate of return and $\bar{R}_M$ is the expected return on the **market portfolio,** the market-value-weighted portfolio of all assets. **Beta,** β_i, is a measure of systematic risk inherent in security i. **Systematic risk** is the nondiversifiable market risk of an asset. The CAPM equation shows that the expected return of security i, R_i, increases in β_i, the greater the market risk, the greater the expected return. Beta is calculated as $Cov(R_i,R_M)/Var(R_M)$, where $Cov(R_i,R_M)$ is the covariance of future returns between security i and the market portfolio and $Var(R_M)$ is the variance of returns of the market portfolio.

Now, suppose that international financial markets are segmented and, as a result, investors can only diversify domestically. In this case, the market portfolio (M) in the CAPM formula would represent the domestic market portfolio, which is often proxied by the S&P 500 Index in the United States. The relevant risk measure in pricing assets will be the beta measured against the domestic market portfolio. In segmented capital markets, the same future cash flows are likely to be priced differently across countries, as they would be viewed as having different systematic risks by investors from different countries.

On the other hand, suppose that international financial markets are fully integrated and, consequently, investors can diversify internationally. In this case, the market portfolio in the CAPM formula will be the "world" market portfolio comprising all assets in the world. The relevant risk measure then should be the beta measured against the world market portfolio. In integrated international financial markets, the same future cash flows will be priced in the same way everywhere. Investors would require, on average, lower expected returns on securities under integration than under segmentation because they can diversify risk better under integration.[3]

EXAMPLE 16.1: A Numerical Illustration Suppose the domestic U.S. beta of IBM is 1.0, that is $\beta_{IBM}^{U.S.} = 1.0$, which is the average beta risk level. In addition, let us assume that the expected return on the U.S. market portfolio is 12 percent, that is, $\bar{R}_{U.S.} = 12\%$, and that the risk-free interest rate, which may be proxied by the U.S. Treasury bill rate, is 6 percent. If U.S. capital markets are segmented from the rest of the world, the expected return on IBM stock will be determined as follows:

$$\begin{aligned}\bar{R}_{IBM} &= R_f + (\bar{R}_{U.S.} - R_f)\,\beta_{IBM}^{U.S.}\\ &= 6 + (12 - 6)\,(1.0) = 12\%.\end{aligned}$$

Considering the domestic beta risk of IBM, investors would require 12 percent return on their investment in IBM stock.

Suppose now that U.S. capital markets are integrated with the rest of the world and that the world beta measure of IBM stock is 0.8, that is, $B_{IBM}^{W} = 0.8$, which is the historical world beta risk of the U.S. stock market index as reported in Exhibit 11.4. If we assume that the risk-free rate is 6 percent and the expected return on the world market portfolio is 12 percent, that is, $R_f = 6\%$ and $\bar{R}_W = 12\%$, we can compute the expected return on IBM stock as follows:

$$\begin{aligned}\bar{R}_{IBM} &= R_f + (\bar{R}_W - R_f)\,\beta_{IBM}^{W}\\ &= 6 + (12 - 6)(0.8) = 10.8\%.\end{aligned}$$

In light of a relatively low world beta measure of 0.8, investors would require a lower return on IBM stock under integration than they would under segmentation.

Obviously, the integration or segmentation of international financial markets has major implications for determining the cost of capital. However, empirical evidence on the issue is less than clear-cut. Increasingly, researchers such as Chan, Karolyi, and Stulz (1992) find it difficult to reject the international version of the CAPM, suggesting that international financial markets are integrated rather than segmented. Another group of researchers, including French and Poterba (1991), however, have documented that investors actually diversify internationally only to a limited extent, suggesting that international financial markets should be more segmented than integrated. In a study examining the integration of the Canadian and U.S. stock markets, on the other hand, Mittoo (1992) found that Canadian stocks cross-listed on U.S. exchanges are priced in an integrated market, and segmentation is predominant for those Canadian stocks that are not cross-listed.

These studies suggest that international financial markets are certainly not segmented anymore, but still are not fully integrated. If international financial markets are less than fully integrated, which is likely to be the case, there can be systematic differences in the cost of capital among countries.

INTERNATIONAL FINANCE IN PRACTICE

The U.S. Welcomes the Alien Invasion

Last year 7.5% of the $2.25 trillion worth of shares traded on the New York Stock Exchange (NYSE) came in the form of American depository receipts (ADRs). This percentage is likely to be even higher this year, helped by new issues from foreign companies, which are expected to surpass the record of 37 new listings set during 1993.

In addition to the NYSE's ADRs, a steady stream of depository receipts (DRs) trade over-the-counter, are listed on other exchanges such as Amex and Nasdaq, or are privately placed under Rule 144A and trade on the Portal system.

The depository receipts marketplace is becoming truly global. Until the late 1980s most DRs represented shares of European companies, but today investors in the United States can place orders domestically for dollar-denominated shares from countries as diverse as Chile, China, India and Mexico.

Investment bankers report the busiest schedule of offerings that they have ever seen in the depository receipts business, although volatility in many emerging markets has caused some concern among underwriters.

European DR issuance is being primarily driven by privatization programmes, notably those being implemented by France and Italy. In Asia, companies from mainland China and Hong Kong need capital to expand against a backdrop of runaway economic growth. And in Latin America the passage of the North American Free Trade Agreement (NAFTA) is expected to spur issuance from Mexico, while a dozen Chilean companies have plans to launch DRs this year. In addition, 1994 should witness the first DRs from countries including Sri Lanka, Pakistan, Peru and Uruguay.

The issuing companies are attracted by the growing demand for international equities in the form of ADRs from investors in the United States, accompanied by European and Asian demand for DRs that trade on exchanges outside the US—often referred to as global depository receipts.

Some companies urgently need to raise fresh capital in quantities unavailable at home. Others simply wish to broaden their investor base, and are being persuaded to set up an ADR programme without raising fresh capital.

But both groups have realized that in the global competition for capital those companies that broaden their investor base by actively courting the foreign investor stand a better chance of achieving a strong share price, and will be in a better position to raise capital as and when needed.

The message is clear. An ADR programme is becoming a necessity in order to gain full access to the US investor. And as the range of foreign shares available in depository receipt form grows many US investors may feel that there is even less of an incentive to hunt for stocks in overseas markets. This effect is magnified by the fact that issuance of depository receipts usually generates a great deal of research and broker interest, and pushes a company's story to the forefront of the many thousands seeking the attention of investors.

There are a range of options available to foreign companies wishing to access the depository receipt market.

DOES THE COST OF CAPITAL DIFFER AMONG COUNTRIES?

It has often been argued that U.S. firms "labored under the burden of heavier capital costs" relative to foreign rivals, especially in Japan and Germany. This argument, of course, implies that capital markets are less than fully integrated. It would be useful to directly compare the cost of capital across countries to see if the argument has any merit.

McCauley and Zimmer (1994) provide a direct comparison of the cost of capital among four major countries, Germany, Japan, the United Kingdom, and the United States. They first estimate the costs of debt and equity capital and then compute the cost of funds as the weighted average cost of capital using the capital structure in each country as the weight. They compute the cost of capital in real terms after adjusting for the inflation rate. In their study, the cost of debt is measured as the real, after-tax rate of interest faced by nonfinancial corporate borrowers. In estimating the cost of equity, McCauley and Zimmer first determine true, economic earnings, adjusting for various distortions like depreciation, inventory profits, and crossholdings

The simplest is the so-called level-one ADR, which entails setting up a programme under which existing domestic shares can be switched into DR form upon demand and trade over-the-counter. Similarly, level-two programmes may be set up under which existing shares can be transformed into DRs—but this time listed on an exchange.

Level-one and level-two programmes lack the benefits which come from the excitement created in the market by an offering of new stock. Nonetheless bankers do not feel that a company should ignore the market if it has no immediate capital-raising needs. "A level-one programme gives companies the chance to stand out," says Joseph Velli, an executive vice-president at Bank of New York, "and helps generate research product and broker interest."

UK companies such as Guinness and Tesco have built up a following by allowing existing shares to trade over-the-counter in the United States in the form of depository receipts. And more recently Telecommunicacoes Brasileiras (Telebras) has also successfully broadened its shareholder base with a level-one programme.

However, the majority of new depository receipt programmes do involve capital-raising. Until the 1980s this typically involved a European company selling ADRs to investors in the United States. But with Latin American and Asian companies doing more offerings, this is increasingly via a global depository receipt (GDR) offering which can tap simultaneously into investor demand from the US, Europe and Asia. Regardless of the terminology, both ADRs and GDRs represent the same basic structure of dollar-denominated securities.

Where capital is being raised, the major decisions a company has to make are whether to place stock privately under 144A or make a public offering; and, if the latter, where to list the depository receipts.

Currently there is a clear trend away from 144A issues toward full registration with the Securities and Exchange Commission.

"Even with a 144A placement, there is still a great deal of disclosure, the same roadshow, and a lot of work leading up to the offering," comments Bill Treut, who heads ADR sales for Latin American at Citibank.

Companies have realized that the accounting reconciliation problem is not as daunting a task as they previously thought. These factors have convinced many of them that it makes sense to take the extra steps needed to do a public offering.

"For particular reasons," Treut says, "some companies feel they have a limited window of opportunity" and can take advantage of the speed of the 144A process. "But without those special factors, the definite trend is toward full registration."

In 1991, $2.29 billion was raised via 144A placements; this rose to $3.83 billion in 1992, but fell back to $2.14 billion last year. Meanwhile, total capital raised via all DRs during 1993 was $9.54 billion, up from $5.26 billion in 1992, and $4.61 billion in 1991. That was preceded by three relatively quiet years in the wake of 1987, when $4.59 billion was raised.

One drawback with 144A placements is that they narrow the institutional investor base down to qualified institutional buyers (QIBs), and totally exclude the retail sector and smaller institutions. Second, liquidity is often not very good on the Portal secondary market trading system, so even the QIBs feel more comfortable buying public stock offerings.

The global trend toward harmonization of accounting standards is also having the effect of bringing more and more foreign companies closer to US accounting principles. This is putting foreign companies in a position where taking the step toward SEC filing for a public ADR issue is less of a challenge.

Source: Michael Marray, *Euromoney*, April 1994, pp. 61–63. Adapted with permission.

of shares, and compare those internationally comparable earnings to the respective national market capitalizations.

The estimated debt and equity costs they compute are presented in Exhibits 16.2 and 16.3, respectively. As Exhibit 16.2 shows, prior to 1982, real debt costs were often negative and divergent among countries, reflecting the distortions of inflation. Since then, debt costs have become similar for U.S., Japanese, and British firms. German firms apparently enjoyed a lower cost of debt during the period 1982–88. Exhibit 16.3 shows that Japanese firms clearly enjoyed a lower cost of equity capital than the other three countries, especially during the period 1986–89. It is noteworthy, however, that the costs of equity of the four countries have converged in the 1990s.

Exhibit 16.4 shows the trend in the capital structure, as measured by the debt-to-equity value ratio, in each of the four countries. Clearly, Germany and Japan have higher debt ratios than the United States and the U.K. There are a few reasons for the higher debt ratios for German and Japanese firms. First, historically, the banking sector in both countries has played a much more important role in corporate financing

EXHIBIT 16.2

Effective Real After-Tax Cost of Debt

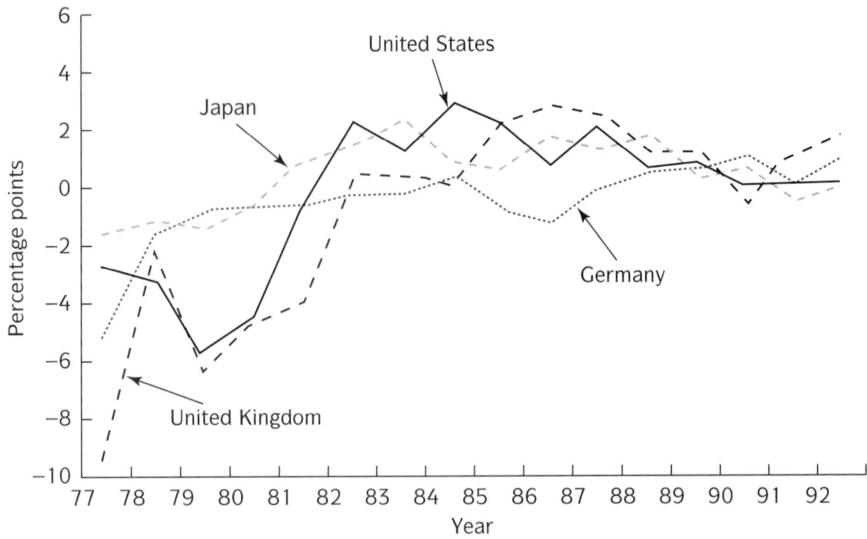

Source: Robert McCauley and Steven Zimmer, "Exchange Rates and International Differences in the Cost of Capital," in Y. Amihud and R. Levich (eds.), *Exchange Rates and Corporate Performance* (Burr Ridge, IL: Irwin, 1994).

EXHIBIT 16.3

Cost of Equity

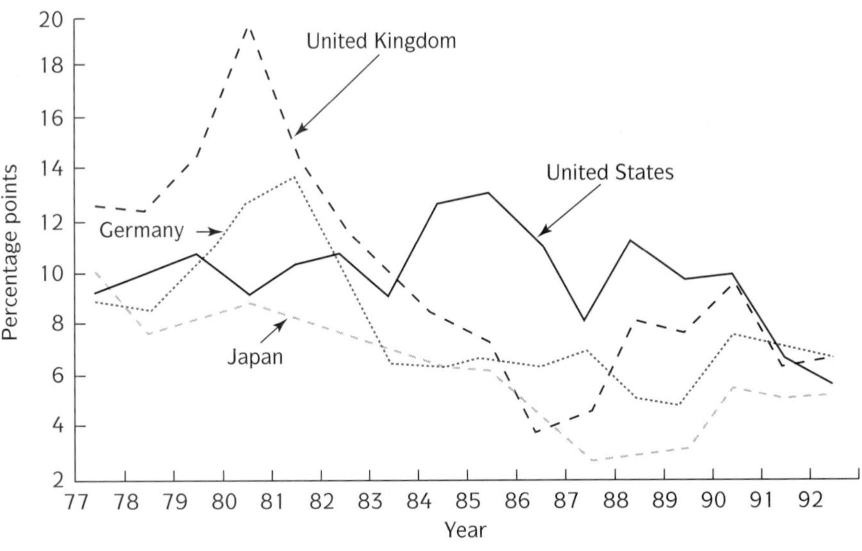

Source: Robert McCauley and Steven Zimmer, "Exchange Rates and International Differences in the Cost of Capital," in Y. Amihud and R. Levich (eds.), *Exchange Rates and Corporate Performance* (Burr Ridge, IL: Irwin, 1994).

than stock markets. Second, both German and Japanese firms could carry high levels of debt without seriously exposing themselves to default risks since banks, which often belong to the same business concern or *keiretsu,* frequently hold bonds as well as stocks of these firms. This fact also tends to reduce the agency problems (or conflict of interest) between bondholders and stockholders.[4] The German and Japanese firms, however, "deleveraged" substantially in recent years, whereas the capital structure of American and British firms stayed relatively stable through time.

EXHIBIT 16.4

Debt-to-Equity Value Ratios

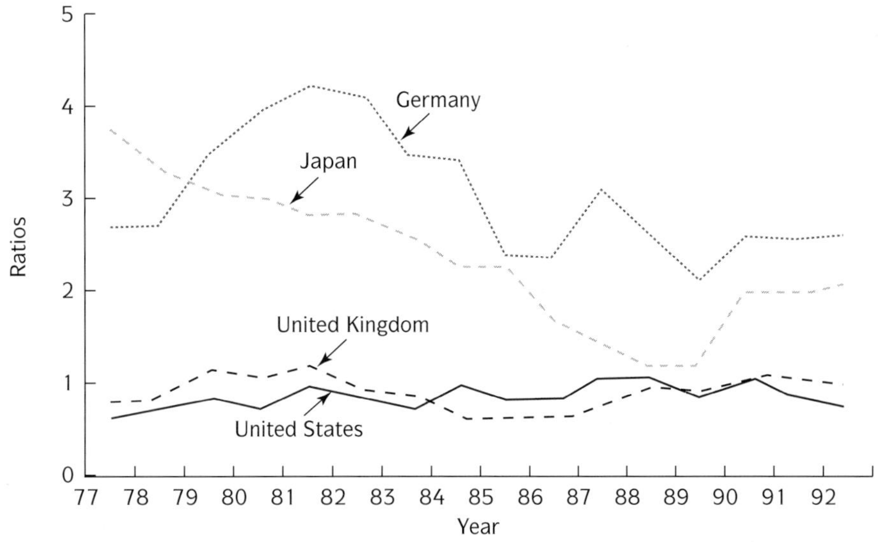

Source: Robert McCauley and Steven Zimmer, "Exchange Rates and International Differences in the Cost of Capital," in Y. Amihud and R. Levich (eds.), *Exchange Rates and Corporate Performance* (Burr Ridge, IL: Irwin, 1994).

EXHIBIT 16.5

Real After-Tax Cost of Funds

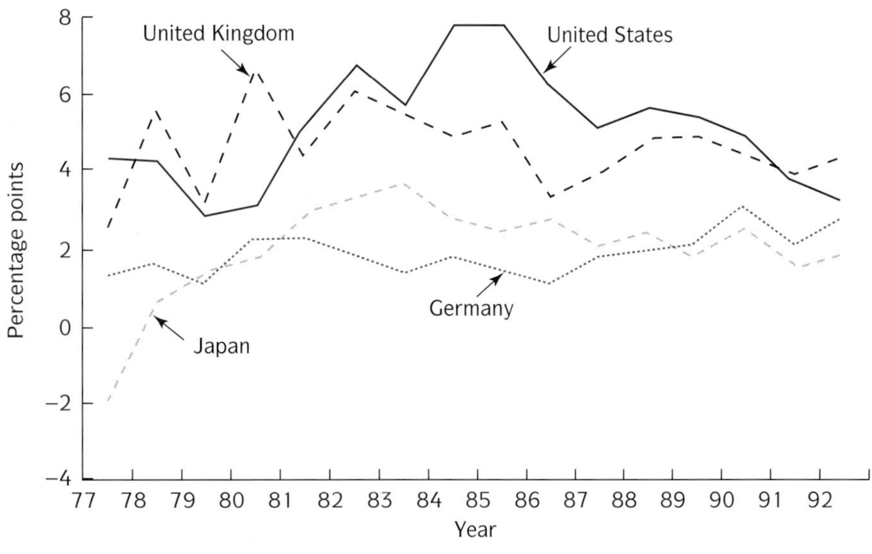

Source: Robert McCauley and Steven Zimmer, "Exchange Rates and International Differences in the Cost of Capital," in Y. Amihud and R. Levich (eds.), *Exchange Rates and Corporate Performance* (Burr Ridge, Ill: Irwin, 1994).

The cost of funds (that is, the weighted average cost of capital) advantages of Japanese and German firms are evident from Exhibit 16.5. The German firms' advantage stemmed mostly from low-cost, short-term debts, whereas the Japanese firms' advantage arose from both low debt and equity costs. Exhibit 16.5, however, also shows that the differential cost of funds among countries is diminishing in the 1990s.

In perfect markets, firms would be indifferent between raising funds abroad or at home. When markets are imperfect, however, international financing can lower the firm's cost of capital. In Chapter 7, for example, we saw that Eurobond financing was typically a less expensive form of debt financing than domestic bond financing. We continue with this line of thinking in this chapter, where we explore ways of lowering the cost of equity capital through internationalizing the firm's ownership structure. Let us first examine the historical experiences of one firm, Novo Industri, that has successfully internationalized its cost of capital by cross-border listings. Our discussion here draws on Stonehill and Dullum (1982).[5]

ILLUSTRATED MINI CASE

Novo Industri

Novo Industri A/S is a Danish multinational corporation that controls about 50 percent of the world industrial enzyme market. The company also produces health care products, including insulin. On July 8, 1981, Novo listed its stock on the New York Stock Exchange, thereby becoming the first Scandinavian company to directly raise equity capital in the United States.

In the late 1970s, Novo management decided that in order to finance the planned future growth of the company, it had to tap into international capital markets. Novo could not expect to raise all the necessary funds exclusively from the Danish stock market, which is relatively small and illiquid. In addition, Novo management felt that the company faced a higher cost of capital than its main competitors, such as Eli Lilly and Miles Lab, because of the segmented nature of the Danish stock market.

Novo thus decided to internationalize its cost of capital in order to gain access to additional sources of capital and, at the same time, lower its cost of capital. Initially, Novo increased the level of financial and technical disclosure, followed by Eurobond issue and the listing of its stock on the London Stock Exchange in 1978. In pursuing its goals further, Novo management decided to sponsor an American depository receipt (ADR) so that U.S. investors could invest in the company's stock using U.S. dollars rather than Danish kroners. Morgan Guarantee issued the ADR shares, which began trading in the over-the-counter (OTC) market in April 1981. On July 8, 1981, Novo

EXHIBIT 16.6

Process of Internationalizing the Capital Structure: Novo

1977:	Novo increased the level of its financial and technical disclosure in both Danish and English versions. Grieveson, Grant and Co, a British stock brokerage firm, started to follow Novo's stock and issued the first professional security analyst report in English. Novo's stock price: DKr200–225.
1978:	Novo raised $20 million by offering convertible Eurobond, underwritten by Morgan Grenfell. Novo listed on the London Stock Exchange.
1980 April:	Novo organized a marketing seminar in New York City promoting its stock to U.S. investors.
1980 December:	Novo's stock price reached DKr600 level; P/E ratio rose to around 16.
1981 April:	Novo ADRs were listed on NASDAQ (5 ADRs = one share) Morgan Guaranty Trust Co. served as the depository bank.
1981 July:	Novo listed on NYSE. Novo stock price reached DKr1400. Foreign ownership increased to over 50% of the shares outstanding. U.S. institutional investors began to hold Novo shares.

Source: Arthur Stonehill and Kare Dullum, *Internationalizing the Cost of Capital* (New York: John Wiley & Sons, 1982).

EXHIBIT 16.7

Novo B's Share Prices Compared to Stock Market Indices

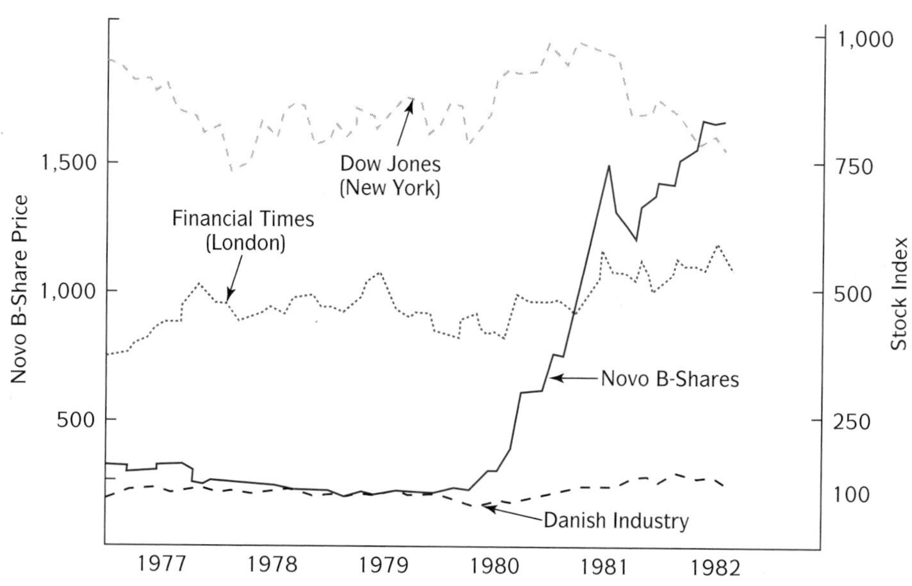

Source: Arthur I. Stonehill and Kare B. Dullum, *Internationalizing the Cost of Capital: The Novo Experience and National Policy Implications* (John Wiley & Sons, 1982), p. 73. Note that Novo A shares are nontradable shares held by the Novo Foundation. Reprinted with permission.

sold 1.8 million ADR shares, raising Dkr. 450 million, and, at the same time, listed its ADR shares on the New York Stock Exchange. The chronology of these events is provided in Exhibit 16.6.

As can be seen from Exhibit 16.7, Novo's stock price reacted very positively to the U.S. listing. Other Danish stocks, though, did not experience comparable price increases. The sharp increase in Novo's stock price indicates that the stock became fully priced internationally upon U.S. listing. This, in turn, implies that the Danish stock market was indeed segmented from the rest of the world. From the experiences of Novo, we can derive the following lesson: *Firms operating in a small, segmented domestic capital market can gain access to new capital and lower the cost of capital by listing their stocks on large, liquid capital markets like the New York and London Stock Exchanges.*

CROSS-BORDER LISTINGS OF STOCKS

As we have seen from the case of Novo Industri, firms can potentially benefit from cross-border listings. As a result, cross-border listings of stocks have become quite popular among major corporations. Exhibit 16.8 shows the extent of cross-border listings on major stock exchanges. The largest contingent of foreign stocks (531 companies at the end of 1995) are listed on the London Stock Exchange. These 531 listings, together with several hundred unlisted foreign issues, accounted for 54 percent of London's average daily turnover of $4.5 billion in 1995. U.S. exchanges attracted the next largest contingent of foreign stocks with 247 on the New York Stock Exchange (NYSE) and 362 on NASDAQ. Exhibit 16.9 provides a partial list of overseas stocks that are listed on the NYSE.

Generally speaking, a company can benefit from cross-border listings of its shares in the following ways:

1. The company can expand its potential investor base, which will lead to a higher stock price and a lower cost of capital.

EXHIBIT 16.8 Distribution of Listings of Foreign Stocks on Major Stock Exchanges

Stock Exchange	1998 Total Turnover ($ Billions)	Foreign Turnover as % of Total	Number of Foreign Companies 1986	1990	1995	1998
New York	7,345	8.5	59	96	247	392
NASDAQ	5,820	3.4	244	256	362	441
London	2,999	54.4	584	613	531	522
Tokyo	867	0.1	52	125	77	52
Paris	615	1.5	195	226	194	178
Frankfurt	1,578	2.3	181	234	235	235
Taiwan	464	0.0	0	0	0	0
Zurich	713	5.2	194	234	233	193
Osaka	250	0.0	0	0	0	0
Madrid	676	0.0	0	2	4	5
Seoul	160	0.0	0	0	0	0
Toronto	322	0.3	51	66	62	49

Sources: G. Andrew Karolyi, "What Happens to Stocks that List Shares Abroad? A Survey of Evidence and its Managerial Implications," University of Western Ontario Working Paper, 1996. London Stock Exchange Fact File, 1999.

EXHIBIT 16.9 Foreign Firms Listed on the New York Stock Exchange (Selected)

Country	Firms
Australia	Broken Hill Prop., Cole Myers, FAI, News Corporation, Western Mining, Westpac
Brazil	Aracruz Celulose, Gerdau, Telebras, Unibanco
Canada	Alcan Aluminum, Avalon, Canadian Pacific, Domtar, Mitel, Northern Telecom, Seagram
China	China Eastern Airlines, Hauneng Power International, Shanghai Petrochemical
Finland	Metso Corp., Nokia Corp., UPM-Kymmene
France	Elf Acquitaine, France Telecom, Rhone Poulenc, Thomson Multimedia, TOTALFina
Germany	Celanese, Deutsche Telecom, DaimlerChrysler, Hoechst, SAP, VEBA
Italy	Bennetton, Fiat, Luxottica, Montedison, Telecom Italia
Japan	Canon, Fuji Photo Film, Japan Air Lines, Kirin Brewery, Kubota, Mitsui Co., NEC, Nissan Motor, Sanyo Electric, Sony, Toyota Motor
Korea	Korea Electric Power, Korea Telecom, Pohang Iron & Steel, SK Telecom
Mexico	Cemex, Impresas ICA, Grupo Televisa, Telefonos de Mexico, Vitro
Netherlands	Aegon, KLM, Philips, Polygram, Royal Dutch Petrol., Unilever, ABN AMRO Holdings
Russia	Tatnet, Rostelecom, Vimpel-Communications
South Africa	ASA Limited
Spain	Banco Bilbao, Banco Central, Banco Santan., Emprosa National, Repsol, Telefon. Nac.
United Kingdom	Attwoods, Barclays, Bass Public, Beazer, BET, British Airways, British Gas, British Petrol., British Steel, British Telecom., Cable & Wireless, Glaxo, Grand Met

Source: *NYSE Factbook*, 1999.

2. Cross-listing creates a secondary market for the company's shares, which facilitates raising new capital in foreign markets.[6]
3. Cross-listing can enhance the liquidity of the company's stock.
4. Cross-listing enhances the visibility of the company's name and its products in foreign marketplaces.

Despite these potential benefits, not every company seeks overseas listings because of the costs.

1. It can be costly to meet the disclosure and listing requirements imposed by the foreign exchange and regulatory authorities.
2. Once a company's stock is traded in overseas markets, there can be volatility spillover from those markets.

EXHIBIT 16.10

Daimler-Benz's Net Profit/Loss (DM bn): German vs. American Accounting Rules

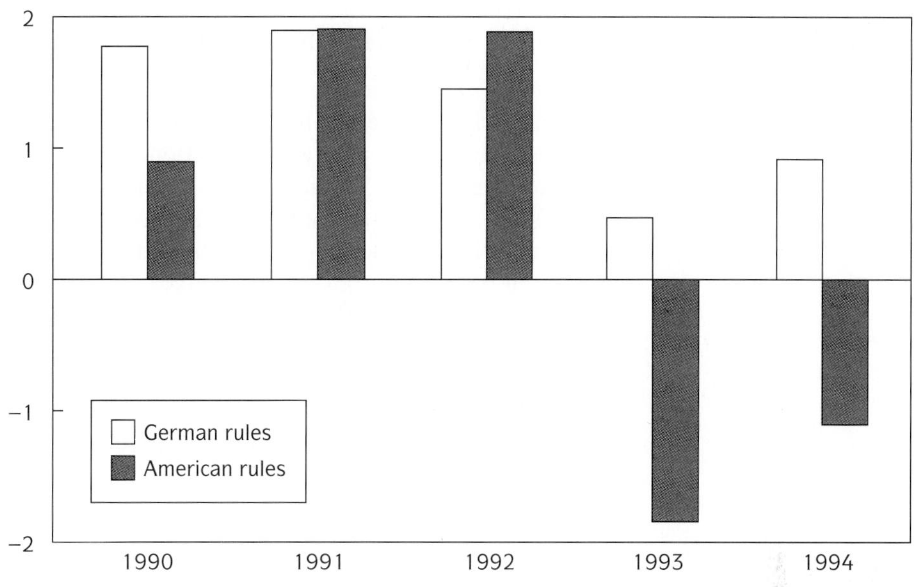

Source: *The Economist,* May 20, 1995.

3. Once a company's stock is made available to foreigners, they might acquire a controlling interest and challenge the domestic control of the company.

According to various surveys, disclosure requirements appear to be the most significant barrier to overseas listings. For example, adaptation to U.S. accounting rules, which is required by the U.S. Security and Exchange Commission (SEC), is found to be the most onerous barrier facing foreign companies that consider NYSE listings. According to a German survey conducted by Glaum and Mandler (1996), one-third of the German sample firms are, in principle, interested in U.S. listings but view the required adaptation of financial statements to the U.S. Generally Accepted Accounting Rules (US-GAAP) as a major obstacle. Daimler-Benz, a German firm listed on the NYSE, employs US-GAAP as well as German accounting law and publishes two versions of consolidated financial statements with different reported earnings.[7] As can be seen from Exhibit 16.10, the company's net earnings were positive by German accounting rules but negative by American rules in 1993 and 1994. In light of the costs and benefits of overseas listings, a foreign listing should be viewed as an investment project to be undertaken if it is judged to have a positive net present value (NPV) and thus adds to the firm's value.

In an extensive survey of the academic literature on the corporate decision to cross-list shares, Karolyi (1996) reports, among other things, that: (1) the share price reacts favorably to cross-border listings; (2) the total postlisting trading volume increases on average, and, for many issues, home-market trading volume also increases; (3) liquidity of trading in shares improves overall; (4) the stock's exposure to domestic market risk is significantly reduced and is associated with only a small increase in global market risk; (5) cross-border listings resulted in a net reduction in the cost of equity capital of 114 basis points on average; and (6) stringent disclosure requirements are the greatest impediment to cross-border listings. A recent study by Miller (1999) also confirms that dual listing can mitigate barriers to international capital flows, resulting in a higher stock price and a lower cost of capital. Considering these findings, cross-border listings of stocks seem to have been, on average, positive NPV projects.

SUPPLEMENTARY MATERIAL

CAPITAL ASSET PRICING UNDER CROSS-LISTINGS[8]

To fully understand the effects of international cross-listings, it is necessary to understand how assets will be priced under the alternative capital market regimes. In this section, we discuss an **International Asset Pricing Model (IAPM)** in a world in which some assets are internationally tradable while others are not. For ease of discussion, we will assume that cross-listed assets are **internationally tradable assets** while all other assets are **internationally nontradable assets.**

It is useful for our purpose to recalibrate the CAPM formula. Noting the definition of beta, the CAPM Equation 16.2 can be restated as:

$$\bar{R}_i = R_f + [(\bar{R}_M - R_f)/Var(R_M)]Cov(R_i,R_M) \qquad (16.3)$$

For our purposes in this chapter, it is best to define $[(\bar{R}_M - R_f)/Var(R_M)]$ as equal to $A^M M$, where A^M is a **measure of aggregate risk aversion** of all investors and is the aggregate market value of the market portfolio.[9] With these definitions, Equation 16.3 can be restated as:

$$\bar{R}_i = R_f + A^M M Cov(R_i,R_M) \qquad (16.4)$$

Equation 16.4 indicates that, given investors' aggregate risk-aversion measure, the expected rate of return on an asset increases as the asset's covariance with the market portfolio increases.

Before we introduce the IAPM with cross-listing, however, let us first discuss the asset pricing mechanism under complete segmentation and integration as benchmark cases. Suppose that there are two countries in the world, the domestic country and the foreign country. In a **completely segmented capital market** where no assets are internationally tradable, they will be priced according to their respective **country systematic risk.** For domestic country assets, the expected asset return is calculated as

$$\bar{R}_i = R_f + A^D D Cov(R_i,R_D) \qquad (16.5)$$

and for foreign country assets, the expected asset return is calculated as

$$\bar{R}_g = R_f + A^F F Cov(R_g,R_F) \qquad (16.6)$$

where $\bar{R}_i(R_g)$ is the current equilibrium expected return on the *i*th (*g*th) domestic (foreign) asset, R_f is the risk-free rate of return that is assumed to be common to both domestic and foreign countries, $A^D(A^F)$ denotes the risk-aversion measure of domestic (foreign) investors, $D(F)$ denotes the aggregate market value of all domestic (foreign) securities, and $Cov(R_i,R_D)[Cov(R_g,R_f)]$ denotes the covariance between the future returns on the *i*th (*g*th) asset and returns on the **domestic (foreign) country market portfolio.**

By comparison, in **fully integrated world capital markets** where all assets are internationally tradable, each asset will be priced according to the **world systematic risk.** For both domestic and foreign country assets

$$R_i = R_f + A^W W cov(R_i,R_W) \qquad (16.7)$$

where A^W is the aggregate risk-aversion measure of world investors, W is the aggregate market value of the **world market portfolio** that comprises both the domestic and foreign portfolios, and $Cov(R_i,R_W)$ denotes the covariance between the future returns of the *i*th security and the world market portfolio.

As we will see shortly, the asset pricing relationship becomes more complicated in **partially integrated world financial markets** where some assets are internationally tradable (that is, those that are cross-listed) while others are nontradable.

To tell the conclusion first, internationally tradable assets will be priced *as if* world financial markets were completely integrated. Regardless of the nationality, a tradable asset will be priced solely according to its world systematic risk as described in Equation 16.7. Nontradable assets, on the other hand, will be priced according to a world systematic risk, reflecting the spillover effect generated by the traded assets, as well as a country-specific systematic risk. Due to the **pricing spillover effect,** nontradable assets will *not* be priced as if world financial markets were completely segmented.

For nontradable assets of the domestic country, the pricing relationship is given by

$$\bar{R}_l = R_f + A^W W Cov^*(R_i,R_W) + A^D D[Cov(R_i,R_D) - Cov^*(R_i,R_D)] \quad (16.8)$$

where $Cov^*(R_i,R_D)$ is the *indirect* covariance between the future returns on the *i*th nontradable asset and the domestic country's market portfolio that is induced by tradable assets. Formally,

$$Cov^*(R_i,R_D) = \sigma_i \sigma_D \rho_{iT} \rho_{TD} \quad (16.9)$$

Where σ_i and σ_D are, respectively, the standard deviations of future returns of the *i*th asset and the domestic country's market portfolio; ρ_{iT} is the correlation coefficient between the *i*th nontradable asset and portfolio *T* of tradable assets, and ρ_{TD} is the correlation coefficient between the returns of portfolio *T* and the domestic country's market portfolio. Similarly, $Cov^*(R_i,R_W)$ is the *indirect* covariance between the *i*th nontradable asset and the world market portfolio. Nontradable assets of the foreign country will be priced in an analogous manner; thus, it is necessary to concentrate only on the pricing of nontradable assets in the domestic country.

Equation 16.8 indicates that nontradable assets are priced according to: (1) the **indirect world systematic risk,** $Cov^*(R_i,R_W)$, and, (2) the *pure* domestic systematic risk, $Cov(R_i,R_D) - Cov^*(R_i,R_D)$, which is the domestic systematic risk, net of the part induced by tradable assets. Despite the fact that nontradable assets are traded only within the domestic country, they are priced according to an indirect world systematic risk as well as a country-specific systematic risk. This partial international pricing of nontradable assets is due to the pricing spillover effect generated by tradable assets. (The asset pricing spillover effect was first expounded in Alexander, Eun, and Janakiramanan, 1987.)

Although nontradable assets are exclusively held by domestic (local) investors, they are priced partially internationally, reflecting the spillover effect generated by tradable assets. As can be inferred from Equation 16.8, nontradable assets will not be subject to the spillover effect and thus be priced solely domestically only if they are not correlated at all to tradable assets. This, of course, is not a very likely scenario. The pricing model also implies that if the domestic and foreign market portfolios can be exactly replicated using tradable assets, all nontradable, as well as tradable, assets will be priced fully internationally as if world financial markets were completely integrated.

The IAPM has a few interesting implications. First, international listing (trading) of assets in otherwise segmented markets directly integrates international capital markets by making these assets tradable. Second, firms with nontradable assets essentially get a **free ride** from firms with tradable assets in the sense that the former indirectly benefit from international integration in terms of a lower cost of capital and higher asset prices, without incurring any associated costs. Appendix 16.A makes this point clear using numerical simulations.

The asset pricing model with nontraded assets demonstrates that the benefits from partial integration of capital markets can be transmitted to the entire economy through the pricing spillover effect. The pricing spillover effect has an important policy implication: *To maximize the benefits from partial integration of capital markets, a country should choose to internationally cross-list those assets that are most highly correlated with the domestic market portfolio.*

Consistent with the theoretical analyses presented above, many firms have indeed experienced a reduction in the cost of capital when their stocks were listed on foreign markets. In their study of foreign stocks listed on U.S. stock exchanges, Alexander, Eun, and Janakiramanan (1989) found that foreign firms from such countries as Australia and Japan experienced a substantial reduction in the cost of capital. Canadian firms, in contrast, experienced a rather modest reduction in the cost of capital upon U.S. listings, probably because Canadian markets were more integrated with U.S. markets than other markets when U.S. listings took place.

THE EFFECT OF FOREIGN EQUITY OWNERSHIP RESTRICTIONS

While companies have incentives to internationalize their ownership structure to lower the cost of capital and increase their market values, they may be concerned, at the same time, with possible loss of corporate control to foreigners. Consequently, governments in both developed and developing countries often impose restrictions on the maximum percentage ownership of local firms by foreigners. In countries like India, Mexico, and Thailand, foreigners are allowed to purchase no more than 49 percent of the outstanding shares of local firms. These countries want to make sure that foreigners do not acquire majority stakes in local companies. France and Sweden impose an even tighter restriction of 20 percent. In Korea, foreigners were allowed to own only 20 percent of the shares of any local firm until recently.

In Switzerland, a local firm can issue two different classes of equity shares, bearer shares and registered shares. Foreigners are often allowed to purchase only bearer shares. In a similar vein, Chinese firms issue A shares and B shares, and foreigners are allowed to hold only B shares. Exhibit 16.11 lists examples of historical restrictions on foreign ownership of local firms for various countries. Obviously, these restrictions are imposed as a means of ensuring domestic control of local firms, especially those that are considered strategically important to national interests.[10]

EXHIBIT 16.11 Restrictions on Equity Ownership by Foreigners: Historical Examples

Country	Restrictions on Foreigners
Australia	10% in banks, 20% in broadcasting, and 50% in new mining ventures.
Canada	20% in broadcasting, and 25% in bank/insurance companies.
China	Foreigners are restricted to B shares; only locals are eligible for A shares.
France	Limited to 20%.
India	Limited to 49%.
Indonesia	Limited to 49%.
Mexico	Limited to 49%.
Japan	Maximum of 25–50% for several major firms; acquisition of over 10% of a single firm subject to approval of the Ministry of Finance.
Korea	Limited to 20%.
Malaysia	20% in banks and 30% in natural resources.
Norway	0% in pulp, paper, and mining, 10% in banks, 20% in industrial and oil shares, and 50% in shipping companies.
Spain	0% in defense industries and mass media. Limited to 50% for other firms.
Sweden	20% of voting shares and 40% of total equity capital.
Switzerland	Foreigners can be restricted to bearer shares.
U.K.	Government retains the veto power over any foreign takeover of British firms.

Source: Various publications of Price Waterhouse.

Pricing-to-Market Phenomenon

Suppose that foreigners, if allowed, would like to buy 30 percent of a Korean firm, but they are constrained to purchase at most 18 percent due to ownership constraints imposed on foreigners. Because the constraint is effective in limiting desired foreign ownership, foreign and domestic investors may face different market share prices. In other words, shares can exhibit a dual pricing or **pricing-to-market (PTM) phenomenon** due to legal restrictions imposed on foreigners.

ILLUSTRATED MINI CASE

Nestlé[11]

The majority of publicly traded Swiss corporations have up to three classes of common stock: (1) registered stock, (2) voting bearer stock, and (3) nonvoting bearer stock. Until recently, foreigners were not allowed to buy registered stocks; they were only allowed to buy bearer stocks. Registered stocks were made available only to Swiss nationals.

In the case of Nestlé, a well-known Swiss multinational corporation that derives more than 95 percent of its revenue from overseas markets, registered shares accounted for about 68 percent of the votes outstanding. This implies that it was practically impossible for foreigners to gain control of the firm. On November 17, 1988, however, Nestlé announced that the firm would lift the ban on foreigners buying registered shares. The announcement was made after the Zurich Stock Exchange closed.

Nestlé's board of directors mentioned two reasons for lifting the ban on foreigners. First, despite the highly multinational nature of its business activities, Nestlé maintained a highly nationalistic ownership structure. At the same time, Nestlé made high-profile cross-border acquisitions, such as Rowntree (U.K.) and Carnation (U.S.). Nestlé's practices thus were criticized as unfair and incompatible with free-market principles. The firm needed to remedy this situation. Second, Nestlé realized that the ban against foreigners holding registered shares had the effect of increasing its cost of capital, negatively affecting its competitive position in the world market.

As Exhibit 16.12 illustrates, prior to the lifting of the ban on foreigners, (voting) bearer shares traded at about twice the price of registered shares. The higher price for

EXHIBIT 16.12

Price Spread between Bearer and Registered Shares of Nestlé

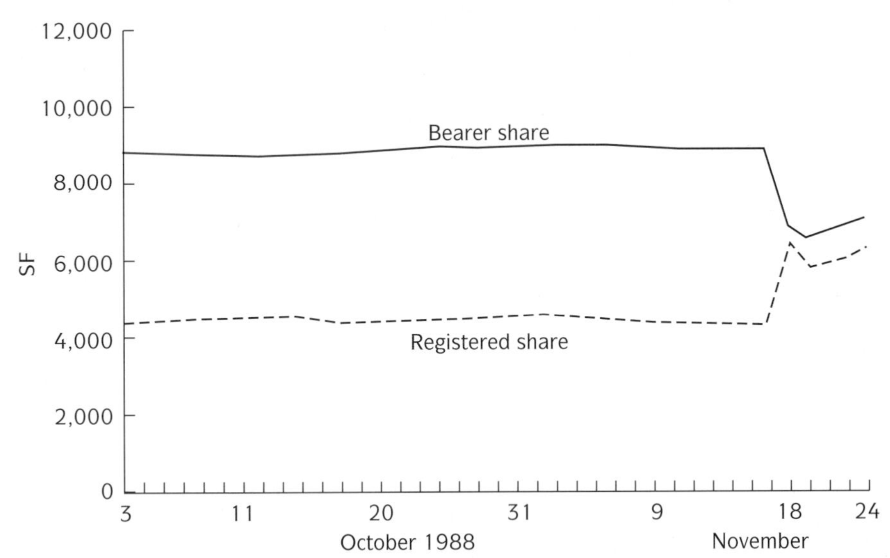

Source: *Financial Times*, November 26, 1988, p. 1. Adapted with permission.

bearer shares suggests that foreigners desired to hold more than they were allowed to in the absence of ownership restrictions imposed on them. When the ban was lifted, however, prices of the two types of shares immediately converged; the price of bearer shares declined by about 25 percent, whereas that of registered shares increased by about 35 percent. Because registered shares represented about two-thirds of the total number of voting shares, the total market value of Nestlé increased substantially when it fully internationalized its ownership structure. This, of course, means that Nestlé's cost of equity capital declined substantially.

In a recent study, Hietala (1989) documented the PTM phenomenon in the Finnish stock market. Finnish firms issue restricted and unrestricted shares, with foreigners allowed to purchase only unrestricted shares. Unrestricted shares accounted for at most 20 percent of the total number of shares of any Finnish firm. Because of this legal restriction, if foreigners desired to hold more than 20 percent of a Finnish firm, dual pricing could result. Indeed, Hietala found that most Finnish firms exhibited the PTM phenomenon, with unrestricted shares trading at roughly a 15 percent to 40 percent premium relative to restricted shares. Recently, Finland abolished restrictions imposed on foreigners altogether. ◗

SUPPLEMENTARY MATERIAL

Asset Pricing under Foreign Ownership Restrictions[12]

In this section, we formally investigate how equilibrium asset prices are determined when foreigners are subject to ownership restrictions on the maximum proportionate ownership of domestic firms. As before, we assume that there are two countries in the world, the domestic country and the foreign country. For simplicity, we assume that the foreign country imposes an ownership constraint on investors from the domestic country, but that the domestic country does not impose any constraints on investors from the foreign country. Consequently, domestic country investors are restricted to holding at most a certain percentage of the shares of any foreign firms, whereas foreign country investors are not restricted in any way from investing in the domestic country.

Since we assume that there are no investment restrictions on domestic shares, both domestic and foreign country investors face the same price for the same domestic asset, which equals the perfect capital market price. As far as domestic assets are concerned, the law of one price prevails. For foreign shares, however, the PTM phenomenon applies.

Specifically, domestic country assets will be priced according to Equation 16.7, the fully integrated world capital market's IAPM. Foreign shares will be priced differently, depending upon whether the investor is from the foreign or domestic country. Investors from the domestic country will pay a premium above and beyond the *perfect market price* that would prevail in the absence of restrictions, whereas investors from the foreign country will receive a discount from the perfect market price. This implies that the domestic country investors would require a lower return on foreign country shares than the foreign country investors.

Eun and Janakiramanan (1988) offer the following solutions for the equilibrium rates of return for foreign asset i from the domestic and the foreign country investors' perspectives, respectively:

$$\bar{R}_i^d = R_f + A^W W Cov(R_i,R_W) - (A^W W - \delta A^D D)[Cov(R_i,R_F) - Cov(R_i,R_S)] \quad (16.10)$$

$$\bar{R}_i^f = R_f + A^W W Cov(R_i,R_W) + [(1 - \delta)A^D D - A^W W][Cov(R_i,R_F) - Cov(R_i,R_S)] \quad (16.11)$$

where δ represents the fraction of the ith foreign firm that domestic country investors as a whole are allowed to own. In the above equations, portfolio S refers to the **substitution portfolio**, which is the portfolio of domestic country assets that is most highly correlated with the foreign market portfolio *F*. Portfolio *S* can thus be regarded as the domestic country investors' best *home-made* substitute for the foreign market portfolio *F*.

According to the above model, the equilibrium rates of return depend critically on (1) the severity of the ownership constraint (δ) and, (2) the ability of domestic country investors to replicate the foreign market portfolio using their domestic assets, which is measured by the **pure foreign market risk,** $Cov(R_i,R_F) - Cov(R_i,R_S)$. In the special case where portfolio *S* is a perfect substitute for the foreign market portfolio *F*, we have $Cov(R_i,R_F) = Cov(R_i,R_S)$. In this event, the foreign asset will be priced as if world capital markets are fully integrated from both the domestic and foreign investors' perspectives, even though an ownership constraint is in force. In general, however, domestic country investors will pay premiums for foreign assets (that is, accept a lower rate of return than the perfect capital market rate) to the extent that they cannot precisely replicate the foreign market portfolio using domestic assets. Foreign country investors, on the other hand, will get a discount (that is, receive a higher rate than the perfect capital market rate).

EXAMPLE 16.2: A Numerical Illustration To illustrate the effect of foreign ownership restrictions on the firm's cost of equity capital, we conduct a numerical simulation using the model economy described in Exhibit 16.13.

Exhibit 16.13 provides the standard deviations and correlation matrix of our model economy. Firms D1 to D4 belong to the domestic country and firms F1 to F4 belong to the foreign country. For simplicity, the correlation matrix reflects the stylized fact that asset returns are typically less correlated between countries than within a country; the pairwise correlation is uniformly assumed to be 0.50 within a country and 0.15 between countries. Both domestic and foreign investors are assumed to have the same aggregate risk-aversion measure, and the risk-free rate is assumed to be 9 percent.

Exhibit 16.14 considers the case in which the foreign country imposes a 20 percent ownership constraint (δ = 20 percent), whereas the domestic country does not impose any constraint on foreign investors. In this case, domestic country assets are priced as if the capital markets were completely integrated. Foreign country assets, however, are priced to market.

In general, the exhibit shows that the firm's cost of capital tends to be higher under the 20 percent ownership constraint than under complete integration. This implies that restricting foreign equity ownership in a firm will have a negative effect on the firm's cost of equity capital. For comparison purposes, we again provide the results obtained under complete segmentation and integration.

EXHIBIT 16.13 Description of the Model Economy

Firm	Expected Future Share Price ($)	Standard Deviation of Share Price ($)	Correlation Matrix						
			D2	D3	D4	F1	F2	F3	F4
D1	100	16	.50	.50	.50	.15	.15	.15	.15
D2	100	20		.50	.50	.15	.15	.15	.15
D3	100	24			.50	.15	.15	.15	.15
D4	100	28				.15	.15	.15.	.15
F1	100	18					.50	.50	.50
F2	100	22						.50	.50
F3	100	26							.50
F4	100	30							

Note: Firms D1 to D4 are from the domestic country, whereas firms F1 to F4 are from the foreign country. The risk-free interest rate is assumed to be 9%. The domestic and foreign country investors are assumed to have the same aggregate (absolute) risk-aversion measure.

EXHIBIT 16.14

International Capital Market Equilibria: The Effect of Foreign Equity Ownership Restrictions

Asset	Complete Segmentation	δ-constraint: $\delta_D = 20\%$ $\delta_r = 20\%$	δ-constraint: $\delta_r = 20\%$	Complete Integration
A. Equilibrium Asset Prices ($)[a]				
D1	81.57	83.04/87.45	85.25	85.25
D2	78.53	80.45/86.22	83.34	83.34
D3	75.30	77.75/85.07	81.41	81.41
D4	71.88	74.86/83.82	79.34	79.34
F1	79.19	86.91/81.12	87.86/80.16	84.01
F2	75.87	85.66/78.31	86.87/77.11	81.99
F3	72.34	84.50/75.38	85.92/73.96	79.94
F4	68.62	83.24/72.28	84.90/70.62	77.76
B. Cost of Equity Capital (%)				
D1	22.59	19.15	17.30	17.30
D2	27.34	22.54	19.99	19.99
D3	32.80	26.24	22.84	22.84
D4	39.12	30.46	26.04	26.04
F1	26.28	21.54	22.40	19.03
F2	31.80	25.34	26.48	21.97
F3	38.24	39.96	32.82	25.09
F4	45.73	47.95	38.85	28.60

[a]The two figures indicate the asset prices for domestic/foreign country investors, respectively.

Specifically, consider foreign firm F1. The exhibit shows that with the 20 percent ownership constraint, the firm's cost of capital is 22.40 percent, which is computed as a weighted average of the required returns by the domestic and foreign country investors in F1. Note that in the absence of the restriction, the firm's cost of capital would have been substantially lower, 19.03 percent. It is also noteworthy that when the PTM phenomenon prevails, the firm's cost of capital depends on which investors, domestic or foreign, supply capital. The exhibit also provides the case where both the domestic and foreign countries impose restrictions at the 20 percent level. Interpretation of this case is left to readers.

THE FINANCIAL STRUCTURE OF SUBSIDIARIES

One of the problems faced by financial managers of multinational corporations is how to determine the financial structure of foreign subsidiaries. According to Lessard and Shapiro (1983), there are three different approaches to determining the subsidiary's financial structure:

1. Conform to the parent company's norm.
2. Conform to the local norm of the country where the subsidiary operates.
3. Vary judiciously to capitalize on opportunities to lower taxes, reduce financing costs and risks, and take advantage of various market imperfections.

Which approach to take depends largely on whether and to what extent the parent company is responsible for the subsidiary's financial obligations. When the parent is fully responsible for the subsidiary's obligations, the independent financial structure of the subsidiary is irrelevant; it is the parent's overall financial structure that becomes relevant. When the parent is legally and morally responsible for the subsidiary's debts, potential creditors will examine the parent's overall financial conditions, not the subsidiary's.

When, however, the parent company is willing to let its subsidiary default, or the parent's guarantee of its subsidiary's financial obligations becomes difficult to enforce across national borders, the subsidiary's financial structure becomes relevant. In this case, potential creditors will examine the subsidiary's financial conditions closely to assess default risk. As a result, the subsidiary should choose its own financial structure to reduce default risk and thus financing costs.

In reality, the parent company cannot let its subsidiary default on its debts without expecting its worldwide operations to be hampered in one way or another. Default by a subsidiary can deplete the parent's reputational capital, possibly increase its own cost of capital, and certainly make it difficult to undertake future projects in the country where default occurred. Various surveys, including one by Robert Stobaugh, strongly suggest that parent firms of MNCs indeed will not allow their subsidiaries to default, regardless of circumstances.

An immediate implication of the parent's legal and moral obligation to honor its subsidiary's debts is that the parent should monitor its subsidiary's financial conditions closely and make sure that the firm's overall financial conditions are not adversely affected by the subsidiary's financial structure. What really matters is the marginal impact that the subsidiary's financial structure may have on the parent's worldwide financial structure. The subsidiary's financial structure should be chosen so that the parent's overall cost of capital can be minimized.

In light of the above discussion, neither the first nor the second approach to determining the subsidiary's financial structure can be deemed appropriate. The first approach, which calls for replicating the parent's financial structure, is not necessarily consistent with minimizing the parent's overall cost of capital. Suppose the subsidiary can locally borrow at a subsidized interest rate because the host government is eager to attract foreign investments. In this situation, the subsidiary should borrow locally and exploit the lower interest rate, even if this means that the subsidiary's debt ratio will exceed the parent's norm. If deemed necessary, the parent can simply lower its own debt ratio. In other words, the distribution of debt between the parent and the subsidiary can be adjusted to take advantage of the subsidized loans. Also, in a special case where the subsidiary is operating in a country that regulates its financial structure, it would be difficult to replicate the parent's norm even if that were desirable.

The second approach, proposed by Stonehill and Stitzil (1969), calls for adopting the local financing norm. In essence, the approach is based on "When in Rome, do as the Romans do." By following the local norm, the firm can reduce the chance of being singled out for criticism. This approach makes sense only when the parent is not responsible for the subsidiary's obligations, and the subsidiary has to depend on local financing due to, say, segmentation of financial markets. Otherwise, it does not make much sense. Suppose each foreign subsidiary conforms to the local financing norm, which reflects the host country's cultural, economic, and institutional environments. Then, the parent firm's worldwide financial structure will be determined strictly in a "residual" manner. The overall financial structure so determined is not likely to be the optimal one that minimizes the parent's overall cost of capital. When the host country's norm reflects, for example, the immature nature of local financial markets, a subsidiary of the MNC with ready access to global financial markets should not slavishly follow the local norm. Doing so means that the MNC gives up its advantage in terms of a lower cost of capital.

This brings us to the third approach, which appears to be the most reasonable and consistent with the goal of minimizing the firm's overall cost of capital. The subsidiary should take advantage of subsidized loans as much as possible whenever available. It should also take advantage of tax deductions of interest payments by borrowing more heavily than is implied by the parent's norm when the corporate income tax rate is higher in the host country than in the home country, unless foreign tax credits are useful.

Apart from the tax factor, political risk is another factor that should be considered in choosing the method of financing the subsidiary. Political risk generally favors local financing over the parent's direct financing. The parent company can renounce the subsidiary's local debt in the event that the subsidiary's assets are expropriated. When the subsidiary is financed by local creditors and shareholders, the chance of expropriation itself can be lowered. When a subsidiary is operating in a developing country, financing from such international development agencies as the World Bank and International Finance Corporation will lower political risk. When the choice is between external debt and equity financing, political risk tends to favor the former. This is the case because the host government tolerates repatriation of funds in the form of interest much better than dividends.

To summarize, since the parent company is responsible, legally and/or morally, for its subsidiary's financial obligations, it has to decide the subsidiary's financial structure considering the latter's effect on the parent's overall financial structure. The subsidiary, however, should be allowed to take advantage of any favorable financing opportunities available in the host country, because that is consistent with the goal of minimizing the overall cost of capital of the parent. If necessary, the parent can adjust its own financial structure to bring about the optimal overall financial structure.

SUMMARY

In this chapter, we have discussed the cost of capital for a multinational firm. Reflecting the trend toward more liberalized and deregulated financial markets, major corporations of the world are internationalizing their capital structure by allowing foreigners to hold their shares and debts.

1. International comparison of the cost of funds indicates that while the costs of funds are converging among major countries in recent years, international financial markets are less than fully integrated. This suggests that firms can increase their market values by judiciously raising capital overseas.
2. When a firm is operating in a segmented capital market, it can reduce the negative effects by cross-listing its stock on foreign stock markets, thereby making the stock internationally tradable.
3. A firm can benefit from international cross-listings in terms of (a) a lower cost of capital and a higher stock price, and (b) access to new sources of capital.
4. When a firm's stock is cross-listed on foreign exchanges in an otherwise segmented capital market, the stock will be priced according to the world systematic risk as if international capital markets were fully integrated. Internationally nontradable assets will be priced according to a country-specific systematic risk and an indirect world systematic risk, reflecting the pricing spillover effect generated by internationally tradable assets.
5. Although the trend is toward more liberal world financial markets, many countries still maintain restrictions on investment by foreigners, especially the maximum percentage ownership of a local firm by foreigners. Under an ownership constraint, foreign and domestic country investors may face different share prices, resulting in the pricing-to-market phenomenon (PTM). PTM generally raises the firm's overall cost of capital.
6. The parent company should decide the financing method for its own subsidiary with a view to minimizing the parent's overall cost of capital. To the extent that the parent is responsible for its subsidiary's financial obligations, the subsidiary's own financial structure is irrelevant.

KEY WORDS

beta, 394
Capital Asset Pricing Model (CAPM), 394
capital structure, 392
completely segmented capital market, 404
cost of capital, 393
country systematic risk, 404
domestic (foreign) country market portfolio, 404
free ride, 405
fully integrated world capital markets, 404
indirect world systematic risk, 405
International Asset Pricing Model (IAPM), 404
internationally nontradable asset, 404
internationally tradable asset, 404
market portfolio, 394
measure of aggregate risk aversion, 404
partially integrated world financial markets, 404
pricing spillover effect, 405
pricing-to-market (PTM) phenomenon, 407
pure foreign market risk, 409
risk aversion measure, 404
substitution portfolio, 408
systematic risk, 394
weighted average cost of capital, 393
world market portfolio, 404

QUESTIONS

1. Suppose that your firm is operating in a segmented capital market. What actions would you recommend to mitigate the negative effects?
2. Explain why and how a firm's cost of capital may decrease when the firm's stock is cross-listed on foreign stock exchanges.
3. Explain the pricing *spillover effect.*
4. In what sense do firms with nontradable assets get a *free ride* from firms whose securities are internationally tradable?
5. Define and discuss *indirect world systematic risk.*
6. Discuss how the cost of capital is determined in segmented vs. integrated capital markets.
7. Suppose there exists a nontradable asset with a perfect positive correlation with a portfolio T of tradable assets. How will the nontradable asset be priced?
8. Discuss what factors motivated Novo Industri to seek U.S. listing of its stock. What lessons can be derived from Novo's experiences?
9. Discuss foreign equity ownership restrictions. Why do you think countries impose these restrictions?
10. Explain the *pricing-to-market phenomenon.*
11. Explain how the premium and discount are determined when assets are priced to market. When would the law of one price prevail in international capital markets even if foreign equity ownership restrictions are imposed?
12. Under what conditions will the foreign subsidiary's financial structure become relevant?
13. Under what conditions would you recommend that the foreign subsidiary conform to the local norm of financial structure?

PROBLEMS

Answer problems 1–3 based on the stock market data given by the following table.

	Correlation Coefficients				
	Telmex	Mexico	World	*SD*(%)	$\bar{R}$(%)
Telmex	1.00	.90	0.60	18	?
Mexico		1.00	0.75	15	14
World			1.00	10	12

The above table provides the correlations among Telmex, a telephone/communication company located in Mexico, the Mexico stock market index, and the world market index, together with the standard deviations (*SD*) of returns and the expected returns ($\bar{R}$).

1. Compute the domestic country beta of Telmex as well as its world beta. What do these betas measure?
2. Suppose the Mexican stock market is segmented from the rest of the world. Using the CAPM paradigm, estimate the equity cost of capital of Telmex.
3. Suppose now that Telmex has made its shares tradable internationally via cross-listing on NYSE. Again using the CAPM paradigm, estimate Telmex's equity cost of capital. Discuss the possible effects of international pricing of Telmex shares on the share prices and the firm's investment decisions.

ENDNOTES

1. Stapleton and Subrahmanyam (1977) pointed out that the firm may alternatively undertake foreign direct investment to mitigate the negative effects of segmented capital markets.
2. In Chapter 17, we distinguish between the cost of equity capital for a levered firm, K_l, and the cost of equity capital for an unlevered firm, K_u.
3. For a detailed discussion of the effect of integration/segmentation on the cost of capital, refer to Cohn and Pringle (1973) and Stulz (1995).
4. Recent evidence, summarized in Stulz (1996), also indicates that the agency costs of managerial discretion are lower in Japan than in the United States. This implies that Japanese managers are less likely to undertake unprofitable investment projects at the expense of existing shareholders. Unless closely monitored by shareholders, the management may pursue corporate empire building for its own interests. Stulz argues that if agency costs are indeed lower in Japan, then the cost of capital can be lower in Japan than the United States even if international financial markets are integrated.
5. Stonehill and Dullum (1982) provides a detailed analysis of the Novo case.
6. In a recent study, Chaplinsky and Ramchand (1995) report that, compared with exclusively domestic offerings, global equity offerings enable firms to raise capital at advantageous terms. In addition, they report that the negative stock price reaction that equity issue often elicits is reduced if firms have a foreign tranche in their offer.
7. Unlike U.S. accounting rules, German accounting rules are driven by tax considerations and creditor protection. For this reason, prudence, not a true and fair view, is the dominant accounting principle. German managers are granted broad discretion in accounting policy, and they try to achieve income smoothing.
8. Readers may skip the theoretical discussion presented in this section and proceed to the numerical example without losing continuity.
9. Here we assume, in fact, that investors' risk-aversion measure is constant.
10. Stulz and Wasserfallen (1995) suggest a theoretical possibility that firms may impose restrictions on foreigners' equity ownership to maximize their market values. They argue that when domestic and foreign investors have differential demand functions for a firm's stocks, the firm can maximize its market value by discriminating between domestic and foreign investors.
11. The Nestlé case was briefly mentioned in Chapter 1. We offer an in-depth analysis of the case here.
12. Readers may proceed to the numerical example without losing continuity.

WEB RESOURCES

www.nyse.com/public/intview/04ix.htm

This site of the New York Stock Exchange (NYSE) provides a comprehensive countrywise list of all non-U.S. companies listed on the NYSE and the standards and procedures for non-U.S. companies to list on the NYSE. Also has links to all the major stock exchanges of the world.

www.nasdaq.com/mktofmkts/nonusoutput a0.stm

This site of NASDAQ provides a comprehensive countrywise list of all non-U.S. companies listed on NASDAQ.

www.pei-intl.com/hmframe.htm

Provides a countrywise economic review.

REFERENCES AND SUGGESTED READINGS

Adler, Michael. "The Cost of Capital and Valuation of a Two-Country Firm." *Journal of Finance* 29 (1974), pp. 119–32.

Alexander, Gordon; Cheol Eun; and S. Janakiramanan. "Asset Pricing and Dual Listing on Foreign Capital Markets: A Note." *Journal of Finance* 42 (1987), pp. 151–58.

_______. "International Listings and Stock Returns: Some Empirical Evidence." *Journal of Financial and Quantitative Analysis* 23 (1988), pp. 135–51.

Bailey, Warren, and Julapa Jagtiani. "Foreign Ownership Restrictions and Stock prices in the Thai Market." *Journal of Financial Economics* 36 (1994), pp. 57–87.

Black, Fisher. "International Capital Market Equilibrium with Investment Barriers." *Journal of Financial Economics* 1 (1974), pp. 337–52.

Bodie, Zvi; Alex Kane; and Alan J. Marcus. *Investments,* 2nd ed. Burr Ridge, IL: Irwin, 1993.

Chaplinsky, Susan, and Latha Ramchand. "The Rationale for Global Equity Offerings." University of Virginia Working Paper, 1995.

Cohn, Richard, and John Pringle. "Imperfections in International Financial Markets: Implications for Risk Premia and the Cost of Capital to Firms." *Journal of Finance* 28 (1973), pp. 59–66.

Errunza, Vihang, and Etienne Losq. "International Asset Pricing under Mild Segmentation: Theory and Test." *Journal of Finance* 40 (1985), pp. 105–24.

Eun, Cheol, and S. Janakiramanan. "A Model of International Asset Pricing with a Constraint on the Foreign Equity Ownership." *Journal of Finance* 41 (1986), pp. 897–914.

French, K., and J. Poterba. "Investor Diversification and International Equity Markets." *American Economic Review* 81 (1991), pp. 222–26.

Glaum, Martin, and Udo Mandler. "Global Accounting Harmonization from a German Perspective: Bridging the GAAP." Europa-Universitaet Viadrina Working Paper, 1996.

Jayaraman, N., K. Shastri, and K. Tandon. "The Impact of International Cross Listings on Risk and Return: The Evidence from American Depository Receipts." *Journal of Banking and Finance* 17 (1993), pp. 91–103.

Karolyi, G. Andrew. "What Happens to Stocks That List Shares Abroad? A Survey of the Evidence and its Managerial Implications." University of Western Ontario Working Paper, 1996.

Lee, Kwang Chul, and Chuck C. Y. Kwok. "Multinational Corporations vs. Domestic Corporations: International Environmental Factors and Determinants of Capital Structure." *Journal of International Business Studies* 19 (1988), pp. 195–217.

Loderer, Claudio, and Andreas Jacobs. "The Nestlé Crash." *Journal of Financial Economics* 37 (1995), pp. 315–39.

McCauley, Robert, and Steven Zimmer. "Exchange Rates and International Differences in the Cost of Capital." In Y. Amihud and R. Levich (eds.), *Exchange Rates and Corporate Performance.* Burr Ridge, IL: Irwin, 1994, pp. 119–48.

Miller, Darius. "The Market Reaction to International Cross-listing: Evidence from Depository Receipts." *Journal of Financial Economics* 51 (1999), pp. 103–123.

Mittoo, Usha. "Additional Evidence on Integration in the Canadian Stock Market." *Journal of Finance* 47 (1992), pp. 2035–54.

Ross, Stephen A.; Randolph W. Westerfield; and Jeffrey F. Jaffee. *Corporate Finance,* 3rd ed. Burr Ridge, IL: Irwin, 1987.

Stapleton, Richard, and Marti Subrahmanyan. "Market Imperfections, Capital Market Equilibrium and Corporation Finance." *Journal of Finance* 32 (1977), pp. 307–21.

———. *Capital Market Equilibrium and Corporate Financial Decisions.* Greenwich, CT: JAI Press, 1980.

Stobaugh, Robert. "Financing Foreign Subsidiaries of U.S.-Controlled Multinational Enterprises." *Journal of International Business Studies* (1970), pp. 43–64.

Stonehill, Arthur, and Kare Dullum. *Internationalizing the Cost of Capital*. New York: John Wiley and Sons, 1982.

Stonehill, Arthur, and Thomas Stitzel. "Financial Structure and Multinational Corporations." *California Management Review* (1969), pp. 91–96.

Stulz, Rene. "On the Effect of Barriers to International Investment." *Journal of Finance* 36 (1981), pp. 923–34.

———. "Pricing Capital Assets in an International Setting: An Introduction." *Journal of International Business Studies* 16 (1985), pp. 55–74.

———. "The Cost of Capital in Internationally Integrated Markets: The Case of Nestlé." *European Financial Management* 1 (1995), pp. 11–22.

———. "Does the Cost of Capital Differ across Countries? An Agency Perspective." *European Financial Management* 2 (1996), pp. 11–22.

Stulz, Rene, and Walter Wasserfallen. "Foreign Equity Investment Restrictions, Capital Flight, and Shareholder Wealth Maximization: Theory and Evidence." *Review of Financial Studies* 8 (1995), pp. 1019–57.

Subrahmanyam, Marti. "On the Optimality of International Capital Market Integration." *Journal of Financial Economics* 2 (1975), pp. 3–28.

APPENDIX 16A

Pricing of Nontradable Assets: Numerical Simulations

To further explain the theoretical results presented in the preceding section, we provide a numerical illustration in which we assume a two-country and eight-firm world as described by Exhibit 16.13 to arrive at the equilibrium stock prices and expected rates of return, or costs of equity capital, under the alternative structures of international capital markets.

Exhibit 16A.1 presents the equilibrium asset prices and the costs of equity capital for each of the eight firms as computed according to the asset pricing models presented earlier. As the exhibit shows, cross-listing of domestic asset D1 on the foreign exchange in an otherwise segmented market decreases the equilibrium cost of equity capital from 22.59 percent (under segmentation) to 17.30 percent upon cross-listing. Clearly, international trading of the asset leads to a decrease in the cost of capital.

Once asset D1 is cross-listed, it will be priced (at $85.25) to yield the same expected rate of return that it would obtain under complete integration. Moreover, when the domestic asset is cross-listed, other domestic assets, which remain internationally nontradable, also experience a decrease in their costs of equity capital. Take asset D2 for example; the cost of capital falls from 27.34 percent under segmentation to 23.72

EXHIBIT 16A.1

International Capital Market Equilibria: The Effect of Cross-Listings

Asset	Complete Segmentation	Cross-Listing Asset D1	Cross-Listing Assets D1 and F1	Complete Integration
A. Equilibrium Asset Prices ($)				
D1	81.57	85.25	85.25	85.25
D2	78.53	80.83	80.37	83.34
D3	75.30	78.06	77.51	81.41
D4	71.88	75.10	74.45	79.34
F1	79.19	78.57	84.01	84.01
F2	75.87	75.11	78.36	81.99
F3	72.34	71.45	75.29	79.94
F4	68.62	67.59	72.02	77.76
B. Cost of Equity Capital (%)				
D1	22.59	17.30	17.30	17.30
D2	27.34	23.72	24.42	19.99
D3	32.80	28.11	19.02	22.84
D4	39.12	33.16	34.32	26.04
F1	26.28	27.28	19.03	19.03
F2	31.80	33.14	27.62	21.97
F3	38.24	29.53	30.97	25.09
F4	45.73	34.28	36.10	28.60

percent after cross-listing asset D1. This reflects the spillover effect generated by asset D1 when it becomes internationally tradable. Additionally, Exhibit 16A.1 shows that when foreign asset F1 is cross-listed in the domestic country, it will lower its own cost of equity capital as well as that of the other foreign firms. The exhibit shows that when F1 is cross-listed, its cost of equity capital falls from 26.28 percent to 19.03 percent, the same as if capital markets were completely integrated. Moreover, other foreign assets that remain internationally nontradable also experience a decrease in their costs of capital as a result of the spillover effect from the cross-listing of F1.

CHAPTER SEVENTEEN

International Capital Budgeting

CHAPTER OUTLINE

In this book, we have taken the view that the fundamental goal of the financial manager is shareholder wealth maximization. Shareholder wealth is created when the firm makes an investment that will return more in a present value sense than the investment costs. Perhaps the most important decisions that confront the financial manager are which capital projects to select. By their very nature, capital projects denote investment in capital assets that make up the productive capacity of the firm. These investments, which are typically expensive relative to the firm's overall value, will determine how efficiently the firm will produce the product it intends to sell, and thus will also determine how profitable the firm will be. In total, these decisions determine the competitive position of the firm in the product marketplace and the firm's long-run survival. Consequently, a valid framework for analysis is important. The generally accepted methodology in modern finance is to use the **net present value (NPV)** discounted cash flow model.

In Chapter 15, we explored why a MNC would make foreign direct investment in another country. In Chapter 16, we discussed the cost of capital for a multinational firm. We saw that a firm that could source funds internationally rather than just domestically could feasibly have a lower cost of capital than a domestic firm because of its greater opportunities to raise funds. A lower cost of capital means that more capital projects will have a positive net present value to the multinational firm. Our objective in this chapter is to detail a methodology for a multinational firm to analyze the investment in a capital project in a foreign land. The methodology we present is based on an analytical framework formalized by Donald Lessard (1985). The APV methodology is an extension of the NPV technique suggested for use in analyzing domestic capital expenditures. As will be seen, the APV methodology facilitates the analysis of special cash flows that are unique to international capital expenditures.

Most readers will already be familiar with NPV analysis and its superiority in comparison to other capital expenditure evaluation techniques as a tool for assisting the financial manager in maximizing shareholder wealth. Therefore, the chapter begins with only a brief review of the basic NPV capital budgeting framework. Next, the basic NPV framework is extended into an *adjusted present value (APV)* model by way of analogy to the Modigliani-Miller equation for the value of a levered firm. Following this, the APV model is extended to make it suitable for use by a MNC analyzing a foreign capital investment. The chapter concludes with an illustrated mini case showing how to implement the APV decision framework.

REVIEW OF DOMESTIC CAPITAL BUDGETING

The basic **net present value (NPV)** capital budgeting equation can be stated as:

$$NPV = \sum_{t=1}^{T} \frac{CF_t}{(1+K)^t} + \frac{TV_T}{(1+K)^T} - C_0 \tag{17.1}$$

where:

CF_t = expected after-tax cash flow for year t,
TV_T = expected after-tax terminal value, including recapture of working capital,
C_0 = initial investment at inception,
K = weighted-average cost of capital,
T = economic life of the capital project in years.

The NPV of a capital project is the present value of all cash inflows, including those at the end of the project's life, minus the present value of all cash outflows. The *NPV rule* is to accept a project if NPV ≥ 0 and to reject it if NPV < 0.[1]

For our purposes, it is necessary to expand the NPV equation. First, however, it is beneficial if we discuss annual cash flows. In capital budgeting, our concern is only with the change in the firm's total cash flows that are attributable to the capital expenditure. CF_t represents the **incremental** change in total firm cash flow for year t resulting from the capital project. Algebraically CF_t can be defined as:

$$\begin{aligned}
CF_t &= (R_t - OC_t - D_t - I_t)(1 - \tau) + D_t + I_t(1 - \tau) && (17.2a)\\
&= NI_t + D_t + I_t(1 - \tau) && (17.2b)\\
&= (R_t - OC_t - D_t)(1 - \tau) + D_t && (17.2c)\\
&= NOI_t(1 - \tau) + D_t && (17.2d)\\
&= (R_t - OC_t)(1 - \tau) + \tau D_t && (17.2e)\\
&= OCF_t(1 - \tau) + \tau D_t && (17.2f)\\
&= \text{nominal after-tax incremental cash flow for year } t
\end{aligned}$$

Equation 17.2a presents a very detailed expression for incremental cash flow that is worth learning so that we can easily apply the model. The equation shows that CF_t is the sum of three flows, or that the cash flow from a capital project goes to three different groups. The first term, as Equation 17.2b shows, is expected income, NI_t, which belongs to the equity holders of the firm. Incremental NI_t is calculated as the after-tax, $(1 - \tau)$, change in the firm's sales revenue, R_t, generated from the project, minus the corresponding operating cash flows (expenses), OC_t, minus project depreciation, D_t, minus interest expense, I_t. (As we discuss later in the chapter, we are only concerned with the interest expense that is consistent with the firm's optimal capital structure and the borrowing capacity created by the project.) The second term represents the fact that depreciation is a *non*cash expense, that is, D_t is removed from the calculation of NI_t only for tax purposes. It is added back because this cash did not actually flow out of the firm in year t. D_t can be viewed as the recapture in year t of a portion of the original investment, C_0, in the project. The last term represents the firm's after-tax payment of interest to debtholders.

Equation 17.2c provides a computationally simpler formula for calculating CF_t. Since I_t $(1 - \tau)$ is subtracted in determining NI_t in Equation 17.2a and then added back, the two cancel out. The first term in Equation 17.2c represents after-tax net operating income, NOI_t $(1 - \tau)$, as stated in Equation 17.2d.

Equation 17.2e provides yet an even simpler formula for calculating CF_t. It shows the result from Equation 17.2c of combining the after-tax value of the depreciation expense, $(1 - \tau)D_t$, with the before-tax value of D_t. The result of this combination is the amount τD_t in Equation 17.2e, which represents the tax saving due to D_t being a tax-deductible item. As summarized in Equation 17.2f, the first term in Equation 17.2e represents after-tax operating cash flow, OCF_t $(1 - \tau)$, and the second term denotes the tax savings from the depreciation expense.[2]

THE ADJUSTED PRESENT VALUE MODEL

To continue on with our discussion, we need to expand the NPV model. To do this, we substitute Equation 17.2f for CF_t in Equation 17.1, allowing us to restate the NPV formula as:

$$\text{NPV} = \sum_{t=1}^{T} \frac{OCF_t(1 - \tau)}{(1 + K)^t} + \sum_{t=1}^{T} \frac{\tau D_t}{(1 + K)^t} + \frac{TV_T}{(1 + K)^T} - C_0 \qquad (17.3)$$

In a famous article, Franco Modigliani and Merton Miller (1963) derived a theoretical statement for the market value of a levered firm (V_l) versus the market value of an equivalent unlevered firm (V_u). They showed that

$$V_l = V_u + \tau\text{Debt} \qquad (17.4a)$$

Assuming the firms are ongoing concerns and the debt the levered firm issued to finance a portion of its productive capacity is perpetual, Equation 17.4a can be expanded as:

$$\frac{NOI(1 - \tau)}{K} = \frac{NOI(1 - \tau)}{K_u} + \frac{\tau I}{i} \qquad (17.4b)$$

where i is the levered firm's borrowing rate, $I = i\text{Debt}$, and K_u is the cost of equity for an **all-equity** financed firm.

Recall from Chapter 16 that the average cost of capital can be stated as:

$$K = (1 - \lambda)K_l + \lambda i(1 - \tau) \qquad (17.5a)$$

where K_l is the cost of equity for a levered firm, and λ is the optimal debt ratio. In their article, Modigliani-Miller showed that K can be stated as:[3]

$$K = K_u(1 - \tau\lambda) \qquad (17.5b)$$

Recall that Equation 17.2a can be simplified to Equation 17.2d. What this implies is that regardless of how the firm (or a capital expenditure) is financed, it will earn the same NOI. From Equation 17.5b, if $\lambda = 0$ (that is, an all-equity financed firm), then $K = K_u$ and $I = 0$; thus in Equation 17.4a $V_l = V_u$. However, if $\lambda > 0$ (that is, a levered firm), then $K_u > K$ and $I > 0$, thus $V_l > V_u$. For Equation 17.4b to hold as an equality, it is necessary to add the present value of the tax savings the levered firm receives. The main result of Modigliani and Miller's theory is that the value of a levered firm is greater than an equivalent unlevered firm earning the same NOI because the levered firm also has tax savings from the tax deductibility of interest payments to bondholders that do not go to the government. The following example clarifies the tax savings to the firm from making interest payments on debt.

EXHIBIT 17.1

Comparison of Cash Flows Available to Investors

	Levered	Unlevered
Revenue	$100	$100
Operating costs	−50	−50
Net operating income	50	50
Interest expense	−10	−0
Earnings before taxes	40	50
Taxes @ .40	−16	−20
Net income	24	30
Cash flow available to investors	$24 + 10 = $34	$ 30

EXAMPLE 17.1: Tax Savings from Interest Payments Exhibit 17.1 provides an example of the tax savings arising from the tax deductibility of interest payments. The exhibit shows a levered and an unlevered firm, each with sales revenue and operating expenses of \$100 and \$50, respectively. The levered firm has interest expense of \$10 and earnings before taxes of \$40, while the unlevered firm enjoys \$50 of before-tax earnings since it does not have any interest expense. The levered firm pays only \$16 in taxes as opposed to \$20 for the unlevered firm. This leaves \$24 for the levered firm's shareholders and \$30 for the unlevered firm's shareholders. Nevertheless, the levered firm has a total of \$34 (= \$24 + \$10) of funds available for investors, while the unlevered firm has only \$30. The extra \$4 comes from the tax savings on the \$10 before-tax interest payment.

By direct analogy to the Modigliani-Miller equation for an unlevered firm, we can convert the NPV Equation 17.3 into the **adjusted present value (APV)** model:

$$APV = \sum_{t=1}^{T} \frac{OCF_t(1-\tau)}{(1+K_u)^t} + \sum_{t=1}^{T} \frac{\tau D_t}{(1+i)^t} + \sum_{t=1}^{T} \frac{\tau I_t}{(1+i)^t} + \frac{TV_T}{(1+K_u)^T} - C_0 \quad (17.6)$$

The APV model is a **value-additivity** approach to capital budgeting. That is, each cash flow that is a source of value is considered individually. Note that in the APV model, each cash flow is discounted at a rate of discount consistent with the risk inherent in that cash flow. The OCF_t and TV_T are discounted at K_u. The firm would receive these cash flows from a capital project regardless of whether the firm was levered or unlevered. The tax savings due to interest, τI_t, are discounted at the before-tax borrowing rate, i, as in Equation 17.4b. It is suggested that the tax savings due to depreciation, τD_t, also be discounted at i because these cash flows are relatively less risky than operating cash flows if tax laws are not likely to change radically over the economic life of the project.[4]

The APV model is useful for a domestic firm analyzing a domestic capital expenditure. If APV ≥ 0, the project should be accepted. If APV < 0, the project should be rejected. Thus, the model is useful for a MNC for analyzing one of its domestic capital expenditures or for a foreign subsidiary of the MNC analyzing a proposed capital expenditure from the subsidiary's viewpoint.

CAPITAL BUDGETING FROM THE PARENT FIRM'S PERSPECTIVE

The APV model as stated in Equation 17.6 is not useful for the MNC in analyzing a foreign capital expenditure of one of its subsidiaries from the MNC's, or parent's, perspective. In fact, it is possible that a project may have a positive APV from the subsidiary's perspective and a negative APV from the parent's perspective. This could happen, for example, if certain cash flows are blocked by the host country from being legally remitted to the parent or if extra taxes are imposed by the host country on foreign exchange remittances. A higher marginal tax rate in the home country may also cause a project to be unprofitable from the parent's perspective. If we assume the MNC owns the foreign subsidiary, but domestic shareholders own the MNC parent, it is the currency of the parent firm that is important because it is that currency into which the cash flows must be converted to benefit the shareholders whose wealth the MNC is attempting to maximize.

Donald Lessard (1985) developed an APV model that is suitable for a MNC to use in analyzing a foreign capital expenditure. The model recognizes that the cash flows will be denominated in a foreign currency and will have to be converted into the currency of the parent. Additionally, Lessard's model incorporates special cash flows that are frequently encountered in foreign project analysis. Using the basic structure of the APV model developed in the previous section, Lessard's model can be stated as:

$$APV = \sum_{t=1}^{T} \frac{\bar{S}_t OCF_t(1-\tau)}{(1+K_{ud})^t} + \sum_{t=1}^{T} \frac{\bar{S}_t \tau D_t}{(1+i_d)^t} + \sum_{t=1}^{T} \frac{\bar{S}_t \tau I_t}{(1+i_d)} + \frac{\bar{S}_T TV_T}{(1+K_{ud})^T} - S_0 C_0 + S_0 RF_0 + S_0 CL_0 - \sum_{t=1}^{T} \frac{\bar{S}_t LP_t}{(1+i_d)^t} \tag{17.7}$$

Several points are noteworthy about Equation 17.7. First, the cash flows are assumed to be denominated in the foreign currency and converted to the currency of the parent at the expected spot exchange rate, $\bar{S}_t$, applicable for year t. The marginal corporate tax rate, τ, is the larger of the parent's or the foreign subsidiary's because the model assumes that the tax authority in the parent firm's home country will give a foreign tax credit for foreign taxes paid *up to* the amount of the tax liability in the home country. Thus, if the parent's tax rate is the larger of the two, additional taxes are due in the home country, which equals the difference between the domestic tax liability and the foreign tax credit. On the other hand, if the foreign tax rate is larger, the foreign tax credit more than offsets the domestic tax liability, so no additional taxes are due. (Foreign tax credits are covered in detail in Chapter 20.) It is also noted that each of the discount rates has the subscript d, indicating that once the foreign cash flows are converted into the parent's home currency, the appropriate discount rates are those of the domestic country.

In Equation 17.7, the OCF_t represent only the portion of operating cash flows available for remittance that can be legally remitted to the parent firm. Cash flows earned in the foreign country that are blocked by the host government from being repatriated do not provide any benefit to the stockholders of the parent firm and are not relevant to the analysis. Additionally, cash flows that are repatriated through circumventing restrictions are not included here.

As with domestic project analysis, it is important to include only incremental revenues and operating costs in calculating the OCF_t. An example will help illustrate the concept. A MNC may presently have a sales affiliate in a foreign country that is supplied by merchandise produced by the parent or a manufacturing facility in a third country. If a manufacturing facility is put into operation in the foreign country to satisfy local demand, sales may be larger overall than with just a sales affiliate if the foreign subsidiary is better able to assess market demand with its local presence. However, the former manufacturing unit will experience **lost sales** as a result of the new foreign manufacturing facility; that is, the new project has *cannibalized* part of an existing project. Thus, incremental revenue is not the total sales revenue of the new manufacturing facility, but rather that amount minus the lost sales revenue. However, if the sales would be lost regardless, say because a competitor who is better able to satisfy local demand is gearing up, then the entire sales revenue of the new foreign manufacturing facility is incremental sales revenue.

Equation 17.7 includes additional terms representing cash flows frequently encountered in foreign projects. The term S_0RF_0 represents the value of accumulated **restricted funds** (of amount RF_0) in the foreign land from existing operations that are freed up by the proposed project. These funds become available only *because* of the proposed project and are therefore available to offset a portion of the initial capital outlay. Examples are funds "whose use is restricted by exchange controls"[5] or funds on which additional taxes would be due in the parent country if they are remitted. RF_0 equals the difference between the face value of these funds and their present value used in the next best alternative. The extended illustration at the end of this chapter will help clarify the meaning of this term.

The term $S_0CL_0 - \sum_{t=1}^{T} \frac{\bar{S}_t LP_t}{(1 + i_d)^t}$ denotes the present value in the currency of the parent firm of the benefit of below-market-rate borrowing in foreign currency. In certain cases, a **concessionary loan** (of amount CL_0) at a below-market rate of interest may be available to the parent firm if the proposed capital expenditure is made in the foreign land. The host country offers this financing in its foreign currency as a means of attracting economic development and investment that will create employment for its citizens. The benefit to the MNC is the difference between the face value of the concessionary loan converted into the home currency and the present value of the similarly converted concessionary loan payments (LP_t) discounted at the MNC's normal domestic borrowing rate (i_d). The loan payments will yield a present value less than the face amount of the concessionary loan when they are discounted at the higher normal rate. This difference represents a subsidy the host country is willing to extend to the MNC if the investment is made. It should be clear that the present value of the loan payments discounted at the normal borrowing rate represents the size of the loan available from borrowing at the normal borrowing rate with a debt service schedule equivalent to that of the concessionary loan.

Recall that to calculate the firm's weighted-average cost of capital, it is necessary to know the firm's optimal debt ratio. When considering a capital budgeting project, it is never appropriate to think of the project as being financed separately from the way the firm is financed, for the project represents a portion of the firm. When the asset base increases because a capital project is undertaken, the firm can handle more debt in its capital structure. That is, the borrowing capacity of the firm has increased because of the project. Nevertheless, the investment and financing decisions are separate. There is an optimal capital structure for the firm; once this is determined, the cost of financing is known and can be used to determine if a project is acceptable. We do not mean to imply that *each* and every capital project is financed with the optimal portions of debt and equity. Rather, some projects may be financed with all debt or all equity or a suboptimal combination. What is important is that in the long run the firm does not stray too far from its optimal capital structure so that overall the firm's assets are financed at the lowest cost. Thus, the interest tax shield term $S_t\tau I_t$ in the APV model recognizes the tax shields of the **borrowing capacity** created by the project *regardless* of how the project is financed. Handling the tax shields in any other way would bias the APV favorably or unfavorably, respectively, if the project was financed by a larger or smaller portion of debt. This is an especially important point in international capital budgeting analysis because of the frequency of large concessionary loans. The benefit of concessionary loans, which are dependent on the parent firm making the investment, is recognized in a separate term.

Generality of the APV Model

Lessard's APV model includes many terms for cash flows frequently encountered in analyzing foreign capital expenditures. However, *all* possible terms are not included in the version presented as Equation 17.7. Nevertheless, the reader should now have the knowledge to incorporate into the basic APV model terms of a more unique nature for specific cash flows encountered in a particular analysis.

For example, there may be tax savings or deferrals that come about because of multinational operations. That is, the MNC may be able to shift revenues or expenses among its affiliates in a way that lowers taxes, or be able to combine profits or affiliates from both low and high tax environments in a manner that results in lower overall taxes. Tax deferrals are possible by reinvesting profits in new capital projects in low-tax countries.

Additionally, through interaffiliate transfer pricing strategies, licensing arrangements, royalty agreements, or other means, the parent firm might be able to repatriate some funds that are meant to be blocked, or restricted, by the host country.[6] These cash flows are the counterpart to the unrestricted funds available for remittance as part of operating cash flows. As with the cash flows arising from tax savings or deferrals, it may be difficult for the firm to accurately estimate the size of these cash flows or their duration. Since these cash flows will exist regardless of how the firm is financed, they should be discounted at the all-equity rate.

One of the major benefits of the APV framework is the ease with which difficult cash flow terms, such as tax savings or deferrals and the repatriation of restricted funds, can be handled. The analyst can first analyze the capital expenditure as if they did not exist. Additional cash flow terms do not need to be explicitly considered unless the APV is negative. If the APV is negative, the analyst can calculate how large the cash flows from other sources need to be to make the APV positive, and then estimate whether these other cash inflows will likely be that large.

Estimating the Future Expected Exchange Rate

The financial manager must estimate the future expected exchange rates, $\bar{S}_t$, in order to implement the APV framework. Chapter 5 provided a wide variety of methods for estimating exchange rates. One quick and simple way to do this is to rely on PPP and estimate the future expected spot rate for year t as:

$$\bar{S}_t = S_0(1 + \pi_d)^t/(1 + \pi_f)^t \tag{17.8}$$

where π_d is the expected long-run annual rate of inflation in the (home) domestic country of the MNC and π_f is the rate in the foreign land.

As noted in Chapter 5, PPP is not likely to hold precisely in reality. Nevertheless, unless the financial manager suspects that there is some systematic long-run bias in using PPP to estimate $\bar{S}_t$ that would result in a systematic over- or underestimate of the series of expected exchange rates, then PPP should prove to be an acceptable tool.

ILLUSTRATED MINI CASE

The Centralia Corporation

The Centralia Corporation is a midwestern manufacturer of small kitchen electrical appliances. The market segment it caters to is the midprice range. It specializes in small and medium-size microwave ovens suitable for small homes, apartment dwellers, or office coffee lounges. In recent years it has been exporting microwave ovens to Spain, where they are sold through a sales affiliate in Madrid. Because of different electrical requirements in Western Europe, the ovens Centralia manufactured for the Spanish market could not be used elsewhere in Europe without an electrical converter. Thus, the sales affiliate concentrated its marketing effort just in Spain. Sales are currently 9,600 units a year and have been increasing at a rate of 5 percent.

Centralia's marketing manager has been keeping abreast of integration activities in the European Union. Since the end of 1992, all obstacles to the free movement of goods, services, people, and capital within the 15 member states of the EU have been removed. Additionally, further integration promises a commonality among member states of rail track size, telephone and electrical equipment, and a host of other items. These developments have led the marketing manager to believe that a substantial number of microwave oven units could be sold throughout the EU and that the idea of a manufacturing facility should be explored.

The marketing and production managers have jointly drawn up plans for a wholly owned manufacturing facility in Zaragoza, which is located about 325 kilometers northeast of Madrid. Zaragoza is located just a couple hundred kilometers from the French border, thus facilitating shipment out of Spain into other EU countries. Additionally, Zaragoza is located close enough to the major population centers in Spain so that internal shipments should not pose a problem. A major attraction of locating the manufacturing facility in Zaragoza, however, is that the Spanish government has promised to arrange for a large portion of the construction cost of the production facility to be financed at a very attractive interest rate if the plant is built there. Any type of industry that will improve the employment situation would be a benefit, as the current unemployment rate in Spain exceeds 19 percent. Centralia's executive committee has instructed the financial manager to determine if the plan has financial merit. If the manufacturing facility is built, Centralia will no longer export units for sale in Europe. The necessary information follows.

On its current exports, Centralia receives $185 per unit, of which $35 represents contribution margin. The sales forecast predicts that 28,000 units will be sold within the EU during the first year of operation and that this volume will increase at the rate of 12 percent per year. All sales will be invoiced in Spanish pesetas. When the plant begins operation, units will be priced at Ptas25,900 each. It is estimated that the current production cost will be Ptas20,500 per unit. The sales price and production costs are expected to keep pace with inflation, which is forecast to be 7 percent per annum for the foreseeable future. By comparison, long-run U.S. inflation is forecast at 3 percent per annum. The current exchange rate is Ptas140/$1.00.

The cost of constructing the manufacturing plant is estimated at Ptas620,000,000. The borrowing capacity created by a capital expenditure of this amount is $1,770,000. The Madrid sales affiliate has accumulated a net amount of Ptas70,000,000 from its operations, which can be used to partially finance the construction cost. The marginal corporate tax rate in Spain and the United States is 35 percent. The accumulated funds were earned under special tax concessions offered during the initial years of the sales operation, and taxed at a marginal rate of 20 percent. If they were repatriated, additional tax at the 35 percent marginal rate would be due, but with a foreign tax credit given for the Spanish taxes already paid.

The Spanish government will allow the plant to be depreciated over an eight-year period. Little, if any, additional investment will be required over that time. At the end of this period, the market value of the facility is difficult to estimate, but Centralia believes that the plant should still be in good condition for its age and that it should therefore have reasonable market value.

One of the most attractive features of the proposal is the special financing the Spanish government is willing to arrange. If the plant is built in Zaragoza, Centralia will be eligible to borrow Ptas450,000,000 at a rate of 6 percent per annum. The normal borrowing rate for Centralia is 8 percent in dollars and 14 percent in pesetas. The loan schedule calls for the principal to be repaid in eight equal installments. In dollar terms, Centralia uses 11 percent as its all-equity cost of capital.

Here is a summary of the key points:

The current exchange rate in American terms is $S_0 = 1/140 = \$0.007143$/Ptas.

$\pi_f = 7\%$.

$\pi_d = 3\%$.

The initial cost of the project in U.S. dollars is
S_0C_0 = (\$0.007143)Ptas620,000,000 = \$4,428,660.

For simplicity, we will assume that PPP holds and use it to estimate future expected spot exchange rates in American terms as:
$\bar{S}_t = .007143(1.03)^t/(1.07)^t$.

The before-tax incremental operating cash flow per unit at $t = 1$ is Ptas25,900 − 20,500 = Ptas5,400. The nominal contribution margin in year t equals Ptas5,400$(1.07)^{t-1}$.

Incremental lost sales in units for year t equals 9,600$(1.05)^t$.

Contribution margin per unit of lost sales in year t equals \$35$(1.03)^t$.

The marginal tax rate, τ, equals the Spanish (or U.S.) rate of 35 percent.

Terminal value will initially be assumed to equal zero.

Straight-line depreciation is assumed; D_t = Ptas77,500,000 = Ptas620,000,000/8 years.

$K_{ud} = 11\%$.

$I_c = 6\%$.

$I_d = 8\%$.

In Exhibit 17.2 the present value of the expected after-tax operating cash flows from Centralia establishing the manufacturing facility in Spain is calculated. Column (a) presents the annual revenue in dollars from operating the new manufacturing facility. These are calculated each year by multiplying the expected quantity of microwave ovens to be sold times the year one unit sales price of Ptas5,400. This product is in turn multiplied by the Spanish price inflation factor of 7 percent. For example, for year $t = 2$ the factor is $(1.07)^{t-1} = (1.07)$. The peseta sales estimates are then converted to dollars at the expected spot exchange rates. Column (b) presents the annual lost sales revenues in dollars that are expected to result if the manufacturing facility is built and the parent firm no longer sells part of its production through the Spanish sales affiliate. These are calculated by multiplying the estimated quantity of lost sales in units by the current contribution margin of \$35 per unit, which is in turn multiplied by a 3 percent U.S. price inflation factor. The incremental dollar operating cash flows are the sum of columns (a) and (b), which are converted to their after-tax value and discounted at K_{ud}. The sum of their present values is \$4,038,144.

The present value of the depreciation tax shields τD_t is calculated in Exhibit 17.3. The tax savings on the annual straight-line depreciation of Ptas77,500,000 is converted to dollars at the expected future spot exchange rates and discounted to the

EXHIBIT 17.2 Calculation of the Present Value of the After-Tax Operating Cash Flows

Year (t)	$\bar{S}_t$	Quantity	$\bar{S}_t$ × Quantity × Ptas5,400 × (1.07^{t-1}) (a) \$	Quantity Lost Sales	Quantity Lost Sales × \$35.00 × $(1.03)^t$ (b) \$	$\bar{S}_tOCF_t$ (a + b) \$	$\frac{\bar{S}_tOCF_t(1-\tau)}{(1+K_{ud})^t}$ \$
1	.006876	28,000	1,039,651	(10,080)	(363,384)	676,267	396,012
2	.006619	31,360	1,199,350	(10,584)	(393,000)	806,350	425,394
3	.006371	35,123	1,383,449	(11,113)	(425,022)	958,427	455,516
4	.006133	39,338	1,595,990	(11,669)	(459,675)	1,136,315	486,542
5	.005904	44,059	1,841,219	(12,252)	(497,120)	1,344,099	518,477
6	.005683	49,346	2,123,921	(12,865)	(537,652)	1,586,270	551,255
7	.005471	55,267	2,450,357	(13,508)	(581,460)	1,868,897	585,110
8	.005266	61,899	2,826,476	(14,184)	(628,875)	2,197,601	619,838
							4,038,144

present at the domestic borrowing rate of 8 percent. The present value of these tax shields is $955,982.

The present value of the benefit of the concessionary loan is calculated in Exhibits 17.4 and 17.5. Exhibit 17.4 finds the present value of the concessionary loan payments in dollars. Since the annual principal payment on the Ptas450,000,000 concessionary loan is the same each year, the interest payments decline as the loan balance declines. For example, during the first year, interest of Ptas27,000,000 (= .06 × Ptas450,000,000) is paid on the full amount borrowed. During the second year interest of Ptas23,625,000 (= .06 × (Ptas450,000,000 − 56,250,000)) is paid on the outstanding balance over year two. The annual loan payment equals the sum of the annual principal payment and the annual interest charge. The sum of their present values in dollars, converted at the expected spot exchange rates, discounted at the domestic borrowing rate of 8 percent, is $2,588,558. This sum represents the size of the equivalent loan available (in dollars) from borrowing at the normal borrowing rate with a debt service schedule equivalent to that of the concessionary loan.

Exhibit 17.5 concludes the analysis of the concessionary loan. It shows the difference between the dollar value of the concessionary loan and the equivalent dollar loan value calculated in Exhibit 17.4. The difference of $625,792 represents the present value of the benefit of the below market rate financing of the concessionary loan.

The present value of the interest tax shields is calculated in Exhibit 17.6. The interest payments in column (b) of Exhibit 17.6 are drawn from column (c) of Exhibit 17.4. That is, we follow a conservative approach and base the interest tax shields on using the concessionary loan interest rate of 6 percent. The concessionary loan of Ptas450,000,000 represents 72.58 percent of the project cost of Ptas620,000,000. By comparison, the borrowing capacity created by the project is $1,770,000, which implies an optimal debt ratio λ for the parent firm of 39.97% = $1,770,000/$4,428,660 of the dollar cost of the project. Thus, only 55 percent (= 39.97%/72.58%) of the interest pay-

EXHIBIT 17.3

Calculation of the Present Value of the Depreciation Tax Shields

Year (t)	$\bar{S}_t$	D_t Ptas	$\frac{\bar{S}_t \tau D_t}{(1+i_d)^t}$ $
1	.006876	77,500,000	172,696
2	.006619	77,500,000	153,927
3	.006371	77,500,000	137,185
4	.006133	77,500,000	122,278
5	.005904	77,500,000	108,993
6	.005683	77,500,000	97,142
7	.005471	77,500,000	86,590
8	.005266	77,500,000	77,172
			955,982

EXHIBIT 17.4

Calculation of the Present Value of the Concessionary Loan Payments

Year (t)	$\bar{S}_t$ (a)	Principal Payment (b) Ptas	I_t (c) Ptas	$\bar{S}_t LP_t$ (a) × (b + c) $	$\frac{\bar{S}_t LP_t}{(1+i_d)^t}$ $
1	.006876	56,250,000	27,000,000	572,427	530,025
2	.006619	56,250,000	23,625,000	528,693	453,269
3	.006371	56,250,000	20,250,000	487,382	386,899
4	.006133	56,250,000	16,875,000	448,476	329,643
5	.005904	56,250,000	13,500,000	411,804	280,267
6	.005683	56,250,000	10,125,000	377,209	237,706
7	.005471	56,250,000	6,750,000	344,673	201,113
8	.005266	56,250,000	3,375,000	313,985	169,636
		450,000,000			2,588,558

EXHIBIT 17.5 **Calculation of the Present Value of the Benefit from the Concessionary Loan**

$$S_0CL_0 - \sum_{t=1}^{T} \frac{\bar{S}_t LP_t}{(1 + i_d)^t} = \$0.007143 \times \text{Ptas}450{,}000{,}000 - 2{,}588{,}558 = \$625{,}792$$

EXHIBIT 17.6

Calculation of the Present Value of the Interest Tax Shields

Year (t)	$\bar{S}_t$ (a)	I_t (b) Ptas	λ/Project Debt Ratio (c)	$\bar{S}_t \cdot 55\tau I_t$ (a × b × c × τ) $	$\frac{\bar{S}_t \cdot 55\tau I_t}{(1+i_d)^t}$ $
1	.006876	27,000,000	0.55	35,738	33,091
2	.006619	23,625,000	0.55	30,102	25,808
3	.006371	20,250,000	0.55	24,835	19,715
4	.006133	16,875,000	0.55	19,923	14,644
5	.005904	13,500,000	0.55	15,343	10,442
6	.005683	10,125,000	0.55	11,077	6,980
7	.005471	6,750,000	0.55	7,109	4,148
8	.005266	3,375,000	0.55	3,421	1,848
					116,676

ments on the concessionary loan should be used to calculate the interest tax shields. At the domestic borrowing rate of 8 percent, the present value of the interest tax shields is $116,676.

To calculate the amount of the freed-up restricted remittances it is first necessary to gross up the after-tax value of the Ptas70,000,000 on which the Madrid sales affiliate has previously paid taxes at the rate of 20 percent. This amount is Ptas87,500,000 = Ptas70,000,000/(1 − .20). The dollar value of this sum at the current spot exchange rate S_0 is $625,013 = $0.007143(Ptas87,500,000). If Centralia decided not to establish a manufacturing facility in Spain, the Ptas70,000,000 should be repatriated to the parent firm. It would be required to pay additional taxes in the U.S. in the amount of $93,752 = (.35 − .20)$625,013. If the manufacturing facility is built, the Ptas70,000,000 should not be remitted to the parent firm. Thus, freed-up funds of $93,752 result from the tax savings, which can be applied to cover a portion of the equity investment in the capital expenditure.

$$\begin{aligned}\text{The APV} &= \$4{,}038{,}144 + 955{,}982 + 625{,}792 + 116{,}676 + 93{,}752 \\ &\quad - 4{,}428{,}660 \\ &= \$1{,}401{,}686.\end{aligned}$$

There appears little doubt that the proposed manufacturing facility will be a profitable venture for Centralia. Had the APV been negative or closer to zero, we would want to consider the present value of the after-tax terminal cash flow. We are quite uncertain as to what this amount might be, and, fortunately, in this case we do not have to base a decision on this cash flow, which is difficult at best to forecast.

RISK ADJUSTMENT IN THE CAPITAL BUDGETING ANALYSIS

The APV model we presented and demonstrated is suitable for use in analyzing a capital expenditure that is of average riskiness in comparison to the firm as a whole. Some projects may be more or less risky than average, however. The *risk-adjusted discount method* is the standard way to handle this situation. This approach requires adjusting the discount rate upward or downward for increases or decreases, respectively, in the systematic risk of the project relative to the firm as a whole. In the APV model presented in Equation 17.16, only the cash flows discounted at K_{ud} incorporate systematic risk; thus, only K_{ud} needs to be adjusted when project risk differs from that of the firm as a whole.[8]

A second way to adjust for risk in the APV framework is the *certainty equivalent method.* This approach extracts the risk premium from the expected cash flows to convert them into equivalent riskless cash flows, which are then discounted at the risk-free rate of interest. This is accomplished by multiplying the risky cash flows by a certainty-equivalent factor that is unity or less. The more risky the cash flow, the smaller is the certainty-equivalent factor. In general, cash flows tend to be more risky the further into the future they are expected to be received. We favor the risk-adjusted discount rate method over the certainty-equivalent approach because we find that it is easier to adjust the discount rate than it is to estimate the appropriate certainty-equivalent factors.[9]

SENSITIVITY ANALYSIS

The way we have approached the analysis of Centralia's expansion into Spain is to obtain a point estimate of the APV through using expected values of the relevant cash flows. The expected values of these inputs are what the financial manager expects to obtain given the information he had at his disposal at the time the analysis was performed. However, each cash flow does have its own probability distribution. Hence, the realized value that may result for a particular cash flow may be different than expected. To examine these possibilities, the financial manager typically performs a sensitivity analysis. In a *sensitivity analysis,* different scenarios are examined by using different exchange rate estimates, inflation rate estimates, and cost and pricing estimates in the calculation of the APV. In essence, the sensitivity analysis allows the financial manager a means to analyze the business risk, economic exposure, exchange rate uncertainty, and political risk inherent in the investment. Sensitivity analysis puts financial managers in a position to more fully understand the implications of planned capital expenditures. It also forces them to consider in advance actions that can be taken should an investment not develop as anticipated.

REAL OPTIONS

Throughout this chapter, we have recommended the APV framework for evaluating capital expenditures in real assets. The APV was determined by making certain assumptions about revenues, operating costs, exchange rates, and the like. This approach treats risk through the discount rate. When evaluated at the appropriate discount rate, a positive APV implies that a project should be accepted and a negative APV implies that it should be rejected. A project is accepted under the assumption that all future operating decisions will be optimal. Unfortunately, the firm's management does not know at the inception date of a project what future decisions it will be confronted with because all information concerning the project has not yet been learned. Consequently, the firm's management has alternative paths, or options, that it can take as new information is discovered. Options pricing theory is useful for evaluating investment opportunities in real assets as well as financial assets, such as foreign exchange that we considered in Chapter 9. The application of options pricing theory to the evaluation of investment options in real projects is known as **real options.**

The firm is confronted with many possible real options over the life of a capital asset. For example, the firm may have a *timing option* about when to make the investment; it may have a *growth option* to increase the scale of the investment; it may have a *suspension option* to temporarily cease production; and, it may have an *abandonment option* to quit the investment early. All of these situations can be evaluated as real options.

In international capital expenditures, the MNC is faced with the political uncertainties of doing business in a foreign host country.[10] For example, a stable political environment for foreign investment may turn unfavorable if a different political party wins power by election—or worse, by political coup. Moreover, an unexpected change in a host country's monetary policy may cause a depreciation in its exchange rate versus the parent firm's home currency, thus adversely affecting the return to the shareholders of the parent firm. These and other political uncertainties make real options analysis ideal for use in evaluating international capital expenditures. Real options analysis, however, should be thought of as an extension of discounted cash flow analysis, not as a replacement of it, as the following example makes clear.

EXAMPLE 17.2: Centralia's Timing Option Suppose that the sales forecast for the first year for Centralia in the illustrated mini case had been for only 20,000 units instead of 28,000. At the lower figure, the APV would have been −$196,900. It is doubtful that Centralia would have entered into the construction of a manufacturing facility in Spain in this event. Suppose further that it is well known that the European Central Bank has been contemplating either tightening or loosening the economy of the European Union through a change in monetary policy that would cause the peseta to either appreciate to Ptas120/$1.00 or depreciate to Ptas160/$1.00 from its current level of Ptas140/$1.00. Under a restrictive monetary policy, the APV would be $232,165, and Centralia would begin operations. On the other hand, an expansionary policy would cause the APV to become an even more negative −$518,700.

Centralia believes that the effect from any change in monetary policy will be known in a year's time. Thus it decides to put its plans on hold until it learns what the ECB decides to do. In the meantime, Centralia can obtain a purchase option for a year on the parcel of land in Zaragoza on which it would build the manufacturing facility by paying the current landowner a fee of Ptas1,000,000, or $7,143.

The situation described is a classic example in which real options analysis is useful in evaluating a capital expenditure. In this situation, the purchase option of Ptas1,000,000 represents the option premium of the real option and the initial investment of Ptas620,000,000 represents the exercise price of the option. Centralia will only exercise its real option if the ECB decides to follow a restrictive policy that would cause the APV to be a positive $232,165. The Ptas1,000,000 seems like a small amount to allow Centralia the flexibility to postpone making a costly capital expenditure until more information is learned. The following example explicitly values the timing option using the binomial options pricing model.

EXAMPLE 17.3: Valuing Centralia's Timing Option In this example, we value the timing option described in the above example using the binomial options pricing model developed in Chapter 9. We use Centralia's 8 percent borrowing cost in dollars and 14 percent borrowing cost in pesetas as our estimates of the domestic and foreign risk-free rates of interest. Depending upon the action of the ECB, the peseta will either appreciate 14 percent to Ptas120/$1.00 or depreciate 14 percent to Ptas160/$1.00 from its current level of Ptas140/$1.00. Thus, $u = 1.14$ and $d = .86$. This implies that the risk-neutral probability of a depreciation is $q = [(1 + i_d)/(1 + i_f) - d]/(u - d) = [(1.08)/(1.14) - .86]/(1.14 - .86) = .31$ and the probability of an appreciation is $1 - q = .69$. Since the timing option will only be exercised if the APV is positive, the value of the timing option is $C = .69(\$232{,}165)/(1.08) = \$148{,}328$. Since this amount is substantially in excess of the $7,143 cost of the purchase option on the land, Centralia should definitely take advantage of the timing option it is confronted with to wait and see what monetary policy the ECB decides to pursue.

SUMMARY

This chapter presents a review of the NPV capital budgeting framework and expands the methodology into the APV model that is suitable for analyzing capital expenditures of a MNC in a foreign land.

1. The NPV capital budgeting framework in a domestic context is reviewed. The NPV is the difference between the present value of the cash inflows and outflows. If NPV ≥ 0 for a capital project, it should be accepted.
2. The annual after-tax cash flow formula was thoroughly defined and presented in a number of variations. This was necessary to expand the NPV model into the APV model.
3. The APV model of capital budgeting was developed by analogy to the Modigliani-Miller formula for the value of a levered firm. The APV model separates the operating cash flows from the cash flows due to financing. Additionally, each cash flow is discounted at a rate of discount commensurate with the inherent risk of the individual cash flow.
4. The APV model was further expanded to make it amenable for use by a MNC parent analyzing a foreign capital project. The cash flows were converted into the parent firm's home currency, and additional terms were added to the model to handle cash flows that are frequently encountered in international capital projects.
5. An illustrated mini case showing how to apply the APV model was presented and solved.

KEY WORDS

adjusted present value (APV), 422
all-equity cost of capital, 422
borrowing capacity, 425
concessionary loan, 425
incremental cash flow, 421
lost sales, 424
net present value (NPV), 420
real option, 431
restricted funds, 425
value-additivity, 423

QUESTIONS

1. Why is capital budgeting analysis so important to the firm?
2. What is the intuition behind the NPV capital budgeting framework?
3. Discuss what is meant by the *incremental* cash flows of a capital project.
4. Discuss the nature of the equation sequence, Equations 17.2a to 17.2f.
5. What makes the APV capital budgeting framework useful for analyzing foreign capital expenditures?
6. Relate the concept of *lost sales* to the definition of incremental cash flows.
7. What problems can enter into the capital budgeting analysis if project debt is evaluated instead of the *borrowing capacity* created by the project?
8. What is the nature of a *concessionary loan* and how is it handled in the APV model?
9. What is the intuition of discounting the various cash flows in the APV model at specific discount rates?
10. In the Modigliani-Miller equation, why is the market value of the levered firm greater than the market value of an equivalent unlevered firm?
11. Discuss the difference between performing the capital budgeting analysis from the parent firm's perspective as opposed to the project perspective.
12. Define the concept of a real option. Discuss some of the various real options a firm can be confronted with when investing in real projects.

PROBLEMS

1. The Alpha Company plans to establish a subsidiary in Greece to manufacture and sell fashion wristwatches. Alpha has total assets of $70 million, of which $45 million is equity financed. The remainder is financed with debt. Alpha considered its current capital structure optimal. The construction cost of the Greek facility in drachmas is estimated at Dr2,400,000,000, of which Dr1,800,000,000 is to be financed at a below-market borrowing rate arranged by the Greek government. Alpha wonders what amount of debt it should use in calculating the tax shields on interest payments in its capital budgeting analysis. Can you offer assistance?
2. The current spot exchange rate is Dr240/$1.00. Long-run inflation in Greece is estimated at 8 percent annually and 4.5 percent in the United States. If PPP is expected to hold between the two countries, what spot exchange should one forecast five years into the future?
3. The Beta Corporation has an optimal debt ratio of 40 percent. Its cost of equity capital is 12 percent and its before-tax borrowing rate is 8 percent. Given a marginal tax rate of 35 percent, calculate (a) the weighted-average cost of capital, and (b) the cost of equity for an equivalent all-equity financed firm.
4. Suppose that in the illustrated mini case in the chapter the APV for Centralia had been −$60,000. How large would the after-tax terminal value of the project need to be before the APV would be positive and Centralia would accept the project?
5. With regards to the Centralia illustrated mini case in the chapter, how would the APV change if:
   a. The forecast of π_d and/or π_f are incorrect?
   b. Depreciation cash flows are discounted at K_{ud} instead of i_d?
   c. The host country did not provide the concessionary loan?

MINI CASE 1

Dorchester, Ltd.

Dorchester, Ltd. is an old-line confectioner specializing in high-quality chocolates. Through its facilities in the United Kingdom, Dorchester manufactures candies that it sells throughout Western Europe and North America (United States and Canada). With its current manufacturing facilities, Dorchester has been unable to supply the U.S. market with more than 225,000 pounds of candy per year. This supply has allowed its sales affiliate, located in Boston, to be able to penetrate the U.S. market no farther west than St. Louis and only as far south as Atlanta. Dorchester believes that a separate manufacturing facility located in the United States would allow it to supply the entire U.S. market and Canada (which presently accounts for 65,000 pounds per year). Dorchester currently estimates initial demand in the North American market at 390,000 pounds, with growth at a 5 percent annual rate. A separate manufacturing facility would, obviously, free up the amount currently shipped to the United States and Canada. But Dorchester believes that this is only a short-run problem. They believe the economic development taking place in Eastern Europe will allow it to sell there the full amount presently shipped to North America within a period of five years.

Dorchester presently realizes £3.00 per pound on its North American exports. Once the U.S. manufacturing facility is operating, Dorchester expects that it will be able to initially price its product at $7.70 per pound. This price would represent an operating profit of $4.40 per pound. Both sales price and operating costs are expected to keep track with the U.S. price level; U.S. inflation is forecast at a rate of 3 percent for the next several years. In the U.K., long-run inflation is expected to be in the 4 to 5 percent range, depending on which economic service one follows. The current spot exchange rate is \$1.50/£1.00. Dorchester explicitly believes in PPP as the best means to forecast future exchange rates.

The manufacturing facility is expected to cost \$7,000,000. Dorchester plans to finance this amount by a combination of equity capital and debt. The plant will increase Dorchester's borrowing capacity by £2,000,000, and it plans to borrow only that amount. The local community in which Dorchester has decided to build will provide \$1,500,000 of debt financing for a period of seven years at 7.75 percent. The principal is to be repaid in equal installments over the life of the loan. At this point, Dorchester is uncertain whether to raise the remaining debt it desires through a domestic bond issue or a Eurodollar bond issue. It believes it can borrow pounds sterling at 10.75 percent per annum and dollars at 9.5 percent. Dorchester estimates its all-equity cost of capital to be 15 percent.

The U.S. Internal Revenue Service will allow Dorchester to depreciate the new facility over a seven-year period. After that time the confectionery equipment, which accounts for the bulk of the investment, is expected to have substantial market value.

Dorchester does not expect to receive any special tax concessions. Further, because the corporate tax rates in the two countries are the same—35 percent in the U.K. and in the United States—transfer pricing strategies are ruled out.

Should Dorchester build the new manufacturing plant in the United States?

MINI CASE 2

Strik-it-Rich Gold Mining Company

The Strik-it-Rich Gold Mining Company is contemplating expanding its operations. To do so it will need to purchase land that its geologists believe is rich in gold. Strik-it-Rich's management believes that the expansion will allow it to mine and sell an additional 2,000 troy ounces of gold per year. The expansion, including the cost of the land, will cost \$500,000. The current price of gold bullion is \$275 per ounce and one-year gold futures are trading at \$291.50 = \$250(1.06). Extraction costs are \$225 per ounce. The firm's cost of capital is 10 percent. At the current price of gold, the expansion appears profitable: NPV = (\$275 − 225) × 2,000/.10 − \$500,000 = \$500,000. Strik-it-Rich's management is, however, concerned with the possibility that large sales of gold reserves by Russia and the United Kingdom will drive the price of gold down to \$240 for the foreseeable future. On the other hand, management believes there is some possibility that the world will soon return to a gold reserve international monetary system. In the latter event, the price of gold would increase to at least \$310 per ounce. The course of the future price of gold bullion should become clear within a year. Strik-it-Rich can postpone the expansion for a year by buying a purchase option on the land for \$25,000. What should Strik-it-Rich's management do?

ENDNOTES

1. The internal rate of return, payback method, and the profitability index are three additional methods for analyzing a capital expenditure. The IRR method solves for the discount rate, that is, the project's IRR, that causes the NPV to equal zero. In many situations a project will have only a single IRR, and the IRR decision rule is to select the project if the IRR $\geq K$. However, under certain circumstances a project will have multiple IRRs, thus causing difficulty in interpreting the simple decision rule if one or more IRRs are less than K. The payback method determines the period of time required for the cumulative cash inflows to "pay back" the initial cash outlay; the shorter the payback period the more acceptable is the project. However, the payback method ignores the time value of money. The profitability index is computed by

dividing the present value of cash inflows by the initial outlay; the larger the ratio, the more acceptable is the project. However, when dealing with mutually exclusive projects, a conflict may arise between the profitability index and the NPV criterion due to the scale of the investments. If the firm is not under a capital rationing constraint, it is generally agreed that conflicts should be settled in favor of the NPV criterion. Overall, the NPV decision rule is considered the superior framework for analyzing a capital budgeting expenditure. See Ross, Westerfield, and Jaffee (1999, Chapter 6) for an overview of the NPV, IRR, payback, and profitability index methods.

2. Annual cash flows might also include incremental working capital funds. These are ignored here to simplify the presentation.
3. To derive Equation 17.5b from Equation 17.5a, it is necessary to know that $K_l = K_u + (1 - \tau)(K_u - i)$ (Debt/Equity).
4. Booth (1982) shows under what circumstances the NPV and APV methods will be precisely equivalent.
5. Lessard (1985, p. 577).
6. Chapter 18 covers interaffiliate transfer pricing strategies, licensing arrangements, and royalty agreements as methods the parent firm might use to repatriate funds restricted by the host country.
7. Booth (1982) shows that tax shields calculated using the concessionary loan rates are also theoretically correct.
8. See Ross, Westerfield, and Jaffee (1999, Chapter 12) for a treatment of capital budgeting using discount rates adjusted for project systematic risk.
9. See Brealey and Myers (1996, Chapter 9 and the chapter appendix) for a more detailed discussion of the certainty equivalent method of risk adjustment.
10. It may be helpful to review the discussion on political risk in Chapter 15.

WEB RESOURCES

www.worldbank.org/html/extdr/business.htm

This site of the World Bank provides information on doing business in the developing world, including information on project financing instruments, risk management instruments, and the like.

REFERENCES AND SUGGESTED READINGS

Ang, James S., and Tsong-Yue Lai. "A Simple Rule for Multinational Capital Budgeting." *The Global Finance Journal* 1 (1989), pp. 71–75.

Booth, Lawrence D. "Capital Budgeting Frameworks for the Multinational Corporation." *Journal of International Business Studies* (Fall 1982), pp. 113–23.

Brealey, Richard A., and Stewart C. Myers. *Principles of Corporate Finance*, 5th ed. New York: McGraw-Hill, 1996.

Coy, Peter. "Exploiting Uncertainty: The Real Options Revolution in Decision Making." *Business Week* (June 7, 1999), pp. 118–124.

Endleson, Michael E. "Real Options: Valuing Managerial Flexibility (A)." *Harvard Business School Note* (March 31, 1994).

Holland, John. "Capital Budgeting for International Business: A Framework for Analysis." *Managerial Finance* 16 (1990), pp. 1–6.

Lessard, Donald R. "Evaluating International Projects: An Adjusted Present Value Approach." In Donald R. Lessard (ed.), *International Financial Management: Theory and Application*, 2nd ed. New York: Wiley, 1985, pp. 570–84.

Luenberger, David G. "Evaluating Real Investment Opportunities." *Investment Science.* New York: Oxford University Press, 1998, pp. 337–43.

Luehrman, Timothy A. "Capital Projects as Real Options: An Introduction." *Harvard Business School Note* (March 22, 1995).

Luehrman, Timothy A. "Investment Opportunities as Real Options: Getting Started on the Numbers." *Harvard Business Review* (July–August 1998) pp. 51–67.

Modigliani, Franco, and Merton H. Miller. "Corporate Income Taxes and the Cost of Capital: A Correction." *American Economic Review* 53 (1963), pp. 433–43.

Ross, Stephen A., Randolph W. Westerfield, and Jeffrey F. Jaffe. *Corporate Finance*, 5th ed. Boston: Irwin/McGraw-Hill, 1999.

Shapiro, Alan C. "Capital Budgeting for the Multinational Corporation." *Financial Management* (Spring 1978), pp. 7–16.

CHAPTER EIGHTEEN

Multinational Cash Management

CHAPTER OUTLINE

Our primary concern in this chapter is with the efficient management of cash within a MNC. We are concerned with the size of cash balances, their currency denominations, and where these cash balances are located among the MNC's affiliates. Efficient cash management techniques can reduce the investment in cash balances and foreign exchange transaction expenses, and it can provide for maximum return from the investment of excess cash. Additionally, efficient cash management techniques result in borrowing at the lowest rate when a temporary cash shortage exists.

The chapter begins with an illustrated mini case that develops a centralized cash management system for a MNC. The system we develop includes interaffiliate netting and a centralized cash depository. The benefits of a centralized system are clearly detailed. A second mini case is used to illustrate transfer pricing strategies and the unbundling of services as two means for a MNC to reposition cash between affiliates and, under certain circumstances, reduce its overall income tax liability. The chapter concludes with a discussion on moving blocked funds from a host country that has imposed foreign exchange restrictions.

MANAGEMENT OF INTERNATIONAL CASH BALANCES

Cash management refers to the investment the firm has in **transaction balances** to cover scheduled outflows of funds during a cash budgeting period and the funds the firm has tied up in precautionary cash balances. **Precautionary cash balances** are necessary in case the firm has underestimated the amount needed to cover transactions. Good cash management also encompasses investing excess funds at the most favorable rate and borrowing at the lowest rate when there is a temporary cash shortage.

Many of the skills necessary for effective cash management are the same regardless of whether the firm has only domestic operations or if it operates internationally. For example, the cash manager of a domestic firm should source funds internationally to obtain the lowest borrowing cost and to place excess funds wherever the greatest return can be earned. Firms with multinational operations, however, regularly deal in more than one currency, and hence the cost of foreign exchange transactions is an important factor in efficient cash management. Moreover, multinational operations require the firm to decide on whether the cash management function should be centralized at corporate headquarters (or elsewhere) or decentralized and handled locally by each affiliate. In this chapter, we make a strong case for centralized cash management.

ILLUSTRATED MINI CASE

Teltrex's Cash Management System

We use a case problem for a company named Teltrex International to illustrate how a centralized cash management system works. Teltrex is a U.S. multinational firm with headquarters in California's Silicon Valley. It manufactures low-priced quartz watches which it markets throughout North America and Europe. In addition to its manufacturing facilities in California, Teltrex has three sales affiliates in Canada, Germany, and the United Kingdom.

The foundation of any cash management system is its cash budget. The **cash budget** is a plan detailing the time and the size of expected cash receipts and disbursements. Teltrex prepares a cash budget in advance for the fiscal year (updating it periodically as the year progresses), using a weekly time interval as the planning frequency. Exhibit 18.1 presents a payments matrix for one week during the cash budget planning horizon; it summarizes all interaffiliate cash receipts and disbursements of Teltrex *and* the receipts from and disbursements to external parties with which Teltrex does business. Exhibit 18.1 is denominated in U.S. dollars, the reporting currency of the parent firm. However, the functional currency of each foreign affiliate is the local currency.

Exhibit 18.1 shows, for example, that the U.S. parent expects to receive the equivalent of $30,000 in Canadian dollars from its Canadian affiliate, the equivalent of $35,000 in deutsche marks from its German affiliate, and the equivalent of $60,000 in British pounds sterling from its affiliate in the United Kingdom. In total, it expects to receive $125,000 from interaffiliate transactions. Additionally, the U.S. parent expects to receive $140,000 from external parties, say, from sales in the United States. In total, the parent expects to receive $265,000 in cash during the week. On the disbursements side, the U.S. parent expects to make payments in dollars in the amounts of

EXHIBIT 18.1 Cash Receipts and Disbursements Matrix for Teltrex ($000)

	Disbursements						
Receipts	U.S.	Canada	Germany	U.K.	External	Total Internal	Total Receipts
U.S.	—	30	35	60	140	125	265
Canada	20	—	10	40	135	70	205
Germany	10	25	—	30	125	65	190
U.K.	40	30	20	—	130	90	220
External	120	165	50	155	—	—	490[a]
Total Internal	70	85	65	130	—	350	—
Total Disbursements	190	250	115	285	530[b]	—	1,370[c]

[a]Total cash disbursed by the U.S. parent firm and its affiliates to external parties.
[b]Total cash received by the U.S. parent firm and its affiliates from external parties.
[c]Balancing check figure.
Note: $350,000 is shifted among the various affiliates; $530,000 − $490,000 = $40,000 = increase in cash balances for Teltrex during the week.

EXHIBIT 18.2 Teltrex's Interaffiliate Cash Receipts and Disbursements Matrix ($000)

	Disbursements					
Receipts	**U.S.**	**Canada**	**Germany**	**U.K.**	**Total Receipts**	**Net[a]**
U.S.	—	30	35	60	125	55
Canada	20	—	10	40	70	(15)
Germany	10	25	—	30	65	0
U.K.	40	30	20	—	90	(40)
Total Disbursements	70	85	65	130	350	0

[a]Net denotes the difference between total receipts and total disbursements for each affiliate.

EXHIBIT 18.3

Teltrex's Interaffiliate Foreign Exchange Transactions without Netting ($000)

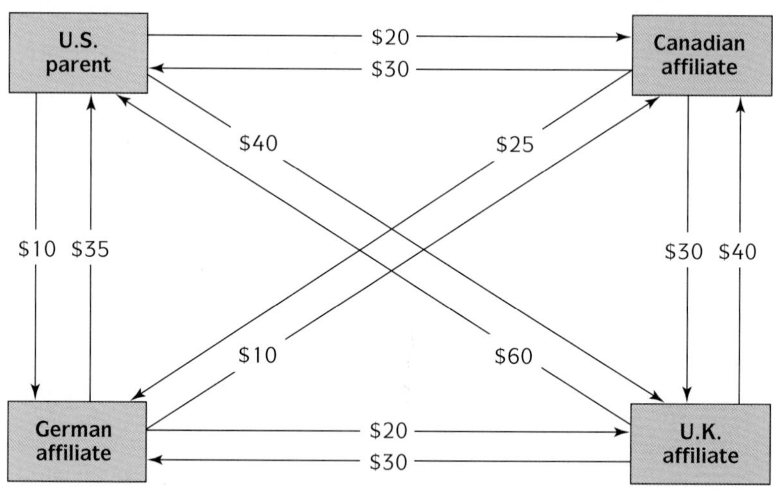

$20,000 to its Canadian affiliate, $10,000 to its German affiliate, and $40,000 to its British affiliate. It also expects to make external disbursements of $120,000 to, say, suppliers for component parts and to cover other operating costs. Analogous cash flows exist for the three affiliates.

Exhibit 18.1 shows that the equivalent of $350,000 in interaffiliate cash flows are expected to flow among the parent and its three affiliates. Note that no increase in cash in the MNC occurs as a result of interaffiliate transactions. Interaffiliate transactions effectively represent taking money out of one pocket of the MNC and putting it into another. However, Teltrex expects to receive the equivalent of $530,000 from external parties and make payments of $490,000 to other external parties. From these external transactions, a net increase of $40,000 in cash among the affiliates is expected during the week.

Netting Systems

Let's first consider the interaffiliate transactions that make up part of Exhibit 18.1. Later we will examine the transactions Teltrex expects to have with external parties. Exhibit 18.2 presents only the portion of Teltrex's receipts and disbursements matrix from Exhibit 18.1 that concerns interaffiliate cash flows.

Exhibit 18.2 shows the amount that each affiliate is to pay and receive from the other. Without a netting policy, 12 foreign exchange transactions will take place among the four affiliates. In general, if there are N affiliates, there will be a maximum of $N(N - 1)$ transactions; in our case $4(4 - 1) = 12$. Exhibit 18.3 diagrams these 12 transactions.

Exhibit 18.3 indicates that the equivalent of $350,000 in funds flows among the four affiliates in 12 foreign exchange transactions. This represents a needless use of administrative time in arranging the transactions and a waste of corporate funds in making the transactions. The cost of transferring funds is in the range of .25 percent to

EXHIBIT 18.4

Bilateral Netting of Teltrex's Interaffiliate Foreign Exchange Transactions ($000)

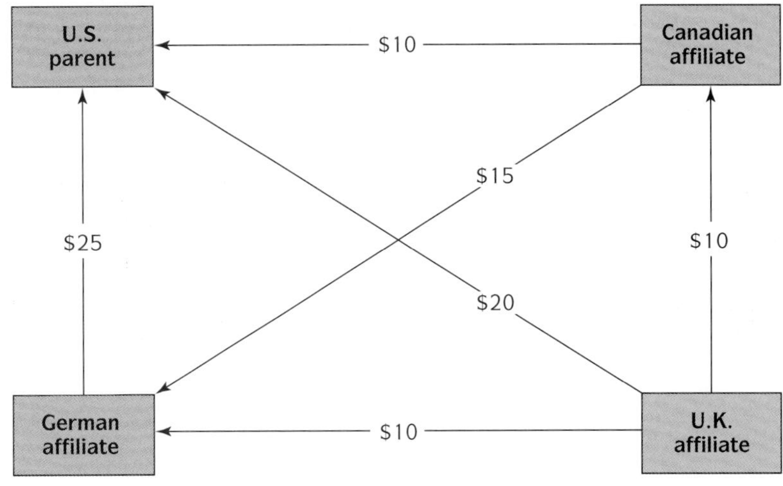

1.5 percent of the transaction; this includes transaction expenses and the opportunity cost of funds tied up in interaffiliate float. If we assume a cost of .5 percent, the cost for transferring $350,000 is $1,750 for the week.

The 12 transactions can be reduced at least by half through bilateral netting. Under a **bilateral netting** system, each pair of affiliates determines the net amount due between them, and only the net amount is transferred. For example, the U.S. parent and the Canadian affiliate would net the $30,000 and the $20,000 to be received from one another. The result is that only one payment is made; the Canadian affiliate pays the U.S. parent an amount equivalent to $10,000. Exhibit 18.4 shows the results of bilateral netting among Teltrex's four affiliates.

From Exhibit 18.4, it can be seen that a total of $90,000 flows among the four affiliates of Teltrex in six transactions. Bilateral netting can reduce the number of foreign exchange transactions among the affiliates to $N(N - 1)/2$, or less. The equivalent of $260,000 in foreign exchange transactions is eliminated through bilateral netting. At .5 percent, the cost of netting interaffiliate foreign exchange transactions is $450, a savings of $1,300 (= $1,750 − 450) over a non-netting system.

Implicit in Exhibit 18.2 is a way to limit interaffiliate transfers to no more than $(N - 1)$ separate foreign exchange transactions. Rather than stop at bilateral netting, the MNC can establish a multilateral netting system. Under a **multilateral netting** system, each affiliate nets all its interaffiliate receipts against all its disbursements. It then transfers or receives the balance, respectively, if it is a net payer or receiver. Recall from Exhibit 18.1 that total interaffiliate receipts will always equal total interaffiliate disbursements. Thus, under a multilateral netting system, the net funds to be received by the affiliates will equal the net disbursements to be made by the affiliates.

Exhibit 18.5 illustrates a multilateral netting system for Teltrex. Because the German affiliate's net receipts equal zero, only two foreign exchange transactions are necessary. The Canadian and Mexican affiliates, respectively, pay the equivalent of $15,000 and $40,000 to the U.S. parent firm. At .5 percent, the cost of transferring $55,000 is only $275 for the week, a savings of $1,475 (= $1,750 − 275) without a multilateral netting system.

Centralized Cash Depository

A multilateral netting system requires a certain degree of administrative structure. At the minimum, there must be a netting center manager who has an overview of the interaffiliate cash flows from the cash budget. The **netting center** manager determines the amount of the net payments and which affiliates are to make or receive them. A netting center does not imply that the MNC has a central cash manager, however. Indeed, the multilateral netting system presented in Exhibit 18.5 suggests that each

EXHIBIT 18.5

Multilateral Netting of Teltrex's Interaffiliate Foreign Exchange Transactions ($000)

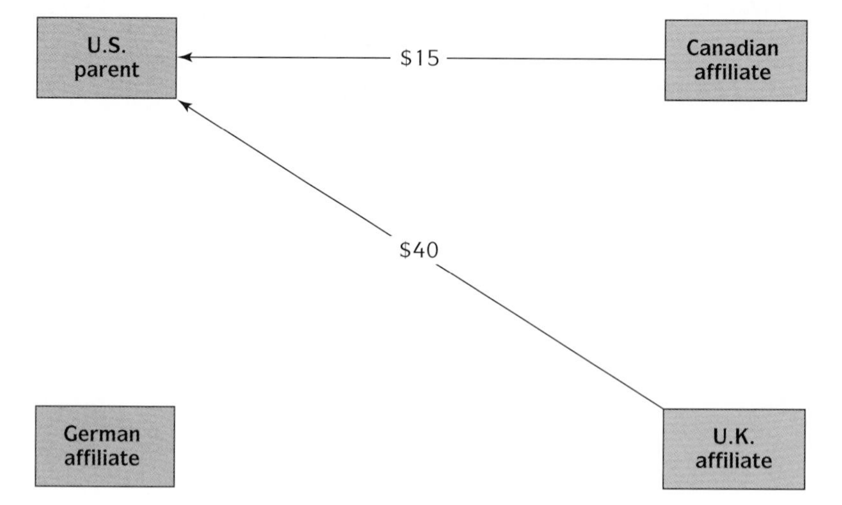

EXHIBIT 18.6

Multilateral Netting of Teltrex's Interaffiliate Foreign Exchange Transactions with a Centralized Depository ($000)

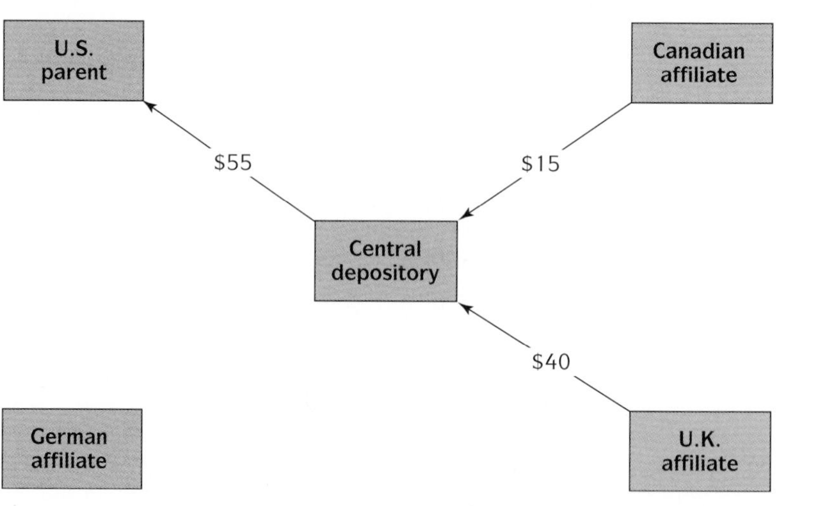

affiliate has a local cash manager who is responsible for investing excess cash and borrowing when there is a temporary cash shortage.

Exhibit 18.6 presents a modified diagram of multilateral netting for Teltrex with the addition of a centralized depository. Under a centralized cash management system, unless otherwise instructed, all interaffiliate payments will flow through the *central cash depository*.

As Exhibit 18.6 shows, the Canadian affiliate remits the equivalent of $15,000 to the central depository and the U.K. affiliate remits the equivalent of $40,000. In turn, the central depository remits $55,000 to the U.S. parent. One might question the wisdom of this system. It appears as if the foreign exchange transactions have doubled from $55,000 in Exhibit 18.5 to $110,000 in Exhibit 18.6. But that is not the case. The Canadian and U.K. affiliates might be instructed to remit to the central depository in U.S. dollars. Alternatively, the central depository could receive the remittances in Canadian dollars and British pounds sterling and exchange them for dollars before transferring the funds to the U.S. parent. (There is the expense of an additional wire transfer, however.)

EXHIBIT 18.7

Expected Net Cash Receipts and Disbursements from Teltrex Transactions with External Parties ($000)

Affiliate	Receipts	Disbursements	Net
United States	$140,000	$120,000	$20,000
Canada	135,000	165,000	(30,000)
Germany	125,000	50,000	75,000
United Kingdom	130,000	155,000	(25,000)
			$40,000

EXHIBIT 18.8

Flow of Teltrex's Net Cash Receipts from Transactions with External Parties with a Centralized Depository ($000)

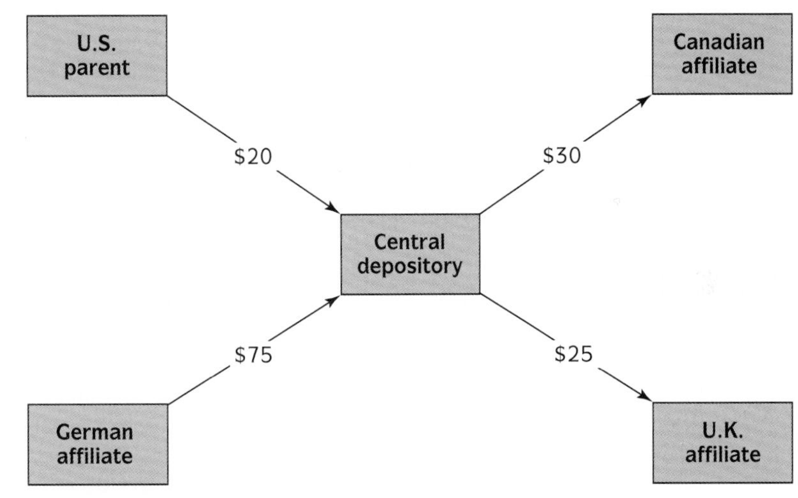

The benefits of a central cash depository derive mainly from the business transactions the affiliates have with external parties. Exhibit 18.7 presents a table showing the net amount of external receipts and disbursements each affiliate of Teltrex is expected to have during the week, as originally presented in Exhibit 18.1.

As Exhibit 18.7 shows, the U.S. parent expects to have net receipts of $20,000 by the end of the week. Analogously, in dollars, the German affiliate expects net receipts of $75,000. The Canadian affiliate expects a cash shortage of $30,000, and the U.K. affiliate expects a cash shortage of $25,000. In total, $40,000 of net receipts are expected for the MNC as a whole.

With a **centralized cash depository**, excess cash is remitted to the central cash pool. Analogously, the central cash manager arranges to cover shortages of cash. The central cash manager has a global view of the MNC's overall cash position and needs. Consequently, there is less of a chance for *mislocated funds*; that is, there is less of a chance for funds being denominated in the wrong currency. Moreover, because of his global perspective, the central cash manager will know the best borrowing and investing rates. A centralized system facilitates *funds mobilization*, where systemwide cash excesses are invested at the most advantageous rates and cash shortages are covered by borrowing at the most favorable rates. Without a centralized cash depository, one affiliate might end up borrowing locally at an unfavorable rate, while another is investing temporary surplus funds locally at a disadvantageous rate. Exhibit 18.8 diagrams the cash payments for Teltrex depicted in Exhibit 18.7, showing the flows to and from the central cash pool.

Exhibit 18.8 shows that the U.S. parent will remit $20,000 of excess cash from transactions with external parties to the central cash pool, and similarly, the German affiliate will remit the $75,000 it has obtained. Both the Canadian and U.K. affiliates will have their cash shortages of $30,000 and $25,000, respectively, covered by the central pool. In total, a net increase of $40,000 is expected at the central cash depository at the end of the week. The diagram shows that a total of $150,000 of cash is expected to flow to ($95,000) and from ($55,000) the cash depository.

SUPPLEMENTARY MATERIAL

BILATERAL NETTING OF INTERNAL AND EXTERNAL NET CASH FLOWS

Up to this point, we have handled the multilateral netting of interaffiliate cash flows (Exhibit 18.6) *and* the net receipts of the affiliates from the transactions with external parties (Exhibit 18.8) as two separate sets of cash flows through the central cash depository. While it was easier to develop the concepts in that manner, it is not necessary, practical, or efficient to do it that way in practice. Instead, the two sets of net cash flows can be bilaterally netted, with the resulting net sums going through the central depository. This will further reduce the number, size, and expense of foreign exchange transactions for the MNC. Exhibit 18.9 calculates the net amount of funds from Teltrex affiliates to flow through the central depository.

Exhibit 18.9 shows the result of netting the cash receipts that would flow through the central cash depository via multilateral netting with the net cash flows that would flow through the central depository as a result of external transactions. As the exhibit shows, the U.S. parent will receive a single payment from the cash pool of $35,000 and the Canadian affiliate will receive $15,000. The German affiliate will remit to the central depository $75,000 and the U.K. affiliate will remit $15,000. In total, the central depository receives $90,000 and disburses $50,000, for an expected net increase in cash of $40,000 for the week. Instead of two separate sets of cash flows totaling $55,000 from the multilateral netting and $150,000 from transactions with external parties, there is only one set of cash flows after the netting totaling $140,000. Thus, there is a savings on foreign exchange transactions of $65,000 for the week. Exhibit 18.10 diagrams the resulting $140,000 of cash flows for Teltrex that are calculated in Exhibit 18.9.

REDUCTION IN PRECAUTIONARY CASH BALANCES

An additional benefit of a centralized cash depository is that the MNC's investment in precautionary cash balances can be substantially reduced without a reduction in its ability to cover unforeseen expenses. To see how this is accomplished, consider the receipts and disbursements each affiliate of Teltrex expected to make with external parties during the week. Assume, for simplicity, that each affiliate will have to make *all* its planned payments to external parties before it receives any cash from other external sources. For example, from Exhibit 18.7, the Canadian affiliate expects to have to pay to external parties the equivalent of $165,000 before it receives any of the expected

EXHIBIT 18.9

Net Cash Flows of Teltrex Affiliates through the Central Cash Depository ($000)

Affiliate	Net Receipts from Multilateral Netting[a]	Net Excess Cash from Transactions with External Parties[b]	Net Flow[c]
United States	$55,000	$20,000	$35,000
Canada	($15,000)	($30,000)	$15,000
Germany	0	$75,000	($75,000)
United Kingdom	($40,000)	($25,000)	($15,000)
			($40,000)

[a]Net receipt from (payment to) the central depository resulting from multilateral netting, as shown in Exhibit 18.2.

[b]Net excess (shortage) of cash to be remitted to (covered by) the central depository, as shown in Exhibit 18.7.

[c]A positive amount in this column denotes a payment to an affiliate from the central cash depository; a negative amount denotes a payment from the affiliate.

EXHIBIT 18.10

Net Cash Flows of Teltrex Affiliates through the Central Cash Depository after Netting Multilateral Netting Payments and Net Payments from External Transactions ($000)

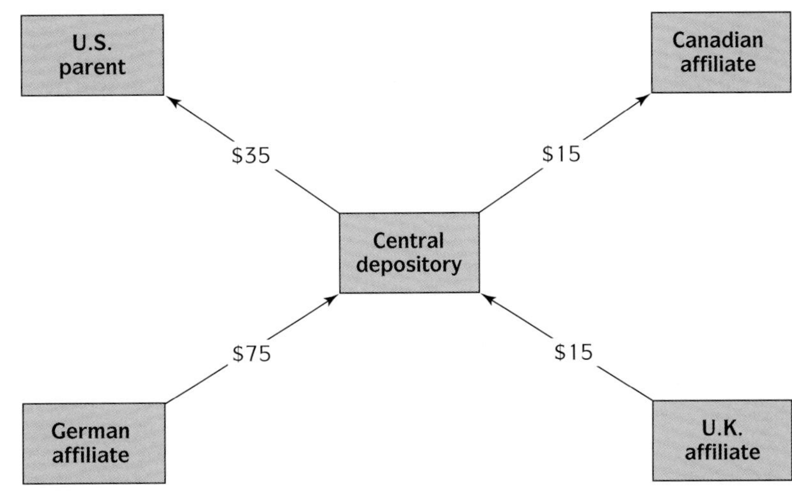

EXHIBIT 18.11

Transaction and Precautionary Cash Balances Held by Each Teltrex Affiliate under a Decentralized Cash Management System

Affiliate	Expected Transactions (a)	Standard Deviation (b)	Expected Needs plus Precautionary (a + 3b)
United States	$120,000	$50,000	$ 270,000
Canada	165,000	70,000	375,000
Germany	50,000	20,000	110,000
United Kingdom	155,000	65,000	350,000
Total	$490,000		$1,105,000

$135,000 in receipts. Thus, the Canadian affiliate will need a transactions balance of $165,000 to cover expected transactions.

As previously mentioned, a firm keeps a precautionary cash balance to cover unexpected transactions during the budget period. The size of this balance depends on how safe the firm desires to be in its ability to meet unexpected transactions. The larger the precautionary cash balance, the greater is the firm's ability to meet unexpected expenses, and the less is the risk of financial embarrassment and loss of credit standing. Assume that cash needs are normally distributed and that the cash needs of one affiliate are independent from the others. If Teltrex follows a conservative policy, it might keep three standard deviations of cash for precautionary purposes, in addition to the cash needed to cover expected transactions for the planning period. Thus, the probability that Teltrex would experience a cash shortage is only .13 of 1 percent; it will have sufficient cash to cover transactions 99.87 percent of the time.

Under a decentralized cash management system, each affiliate would hold its own transaction balance and precautionary cash. Exhibit 18.11 shows the total cash held for transactions and precautionary purposes by each affiliate and by Teltrex as a whole.

As can be seen from Exhibit 18.11, Teltrex needs the equivalent of $490,000 in cash to cover expected transactions and an additional $615,000 in precautionary balances to cover unexpected expenses, for a total of $1,105,000. A centralized cash management system will greatly reduce the investment in precautionary cash balances. Under a centralized system, the amount of cash held by the MNC is viewed as a portfolio. Each affiliate will continue to hold cash sufficient to cover its expected cash transactions, but the precautionary cash balances are held by the central cash manager at the central cash depository. In the event one of the affiliates experiences a cash shortage, funds would be wired from precautionary cash held in the central cash pool.

From portfolio theory, the standard deviation of the portfolio of cash held by the centralized depository for N affiliates is calculated as:[1]

$$\text{Portfolio Std. Dev.} = \sqrt{(\text{Std. Dev. Affiliate } 1)^2 + \cdots + (\text{Std. Dev. Affiliate } N)^2}$$

For our example,

$$\text{Portfolio Std. Dev.} = \sqrt{(\$50{,}000)^2 + (\$70{,}000)^2 + (\$20{,}000)^2 + (\$65{,}000)^2}$$

$$= \$109{,}659.$$

Thus under a centralized system, only \$328,977 (= 3 × \$109,659) needs to be held for precautionary purposes by Teltrex's central cash manager. A total of \$818,977 (= \$490,000 + \$328,977) is held by Teltrex. The reduction in precautionary cash balances under the centralized system is \$286,023 (= \$1,105,000 − \$818,977), a sum that most likely can be used more profitably elsewhere, rather than standing by as a potential safety net.

CASH MANAGEMENT SYSTEMS IN PRACTICE

Multilateral netting is an efficient and cost-effective mechanism for handling interaffiliate foreign exchange transactions. The United States, the United Kingdom, Canada, Germany, Switzerland, Hong Kong, and Singapore do not have any restrictions on netting.[2] Not all countries allow MNCs the freedom to net payments, however. Some countries, such as Belgium, the Netherlands, Italy, Ireland, and Finland, require permission (which is typically granted) to net payments. And other countries, such as Austria, the Philippines, and Spain, limit netting, allowing interaffiliate transactions to be settled only on a gross basis. That is, all receipts for a settlement period must be grouped into a single large receipt and all disbursements must be grouped into a single large payment. The reason for requiring gross settlement is precisely the opposite of the reason that MNCs desire to net. By limiting netting, more needless foreign exchange transactions flow through the local banking system, thus generating income for the local banks that handle them.

A study by Collins and Frankle (1985) surveyed the cash management practices of the *Fortune* 1000 firms. The researchers received a 22 percent response rate from their questionnaire. Of the responding firms, 163 were involved in international operations. Thirty-five percent of the international respondents reported using some type of intracorporate netting and 23 percent had centralized funds concentration.

In another study, Bokos and Clinkard (1983) found that the most frequently cited benefits of a multilateral netting system were:

1. The decrease in the expense associated with funds transfer, which in some cases can be over \$1,000 for a large international transfer of foreign exchange.
2. The reduction in the number of foreign exchange transactions and the associated cost of making fewer but larger transactions.
3. The reduction in intracompany float, which is frequently as high as five days even for wire transfers.
4. The savings in administrative time.
5. The benefits that accrue from the establishment of a formal information system, which serves as the foundation for centrally managing transaction exposure and the investment of excess funds.

Bokos and Clinkard note that several international banks offer multilateral netting software packages that calculate the net currency positions of each affiliate. Some packages integrate the netting function with foreign exchange exposure management. In a recent article, Srinivasin and Kim (1986) develop a sophisticated network optimization approach for netting interaffiliate cash payments that is computationally efficient and visually appealing.

The International Finance in Practice box on, page 448, illustrates the use of many of the cash management techniques discussed in the first part of this chapter.

TRANSFER PRICING AND RELATED ISSUES

Within a large business firm with multiple divisions, goods and services are frequently transferred from one division to another. The process brings into question the **transfer price** that should be assigned, for bookkeeping purposes, to the goods or services as they are transferred between divisions. Obviously, the higher the transfer price, the larger will be the gross profits of the transferring division relative to the receiving division. Even within a domestic firm, it is difficult to decide on the transfer price. Within a MNC, the decision is further compounded by exchange restrictions on the part of the host country where the receiving affiliate is located, a difference in income tax rates between the two countries, and import duties and quotas imposed by the host country.

ILLUSTRATED MINI CASE

Mintel Products Transfer Pricing Strategy

Low versus High Markup Policy

Mintel Products, Inc., manufactures goods for sale in the United States and overseas. Finished goods are transferred from the parent firm to its wholly owned sales affiliate for overseas retail sale. Mintel's financial manager, Hilary Van Kirk, has decided that the firm's transfer pricing strategy should be reevaluated as part of a routine review of the operations of the sales affiliate. Van Kirk has decided to explore both a low and a high markup policy. The analysis is to be done in U.S. dollars. She notes that both the parent firm and the sales affiliate have a 40 percent income tax rate, that the variable production cost of one unit is $1,500, and that the unit retail sales price charged by the sales affiliate to the final customer is $3,000. As a first step in her analysis, Van Kirk prepares Exhibit 18.12. The upper portion of the exhibit presents the analysis of a low markup policy, where the transfer price is set at $2,000. The lower portion of the exhibit analyzes the effect of a high markup policy, where the transfer price is $2,400 per unit.

Van Kirk notices from Exhibit 18.12 that the low markup policy results in larger pretax income, income taxes, and net income per unit in the selling country. On the other hand, the high markup policy has the opposite effect, that is, higher taxable income, income taxes, and net profit per unit in the manufacturing country. She also notes that because the income tax rates are the same in both countries, the consolidated results are identical regardless of whether the MNC follows a low or high transfer pricing scheme.

Exchange Restrictions

Van Kirk wonders if Mintel should be indifferent between the low and high markup policies, since the consolidated results are the same. She reasons, however, that if the distribution country imposes exchange restrictions limiting or blocking the amount of profits that can be repatriated to the manufacturing parent, Mintel would no longer be indifferent between the two markup policies. It obviously would prefer the high markup policy. According to Exhibit 18.12, the higher markup allows $240 per unit to be

INTERNATIONAL FINANCE IN PRACTICE

Disciplining European Cash: Currency Volatility Spurs Proactive Cash Management

Since 1992, international executives have focused mainly on adapting currency management techniques to the more volatile, riskier foreign-exchange market. But there's another, more subtle lesson to be learned from the new turbulence in currency markets: Sloppy cash management in Europe has become an unaffordable luxury.

This has not gone unnoticed. Many U.S. companies operating in Europe are seriously rethinking their cash management policies. Financial managers are more aware than ever of the need to monitor European cash positions closely. "The events of the last year have been a wake-up call," says Leonard Stolk, vice president at ABN AMRO Bank N.V. in Amsterdam. This is particularly true for U.S. and Asian firms.

Getting informed

The biggest reaction of rudely awakened senior executives has been to start managing cash proactively. For that to work, companies must have timely, comprehensive information on European cash positions. Many multinationals are therefore moving to centralize cash management, introducing more precision in handling and tracking cash positions, relying more on local-currency borrowing, and accelerating the remittance schedule of overseas cash balances.

John Perrotti, vice president and controller at Gleason Corp., readily acknowledges the "need to be more proactive in foreign exchange and cash management." Gleason, a $150 million Rochester, N.Y., multinational, derives more than two-thirds of its revenues from overseas. In 1992 only 32 percent of Gleason's revenues were generated in the Americas (South America included), with the remainder in Europe (25 percent of total) and the Asia-Pacific region. Gleason has machine-parts manufacturing, sales and service operations in the U.K., Germany, Italy and Belgium; it is setting up a direct affiliate in Spain (switching over from a local dealer).

"More and more of our European customers pay in their local currency," says Mr. Perrotti. This plus the currency markets' new volatility has increased Gleason's exposure and risk, making more disciplined cash management a must. "Our policy is to repatriate as much as we can," says Mr. Perrotti.

Last year cash from the U.K. operation was brought back to the U.S. as dividends at an exchange rate locked in at $1.90. (The rest of the European subs are either cash break-even or net debtors.) "That generated net savings to the company of $2 million," says Mr. Perrotti. Cash is not remitted blindly, however. Other factors, such as a sub's cash needs vs. cash needs in the U.S. and the tax impact, are also carefully considered.

Gleason has further shifted to using local borrowing facilities to help tighten cash management. With European interest rates more fluid, "we borrow more in the local currencies," says Mr. Perrotti. "We're also becoming more

repatriated to the parent that otherwise may have been blocked. This amount represents the $400 higher markup minus the $160 additional taxes paid in the parent country.

Van Kirk notes that the low markup policy is disadvantageous from the host country's perspective. If the transferring affiliate attempts to reposition funds by changing from the low to the high markup policy, the exchange controls have been partially bypassed and there is a loss of tax revenue in the host country. Thus, the host country may take measures to enforce a certain transfer price. She decides she needs to brush up on how this might be accomplished and also to consider the effect of a difference in income tax rates between the two affiliates.

Differential Income Tax Rates

As a second step, Van Kirk prepares Exhibit 18.13, which examines the low versus high markup policies when the tax rate in the transferring country is assumed to be 25 percent, or 15 percent less than the marginal tax rate of 40 percent in the receiving country.

Van Kirk notes from Exhibit 18.13 that the consolidated *taxable* income is $1,100 under both markup policies. However, Mintel would no longer be indifferent when sensitive to local sourcing as a way of protecting local revenue flows."

Speedy repatriation

Advanced Logic Research, a $230 million Irvine, Calif., company, has also accelerated its remittance schedule. The company has two subsidiaries, in the U.K. and Germany, plus sales and marketing affiliates throughout Europe. Sales to the continent account for some 20 percent of the total, according to treasurer Vick Sial. Since all manufacturing is done in the U.S., Advanced Logic has no foreign cost structure to offset local-currency revenue naturally. So cash balances are remitted quickly to the U.S. in the form of intercompany payments to prevent a buildup of cash pools in volatile currencies.

But accelerated remittance is often easier said than done, since trade terms and collections practices can vary dramatically from one country to another. To speed up repatriation, companies must become familiar with each subsidiary's cash management environment, advises Dan Perkins, manager of Arthur Andersen's treasury consulting practice. For example, a company may have subsidiaries in the U.K., France and Italy. The U.S. parent sells product to the subs on 30-day terms. They then sell the product to local customers on 30-day terms in the U.K., 60-day in France, and 180-day in Italy. At the end of the 30-day period, the parent does not see the cash from the Italian and French subs and is effectively financing them and their customers.

"The U.S. parent can do one of two things," says Mr. Perkins. It can extend its own credit terms to match local market practice or require payment in 30 days and force the sub to borrow locally to finance its sales. The latter allows quick remittance of the funds back to the U.S.

Borrowing dollars may be cheaper in absolute terms, but there are benefits to setting up foreign credit facilities. (In any event, the interest expense should be factored into the subsidiary's margins and pricing to give the parent a true picture of profitability.) Local banking relations are a big step in developing the company's European business. Plus, the local-currency borrowing can act as a natural offset to local-currency revenues in case of devaluation.

The next generation

The sophistication of cash management is often a function of the size of the cash flow. Nordson Corp. of Westlake, Ohio, has taken proactive cash management a step further by instituting an intracompany netting system. The system, which senior treasury analyst Neechu Mei put in place two years ago, has helped the $600 million (60 percent international) machinery manufacturer to navigate the storm in the European currency markets.

How? It has developed a steady, centralized flow of information. The company has subsidiaries in almost every Western European country. That means its cash position is supersensitive to "rock and roll" currencies. "Subsidiaries file a monthly cash report," explains Ms. Mei. The report shows each sub's net cash position. Intracompany invoices are netted once a month. The U.S. parent buys and sells the local currencies, using forward contracts to hedge.

The netting system reduces the company's transaction cost, but more important, it allows Ms. Mei to monitor subsidiary exposure closely. It also enables the U.S. parent to use a system of intercompany loans to reduce the cost of borrowing. The monthly cash reports are studied carefully at the central treasury. If a large position is being accumulated, the parent can move it where it is most needed or remit it to the U.S.

Source: Excerpted from Nilly Landau, "Disciplining European Cash: Currency Volatility Spurs Protective Cash Management," *International Business*, December 1993, pp. 30 and 32. Used by permission.

there is a differential in the income tax rates. In the absence of governmental restrictions on the transfer price, the MNC would prefer a high markup policy when the tax rate in the parent country is lower than the tax rate in the receiving country. Consolidated net income for Mintel would be $60 [= ($2,000 − 2,400) × (.25 − .40)] per unit greater under the high versus the low markup policy. The high markup policy results in $400 per unit of taxable income being shifted from the receiving country to the transferring country, where it is taxed at a 15 percent lower rate. Consequently, the consolidated income taxes paid by Mintel drop from $395 to $335 per unit.

If the tax rate in the receiving country is lower than in the parent country, it is not clear that a low markup policy should be pursued. Van Kirk recalls that U.S. MNCs are taxed on their worldwide income. Hence, income repatriated to the U.S. parent from a receiving country with a low tax rate would be "grossed up" to its pretax amount so that U.S. taxes could be figured. A credit for the taxes paid in the receiving country would be given against taxes owed in the United States. Thus, pursuing a low markup policy would not result in a dollar tax savings if net income was to be repatriated. However, if the net income of the foreign subsidiary was to be reinvested in the host country, the low markup policy would result in a tax savings and allow more funds for

EXHIBIT 18.12

Low versus High Transfer Pricing Strategy between Mintel Affiliates with the Same Income Tax Rate

	Manufacturing Affiliate	Sales Affiliate	Consolidated Company
Low Markup Policy			
Sales revenue	$2,000	$3,000	$3,000
Cost of goods sold	1,500	2,000	1,500
Gross profit	500	1,000	1,500
Operating expenses	200	200	400
Taxable income	300	800	1,100
Income taxes (40%)	120	320	440
Net income	180	480	660
High Markup Policy			
Sales revenue	$2,400	$3,000	$3,000
Cost of goods sold	1,500	2,400	1,500
Gross profit	900	600	1,500
Operating expenses	200	200	400
Taxable income	700	400	1,100
Income taxes (40%)	280	160	440
Net income	420	240	660

reinvestment. Nevertheless, this would only be temporary, Van Kirk reasons. At some point, profitable investment opportunities would be exhausted, and the parent firm and its stockholders would desire some return on the investment made—and this means repatriation.

Regulations Affecting Transfer Prices

Van Kirk believes that governmental authorities within a host country would be quite aware of the motives of MNCs to use transfer pricing schemes to move blocked funds or evade tax liabilities. After doing some research, she learns that most countries have regulations controlling transfer prices. In the United States, Section 482: Allocation of Income and Deductions Among Taxpayers of the U.S. Internal Revenue Code stipulates that the transfer price must reflect an *arm's-length price*, that is, a price the selling affiliate would charge an unrelated customer for the good or service. The Internal Revenue Service (IRS) . . . "may distribute, apportion, or allocate gross income, deductions, credits, or allowances between or among such organizations . . . [if it is] necessary in order to prevent evasion of taxes or clearly to reflect the income of any such organizations . . ." Moreover, in the event of conflict, the burden of proof lies with the taxpayer to show that the IRS has unreasonably established the transfer price and determined taxable income.

She learns that there are three basic methods prescribed by the IRS, and recognized internationally, for establishing arm's-length prices of tangible goods. The method considered the best is to use a *comparable uncontrolled price* between unrelated firms. While this method seems reasonable and theoretically sound, it is difficult to use in practice because many factors enter into the pricing of goods and services between two business enterprises. The Code allows for some adjustments because differences in the terms of sale, the quantity sold, quality differences, and the date of sale are all factors that can realistically affect the sale price among various customers. Thus, what is a reasonable price for one customer may not be reasonable for another. The next best method is the *resale price* approach, which can be used if, among other things, there is no comparable uncontrolled sales price. Under this method, the price at which the good is resold by the distribution affiliate is reduced by an amount sufficient to cover overhead costs and a reasonable profit. However, it may be difficult to determine the value added by the distribution affiliate. The third method is the *cost-plus* approach, where an appropriate profit is added to the cost of the manufacturing affiliate. This method

EXHIBIT 18.13

Low versus High Transfer Pricing Strategy between Mintel Affiliates with Differential Income Tax Rates

	Manufacturing Affiliate	Sales Affiliate	Consolidated Company
Low Markup Policy			
Sales revenue	$2,000 →	$3,000	$3,000
Cost of goods sold	1,500	→ 2,000	1,500
Gross profit	500	1,000	1,500
Operating expenses	200	200	400
Taxable income	300	800	1,100
Income taxes (25%/40%)	75	320	395
Net income	225	480	705
High Markup Policy			
Sales revenue	$2,400 →	$3,000	$3,000
Cost of goods sold	1,500	→ 2,400	1,500
Gross profit	900	600	1,500
Operating expenses	200	200	400
Taxable income	700	400	1,100
Income taxes (25%/40%)	175	160	335
Net income	525	240	765

assumes that the manufacturing cost is readily accountable. Additionally, a group of methods collectively referred to as *fourth methods* can be applied to approximate arm's-length prices when the three basic methods are not applicable. The fourth methods include those based on financial and economic models and econometric techniques. The comparable uncontrolled price method and fourth methods are used for determining an arm's-length transfer price for intangible goods, whereas cost methods are used for pricing services.

The Organization for Economic Co-Operation and Development Model Tax Convention sets out the same methods as the IRS Code for use by member countries. Van Kirk concludes that all methods present operational difficulties of some type and are also difficult for the taxing authority to evaluate. Thus, transfer pricing manipulation cannot be completely controlled and the potential exists for maneuverability by the MNC to reposition funds or reduce its tax liability.

The International Finance in Practice box on pages 454–456 discusses the complexities MNCs face in attempting to satisfy governmental authorities in transfer pricing disputes.

Import Duties

After some reflection, Van Kirk concludes that import duties are another factor that need to be considered. When a host country imposes an *ad valorem* import duty on goods shipped across its borders from another country, the import tax raises the cost of doing business within the country. An ad voloreum duty is a percentage tax levied at customs on the assessed value of the imported goods. She reasons that an import tax will affect the transfer pricing strategy a MNC uses, but that in general, the income tax will have the greatest after-tax effect on consolidated net income. To analyze the effect of an import duty on Mintel, she prepares Exhibit 18.14, which shows the low versus high transfer price alternatives presented in Exhibit 18.13 with the imposition of a 5 percent import duty by the receiving country.

Comparison of Exhibits 18.13 and 18.14 shows Van Kirk that under the low markup policy, Mintel would receive $60 less (= $645 − 705) per unit if a 5 percent import duty was imposed by the host country. The $60 represents the after-tax cost of the $100 import duty on the $2,000 per unit transfer price cost of the good. Mintel would still prefer the high markup policy as before, however, as it results in an increase

EXHIBIT 18.14

Low versus High Transfer Pricing Strategy between Mintel Affiliates with Differential Income Tax Rates and a 5 Percent Import Duty

	Manufacturing Affiliate	Sales Affiliate	Consolidated Company
Low Markup Policy			
Sales revenue	$2,000	$3,000	$3,000
Cost of goods sold	1,500	2,000	1,500
Import duty (5%)	—	100	100
Gross profit	500	900	1,400
Operating expenses	200	200	400
Taxable income	300	700	1,000
Income taxes (25%/40%)	75	280	355
Net income	225	420	645
High Markup Policy			
Sales revenue	$2,400	$3,000	$3,000
Cost of goods sold	1,500	2,400	1,500
Import duty (5%)	—	120	120
Gross profit	900	480	1,380
Operating expenses	200	200	400
Taxable income	700	280	980
Income taxes (25%/40%)	175	112	287
Net income	525	168	693

in net income from $645 to $693 per unit. The difference in the net incomes between the two markup policies is only $48, in comparison to $60 without the 5 percent import tax. The loss of $12 represents the after-tax cost of an additional $20 of import duty per unit when the transfer price is $2,400 instead of $2,000 per unit.

Unbundling Fund Transfers

As Van Kirk knows, host countries are well aware of transfer pricing schemes used by MNCs to evade taxes within its borders or to avoid exchange restrictions. She wonders if there are ways to avoid suspicion from host country governmental authorities, and the administrative hassle likely to arise from such an inquiry, when the firm is merely trying to repatriate a sufficient amount of funds from a foreign affiliate to make the investment worthwhile. To learn more about transfer pricing strategies and related issues, she decides to attend a one-day seminar on the topic she saw advertised by a professional organization to which she belongs. She hopes it is beneficial, as the registration fee is $500 for the day!

As it turns out the money was well spent. In addition to making the acquaintance of financial managers from other companies, one thing Van Kirk learned at the conference was that a MNC is likely to fare better if, instead of lumping all costs into a single transfer price, the parent firm unbundled the package to recognize the cost of the physical good and each service separately that it provides the affiliate. A detailing of the charges makes it easier, if ever necessary, to present and support to the taxing authority of a host country that each charge is legitimate and can be well substantiated. For instance, in addition to charging for the cost of the physical good, the parent firm could charge a fee for technical training of the affiliate's staff, a share of the cost of worldwide advertising or other corporate overhead, or a royalty or licensing fee as payment for use of well-recognized brand names, technology, or patents. The royalty or licensing fee represents remuneration for expense previously incurred by the parent for development or having made the product one that is desirable to own.

As a final step in her analysis, Van Kirk prepares Exhibit 18.15, which reproduces the low versus high markup policy analysis for Mintel with differential income tax rates presented in Exhibit 18.13. In addition, Exhibit 18.15 shows that a $2,000 transfer price and $400 per unit charge for royalties and fees results in the same consolidated

EXHIBIT 18.15

Low versus High Transfer Pricing Strategy for Mintel with Low Transfer Price and Additional Royalty Charge with Differential Income Tax Rates

	Manufacturing Affiliate	Sales Affiliate	Consolidated Company
Low Markup Policy			
Sales revenue	$2,000	$3,000	$3,000
Cost of goods sold	1,500	2,000	1,500
Gross profit	500	1,000	1,500
Operating expenses	200	200	400
Taxable income	300	800	1,100
Income taxes (25%/40%)	75	320	395
Net income	225	480	705
High Markup Policy			
Sales revenue	$2,400	$3,000	$3,000
Cost of goods sold	1,500	2,400	1,500
Gross profit	900	600	1,500
Operating expenses	200	200	400
Taxable income	700	400	1,100
Income taxes (25%/40%)	175	160	335
Net income	525	240	765
Low Markup Policy and Royalty			
Sales revenue	$2,000	$3,000	$3,000
Royalty and fee income	400	—	—
Cost of goods sold	1,500	2,400	1,500
Gross profit	900	600	1,500
Operating expenses	200	200	400
Taxable income	700	400	1,100
Income taxes (25%/40%)	175	160	335
Net income	525	240	765

net income of $765 as does the high markup policy with a $2,400 transfer price. By comparison, the low markup policy only provides $705 per unit consolidated net income. This is the case, regardless of whether a portion of the $480 net income of the sales affiliate is repatriated to the manufacturing affiliate as a dividend, because the tax rate in the distribution country is higher. As Van Kirk learned at the conference, the strategy of recognizing specific services may be acceptable to the host government, whereas the high markup policy may not, if $2,400 appears to be more than an arm's-length price for the transferred good. ◗

Miscellaneous Factors

Transfer pricing strategies may be beneficial when the host country restricts the amount of foreign exchange that can be used for importing specific goods. In this event, a lower transfer price allows a greater quantity of the good to be imported under a quota restriction. This may be a more important consideration than income tax savings, if the imported item is a necessary component needed by an assembly or manufacturing affiliate to continue or expand production.

Transfer prices also have an effect on how divisions of a MNC are perceived locally. A high markup policy leaves little net income to show on the affiliate's books. If the parent firm expects the affiliate to be able to borrow short-term funds locally in the event of a cash shortage, the affiliate may have difficulty doing so with unimpressive financial statements. On the other hand, a low markup policy makes it appear, at least superficially, as if affiliates, rather than the parent firm, are contributing a larger portion to consolidated earnings. To the extent that financial markets are

INTERNATIONAL FINANCE IN PRACTICE

Taking Shelter As Congress Ponders New Tax Breaks, Firms Already Find Plenty

WASHINGTON—Congress is putting the final touches on a bill that would award corporate America billions of dollars in new tax breaks. But corporate America has already found plenty of breaks in current tax laws.

Thirteen years after Congress passed a tax-reform law intended to make every company pay its fair share, government and corporate records show that many profitable U.S. corporations are again paying little or no federal income tax.

The top federal income-tax rate for corporations is 35%. On paper. Yet even as they brag to shareholders about rising profits, companies are finding legal ways to reduce the amount of pretax income they report to the Internal Revenue Service. They establish financial subsidiaries in tax havens. They indulge in tax shelters so complex government auditors can't always understand them. They shift profits to low-tax countries by manipulating prices when doing business with their own overseas branches. And they take full advantage of the tax breaks that Congress has awarded over the years, while dispatching lobbyists to plead for still more.

Scot-free

Out of 2.3 million U.S. corporations, more than half paid no federal income tax at all between 1989 and 1995, according to a General Accounting Office study using the most recent IRS data available. Many of these were mom-and-pop operations. But four of every 10 companies with more than $250 million in assets or $50 million in gross receipts paid less than $100,000 to Uncle Sam in 1995. "You could probably make the case that a lot of small companies don't make much money," says Sen. Byron Dorgan, a North Dakota Democrat who has made a pet cause out of fighting corporate tax avoidance. "But it's pretty hard to make the case that a lot of large companies aren't making a lot of money."

Yet that's exactly the case many large companies are trying to make to the IRS, at a time when the U.S. is enjoying an extended economic boom and the stock market is constantly flirting with new records. Sure, after long years of deficits, the economy is producing big federal budget surpluses—$3 trillion projected over the next decade. But the bulk of that revenue is coming from individuals, not companies. "Revenues in general have really been skyrocketing, and the big action has been on the individual side," says Alan Auerbach, professor of law and economics at the University of California at Berkeley. "If you ask how much of this surplus has been on the corporate side, the answer is not much."

Tax bills

Annual federal revenue from personal income taxes is up 60% over the past six years, while revenue from corporate income taxes has increased just 30%. For the five years through calendar 1998, the government calculates that corporate profits increased 43%.

Companies aren't satisfied, though. In the $792 billion tax-cut bill the House just passed, corporate lobbyists have persuaded lawmakers to include $100 billion in tax cuts for business over 10 years. The Senate bill has about $50 billion in tax cuts for corporate America over 10 years.

One break, estimated to cut corporate tax bills by a total of $25 billion over a decade, would let global companies deduct from their U.S. returns more of the interest they pay abroad. Another, which would save companies $10 billion over the next 10 years and even more after being fully implemented in 2009, would repeal the corporate alternative-minimum tax. That tax was established in its current form in 1986 to make sure that profitable companies pay at least some taxes even if they have lots of deductions and credits.

Archer's view

Texas GOP Rep. Bill Archer, chairman of the House Ways and Means Committee, is skeptical that profitable corporations are really getting off easy. The alternative-minimum tax, he says, is a "job destroyer" because it punishes growing companies by making them pay taxes even if they deserve deductions for buying new equipment. And, he argues, reducing the tax burden on U.S.-based multinationals would make them less likely to merge with foreign companies and move their headquarters overseas, where they would pay even less to the IRS.

"If we don't do something to prevent our corporations from being gobbled up by foreign companies, we'll surely end up with less tax revenues," Mr. Archer says.

But the fact is that companies these days are already paying a smaller share of their profits to the federal government—31% in 1998, compared with 41% in 1989, the peak of the last business cycle, according to data in the newest Economic Report of the President.

That doesn't mean they are doing anything illegal. For the most part, executives are just using every bit of flexibility in the tax code to maximize their write-offs and minimize their taxable income, even as they play up their profits to investors.

Few companies release tax returns to the public. In annual reports, however, they tell shareholders how much they made before taxes and how much federal tax they must pay immediately, figures the GAO uses to calculate a company's effective tax rate. Although it's an imperfect method, the GAO considers it the most accurate because it excludes taxes that the companies report to shareholders, but can put off paying for years.

Take General Motors Corp., the largest corporation in the U.S. as measured by revenue. It reported $4.61 billion in worldwide pretax income in its 1998 annual report. "Your company is in better financial shape than it has been in many years," Chairman John F. Smith Jr. assured shareholders in June. But for 1998, the auto maker owed the IRS just $36 million—0.8% of its global pretax income. The same year, GM paid about two-thirds that much in compensation to Mr. Smith and his four top lieutenants—a total of $23.9 million for their salaries, bonuses, stock options and other remuneration.

Why was GM's tax bill so small? First, the company paid lots of taxes overseas, which can be credited against U.S. taxes. "When the day is done, we pay taxes that are equivalent to a statutory U.S. tax rate," says Mark Tanner, a GM spokesman. "We pay taxes to various governments overseas, and we're allowed to take credits for that. It's very difficult to compare a global company like GM to an individual company or individual person who has all of his or her operations or income in the U.S."

Indeed, GM reported to its shareholders that 27% of its pretax income—$1.23 billion—came from U.S. operations last year, although more than half of its car and truck production was here. (Mr. Tanner points out that vehicle-output figures ignore other GM businesses such as locomotives and financial services.) But only 13% of GM's current tax payments for 1998 went to federal, state or local tax collectors. The rest was paid to foreign governments. The company told shareholders it paid only 2.9% of U.S. profits to the federal government in current taxes.

Then there's the difference between the amount the company reported to its shareholders, whom it wants to impress with high profits, and the amount the company reported to the IRS, which it hopes to keep at bay. GM won't release its tax returns. But, among other things, such differences usually reflect the fact that tax laws allow companies to write off investments in equipment more rapidly than shareholder accounting methods do. In GM's case, there were also tax credits left over from the early 1990s, when the company ran huge losses and logged large employee-benefit payments on its books. GM won't say how much of a credit it claimed for those or other items in 1998.

GM points out that on top of the tax payments it made last year, it owed $145 million that it was allowed to defer. Assuming it eventually pays those taxes, it effective tax rate would rise to 14.7% for last year. But money paid tomorrow doesn't hurt as much as money paid today. To have $145 million for the IRS five years from now, for example, GM would need to set aside just $114 million now in an investment paying 5% interest.

Delay and accelerate

Congress has intentionally created ways for companies to put off tax payments and to collect tax credits that reduce future IRS bills. The tax code also lets companies take deductions for using up their equipment faster than it actually ages, a practice called accelerated depreciation.

Enron Corp. had $197 million of pretax income from its U.S. operations last year but, because of a variety of tax strategies, owed just 15% of that to the federal government. The company also had deferred tax credits, which reduced its effective federal tax rate to 8%. (Deferred credits, of course, are worth less than current credits, the same way deferred taxes hurt less than current taxes.) "Any taxpayer—a company or an individual—is going to make sure they pay what is legally required and not more," says Steve Kean, an Enron executive vice president.

"A company like ours that is making significant investments and is growing substantially is going to see lower effective tax rates," Mr. Kean continues. "But those investments and the growth they produce certainly add to the tax base and create additional tax revenues in the long run."

The corporate provisions of the 1986 Tax Reform Act passed partly because of popular outrage over reports that some big companies were paying less in taxes than their janitors were paying. Robert McIntyre, director of Citizens for Tax Justice, a group funded partly by organized labor, attracted a lot of media attention at the time with a report showing that 128 out of 250 large, profitable companies paid no federal income tax at all.

Tax reform lowered the top tax rates for companies and individuals, but eliminated many loopholes that the wealthy and corporations had used to avoid paying the statutory rates. The top corporate income-tax rate was lowered to 34% from 46%, then raised to 35% in 1993.

The reform has had some effect; corporate rate income taxes will provide 10% of total federal revenue this fiscal year, up from 8% in 1986.

But corporate tax payments aren't keeping pace with corporate profits, and critics of the system argue that a major reason is that companies are becoming more global, creating vast opportunities to shift to lower-tax countries, while moving their tax deductions to the U.S.

Transfer pricing

One way to do this is by playing with the price that one branch of the company charges another branch for goods and services. Say a U.S.-based company makes computers with parts from its subsidiary in a low-tax East Asian country. It can reduce its reported U.S. income—and increase its subsidiary's profit—by overpaying for those components. Or it can undercharge for exports to its overseas operations. Either way, the overall company can

(continued)

show a healthy profit while telling the IRS that not much of it is earned in the U.S.

Since overseas profits are taxed only when they come back to the U.S., the company can put off paying a chunk of its federal tax bill. And foreign companies with U.S. subsidiaries can minimize U.S. taxes because their non-U.S. profits aren't subject to U.S. tax.

The IRS estimates that transfer-pricing abuses cost the government $2.8 billion in lost revenue each year. Other estimates are much higher. Finance professors John S. Zdanowicz and Simon J. Pak of Florida International University in Miami believe that such methods led to $35.6 billion in lost federal revenue in 1998, with more companies joining the party each year. "Now that we've become a global economy, the idea is to shift income to countries where the net impact is to pay the lowest taxes," says Prof. Zdanowicz.

Tax watchers debate the accuracy of Florida International's lost-revenue estimates, but the study's anecdotal evidence is eye-catching. Combing through anonymous Customers records, the researchers found $18,000 dot-matrix printers being imported from Japan and $2,600 radial tires coming from Indonesia. And somebody in the U.S. is exporting $12,000 helicopters to Italy and $135 howitzers to South Africa.

Corporations also take advantage of federal rules that let them shift profits to financial subsidiaries set up in low-tax locales such as Liechtenstein. The practice came about in 1996 after the Treasury allowed companies to choose whether a distant financial subsidiary would be considered part of the U.S. operation or part of a foreign branch. Treasury officials didn't foresee that this allowed U.S. companies to shift income to the financing unit, minimizing both U.S. and foreign taxes.

Here's how it typically works: The U.S. company sets up a financing arm, called a hybrid, in Liechtenstein, and tells the IRS that for U.S. tax purposes, it is part of the company's German manufacturing operation. The Liechtenstein company lends money to the German subsidiary at a very high interest rate, in essence moving some German profits to Liechtenstein. German authorities tax only the German subsidiary, as does the U.S. The profits in Liechtenstein escape high tax rates and still show up on the parent corporation's bottom line for shareholders. Treasury officials have tried to close the loophole, but the agency backed down last month under pressure from Congress and lobbyists.

Congressional staffers estimate that the practice will cost the government $10 billion over 10 years. "This thing is new and a lot of companies aren't doing it yet," says Mr. McIntyre of Citizens for Tax Justice. "But they're all going to do it if it works."

In the post-tax-reform world, companies are finding all sorts of complex new tax shelters, whose legality is tested only if IRS auditors can find them in corporate tax returns. "The proliferation of corporate tax shelters presents an unacceptable and growing level of tax-avoidance behavior," the Treasury said in a recent study.

Companies know that the safest tax savings come from Congress itself, and, with tax-reform enthusiasm fading, lawmakers are again bestowing valuable favors on business. The House bill, which President Clinton has vowed to veto, is bedecked with narrow tax breaks for companies that produce everything from plastic fishing-tackle boxes to steel. House and Senate negotiators will try to come up with a compromise this week.

But business lobbyists would have liked more than either the House or the Senate provides. Explains Dorothy Coleman, tax-policy director for the National Association of Manufacturers: "We thought that with the surpluses as large as projected, about one-third of the tax cuts should go to business."

Source: Michael M. Phillips, "Taking Shelter," *The Wall Street Journal,* August 4, 1999, pp. A1ff. Reprinted by permission of *The Wall Street Journal.* © 1999 Dow Jones & Company, Inc. All rights reserved worldwide.

inefficient, or securities analysts do not understand the transfer pricing strategy being used, the market value of the MNC may be lower than is justified.

Obviously, transfer pricing strategies have an effect on international capital expenditure analysis. A very low (high) markup policy makes the APV of a subsidiary's capital expenditure appear more (less) attractive. Consequently, in order to obtain a meaningful analysis, arm's-length pricing should be used in the APV analysis to determine after-tax operating income, regardless of the actual transfer price employed. A separate term in the APV analysis can be used to recognize tax-savings from transfer pricing strategies. This was the recommended approach detailed in Chapter 17.

BLOCKED FUNDS

For a variety of reasons, a country may find itself short of foreign currency reserves, and thus impose exchange restrictions on its own currency, limiting its conversion into other currencies so as not to further reduce scarce foreign currency reserves. When a country enforces exchange controls, the remittance of profits from a subsidiary firm to its foreign parent is blocked. The blockage may be only temporary, or it may be for a considerable period of time. A lengthy blockage is detrimental to a MNC. Without the ability to repatriate profits from a foreign subsidiary, the MNC might as well not even have the investment as returns are not being paid to the stockholders of the MNC.

Prior to making a capital investment in a foreign subsidiary, the parent firm should investigate the potential of future funds blockage. This is part of the capital expenditure analysis outlined in Chapter 17. The APV framework developed in that chapter only considers the expected operating cash flows that are available for repatriation.

Unexpected funds blockage after an investment has been made, however, is a political risk with which the MNC must contend. Thus, the MNC should be familiar with methods for moving blocked funds so as to benefit its stockholders. Several methods for moving blocked funds have already been discussed in this chapter and others. For example, transfer pricing strategies and unbundling services are methods the MNC might be able to use to move otherwise blocked funds. These methods were covered earlier in this chapter. Parallel and back-to-back loans discussed in Chapter 10 may also be used to reposition blocked funds. Moreover, in Chapter 13, leading and lagging of payments were discussed primarily as a means of controlling transaction exposure. However, leading and lagging payments may be used as a strategy for repositioning funds within a MNC. Additional strategies that may be useful for moving blocked funds are *export creation* and *direct negotiation*.

Export creation involves using the blocked funds of a subsidiary in the country in which they are blocked to pay for exports that can be used to benefit the parent firm or other affiliates. Thus, instead of using repatriated funds to pay for goods or services that will benefit the MNC, blocked funds are used. Examples include: using consulting firms located in the host country where funds are blocked, instead of a firm in the parent country, to provide necessary consulting work that benefits the MNC; transferring personnel from corporate headquarters to the subsidiary offices where they will be paid in the blocked local currency; using the national airlines of the host country when possible for the international travel of all MNC executives, where the reservations and fare payments are made by the subsidiary; and holding business conferences in the host country, instead of elsewhere, where the expenses are paid by the local subsidiary. All of these possibilities not only benefit the MNC, since these goods and services are needed, but they also benefit various industries within the host country.

Host countries desire to attract foreign industries that will most benefit their economic development and the technical skills of its citizens. Thus, foreign investment in the host country in industries that produce export goods, such as automobiles or electronic equipment, or in industries that will attract tourists, such as resort hotels, is desirable. This type of investment provides good employment and training for the country's citizens and is also a source, rather than a use, of foreign exchange. The host country should not expect a MNC to make beneficial investment within its borders if it is not likely to receive an appropriate return. Consequently, MNCs in desirable industries may be able to convince the host country government through direct negotiation that funds blockage is detrimental to all.

SUMMARY

This chapter discussed cash management in the multinational firm. Special attention was given to the topics of multilateral netting and transfer pricing policy. Illustrated case problems were used to show the benefits of centralized cash management and to examine transfer pricing strategies.

1. A multilateral netting system is beneficial in reducing the number of and the expense associated with interaffiliate foreign exchange transactions.

2. A centralized cash pool assists in reducing the problem of mislocated funds and in funds mobilization. A central cash manager has a global view of the most favorable borrowing rates and most advantageous investment rates.
3. A centralized cash management system with a cash pool can reduce the investment the MNC has in precautionary cash balances, saving the firm money.
4. Transfer pricing strategies are a means to reposition funds within a MNC and a possible technique for reducing tax liabilities and removing blocked funds from a host country that has imposed foreign exchange restrictions.
5. Unbundling fund transfers, export creation, and direct negotiation are other means for removing blocked funds from a host country that is enforcing foreign exchange restrictions.

KEY WORDS

bilateral netting, 441
cash budget, 439
cash management, 438
centralized cash depository, 443
multilateral netting, 441
netting center, 441
precautionary cash balances, 438
transaction balances, 438
transfer price, 447

QUESTIONS

1. Describe the key factors contributing to effective cash management within a firm. Why is the cash management process more difficult in a MNC?
2. Discuss the pros and cons of a MNC having a centralized cash manager handle all investment and borrowing for all affiliates of the MNC versus each affiliate having a local manager who performs the cash management activities of the affiliate.
3. How might a MNC use transfer pricing strategies? How do import duties affect transfer pricing policies?
4. What are the various means the taxing authority of a country might use to determine if a transfer price is *reasonable*?
5. Discuss how a MNC might attempt to repatriate blocked funds from a host country.

PROBLEMS

1. Affiliate A sells 5,000 units to Affiliate B per year. The marginal income tax rate for Affiliate A is 25 percent and the marginal income tax rate for Affiliate B is 40 percent. The transfer price per unit is currently \$2,000, but it can be set at any level between \$2,000 and \$2,400. Derive a formula to determine how much annual after-tax profits can be increased by selecting the optimal transfer price.
2. Affiliate A sells 5,000 units to Affiliate B per year. The marginal income tax rate for Affiliate A is 25 percent and the marginal income tax rate for Affiliate B is 40 percent. Additionally, Affiliate B pays a tax-deductible tariff of 5 percent on imported merchandise. The transfer price per unit is currently \$2,000, but it can be set at any level between \$2,000 and \$2,400. Derive (a) a formula to determine the effective marginal tax rate for Affiliate B and, (b) a formula to determine how much annual after-tax profits can be increased by selecting the optimal transfer price.

MINI CASE 1

Efficient Funds Flow at Eastern Trading Company

The Eastern Trading Company of Singapore purchases spices in bulk from around the world, packages them into consumer-size quantities, and sells them through sales affiliates in Hong Kong, the United Kingdom, and the United States. For a recent month, the following payments matrix of interaffiliate cash flows, stated in Singapore dollars, was forecasted. Show how Eastern Trading can use multilateral netting to minimize the foreign exchange transactions necessary to settle interaffiliate payments. If foreign exchange transactions cost the company .5 percent, what savings results from netting?

Eastern Trading Company Payments Matrix (S$000)

	Disbursements				
Receipts	**Singapore**	**Hong Kong**	**U.K.**	**U.S.**	**Total Receipts**
Singapore	—	40	75	55	170
Hong Kong	8	—	—	22	30
U.K.	15	—	—	17	32
U.S.	11	25	9	—	45
Total disbursements	34	65	84	94	277

MINI CASE 2

Eastern Trading Company's Optimal Transfer Pricing Strategy

The Eastern Trading Company of Singapore ships prepackaged spices to Hong Kong, the United Kingdom, and the United States, where they are resold by sales affiliates. Eastern Trading is concerned with what might happen in Hong Kong now that control has been turned over to China. Eastern Trading has decided that it should reexamine its transfer pricing policy with its Hong Kong affiliate as a means of repositioning funds from Hong Kong to Singapore. The following table shows the present transfer pricing scheme, based on a carton of assorted, prepackaged spices, which is the typical shipment to the Hong Kong sales affiliate. What do you recommend that Eastern Trading should do?

Eastern Trading Company Current Transfer Pricing Policy with Hong Kong Sales Affiliate

	Singapore Parent	Hong Kong Affiliate	Consolidated Company
Sales revenue	S$300	S$500	S$500
Cost of goods sold	200	300	200
Gross profit	100	200	300
Operating expenses	50	50	100
Taxable income	50	150	200
Income taxes (31%/16.5%)	16	25	41
Net income	34	125	159

MINI CASE 3

Eastern Trading Company's New MBA

The Eastern Trading Company of Singapore presently follows a decentralized system of cash management where it and its affiliates each maintain their own transaction and precautionary cash balances. Eastern Trading believes that it and its affiliates' cash needs are normally distributed and independent from one another. It is corporate policy to maintain two and one-half standard deviations of cash as precautionary holdings. At this level of safety there is a 99.37 percent chance that each affiliate will have enough cash holdings to cover transactions.

A new MBA hired by the company claims that the investment in precautionary cash balances is needlessly large and can be reduced substantially if the firm converts to a centralized cash management system. Use the projected information for the current month, which is presented below, to determine the amount of cash Eastern Trading needs to hold in precautionary balances under its current decentralized system and the level of precautionary cash it would need to hold under a centralized system. Was the new MBA a good hire?

Affiliate	Expected Transactions	One Standard Deviation
Singapore	S$125,000	S$40,000
Hong Kong	60,000	25,000
United Kingdom	95,000	40,000
United States	70,000	35,000

ENDNOTES

1. The standard deviation formula assumes that interaffiliate cash flows are uncorrelated with one another.
2. Bokos and Clinkard (1983) provide this list of countries allowing and having restrictions on netting.

WEB RESOURCES

cibs.tamu.edu/eden/tp.websites.htm

This site provides links to international tax and transfer pricing information Websites.

www.office.com/global/tools

This site provides a discussion of the purpose, preparation, and analysis of cash budgets.

REFERENCES AND SUGGESTED READINGS

Allman-Ward, Michele. "Globalization and the Cash/Treasury Manager." *Journal of Cash Management* 12 (1992), pp. 26–34.

Bogusz, Robert J. "The Renaissance of Netting." *Journal of Cash Management* 13 (1993), pp. 10–17.

Bokos, W. J., and Anne P. Clinkard. "Multilateral Netting." *Journal of Cash Management* 3 (1983), pp. 24–34.

Burns, Jane O. "Transfer Pricing Decisions in U.S. Multinational Corporations." *Journal of International Business Studies* 11 (1980), pp. 23–39.

Collins, J. Markham, and Alan W. Frankle. "International Cash Management Practices of Large U.S. Firms." *Journal of Cash Management* 5 (1985), pp. 42–48.

Diewert, W. Erwin. "Transfer Pricing and Economic Efficiency." In Alan M. Rugman and Lorraine Eden, eds., *Multinationals and Transfer Pricing*. New York: St. Martins, 1985.

Griffiths, Susan. "International Pooling—Getting the Story Straight." *Journal of Cash Management* 12 (1992), pp. 5–7.

International Transfer Pricing. New York: Business International Corporation and Ernst and Young, 1991.

Pagar, Jill C., and J. Scott Wilkie. *Transfer Pricing Strategy in a Global Economy*. Amsterdam: IBFD Publications, 1993.

Prusa, Thomas J. "An Incentive Compatible Approach to Transfer Pricing." *Journal of International Economics* 28 (1990), pp. 155–72.

Shapiro, Alan C. "Payments Netting in International Cash Management." *Journal of International Business Studies* 9 (1978), pp. 51–58.

Srinivasin, Venkat, and Yong H. Kim. "Payments Netting in International Cash Management: A Network Optimization Approach." *Journal of International Business Studies* 17 (1986), pp. 1–20.

Tang, Roger Y. W. *Transfer Pricing in the 1990s: Tax and Management Perspectives*. Westport, CT: Quorum Books, 1993.

Tawfik, Mohamed Sherih. *An Optimal International Transfer Pricing System: A Nonlinear Multiobjective Approach*. Ph.D. dissertation, Pennsylvania State University, 1982.

Tax Aspects of Transfer Pricing within Multinational Enterprises: The United States Proposed Regulations. Paris: Organization for Economic Co-Operation and Development, 1993.

U.S. Internal Revenue Code. Chicago: Commerce Clearing House, 1993.

CHAPTER NINETEEN

Exports and Imports

CHAPTER OUTLINE

To help protect elephants and rhinos against poachers, the Ugandan government needed 18 helicopters. Unfortunately, it did not have the $25 million needed to cover the cost. In stepped Gary Pacific, the head of countertrade for McDonnell Douglas Helicopters. He helped Uganda set up several local factories that are able to generate hard currency. One was a plant to catch and process Nile perch and another was a factory for making passion fruit and pineapple concentrate from fresh fruit. Additionally, Pacific found buyers for the output of these plants. After 14 months, Uganda had earned enough hard currency to start receiving the helicopters it needed.[1]

Foreign trade is obviously important for a country. In modern times, it is virtually impossible for a country to produce domestically everything its citizens need or demand. Even if it could, it is unlikely that it could produce all items more efficiently than producers in other countries. Without international trade, scarce resources are not put to their best uses. As the opening example illustrates, countries and firms will take even exotic steps to clinch a deal.

International trade is more difficult and risky, however, than domestic trade. In foreign trade, the exporter may not be familiar with the buyer, and thus not know if the importer is a good credit risk. If merchandise is exported abroad and the buyer does not pay, it may prove difficult, if not impossible, for the exporter to have any legal recourse. Additionally, political instability makes it risky to ship merchandise abroad to certain parts of the world. From the importer's perspective, it is risky to make advance payment for goods that may never be shipped by the exporter.

The present chapter deals with these issues and others. The chapter begins with an example of a simple yet typical foreign trade transaction. The mechanics of the trade are discussed, delineating the institutional arrangements that have been developed over time to facilitate international trade in light of the risks we have identified. The three basic documents needed in a foreign trade transaction—a letter of credit, a time draft, and a bill of lading—are discussed in detail. It is shown how a time draft becomes a banker's acceptance, a negotiable money market instrument.

The second part of the chapter discusses the role of the Export-Import Bank, an independent government agency founded to offer competitive assistance to U.S.

exporters through loans, financial guarantees, and credit insurance. The chapter concludes with a discussion of various types of countertrade transactions, which include such trades as the Ugandan-McDonnell Douglas helicopter deal. Countertrade transactions can collectively be defined as foreign trade transactions in which the seller provides the buyer with goods or services in return for a reciprocal promise from the seller to purchase goods or services from the buyer.

A TYPICAL FOREIGN TRADE TRANSACTION

To understand the mechanics of a typical foreign trade transaction, it is best to use an illustration. Consider a U.S. importer, who is an automobile dealer, and who desires to purchase automobiles from a Japanese exporter, the manufacturer. The two do not know one another and are obviously separated by a great distance. If the Japanese manufacturer could have his way, he would have the U.S. importer pay *cash in advance* for the shipment, since he is unfamiliar with the creditworthiness of the auto dealer.

If the auto dealer could have his way, he ideally would prefer to receive the cars on consignment from the auto manufacturer. In a *consignment* sale, the exporter retains title to the merchandise that is shipped. The importer only pays the exporter once he sells the merchandise. If the importer cannot sell the merchandise, he returns it to the exporter. Obviously, the exporter bears all the risk in a consignment sale. Second best for the auto dealer would be to receive the car shipment on credit and then to make payment, thus not paying in advance for an order that might not ever be received.

How can the situation be reconciled so that the foreign trade transaction is satisfactory for both the exporter and the importer? Fortunately for the auto dealer and the auto manufacturer, they are not the first two parties faced with such a dilemma. Over the years, an elaborate process has evolved for handling just this type of foreign commerce transaction. Exhibit 19.1 presents a schematic of the process that is typically followed in foreign trade. Working our way through Exhibit 19.1 in a narrative fashion will allow us to understand the mechanics of a trade and also the three major documents involved.

Exhibit 19.1 begins with (1) the U.S. importer placing an order with the Japanese exporter, asking if he will ship automobiles under a letter of credit. If the auto manufacturer agrees to this, he will inform the U.S. importer of the price and the other terms of sale, including the credit terms. For discussion purposes, we will assume the length of the credit period is 60 days. The U.S. importer will (2) apply to his bank for a letter of credit for the merchandise he desires to purchase, providing his bank with the terms of the sale.

A **letter of credit (L/C)** is a guarantee from the importer's bank that it will act on behalf of the importer and pay the exporter for the merchandise if all relevant documents specified in the L/C are presented according to the terms of the L/C. In essence, the importer's bank is substituting its creditworthiness for that of the unknown U.S. importer.

The L/C is (3) sent via the importer's bank to the exporter's bank. Once the L/C is received, the exporter's bank will (4) notify the exporter. The Japanese exporter will (5) then ship the cars.

After shipping the automobiles, the Japanese exporter will (6) present to his bank a (60-day) time draft, drawn according to the instructions in the L/C, the bill of lading, and any other shipping documents that are required, such as the invoice and a packing list. A **time draft** is a written order instructing the importer or his agent, the importer's bank, to pay the amount specified on its face on a certain date (that is, the end of the credit period in a foreign trade transaction). A **bill of lading (B/L)** is a

EXHIBIT 19.1 Process of Typical Foreign Trade Transaction

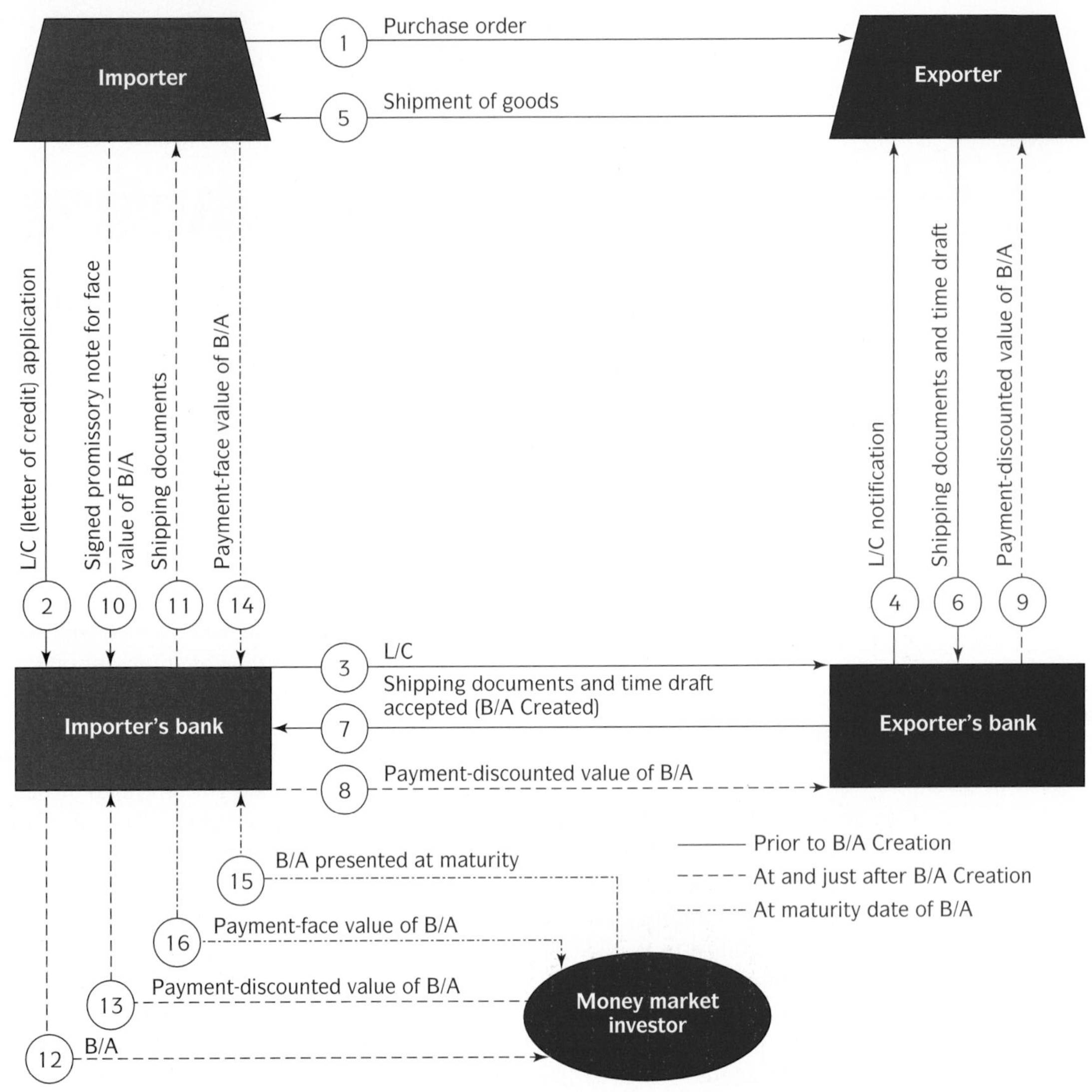

Source: Adapted from *Instruments of the Money Market*, Federal Reserve Bank of Richmond, 1986. Used by permission.

document issued by the common carrier specifying that it has received the goods for shipment; it can serve as title to the goods. The exporter's bank (7) presents the shipping documents and the time draft to the importer's bank. After taking title to the goods via the bill of lading, the importer's bank accepts the time draft, creating at this point a **banker's acceptance (B/A)**, a negotiable money market instrument for which a secondary market exists. The importer's bank charges an acceptance commission, which is deducted at the time of final settlement. The acceptance commission is based on the term to maturity of the time draft and the creditworthiness of the importer.

One of several things can happen with the B/A. It can be returned to the Japanese exporter, who will hold it for 60 days and then present it for payment to the importer's bank at maturity. Should the exporter suddenly find he needs funds prior to the maturity date, the B/A can be sold at a discount in the money market. Since their risks are similar, banker's acceptances trade at rates similar to rates for negotiable bank certificates of deposit. Alternatively, as in Exhibit 19.1, the Japanese exporter could instruct its bank to have the B/A (8) discounted by the importer's bank and (9) pay that amount to it. Analogously, the exporter's bank may decide to hold the B/A to maturity as an investment, and pay the Japanese exporter the discounted equivalent.

The U.S. importer (10) signs a (60-day) promissory note with his bank for the face value of the banker's acceptance, due on the maturity date of the B/A. In return, the exporter's bank (11) provides the auto dealer with the shipping documents needed to take possession of the automobiles from the common carrier.

If the B/A is not held by the Japanese exporter or the exporter's bank, the importer's bank may hold it for 60 days until maturity when it will collect the face value from the U.S. importer via the promissory note. Alternatively, as in Exhibit 19.1, the importer's bank may (12) sell the B/A in the money market to an investor at a (13) discount from face value. At maturity, the importer's bank will (14) collect the face value of the B/A via the promissory note from the U.S. importer, the money market investor will (15) present the B/A for payment to the importer's bank, and the importer's bank will (16) pay the face value of the B/A to the investor. In the event of default by the U.S. importer, the importer's bank will seek recourse against the importer. B/As usually have maturities ranging from 30 to 180 days; as such they are only short-term sources of trade financing.

EXAMPLE 19.1: Cost Analysis of a Banker's Acceptance As mentioned in the previous discussion of the schematic describing a typical foreign trade transaction, the exporter may hold the B/A to maturity and collect payment at that time. Alternatively, the exporter may discount the B/A with the importer's bank or sell it at a discount in the money market.

Suppose the face amount of the promissory note is \$1,000,000 and the importer's bank charges an acceptance commission of 1.5 percent. Since the note is for 60 days, the exporter will receive $\$997{,}500 = \$1{,}000{,}000 \times [1 - (.015 \times 60/360)]$ if he decides to hold the B/A until maturity. Thus, the acceptance commission is \$2,500.

If 60-day B/A rates are 5.25 percent and the exporter discounts the B/A with the importer's bank, he will receive $\$988{,}750 = \$1{,}000{,}000 \times [1 - ([.0525 + .0150] \times 60/360)]$. Thus, the importer's bank receives a discount rate of interest of 6.75 percent = 5.25 + 1.50 percent on its investment. At maturity the importer's bank will receive \$1,000,000 from the importer. The bond equivalent yield it receives on its investment (which is figured on the actual number of days in a year instead of a 360-day banker's year) is 6.92 percent, or $.0692 = (\$1{,}000{,}000/\$988{,}750 - 1) \times 365/60$.

The exporter pays the acceptance commission regardless of whether he discounts the B/A or holds it to maturity, hence it is not marginal to a decision to discount the B/A. The bond equivalent rate the exporter receives from discounting the B/A is 5.38 percent, or $.0538 = (\$997{,}500/\$988{,}750 - 1) \times 365/60$. If the exporter's opportunity cost of capital is greater than 5.38 percent compounded bi-monthly (an effective annual rate of 5.5 percent), discounting makes sense; if not, the exporter should hold the B/A to maturity.

FORFAITING

Forfaiting is a type of medium-term trade financing used to finance the sale of capital goods. Forfaiting involves the sale of promissory notes signed by the importer in favor of the exporter. The *forfait*, usually a bank, buys the notes at a discount from face value from the exporter. In this way, the exporter receives payment for the export and does not have to carry the financing. The forfait does not have recourse against the exporter in the event of default by the importer. The promissory notes are typically structured to extend out in a series over a period of from three to seven years, with a note in the series maturing every six months. Since forfaiting transactions are typically used to finance capital goods, they usually are for amounts of $500,000 or more. Forfaiting began in Switzerland and Germany, but it has now spread throughout most of Western Europe and into the United States. Forfait transactions are typically denominated in Swiss francs, deutsche marks, and U.S. dollars.

GOVERNMENT ASSISTANCE IN EXPORTING

Success in international trade is fundamentally important for a country. Success in exporting implies that there is demand for a country's products, that its labor force is benefiting from employment, and that some resources are used for technological advancement. To be successful in international trade requires a country's export-oriented firms to be good marketers, that is, to be competitive in terms of product offerings, promotion, price, delivery capability, and service provided to importers. Equally important, however, is for firms to be competitive in terms of extending credit to importers.

Because of the benefits that accrue from exporting, the governments of most developed countries offer competitive assistance to domestic exporters in the form of subsidized credit that can be extended to importers. Also, credit insurance programs that guarantee financing extended by private financial institutions are common. In this section, we discuss the main features of programs available to U.S. exporters.

The Export-Import Bank and Affiliated Organizations

In 1934, the **Export-Import Bank (Eximbank) of the United States** was founded, and subsequently chartered in 1945, as an independent government agency to facilitate and finance U.S. export trade. Eximbank's purpose is to provide financing in situations where private financial institutions are unable or unwilling to because: (1) the loan maturity is too long; (2) the amount of the loan is too large; (3) the loan risk is too great; or (4) the importing firm has difficulty obtaining hard currency for payment.

To meet its objectives, Eximbank provides service through three types of programs: direct loans to foreign borrowers, loan guarantees, and credit insurance.[2]

Through its *Extended Term Program* (beyond five years), Eximbank will facilitate direct credit to foreign buyers of U.S. exports with a contract value in excess of about $10 million, and which generally involve multiple U.S. suppliers. Eximbank will arrange financing for up to 85 percent of the contract value through a combination of direct loans from Eximbank and private sources, or alternatively provide a financial guarantee for a loan from a private source covering up to 85 percent of the contract value. The *Private Export Funding Corporation (PEFCO)*, established in 1970 by a group of commercial banks and industrial corporations, frequently cooperates in loans with the Eximbank under this program, especially when fixed-rate credit is extended.

Eximbank offers three separate packages through its *Medium and Short Term Programs*. Through its *Medium Term Credit Program*, Eximbank will extend below-market-rate direct credit to a foreign importer in an amount up to 85 percent of the contract value for a period of one to five years, in cases "where the U.S. exporter is encountering subsidized, foreign officially supported export credit competition."[3] Through its *Commercial Bank Guarantee Program*, Eximbank will guarantee, for a period of one-half to five years, 100 percent coverage on political risks only, and up to 85 percent of the contract value on loans extended to foreign importers of U.S. goods. Through its *Short and Medium-Term Credit Insurance Program*, Eximbank offers credit insurance policies that provide 100 percent coverage on political risks and 90 percent on commercial risks on trade credit extended by a U.S. exporter to a foreign importer. The credit limit is discretionary for multiple-buyer policies, and up to 85 percent for single-buyer policies. Approval by the *Federal Credit Insurance Association (FCIA)* is frequently a prerequisite. The FCIA was formed in 1961 by a group of private insurance companies to act in cooperation with the Eximbank to extend credit insurance to U.S. exporters against the default on payment by foreign importers on accounts receivables due to commercial and political risk.

In the United Kingdom, the *Exports Credits Guarantee Department (ECGD)* performs functions similar to those of the Eximbank and FCIA. Formed in 1919, the ECGD provides assistance to exporters through direct insurance coverage against nonpayment by the importer due to commercial and political risks and by guaranteeing bank loans to foreign borrowers. The exporter, who is considered to be the true beneficiary, pays to ECGD the guaranteed bank loan insurance premium.

COUNTERTRADE

Countertrade is an umbrella term used to describe many different types of transactions, each "in which the seller provides a buyer with goods or services and promises in return to purchase goods or services from the buyer."[4] Countertrades may or may not involve the use of money. If money is not exchanged, the trade is a type of barter. Regardless, countertrade usually results in a two-way flow of commodities.

Countertrade arrangements can be traced back to prehistoric times and they have been used throughout history whenever money was scarce. While it is difficult to determine the exact volume of countertrade, the practice is nevertheless widespread. According to Hammond (1990), some estimates put countertrade at only 5 percent of total world trade, whereas other estimates are as high as 40 percent. Moreover, countertrade transactions are not accounted for in official trade statistics. By the year 2000, the IMF, the World Bank, and the U.S. Department of Commerce estimate that as much as half of all international trade transactions will be conducted as countertrade.[5] Most recently, a surge of countertrade activity occurred in the 1980s, when the Third World debt crisis left the debtor countries without sufficient foreign exchange reserves or bank lines of credit to carry on normal commerce.[6]

Forms of Countertrade

Hennart (1989) identifies six forms of countertrade: barter, clearing arrangement, switch trading, buy-back, counterpurchase, and offset. The first three do not involve the use of money, whereas the latter three do.

Barter is the direct exchange of goods between two parties. While money does not exchange hands in a barter transaction, it is common to value the goods each party exchanges in an agreed-upon currency. It is often necessary to place a monetary value on the goods for accounting, taxation, and insurance purposes.

Hammond (1990) describes barter as "a rather primitive way to do business. It fosters bilateral trade which, in turn, under mercantilist economies and imperialistic policies, fostered a tight system of colonial dependency with protected markets and captive sources of raw materials." He notes that barter flourished until after World War II when the Bretton Woods fixed exchange rate system was established that provided for currency convertibility and fostered free trade.

Today, barter transactions are typically one-time exchanges of merchandise that take place when circumstances warrant. Schaffer (1989) describes a modern example of barter that took place between General Electric (GE) and Rumania. GE had agreed to sell Rumania a turbine generator for cash. The Rumanian loan financing subsequently fell through, and in order to complete the deal, GE agreed to accept Rumanian products, which it in turn sold for cash through its trading company.

A *clearing arrangement* (also called a bilateral clearing agreement) is a form of barter in which the counterparties (governments) contract to purchase a certain amount of goods and services from one another. Both parties set up accounts with each other that are debited whenever one country imports from the other. At the end of an agreed-upon period of time, any account imbalances are settled for hard currency, or by the transfer of goods. The clearing arrangement introduces the concept of credit to barter transactions, and means bilateral trade can take place that does not have to be immediately settled. Account balances are periodically determined and any trade imbalances are settled in an agreed-upon currency. Anyane-Ntow and Harvey (1995) note that bilateral clearing agreements have usually taken place between Third World and Eastern European countries. They cite the 1994 agreement between China and Saudi Arabia with a $1 billion target as an example.

A *switch trade* is the purchase by a third party of one country's clearing agreement imbalance for hard currency, which is in turn resold. The second buyer uses the account balance to purchase goods and services from the original clearing agreement counterparty who had the account imbalance. Anyane-Ntow and Harvey (1995) give the example of a switch trade when the United States exported fertilizers to Pakistan through a Rumanian-Pakistani clearing agreement.

A *buy-back transaction* involves a technology transfer via the sale of a manufacturing plant. As part of the transaction, the seller agrees to purchase a certain portion of the plant output once it is constructed. As Hennart (1989) notes, money enters into the agreement in two ways. First, the plant buyer borrows hard currency in the capital market to pay the seller for the plant. Second, the plant seller agrees to purchase enough of the plant output over a period of time to enable the buyer to pay back the borrowed funds. A buy-back transaction can be viewed as a form of direct investment in the purchasing country. Examples of buy-back transactions include Japan's agreements with Taiwan, Singapore, and Korea to exchange computer chip production equipment for a certain percentage of the output.[7]

A *counterpurchase* is similar to a buy-back transaction, but with some notable differences. The two counterparties are usually an Eastern importer and a Western exporter of technology. The major difference between a buy-back and a counterpurchase transaction is that in the latter, the merchandise the Western buyer agrees to purchase is unrelated and has not been produced on the exported equipment. The seller agrees to purchase goods from a list drawn up by the importer at prices set by the importer. Goods on the list are frequently items for which the buyer does not have a ready market. As an example of a counterpurchase, Anyane-Ntow and Harvey (1995) cite the agreement to exchange Italian industrial equipment for Indonesian rubber.

An *offset transaction* can be viewed as a counterpurchase trade agreement involving the aerospace/defense industry. Offset transactions are reciprocal trade agreements between an industrialized country and a country that has defense and/or aerospace industries. Hammond (1990) cites the example of the sale of F-16 jet fighters manufactured by General Dynamics to Turkey and Greece in exchange for olives, hydroelectric power projects, the promotion of tourism, and aircraft coproduction.

Some Generalizations about Countertrade

Why have countertrade transactions become so prominent in international trade in the 1980s and 1990s? Arguments both for and against countertrade transactions can be made. Hammond (1990) notes that there are both negative and positive incentives for a country to be in favor of countertrade. Negative incentives are those that are forced upon a country or corporation whether or not it desires to engage in countertrade. They include the conservation of cash and hard currency, the improvement of trade imbalances, and the maintenance of export prices. Positive reasons from both the country and corporate perspectives include enhanced economic development, increased employment, technology transfer, market expansion, increased profitability, less costly sourcing of supply, reduction of surplus goods from inventory, and the development of marketing expertise.

Those against countertrade transactions claim that such transactions tamper with the fundamental operation of free markets, and therefore, resources are used inefficiently. Opponents claim that transaction costs are increased, that multilateral trade is restricted through fostering bilateral trade agreements, and that, in general, transactions that do not make use of money represent a step backwards in economic development.

Hennart (1989) empirically studied all 1,277 countertrade contracts between June 1983, and December 31, 1986, that were reported in *Countertrade Outlook*. Of these transactions, 694 were clearing arrangements, 171 were classified as barters, 298 as counterpurchases, 71 as buy-backs, and 43 as offsets. The countries involved were classified into the World Bank categories of: Developed, Organization of Petroleum Exporting Countries (OPEC) Members, Centrally Planned Economies (CPE), Middle-Income, and Low-Income.

Hennart found that each country grouping had a propensity to engage in certain types of countertrade transactions. OPEC, middle-income, and low-income countries used more counterpurchases, CPEs more buy-backs, and developed and middle-income countries engaged in more offsets. Barter was most common between two middle-income countries, between developed and middle-income countries, and between middle-income countries and CPEs.

Hennart claims the high frequency of buy-backs among CPEs is consistent with their use as a substitute for foreign direct investment. The reasons that CPEs and low-income countries do not actively engage in offset transactions are twofold: CPEs are not allowed to purchase Western weapons, and low-income developing countries cannot afford sophisticated weapons systems typically sold via offset transactions. Barter between two middle-income countries (the most frequent) is consistent with the two countries desiring to avoid the repayment of external debt. The absence of barter between OPEC countries and between developed countries is consistent with the use of barter to bypass cartels and commodity arrangements. The analysis of Marin and Schnitzer (1995) is consistent with Hennart's conclusions.

Whether countertrade transactions are good or bad for the global economy, it appears certain that they will increase in the near future as world trade increases.

SUMMARY

Export and import transactions and trade financing are the main topics discussed in this chapter.

1. Conducting international trade transactions is difficult in comparison to domestic trades. Commercial and political risks enter into the equation, which are not factors in domestic trade. Yet it is important for a country to be competitively strong in international trade in order for its citizens to have the goods and services they need and demand.
2. A typical foreign trade transaction requires three basic documents: letter of credit, time draft, and bill of lading. A time draft can become a negotiable money market instrument called a banker's acceptance.
3. Forfaiting, in which a bank purchases at a discount from an importer a series of promissory notes in favor of an exporter, is a medium-term form of trade financing.
4. The Export-Import Bank provides competitive assistance to U.S. exporters through direct loans to foreign importers, loan guarantees, and credit insurance to U.S. exporters.
5. Countertrade transactions are gaining renewed prominence as a means of conducting international trade transactions. There are several types of

countertrade transactions, only some of which involve the use of money. In each type, the seller provides the buyer with goods or services in return for a reciprocal promise from the seller to purchase goods or services from the buyer.

KEY WORDS

banker's acceptance (B/A), 464
bill of lading (B/L), 463
countertrade, 467
Export-Import Bank (Eximbank) of the United States, 466
forfaiting, 465
letter of credit (L/C), 463
time draft, 463

QUESTIONS

1. Discuss some of the reasons why international trade is more difficult and risky from the exporter's perspective than is domestic trade.
2. What three basic documents are necessary to conduct a typical foreign commerce trade? Briefly discuss the purpose of each.
3. How does a time draft become a banker's acceptance?
4. What is a forfaiting transaction?
5. What is the purpose of the Export-Import Bank?
6. Do you think that a country's government should assist private business in the conduct of international trade through direct loans, loan guarantees, and/or credit insurance?
7. Briefly discuss the various types of countertrade.
8. Discuss some of the pros and cons of countertrade from the country's perspective and the firm's perspective.

PROBLEMS

1. Assume the time from acceptance to maturity on a $2,000,000 banker's acceptance is 90 days. Further assume that the importing bank's acceptance commission is 1.25 percent and that the market rate for 90-day B/As is 7 percent. Determine the amount the exporter will receive if he holds the B/A until maturity and also the amount the exporter will receive if he discounts the B/A with the importer's bank.
2. The time from acceptance to maturity on a $1,000,000 banker's acceptance is 120 days. The importer's bank's acceptance commission is 1.75 percent and the market rate for 120-day B/As is 5.75 percent. What amount will the exporter receive if he holds the B/A until maturity? If he discounts the B/A with the importer's bank? Also determine the bond equivalent yield the importer's bank will earn from discounting the B/A with the exporter. If the exporter's opportunity cost of capital is 11 percent, should he discount the B/A or hold it to maturity?

MINI CASE

American Machine Tools, Inc.

American Machine Tools is a midwestern manufacturer of tool-and-die-making equipment. The company has had an inquiry from a representative of the Estonian government about the terms of sale for a $5,000,000 order of machinery. The sales manager spoke with the Estonian representative, but he is doubtful that the Estonian government will be able to obtain enough hard currency to make the purchase. While the U.S. economy has been growing, American Machine Tools has not had a very good year. An additional $5,000,000 in sales would definitely help. If something cannot be arranged, the firm will likely be forced to lay off some of its skilled workforce.

Is there a way that you can think of that American Machine Tools might be able to make the machinery sale to Estonia?

ENDNOTES

1. This example is from the 1992 article by Shelley Neumeier, entitled "Why Countertrade Is Getting Hot," in *Fortune* magazine.
2. Much of the discussion in this section on the Export-Import Bank is drawn from *A Handbook on Financing U.S. Exports*, 4th ed. (1984), published by the Machinery and Allied Products Institute.
3. See *A Handbook on Financing U.S. Exports*, p. 6.
4. Definition from Hennart (1990).
5. See Anyane-Ntow and Harvey (1995, p. 47) for this estimate.
6. See Chapter 6 for a discussion of the extent and severity of the Third World debt crisis.
7. See Anyane-Ntow and Harvey (1995, p. 48).

WEB RESOURCES

Gopher://gopher.umsl.edu:70/11/library/govdocs/expguide

(no http://)

A comprehensive guide to exporting that is designed to help U.S. firms learn the costs and risks associated with exporting and develop a strategy for exporting. The Website also includes an export glossary.

www.countertrade.org/

Official site of the American Countertrade Association (ACA). The ACA provides a forum for companies involved in countertrade and a resource for companies exploring the possibilities held by countertrade.

www.exim.gov/

Website of the Export-Import Bank of the United States (Eximbank). The site provides details of the Eximbank and its services.

www.eximbankindia.com

Website of the Export-Import Bank of India. The EXIM India was set up in 1982 to finance, facilitate and promote India's international trade. It is the counterpart of the Eximbank of the United States. There are several Websites providing information about various countries' export-import banks.

www.ita.doc.gov/bems/

Big emerging markets information resource page, a service of the U.S. Department of Commerce. The site provides information on exporting from the U.S. to the big emerging markets. It also provides updates on the Asian financial crisis.

REFERENCES AND SUGGESTED READINGS

Anyane-Ntow, Kwabena, and Santhi C. Harvey. "A Countertrade Primer." *Management Accounting* (April 1995), pp. 47–50.

Celi, Louis J., and I. James Czechowicz. *Export Financing: A Handbook of Sources and Techniques*. Morristown, N.J.: Financial Executives Research Foundation, 1985.

Edwards, Burt. *Getting Paid for Exports*. Brookfield, VT: Gower, 1990.

Francis, Dick. *The Countertrade Handbook*. New York: Quorum Books, 1987.

Guild, Ian, and Rhodri Harris. *Forfaiting*. New York: Universe Books, 1986.

Hammond, Grant T. *Countertrade, Offsets and Barter in International Political Economy*. New York: St. Martin's Press, 1990.

Hill, Eric. "Bankers Acceptances." In *Instruments of the Money Market*, 6th ed., Timothy Q. Cook and Timothy D. Rowe, eds. Richmond, VA: Federal Reserve Bank of Richmond, 1986.

Hennart, Jean-Francois. "Some Empirical Dimensions of Countertrade." *Journal of International Business Studies* (Second Quarter, 1989), pp. 243–70.

Knight, Martin; James Ball; and Andrew Inglis-Taylor, eds. *Export Finance*. London: Euromoney Publications, 1988.

Machinery and Allied Products Institute. *A Handbook on Financing U.S. Exports*, 4th ed. Washington, D.C.: Machinery and Allied Products Institute, 1984.

Marin, Dalia, and Monika Schnitzer. "Tying Trade Flows: A Theory of Countertrade with Evidence." *The American Economic Review* 85 (1995), pp. 1047–64.

Neumeir, Shelley. "Why Countertrade Is Getting Hot," *Fortune*, June 29, 1992, p. 25.

Rodriguez, Rita M. *The Export-Import Bank at Fifty.* Lexington, MA: Lexington Books, 1987.

Schaffer, Matt. *Winning the Countertrade War*. New York: John Wiley and Sons, 1989.

CHAPTER TWENTY

International Tax Environment

CHAPTER OUTLINE

The purpose of this chapter is to provide a brief introduction to the international tax environment that will be useful to multinational firms in their tax planning and also informative to investors in international financial assets. Tax regulation is a complex topic at the domestic level. It is obviously a much more complex topic at the international level. Hence, this chapter is designed to serve only as an introduction.

The chapter begins with a discussion of the two main objectives of taxation: tax neutrality and tax equity. After this theoretical foundation has been established, the main types of taxation are discussed. Next follows discussions of how taxes are typically levied throughout the world, the purpose of foreign tax credits, and tax treaties between nations. The chapter concludes by examining various types of organizational structures that exist for reducing tax liabilities. Since it is not possible to thoroughly address taxation from the viewpoint of all national taxpayers, by necessity the perspective is from the U.S. taxpayer's viewpoint when the discussion needs to be country specific.

Some taxation issues have been introduced earlier in other chapters because a thorough presentation of the topic under discussion required it. For example, Chapter 17 on international capital budgeting required some elementary knowledge of the concepts of worldwide taxation of active foreign-source income and foreign tax credits applied against a MNC's domestic tax liability. This topic will be revisited in this chapter to provide a more detailed and structured understanding of these issues. Additionally, Chapter 18 on multinational cash management investigated the viability of transfer pricing strategies for reducing a MNC's tax liability. Because this topic was covered sufficiently in Chapter 18, it is given only minor treatment in this chapter.

THE OBJECTIVES OF TAXATION

Two basic objectives of taxation have to be discussed to help frame our thinking about the international tax environment: tax neutrality and tax equity.

Tax Neutrality

Tax neutrality has its foundations in the principles of economic efficiency and equity. Tax neutrality is determined by three criteria. **Capital-export neutrality** is the criterion that an ideal tax should be effective in raising revenue for the government and not have any negative effects on the economic decision-making process of the taxpayer. That is, a good tax is one that is efficient in raising tax revenue for the government and does not prevent economic resources from being allocated to their most appropriate use no matter where in the world the highest rate of return can be earned. Obviously, capital-export neutrality is based on worldwide economic efficiency.

A second neutrality criterion is **national neutrality**. That is, taxable income is taxed in the same manner by the taxpayer's national tax authority regardless of where in the world it is earned. In theory, national tax neutrality is a commendable objective, as it is based on the principle of equality. In practice, it is a difficult concept to apply. In the United States, for example, foreign-source income is taxed at the same rate as U.S.-earned income and a foreign tax credit is given against taxes paid to a foreign government. However, the foreign tax credit is limited to the amount of tax that would be due on that income if it were earned in the United States. Thus, if the tax rate paid on foreign-source income is greater than the U.S. tax rate, part of the credit may go unused. Obviously, if the U.S. tax authority did not limit the foreign tax credit to the equivalent amount of U.S. tax, U.S. taxpayers would end up subsidizing part of the tax liabilities of U.S. MNCs' foreign earned income.

The third neutrality criterion is **capital-import neutrality**. To illustrate, this criterion implies that the tax burden a host country imposes on the foreign subsidiary of a MNC should be the same regardless in which country the MNC is incorporated and the same as that placed on domestic firms. Implementing capital-import neutrality means that if the U.S. tax rate were greater than the tax rate of a foreign country in which a U.S. MNC earned foreign income, additional tax on that income above the amount paid to the foreign tax authority would *not* be due in the United States. The concept of capital-import neutrality, like national neutrality, is based on the principle of equality, and its implementation provides a level competitive playing field for all participants in a single marketplace, at least with respect to taxation. Nevertheless, implementing capital-import neutrality means that a sovereign government follows the taxation policies of foreign tax authorities on the foreign-source income of its resident MNCs and that domestic taxpayers end up paying a larger portion of the total tax burden. Obviously, the three criteria of tax neutrality are not always consistent with one another.

Tax Equity

The underlying principle of **tax equity** is that all similarly situated taxpayers should participate in the cost of operating the government according to the same rules. Operationally, this means that regardless of the country in which an affiliate of a MNC earns taxable income, the same tax rate and tax due date apply. A dollar earned by a foreign affiliate is taxed under the same rules as a dollar earned by a domestic affiliate of the MNC. The principle of tax equity is difficult to apply; as we will see in a later section, the organizational form of a MNC can affect the timing of a tax liability.

TYPES OF TAXATION

This section discusses the three basic types of taxation that national governments throughout the world use in generating revenue: income tax, withholding tax, and value-added tax.

Income Tax

Many countries in the world obtain a significant portion of their tax revenue from imposing an **income tax** on personal and corporate income. An income tax is a **direct tax**, that is, one that is paid directly by the taxpayer on whom it is levied. The tax is levied on **active income**, that is, income that results from production by the firm or individual or from services that have been provided.

One of the best guides detailing corporate income tax regulations in most countries is the PriceWaterhouseCoopers annual *Corporate Taxes: Worldwide Summaries*. Exhibit 20.1 is derived from the PriceWaterhouseCoopers summaries. It lists the normal, standard, or representative upper-end marginal income tax rates for domestic nonfinancial corporations for 123 countries. As the exhibit shows, national tax rates vary from a low of zero percent in such tax haven countries as Bahrain, Bermuda, the British Virgin Islands, and the Cayman Islands to well over 40 percent in many countries. The current U.S. marginal tax rate of 35 percent is positioned pretty well in the middle of the rates assessed by the majority of countries.

Withholding Tax

A **withholding tax** is a tax levied on passive income earned by an individual or corporation of one country within the tax jurisdiction of another country. **Passive income** includes dividends and interest income, and income from royalties, patents, or copyrights paid to the taxpayer. A withholding tax is an **indirect tax**, that is, a tax that is borne by a taxpayer who did not directly generate the income that serves as the source of the passive income. The tax is withheld from payments the corporation makes to the taxpayer and turned over to the local tax authority. The withholding tax assures the local tax authority that it will receive the tax due on the passive income earned within its tax jurisdiction.

Many countries have **tax treaties** with one another specifying the withholding tax rate applied to various types of passive income. Exhibit 20.2 lists the *basic* withholding tax rates the U.S. imposes on other countries through its tax treaties with them. For specific types of passive income, the tax rates may be different from those presented in the exhibit.[1] Withholding tax rates imposed through tax treaties are bilateral; that is, through negotiation two countries agree to impose the same tax rate on one another on the same category of passive income.

Note from Exhibit 20.2 that withholding tax rates vary by category of passive income from zero to 30 percent. It is also noteworthy that withholding tax rates vary significantly among countries within an income category. For example, the United States withholds 0 percent on interest income from taxpayers residing in most Western European countries, but 30 percent from taxpayers residing in Pakistan. The exhibit also shows that the United States withholds 30 percent of passive income from taxpayers that reside in countries with which it does not have withholding tax treaties. Exhibit 20.2 also indicates that dividend income received from portfolio investment (less than a 10 percent equity ownership position) in a foreign firm is taxed at withholding tax rates that are frequently higher than the rates applied to investors with a substantial (at least 10 percent) ownership share.

Value-Added Tax

A **value-added tax (VAT)** is an indirect national tax levied on the value added in the production of a good (or service) as it moves through the various stages of production.

EXHIBIT 20.1 Corporate Percentage Income Tax Rates from Certain Countries[a]

Country	Tax Rate	Country	Tax Rate	Country	Tax Rate	Country	Tax Rate
Antigua & Barbuda	40	Dominican Republic	25	Lithuania	29	Russian Federation	35
Argentina	35	Ecuador	0	Loas	45	Saudi Arabia	45
Australia	36	Egypt	42	Luxembourg	37.45	Senegal	35
Austria	34	Estonia	26	Macau	15.75	Singapore	26
Azerbaijan	30	Faroe Islands	27	Malawi	38	Slovak Republic	40
Bahamas	0	Fiji	35	Malaysia	28	Slovenia	25
Bahrain	0	Finland	28	Malta	35	Solomon Islands	35
Barbados	40	France	40.33	Mauritius	35	South Africa	30
Belgium	39	Germany	30	Mexico	35	Spain	35
Bermuda	0	Ghana	35	Monaco	33.33	Sri Lanka	39.88
Bolivia	25	Greece	35	Morocco	35	St. Lucia	33.33
Botswana	25	Guatemala	25	Mozambique	35	Sweden	28
Brazil	15	Guyana	35	Myanmar	30	Switzerland	26∓
British Virgin Islands[b]	15/0	Hong Kong	16	Namibia	40	Tahiti	40
Brunei Darussalam	30	Hungary	18	Netherlands Antilles	44.85	Taiwan	25
Bulgaria	34.3	India	35	Netherlands	35	Tanzania	30
Cambodia	20	Indonesia	30	New Caledonia	30	Thailand	30
Cameroon	38.5	Iran	58.6	New Zealand	33	Trinidad & Tobago	35
Canada	44.6	Ireland	32	Nigeria	30	Turkey	40.37
Cayman Islands	0	Isle of Man	20	Norway	28	Uganda	30
Channel Islands, Guernsey	20	Israel	36	Oman	25	Ukraine	30
Channel Islands, Jersey	20	Italy	37	Panama	30	United Arab Emirates[c]	
Chile	15	Ivory Coast	35	Papau New Guinea	25	United Kingdom	30
China	33	Jamaica	33.33	Paraguay	30	United States	35
Colombia	35	Japan	34.5	Peru	30	Uruguay	30
Congo	45	Kazakstan	30	Philippines	32	Uzbekistan	33
Costa Rica	30	Kenya	32.5	Poland	32	Venezuela	34
Croatia	35	Korea	30.8	Portugal	37.4	Vietnam	25
Cyprus	25	Kuwait	55	Puerto Rico	23.8	Zambia	35
Czech Republic	35	Latvia	25	Qatar	35	Zimbabwe	35
Denmark	32	Liechtenstein	20	Romania	38		

[a]The table lists normal, standard, or representative upper-end marginal tax rates for nonfinancial corporations.
[b]In the British Virgin Islands, a nonresident company incorporated as an international business company is tax exempt.
[c]Tax decrees have not been enforced, except for oil-producing companies where the tax rate is set by the ruler of each Emirate.

Source: Derived from PriceWaterhouseCoopers, *Corporate Taxes: Worldwide Summaries*, 1999.

EXHIBIT 20.2

U.S. Tax Treaty Percentage Withholding Tax Rates with Selected Countries[a]

Country	Dividends: Investment Portfolio	Dividends: Substantial Holdings[b]	Interest[c]	Royalties[d]
Nontreaty countries	30	30	30	30
Australia	15	15	10	10
Austria	15	5	0	0
Barbados	15	5	5	5
Belgium	15	5	15	0
Bermuda	30	30	30	30
Canada	15	5	10	0
China, People's Republic of	10	10	10	10
Commonwealth of Independent States	30	30	0	0
Cyprus	15	5	10	0
Czech Republic	15	5	0	10
Denmark	15	5	0	0
Egypt	15	5	15	0
Finland	15	5	0	5
France	15	5	0	5
Germany	15	5	0	0
Greece	30	30	0	0
Hungary	15	5	0	0
Iceland	15	5	0	0
India	25	15	15	10
Indonesia	15	10	10	10
Ireland, Republic of	15	5	0	0
Israel	25	12.5	10	15
Italy	15	5	15	10
Jamaica	15	10	12.5	10
Japan	15	10	10	10
Korea, Republic of	15	10	12	15
Kazakhstan	15	5	0	10
Luxembourg	7.5	5	0	0
Mexico	15	5	15	10
Morocco	15	10	15	10
Netherlands	15	5	0	0
Netherlands Antilles	30	30	0	30
New Zealand	15	15	10	10
Norway	15	15	0	0
Pakistan	30	15	30	0
Philippines	25	20	15	15
Poland	15	5	0	10
Portugal	15	10	0	10
Romania	10	10	10	15
Russia	10	5	0	0
Slovak Republic	15	5	0	10
South Africa	15	5	0	0
Spain	15	10	0	10
Sweden	15	5	0	0
Switzerland	15	5	5	0
Thailand	15	10	10	10
Trinidad and Tobago	30	30	30	15
Tunisia	20	14	0	15
Turkey	20	15	10	5
United Kingdom	15	5	0	0

[a]The exhibit shows the basic treaty withholding tax rates; see the original source for exceptions and rates that apply to special situations.

[b]These rates apply where the recipient corporation owns at least 10% of the outstanding voting shares of the payer corporation.

[c]"Portfolio interest" (received from certain debt obligations issued after July 18, 1984) and interest paid by banks and insurance companies to specified foreign taxpayers are exempt from tax.

[d]In many treaties, industrial royalties, motion picture royalties, and other copyright royalties may be subject to withholding at different rates.

Source: PriceWaterhouseCoopers, *Corporate Taxes: Worldwide Summaries*, 1999, pp. 760–63. Used by permission.

There are several ways to implement a VAT. The "subtraction method" is frequently followed in practice.

EXAMPLE 20.1: Value-Added Tax Calculation As an example of the subtraction method of calculating VAT, consider a VAT of 15 percent charged on a consumption good that goes through three stages of production. Suppose that Stage 1 is the sale of raw materials to the manufacturer at a cost of DM100 per unit of production. Stage 2 results in a finished good shipped to retailers at a price of DM300. Stage 3 is the retail sale to the final consumer at a price of DM380. DM100 of value has been added in Stage 1, resulting in a VAT of DM15. In Stage 2 the VAT is 15 percent of DM300, or DM45, with a credit of DM15 given against the value added in Stage 1. In Stage 3, an additional VAT of DM12 is due on the DM80 of value added by the retailer. Since the final consumer pays a price of DM380, he effectively pays the total VAT of DM57 (= DM15 + DM30 + DM12), which is 15 percent of DM380. Obviously, a VAT is the equivalent of imposing a national sales tax. Exhibit 20.3 summarizes the VAT calculation.

In many European countries (especially the EU) and also Latin American countries, VAT has become a major source of taxation on private citizens. Many economists prefer a VAT in place of a personal income tax because the latter is a disincentive to work, whereas a VAT discourages unnecessary consumption. A VAT fosters national saving, whereas an income tax is a disincentive to save because the returns from savings are taxed. Moreover, national tax authorities find that a VAT is easier to collect than an income tax because tax evasion is more difficult. Under a VAT, each stage in the production process has an incentive to obtain documentation from the previous stage that the VAT was paid in order to get the greatest tax credit possible. Of course, some argue that the cost of record keeping under a VAT system imposes an economic hardship on small businesses.

A problem with a VAT, especially in the EU, is that not all countries impose the same VAT tax rate. For example, in Denmark the VAT rate is 25 percent, but in Germany it is only 16 percent. Consequently, consumers who reside in a high-VAT country can purchase goods less expensively by simply shopping across the border in a lower VAT country. Indeed, *The Wall Street Journal* reports that Danish customers frequently *demand* the lower German VAT rate on their purchases in Denmark![2] This problem should eventually be resolved, or at least mitigated, in the EU countries as it is expected that a harmonization in VAT rates among member states will occur. The International Finance in Practice box on pages 480–481 presents an interesting discussion of VAT.

NATIONAL TAX ENVIRONMENTS

The international tax environment confronting a MNC or an international investor is a function of the tax jurisdictions established by the individual countries in which the

EXHIBIT 20.3

Value-Added Tax Calculation

Production Stage	Selling Price	Value Added	Incremental VAT
1	DM100	DM100	DM15
2	DM300	DM200	DM30
3	DM380	DM 80	DM12
			Total VAT DM57

INTERNATIONAL FINANCE IN PRACTICE

The Rise and Rise of VAT

Winston Churchill famously remarked that "there is no such thing as a good tax." Faced with a two percentage-point rise in the standard rate of value-added tax (VAT)—from 18.6% to 20.6%—earlier this month, many of the French will doubtless agree with him. France is, after all, already one of Europe's most heavily taxed countries. But leaving aside the question of whether more taxes (rather than bigger spending cuts) is the best way to cut France's budget deficit, the decision to get most of the new revenue from VAT makes sense.

VAT is paid throughout the production process—from the factory all the way through to the shop, with each intermediary (except the consumer) being able to claim back the tax paid. Its cousin, the retail-sales tax, which is used at the state level in America, is levied only at the time of sale to the consumer. Both are consumption taxes, levied when people spend money rather than when they earn it—as income taxes are.

Consumption taxes are usually hailed as an efficient means of taxation. A consumption tax is less likely to distort economic behavior than income taxes. With high marginal rates of income tax, individuals may have less incentive to work hard. With a consumption tax, their extra income is not taxed until it is spent. Consumption taxes can also be levied on a wide base. In theory, people should be taxed on everything they buy; in practice, things are a little more complicated. Many countries have numerous exemptions from VAT; others tax some goods at lower rates. The wider the tax base, the lower the tax rate needed to raise a given amount of revenue.

The main argument against consumption taxes is a political one. Personal allowances and higher rates for higher incomes mean that income taxes are progressive: the marginal rate of taxation (the rate people pay on the last dollar they earn) is always higher than the average rate. Consumption taxes, in contrast, are generally levied at a constant rate. This means that poor people, who consume a higher share of their current income than rich people, suffer—so consumption taxes are "unfair". This is true, though many economists argue that the most efficient response of a government should be to give poorer people benefits in cash rather than to distort the tax system.

Over the past 30 years, industrial countries have gradually shifted towards general consumption taxes. According to a new report by the Organisation for Economic Co-operation and Development (OECD) on consumption taxes, rich countries raised an average of only 3.5% of GDP from general consumption taxes in 1965. Three decades later the amount has doubled, to 7.0% (see chart).

Although countries still raise substantial amounts of money from some specific consumption taxes (especially on harmful goods such as alcohol or tobacco), part of this increase is due to a shift from specific taxes (such as excise taxes and import duties) to general ones such as VAT. The average amount of money raised from specific consumption taxes in OECD countries has fallen from 6% of GDP in 1965 to around 4% today. Half the increases in total tax revenue since 1965 has come from general consumption taxes, which now make up nearly a fifth of tax revenue in industrial countries.

VAT has become especially popular. In the 1960s only nine countries in the world levied VAT; now more than 90

MNC does business or in which the investor owns financial assets. There are two fundamental types of tax jurisdiction: the *worldwide* and the *territorial*. Unless some mechanism were established to prevent it, double taxation would result if all nations were to follow both methods simultaneously.

Worldwide Taxation

The **worldwide** or **residential** method of declaring a national tax jurisdiction is to tax national residents of the country on their worldwide income no matter in which country it is earned. The national tax authority, according to this method, is declaring its tax jurisdiction over people and businesses. A MNC firm with many foreign affiliates would be taxed in its home country on its income earned at home and abroad. Obviously, if the host countries of the foreign affiliates of a MNC also tax the income earned within their territorial borders, the possibility of double taxation exists, unless a mechanism is established to prevent it.

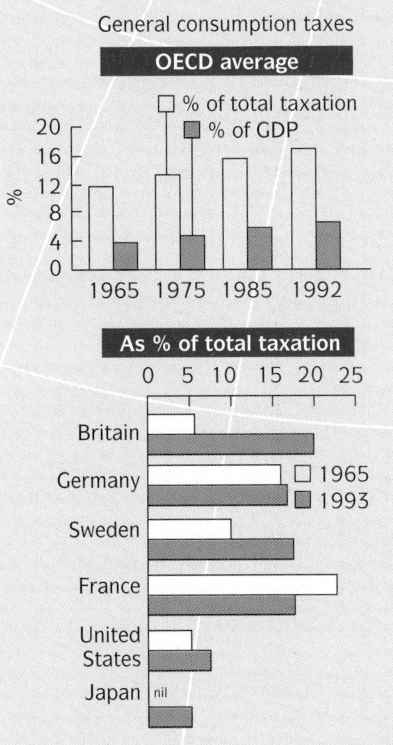

do. Of the OECD countries, only America and Australia do not use value-added taxes. In the developing world, too, VAT has become the consumption tax of choice. All Latin American countries now have VAT, as do the ex-communist economies of Eastern Europe.

In principle there is little economic difference between VAT and the American system of retail-sales taxes. Levied at the same rates, and covering the same number of goods and services (ideally all), both taxes should raise the same amount of money. However the different ways in which they are collected makes VAT more efficient. Under a retail-sales tax system, producers, wholesalers and retailers do not pay tax when they buy or sell from one another. VAT, in contrast, is paid throughout the production chain; registered intermediaries (but not the final consumer) reclaim VAT by presenting a set of invoices to the tax authorities.

This makes VAT much harder to avoid. While a good is being produced, sellers have an interest in proving they have paid the tax on their inputs in order to reduce the tax liability on their sales. With a retail-sales tax system, in contrast, the burden of collecting the tax lies entirely with the final seller of the good. If he fails to charge it, the tax on the whole value-added is lost. As the tax rises, the incentive to avoid it increases.

By limiting such incentives, governments can set VAT at higher rates than they could retail-sales taxes. It is no coincidence that sales taxes in America are, on average, below 8%, compared with a total OECD average for general consumption taxes of nearer 20%. Most economists reckon that 10% is the highest level at which a sales tax can be set without large-scale attempts at evasion. So, for countries which have high revenue requirements, VAT makes more sense.

Nonetheless, VAT rates are generally higher than they need be. Some services, such as financial services or insurance, are exempted by almost all countries, largely because it is difficult to work out exactly what the tax should be levied on. But usually the list of exemptions, or goods subject to lower rates, goes much further. In France many foods, medicine and books are taxed at the lower rate of 5.5%. Newspapers are taxed at only 2.1%.

Widening a VAT base is not popular—as Kenneth Clarke, Britain's chancellor found out when he tried to introduce VAT on fuel. On the other hand, any Frenchman who groans at the breakfast table at the thought of a 20.6% VAT rate should consider carefully the croissant on his plate and the newspaper in his hands.

Source: © 1995 The Economist Newspaper Group, Inc. Reprinted with permission.

Territorial Taxation

The **territorial** or **source** method of declaring a tax jurisdiction is to tax all income earned within the country by any taxpayer, domestic or foreign. Hence, regardless of the nationality of a taxpayer, if the income is earned within the territorial boundary of a country, it is taxed by that country. The national tax authority, according to this method, is declaring its tax jurisdiction over transactions conducted within its borders. Consequently, local firms and affiliates of foreign MNCs are taxed on the income earned in the *source* country. Obviously, if the parent country of the foreign affiliate also levies a tax on worldwide income, the possibility of double taxation exists, unless a mechanism is established to prevent it.

Foreign Tax Credits

The typical approach to avoiding double taxation is for a nation not to tax foreign-source income of its national residents. An alternative method, and the one the United States follows, is to grant to the parent firm **foreign tax credits** against U.S. taxes for taxes paid to foreign tax authorities on foreign-source income.[3] In general, foreign tax credits are categorized as direct or indirect. A *direct* foreign tax credit is computed for direct taxes paid on active foreign-source income of a foreign branch of a U.S. MNC or on the indirect withholding taxes withheld from passive income distributed by the foreign subsidiary to the U.S. parent. For foreign subsidiaries of U.S. MNCs, an *indirect* foreign tax credit is computed for income taxes *deemed paid* by the subsidiary. The deemed-paid tax credit corresponds to the portion of the distribution of earnings available for distribution that were actually distributed. For example, if a wholly owned foreign subsidiary pays out dividends equal to 50 percent of the earnings available for distribution, the deemed-paid tax credit is 50 percent of the foreign income taxes paid by the foreign subsidiary.

In a given tax year, an *overall limitation* applies to foreign tax credits; that is, the maximum total tax credit is limited to the amount of tax that would be due on the foreign-source income if it had been earned in the United States. The maximum tax credit is figured on worldwide foreign-source income; losses in one country can be used to offset profits in another. Excess tax credits for a tax year can be carried back two years and forward five years. Examples of calculating foreign tax credits for U.S. foreign branch and subsidiary operations are provided in the next section. Value-added taxes paid may not be included in determining the amount of the foreign tax credit, but they are nevertheless indirectly expensed as part of the cost of a good or service.

Individual U.S. investors may take a tax credit for the withholding taxes deducted from the dividend and interest income they received from the foreign financial assets in their portfolios.

ORGANIZATIONAL STRUCTURES FOR REDUCING TAX LIABILITIES

Countries differ in how they tax foreign-source income of their domestic MNCs. Additionally, regardless of the twin objectives of tax neutrality and tax equity, different forms of structuring a multinational organization within a country can result in different tax liabilities for the firm. Thus, it behooves management to be familiar with the different organizational structures that can be useful at various stages in the life cycle of the MNC for reducing tax liabilities. The following discussion on MNC organizational structure relates to U.S. tax regulations.

Branch and Subsidiary Income

An overseas affiliate of a U.S. MNC can be organized as a branch or a subsidiary. A **foreign branch** is not an independently incorporated firm separate from the parent; it is an extension of the parent. Consequently, active or passive foreign-source income earned by the branch is consolidated with the domestic-source income of the parent for determining the U.S. tax liability, regardless of whether or not the foreign-source income has been repatriated to the parent. A **foreign subsidiary** is an affiliate organization of the MNC that is independently incorporated in the foreign country, and one in which the U.S. MNC owns at least 10 percent of the voting equity stock. A foreign subsidiary in which the U.S. MNC owns more than 10 but less than 50 percent of the voting equity is a *minority foreign subsidiary* or an *uncontrolled foreign corporation*. Active and passive foreign-source income derived from a minority foreign subsidiary is taxed in the United States only when remitted to the U.S. parent firm via a dividend. A foreign subsidiary in which the U.S. MNC owns more than 50 percent of the voting equity is a *controlled foreign corporation*. Active foreign-source income from a controlled foreign corporation is taxed in the United States only as remitted to the U.S. parent, but passive income is taxed in the United States as earned, even if it has not been repatriated to the parent.

A more detailed discussion on controlled foreign corporations is reserved for later in this section.

EXAMPLE 20.2: Foreign Tax Credit Calculations Exhibit 20.4 presents examples of calculating the foreign tax credits for both a foreign branch and a wholly owned foreign subsidiary of a U.S. MNC in the host countries of Finland, Germany, and the Czech Republic. The examples use the actual domestic marginal income tax rates presented in Exhibit 20.1 and the withholding tax rates presented in Exhibit 20.2. Additionally, it is necessary to know that Germany taxes foreign branch income at a rate of 40 percent, whereas Finland and the Czech Republic tax foreign branch income at the same rate as domestic taxable income. The examples show the total tax liability for $100 of foreign taxable income when any excess foreign tax credits can be used and when they cannot. The examples assume that *all* after-tax foreign-source income available for remittance is immediately remitted to the U.S. parent.

Exhibit 20.4 indicates that when the U.S. MNC can use the full excess tax credits, the total tax liability is $35 per $100 of foreign taxable income, or 35 percent, the same amount due on $100 of taxable income earned in the United States. This is true: (1) regardless in which country the foreign affiliate is located; (2) whether the foreign affiliate is established as a branch or a subsidiary; and (3) regardless of the size of the income tax and withholding tax rates. A MNC that consistently generates excess foreign tax credits will never be able to use them in the allowable time. Thus, the more typical situation is that excess foreign tax credits go unused.

When excess tax credits go unused, the foreign tax liability for a branch is greater than the corresponding U.S. tax liability when the foreign income tax rate is greater than the U.S. rate of 35 percent. For a foreign subsidiary, the foreign tax liability is greater than the corresponding U.S. tax liability when: [foreign

EXHIBIT 20.4 Examples of Calculating U.S. Foreign Tax Credits for Branch and Subsidiary Operations

	Finland		Germany		Czech Republic	
	Branch	Subsidiary	Branch	Subsidiary	Branch	Subsidiary
Foreign income tax rate	28%	28%	40%	30%	35%	35%
Withholding tax rate	N/A	5%	N/A	5%	N/A	5%
Taxable income	100	100	100	100	100	100
Foreign income tax	−28	−28	−40	−30	−35	−35
Net available for remittance	72	72	60	70	65	65
Withholding tax[a]	0	−4	0	−4	0	−3
Net cash to U.S. parent	72	68	60	56	61	62
Gross-up: Income tax	28	28	40	30	39	35
Gross-up: Withholding tax	0	4	0	4	0	3
U.S. taxable income	100	100	100	100	100	100
U.S. income tax at 35%	35	35	35	35	35	35
Less foreign tax credit:						
Income tax	−28	−28	−40	−30	−39	−35
Withholding tax	0	−4	0	−4	0	−3
Net U.S. tax (excess credit)	7	3	(5)	1	(4)	(3)
Total tax: Excess credit used	35	35	35	35	35	35
Total tax: Excess credit not used	35	35	40	35	39	38

[a]100 percent of the funds available for remittance are assumed to be declared as dividends.

income tax rate + withholding tax rate − (foreign income tax rate × withholding tax rate)] is greater than the U.S. income tax rate of 35 percent. To illustrate, a foreign subsidiary in the Czech Republic for which excess foreign tax credits cannot be used has a total tax liability of: $.35 + .05 - (.35 \times .05) = .3825$, or 38.25 percent versus 35 percent in the United States.

This example suggests that the management of a MNC should be aware of the current tax rates levied by various host countries when deciding where to locate foreign affiliate operations. Moreover, the exhibit indicates that there can be a difference in the tax liability due on foreign-source income depending upon the organizational structure selected for the foreign affiliate. Thus, the management of a MNC must be aware of any differences in the taxation of income by a particular host country when deciding whether to organize a foreign operation as a branch or subsidiary. For example, new foreign affiliates frequently experience operating losses in the early years of operation. If this situation is expected, it may be beneficial for a U.S. MNC to originally establish overseas operations as a foreign branch of the parent because branch operating losses are consolidated with the parent firm's earnings for tax purposes. Alternatively, when foreign-source income is to be reinvested abroad to expand foreign operations, it may be preferable to organize as a minority foreign subsidiary if the foreign income tax rate is less than the U.S. income tax rate because the tax liability in the United States can be deferred until the subsidiary remits a dividend to the U.S. parent.

Payments to and from Foreign Affiliates

In Chapter 18, we discussed transfer pricing strategies that may help a U.S. MNC to minimize its global tax liability. Since the discussion there was sufficient, we will only recap the major points in this chapter. Recall that a *transfer price* was the accounting value assigned to a good or service as it was transferred from one affiliate to another. We learned that the higher the transfer price, the larger will be the gross profits of the transferring division relative to the receiving division. Consequently, it is beneficial to follow a high markup policy on transferred goods and services from the parent to a foreign affiliate when the income tax rate in the host country is greater than the tax rate in the parent country because there will be less taxable income remaining in the high-tax host country. However, when the parent country has the higher tax rate, it is not instantly clear that a low markup policy should be pursued. Since U.S. MNCs are taxed on their worldwide income, earnings repatriated to the United States from a low-tax host country would be grossed up to figure the additional tax due in the United States. However, if foreign-source retained earnings were needed for reinvestment in the host country, a low markup policy would result in a tax savings (assuming, of course, that undistributed profits are not highly taxed by the host country).

We also learned from Chapter 18 that governmental authorities are quite aware of transfer pricing schemes used by MNCs to reduce their worldwide tax liability, and most countries have regulations controlling transfer prices. These regulations typically state that the transfer price must reflect an *arm's-length price*, that is, a price the selling affiliate would charge an unrelated customer for the good or service. However, an arm's-length price is frequently difficult to establish and evaluate; thus, there exists a window of opportunity for some maneuverability by a MNC to use transfer pricing strategies to reduce its worldwide tax liability.

Tax Havens

A **tax haven** country is one that has a low corporate income tax rate and low withholding tax rates on passive income. Some major tax haven countries, which are suggested by the income tax rates presented in Exhibit 20.1, are the Bahamas, Bahrain, Bermuda, British Virgin Islands, Cayman Islands, Channel Islands (Guernsey and

Jersey), Hong Kong, and the Isle of Man. Additionally, in Hong Kong and Panama, foreign-source income is exempt from taxation.

In Ireland and the Netherlands Antilles, special tax incentives or tax holidays are granted for businesses that will earn hard currency or develop export markets. In Puerto Rico, certain businesses are granted a reduced flat income tax rate of 7 percent applicable to industrial development income, which in some areas may be further reduced to 2 percent. In Liechtenstein and in many instances in Switzerland, holding companies are exempt from certain income taxes. Similarly, in Luxembourg, a foreign company is subject to taxation only if it has a permanent establishment in the country.

Tax havens were once useful as locations for a MNC to establish a wholly owned "paper" foreign subsidiary that in turn would own the operating foreign subsidiaries of the MNC. Hence, when the tax rates in the host countries of the operating affiliates were lower than the tax rate in the parent country, dividends could be routed through the tax haven affiliate for use by the MNC, but the taxes due on them in the parent country could continue to be deferred until a dividend was declared by the tax haven subsidiary. These days the benefit of a tax haven subsidiary for U.S. MNCs has been greatly reduced by two factors: One is that the present corporate income tax rate in the United States is not especially high in comparison to most non-tax-haven countries, thus eliminating the need for deferral; the second factor is that the rules governing controlled foreign corporations (the topic to be discussed next) have effectively eliminated the ability to defer passive income in a tax haven foreign subsidiary.

Controlled Foreign Corporation

The Tax Reform Act of 1986 created a new type of foreign subsidiary called a controlled foreign corporation. The purpose of the reform was to prevent the tax deferral of certain income in tax haven countries and to raise taxes by reducing the benefit gained by U.S. MNCs from foreign tax credits. A **controlled foreign corporation (CFC)** is a foreign subsidiary that has more than 50 percent of its voting equity owned by U.S. shareholders. A U.S. shareholder is any U.S. citizen, resident, partnership, corporation, trust, or estate that owns (or indirectly controls) 10 percent or more of the voting equity of the CFC. Thus, six nonaffiliated U.S. shareholders each owning exactly 10 percent of the voting equity would be required for a foreign corporation to be designated a CFC. Alternatively, a wholly owned subsidiary of a U.S. MNC would be a CFC.

The undistributed income of a minority foreign subsidiary of a U.S. MNC is tax deferred until it is remitted via a dividend. This rule is modified for Subpart F income of CFCs, which is subject to immediate taxation. **Subpart F income** includes income of a type that is relatively easy to transfer between countries and that is subject to a low foreign tax levy. Special rules apply for calculating foreign tax credits for CFCs. Much Subpart F income can be classified into four distinct categories or "baskets" of income: passive income, high withholding tax interest, financial services income, and shipping income. The allowable foreign tax credit limit is figured separately for each basket. Operating income of the CFC goes into the overall basket. The result is that high taxes paid in one country on income classified into one basket cannot be used to offset low taxes paid in another country on income classified into a different basket. This procedure results in more excess foreign tax credits, which are unlikely to be completely used.

Foreign Sales Corporation

The Tax Reform Act of 1984 created the **foreign sales corporation (FSC)** as a special vehicle for encouraging the exporting of U.S. property. A FSC is a foreign corporation established as an affiliate of a U.S. corporation for the purpose of "buying" from the U.S. corporation property for resale and use abroad. A FSC may only be established in a possession of the United States or in a foreign country that has an agreement with the U.S. Internal Revenue Service, which contains an exchange of tax information program. Additionally, to qualify as a FSC, a corporation must maintain an adequate foreign presence and meet certain foreign management requirements. Foreign trade income (FTI) allowable for tax exemption must come from foreign trade gross receipts derived from: the sale or exchange of export property; the lease or rental of export property, or related incidental services; or fees from engineering, architectural, or managerial services.

Two important and related benefits exist from the establishment of a FSC. One benefit is that a *portion* of the total foreign trade income of a FSC is exempt from U.S. taxation; the other portion is fully taxable. If the FSC uses arm's-length transfer pricing, 30 percent of FTI is exempt from taxation. Alternatively, if administrative transfer pricing rules are used, 15/23 of FTI is tax exempt. The second benefit of a FSC is that the transfer price between the FSC and its U.S.-related supplier does *not* have to be an arm's-length price. Administrative pricing rules exist that allow the FSC to select (if more advantageous) an artificially low transfer price that increases the profit of the FSC at the expense of the U.S.-related supplier (for example, a parent corporation). The net result is that since only a portion of the FTI of the FSC is taxable, the increase in taxes paid by the FSC from shifting profit to it via the transfer pricing strategy is less than the tax savings realized by the U.S. parent from having lower taxable income via the advantageous transfer price.

SUMMARY

This chapter provided a brief introduction to the international tax environment that confronts MNCs and investors in international financial assets.

1. The twin objectives of taxation are tax neutrality and tax equity. Tax neutrality has its foundations in the principles of economic efficiency and equity. Tax equity is the principle that all similarly situated taxpayers should participate in the cost of operating the government according to the same rules.
2. The three basic types of taxation are income tax, withholding tax, and value-added tax. Corporate income tax rates from many countries were listed and compared. Similarly, the withholding tax rates for certain countries for various types of foreign-source income for which the U.S. has bilateral tax treaties were listed and compared.
3. Nations often tax the worldwide income of resident taxpayers and also the income of foreign taxpayers doing business within their territorial boundaries. If countries simultaneously apply both methods, double taxation will result unless a mechanism is established to prevent it. The concept of the foreign tax credit as a means to eliminate double taxation was developed. Examples were presented from the perspective of a U.S. MNC showing the calculation of the foreign tax credits for branch and subsidiary operations in three countries with different corporate income tax rates.
4. Different forms of organizational structure can affect the tax liability of a MNC. Specifically, there are differences in taxation between branch and subsidiary operations. Transfer pricing strategies, subsidiary operations in tax haven countries, foreign-controlled corporations, and foreign sales corporations, were also defined and discussed.

KEY WORDS

active income, 476
capital-export neutrality, 475
capital-import neutrality, 475
controlled foreign corporation (CFC), 485
direct tax, 476
foreign branch, 482
foreign sales corporation (FSC), 485
foreign subsidiary, 482
foreign tax credits, 481
indirect income, 476

income tax, 476
national neutrality, 475
passive income, 476
residential taxation, 480
source taxation, 481
Subpart F income, 485
tax equity, 475
tax haven, 484
tax neutrality, 475
tax treaty, 476
territorial taxation, 481
value-added tax (VAT), 476
withholding tax, 476
worldwide taxation, 480

QUESTIONS

1. Discuss the twin objectives of taxation. Be sure to define the key words.
2. Compare and contrast the three basic types of taxation that governments levy within their tax jurisdiction.
3. Show how double taxation on a taxpayer may result if all countries were to tax the worldwide income of their residents and the income earned within their territorial boundaries.
4. What methods do taxing authorities use to eliminate or mitigate the evil of double taxation?
5. There is a difference in the tax liability levied on foreign-source income depending upon whether a foreign branch or subsidiary form of organizational structure is selected for a foreign affiliate. Please elaborate on this statement.

PROBLEMS

1. There are three production stages required before a pair of skis produced by Innsbruck Fabrication can be sold at retail for $2,300. Fill in the following table to show the value added at each stage in the production process and the incremental and total VAT. The Austrian VAT rate is 20 percent.

Production Stage	Selling Price	Value Added	Incremental VAT
1	$ 450		
2	$1,900		
3	$2,300		
			Total VAT

MINI CASE

Sigma Corp.'s Location Decision

Sigma Corporation of Boston is contemplating establishing an affiliate operation in the Mediterranean. Two countries under consideration are Spain and Cyprus. Sigma intends to repatriate all after-tax foreign-source income to the United States. At this point, Sigma is not certain whether it would be best to establish the affiliate operation as a branch operation or a wholly owned subsidiary of the parent firm.

In Cyprus, the marginal corporate tax rate is 25 percent. Foreign branch profits are taxed at the same rate. In Spain, corporate income is taxed at 35 percent, the same rate as in the United States. Additionally, foreign branch income in Spain is also taxed at 35 percent. The U.S. withholding tax treaty rates on dividend income are 5 percent with Cyprus and 10 percent with Spain.

The financial manager of Sigma has asked you to help him determine where to locate the new affiliate and which organization structure to establish. The location decision will be largely based on whether the total tax liability would be smallest for a foreign branch or a wholly owned subsidiary in Cyprus or Spain.

ENDNOTES

1 See the 1999 PriceWaterhouseCoopers *Corporate Taxes: Worldwide Summaries* for exceptions to the basic withholding tax rates.

2. See Horwitz (1993).

3. In general, as Kuntz and Peroni (1994) note, the United States claims only a "limited taxing jurisdiction over nonresident alien individuals and foreign corporations. Foreign persons pay U.S. taxes only on income that has a sufficient nexus with the U.S."

WEB RESOURCES

www.clnewsnet.com/tnn/hotsites/intnatl.html

This Website is managed by PriceWaterhouseCoopers. From this site one can link to the Website of the tax authority in many countries. Additionally, current international tax news is provided.

www.tax.kpmg.net

KPMG International, a global professional advisory firm, manages this Website. A useful corporate tax survey that compares tax rates for 60 countries can be downloaded from this site.

REFERENCES AND SUGGESTED READINGS

Bischel, Jon E., and Robert Feinscheiber. *Fundamentals of International Taxation*, 2nd ed. New York: Practicing Law Institute, 1985.

Gamme, Malcolm, and Bill Robinson. *Beyond 1992: A European Tax System, Proceedings of the Fourth Institute for Fiscal Studies Residential Conference*. London: Chameleon Press, July 1989.

Horst, Thomas. "American Taxation of Multinational Firms." *American Economic Review* (July 1977), pp. 376–89.

Horwitz, Tony. "Continental Shift: Europe's Borders Fade and People and Goods Can Move Freely." *The Wall Street Journal*, May 18, 1993.

Isenbergh, Joseph. *International Taxation: U.S. Taxation of Foreign Taxpayers and Foreign Income*, Vols. I and II. Boston: Little, Brown, 1990.

Jones, Sally M., and Ray M. Sommerfeld. *Federal Taxes and Management Decisions*. Burr Ridge, IL: Irwin, 1995–96.

Kaplan, Richard L. *Federal Taxation of International Transactions: Principles, Planning and Policy*. St. Paul, MN: West, 1988.

Kopits, George, ed. *Tax Harmonization in the European Community: Policy Issues and Analysis*. International Monetary Fund Occasional Paper, No. 94, Washington, D.C., June 1992.

Kuntz, Joel D., and Robert J. Peroni. *U.S. International Taxation*, Vols. I and II. Boston: Warren, Gorham and Lamont, 1994.

Metcalf, Gilbert E. "Value-Added Taxation: A Tax Whose Time Has Come?" *Journal of Economic Perspectives* 9 (1995), pp. 121–40.

Pratt, James W., and William N. Kulsrud. *Corporate, Partnership, Estate, and Gift Taxation*. Burr Ridge, IL: Irwin Taxation Series, 1996.

PriceWaterhouseCoopers. *Corporate Taxes: Worldwide Summaries*. New York: John Wiley and Sons, Inc., 1999.

U.S. Internal Revenue Code, Part III. Income From Sources Without the United States. Chicago: Commerce Clearing House, 1993.

GLOSSARY

Active Income Income which results from production or services provided by an individual or corporation.

Adjusted Present Value (APV) A present value technique which discounts a firm's cash flows at different rates depending on the risk of the cash flows.

Agency Market A market in which the broker takes the client's order through the agent, who matches it with another public order.

All-Equity Cost of Capital The required return on a company's stock in the absence of debts.

All-in-Cost All costs of a swap, which are interest expense, transaction cost, and service charges.

American Depository Receipt (ADR) A certificate of ownership issued by a U.S. bank representing a multiple of foreign shares that are deposited in a U.S. bank. ADRs can be traded on the organized exchanges in the U.S. or in the OTC market.

American Option An option which can be exercised at any time during the option contract.

Arbitrage The act of simultaneously buying and selling the same or equivalent assets or commodities for the purpose of making certain, guaranteed profits.

Ask Price *See* Offer Price.

Back-to-Back Loan A loan involving two parties—two companies located in different countries. Each company borrows funds in its capital market and re-lends to the other company.

Balance of Payments A country's record of international transactions presented in a double-entry bookkeeping form.

Balance Sheet Hedge Intended to reduce translation exposure of a MNC by eliminating the mismatch of exposed net assets and exposed net liabilities denominated in the same currency.

Bank Capital Adequacy The amount of equity capital and other securities a bank holds as reserves against risky assets to reduce the probability of a bank failure.

Banker's Acceptance (B/A) A negotiable money market instrument for which a secondary market exists and is issued by the Importer's Bank once the bill of lading and time draft are accepted. It is essentially a promise that the bank will pay the draft when it matures.

Basle Accord Established in 1988 by the Bank for International Settlements, this act established a framework to measure bank capital adequacy for banks in the Group of Ten and Luxembourg.

Bearer Bond A bond in which ownership is demonstrated through possession of the bond.

Bid Price The price at which dealers will buy a financial asset.

Bilateral Netting A system in which a pair of affiliates determines the net amount due between them and only this amount is transferred.

Bill of Lading (B/L) In exporting, a document issued by a common carrier specifying that it has received goods for shipment and which can also serve as title to the goods.

Bimetallism A double standard maintaining free coinage for both gold and silver.

Brady Bonds Loans converted into collateralized bonds with a reduced interest rate devised to resolve the international debt crisis in the late 1980s. Named after the U.S. Treasury Secretary Charles Brady.

Bretton Woods System An international monetary system created in 1944 to promote postwar exchange rate stability and coordinate international monetary policies. Otherwise known as the gold-exchange system.

Call Market A market in which market and limit orders are accumulated and executed at specific intervals during the day.

Call Option An option to "buy" an underlying asset at a specified price.

Capital Account Balance of payment entry capturing all sales and purchases of financial assets, real estate, and businesses.

Capital-Export Neutrality The idea that an ideal tax is one which is effective in raising revenue for the government and, at the same time, does not prevent economic resources from being deployed most efficiently no matter where in the world the highest return can be earned.

Capital-Import Neutrality The idea that an ideal tax burden imposed by a host country on a foreign subsidiary of a MNC should be the same regardless of which country the MNC is incorporated in and should be the same burden as placed on domestic firms.

Cash Budget In cash management, a plan which details the time and size of expected receipts and disbursements.

Cash Management The handling of cash within a firm such as the investment a firm has in transaction balances, funds tied up in precautionary cash balances, investment of excess funds at the most favorable rate, and borrowing at the lowest rate when there is a temporary cash shortage.

Central Cash Depository In a MNC, it is a central cash pool in which excess cash from affiliates is collected and invested or used to cover system-wide shortages of cash.

Closed-End Country Fund (CECF) A country fund (fund invested exclusively in the securities of one country) which issues a given number of shares that are traded on the host country exchange as if it were an individual stock. These shares are not redeemable at the underlying net asset value set in the home market.

Competitive Effect Refers to the effect of exchange rate changes on the firm's competitive position, which, in turn, affects the firm's operating cash flows.

Composite Currency Bond A bond denominated in a currency basket such as ECU, instead of a single currency. Also called *Currency Cocktail Bonds.*

Concessionary Loan A loan below the market interest rate offered by the host country to a parent MNC to encourage capital expenditures in the host country.

Contingent Claim Security *See* Derivative Security.

Contingent Exposure The risk due to uncertain situations in which a firm does not know if it will face exchange risk exposure in the future.

Continuous Market A market in which market and limit orders can be executed any time during business hours.

Controlled Foreign Corporation (CFC) A foreign subsidiary in which U.S. shareholders own more than 50 percent of the voting equity stock.

Conversion Effect Refers to the fact that the dollar amount converted from a given cash flow from foreign operation will be affected by exchange rate changes.

Convertible Bond A bond which can be exchanged for a pre-determined number of equity shares of the issuer.

Counterparty One of the two parties involved in financial contracts who agrees to exchange cash flows on particular terms.

Countertrade Transactions in which parties exchange goods or services. If these transactions do not involve an exchange of money, they are a type of barter.

Country Risk In banking and investment, it is the probability that unexpected events in a country will influence its ability to repay loans and repatriate dividends. It includes political and credit risks.

Covered Interest Arbitrage A situation which occurs when IRP does not hold, thereby allowing certain arbitrage profits to be made without the arbitrageur investing any money out of pocket or bearing any risk.

Cross Exchange Rate An exchange rate between a currency pair where neither currency is the U.S. dollar.

Cross-Currency Interest Rate Swap Typically called a "currency swap." One counterparty exchanges the debt service obligations of a bond denominated in one currency for the debt service obligations of the other counterparty which are denominated in another currency.

Cross-hedging Involves hedging a position in one asset by taking a position in another asset.

Cumulative Translation Adjustment (CTA) Used in the current rate method of translating foreign currency financial statements, this equity account allows balancing of the balance sheet by accounting for translation gains and losses.

Currency board An extreme form of the fixed exchange rate regime under which local currency is fully backed by the U.S. dollar or another chosen standard currency.

Currency Swap One counter party exchanges the debt service obligations of a bond denominated in one currency for the debt service obligations of the other counter party denominated in another currency.

Current Account Balance of payment entry representing the exports and imports of goods and services, and unilateral transfer.

Current/Noncurrent Method In dealing with foreign currency translation, the idea that current assets and liabilities are converted at the current exchange rate while non-current assets and liabilities are translated at the historical exchange rates.

Current Rate Method In dealing with foreign currency translation, the idea that all balance sheet accounts are translated at the current exchange rate except stockholder's equity which is translated at the exchange rate on the date of issuance.

Dealer Market A market in which the broker takes the trade through the dealer, who participates in trades as a principal.

Debt for Equity Swap The sale of sovereign debt for U.S. dollars to investors desiring to make equity investment in the indebted nation.

Derivative Security A security whose value is contingent upon the value of the underlying security. Examples are futures, forward, and options contracts.

Direct Tax A tax paid directly by the taxpayer on whom the tax is levied.

Diversification of the Market A strategy for managing operating exposure in which a firm diversifies the market for its product. Thus, exchange rate changes in one country may be offset by opposite exchange rate changes in another.

Draft A written order instructing the importer or his agent to pay the amount specified on its face at a certain date.

Dual Currency Bond A straight fixed-rate bond which pays coupon interest in the issue currency, but at maturity pays the principal in a currency other than the issue currency.

Economic Exposure The possibility that cash flows and the value of the firm may be affected by unanticipated changes in the exchange rates.

Edge Act Bank Federally chartered subsidiaries of U.S. banks which may engage in the full range of international banking operations. These banks are located in the United States.

Efficient Market Hypothesis Hypothesis stating that financial markets are informationally efficient in that the current asset prices reflect all the relevant and available information.

Elasticity of Demand A measure of the sensitivity of demand for a product with respect to its price.

EURIBOR The rate at which interbank deposits of the euro are offered by one prime bank to another in countries that comprise the EMU as well as prime banks in non-EMU EU countries and major prime banks in non-EU countries.

Euro The common European currency introduced in 1999 of the 11 countries of the EU that comprise the EMU.

Eurobond A bond issue denominated in a particular currency but sold to investors in national capital markets other than the issuing country.

Eurocurrency A time deposit of money in an international bank located in a country other than the country which issues the currency.

European Central Bank (ECB) The central bank of the 11 countries that comprise the EMU, responsible for maintaing price stability via monetary policy.

European Currency Unit (ECU) A basket currency made up of a weighted average of the currencies of the 12 members of the European Union. The precursor of the euro.

European Monetary System (EMS) Replaced the snake in 1979. A system to establish monetary stability in Europe and promote European economic and political unification.

European Monetary Union (EMU) The monetary union of 11 countries of the EU that irrevocably fixed their exchange rates and use the common euro currency.

European Option An option which can be exercised only at the maturity date of the contract.

European Union (EU) A regional economic integration in Western Europe, currently with 15 member states, in which all barriers to the free flow of goods, capital, and people have been removed. EU plans to complete economic unification including a single currency.

Exchange Rate Mechanism (ERM) The procedure, prior to the introduction of the euro, by which EMS member countries collectively manage their exchange rates based on a parity grid system, a system of par values between ERM countries.

Exchange rate pass-through The relationship between exchange rate changes and the price adjustments of internationally traded goods.

Exercise Price The prespecified price paid or received when an option is exercised.

Export-Import Bank (Eximbank) of the United States Chartered in 1945, it is an independent government agency which facilitates and finances U.S. export trade by financing exports in situations where private financial institutions are unable or unwilling to provide financing.

Exposure Coefficient The coefficient obtained from regressing the home currency value of assets on the foreign exchange rate under consideration. This provides a measure of the firm's economic exposure to currency risk.

Exposure Netting Hedging only the net exposure by firms which have both payables and receivables in foreign currencies.

Financial Hedges Refers to hedging exchange risk exposure using financial contracts such as currency forward and options contracts.

Fisher Effect Theory stating that the nominal interest rate is the sum of the real interest rate and the expected inflation rate.

Flexible Sourcing Policy A strategy for managing operating exposure which involves sourcing from areas where input costs are low.

Floating Rate Note Medium-term bonds which have their coupon payments indexed to a reference rate such as the three-month U.S. dollar LIBOR.

Foreign Branch An overseas affiliate of an MNC which is not an independently incorporated firm but is rather an extension of the parent.

Foreign Direct Investment (FDI) Investment in a foreign country that gives the MNC a measure of control.

Foreign Exchange Risk The risk of facing uncertain future exchange rates.

Foreign Sales Corporation (FSC) A foreign corporation established as an affiliate of a U.S. corporation for the purpose of buying from the U.S. corporation property for resale.

Foreign Subsidiary An affiliate organization of an MNC which is independently incorporated in a foreign country.

Foreign Tax Credit Used to avoid double taxation on a parent firm with foreign subsidiaries. It is the credit given to the parent firm against taxes due in the host country based on the taxes paid to foreign tax authorities on foreign-source income.

Forfaiting A form of medium-term trade financing used to finance exports in which the exporter sells promissory notes to a bank at a discount, thereby freeing the exporter from carrying the financing.

Forward Market Hedge A method of hedging exchange risk exposure in which a foreign currency contract is sold or bought forward.

Forward Market A market for trading foreign exchange contracts initiated today but to be settled at a future date.

Forward Parity Theory stating that the forward premium or discount is equal to the expected change in the exchange rate between two currencies.

Forward Premium/Discount The amount over (under) the spot exchange rate for a forward rate which is often expressed as an annualized percent deviation from the spot rate.

Forward Rate Agreement An interbank contract that is used to hedge the interest rate risk in mismatched deposits and credits.

Functional Currency For a foreign subsidiary of a MNC, it is the currency of the primary economic environment in which the entity operates. This is typically the local currency of the country in which the entity conducts most of its business.

Currency Futures A standardized foreign exchange contract with a future delivery date that is traded on organized exchanges.

General Agreement on Tariffs and Trade (GATT) A multilateral agreement between member countries to promote international trade. The GATT played a key role in reducing international trade barriers.

Gold Exchange Standard A monetary system in which countries hold most of their reserves in the form of a currency of a particular country. That country is on the gold standard.

Gold Standard A monetary system in which currencies are defined in terms of their gold content. The exchange rate between a pair of currencies is determined by their relative gold contents.

Gresham's Law Under the bimetallic standard, the abundant metal was used as money while the scarce metal was driven out of circulation, based on the fact that the ratio of the two metals was officially fixed.

Hedging via the Invoice Currency A method of hedging exchange risk exposure by invoicing in terms of the home currency of the firm.

Home Bias In portfolio holdings, the tendency of an investor to hold a larger portion of the home country securities than is optimum for diversification of risk.

Income Tax A direct tax levied on the active income of an individual or corporation.

Indirect Tax A tax levied on a taxpayer's income which was not directly generated by the taxpayer and serves as passive income for the taxpayer.

Initial Margin An initial collateral deposit needed to establish an asset position.

Interest Rate Parity (IRP) An arbitrage equilibrium condition holding that the interest rate differential between two countries should be equal to the forward exchange premium or discount. Violation of IRP gives rise to profitable arbitrage opportunities.

International Banking Facility (IBF) Banking operation within domestic U.S. banks that act as foreign banks in the U.S. and, as such, are not bound by domestic reserve requirements or FDIC insurance requirements. They seek deposits from non-U.S. citizens and can make loans only to foreigners.

International Fisher Effect A theory stating that the expected change in the spot exchange rate between two countries is the difference in the interest rates between the two countries.

International Monetary System The institutional framework within which international payments are made, movements of capital are accommodated, and exchange rates among currencies are determined.

Intrinsic Value The immediate exercise value of an American option.

Jamaica Agreement International monetary agreement in January 1976 by which flexible exchange rates were accepted and gold was abandoned as an international reserve asset.

J-curve Effect Refers to the initial deterioration and eventual improvement of the trade balance following a depreciation of a country's currency.

Law of one price The requirement that similar commodities or securities should be trading at the same or similar prices.

Lead/Lag Strategy Reducing transaction exposure by paying or collecting foreign financial obligations early (lead) or late (lag) depending on whether the currency is hard or soft.

Letter of Credit (L/C) A guarantee from the Importer's Bank that it will act on behalf of the importer and pay the exporter for merchandise if all documentation is in order.

Limit Order An order away from the market price which is held until it can be executed at the desired price.

Liquidity The ability of securities to be bought and sold quickly at close to the current quoted price.

London Interbank Offered Rate (LIBOR) The interbank interest rate at which a bank will offer Eurocurrency deposits to another bank in London. LIBOR is often used as the basis for setting Eurocurrency loan rates. The loan rate is determined by adding a risk premium to LIBOR.

Louvre Accord An agreement in 1987, prompted by the dollar's decline, in which the G-Seven countries (i) cooperate to achieve greater exchange rate stability and (ii) consult and coordinate their macroeconomic policies.

Maastricht Treaty Treaty signed in December 1991 states that the European Union will irrevocably fix exchange rates among member countries by January 1999 and introduce a common European currency which will replace individual national currencies.

Maintenance Margin Collateral needed to maintain an asset position.

Managed Float System Established by the Louvre Accord in 1987, it allows the G-7 countries to jointly intervene in the exchange market to correct over- or under-valuation of currencies.

Market Completeness A market is complete if each state of the economy is matched by security payoff.

Market Imperfections Various frictions, such as transaction costs and legal restrictions, that prevent the markets from functioning perfectly.

Market Order An order executed at the best price available (market price) when the order is received in the market.

Marking-to-Market The process of establishing daily price gains and losses in the futures market by the change in the settlement price of the futures contract.

Merchant Bank Banks which perform traditional commercial banking as well as investment banking activities.

Monetary/Nonmonetary Method In dealing with foreign currency translation, the idea that monetary balance sheet accounts such as accounts receivable are translated at the current exchange rate while non-monetary balance sheet accounts such as stockholder's equity are converted at the historical exchange rate.

Money Market Hedge A method of hedging transaction exposure by borrowing and lending in the domestic and foreign money markets.

Multilateral Netting A system in which all affiliates each net their individual interaffiliate receipts against all their disbursements and transfer or receive the balance, respectively, if it is a net payer or receiver.

Multinational Corporation (MNC) Refers to a firm that has business activities and interests in multiple countries.

National Neutrality The idea that an ideal tax on taxable income would tax all income in the same manner by the taxpayer's national tax authority regardless of where in the world it is earned.

Negotiable Certificate of Deposit (NCD) A negotiable bank time deposit.

Net Present Value (NPV) A capital budgeting method in which the present value of cash outflows is subtracted from the present value of expected future cash inflows to determine the net present value of an investment project.

Netting Center In multilateral netting, it determines the amount of net payments and which affiliates are to make or pay them.

North American Free Trade Agreement (NAFTA) Created in 1994, it includes the U.S., Canada, and Mexico as members in a free trade area. NAFTA aims to eliminate tariffs and import quotas over a 15-year period.

Notional Principal A reference amount of principal used for determining payments under various derivative contracts.

Offer Price The price at which a dealer will sell a financial asset.

Offshore Banking Center A country in which the banking system is organized to allow external accounts beyond the normal economic activity of the country. Their primary function is to seek deposits and grant loans in currencies other than the host country currency.

Open Interest The total number of short or long contracts outstanding for a particular delivery month in the derivative markets.

Operating Exposure The extent to which the firm's operating cash flows will be affected by random changes in the exchange rates.

Operational Hedges Long-term, operational approaches to hedging exchange exposure which include diversification of the market and flexible sourcing.

Optimum currency area A geographical area that is suitable for sharing a common currency by virtue of a high degree of factor mobility within the area.

Option A contract giving the owner the right, but not the obligation, to buy or sell a given quantity of an asset at a specified price at some date in the future.

Options Market Hedge Use of put and call options to limit the downside risk of transaction exposure while preserving the upside potential. The price of such flexibility is the option premium.

Over-the-Counter (OTC) Market Trading market in which there is no central marketplace; instead, buyers and sellers are linked via a network of telephones, telex machines, computers, and automated dealing systems.

Par Value The nominal or face value of stocks or bonds.

Parallel Loan A loan involving four parties—two parents firms located in different countries and two foreign subsidiaries. The parent firms borrow in their capital markets and relend to the other's subsidiary.

Passive Income Income not directly generated by an individual or corporation, such as interest income, royalty income, and copyright income.

Plaza Accord G-5 agreement in 1985 that depreciation of the dollar is desirable to correct the U.S. trade deficits.

Political Risk Potential losses to the parent firm resulting from adverse political developments in the host country.

Portfolio Risk Diversification Portfolio risk is minimized by investing in multiple securities which do not have strong correlations between one another.

Precautionary Cash Balance Emergency funds a firm maintains in case it has underestimated its transaction cash balance.

Price-Specie-Flow Mechanism Under the gold standard, it is the automatic correction of payment imbalances between countries. This is based on the fact that, under the gold standard, the domestic money stock rises or falls as the country experiences inflows or outflows of gold.

Primary Market The market in which new security issues are sold to investors. In selling the new securities, investment bankers can play a role either as a broker or a dealer.

Privatization Act of a country divesting itself of ownership and operation of business ventures by turning them over to the free market system.

Product Differentiation Creating a perception among consumers that a firm's product(s) are different from those offered by competitors, thereby reducing price sensitivity of demand.

Purchasing Power Parity (PPP) A theory stating that the exchange rate between currencies of two countries should be equal to the ratio of the countries' price levels of a commodity basket.

Put An option to sell an underlying asset at a prespecified price.

Quality Spread Differential (QSD) The difference between the fixed interest rate spread differential and the floating interest rate spread differential of the debt of two counterparties of different creditworthiness. A positive QSD is necessary condition for an interest swap to occur which ensures the swap will be beneficial to both parties.

Quantity Theory of Money An identity stating that for each country, the general price level times the aggregate output should be equal to the money supply times the velocity of money.

Random Walk Hypothesis A hypothesis stating that in an efficient market, asset prices change randomly (i.e. independently of historical trends), or follow a "random walk." Thus, the expected future exchange rate is equivalent to the current exchange rate.

Real Exchange Rate Measures the degree of deviation from PPP over a period of time, assuming PPP held at the beginning of the period.

Real Option The application of options pricing theory to the evaluation of investment options in real projects.

Registered Bond A bond whose ownership is demonstrated by associating the buyer's name with the bond in the issuer's records.

Reinvoice Center A central financial subsidiary of a multinational corporation where intrafirm transaction exposure is netted, and the residual exposure is managed.

Reporting Currency The currency in which a MNC prepares its consolidated financial statements. Typically this is the currency in which the parent firm keeps its books.

Residential Taxation *See* Worldwide Taxation.

Reversing Trade A trade in either the futures or forward market that will neutralize a position.

Secondary Market A market in which investors buy and sell securities to other investors; the original issuer is not involved in these trades. This market provides marketability and valuation of the securities.

Sharpe Performance Measure (SHP) A risk-adjusted performance measure for a portfolio which gives the excess return (above the risk-free interest rate) per standard deviation risk.

Shelf Registration Allows bond issuer to pre-register a securities issue which will occur at a later date.

Single-Currency Interest Rate Swap Typically called an "interest rate swap." There are many variants; however, all involve swapping interest payments on debt obligations that are denominated in the same currency.

Smithsonian Agreement In December 1971, the G-10 countries agreed to devalue the U.S. dollar against gold and most major currencies in an attempt to save the Bretton Woods system.

Snake European version of fixed exchange rate system which appeared as the Bretton Woods system declined.

Source Taxation *See* Territorial Taxation.

Special Drawing Rights (SDR) An artificial international reserve created by the International Monetary Fund (IMF) which is a currency basket currently comprised of five major currencies.

Specialist On exchange markets in the U.S., each stock is represented by a specialist who makes a market by holding an inventory of the security.

Spot (Exchange) Rate Price at which foreign exchange can be sold or purchased for immediate (within two business days) delivery.

Straight Fixed-Rate Bond Bonds with a specified maturity date that have fixed coupon payments.

Striking Price *See* Exercise Price.

Stripped Bond A synthetic zero coupon bond created by an investment bank via selling the rights to a specific coupon payment or the bond principal of a coupon bond, typically a U.S. Treasury bond.

Subpart F Income Income of controlled foreign corporations which is subject to immediate U.S. taxation and includes income that is relatively easy to transfer between countries and is subject to a low foreign tax levy.

Swap Bank A generic term to describe a financial institution which facilitates currency and interest rate swaps between counterparties.

Swap Broker Function of a swap bank in which it matches counterparties but does not assume any risk of the swap; however, it does receive a commission for this service.

Swap Dealer Function of a swap bank in which it makes a market in one or the other side of a currency or interest rate swap.

Swap Transaction The simultaneous spot sale (purchase) of an asset against a forward purchase (sale) of an approximately equal amount of the asset.

Syndicate A group of Eurobanks banding together to share the risk of lending Eurocredits.

Tax Equity The idea that all similarly situated taxpayers should participate in the cost of operating the government according to the same rules.

Tax Haven A country which has a low corporate income tax rate and low withholding tax rates on passive income.

Tax Neutrality A principle in taxation, holding that taxation should not have a negative effect on the decision-making process of taxpayers.

Technical Analysis A method of predicting the future behavior of asset prices based on their historical patterns.

Temporal Method In dealing with foreign currency translation, the idea that current and noncurrent monetary accounts as well as accounts which are carried on the books at current value are converted at the current exchange rate. Accounts carried on the books at historical cost are translated at the historical exchange rate.

Territorial Taxation A method of declaring tax jurisdiction in which all income earned within a country by any taxpayer, domestic or foreign, is taxed.

Theory of Comparative Advantage An argument which supports the existence of international trade. This theory states that it is mutually beneficial for countries to specialize in production of goods for which they can produce most efficiently and then engage in trade.

Time Draft A written order instructing the importer or the importer's bank to pay a specific sum of money on a certain date. Used in import-export trade financing.

Tobin tax A tax on the international flow of hot money proposed by Professor Tobin for the purpose of discouraging cross-border financial speculation.

Transaction Cash Balance Funds a firm has marked to cover scheduled outflows during a cash budgeting period.

Transaction Exposure The potential change in the value of financial positions due to changes in the exchange rate between the inception of a contract and the settlement of the contract.

Transfer Price The price assigned, for bookkeeping purposes, to the receiving division within a business for the cost of transferring goods and services from another division.

Translation Exposure The effect of an unanticipated change in the exchange rates on the consolidated financial reports of a MNC.

Triangular Arbitrage The process of trading U.S. dollars for a second currency and subsequently trading this for a third currency. This third currency is then traded for U.S. dollars. The purpose of such trading is to earn arbitrage profit via trading from the second currency to the third.

Triffin Paradox Under the gold exchange standard, the reserve-currency country should run a balance of payments deficit, but this can decrease confidence in the reserve currency and lead to the downfall of the system.

Universal Bank International banks which provide such services as consulting in foreign exchange hedging strategies, interest rate and currency swap financing, and international cash management.

Value at Risk An analysis which provides a confidence interval on the probability of maximum loss that can occur during a given period of time.

Value-Added Tax (VAT) An indirect national tax which is levied on the value added in the production of a good or service as it moves through the various stages of production.

Withholding Tax An indirect tax levied on passive income earned by an individual or corporation of one country within the tax jurisdiction of another country.

World Beta A measure of the sensitivity of an asset or portfolio to the world market movements. This is a measure of the world systematic risk.

World Equity Benchmark Shares (WEBS) WEBS are exchange-traded, open-end country funds designed to closely track national stock market indices. WEBS are traded on the American Stock Exchange (AMEX).

World Trade Organization (WTO) Permanent international organization created by the Uruguay Round to replace GATT. The WTO will have power to enforce international trade rules.

Worldwide Taxation A method of declaring national tax jurisdiction in which national residents of the country are taxed on their world-wide income regardless of which country it is earned in.

Yankee Bond (Stock) Bond (stock) directly sold to U.S. investors by foreign companies.

Zero Coupon Bond A bond that pays no coupon interest and simply returns the face value at maturity.

INDEX

499

I

J

N

Category 1
Antigua & Barbuda
Argentina
The Bahamas
Barbados
Belize
Djibouti
Dominica
Grenada
Iraq
Liberia
Lithuania
Marshall Islands
Fed. States of Micronesia
Nigeria
Oman
Panama
St. Kitts & Nevis
St. Lucia
St. Vincent and the Grenadines
Syrian Arab Republic

Category 2
Benin
Burkina Faso
Cameroon
C. African Republic
Chad
Comoros
Congo
Côte d'Ivoire
Equatorial Guinea
Gabon
Mali
Niger
Senegal
Togo

Category 3
Bangladesh
Bhutan
Bosnia and Herzegovina
Brunei Darussalam
Burundi
Cape Verde
Cyprus
Czech Republic
Estonia
Fiji
Iceland
Jordan
Kiribati
Kuwait
Libya
Lesotho
Malta
Morocco
Myanmar
Namibia
Nepal
San Marino
Seychelles
Slovak Republic
Solomon Islands
Swaziland
Thailand
Tonga
Vanuatu
Western Samoa

Category 4
Austria
Belgium
Finland
France
Germany
Ireland
Italy
Luxembourg
Netherlands
Portugal
Spain

Category 5
Bahrain
Qatar
Saudi Arabia
United Arab Emirates
Chile
Nicaragua

Category 6
Algeria
Angola
Belarus
Brazil
Cambodia
China, P.R.
Colombia
Costa Rica
Croatia
Dominican Republic
Ecuador
Egypt
El Salvador
Eritrea
Georgia
Greece
Guinea-Bissau
Honduras
Hungary
Indonesia
Iran, I.R. of
Israel
Korea
Kyrgyz Rep.
Latvia
Macedonia, FYR of
Malaysia
Maldives
Mauritius
Norway
Pakistan
Poland
Russia
Singapore
Slovenia
Sri Lanka
Sudan
Suriname Tunisia
Turkmenistan
Turkey
Ukraine
Uruguay
Uzbekistan
Venezuela
Vietnam

Category 7
Afghanistan, Islamic State of
Albania
Armenia
Australia
Azerbaijan
Bolivia
Bulgaria
Canada
Denmark
Ethiopia
Gambia, The
Ghana
Guatemala
Guinea
Guyana
Haiti
India
Jamaica
Japan
Kazakhstan
Kenya
Lao P.D. Rep
Lebanon
Madagascar
Malawi
Mauritania
Mexico
Moldova
Mongolia
Mozambique
New Zealand
Papua New Guinea
Paraguay
Peru
Philippines
Romania
Rwanda
São Tomé and Príncipe
Sierra Leone
Somalia
South Africa
Sweden
Switzerland
Tajikistan, Rep. of
Tanzania
Trinidad and Tobago
Uganda
United Kingdom
United States
Yemen, Republic of
Zaïre
Zambia
Zimbabwe

Exchange Rat

SOURCE: *International Financial Statistics*, Au